P9-DWG-795

THE GREATEST MILITARY GAMBLE
OF WORLD WAR II, AND ALMOST
THE GREATEST DISASTER.

ARNHEM

where the most prestigious Allied generals
gambled with their reputations and the lives
of their finest troops.

ARNHEM

where Germany's most brilliant military
commander was called back into service by
Hitler to achieve a miracle—and came close
to succeeding.

ARNHEM

where over twice as many Allied soldiers fell
than at Normandy, and where feats of near-
incredible heroism were commonplace.

ARNHEM

where a war that was almost won was almost
lost.

A BRIDGE TOO FAR

CORNELIUS RYAN

POPULAR LIBRARY • NEW YORK

All POPULAR LIBRARY books are carefully selected by the POPULAR LIBRARY Editorial Board and represent titles by the world's greatest authors.

POPULAR LIBRARY EDITION

Copyright © 1974 by Cornelius Ryan

Library of Congress Catalog Card Number: 74-3252

Published by arrangement with Simon & Schuster, Inc.

PRINTED IN THE UNITED STATES OF AMERICA

All rights reserved including the right of reproduction in whole or in part in any form.

FOR THEM ALL

MAPS BY RAFAEL PALACIOS

The photographs in this book are from the collection of the author, who gratefully acknowledges the assistance of the Imperial War Museum in London, the U.S. Department of Defense, the Dutch Historical Military Archives, the Dutch Municipal Archives, and the many individuals who provided photographs of events and themselves.

CONTENTS

✸

CONTENTS

8

On the narrow corridor that would carry the armored drive, there were five major bridges to take. They had to be seized intact by airborne assault. It was the fifth, the crucial bridge over the Lower Rhine at a place called Arnhem, sixty-four miles behind the German lines, that worried Lieutenant General Frederick Browning, Deputy Commander, First Allied Airborne Army. Pointing to the Arnhem bridge on the map he asked, "How long will it take the armor to reach us?" Field Marshal Montgomery replied briskly, "Two days." Still looking at the map, Browning said, "We can hold it for four." Then he added, "But, sir, I think we might be going a bridge too far."

> The final conference at Montgomery's Head-
> quarters on Operation Market-Garden, Sep-
> tember 10, 1944, as recalled by participants.
> The quotes come from Major General Roy E.
> Urquhart's memoirs, *Arnhem*.

FOREWORD

OPERATION MARKET-GARDEN

September 17–24, 1944

Shortly after 10 A.M. on Sunday, September 17, 1944, from airfields all over southern England the greatest armada of troop-carrying aircraft ever assembled for a single operation took to the air. In this, the 263rd week of World War II, the Supreme Allied Commander, General Dwight David Eisenhower, unleashed Market-Garden, one of the most daring and imaginative operations of the war. Surprisingly, Market-Garden, a combined airborne and ground offensive, was authored by one of the most cautious of all the Allied commanders, Field Marshal Bernard Law Montgomery.

Market, the airborne phase of the operation, was monumental: it involved almost five thousand fighters, bombers, transports and more than 2500 gliders. That Sunday afternoon, at exactly 1:30 P.M., in an unprecedented daylight assault, an entire Allied airborne army, complete with vehicles and equipment, began dropping behind the German lines. The target for this bold and historic invasion from the sky: Nazi-occupied Holland.

On the ground, poised along the Dutch-Belgian border, were the Garden forces, massed tank columns of the British Second Army. At 2:35 P.M., preceded by artillery and led by swarms of rocket-firing fighters, the tanks began a dash up the backbone of Holland along a strategic route the paratroopers were already fighting to capture and hold open.

Montgomery's ambitious plan was designed to sprint the troops and tanks through Holland, springboard across the Rhine and into Germany itself. Operation Market-Garden, Montgomery reasoned, was the lightning stroke needed to topple the Third Reich and effect the end of the war in 1944.

Part One

✿

THE RETREAT

✿

1 ✺

In the thousand-year-old Dutch village of Driel, people listened intently. Even before dawn, restless sleepers woke and lights came on behind shuttered windows. Initially there was only a sense of something unaccountable taking place somewhere beyond the immediate, physical surroundings. Gradually vague impressions took form. In the far distance came a muted, continuous mutter.

Barely audible, but persistent, the sound reached the village in waves. Unable to identify the subtle noise, many listened instinctively for some change in the flow of the nearby Lower Rhine. In Holland, half of which lies below sea level, water is the constant enemy, dikes the major weapon in a never-ending battle that has gone on since before the eleventh century. Driel, sitting in a great bend of the Lower Rhine, southwest of Arnhem, capital of Gelderland, has an ever-present reminder of the struggle. A few hundred yards to the north, protecting the village and the region from the restless 400-yard-wide river, a massive dike, topped by a road, rises at places more than twenty feet high. But this morning the river gave no cause for alarm. The Neder Rijn swept peacefully toward the North Sea at its customary speed of two miles per hour. The sounds reverberating off the stone face of the protective dike came from another, far more ruthless, enemy.

As the sky lightened and the sun began to burn off the mist, the commotion grew louder. From roads due east of Driel the villagers could clearly hear the sound of traffic—traffic that seemed to grow heavier by the minute. Now their uneasiness turned to alarm, for there was no doubt about the identity of the movement: in this fifth year of World War II and after fifty-one months of Nazi occupation, everyone recognized the rumble of German convoys.

Even more alarming was the size of the procession. Some people later recalled that only once before had they heard such a flow of traffic—in May, 1940, when the Germans had invaded the Netherlands. At that time, swarming across the Reich frontier ten to fifteen miles from Driel, Hitler's mechanized armies had reached the main highways and spread swiftly throughout the country. Now, over those same roads convoys seemed once more to be moving endlessly.

Strange sounds came from the nearest main road—a two-lane highway connecting Arnhem, on the northern bank of the Lower Rhine, with the eighth-century city of Nijmegen, on the broad river Waal, eleven miles to the south. Against the low background throb of engines, people could plainly identify individual noises which seemed curiously out of place in a military convoy—the scrape of wagon wheels, the whir of countless bicycles and the slow, unpaced shuffling of feet.

What kind of convoy could this be? And, more important, where was it heading? At this moment in the war Holland's future could well depend on the answer to that question. Most people believed the convoys carried heavy reinforcements—either pouring into the country to bolster the German garrison or rushing south to halt the Allied advance. Allied troops had liberated northern France with spectacular speed. Now they were fighting in Belgium and were said to be close to the capital, Brussels, less than one hundred miles away. Rumors persisted that powerful Allied armored units were driving for the Dutch border. But no one in Driel could tell for sure exactly the direction the convoys were taking. Distance and the diffusion of sound made that impossible. And because of the nightly curfew the villagers were unable to leave their houses to investigate.

Plagued by uncertainty, they could only wait. They could not know that shortly before dawn the three young soldiers who constituted little Driel's entire German garrison had left the village on stolen bicycles and pedaled off into the mist. There was no longer any military authority in the village to enforce the curfew regulations.

Unaware, people kept to their homes. But the more curious among them were too impatient to wait and decided to risk using the telephone. In her home at 12 Honingveldsestraat, next to her family's jam-and-preserves factory, young Cora Baltussen called friends in Arnhem. She could scarcely believe their eyewitness report. The convoys were *not* heading south to the western front. On this misty morning, September 4, 1944, the Germans and their supporters appeared to be fleeing from Holland, traveling in anything that would move.

The fighting that everyone had expected, Cora thought, would now pass them by. She was wrong. For the insignificant village of Driel, untouched until now, the war had only begun.

2 ✻

FIFTY MILES SOUTH, in towns and villages close to the Belgian border, the Dutch were jubilant. They watched incredulously as the shattered remnants of Hitler's armies in northern France and Belgium streamed past their windows. The collapse seemed infectious; besides military units, thousands of German civilians and Dutch Nazis were pulling out. And for these fleeing forces all roads seemed to lead to the German border.

Because the withdrawal began so slowly—a trickle of staff cars and vehicles crossing the Belgian frontier—few Dutch could tell exactly when it had started. Some believed the retreat began on September 2; others, the third. But by the fourth, the movement of the Germans and their followers had assumed the characteristics of a rout, a frenzied exodus that reached its peak on September 5, a day later to be known in Dutch history as *Dolle Dinsdag*, "Mad Tuesday."

Panic and disorganization seemed to characterize the German flight. Every kind of conveyance was in use. Thronging the roads from the Belgian border north to Arnhem and beyond were trucks, buses, staff cars, half-track vehicles, armored cars, horse-drawn farm carts and civilian automobiles running on charcoal or wood. Everywhere throughout the disorderly convoys were swarms of tired, dusty soldiers on hastily commandeered bicycles.

There were even more bizarre forms of transportation. In the town of Valkenswaard, a few miles north of the Belgian frontier, people saw heavily laden German troopers laboriously pushing along on children's scooters. Sixty miles away, in Arnhem, crowds standing on the Amsterdamseweg watched as a massive black-and-silver hearse pulled by two plodding farm horses passed slowly by. Crowded in the casket space in back were a score of disheveled, exhausted Germans.

Trudging in these wretched convoys were German soldiers from many units. There were Panzer troops, minus tanks, in their black battle suits; Luftwaffe men, presumably all that remained of German air force units that had been shattered in either France or Belgium; Wehrmacht soldiers from a score of divisions; and Waffen SS troops, their skull-and-crossbones insignia a macabre identification. Looking at these apparently leaderless, dazed troops moving aimlessly along, young Wilhelmina Coppens in St. Oedenrode thought that "most of them had no idea where they were or even where they were going." Some soldiers, to the bitter amusement of Dutch bystanders, were so disoriented that they asked for directions to the German frontier.

In the industrial town of Eindhoven, home of the giant Philips electrical works, the population had heard the low sound of artillery fire from Belgium for days. Now, watching the dregs of the beaten German army thronging the roads, people expected Allied troops to arrive within hours. So did the Germans. It appeared to Frans Kortie, twenty-four-year-old employee in the town's finance department, that these troops had no intention of making a stand. From the nearby airfield came the roar of explosions as engineers blew up runways, ammunition dumps, gasoline storage tanks and hangars; and through a pall of smoke drifting across the town, Kortie saw squads of troops rapidly working to dismantle heavy antiaircraft guns on the roofs of the Philips buildings.

All through the area, from Eindhoven north to the city of Nijmegen, German engineers were hard at work. In the Zuid Willemsvaart Canal running below the town of Veghel, Cornelis de Visser, an elementary-school teacher, saw a heavily loaded barge blown skyward, shooting out airplane engine parts like a deadly rain of shrapnel. Not far away, in the village of Uden, Johannes de Groot, forty-five-year-old car-body builder, was watching the retreat with his family when Germans set fire to a former Dutch barracks barely 300 yards from his home. Minutes later heavy bombs stored in the building exploded, killing four of de Groot's children, aged five to eighteen.

In places such as Eindhoven, where school buildings were set ablaze, fire brigades were prevented from operating and whole blocks were burned down. Still, the sappers, in contrast to the fleeing columns on the roads, gave evidence of following some definite plan.

The most frantic and confused among the escapees were the civilians, German, Dutch, Belgian and French Nazis. They got no sympathy from the Dutch. To farmer Johannes Hulsen at St. Oedenrode, they looked "scared stiff"; and they had reason to be, he thought with satisfaction, for with the Allies "snapping at their heels these traitors knew it was *Bijltjesdag* ['Hatchet Day']."

The frantic flight of Dutch Nazis and German civilians had been triggered by the *Reichskommissar* in Holland, the notorious fifty-two-year-old Dr. Arthur Seyss-Inquart, and by the ambitious and brutal Dutch Nazi Party leader, Anton Mussert. Nervously watching the fate of the Germans in France and Belgium, Seyss-Inquart on September 1 ordered the evacuation of German civilians to the east of Holland, closer to the Reich border. The fifty-year-old Mussert followed suit, alerting members of his Dutch Nazi Party. Seyss-Inquart and Mussert were themselves among the first to leave: they moved from The Hague east to Apeldoorn, fifteen miles north of Arnhem.° Mussert rushed his family even closer to the Reich, moving them into the frontier region at Twente, in the province of Overijssel. At first most of the German and Dutch civilians moved at a leisurely pace. Then a sequence of events produced bedlam. On September 3 the British captured Brussels. The next day Antwerp fell. Now, British tanks and troops were only miles from the Dutch border.

On the heels of these stunning victories, the aged Queen of the Netherlands, Wilhelmina, told her people in a radio broadcast from London that liberation was at hand. She announced that her son-in-law, His Royal Highness Prince Bernhard, had been named Commander in Chief of the Netherlands Forces and would also assume leadership of all underground resistance groups. These factions, comprising three distinct organizations ranging politically from the left to the extreme right, would now be grouped together and officially known as *Binnenlandse Strijdkrachten* (Forces of the Interior). The thirty-three-year-old Prince Bernhard, husband of Princess Juliana, heir to the throne, followed the Queen's announcement with one of his own. He asked the underground to have armlets ready "displaying in distinct letters the word 'Orange,'" but not to use them "without my order." He warned them to "refrain in the enthusiasm of the moment from premature and independent actions, for these would compromise yourselves and the military operations underway."

° Seyss-Inquart was terrified. At Apeldoorn, he took to his underground headquarters—a massive concrete and brick bunker constructed at a cost of more than $250,000—complete with conference rooms, communications and personal suites. It still exists. Scratched on the concrete exterior near the entrance are the figures "6 1/4," the nickname for the hated commissioner. The Netherlanders couldn't resist it; in Dutch, Seyss-Inquart and "6 1/4" sound almost the same—*zes en een kwart*.

Next, a special message was broadcast from General Dwight D. Eisenhower, Supreme Commander of the Allied Forces, confirming that freedom was imminent. "The hour of liberation the Netherlands have awaited so long is now very near," he promised. And within a few hours these broadcasts were followed by the most optimistic statement of all, from the prime minister of the Dutch government in exile, Pieter S. Gerbrandy. He told his listeners, "Now that the Allied armies, in their irresistible advance, have crossed the Netherlands frontier . . . I want all of you to bid our Allies a hearty welcome to our native soil. . . ."

The Dutch were hysterical with joy, and the Dutch Nazis fled for their lives. Anton Mussert had long boasted that his party had more than 50,000 Nazis. If so, it seemed to the Dutch that they all took to the roads at the same time. In scores of towns and villages all over Holland, Nazi-appointed mayors and officials suddenly bolted—but often not before demanding back pay. The mayor of Eindhoven and some of his officials insisted on their salaries. The town clerk, Gerardus Legius, thought their posture ridiculous, but he didn't even feel badly about paying them off. Watching them scurry out of town "on everything with wheels" he wondered: "How far can they get? Where can they go?" There was also a run on the banks. When Nicolaas van de Weerd, twenty-four-year-old bank clerk, got to work in the town of Wageningen on Monday, September 4, he saw a queue of Dutch Nazis waiting outside the bank. Once the doors were opened they hurriedly closed accounts and emptied safety deposit boxes.

Railway stations were overrun by terrified civilians. Trains leaving for Germany were crammed to capacity. Stepping off a train on its arrival in Arnhem, young Frans Wiessing was engulfed by a sea of people fighting to get aboard. So great was the rush that after the train left, Wiessing saw a mountain of luggage lying abandoned on the platform. In the village of Zetten, west of Nijmegen, student Paul van Wely watched as Dutch Nazis crowding the railroad station waited all day for a Germany-bound train, which never arrived. Women and children were crying and to Van Wely "the waiting room looked like a junk store full of tramps." In every town there were similar incidents. Dutch collaborators fled on anything that would move. Municipal architect Willem Tiemans, from his office window near the great Arnhem bridge, watched as Dutch Nazis "scrambled like mad" to get onto a barge heading up the Rhine for the Reich.

Hour after hour the traffic mounted, and even during darkness it went on. So desperate were the Germans to reach safety that on the nights of September 3 and 4, in total disregard of Allied air attacks, soldiers set up searchlights at some crossroads and many overloaded vehicles crawled by, headlights blazing. German officers seemed to have lost control. Dr. Anton Laterveer, a general practitioner in Arnhem, saw soldiers throwing away rifles —some even tried to sell their weapons to the Dutch. Joop Muselaars, a teen-ager, watched a lieutenant attempt to stop a virtually empty army vehicle, but the driver, ignoring the command, drove on through. Furious, the officer fired his pistol irrationally into the cobblestones.

Everywhere soldiers tried to desert. In the village of Eerde, Adrianus Marinus, an eighteen-year-old clerk, noticed a soldier jumping off a truck. He ran toward a farm and disappeared. Later Marinus learned that the soldier was a Russian prisoner of war who had been conscripted into the Wehrmacht. Two miles from Nijmegen, in the village of Lent on the northern bank of the Waal, Dr. Frans Huygen, while making his rounds, saw troops begging for civilian clothing, which the villagers refused. In Nijmegen deserters were not so abject. In many cases they demanded clothing at gunpoint. The Reverend Wilhelmus Peterse, forty-year-old Carmelite, saw soldiers hurriedly remove uniforms, change to suits and set off on foot for the German border. "The Germans were totally fed up with the war," recalls Garrit Meme-link, Arnhem's Chief Forestry Inspector. "They were doing their damnedest to evade the military police."

With officers losing control, discipline broke down. Unruly gangs of soldiers stole horses, wagons, cars and bicycles. Some ordered farmers at gunpoint to haul them in their wagons toward Germany. All through the convoys the Dutch saw trucks, farm wagons, hand carts—even perambulators pushed by fleeing troops—piled high with loot filched from France, Belgium and Luxembourg. It ranged from statuary and furniture to lingerie. In Nijmegen soldiers tried to sell sewing machines, rolls of cloth, paintings, typewriters—and one soldier even offered a parrot in a large cage.

Among the retreating Germans there was no shortage of alcohol. Barely five miles from the German border in the town of Groesbeek, Father Herman Hoek watched horse-drawn carts loaded down with large quantities of wines and liquors. In Arnhem, the Reverend Reinhold Dijker spotted boisterous Wehrmacht troops on a truck drinking from a huge vat of wine which they had apparently brought all the way from France. Sixteen-year-old Agatha Schulte, daughter of the chief pharmacist of Arnhem's municipal hospital, was convinced that most of the soldiers she saw were drunk. They were throwing handfuls of French and Belgian coins to the youngsters and trying to sell bottles of wine, champagne and cognac to the adults. Her mother, Hendrina Schulte, vividly recalls seeing a German truck carrying another kind of booty. It was a large double bed—and in the bed was a woman.°

Besides the columns straggling up from the south, heavy German and civilian traffic was coming in from western Holland and the coast. It flooded through Arnhem and headed east for Germany. In the prosperous Arnhem suburb of Oosterbeek, Jan Voskuil, a thirty-eight-year-old chemical engineer, was hiding out at the home of his father-in-law. Learning that he was on a list of Dutch hostages to be arrested by the Germans, he had fled from his home in the town of Geldermalsen, twenty miles away, bringing his wife, Bertha, and their nine-year-old son. He had arrived in Oosterbeek just in time to see the evacuation. Jan's

---

° "Scenes were witnessed which nobody would ever have deemed possible in the German army," writes Walter Goerlitz, the German historian, in his *History of the German General Staff.* "Naval troops marched northward without weapons, selling their spare uniforms . . . They told people that the war was over and they were going home. Lorries loaded with officers, their mistresses and large quantities of champagne and brandy contrived to get get back as far as the Rhineland, and it was necessary to set up special courts-martial to deal with such cases."

father-in-law told him not to "worry anymore about the Germans; you won't have to 'dive' now." Looking down the main street of Oosterbeek, Voskuil saw "utter confusion." There were dozens of German-filled trucks, nose-to-tail, "all dangerously overloaded." He saw soldiers "on bicycles, pedaling furiously, with suitcases and grips looped over their handlebars." Voskuil was sure that the war would be over in a matter of days.

In Arnhem itself, Jan Mijnhart, sexton of the Grote Kerk—the massive fifteenth-century Church of St. Eusebius with a famed 305-foot-high tower—saw the *Moffen* (a Dutch nickname for the Germans, equivalent to the English "Jerry") filing through the town "four abreast in the direction of Germany." Some looked old and sick. In the nearby village of Ede an aged German begged young Rudolph van der Aa to notify his family in Germany that they had met. "I have a bad heart," he added, "and probably won't live much longer." Lucianus Vroemen, a teen-ager in Arnhem, noticed the Germans were exhausted and had "no fighting spirit or pride left." He saw officers trying, with little or no success, to restore order among the disorganized soldiers. They did not even react to the Dutch, who were yelling, "Go home! The British and Americans will be here in a few hours."

Watching the Germans moving east from Arnhem, Dr. Pieter de Graaff, forty-four-year-old surgeon, was sure he was seeing "the end, the apparent collapse of the German army." And Suze van Zweden, high-school mathematics teacher, had a special reason to remember this day. Her husband, Johan, a respected and well-known sculptor, had been in Dachau concentration camp since 1942 for hiding Dutch Jews. Now he might soon be freed, for obviously the war was nearly over. Suze was determined to witness this historic moment—the departure of the Germans and the arrival of the Allied liberators. Her son Robert was too young to realize what was happening but she decided to take her daughter Sonja, aged nine, into town. As she dressed Sonja, Suze said, "This is something you have to see. I want you to try and remember it all your life."

Everywhere the Dutch rejoiced. Dutch flags made their appearance. Enterprising merchants sold orange buttons and large stocks of ribbon to the eager crowds. In the village of Renkum there was a run on the local drapery shop, where manager Johannes Snoek sold orange ribbon as fast as he could cut it. To his amazement, villagers fashioned bows then and there and proudly pinned them on. Johannes, who was a member of the underground, thought "this was going a bit too far." To protect the villagers from their own excesses, he stopped selling the ribbon. His sister Maria, caught up in the excitement, noted happily in her diary that there was "a mood in the streets almost as though it was *Koninginnedag*, the Queen's birthday." Cheering crowds stood on sidewalks yelling, "Long live the Queen!" People sang the "Wilhelmus" (the Dutch national anthem) and "Oranje Boven!" ("Orange Above All!"). Cloaks flying, Sisters Antonia Stranzky and Christine van Dijk from St. Elisabeth's Hospital in Arnhem cycled down to the main square, the Velperplein, where they joined crowds on the terraces of cafés who were sipping coffee and eating potato pancakes as the Germans and Dutch Nazis streamed by.

At St. Canisius Hospital in Nijmegen, Sister M. Dosithèe Symons saw nurses dance with joy in the convent corridors. People brought out long-hidden radios and, while watching the retreat flood by their windows, listened openly for the first time in long months to the special Dutch service, Radio Orange, from London's BBC. So excited by the broadcasts was fruit grower Joannes Hurkx, in St. Oedenrode, that he failed to spot a group of Germans back of his house stealing the family bicycles.

In scores of places schools closed and work came to a halt. Employees at the cigar factories in Valkenswaard promptly left their machines and crowded into the streets. Streetcars stopped running in The Hague, the seat of government. In the capital, Amsterdam, the atmosphere was tense and unreal. Offices closed, and trading ceased on the stock exchange. Military units suddenly disappeared from the main thoroughfares, and the central station was mobbed by Germans and Dutch Nazis. On the outskirts of Amsterdam, Rotterdam and The Hague, crowds carrying flags and flowers stood along main roads leading into the cities—hoping to be the first to see British tanks coming from the south.

Rumors grew with every hour. Many in Amsterdam believed that British troops had already freed The Hague, near the coast about thirty miles to the southwest. In The Hague people thought the great port of Rotterdam, fifteen miles away, had been liberated. Rail travelers got a different story every time their trains stopped. One of them, Henri Peijnenburg, a twenty-five-year-old resistance leader traveling from The Hague to his home in Nijmegen, a distance of less than eighty miles, heard at the beginning of his journey that the British had entered the ancient border city of Maastricht. In Utrecht he was told they had reached Roermond. Then, in Arnhem he was assured that the British had taken Venlo, a few miles from the German border. "When I finally got home," he recalls, "I expected to see the Allies in the streets, but all I saw were the retreating Germans." Peijnenburg felt confused and uneasy.

Others shared his concern—especially the underground high command meeting secretly in The Hague. To them, tensely watching the situation, Holland seemed on the threshold of freedom. Allied tanks could easily slice through the country all the way from the Belgian border to the Zuider Zee. The underground was certain that the "gateway"—through Holland, across the Rhine and into Germany—was wide open.

The resistance leaders knew the Germans had virtually no fighting forces capable of stopping a determined Allied drive. They were almost scornful of the one weak and undermanned division composed of old men guarding coastal defenses (they had been sitting in concrete bunkers since 1940 without firing a shot), and of a number of other low-grade troops, whose combat capabilities were extremely doubtful, among them Dutch SS, scratch garrison troops, convalescents and the medically unfit—these last grouped into units aptly known as "stomach" and "ear" battalions, because most of the men suffered from ulcers or were hard of hearing.

To the Dutch the Allied move seemed obvious, invasion imminent. But its success depended on the speed of British forces driving from the south, and about this the underground high command was puzzled: they were unable to determine the precise extent of the Allied advance.

Checking on the validity of Prime Minister Gerbrandy's statement that Allied troops had already crossed the frontier was no simple matter. Holland was small—only about two thirds the size of Ireland—but it had a dense population of more than nine million, and as a result the Germans had difficulty controlling subversive activity. There were underground cells in every town and village. Still, transmitting information was hazardous. The principal, and most dangerous, method was the telephone. In an emergency, using complicated circuitry, secret lines and coded information, resistance leaders could call all over the country. Thus, on this occasion, underground officials knew within minutes that Gerbrandy's announcement was premature: British troops had not crossed the border.

Other Radio Orange broadcasts further compounded the confusion. Twice in a little more than twelve hours (at 11:45 P.M. on September 4 and again on the morning of September 5) the Dutch Service of the BBC announced that the fortress city of Breda, seven miles from the Dutch-Belgian border, had been liberated. The news spread rapidly. Illegal, secretly printed newspapers promptly prepared liberation editions featuring the "fall of Breda." But the Arnhem regional resistance chief, thirty-eight-year-old Pieter Kruyff, whose group was one of the nation's most highly skilled and disciplined, seriously doubted the Radio Orange bulletin. He had his communications expert Johannes Steinfort, a young telephone-company instrument maker, check the report. Quickly tying in to a secret circuit connecting him with the underground in Breda, Steinfort became one of the first to learn the bitter truth: the city was still in German hands. No one had seen Allied troops, either American or British.

Because of the spate of rumors, many resistance groups hurriedly met to discuss what should be done. Although Prince Bernhard and SHAEF (Supreme Headquarters Allied Expeditionary Forces) had cautioned against a general uprising, some underground members had run out of patience. The time had come, they believed, to directly confront the enemy and thus aid the advancing Allies. It was obvious that the Germans feared a general revolt. In the retreating columns, the underground noted, sentries were now sitting on the fenders of vehicles with rifles and submachine guns at the ready. Undeterred, many resistance men were eager to fight.

In the village of Ede, a few miles northwest of Oosterbeek, twenty-five-year-old Menno "Tony" de Nooy tried to persuade the leader of his group, Bill Wildeboer, to attack. It had long been planned, Tony argued, that the group should take over Ede in the event of an Allied invasion. The barracks at Ede, which had been used to train German marines, were now practically empty. De Nooy wanted to occupy the buildings. The older Wildeboer, a former sergeant major in the Dutch Army, disagreed. "I don't trust this situation," he told them. "The time is not yet ripe. We must wait."

Not all resistance movements were held in check. In Rotterdam, underground members occupied the offices of the water-supply company. Just over the Dutch-Belgian border in the village of Axel, the town hall with its ancient ramparts was seized and hundreds of German soldiers surrendered to the civilian fighters. In many towns Dutch Nazi officials were captured as they tried to bolt. West of Arnhem, in the village of Wolfheze, noted principally for its hospital for the mentally ill, the district police commissioner was seized in his car. He was locked up temporarily in the nearest available quarters, the asylum, for delivery to the British "when they arrived."

These were the exceptions. In general, underground units remained calm. Yet, everywhere they took advantage of the confusion to prepare for the arrival of Allied forces. In Arnhem, Charles Labouchère, forty-two, descendant of an old French family and active in an intelligence unit, was much too busy to bother about rumors. He sat, hour after hour, by the windows of an office in the neighborhood of the Arnhem bridge and, with a number of assistants, watched German units heading east and northeast along the Zevenaar and Zutphen roads toward Germany. It was Labouchère's job to estimate the number of troops and, where possible, to identify the units. The vital information he noted down was sent to Amsterdam by courier and from there via a secret network to London.

In suburban Oosterbeek, young Jan Eijkelhoff, threading his way unobtrusively through the crowds, cycled all over the area, delivering forged food ration cards to Dutchmen hiding out from the Germans. And the leader of one group in Arnhem, fifty-seven-year-old Johannus Penseel, called "the Old One," reacted in the kind of wily manner that had made him a legend among his men. He decided the moment had come to move his arsenal of weapons. Openly, with German troops all about, he and a few hand-picked assistants calmly drove up in a baker's van to the Municipal Hospital, where the weapons were hidden. Quickly wrapping the arms in brown paper they transported the entire cache to Penseel's home, whose basement windows conveniently overlooked the main square. Penseel and his coleader, Toon van Daalen, thought it was a perfect position from which to open fire on the Germans when the time came. They were determined to live up to the name of their militant subdivision—*Landelyke Knokploegen* ("Strong-arm Boys").

Everywhere men and women of the vast underground army poised for battle; and in southern towns and villages, people who believed that parts of Holland were already free ran out of their homes to welcome the liberators. There was a kind of madness in the air, thought Carmelite Father Tiburtius Noordermeer as he observed the joyful crowds in the village of Oss, southeast of Nijmegen. He saw people slapping one another on the back in a congratulatory mood. Comparing the demoralized Germans on the roads with the jubilant Dutch spectators, he noted "wild fear on the one hand and crazy, unlimited, joy on the other." "Nobody," the stolid Dutch priest recalled, "acted normally."

Many grew more anxious as time passed. In the drugstore on the main street in Oosterbeek, Karel de Wit was worried. He told his wife and chief pharmacist, Johanna, that he couldn't understand why Allied planes had not attacked the German traffic. Frans Schulte, a retired Dutch major, thought the general enthusiasm was premature. Although his brother and sister-in-law were overjoyed at what appeared to be a German debacle, Schulte was not convinced. "Things may get worse," he warned. "The Germans are far from beaten. If the Allies try to cross the Rhine, believe me, we may see a major battle."

✵ 3 ✵

Hitler's crucial measures were already underway. On September 4 at the Führer's headquarters deep in the forest of Görlitz, Rastenburg, East Prussia, sixty-nine-year-old Field Marshal Gerd von Rundstedt prepared to leave for the western front. He had not expected a new command.

Called abruptly out of enforced retirement, Von Rundstedt had been ordered to Rastenburg four days before. On July 2, two months earlier, Hitler had fired him as Commander in Chief West (or, as it was known in German military terms, OB West—*Oberbefehlshaber* West) while Von Rundstedt, who had never lost a battle, was trying to cope with the aftermath of Germany's greatest crisis of the war, the Allied invasion of Normandy.

The Führer and Germany's most distinguished soldier had never agreed on how best to meet that threat. Before the invasion, appealing for reinforcements, Von Rundstedt had bluntly informed Hitler's headquarters (OKW—Oberkommando der Wehrmacht)* that the Western Allies, superior in men, equipment and planes, could "land anywhere they want to." Not so, Hitler declared. The Atlantic Wall, the partly completed coastal

* Armed Forces High Command

fortifications which, Hitler boasted, ran almost three thousand miles from Kirkenes (on the Norwegian-Finnish frontier) to the Pyrenees (on the Franco-Spanish border) would make "this front impregnable against any enemy." Von Rundstedt knew only too well that the fortifications were more propaganda than fact. He summed up the Atlantic Wall in one word: "Humbug."

The legendary Field Marshal Erwin Rommel, renowned for his victories in the North African deserts in the first years of the war and sent by Hitler to command Army Group B under Von Rundstedt, was equally appalled by the Führer's confidence. To Rommel, the coastal defenses were a "figment of Hitler's *Wolkenkuckkucksheim* [cloud cuckoo land]." The aristocratic, tradition-bound Von Rundstedt and the younger, ambitious Rommel found themselves, probably for the first time, in agreement. On another point, however, they clashed. With the crushing defeat of his Afrika Korps by Britain's Montgomery at El Alamein in 1942 always in his mind, and well aware of what the Allied invasion would be like, Rommel believed that the invaders must be stopped on the beaches. Von Rundstedt icily disagreed with his junior—whom he sarcastically referred to as the "Marschall Bubi" ("Marshal Laddie"); Allied troops should be wiped out *after* they landed, he contended. Hitler backed Rommel. On D Day, despite Rommel's brilliant improvisations, Allied troops breached the "impregnable" wall within hours.

In the terrible days that followed, overwhelmed by the Allies, who enjoyed almost total air supremacy over the Normandy battlefield, and shackled by Hitler's "no withdrawal" orders ("Every man shall fight and fall where he stands"), Von Rundstedt's straining lines cracked everywhere. Desperately he plugged the gaps, but hard as his men fought and counterattacked, the outcome was never seriously in doubt. Von Rundstedt could neither "drive the invaders into the sea" nor "annihilate them" (the words were Hitler's).

On the night of July 1, at the height of the Normandy battle, Hitler's chief of staff, Field Marshal Wilhelm Keitel, called Von Rundstedt and plaintively asked, "What shall we do?" Characteristically blunt, Von Rundstedt snapped, "End the war, you fools. What else can you do?" Hitler's comment on hearing the remark was mild. "The old man has lost his nerve and can't master the situation any longer. He'll have to go." Twenty-four hours later, in a polite handwritten note, Hitler informed Von Rundstedt that, "in consideration of your health and of the increased exertions to be expected in the near future," he was relieved of command.

Von Rundstedt, the senior and most dependable field marshal in the Wehrmacht, was incredulous. For the five years of war his military genius had served the Third Reich well. In 1939, when Hitler cold-bloodedly attacked Poland, thereby igniting the conflict that eventually engulfed the world, Von Rundstedt had clearly demonstrated the German formula for conquest—*Blitzkrieg* ("lightning war")—when his Panzer spearheads reached the outskirts of Warsaw in less than a week. One year later, when Hitler turned west and with devastating speed overwhelmed most of western Europe, Von Rundstedt was in charge of an entire Panzer army. And in 1941 he was in the forefront again when Hitler attacked Russia. Now, outraged at the jeopardy to his career and reputation, Von Rundstedt told his chief of staff, Major General Gunther Blumentritt, that he had been "dismissed in disgrace by an amateur strategist." That "Bohemian corporal," he fumed, had used "my age and ill health as an excuse to relieve me in order to have a scapegoat." Given a free hand, Von Rundstedt had planned a slow withdrawal to the German frontier, during which, as he outlined his plans to Blumentritt, he would have "exacted a terrible price for every foot of ground given up." But, as he had said to his staff many times, because of the constant "tutelage from above," about the only authority he had as OB West was "to change the guard in front of the gate."°

From the moment of his recall and his arrival at the end of

° "Von Rundstedt was hurt by the implication in Hitler's letter that he had 'requested' relief," the late General Blumentritt told me in an interview. "Some of us at Headquarters actually thought he had, but this was not so. Von Rundstedt denied that he had ever asked to be relieved—or that he had ever thought of doing so. He was extremely angry—so angry in fact that he swore he would never again take a command under Hitler. I knew he did not mean it for, to Von Rundstedt, military obedience was unconditional and absolute."

August at the Rastenburg *Wolfsschanze* ("Wolf's Lair"), as it was named by Hitler, Von Rundstedt, at the Führer's invitation, attended the daily briefing conference. Hitler, according to the Deputy Chief of Operations General Walter Warlimont, greeted his senior field marshal warmly, treating him with "unwonted diffidence and respect." Warlimont also noted that throughout the long sessions Von Rundstedt simply sat "motionless and mono-syllabic."° The precise, practical field marshal had nothing to say. He was appalled by the situation.

The briefings clearly showed that in the east the Red Army now held a front more than 1,400 miles long, from Finland in the north to the Vistula in Poland, and from there to the Carpathian Mountains in Rumania and Yugoslavia. In fact, Russian armor had reached the borders of East Prussia, barely a hundred miles from the Führer's headquarters.

In the west Von Rundstedt saw that his worst fears had been realized. Division after division was now destroyed, the entire German line thrown helplessly back. Rear-guard units, although surrounded and cut off, still clung to vital ports such as Dunkirk, Calais, Boulogne, Le Havre, Brest, Lorient and St. Nazaire, forcing the Allies to continue bringing supplies in from the distant invasion beaches. But now, with the sudden, stunning capture of Antwerp, one of Europe's greatest deep seaports, the Allies might well have solved their supply problem. Von Rundstedt noted, too, that the tactic of *Blitzkrieg*, perfected by himself and others, was being borrowed with devastating effect by Eisenhower's armies. And Field Marshal Walter Model, the fifty-four-year-old new Commander in Chief, West (he took over on August 17), was clearly unable to bring order out of the chaos. His front had been ripped apart, slashed in the north by tanks of the British Second Army and the U.S. First Army driving through Belgium toward Holland; and, south of the Ardennes, armored columns of the U.S. Third Army under General George S. Patton were heading for Metz and the Saar. To Von Rundstedt the situation was no longer merely ominous. It was cataclysmic.

° Warlimont, *Inside Hitler's Headquarters, 1939–45*, p. 477.

THE FRONT, SEPT. 14, 1944

RHINE R.
Bonn
Arnberg
VON RUNDSTEDT'S OB WEST
Koblenz
MOSEL R.

BLASCOWITZ'S AG G

S A A R
Saarbrücken

GERMAN SEVENTH ARMY
BITTRICH'S II SS PANZER CORPS

S I E G F R I E D   L I N E

Trier

MOSELLE R.

Malmédy
Liège
Bastogne

HODGES' U.S. FIRST ARMY
MEUSE R.

BRADLEY'S U.S. 12TH AG

Luxembourg

Metz

PATTON'S U.S. THIRD ARMY

Verdun
MEUSE R.

F R A N C E

Reims
N
Paulacias
Miles
50
0

He had time to dwell on the inevitability of the end. Almost four days elapsed before Hitler allowed Von Rundstedt a private audience. During his wait the Field Marshal stayed in the former country inn reserved for senior officers in the center of the vast headquarters—a barbed-wire-enclosed enclave of wooden huts and concrete bunkers built over a catacomb of underground installations. Von Rundstedt vented his impatience at the delay on Keitel, the chief of staff. "Why have I been sent for?" he demanded. "What sort of game is going on?" Keitel was unable to tell him. Hitler had given Keitel no particular reason, short of an innocuous mention of the Field Marshal's health. Hitler seemed to have convinced himself of his own manufactured version for Von Rundstedt's dismissal on "health grounds" back in July. To Keitel, Hitler had merely said, "I want to see if the old man's health has improved."

Twice Keitel reminded the Führer that the Field Marshal was waiting. Finally, on the afternoon of September 4, Von Rundstedt was summoned to Hitler's presence, and, uncharacteristically, the Führer came to the point immediately. "I would like to entrust you once more with the western front."

Stiffly erect, both hands on his gold baton, Von Rundstedt merely nodded. Despite his knowledge and experience, his distaste for Hitler and the Nazis, Von Rundstedt, in whom the Prussian military tradition of devotion to service was ingrained, did not decline the appointment. As he was later to recall, "it would have been useless to protest anyway."[*]

Almost cursorily, Hitler outlined Von Rundstedt's task. Once more Hitler was improvising. Before D Day he had insisted that the Atlantic Wall was invulnerable. Now, to Von Rundstedt's dismay, the Führer stressed the impregnability of the West-wall—the long-neglected, unmanned but still formidable frontier fortifications better known to the Allies as the Siegfried Line.

---

[*] According to Walter Goerlitz, editor of *The Memoirs of Field Marshal Keitel* (Chapter 10, p. 347), Von Rundstedt said to Hitler, "My Führer, whatever you may command, I will do my duty to my last breath." My version of Von Rundstedt's reaction is based on the recollections of his former chief of staff, Major General Blumentritt. "I said nothing," Von Rundstedt told him. "If I'd opened my mouth, Hitler would have talked 'at me' for three hours."

Von Rundstedt, Hitler ordered, was not only to stop the Allies as far west as possible, but to counterattack for, as the Führer saw it, the most dangerous Allied threats were no more than "armored spearheads." Clearly, however, Hitler was shaken by the capture of Antwerp. Its vital port was to be denied the Allies at all costs. Thus, since the other ports were still in German hands, Hitler said, he fully expected the Allied drive to come to a halt because of overextended supply lines. He was confident that the western front could be stabilized and, with the coming of winter, the initiative regained. Hitler assured Von Rundstedt that he was "not unduly worried about the situation in the west."

It was a variation of a monologue Von Rundstedt had heard many times in the past. The Westwall, to Hitler, had now become an *idée fixe*, and Von Rundstedt once again was being ordered "not to give an inch," and "to hold under all conditions."

By ordering Von Rundstedt to replace Field Marshal Model, Hitler was making his third change of command of OB West within two months—from Von Rundstedt to Field Marshal Gunther von Kluge, to Model, and now once again to Von Rundstedt. Model, in the job just eighteen days, would now command only Army Group B under Von Rundstedt, Hitler said. Von Rundstedt had long regarded Model with less than enthusiasm. Model, he felt, had not earned his promotion the hard way; he had been elevated to the rank of field marshal too quickly by Hitler. Von Rundstedt thought him better suited to the job of a "good regimental sergeant major." Still, the Field Marshal felt that Model's position made little difference now. The situation was all but hopeless, defeat inevitable. On the afternoon of September 4, as he set out for his headquarters near Koblenz, Von Rundstedt saw nothing to stop the Allies from invading Germany, crossing the Rhine and ending the war in a matter of weeks.

On this same day in Wannsee, Berlin, Colonel General Kurt Student, fifty-four-year-old founder of Germany's airborne forces, emerged from the backwater to which he had been relegated for three long years. For him, the war had begun with great promise. His paratroops, Student felt, had been chiefly responsible for the capture of Holland in 1940, when some 4,000 of them dropped on the bridges of Rotterdam, Dordrecht and Moerdijk, holding the vital spans open for the main German invasion force. Student's losses had been incredibly low—only 180 men. But the situation was different in the 1941 airborne assault of Crete. There, losses were so high—more than a third of the 22,000-man force—that Hitler forbade all future airborne operations. "The day of parachute troops is over," the Führer said, and the future had dimmed for Student. Ever since, the ambitious officer had been tied to a desk job as commander of an airborne-training establishment, while his elite troopers were used strictly as infantry. With shattering abruptness, at precisely 3 P.M. on this critical September 4, Student emerged into the mainstream once again. In a brief telephone call, Colonel General Alfred Jodl, Hitler's operations chief, ordered him to immediately organize an army, which the Führer had designated as the "First Parachute Army." As the astounded Student listened, it occurred to him that "it was a rather high-sounding title for a force that didn't exist."

Student's troopers were scattered all over Germany, and apart from a few seasoned, fully equipped units, they were green recruits armed only with training weapons. His force of about ten thousand had almost no transportation, armor or artillery. Student didn't even have a chief of staff.

Nevertheless, Student's men, Jodl explained, were urgently needed in the west. They were to "close a gigantic hole" between Antwerp and the area of Liège-Maastricht by "holding a line along the Albert Canal." With all possible speed, Student was ordered to rush his forces to Holland and Belgium. Weapons and equipment would be issued at the "railheads of destination." Besides his paratroopers, two divisions had been earmarked for his new "army." One of them, the 719th, Student soon learned, was "made up of old men stationed along the Dutch coast who had not as yet fired a single shot." His second division, the 176th, was even worse. It consisted of "semi-invalids and convalescents who, for convenience, had been grouped together in separate battalions according to their various ailments." They even had special "diet" kitchens for those suffering from stomach trouble. Besides these units, he would get a grab bag of other forces scattered in Holland and Belgium—Luftwaffe troops, sailors and antiaircraft crews—and twenty-five tanks. To Student, the expert in paratroop warfare and supertrained airborne shock troops, his makeshift army was a "grotesque improvisation on a grand scale." Still, he was back in the war again.

All through the afternoon, by telephone and teletype, Student mustered and moved his men out. It would take at least four days for his entire force to reach the front, he estimated. But his toughest and best troops, rushed in special trains to Holland in what Student called a "blitz move," would be in position on the Albert Canal, as part of Model's Army Group B, within twenty-four hours.

Jodl's call and the information he himself had since gathered alarmed Student. It seemed apparent that his most seasoned group—the 6th Parachute Regiment plus one other battalion, together totaling about three thousand men—probably constituted the only combat-ready reserve in the whole of Germany. He found the situation ominous.

Frantically, Field Marshal Walter Model, Commander in Chief, West, tried to plug the yawning gap east of Antwerp and halt the disorderly retreat from Belgium into Holland. As yet no news of Von Rundstedt's appointment as his successor had reached him. His forces were so entangled, so disorganized that Model had all but lost control. He no longer had contact with the second half of his command, Army Group G in the south. Had General Johannes Blaskowitz, its commander, successfully withdrawn from France?

Model wasn't sure. To the harassed Field Marshal the predicament of Army Group G was secondary. The crisis was clearly in the north.

With dispatch and ferocity, Army Group B had been split in two by armored columns of the British and Americans. Of the two armies composing Army Group B, the Fifteenth was bottled up, its back to the North Sea, roughly between Calais and a point northwest of Antwerp. The Seventh Army had been almost destroyed, and thrown back toward Maastricht and Aachen. Between the two armies lay a 75-mile gap and the British had driven through it straight to Antwerp. Plunging along the same route were Model's own demoralized, retreating forces.

In a desperate effort to halt their flight, Model issued an emotional plea to his troops.

. . . With the enemy's advance and the withdrawal of our front, several hundred thousand soldiers are falling back—army, air force and armored units—troops which must re-form as planned and hold in new strong points or lines.

In this stream are the remnants of broken units which, for the moment, have no set objectives and are not even in a position to receive clear orders. Whenever orderly columns turn off the road to reorganize, streams of disorganized elements push on. With their wagons move whispers, rumors, haste, endless disorder and vicious self-interest. This atmosphere is being brought back to the rear areas, infecting units still intact and in this moment of extreme tension must be prevented by the strongest means.

I appeal to your honor as soldiers. We have lost a battle, but I assure you of this: We will win this war! I cannot tell you more at the present, although I know that questions are burning on your lips. Whatever has happened, never lose your faith in the future of Germany. At the same time you must be aware of the gravity of the situation. This moment will and should separate men from weaklings. Now every soldier has the same responsibility. When his commander falls, he must be ready to step into his shoes and carry on . . .

There followed a long series of instructions in which Model "categorically" demanded that retreating troops should immediately "report to the nearest command point," instill in others "confidence, self-reliance, self-control and optimism," and repudiate "stupid gossip, rumors and irresponsible reports." The enemy, he said, was "not everywhere at once" and, indeed, "if all the tanks reported by rumormongers were counted, there would have to be a hundred thousand of them." He begged his men not to give up important positions or demolish equipment, weapons or installations "before it is necessary." The astonishing document wound up by stressing that everything depended on "gaining time, which the Führer needs to put new weapons and new troops into operation."

Virtually without communications, depending for the most part on radio, Model could only hope that his Order of the Day reached all his troops. In the confusion he was not even sure of the latest position of his disorganized and shattered units; nor did he know precisely how far Allied tanks and troops had advanced. And where was the *Schwerpunkt* (main thrust) of the Allied drive—with the British and Americans in the north heading for the Siegfried Line and thence across the Rhine and into the Ruhr? Was it with Patton's massive U.S. Third Army driving for the Saar, the Siegfried Line and over the Rhine into Frankfurt?

Model's dilemma was the outgrowth of a situation that had occurred nearly two months earlier at the time of Von Rundstedt's dismissal and Hitler's swift appointment of Von Kluge as the old Field Marshal's successor. On sick leave for months from his command in Russia, Von Kluge happened to be making a courtesy call on the Führer at the precise moment when Hitler decided to dismiss Von Rundstedt. With no preamble, and possibly because Von Kluge happened to be the only senior officer in sight, Hitler had named the astonished Von Kluge Commander in Chief, West.

Von Kluge, a veteran front commander, took over on July 4. He was to last forty-four days. Exactly as predicted by Von Rundstedt, the Allied breakout occurred. "The whole western front has been ripped open," Von Kluge informed Hitler. Overwhelmed by the Allied tide pouring across France, Von Kluge, like Von

Rundstedt before him, found his hands tied by Hitler's insistent "no withdrawal" orders. The German armies in France were encircled and all but destroyed. It was during this period that another convulsion racked the Third Reich—an abortive assassination attempt on Hitler's life.

During one of the endless conferences at the Führer's headquarters, a time bomb in a briefcase, placed by Colonel Claus Graf von Stauffenberg beneath a table close to Hitler, exploded, killing and wounding many in the room. The Führer escaped with minor injuries. Although only a small elite group of officers were involved in the plot, Hitler's revenge was barbaric. Anyone connected with the plotters, or with their families, was arrested; and many individuals, innocent or not, were summarily executed.° Some five thousand people lost their lives. Von Kluge had been indirectly implicated, and Hitler also suspected him of trying to negotiate a surrender with the enemy. Von Kluge was replaced by Model and ordered to report immediately to the Führer. Before leaving his headquarters the despairing Von Kluge wrote a letter to Hitler. Then, en route to Germany, he took poison.

When you receive these lines I shall be no more [he wrote to the Führer]. *. . . I did everything within my power to be equal to the situation . . . Both Rommel and I, and probably all the other commanders here in the west with experience of battle against the Anglo-Americans, with their preponderance of material, foresaw the present developments. We were not listened to. Our appreciations were not dictated by pessimism, but from sober knowledge of the facts. I do not know whether Field Marshal Model, who has been proved in every sphere, will master the situation. From my heart I hope so. Should it not be so, however, and your new weapons . . . not succeed, then, my Führer, make up your mind to end the war. It is time to put an end to this frightfulness. . . . I have always admired your greatness . . . and*

° Hitler took advantage of his most senior officer, Von Rundstedt, once again by making him President of the Court of Honor that passed judgment on the officers suspected. Von Rundstedt quietly acceded to the Führer's request. "If I had not," he later explained, "I too might have been considered a traitor." Von Rundstedt's explanation has never satisfied many of his brother generals, who privately denounced him for bending to Hitler's request.

your iron will . . . Show yourself now also great enough to put an end to this hopeless struggle. . . .

Hitler had no intention of conceding victory to the Allies, even though the Third Reich that he had boasted would last a millennium was undermined and tottering. On every front he was attempting to stave off defeat. Yet each move the Führer made seemed more desperate than the last.

Model's appointment as OB West had not helped. Unlike Von Rundstedt or, briefly, Von Kluge, Model did not have the combat genius of Rommel as support. After Rommel was badly wounded by a strafing Allied plane on July 17, no one had been sent to replace him.° Model did not at first appear to feel the need. Confident that he could right the situation, he took on Rommel's old command as well, becoming not only OB West but also Commander of Army Group B. Despite Model's expertise, the situation was too grave for any one commander.

At this time Army Group B was battling for survival along a line roughly between the Belgian coast and the Franco-Luxembourg border. From there, south to Switzerland, the remainder of Model's command—Army Group G under General Blaskowitz—had already been written off. Following the second Allied invasion on August 15, by French and American forces in the Marseilles area, Blaskowitz' group had hurriedly departed southern France. Under continuous pressure they were now falling back in disarray to the German border.

Along Model's disintegrating northern front, where Allied armor had torn the 75-mile-wide gap in the line, the route from Belgium into Holland and from there across Germany's vulnerable northwest frontier lay open and undefended. Allied forces driving into Holland could outflank the Siegfried Line where the massive belt of fortifications extending along Germany's frontiers from Switzerland terminated at Kleve on the Dutch-German

° Rommel, who was also suspected by Hitler of being involved in the assassination attempt, died three months later. While convalescing at his home, Hitler gave him a choice: stand trial for treason or commit suicide. On October 14, Rommel swallowed cyanide, and Hitler announced that the Reich's most popular field marshal had "died of wounds sustained on the battlefield."

border. By turning this northern tip of Hitler's Westwall and crossing the Rhine, the Allies could swing into the Ruhr, the industrial heart of the Reich. That maneuver might well bring about the total collapse of Germany.

Twice in seventy-two hours Model appealed desperately to Hitler for reinforcements. The situation of his forces in the undefended gap was chaotic. Order had to be restored and the breach closed. Model's latest report, which he had sent to Hitler in the early hours of September 4, warned that the crisis was approaching and unless he received a minimum of "twenty-five fresh divisions and an armored reserve of five or six panzer divisions," the entire front might collapse, thereby opening the "gateway into northwest Germany."

Model's greatest concern was the British entry into Antwerp. He did not know whether the huge port, the second-largest in Europe, was captured intact or destroyed by the German garrison. The city of Antwerp itself, lying far inland, was not the crux. To use the port, the Allies needed to control its seaward approach, an inlet 54 miles long and 3 miles wide at its mouth, running into Holland from the North Sea past Walcheren Island and looping alongside the South Beveland peninsula. So long as German guns commanded the Schelde estuary, the port of Antwerp could be denied the Allies.

Unfortunately for Model, apart from antiaircraft batteries and heavy coastal guns on Walcheren Island, he had almost no forces along the northern bank. But on the other side of the Schelde and almost isolated in the Pas de Calais was General Gustav von Zangen's Fifteenth Army—a force of more than 80,000 men. Though pocketed—the sea lay behind them to the north and west, and Canadians and British were pressing in from the south and east—they nevertheless controlled most of the southern bank of the estuary.

By now, Model believed, British tanks, exploiting the situation, would surely be moving along the northern bank and sweeping it clear. Before long the entire South Beveland peninsula could be in their hands and sealed off from the Dutch mainland at its narrow base north of the Belgian border, barely 18 miles from Antwerp. Next, to open the port, the British would turn on the trapped Fifteenth Army and clear the southern bank. Von Zangen's forces had to be extricated.

Late in the afternoon of September 4 at Army Group B's headquarters southeast of Liège in the village of La Chaude Fontaine, Model issued a series of orders. By radio he commanded Von Zangen to hold the southern bank of the Schelde and reinforce the lesser ports of Dunkirk, Boulogne and Calais, which Hitler had earlier decreed were to be held with "fanatical determination as fortresses." With the remainder of his troops the hapless Von Zangen was to attack northeast into the avalanche of British armor. It was a desperate measure, yet Model saw no other course. If Von Zangen's attack was successful, it might isolate the British in Antwerp and cut off Montgomery's armored spearheads driving north. Even if the attack failed, Von Zangen's effort might buy time, slowing up the Allied drive long enough for reserves to arrive and hold a new front along the Albert Canal.

Exactly what reinforcements were on the way, Model did not know. As darkness fell he finally received Hitler's answer to his pleas for new divisions to stabilize the front. It was the terse news of his replacement as Commander in Chief, West, by Field Marshal von Rundstedt. Von Kluge had lasted forty-four days as OB West, Model barely eighteen. Normally temperamental and ambitious, Model reacted calmly on this occasion. He was more aware of his shortcomings as an administrator than his critics believed.* Now he could concentrate on the job he knew best:

---

* Twice Model informed Hitler of his inability to command both OB West and Army Group B. "We rarely saw him," OB West's Chief of Staff Blumentritt recalled. "Model hated paper work and spent most of his time in the field." Lieutenant General Bodo Zimmermann, OB West's operations chief, wrote after the war (OCMH MS 308, pp. 153–154) that though Model "was a thoroughly capable soldier," he often "demanded too much and that too quickly," hence "losing sight of what was practically possible." He had a tendency to "dissipate his forces," added Zimmermann, and "staff work suffered under his too-frequent absences and erratic, inconsistent demands."

being a front-line commander, solely in charge of Army Group B.
But, among the flurry of frantic orders Model issued on this last
day as OB West, one would prove momentous. It concerned the
relocation of his II SS Panzer Corps.

The commander of the Corps, fifty-year-old Obergruppen-
führer (Lieutenant General) Wilhelm Bittrich, had been out of
touch with Model for more than seventy-two hours. His forces,
fighting almost continuously since Normandy, had been badly
mauled. Bittrich's tank losses were staggering, his men short on
ammunition and fuel. In addition, because of the breakdown of
communications, the few orders he had received by radio were
already out of date when Bittrich got them. Uncertain of the
enemy's movements and badly in need of direction, Bittrich set
out on foot to find Model. He finally located the Field Marshal at
Army Group B headquarters near Liège. "I had not seen him
since the Russian front in 1941," Bittrich later recalled. "Monocle
in his eye, wearing his usual short leather coat, Model was standing looking at a map and snapping out commands one after the
other. There was little time for conversation. Pending official
orders, which would follow, I was told to move my Corps headquarters north into Holland." With all possible speed Bittrich was
directed to "supervise the refitting and rehabilitation of the 9th
and 10th SS Panzer divisions." The battered units, Model told
him, were to "slowly disengage from the battle and immediately
head north."[*]

The almost unknown Bittrich could hardly foresee the critical

---

[*] Understandably perhaps, German records of this period are vague and often
inexplicable. Commands were issued, never received, re-sent, countermanded or
changed. Considerable confusion exists about Model's order. According to Army
Group B's war diary, movement orders for the 9th and 10th SS Panzer divisions
were sent on the night of September 3. If so, they were never received. Also, it
is recorded that Bittrich received his instructions forty-eight hours later to supervise
the regrouping and rehabilitation of not only the 9th but the 2nd and 116th Panzer
units. Curiously, the 10th is not mentioned. I can find no evidence that either the
2nd or 116th ever reached the Arnhem area. (It appears they continued fighting at
the front.) According to Bittrich's own papers and logs, he received Model's orders
orally on September 4 and duly directed only the 9th and 10th to proceed north.
Both units, according to their commanders, began slowly withdrawing on September 5–6.

role his 9th and 10th SS Panzer divisions would play within the next two weeks. The site Model chose for Bittrich was in a quiet zone, at this point some seventy-five miles behind the front. By a historic fluke, the area included the city of Arnhem.

✣ 4 ✣

THE HEADLONG RETREAT of the Germans out of Holland was slowing, although few of the jubilant Dutch realized it as yet. From the Belgian border north to Arnhem, roads were still choked, but there was a difference in the movement. From his post in the Provincial Building above the Arnhem bridge, Charles Labouchère saw no letup in the flood of vehicles, troops and Nazi sympathizers streaming across the bridge. But a few blocks north of Labouchère's location, Gerhardus Gysbers, a seller of antique books, saw a change take place. German troops entering Arnhem from the west were not moving on. The compound of the Willems Barracks next to Gysbers' home and the streets in the immediate vicinity were filling with horse-drawn vehicles and disheveled soldiers. Gysbers noted Luftwaffe battalions, antiaircraft personnel, Dutch SS and elderly men of the 719th Coastal Division. It was clear to Arnhem's resistance chief, Pieter Kruyff, that this was no temporary halt. These troops were not heading back into Germany. They were slowly regrouping; some horse-drawn units of the 719th were starting to move south. Kruyff's chief of intelligence for the Arnhem region, thirty-three-year-old Henri Knap, unobtrusively cycling through the area, spotted the subtle change, too. He was puzzled. He wondered if the optimistic broadcasts from London were false. If so, they were cruel deceptions. Everywhere he saw the Dutch rejoicing. Everyone knew that Montgomery's troops had taken Antwerp. Surely Holland would be liberated within hours. Knap could see the Germans were re-organizing. While they still had little strength, he knew that if the British did not come soon that strength would grow.

In Nijmegen, eleven miles to the south, German military police were closing off roads leading to the German frontier. Elias Broekkamp, a wine importer, saw some troops moving north toward Arnhem, but the majority were being funneled back and traffic was being broken up, processed and fanned out. As in Arnhem, the casual spectator seemed unaware of the difference. Broekkamp observed Dutch civilians laughing and jeering at what they believed to be the Germans' bewildering predicament.

In fact the predicament was growing much less. Nijmegen was turning into a troop staging area, once more in the firm control of German military.

Farther south, in Eindhoven, barely ten miles from the Belgian border, the retreat had all but stopped. In the straggling convoys moving north there were now more Nazi civilians than troops. Frans Kortie, who had seen the Germans dismantling antiaircraft guns on the roofs of the Philips factories, noted a new development. In a railway siding near the station he watched a train pulling flatcars into position. On the cars were heavy antiaircraft guns. Kortie experienced a feeling of dread.

Far more disheartening for observant Dutch was the discovery that reinforcements were coming in from Germany. In Tilburg, Eindhoven, Helmond and Weert, people saw contingents of fresh troops arrive by train. Unloaded quickly and formed up, they set out for the Dutch-Belgian border. They were not regular Wehr-macht soldiers. They were seasoned, well-equipped and disci-plined, and their distinctive helmets and camouflaged smocks instantly identified them as veteran German paratroopers.

❊ 5 ❊

B Y LATE AFTERNOON of September 5 Colonel General Kurt Student's first paratroop formations were digging in at points along the north side of Belgium's Albert Canal. Their haste was almost frantic. Student, on his arrival at noon, had discovered that Model's "new German line" was strictly the 80-foot-wide water barrier itself. Defense positions had not been prepared. There were no strong points, trenches or fortifications. And, to make matters worse for the defenders, Student noted, "almost everywhere the southern bank dominated the northern side." Even the bridges over the canal were still standing. Only now were engineers placing demolition charges. In all the confusion no one apparently had ordered the crossings destroyed.

Nevertheless, Student's timetable was well planned. The "blitz move" of his airborne forces was a spectacular success. "Considering that these paratroopers were rushed in from all over Germany, from Güstrow in Mecklenburg to Bitsch in Lothringen," he later recalled, "and arms and equipment, brought in from still other parts of Germany, were waiting for them at the railheads, the speed of the move was remarkable." Student could only admire "the astonishing precision of the general staff and the entire German organization." Lieutenant General Karl Sievers' 719th Coastal Division had made good time, too. Student was heartened to see their columns heading for positions north of Antwerp "clattering down the roads to the front, their transports and artillery pulled by heavy draft horses."° Hour by hour, his

° Despite the confusion, horse-lover Student took the time to note in his diary that "these huge animals were Clydesdale, Percheron, Danish and Frisian types."

hastily formed First Parachute Army was arriving. Also, by extraordinary good fortune, help had come from a most unexpected source.

The headlong retreat from Belgium into Holland had been slowed and then virtually stopped by the doggedness and ingenuity of one man: Lieutenant General Kurt Chill. Because his 85th Infantry Division was almost totally destroyed, Chill had been ordered to save whatever remained and move back into Germany. But the strong-willed general, watching the near-panic on the roads and prompted by Model's Order of the Day, decided to disregard orders. Chill concluded that the only way to avert catastrophe was to organize a line along the Albert Canal. He welded what remained of his 85th Division with the remnants of two others and quickly dispersed these men to strategic points on the northern bank of the canal. Next, he turned his attention to the bridges and set up "reception centers" at their northern exits. In twenty-four hours Chill succeeded in netting thousands of servicemen from nearly every branch of the German armed forces. It was a "crazy-quilt mob,"* including Luftwaffe mechanics, military-government personnel, naval coastal units and soldiers from a dozen different divisions, but these stragglers, armed at best with rifles, were already on the canal when Student arrived.

Student called Chill's virtuoso performance in halting the near-rout "miraculous." With remarkable speed he had established a defense line of sorts, helping to buy a little time for all of Student's forces to arrive. This would still take several days. Even with the boost from Chill, Student's patchwork First Parachute Army might total at best 18,000–20,000 men, plus some artillery,

---

Contrary to general belief, Hitler's armies, unlike the Allies', were never totally motorized. Even at the pinnacle of German strength more than 50 percent of their transport was horse-drawn.

* Charles B. MacDonald, *The Siegfried Line Campaign*, p. 124. Published in the official U.S. Army History series, MacDonald's volume and Martin Blumenson's *Breakout and Pursuit* together give the most accurate military picture of the German debacle in the west and the events that followed. Another valuable work on the period, more vivid perhaps because it was written shortly after the war, is Milton Shulman's *Defeat in the West*.

antiaircraft guns and twenty-five tanks—hardly the equivalent of an American division. And racing toward this scanty force—so thin that Student could not even man the 75-mile Antwerp-Maastricht gap, let alone close it—were the awesome armored forces of the British Second Army and part of the U.S. First Army. Student was outgunned and outnumbered; about all that stood between him and disaster was the Albert Canal itself.

At what point along it would the enemy attack? Student's line was vulnerable everywhere, but some areas were more critical than others. He was particularly concerned about the sector north of Antwerp, where the weak 719th Coastal Division was only now taking up position. Was there still time to take advantage of the 80-foot-wide water barrier and turn it into a major defense line that would delay the Allies long enough for additional reinforcements to reach the canal? This was Student's greatest hope.

He expected to be attacked at any moment, yet there were still no reports of Allied armor. Student was particularly surprised that there was almost no enemy contact north of Antwerp. He had by now expected that British tanks, after capturing the city, would strike north, cut off the Beveland peninsula, and smash into Holland. It seemed to Student that the British had slowed down. But why?

Four times in eighteen days the vast complex of the German Supreme Headquarters in the West had been forced to move. Bombed, shelled, almost overrun by Allied tanks, OB West had finally come to a halt behind the borders of the Reich. And shortly after 2 P.M. on September 5 the new commander in chief found his headquarters in the little town of Aremberg near Koblenz.

Tired and irritable after his long journey, Field Marshal Gerd von Rundstedt dispensed with the usual military courtesies and fanfare that often accompanied a German change of command. Immediately he plunged into a series of staff conferences that were to last long into the evening. Officers not personally acquainted with the field marshal were startled by the speed of his takeover. To older hands, it was as though he had never been away. For everyone, the very presence of Von Rundstedt brought feelings of relief and renewed confidence.

Von Rundstedt's task was formidable, his problems were massive. He must produce, as quickly as possible, a strategic blueprint for the 400-mile western front running from the North Sea all the way to the Swiss border—a plan which Field Marshal Model had candidly found beyond his capability. With the battered forces at Von Rundstedt's disposal—Army Group B in the north and G in the south—he was expected to hold everywhere and even to counterattack, as Hitler had directed. Simultaneously, to stave off invasion of the Reich, he was to make a reality of Hitler's "impregnable" Siegfried Line—the long-obsolete, unfinished concrete fortifications which had lain neglected, unmanned, and stripped of guns since 1940. There was more, but on this afternoon Von Rundstedt gave first priority to the immediate problems. They were far worse than even he had anticipated.

The picture was bleak. Before his dismissal by Hitler in July, Von Rundstedt had command of sixty-two divisions. Now his operations chief, Lieutenant General Bodo Zimmermann, produced an ominous balance sheet. In the two army groups, he told the Field Marshal, there were "forty-eight 'paper' divisions, fifteen panzer divisions and four brigades with almost no tanks." So weak in men, equipment and artillery were these forty-eight divisions, Zimmermann said, that in his view they constituted "a combat power equivalent to only twenty-seven divisions." This force was less than "half the strength of the Allies." Von Rundstedt learned that his staff believed Eisenhower had at least sixty divisions, completely motorized and at full strength. (This estimate was wrong. Eisenhower had, at this moment, forty-nine divisions on the Continent.)

As for German panzer forces, they were virtually nonexistent. Along the entire front, against the Allies' estimated strength of more than two thousand tanks, there were only one hundred panzers left. The Luftwaffe had been virtually destroyed; above the battlefield, the Allies had complete aerial supremacy. Von Rundstedt's own grim summation was that in troops, most of whom were exhausted and demoralized, he was outnumbered more than 2 to 1; in artillery by 2½ guns to 1; in tanks, 20 to 1; and in planes, 25 to 1.° Besides there were grave shortages in gasoline, transportation and ammunition. Von Rundstedt's new chief of staff, General Siegfried Westphal, was later to recall, "The situation was desperate. A major defeat anywhere along the front—which was so full of gaps that it did not deserve the name—would lead to catastrophe if the enemy were to fully exploit the opportunities."

Lieutenant General Blumentritt, fully agreeing with Westphal's view, was even more specific.† In his opinion, if the Allies mounted "a major thrust resulting in a breakthrough anywhere," collapse would follow. The only capable troops Von Rundstedt had were those facing General George S. Patton's U.S. Third Army driving toward Metz and heading for the industrial region of the Saar. These forces might delay Patton, but they were not strong enough to stop him. Rather than waste precious time, it seemed to Blumentritt that the Allies would strike where the Germans were weakest—by attempting a powerful thrust in the north to cross the Rhine and move into the Ruhr. That drive, he believed, might be given priority by the Americans and the British, because, as he later put it, "He who holds northern Germany, holds Germany."

° German losses in men and matériel had been staggering. In the ninety-two days since the invasion of Normandy, 300,000 German troops had been killed or wounded or were missing; another 200,000 were surrounded, holding "last-ditch fortresses" such as ports or in the Channel Islands. Some 53 German divisions had been destroyed, and strewn across France and Belgium were vast quantities of matériel including at least 1,700 tanks, 3,500 guns, thousands of armored vehicles and horse-drawn or motorized transports and mountains of equipment and supplies ranging from small arms to vast ammunition dumps. The casualties included two field marshals and more than twenty generals.

† To Von Rundstedt's annoyance, General Blumentritt, who had long been his chief of staff and most trusted confidant, was replaced by General Westphal on September 5 and ordered back to Germany. Von Rundstedt protested the change, to no avail. Blumentritt did, however, attend the early conferences in Aremberg and did not leave the headquarters until September 8.

Von Rundstedt had already reached the same conclusion. Seizing the Ruhr was undoubtedly the major Allied objective. The British and Americans in the north were driving in that direction, toward the frontier at Aachen. There was little to stop them from penetrating the unmanned, outdated Siegfried Line, crossing Germany's last natural barrier, the vital Rhine, and striking into the Reich's industrial heart.

Von Rundstedt's analytical mind had seized on one more fact. Eisenhower's skilled and highly trained airborne forces, used so successfully in the Normandy invasion, had disappeared off German situation maps. They were not being used as infantry. Obviously these forces had been withdrawn, preparatory to another airborne operation. But where and when? It was logical that an airborne drop would coincide with a drive on the Ruhr. In Von Rundstedt's view such an attack might come at either of two key areas: behind the Westwall fortifications, or east of the Rhine to seize bridgeheads. In fact, Field Marshal Model, several days earlier, had expressed the same fear in a message to Hitler, stressing the possibility as an "acute threat." Equally, Von Rundstedt could not discount the possibility of the entire Allied front moving forward simultaneously toward the Ruhr *and* the Saar with airborne troops committed at the same time. The Field Marshal could see no solution to any of these impending threats. Allied opportunities were too many and too varied. His only option was to try to bring order out of chaos and to buy time by outguessing Allied intentions, if he could.

Von Rundstedt did not underestimate Eisenhower's intelligence of the German predicament. But, he pondered, was the Allied command really aware how desperate the situation was? The truth was that he was fighting, as he put it to Blumentritt, with "rundown old men" and the pillboxes of the Westwall would be "absolutely useless against an Allied onslaught." It was "madness," he said, "to defend these mouse holes for reasons of prestige." Nevertheless, the ghostly Siegfried Line must be given substance, its fortifications readied and manned. Tersely, Von

Rundstedt told his staff: "We must somehow hold for at least six weeks."

Studying each aspect of the situation confronting him, diagraming possible Allied moves and weighing each alternative, he noted that the most vigorous attacks were still being made by Patton, heading for the Saar. In the north British and American pressure was noticeably less. Von Rundstedt thought he detected an absence of movement, almost a pause, in that area. Turning his attention to Montgomery's front, as Blumentritt was later to remember, Von Rundstedt concentrated on the situation at Antwerp. He was intrigued by reports that, for more than thirty-six hours now, the British had mounted no drive north from the city, nor had they cut the South Beveland peninsula. Obviously, Antwerp's great harbor facilities would solve Allied supply problems. But they could not use the port if both sides of the 54-mile-long estuary leading to it remained in German hands. To the Field Marshal, it seemed clear that the letup he had noted was real; a definite Allied slowdown had occurred, particularly in Montgomery's area.

Throughout his career, Von Rundstedt had closely studied British military tactics; he had also, to his own misfortune, been able to observe American warfare at first hand. He had found the Americans more imaginative and daring in the use of armor, the British superb with infantry. In each case, however, commanders made the difference. Thus, Von Rundstedt considered Patton a far more dangerous opponent than Montgomery. According to Blumentritt, Von Rundstedt viewed Field Marshal Montgomery as "overly cautious, habit-ridden and systematic." Now the Field Marshal weighed the significance of Montgomery's tardiness. With the other Channel ports still in German hands, Von Rundstedt saw Antwerp as essential to Eisenhower's advance—so why had Montgomery not moved for thirty-six hours and apparently failed to secure the second-largest port in Europe? There could be only one reason: Montgomery was not ready to continue the attack. Von Rundstedt was certain that he would not depart from

VON RUNDSTEDT'S PLAN:
ESCAPE OF VON ZANGEN'S
FIFTEENTH ARMY BEGINS
SEPT. 6, 1944

0   Miles   15

SCHOUWEN

NORTH
SEA

N

NORTH
BEVELAND

WALCHEREN

Flushing

Breskens

SOUTH
BEVELAND

SCHELDE ESTUARY

VON ZANGEN'S HQ.

Axel

HOLLAND
BELGIUM

Bruges

FIFTEENTH ARMY POCKET, SEPT. 5, 1944

CANADIAN
FIRST ARMY

Ghent

Rotterdam

LOWER RHINE

WAAL R.

Dordrecht

MAAS R.

Vught

WILHELMINA CANAL

Breda

Tilburg

Bergen op Zoom

Woensdrecht

HOLLAND
BELGIUM

THE GREAT MISTAKE:
BRITISH FAIL TO CUT
ESCAPE ROUTE OF
VON ZANGEN'S
FIFTEENTH ARMY

FRONT LINE SEPT. 5, 1944

MEUSE - ESCAUT CANAL

Antwerp

ALBERT CANAL

SCHELDE R.

BRITISH
SECOND ARMY

palacios

habit. The British would never attack until the meticulous, detail-minded Montgomery was fully prepared and supplied. The answer therefore, Von Rundstedt reasoned, was that the British had overextended themselves. This was not a pause, Von Rundstedt told his staff. Montgomery's pursuit, he was convinced, had ground to a halt.

Quickly, Von Rundstedt turned his attention to Model's orders of the previous twenty-four hours. Because now, if his theory was right, Von Rundstedt saw a chance not only to deny the port of Antwerp to the Allies but, equally important, to save General Von Zangen's trapped Fifteenth Army, a force of more than 80,000 men—men that Von Rundstedt desperately needed.

From Model's orders he saw that, while Von Zangen had been told to hold the southern bank of the Schelde and reinforce the Channel ports, he had also been ordered to attack with the remainder of his troops northeast into the flank of the British drive—an attack scheduled to take place on the morning of the sixth. Without hesitation, Von Rundstedt canceled that attack. Under the circumstances, he saw no merit to it. Besides, he had a bolder, more imaginative plan. The first part of Model's orders could stand, because now holding the Channel ports was more important than ever. But instead of attacking northeast, Von Zangen was ordered to evacuate his remaining troops by sea, across the waters of the Schelde to the island of Walcheren. Once on the northern bank of the estuary, Von Zangen's troops could march eastward along the one road running from Walcheren Island, across the South Beveland peninsula until they reached the Dutch mainland north of Antwerp. Because of Allied air power, ferrying operations across the 3-mile mouth of the Schelde, between the ports of Breskens and Flushing, would have to take place at night. Nevertheless, with luck, a good portion of the Fifteenth Army might be safely withdrawn within two weeks. Von Rundstedt knew that the plan was hazardous, but he saw no other course, for, if successful, he would have almost an entire German army, battered though it might be, at his disposal. More than that he would still—unbelievably—control the vital port of

Antwerp. But the success of the operation would depend entirely on Von Rundstedt's hunch that Montgomery's drive had indeed come to a halt.

Von Rundstedt was sure of it. Further, he was banking on it that Montgomery's slowdown held a far deeper significance. Because of overextended communications and supply lines, he was convinced, the Allied breakneck pursuit had reached its limit. At the close of the conference, as Blumentritt was later to recall, "Von Rundstedt looked at us and suggested the incredible possibility that, for once, Hitler might be right."

Hitler's and Von Rundstedt's estimates of the situation, although only partly correct, were far more accurate than either realized. The precious time Von Rundstedt needed to stabilize his front was being provided by the Allies themselves. The truth was that the Germans were losing faster than the Allies could win.

✻ 6 ✻

Even as Von Rundstedt gambled desperately to save the trapped Fifteenth Army, Major General George Philip Roberts, commander of the British 11th Armored Division, 150 miles away in Antwerp, was jubilantly informing his superiors of a startling development. His men had captured not only the city but the huge port as well.

Together with the Guards Armored Division, Roberts' tanks had made an extraordinary dash of more than 250 miles in just five days. The spearhead of Lieutenant General Miles C. Dempsey's great British Second Army had been ordered by Lieutenant General Brian Horrocks, XXX Corps commander, to "keep going like mad." Leaving the Guards to capture Brussels, Roberts' division bypassed the city and in the early hours of September 4, with the courageous help of the Belgian underground, entered Antwerp. Now, some thirty-six hours later, after clearing the deep-sea complex of a stunned and panic-stricken enemy, Roberts reported that his men had captured Antwerp's huge 1,000-acre harbor area intact. Warehouses, cranes, bridges, 3½ miles of wharves, quays, locks, drydocks, rolling stock—and, unbelievably, even the all-important electrically controlled sluice gates, in full working order—had been seized.

German plans to demolish the port had failed. Explosives had been placed on major bridges and other key installations, but, overwhelmed by the spectacular speed of the British and resistance groups (among them Belgian engineers who knew exactly where the demolitions were planted), the disorganized German garrison never had a chance to destroy the vast harbor facilities.

The thirty-seven-year-old Roberts had brilliantly executed his orders. Unfortunately, in one of the greatest miscalculations of the European war, no one had directed him to take advantage of the situation—that is, strike north, grab bridgeheads over the Albert Canal in the northern suburbs, and then make a dash for the base of the South Beveland peninsula only eighteen miles away. By holding its 2-mile-wide neck, Roberts could have bottled up German forces on the isthmus, preparatory to clearing the vital northern bank. It was a momentous oversight.[*] The port of Antwerp, one of the war's major prizes, was secured; but its approaches, still held by the Germans, were not. This great facility, which could have shortened and fed Allied supply lines all

---

[*] The late B. H. Liddell Hart, the celebrated British historian, in his *History of the Second World War* wrote: "It was a multiple lapse—by four commanders from Montgomery downwards . . ." Charles B. MacDonald, the American historian in *The Mighty Endeavor*, agrees with Liddell Hart. He called the failure "one of the greatest tactical mistakes of the war." The best and most detailed account on the cost of Antwerp is undoubtedly R. W. Thompson, *The 85 Days*, and I agree with him that one of the main reasons for the missed opportunity was "weariness." Men of the 11th Armored, he wrote, "slept where they sat, stood or lay, drained of emotion, and in utter exhaustion." If we accept his theory it is doubtful that Roberts' 11th could have continued its drive with the same vigor. Nevertheless, Antwerp and its vital approaches, argues Thompson, might have been taken with ease "had there been a commander following the battle, hour by hour, day by day, and with the flexibility of command to see the prospect."

along the front, was useless. Yet nobody, in the heady atmosphere of the moment, saw this oversight as more than a temporary condition. Indeed, there seemed no need to hurry. With the Germans reeling, the mop-up could take place at any time. The 11th Armored, its assignment completed, held its positions awaiting new orders.

The magnificent drive of Dempsey's armored forces in the north, equaling that of Patton's south of the Ardennes, had run its course, though at this moment few realized it. Roberts' men were exhausted, short on gasoline and supplies. The same was true of the remainder of General Brian Horrocks' XXX Corps. Thus, on this same afternoon, the relentless pressure that had thrown the Germans back in the north, shattered and demoralized, suddenly relaxed. The blunder at Antwerp was compounded as the British came to a halt to "refit, refuel, and rest."

General Horrocks, the XXX Corps's capable and dynamic commander, was not even thinking about Antwerp.° Like Field Marshal Montgomery, commander of the British 21st Army Group, his attention was focused on another target: the crossing of the Rhine and a swift end to the war. Only a few hours earlier, elated at the verve and dash of his armies, Montgomery had cabled the Supreme Commander, General Dwight D. Eisenhower: "We have now reached a stage where a really powerful and full-blooded thrust towards Berlin is likely to get there and thus end the war."

In London, His Royal Highness, the Prince of the Netherlands conferred with Queen Wilhelmina and then telephoned his wife,

---

° Horrocks, in his memoirs, gives a very frank explanation. "My excuse is that my eyes were fixed entirely on the Rhine and everything else seemed of subsidiary importance. It never entered my head that the Schelde would be mined and that we would not be able to use Antwerp until the channel had been swept and the Germans cleared from the coastlines on either side. . . . Napoleon would, no doubt, have realized these things but Horrocks didn't." He also readily admits there was little opposition ahead of him and "we still had 100 miles of petrol per vehicle and one further day's supply within reach." There would have been "considerable risk" but "I believe that if we had taken the chance and carried straight on with our advance, instead of halting in Brussels, the whole course of the war in Europe might have been changed."

the Princess Juliana, in Canada. He urged her to fly immediately to England, ready to return to the Netherlands the moment the country was freed. Their long exile was about to end. The liberation, when it came, would be swift. They must be ready. Yet Bernhard was uneasy.

Over the past seventy-two hours messages reaching him from the resistance had again and again underscored the German panic in Holland and repeated the news that the retreat, begun on September 2, was still in progress. Now, on the fifth, underground leaders reported that although the Germans were still disorganized, the exodus appeared to be slowing down. Bernhard had also heard from the Dutch Prime Minister in exile. Prime Minister Gerbrandy was somewhat embarrassed. Obviously his September 3 broadcast was premature; Allied troops had most certainly not crossed the Dutch border as yet. The Prince and the Prime Minister pondered the reason. Why had the British not moved? Surely, from the underground messages they received, the situation in Holland was clear.

Bernhard had little military training and was dependent on his own advisers, yet he was puzzled.° If the Germans were still disorganized and, as his resistance leaders believed, a "thrust by a few tanks" could liberate the country "in a matter of hours"— why, then, didn't the British proceed? Perhaps Montgomery disbelieved the reports of the Dutch resistance because he considered them amateurish or unreliable. Bernhard could find no other explanation. Why else would the British hesitate, instead of instantly crossing the border? Although he was in constant touch

° The young Prince, although named Commander in Chief of the Netherlands Forces by the Queen, was quite frank in interviews with the author regarding his military background. "I had no tactical experience," he told me, "except for a course at the War College before the war. I followed this up with courses in England, but most of my military knowledge was learned in a practical way by reading and by discussions with my officers. However, I never considered myself experienced enough to make a tactical decision. I depended on my staff, who were very well qualified." Nevertheless Bernhard took his job very seriously. In his meticulously kept personal diary for 1944, which he kindly placed at my disposal, he recorded in minuscule handwriting each movement, almost minute by minute, from telephone calls and military conferences to official functions. During this period, based on his own notations, I would estimate that his average working day was about sixteen hours.

with his ministers, the United States ambassador at large, Anthony Biddle, and Eisenhower's chief of staff, Bedell Smith, and as a result was well aware that, at this moment, the advance was so fluid that the situation was changing almost hour by hour, nevertheless Bernhard thought he would like firsthand information. He made a decision: he would request permission of SHAEF to fly to Belgium and see Field Marshal Montgomery himself as soon as possible. He had every faith in the Allied high command and, in particular, Montgomery. Still, if something was wrong, Bernhard had to know.

At his spartan, tented headquarters in the Royal Palace Gardens at Laeken, a few miles from the center of Brussels, Field Marshal Bernard Law Montgomery impatiently waited for an answer to his coded "Personal for Eisenhower Eyes Only" message. Its urgent demand for a powerful and full-blooded thrust to Berlin was sent in the late hours of September 4. Now, by midday on September 5, the brusque, wiry fifty-eight-year-old hero of El Alamein waited for a reply and impatiently fretted about the future course of the war. Two months before the invasion of Normandy he had said, "If we do our stuff properly and no mistakes are made, then I believe that Germany will be out of the war this year." In Montgomery's unalterable opinion, a momentous strategic mistake had been made just before the Allies captured Paris and crossed the Seine. Eisenhower's "broad-front policy"—moving his armies steadily forward to the borders of the Reich, then up to the Rhine—may have been valid when planned before the invasion, but with the sudden disorderly collapse of the Germans, the Britisher believed, it was now obsolete. As Montgomery put it, that strategy had become "unstitched." And all his military training told him "we could not get away with it and . . . would be faced with a long winter campaign with all that that entailed for the British people."

On August 17 he had proposed to General Omar N. Bradley,

the U.S. 12th Army Group commander, a single-thrust plan. Both his own and Bradley's army group should stay "together as a solid mass of forty divisions, which would be so strong that it need fear nothing. This force should advance northeastward." Montgomery's 21st Army Group would clear the Channel coast, and secure Antwerp and southern Holland. Bradley's U.S. 12th Army Group, its right flank on the Ardennes, would head for Aachen and Cologne. The basic objective of Montgomery's proposed drive was to "secure bridgeheads over the Rhine before the winter began and to seize the Ruhr quickly." In all probability, he theorized, it would also end the war. Montgomery's plan called for three of Eisenhower's four armies—the British Second, the U.S. First and the Canadian First. The fourth, Patton's U.S. Third Army, at this moment making headlines around the world for its spectacular advances, Montgomery dismissed. He calmly suggested it should be brought to a halt.

Some forty-eight hours later Montgomery learned that Bradley, who he had believed was responsive to his own idea, actually favored an American thrust, a Patton drive toward the Rhine and Frankfurt. Eisenhower rejected both plans; he was not prepared to change his strategic concept. The Supreme Commander wanted to remain flexible enough to thrust both to the Ruhr and the Saar as the occasion permitted. To Montgomery, this was no longer the "broad-front policy" but a double-thrust plan. Everybody now, he felt, was "going his own way"—especially Patton, who seemed to be allowed enormous latitude. Eisenhower's determination to persist in his original concept revealed quite clearly, in Montgomery's opinion, that the Supreme Commander was "in fact, completely out of touch with the land battle."

Montgomery's view was based on a recent development which angered him and, he felt, demeaned his own role. He was no longer the over-all coordinator of the land battle. On September 1 Eisenhower had personally taken over command. Because the Supreme Commander believed Montgomery "a master of the set battle piece," he had given the British general operational control of the D-Day assault and the initial period of fighting thereafter.

Thus, General Omar N. Bradley's 12th Army Group was under Montgomery. Press stories appearing in the United States at the end of August revealing that Bradley's army group still operated under Montgomery created such a public furor that Eisenhower was promptly ordered by General George C. Marshall, U.S. Chief of Staff, to "immediately assume direct command" of all ground forces. American armies reverted back to their own command. The move caught Montgomery off base. As his chief of staff, General Francis de Guingand, later put it: "Montgomery . . . never, I believe, thought that the day would come so soon. Possibly he hoped that the initial command set up was there to stay for a long time. He was, I think, apt to give insufficient weight to the dictates of prestige and national feelings, or to the increasing contribution of America, in both men and arms . . . it was obvious, however, to most of us that it would have been an impossible situation for a British general and a British headquarters to retain command of these more numerous American formations indefinitely."° It may have been obvious to his staff but not to Montgomery. He felt publicly humiliated.†

It was hardly a secret that Monty and his superior, Sir Alan Brooke, Chief of the Imperial General Staff, were highly critical of Eisenhower. Both men considered him ambivalent and indecisive. In a letter to Montgomery on July 28, Brooke commented that Eisenhower had only "the very vaguest conception of war!" On another occasion he summarized the Supreme Commander as "a most attractive personality," but with "a very, very limited brain from a strategic point of view." Montgomery, never a man to mince words, saw "right from the beginning that Ike had simply no experience for the job," and while history, he felt, would record Eisenhower "as a very good Supreme Commander, as a field commander he was very bad, very bad."‡ Angrily, Montgomery began promoting the idea of an over-all "Land

---

° Major General Francis de Guingand, *Generals at War*, pp. 100–101.
† Montgomery and the British public, as outraged as he, were somewhat mollified when George VI, at Churchill's strong urging, made Montgomery a field marshal on September 1.
‡ Author's interview with Field Marshal Montgomery.

Forces Commander," a post sandwiched between the army groups and Eisenhower. He knew just the man for the job—himself. Eisenhower was well aware of the underground campaign. He remained calm. The Supreme Commander was, in his way, as obstinate as Montgomery. His orders from General Marshall were clear and he had no intention of entertaining the idea of any overall ground commander other than himself.

Montgomery had no opportunity to discuss his single-thrust plan or his thoughts about a land-forces commander directly with Eisenhower until August 23, when the Supreme Commander came to lunch at 21st Army Group headquarters. Then the fractious Montgomery, with extraordinary tactlessness, insisted on a private conversation with the Supreme Commander. He demanded that Eisenhower's chief of staff, General Bedell Smith, be excluded from the conference. Smith left the tent, and for an hour Eisenhower, grimly keeping his temper, was lectured by his subordinate on the need for "a firm and sound plan." Montgomery demanded that Eisenhower "decide where the main effort would be" so that "we could be certain of decisive results quickly." Again and again he pressed for the "single thrust," warning that if the Supreme Commander continued the "broad-front strategy with the whole line advancing and everyone fighting all the time, the advance would inevitably peter out." If that happened, Montgomery warned, "the Germans would gain time to recover, and the war would go on all through the winter and well into 1945. If we split the maintenance," Montgomery said, "and advance on a broad front we shall be so weak everywhere we'll have no chance of success." To his mind there was only one policy: "to halt the right and strike with the left, or halt the left and strike with the right." There could only be one thrust and everything should support it.

Eisenhower saw Montgomery's proposal as a gigantic gamble. It might produce speedy and decisive victory. It might instead result in disaster. He was not prepared to accept the risks involved. Nevertheless he found himself caught between Montgomery on one side and Bradley and Patton on the other—each advocating "the main thrust," each wanting to be entrusted with it.

Up to this point, Montgomery, notorious for his slow-moving, if successful, tactics, had yet to prove that he could exploit a situation with the speed of Patton; and at this moment Patton's army, far ahead of everyone else, had crossed the Seine and was racing toward Germany. Diplomatically, Eisenhower explained to Montgomery that, whatever the merits of a single thrust, he could hardly hold back Patton and stop the U.S. Third Army in its tracks. "The American people," said the Supreme Commander, "would never stand for it, and public opinion wins wars." Montgomery heatedly disagreed. "Victories win wars," he announced. "Give people victory and they won't care who won it."

Eisenhower was not impressed. Although he did not say so at the time, he thought Montgomery's view was "much too narrow," and that the Field Marshal did not "understand the over-all situation." Eisenhower explained to Montgomery that he wanted Patton to continue eastward so that a link-up might be effected with the American and French forces advancing from the south. In short, he made it quite clear that his "broad-front policy" would continue.

Montgomery turned for the moment to the subject of a land commander. "Someone must run the land battle for you." Eisenhower, Montgomery declared, should "sit on a very lofty perch in order to be able to take a detached view of the whole intricate problem, which involves land, sea, air, et cetera." He retreated from arrogance to humility. If the matter of "public opinion in America was involved," Montgomery declared, he would gladly "let Bradley control the battle and serve under him."

Eisenhower quickly dismissed the suggestion. Placing Bradley over Montgomery would be as unacceptable to the British people as the reverse would be to the Americans. As for his own role he could not, he explained, deviate from the plan to take personal control of the battle. But, in seeking a solution to some of the immediate problems, he was ready to make some concessions to Montgomery. He needed the Channel ports and Antwerp. They were vital to the entire Allied supply problem. Thus, for the moment, Eisenhower said, priority would be given to the 21st Army Group's northern thrust. Montgomery could use the Allied First Airborne Army in England—at the time SHAEF's only reserve. Additionally, he could have the support of the U.S. First Army moving on his right.

Montgomery had, in the words of General Bradley, "won the initial skirmish," but the Britisher was far from satisfied. It was his firm conviction that Eisenhower had missed the "great opportunity." Patton shared that view—for different reasons—when the news reached him. Not only had Eisenhower given supply priority to Montgomery at the expense of the U.S. Third Army, but he had also rejected Patton's proposed drive to the Saar. To Patton, it was "the most momentous error of the war."

In the two weeks since this clash of personalities and conflicting military philosophies had taken place, much had happened. Montgomery's 21st Army Group now rivaled Patton's in speed. By September 5, with his advance units already in Antwerp, Montgomery was more convinced than ever that his single-thrust concept was right. He was determined to reverse the Supreme Commander's decision. A crucial turning point in the conflict had been reached. The Germans, Montgomery was convinced, were teetering on the verge of collapse.

He was not alone in this view. On nearly every level of command, intelligence officers were forecasting the imminent end of the war. The most optimistic estimate came from the Combined Allied Intelligence Committee in London. The German situation had deteriorated to such an extent that the group believed the enemy incapable of recovery. There was every indication, their estimate said, that "organized resistance under the control of the German high command is unlikely to continue beyond December 1, 1944, and . . . may end even sooner." Supreme Headquarters shared this optimism. At the end of August, SHAEF's intelligence summary declared that "the August battles have done it and the enemy in the west has had it. Two and one half months of bitter fighting have brought the end of the war in Europe in sight, almost within reach." Now, one week later, they considered the

German army "no longer a cohesive force but a number of fugitive battle groups, disorganized and even demoralized, short of equipment and arms." Even the conservative director of military operations at the British War Office, Major General John Kennedy, noted on September 6 that "If we go at the same pace as of late, we should be in Berlin by the 28th. . . ."

In this chorus of optimistic predictions there seemed only one dissenting voice. The U.S. Third Army's intelligence chief, Colonel Oscar W. Koch, believed the enemy still capable of waging a last-ditch struggle and warned that "barring internal upheaval in the homeland and the remote possibility of insurrection within the Wehrmacht . . . the German armies will continue to fight until destroyed or captured."* But his own intelligence officer's cautious appraisal meant little to the Third Army's ebullient commander, Lieutenant General George S. Patton. Like Montgomery in the north, Patton in the south was now only one hundred miles from the Rhine. He too believed the time had come, as Montgomery had put it, "to stick our neck out in a single deep thrust into enemy territory," and finish off the war. The only difference lay in their views of who was to stick out his neck. Both commanders, flushed with victory and bidding for glory, now vied for that opportunity. In his zeal, Montgomery had narrowed his rivalry down to Patton alone: a British field marshal in charge of an entire army group was trying to outrace an American lieutenant general in charge of a single army.

But all along the front the fever of success gripped battle commanders. After the spectacular sweep across France and Belgium and with evidence of German defeat all around, men now confidently believed that nothing could stop the victorious surge from continuing through the Siegfried Line and beyond, into the heart of Germany. Yet, keeping the enemy off balance and disorganized demanded constant, unremitting Allied pressure. Supporting that pressure had now produced a crisis that few seemed aware of. The heady optimism bordered on self-deception

* For a more detailed version of Allied intelligence estimates see Dr. Forrest C. Pogue, *The Supreme Command*, pp. 244–45.

for, at this moment, Eisenhower's great armies, after a hectic dash of more than two hundred miles from the Seine, were caught up in a gigantic maintenance and supply problem. After six weeks of almost nonstop advance against little opposition, few noted the sudden loss of momentum. But as the first tanks approached Germany's threshold and at places began probing the Westwall itself, the advance began to slow. The Allied pursuit was over, strangled by its own success.

The chief problem crippling the advance was the lack of ports. There was no shortage of supplies, but these were stockpiled in Normandy, still being brought in across the beaches or through the only workable port, Cherbourg—some 450 miles behind the forward elements. Supplying four great armies in full pursuit from that far back was a nightmarish task. A lack of transportation added to the creeping paralysis. Rail networks, bombed in preinvasion days or destroyed by the French underground, could not be repaired fast enough. Gasoline pipelines were only now being laid and extended. As a result, everything from rations to gasoline was being hauled by road, and there was a frustrating shortage of trucks.

To keep abreast of the pursuit which, day by day, pushed farther east, every kind of vehicle was being pressed into service. Artillery, antiaircraft guns and spare tanks had been unloaded from their conveyors and left behind so that the conveyors could be used to carry supplies. Divisions had been stripped of their transport companies. The British had left one entire corps west of the Seine so that its transport could service the rest of the speeding army. Montgomery's difficulties mounted with the discovery that 1,400 British three-ton trucks were useless because of faulty pistons.

Now, in herculean efforts to keep the pursuit going without pause, a ceaseless belt of trucks—the "Red Ball Express"—hammered east, delivered their supplies and then swung back to the west for more, some convoys often making a grueling round trip of between six and eight hundred miles. Even with all available transport moving around the clock and with commanders in the field applying the most stringent economies, the supply demands of the armies could not be met. Taxed beyond its capabilities, the makeshift supply structure had almost reached the breaking point.

Besides the acute transportation problem, men were tired, equipment worn out after the catapultlike advance from Normandy. Tanks, half-tracks and vehicles of every description had been driven so long without proper maintenance that they were breaking down. Overshadowing everything was a critical shortage of gasoline. Eisenhower's armies, needing one million gallons per day, were receiving only a fraction of that amount.

The effect was critical. In Belgium, as the enemy fled before it, an entire corps of the U.S. First Army was halted for four days, its tanks dry. Patton's U.S. Third Army, more than a hundred miles ahead of everyone else, and meeting little opposition, was forced to halt for five days on the Meuse, because armored columns were out of gas. Patton was furious when he discovered that of the 400,000 gallons of gasoline ordered, he had received only 32,000 due to priority cutbacks. He promptly ordered his leading corps commander: "Get off your fanny as fast as you can and move on until your engines run dry, then get out and walk, goddammit!" To his headquarters staff, Patton raged that he was "up against two enemies—the Germans and our own high command. I can take care of the Germans, but I'm not sure I can win against Montgomery and Eisenhower." He tried. Convinced that he could bludgeon his way into Germany in a matter of days, Patton furiously appealed to Bradley and Eisenhower. "My men can eat their belts," he stormed, "but my tanks have gotta have gas."

The crushing defeat of the Germans in Normandy and the systematic and speedy annihilation of their forces following the breakout had caused the logistic crisis. On the assumption that the enemy would hold and fight on the various historic river lines, invasion planners had anticipated a more conservative advance. A pause for regrouping and massing of supplies, it was assumed, would take place after the Normandy beachhead had been secured and Channel ports captured. The lodgment area was expected to lie west of the river Seine which, according to the projected timetable, would not be reached until September 4 (D plus 90 days). The sudden disintegration of the enemy's forces and their headlong flight eastward had made the Allied timetable meaningless. Who could have foreseen that by September 4 Allied tanks would be two hundred miles east of the Seine and in Antwerp? Eisenhower's staff had estimated that it would take approximately eleven months to reach the German frontier at Aachen. Now, as tank columns approached the Reich, the Allies were almost seven months ahead of their advance schedule. That the supply and transportation system, designed for a much slower rate of progress, had stood up to the strain of the hectic pursuit at all was close to miraculous.

Yet, in spite of the critical logistic situation, no one was ready to admit that the armies must soon halt or that the pursuit was over. "Every commander from division upwards," Eisenhower later wrote, was "obsessed with the idea that with only a few more tons of supply, he could rush right on and win the war. . . . Each commander, therefore, begged and demanded priority over all others, and it was quite undeniable that in front of each were opportunities for quick exploitation that made the demands completely logical." Still, the optimism had infected even the Supreme Commander. It was obvious that he believed the impetus of the advance could be maintained long enough for the Allied armies to overrun the Siegfried Line before the Germans had a chance to defend it, for he saw signs of "collapse" on the "entire front." On September 4 he directed that Bradley's "12th Army Group will capture the Saar and the Frankfurt area." Montgomery's "21st Army Group will capture the Ruhr and Antwerp."

Even Patton seemed appeased by the announcement. Now he was sure that, given adequate supplies, his powerful U.S. Third Army could, by itself, reach the industrial Saar and then dash on all the way to the Rhine.° And in the unparalleled atmosphere of

° Patton's weekly press conferences were always newsworthy, but especially memorable for the General's off-the-record remarks, which, because of his colorful vocabulary, could never have been printed anyway. That first week of September, as a war correspondent for the London *Daily Telegraph*, I was present when, in victory that prevailed, Montgomery, with his coded message of September 4, once again doggedly pressed his case. This time he went far beyond his proposal of August 17 and his conversation with Eisenhower on August 23. Convinced that the Germans were broken, the commander of the British 21st Army Group believed that he could not only reach the Ruhr but race all the way to Berlin itself.

In his nine-paragraph message to Eisenhower, Montgomery spelled out again the reasons that convinced him that the moment had come for a "really powerful and full-blooded thrust." There were two strategic opportunities open to the Allies, "one via the Ruhr and the other via Metz and the Saar." But, he argued, because "we have not enough resources, two such drives could not be maintained." There was a chance for only one—his. That thrust, the northern one "via the Ruhr," was, in Montgomery's opinion, "likely to give the best and quickest results." To guarantee its success, Monty's single thrust would need "all the maintenance resources . . . without qualification." He was now clearly impatient of any other considerations. He was going on record both as to the worth of his own plan and his skill and belief in himself as the one man to carry it off. Other operations would have to get along with whatever logistic support remained. There could be no compromise, he warned the Supreme Commander. He dismissed the possibility of two drives, because "it would split our maintenance resources so that neither thrust is full-blooded" and as a result "prolong the war." As Montgomery saw the problem it was "very simple and clear-cut." But time was of "such vital importance . . . that a decision is required at once."

Acrid and autocratic, the most popular British commander since Wellington was obsessed by his own beliefs. Considering the acute logistic situation, he reasoned that his single-thrust theory was now more valid than it had been two weeks before. In

---

typical fashion, he expounded on his plans for the Germans. In his high-pitched voice and pounding the map, Patton declared that, "Maybe there are five thousand, maybe ten thousand, Nazi bastards in their concrete foxholes before the Third Army. Now, if Ike stops holding Monty's hand and gives me the supplies, I'll go through the Siegfried Line like shit through a goose."

his intractable way—and indifferent as to how the tone of his message might be received—Montgomery was not merely suggesting a course of action for the Supreme Commander; the Field Marshal was dictating one. Eisenhower must halt all other armies in their tracks—in particular Patton's—so that all resources could be put behind his single drive. And his Signal No. M-160 closed with a typical example of Montgomery's arrogance. "If you are coming this way perhaps you would look in and discuss it," he proposed. "If so, delighted to see you lunch tomorrow. Do not feel I can leave this battle just at present." That his closing words bordered on the insolent seemed not to occur to Montgomery in his anxiety that this last chance to finish off the Germans must not be lost. Limpetlike, he clung to his single-thrust plan. For now he was sure that even Eisenhower must realize that the time had come to strike the final blow.

In the bedroom of his villa at Granville on the western side of the Cherbourg peninsula, the Supreme Commander read Montgomery's Signal No. M-160 with angry disbelief. The fifty-five-year-old Eisenhower thought Montgomery's proposal "unrealistic" and "fantastic." Three times Montgomery had nagged him to exasperation about single-thrust schemes. Eisenhower thought he had settled the strategy conflict once and for all on August 23. Yet, now Montgomery was not only advocating his theory once again but was proposing to rush all the way to Berlin. Usually calm and congenial, Eisenhower now lost his temper. "There isn't a single soul who believes this can be done, except Montgomery," he exploded to members of his staff. At this moment, to Eisenhower's mind, the most urgent matter was the opening of the Channel ports, especially Antwerp. Why could Montgomery not understand that? The Supreme Commander was only too well aware of the glittering opportunities that existed. But, as he told the Deputy Supreme Commander, Marshal of the Royal Air Force Sir Arthur Tedder, and SHAEF's assistant chief of staff

Lieutenant General Frederick Morgan, for Montgomery "to talk of marching to Berlin with an army which is still drawing the great bulk of its supplies over the beaches is fantastic."

The Field Marshal's message could hardly have come at a worse time. The Supreme Commander was propped up in bed, his right knee in a cast, as a consequence of an injury of which Montgomery, at the moment, was unaware. Eisenhower had more cause than this, however, to be edgy. Leaving the main body of SHAEF in London, he had come to the Continent to take personal control on September 1, four days earlier. His small advance command headquarters at Jullouville near Granville was totally inadequate. Because of the phenomenal movement of his armies, Eisenhower was stranded more than four hundred miles from the front—and there were, as yet, no telephone or teletype facilities. Except for radio and a rudimentary courier system, he was unable to communicate immediately with his commanders in the field. The physical injury which added to these tactical discomforts had occurred after one of his routine flying visits to his principal commanders. On September 2, returning from a conference at Chartres with senior American generals, Eisenhower's plane, because of high winds and bad visibility, had been unable to land at the headquarters' airfield. Instead, it had put down—safely—on the beach near his villa. But then, trying to help the pilot pull the plane away from the water's edge, Eisenhower had badly wrenched his right knee. Thus, at this vital juncture in the war, as the Supreme Commander tried to take control of the land battle and with events happening so fast that immediate decisions were necessary, Eisenhower was physically immobilized.

Although Montgomery—or, for that matter, Bradley and Patton—might feel that Eisenhower "was out of touch with the land battle," only distance made that argument valid. His excellent, integrated Anglo-American staff was much more cognizant of the day-to-day situation in the field than his generals realized. And while he expected combat commanders to display initiative and boldness, only the Supreme Commander and his staff could view the over-all situation and make decisions accordingly. But it was true that, in this transitional period, while Eisenhower was assuming personal control, there appeared to be a lack of clear-cut direction, due in part to the complexity of the Supreme Commander's role. Coalition command was far from easy. Yet, Eisenhower, maintaining a delicate balance, and following to the letter the plans of the Combined Chiefs of Staff, made the system work. In the interest of Allied amity, he might modify strategy, but Eisenhower had no intention of throwing caution to the winds and allowing Montgomery, as the Supreme Commander later put it, to make a "single, knifelike drive toward Berlin."°

He had been more than tolerant with Montgomery, granting him concession after concession, often incurring the anger of his own American generals. Yet, it seemed that Monty "always wanted everything and he never did anything fast in his life."† Eisenhower said he understood Montgomery's peculiarities better than the Britisher realized. "Look, people have told me about his boyhood," Eisenhower recalled, "and when you have a contest between Eton and Harrow on one side and some of the lesser schools on the other, some of these juniors coming into the army

---

° In all fairness to Montgomery, it must be said that he, himself, never used this phrase. His idea was to throw forty divisions together and drive toward Berlin—certainly no knifelike thrust—but he has been credited with the remark and in my opinion it hurt his cause at SHAEF during the many strategic meetings that took place.

† To the author. In a taped interview, President Eisenhower almost relived for me his emotions at the time of this bitter argument with Montgomery. When I told him I had interviewed the Field Marshal, Eisenhower cut me short and said, "You don't have to tell me what he told you—he said I knew nothing about war—right? Look, I'm interested only in getting this thing down truthfully and logically, because any historian has to make deductions. . . . Personally, I don't believe I would put too much weight on what generals remember, including me. Because memory is a fallible thing . . . Goddammit, I don't know what you heard in Britain, but the British have never understood the American system of command. . . . When the whole damned thing [WW II] was done . . . I never heard from the British any goldarn paeans of praise. And you're not going to hear it now, particularly from people like Montgomery. . . . His associates—they've said things about him that I would never dream of repeating. . . . I don't care if he goes down as the greatest soldier in the world. He isn't, but if he goes down that way it's all right with me. . . . He got so damn personal to make sure that the Americans and me, in particular, had no credit, had nothing to do with the war, that I eventually just stopped communicating with him . . . I was just not interested in keeping up communications with a man that just can't tell the truth." The reader is urged to remember that never, during the war, did the Supreme Commander publicly discuss the Field Marshal, and his views expressed here are revealed for the first time.

felt sort of inferior. The man, all his life, has been trying to prove that he was somebody." Clearly, however, the Field Marshal's views reflected his British superiors' beliefs on how the Allies should proceed.

Understandable as this might be, Montgomery's arrogance in presenting such views invariably set American commanders' teeth on edge. As Supreme Commander, armed by the Combined Chiefs of Staff with sweeping powers, Eisenhower had one prime concern: to hold the Allies together and win the war swiftly. Although some of SHAEF's staff, including many Britishers, considered Montgomery insufferable and said so, Eisenhower never commented on him except in private to his chief of staff, Bedell Smith. But, in fact, the Supreme Commander's exasperation with Montgomery went far deeper than anyone knew. Eisenhower felt that the Field Marshal was "a psychopath . . . such an egocentric" that everything he had ever done "was perfect . . . he never made a mistake in his life." Eisenhower was not going to let him make one now. "Robbing the American Peter who is fed from Cherbourg," he told Tedder, "will certainly not get the British Paul to Berlin."

Nevertheless, Eisenhower was deeply disturbed at the widening rift between him and Britain's favorite general. Within the next few days, the Supreme Commander decided, he would meet with Montgomery in an effort to clarify what he considered to be a misunderstanding. Once more he would attempt to spell out his strategy and hope for agreement, however grudgingly it might come. In the interim before the meeting, he made one thing clear. He firmly rejected Montgomery's single-thrust plan and his bid for Berlin. On the evening of September 5, in a coded message to the Field Marshal, he said, "While agreeing with your conception of a powerful and full-blooded thrust toward Berlin, I do not agree that it should be initiated at this moment to the exclusion of all other maneuvers." As the Supreme Commander saw it, "the bulk of the German army in the west has now been destroyed," and that success should be exploited "by promptly breaching the Siegfried Line, crossing the Rhine on a wide front and seizing the

Saar and the Ruhr. This I intend to do with all possible speed."
These moves, Eisenhower believed, would place a "strangle hold
on Germany's main industrial areas and largely destroy her
capacity to wage war. . . ." Opening the ports of Le Havre and
Antwerp was essential, Eisenhower went on, before any "powerful thrust" into Germany could be launched. But, at the moment,
Eisenhower emphasized, "no relocation of our present resources
would be adequate to sustain a thrust to Berlin. . . ."

Eisenhower's decision took thirty-six hours to reach Montgomery, and then only the last half of the message arrived. The
concluding two paragraphs were received by Montgomery at 9
A.M. on the morning of September 7. The opening section did not
arrive until September 9, another forty-eight hours later. As
Montgomery saw it, Eisenhower's communication was one more
confirmation that the Supreme Commander was "too far removed
from the battle."

From the first fragment of the message that Montgomery received, it was abundantly clear that Eisenhower had rejected his
plan, for it contained the sentence, "No relocation of our present
resources would be adequate to sustain a thrust to Berlin." Montgomery immediately sent off a message disagreeing heatedly.

With the slackening of the pursuit, Montgomery's worst fears
were being realized. German opposition was stiffening. In his
message, focusing in particular on the shortage of supplies, Montgomery claimed that he was getting only half his requirements,
and "I cannot go on for long like this." He refused to be diverted
from his plan to drive to Berlin. The obvious necessity of immediately opening up the vital port of Antwerp was not even mentioned in his dispatch, yet he stressed that "as soon as I have a Pas
de Calais port working, I would then require about 2,500 additional three-ton lorries, plus an assured airlift averaging about
1,000 tons a day to enable me to get to the Ruhr and finally
Berlin." Because it was all "very difficult to explain," the Field

Marshal "wondered if it was possible" for Eisenhower to come and see him. Unshaken in his conviction that the Supreme Commander's decision was a grave error and confident that his own plan would work, Montgomery refused to accept Eisenhower's rejection as final. Yet he had no intention of flying to Jullouville in an attempt to change Eisenhower's mind. Such diplomacy was not part of his makeup, although he was fully aware that the only hope of selling his proposal was via a face-to-face meeting with the Supreme Commander. Outraged and seething, Montgomery awaited a reply from Eisenhower. The British Field Marshal was in near-seclusion, impatient and irritable, at the moment when Prince Bernhard arrived at the headquarters to pay his respects.

Bernhard had arrived in France on the evening of the sixth. With a small staff, three jeeps, his Sealyham terrier Martin and a bulging briefcase containing Dutch underground reports, he and his party flew to the Continent, guarded by two fighter planes, in three Dakotas with Bernhard at the controls of one. From the airfield at Amiens they drove to Douai, fifty miles north, and early on the seventh set out for Belgium and Brussels. At the Laeken headquarters the Prince was met by General Horrocks, introduced to Montgomery's staff and ushered into the presence of the Field Marshal. "He was in a bad humor and obviously not happy to see me," Bernhard recalled. "He had a lot on his mind, and the presence of royalty in his area was understandably a responsibility that he could easily do without."

The Field Marshal's renown as the greatest British soldier of the war had made him, in Bernhard's words, "the idol of millions of Britishers." And the thirty-three-year-old Prince was in awe of Montgomery. Unlike Eisenhower's relaxed, almost casual manner, Montgomery's demeanor made it difficult for Bernhard to converse easily with him. Sharp and blunt from the outset, Montgomery made it clear that Bernhard's presence in his area "worried" him. With justification untempered by tact or explanation, Montgomery told the Prince that it would be unwise for Bernhard to visit the headquarters of the Dutch unit—the Princess Irene Brigade—attached to the British Second Army, quartered in the area around Diest, barely ten miles from the front line. Bernhard, who, as Commander in Chief of the Netherlands Forces, had every intention of visiting Diest, for the moment did not respond. Instead, he began to discuss the Dutch resistance reports. Montgomery overrode him. Returning to the matter, he told the Prince, "You must not live in Diest. I cannot allow it." Irked, Bernhard felt compelled to point out that he was "serving directly under Eisenhower and did not come under the Field Marshal's command." Thus, from the start, as Bernhard remembers the meeting, "rightly or wrongly, we got off on the wrong foot." (Later, in fact, Eisenhower backed Montgomery regarding Diest, but he did say that Bernhard could stay in Brussels "close to 21st Army Group headquarters, where your presence may be needed.")

Bernhard went on to review the situation in Holland as reflected in the underground reports. Montgomery was told of the retreat and disorganization of the Germans, which had been going on since September 2, and of the makeup of the resistance groups. To the best of his knowledge, Bernhard said, the reports were accurate. Montgomery, according to the Prince, retorted, "I don't think your resistance people can be of much use to us. Therefore, I believe all this is quite unnecessary." Startled by the Field Marshal's bluntness, Bernhard "began to realize that Montgomery apparently did not believe *any* of the messages coming from my agents in Holland. In a way, I could hardly blame him. I gathered he was a bit fed up with misleading information that he had received from the French and Belgian resistance during his advance. But, in this instance, I knew the Dutch groups involved, the people who were running them and I knew the information was, indeed, correct." He persisted. Showing the Field Marshal the message file and quoting from report after report, Bernhard posed a question: "In view of this, why can't you attack right away?"

"We can't depend on these reports," Montgomery told him. "Just because the Dutch resistance claim the Germans have been retreating from September 2 doesn't necessarily mean they are still retreating." Bernhard had to admit the retreat "was slowing down," and there were "signs of reorganization." Still, in his opinion, there was valid reason for an immediate attack.

Montgomery remained adamant. "Anyway," he said, "much as I would like to attack and liberate Holland, I can't do it because of supplies. We are short of ammunition. We are short of petrol for the tanks and if we did attack, in all probability they would become stranded." Bernhard was astounded. The information he received in England from both SHAEF and his own advisers had convinced him that the liberation of Holland would be accomplished in a matter of days. "Naturally I automatically assumed that Montgomery, commander on the spot, knew the situation better than anyone else," Bernhard later said. "Yet we had absolutely every detail on the Germans—troop strength, the number of tanks and armored vehicles, the position of antiaircraft guns—and I knew, apart from immediate front-line opposition, that there was little strength behind it. I was sick at heart, because I knew that German strength would grow with each passing day. I was unable to persuade Montgomery. In fact, nothing I said seemed to matter."

Then Montgomery made an extraordinary disclosure. "I am just as eager to liberate the Netherlands as you are," he said, "but we intend to do it in another, even better way." He paused, thought a moment and then, almost reluctantly, said, "I am planning an airborne operation ahead of my troops." Bernhard was startled. Instantly a number of questions came to his mind. In what area were the drops planned? When would the operation take place? How was it being developed? Yet he refrained from asking. Montgomery's manner indicated he would say no more. The operation was obviously still in the planning stage and the Prince's impression was that only the Field Marshal and a few of his staff officers knew of the plan. Although he was given no more details, Bernhard was now hopeful that the liberation of Holland, despite Montgomery's earlier talk of lack of supplies, was imminent. He must be patient and wait. The Field Marshal's reputation was awesome. Bernhard believed in it and in the man himself. The Prince felt a renewal of hope, for "anything Montgomery did, he would do well."

Eisenhower, acceding to Montgomery's request, set Sunday, September 10, as the date for a meeting. He was not particularly looking forward to his meeting with Montgomery and the usual temperamental arguments he had come to expect from the Field Marshal. He was, however, interested in learning what progress had been made in one aspect of the Montgomery operation. Although the Supreme Commander must approve all airborne plans, he had given Montgomery tactical use of the First Allied Airborne Army and permission to work out a possible plan involving that force. He knew that Montgomery, at least since the fourth, had been quietly exploring the possibility of an airborne operation to seize a bridgehead across the Rhine.

Ever since the formation of the First Allied Airborne Army under its American commander, Lieutenant General Lewis Hyde Brereton, six weeks earlier, Eisenhower had been searching for both a target and a suitable opportunity to employ the force. To that end he had been pressing Brereton and the various army commanders to develop bold and imaginative airborne plans calling for large-scale mass attacks deep behind the enemy's lines. Various missions had been proposed and accepted, but all had been canceled. In nearly every case the speeding land armies had already arrived at the objectives planned for the paratroops.

Montgomery's original proposal had called for units of Brereton's airborne force to grab a crossing west of the town of Wesel, just over the Dutch-German border. However, heavy antiaircraft defenses in that area had forced the Field Marshal to make a change. The site he then chose was farther west in Holland: the Lower Rhine bridge at Arnhem—at this juncture more than seventy-five miles behind the German front lines.

By September 7, Operation Comet, as the plan was called, was in readiness; then bad weather, coupled with Montgomery's concern about the ever-increasing German opposition his troops were encountering, forced a postponement. What might have succeeded on the sixth or seventh seemed risky by the tenth. Eisenhower too was concerned; for one thing he felt that the launching of an airborne attack at this juncture would mean a delay in opening the port of Antwerp. Yet the Supreme Commander remained fascinated by the possibilities of an airborne attack.

The abortive operations, some of them canceled almost at the last minute, had created a major problem for Eisenhower. Each time a mission reached the jump-off stage, troop-carrier planes, hauling gasoline to the front, had to be grounded and made ready. This loss of precious air-supply tonnage brought cries of protest from Bradley and Patton. At this moment of relentless pursuit, the airlift of gasoline, they declared, was far more vital than airborne missions. Eisenhower, anxious to use the paratroopers and urged by Washington to do so—both General Marshall and General Henry H. Arnold, commander of the U.S. Army air forces, wanted to see what Brereton's new Allied Airborne Army could accomplish—was not prepared to ground his highly trained airborne divisions. On the contrary, he was insisting that they be used at the earliest opportunity.[*] In fact, it might be a way to catapult his troops across the Rhine at the very moment when the pursuit was slowing down. But on this morning of September 10, as he flew to Brussels, all other considerations were secondary in his mind to the opening of the vital port of Antwerp.

Not so Montgomery. Anxious and determined, he was waiting at Brussels airport as Eisenhower's plane touched down. With characteristic preciseness, he had honed and refined his arguments preparatory to the meeting. He had talked with General Miles C. Dempsey of the British Second Army, and Lieutenant General Frederick Browning, commander of the British I Airborne Corps, who was also deputy chief of the First Allied Airborne Army. Browning was waiting in the wings for the outcome of the conference. Dempsey, concerned at the ever-stiffening enemy resist-

[*] Pogue, *The Supreme Command*, p. 280.

ance before him and aware from the intelligence reports that new units were moving in, asked Montgomery to abandon the plan for an airborne attack on the bridge at Arnhem. Instead, he suggested concentrating on seizing the Rhine crossing at Wesel. Even in conjunction with an airborne mission, Dempsey contended, the British Second Army probably was not strong enough to drive due north to Arnhem by itself. It would be better, he believed, to advance in conjunction with the U.S. First Army northeast toward Wesel.

A drive into Holland was, in any case, now imperative. The British War Office had informed Montgomery that V-2's—the first German rockets—had landed in London on September 8. Their launch sites were believed to be somewhere in western Holland. Whether before or after receiving this information, Montgomery altered his plans. Operation Comet, as originally devised, called for only a division and a half—the British 1st Airborne and the Polish 1st Parachute Brigade; that force was too weak to be effective, he believed. As a result, he canceled Comet. In its place, Montgomery came up with an even more ambitious airborne proposal. As yet, only a few of the Field Marshal's upper-echelon officers knew about it and, apprehensive of General Bradley's influence with Eisenhower, they had taken great pains to see that no hint of the plan reached American liaison officers at the British headquarters. Like Eisenhower, Lieutenant General Browning and the headquarters of the First Allied Airborne Army in England were, at this moment, unaware of Montgomery's new airborne scheme.

Because of his injured knee, Eisenhower was unable to leave his plane, and the conference was held on board. Montgomery, as he had done on August 23, determined who should be present at the meeting. The Supreme Commander had brought his deputy, Air Chief Marshal Sir Arthur Tedder, and an assistant chief of staff, Lieutenant General Sir Humphrey Gale, in charge of administration. Curtly, Montgomery asked that Eisenhower exclude Gale from the conference while insisting that his own administrative and supply chief, Lieutenant General Miles Graham, remain. Another, less acquiescent superior might well have taken issue with Montgomery's attitude. Eisenhower patiently granted the Field Marshal's demand. General Gale left.

Almost immediately Montgomery denounced the Supreme Commander's broad-front policy. Constantly referring to a sheaf of Eisenhower's communications that had arrived during the previous week, he called attention to the Supreme Commander's inconsistencies in not clearly defining what was meant by "priority." He argued that his 21st Army Group was not getting the "priority" in supplies promised by Eisenhower; that Patton's drive to the Saar was being allowed to proceed at the expense of Montgomery's forces. Calmly Eisenhower answered that he had never meant to give Montgomery "absolute priority" to the exclusion of everyone else. Eisenhower's strategy, Montgomery reiterated, was wrong and would have "dire consequences." So long as these two "jerky and disjointed thrusts were continued," with supplies split between himself and Patton, "neither could succeed." It was essential, Montgomery said, that Eisenhower decide between him and Patton. So fierce and unrestrained was Montgomery's language that Eisenhower suddenly reached out, patted Montgomery's knee and told him, "Steady, Monty! You can't speak to me like that. I'm your boss." Montgomery's anger vanished. "I'm sorry, Ike," he said quietly.*

The uncharacteristic but seemingly genuine apology was not the end of the matter. Doggedly, though with less acrimony, Montgomery continued to argue for his "single thrust." Eisenhower listened intently and with sympathy to the arguments, but his own view remained unchanged. His broad-front advance would continue. He told Montgomery clearly why. As Eisenhower was later to recall,† he said, "What you're proposing is this—if I give you all of the supplies you want, you could go straight to Berlin—right straight to Berlin? Monty, you're nuts.

---

* In his memoirs, Montgomery, in discussing the meeting, says that "we had a good talk." But he does state that, during these days of strategy arguments, "Possibly I went a bit far in urging on him my own plan, and did not give sufficient weight to the heavy political burden he bore. . . . Looking back on it all I often wonder if I paid sufficient heed to Eisenhower's notions before refuting them. I think I did. Anyhow . . . I never cease to marvel at his patience and forbearance. . . ."

† To the author.

You can't do it. What the hell! If you try a long column like that in a single thrust you'd have to throw off division after division to protect your flanks from attack. Now suppose you did get a bridge across the Rhine. You couldn't depend for long on that one bridge to supply your drive. Monty, you can't do it."

Montgomery, according to Eisenhower, replied, "I'll supply them all right. Just give me what I need and I'll reach Berlin and end the war."

Eisenhower's rejection was firm. Antwerp, he stressed, must be opened before any major drive into Germany could even be contemplated. Montgomery then played his trump card. The most recent development—the rocket attack on London from sites in the Netherlands—necessitated an immediate advance into Holland. He knew exactly how such a drive should begin. To strike into Germany, Montgomery proposed to use almost the entire First Allied Airborne Army in a stunning mass attack.

His plan was an expanded, grandiose version of Operation Comet. Montgomery now wanted to use three and a half divisions—the U.S. 82nd and 101st, the British 1st Airborne and the Polish 1st Parachute Brigade. The airborne forces were to seize a succession of river crossings in Holland ahead of his troops, with the major objective being the Lower Rhine bridge at Arnhem. Anticipating that the Germans would expect him to take the shortest route and drive northeast for the Rhine and the Ruhr, Montgomery had deliberately chosen a northern "back door" route to the Reich. The surprise airborne attack would open a corridor for the tanks of his British Second Army, which would race across the captured bridges to Arnhem, over the Rhine and beyond. Once all this was accomplished, Montgomery could wheel east, outflank the Siegfried Line, and dash into the Ruhr.

Eisenhower was intrigued and impressed. It was a bold, brilliantly imaginative plan, exactly the kind of mass attack he had been seeking for his long-idle airborne divisions. But now the Supreme Commander was caught between the hammer and the anvil: if he agreed to the attack, the opening of Antwerp would temporarily have to be delayed and supplies diverted from Patton. Yet, Montgomery's proposal could revitalize the dying advance and perhaps propel the pursuit across the Rhine and into the Ruhr. Eisenhower, fascinated by the audaciousness of the plan, not only gave his approval,° but insisted that the operation take place at the earliest possible moment.

Yet the Supreme Commander stressed that the attack was a "limited one." And he emphasized to Montgomery that he considered the combined airborne-ground operation "merely an extension of the northern advance to the Rhine and the Ruhr." As Eisenhower remembered the conversation, he said to Montgomery, "I'll tell you what I'll do, Monty. I'll give you whatever you ask to get you over the Rhine because I want a bridgehead . . . but let's get over the Rhine first before we discuss anything else." Montgomery continued to argue, but Eisenhower would not budge. Frustrated, the Field Marshal had to accept what he called a "half measure," and on this note the conference ended.

After Eisenhower's departure, Montgomery outlined the proposed operation on a map for Lieutenant General Browning. The elegant Browning, one of Britain's pioneer airborne advocates, saw that the paratroopers and glider-borne forces were being called upon to secure a series of crossings—five of them major bridges including the wide rivers of the Maas, the Waal and the Lower Rhine—over a stretch approximately sixty-four miles long between the Dutch border and Arnhem. Additionally, they were charged with holding open the corridor—in most places a single highway running north—over which British armor would drive. All of the bridges had to be seized intact if the armored dash was to succeed. The dangers were obvious, but this was precisely the kind of surprise assault for which the airborne forces had been trained. Still, Browning was uneasy. Pointing to the most northern bridge over the Lower Rhine at Arnhem, he asked, "How long will it take the armor to reach us?" Montgomery replied briskly, "Two days." Still intent on the map, Browning said, "We can hold it for four." Then he added, "But sir, I think we might be going a bridge too far."

° Eisenhower told Stephen E. Ambrose, according to his book, *The Supreme Commander*, p. 518 fn.: "I not only approved . . . I insisted upon it. What we needed was a bridgehead over the Rhine. If that could be accomplished, I was quite willing to wait on all other operations. . . ."

THE PRIZE
The most northern of all crossings to be seized by Anglo-American and Polish airborne forces was the Arnhem bridge over the Lower Rhine. Assigned to Major General Urquhart's British 1st Airborne Division and Major General Sosabowski's Polish 1st Parachute Brigade, it was the key to Montgomery's plan to end the war in 1944. Photo shows bridge with long boulevards stretching back to the concert hall complex, Musis Sacrum (left foreground).

The Bridges: *Urquhart's men were also to capture the Arnhem railroad crossing and the pontoon bridge. The Germans blew up the former, and the middle section of the latter was found missing. Mystery surrounds RAF photo of pontoon bridge* [LEFT] *taken eleven days before attack: were Germans replacing or removing the center? No one could tell, but attack was ordered just the same.*

Major General Gavin's 82nd Airborne swiftly captured the 1500-foot-long Grave bridge over the Maas River [OPPOSITE TOP] *and, among others, the Heumen Canal bridge* [OPPOSITE CENTER]. *But due to confusion in orders and quick German reaction, they failed to capture on the first day Nijmegen bridge, over the Waal* [BELOW], *eleven miles from Arnhem. Crossing fell in combined Anglo-American attack on the 19th when the 82nd made a daring river assault which has been called a "second Omaha Beach landing."*

South of 82nd's positions, Major General Taylor's 101st Airborne captured all bridges but one: the crossing at Son [BELOW] was blown up, throwing Market-Garden's schedule off by 36 hours.

Eisenhower and Montgomery were bitterly opposed on war strategy. Montgomery thought Supreme Commander indecisive with "no experience for the job"; Eisenhower considered Britain's popular Field Marshal "an egocentric who never made a mistake in his life."

New chief of First Allied Airborne Army, Lieutenant General Brereton, had never commanded paratroops before. He was in disagreement with British deputy, Lieutenant General Browning. Hours before attack planning began, Brereton received a letter of resignation from Browning.

Browning, Britain's foremost airborne authority, withdrew his resignation when named to command Market-Garden. He had never had operational control of an airborne corps before.

(*Left to right*) *Major General Adair, commander of Guards Armored Division; Field Marshal Montgomery; Lieutenant General Horrocks, whose XXX Corps tanks and infantry would make drive; and Major General Roberts, whose Eleventh Armored captured Antwerp but was halted to "refuel, refit and rest," thus allowing bulk of German Fifteenth Army to reach Holland and participate in Market-Garden offensive.*

[BELOW LEFT] *Major General Taylor, commander of the U.S. 101st Airborne, meets with Lieutenant General Ritchie, of 12th British Corps; and* [RIGHT] *General Dempsey, chief of Second British Army, confers with Major General Gavin, U.S. 82nd Airborne commander.*

Dutch intelligence man Henri Knap [TOP LEFT] with Arnhem underground chief Pieter Kruyff [RIGHT] warned London of Panzer divisions in Arnhem area on September 14th. · [CENTER] Major Brian Urquhart, Browning's intelligence chief, also spotted German tanks on RAF reconnaissance photos. Warnings went unheeded. · [LOWER LEFT] Major General "Roy" Urquhart, commander of British 1st Airborne, though veteran combat leader, was commanding paratroop division for first time. He was not only unaware of German armor but was forced to land his units from six to eight miles from crucial Arnhem bridge. Hardly had the attack begun than communications failed, and General Urquhart, cut off from headquarters behind German lines, was forced to hide out for 39 vital hours.

With Urquhart "missing," Brigadier Hicks [TOP LEFT] was forced to lead the division. · When 4th Parachute Brigade landed, September 18th, Brigadier Hackett [ABOVE RIGHT], because of seniority, challenged Hicks over division command. · Urquhart's Chief of Staff, Colonel Mackenzie [CENTER LEFT], calmed down arguing brigadiers · Meanwhile, unaware of true situation in Arnhem, General Sosabowski [CENTER RIGHT] and his Polish 1st Parachute Brigade were delayed more than two days because of bad weather. · Brigadier Lathbury [BELOW], commander of 1st Parachute Brigade, should have assumed division leadership, but was wounded and, like General Urquhart, considered "missing."

Holding northern approaches to Arnhem bridge and outnumbered by at least 10 to 1, Colonel John Frost [LEFT], with his men, in one of history's greatest feats of arms, held off elements of two German Panzer divisions. · Another bridge hero, Captain Eric Mackay [CENTER, AS HE IS TODAY], though almost out of ammunition, actually called on Germans to surrender. Wounded and captured, Mackay [BELOW, AT TILLER] refused to give up; he escaped and floated downstream to Nijmegen with companions.

*Irish Guards tank group
led the armored breakout
from Dutch-Belgian
border. Shown here are
its commander, Colonel
J. O. E. Vandeleur [ABOVE
LEFT], and his cousin
Giles, a battalion
commander [ABOVE
RIGHT]. [RIGHT] The two
men as they appeared in
1944. The Germans
succeeded in halting
Vandeleur's tanks barely
six miles short of Frost's
men on Arnhem bridge.*

RAF Flight Lieutenant Love [TOP], *ground-to-air communications officer during tank drive, wondered why he had volunteered for job.* · *Lord Wrottesley* [LEFT CENTER], *who made first contact with Urquhart's isolated troops.* · *Lieutenant Hay* [RIGHT CENTER], *whose "Phantom" radio unit finally contacted ground forces for Urquhart.* · *Colonel Chatterton* [RIGHT], *Glider Pilot Regiment commander, who pressed for a daring glider coup-de-main on Arnhem bridge. Had his plan been adopted, the bridge might have been taken within hours. Instead, Chatterton was called "an assassin and a bloody murderer" for suggesting the idea.*

In his division's last stand at Oosterbeek, Major Cain [ABOVE LEFT], though wounded again and again, continued to fight back against enemy tanks. · Miss Clair Miller [ABOVE RIGHT], of London's Hobson & Sons Ltd., made Browning's Pegasus flag, contrary to the Arnhem myth that it was the work of his wife, novelist Daphne du Maurier. Miss Miller also sewed 500 tiny compasses into troopers' uniforms, which later aided many in making an escape. · Major Lonsdale [BELOW LEFT], whose "Lonsdale Force" held out to the very end.

In the Anglo-American attack on Nijmegen bridge, 82nd Airborne's Major Cook [ABOVE RIGHT] led the unprecedented crossing of Waal River to seize bridge's northern end. · Simultaneously Lieutenant Colonel Vandervoort [ABOVE LEFT], together with British forces, attacked southern approaches.

Military Cross winner Lieutenant Gorman [ABOVE LEFT] had his "doubts" about the entire operation. He felt that no one was moving fast enough to rescue Frost's men on Arnhem bridge. · Lieutenant Wierzbowski [ABOVE RIGHT] was sent with a company to capture the bridge at Best, which was believed to be "lightly held." The area actually contained more than 1,000 German troops of the forgotten Fifteenth Army and in the end involved an entire regiment of the 101st Airborne.

Lieutenant Glover [ABOVE LEFT], who took his pet chicken, Myrtle, on the Arnhem jump. "Myrtle, the parachick" was killed and in the midst of the fighting was given a formal burial. · Major Deane-Drummond [ABOVE RIGHT], second in command, 1st Airborne Division Signals, had doubts that his communications would work, but like everyone else was "swept along with the prevailing attitude," which was "For God's sake, don't rock the boat." · Colonel Tucker [RIGHT], 504th regimental commander, whose units crossed Waal River, was appalled at slowness of British tanks. He had expected a special task force to make the eleven-mile dash to Arnhem and relieve bridge defenders. Instead, Tucker said, the British "stopped for tea."

Fired by Hitler after the Normandy débâcle, Von Rundstedt [LEFT], the Reich's most competent Field Marshal, was recalled in September. The situation on the western front was so catastrophic that Von Rundstedt believed the Allies could invade the Reich and end the war within two weeks. His strategy in saving Fifteenth Army was major factor in defeating Montgomery's Market-Garden plan. Field Marshal Model [BELOW], whom Von Rundstedt called a "good regimental sergeant major," had been unable to halt Allied drive across western Europe, but by chance had moved the II SS Panzer Corps into the Arnhem area days before the airborne attack. Captured Market-Garden plans were in his hands within 48 hours, but, incredibly, Model refused to believe them.

II SS Panzer Corps commander, Lieutenant General Bittrich (shown above as he is today and in 1944), knew nothing of captured Market-Garden plans, but correctly deduced that main objective was Arnhem bridge.

The Reich's airborne expert, Colonel General Student (today and in 1944), was stunned by size of airborne drop and "only wished I had had such forces at my disposal."

The British landed virtually amidst two Panzer divisions in the Arnhem area, to the surprise of their commanders: Lieutenant Colonel Harzer (above as he is today and in 1944) of 9th SS "Hohenstaufen" Division; Major General Harmel (below) of 10th SS "Frundsberg" Division.

Double agent "King Kong" Lindemanns [RIGHT] crossed front lines to inform Germans of British ground attack on September 17th. Contrary to British newspaper reports after the war, Lindemanns knew nothing about scope of airborne attack.

Luftwaffe General Dessloch [ABOVE LEFT] was so worried about possibility of airborne attack that he refused to visit Model. The battalion of Major Krafft [ABOVE RIGHT] was by chance in position on the edge of British drop zones.

The first man at Model's headquarters in Tafelberg Hotel to learn of airborne drop barely two miles away was Lieutenant Sedelhauser [RIGHT]. "They are dropping in our laps," he was told.

Prince Bernhard [ABOVE] shown as he arrived in liberated Eindhoven and [OPPOSITE] as he is today. Neither Bernhard nor his general staff were consulted about terrain difficulty in the Market-Garden plan until it was too late, and detailed information which the Prince had from Dutch underground sources regarding German armor in Arnhem was discounted.

*Expecting liberation, the Dutch in Oosterbeek found them-
selves caught up in brutal battle. "Montgomery will be here
soon," optimistic Britishers told 17-year-old Anje van Maanen*
[LEFT]. · *Jan Voskuil* [ABOVE] *could not rid himself of a "feeling of hopelessness."*
· *Hendrika van der Vlist* [BELOW] *wrote in her diary that Oosterbeek had become
"one of the bloodiest battlefields."*

Kate ter Horst [ABOVE LEFT] *with son Michiel during war and* [RIGHT] *with husband, Jan, as they are today, courageously made her home available to British wounded. At one time during battle more than 300 casualties crowded the house. A former Dutch captain, Jan could not understand why the British failed to use Driel ferry* [BELOW] *to cross the Rhine. In Market-Garden planning the ferry was completely overlooked.*

The embryo concept (which thereafter would bear the code name "Operation Market-Garden"—"Market" covering the airborne drop and "Garden" for the armored drive) was to be developed with the utmost speed, Montgomery ordered. He insisted that the attack had to be launched in a few days. Otherwise, he told Browning, it would be too late. Montgomery asked: "How soon can you get ready?" Browning, at this moment, could only hazard a guess. "The earliest scheduling of the operation would be the fifteenth or sixteenth,"° he told the Field Marshal.

Carrying Montgomery's skeleton plan and weighed with the urgency of preparing for such a massive mission in only a few days, Browning flew back to England immediately. On landing at his Moor Park Golf Course base near Rickmansworth on the outskirts of London, he telephoned the First Allied Airborne headquarters, twenty miles away, and notified the commander, Lieutenant General Brereton, and his chief of staff, Brigadier General Floyd L. Parks. The time was 2:30 P.M., and Parks noted that Browning's message contained "the first mention of 'Market' at this headquarters."

The airborne commanders were not the only officers caught unaware. Montgomery's daring plan so impressed and surprised the Field Marshal's greatest critic, General Omar N. Bradley, that he later recalled, "Had the pious, teetotalling Montgomery wobbled into SHAEF with a hangover, I could not have been more astonished. . . . Although I never reconciled myself to the venture, I nevertheless freely concede that it was one of the most imaginative of the war."†

It was, but Montgomery remained unhappy. He now prodded

° Minutes of the first planning meeting, First Allied Airborne Army operational file 1014–1017.

† General Omar N. Bradley, A Soldier's Story, p. 416. Bradley also added, "I had not been brought into the plan. In fact, Montgomery devised and sold it to Ike several days before I even learned of it from our own liaison officer at 21st Army Group."

the Supreme Commander even further, reverting to the cautious, perfectionist thinking that was characteristic of his military career. Unless the 21st Army Group received additional supplies and transport for the "selected thrust," Montgomery warned Eisenhower, Market-Garden could not be launched before September 23 at the earliest, and might even be delayed until September 26. Browning had estimated that Market could be ready by the fifteenth or sixteenth, but Montgomery was concerned about Garden, the land operation. Once again he was demanding what he had always wanted: absolute priority, which to his mind would guarantee success. Eisenhower noted in his desk diary for September 12: "Monty's suggestion is simple—'give him everything.'" Fearing that any delay might jeopardize Market-Garden, Eisenhower complied. He promptly sent his chief of staff, General Bedell Smith, to see Montgomery; Smith assured the Field Marshal of a thousand tons of supplies per day plus transport. Additionally, Montgomery was promised that Patton's drive to the Saar would be checked. Elated at the "electric" response—as the Field Marshal called it—Montgomery believed he had finally won the Supreme Commander over to his point of view.

Although opposition before Montgomery's troops had stiffened, he believed that the Germans in Holland, behind the hard crust of their front lines, had little strength. Allied intelligence confirmed his estimate. Eisenhower's headquarters reported "few infantry reserves" in the Netherlands, and even these were considered to be "troops of low category." The enemy, it was thought, was still "disorganized after his long and hasty retreat . . . and though there might be numerous small bodies of Germans in the area," they were hardly capable of any great organized resistance. Montgomery now believed he could quickly crack the German defenses. Then, once he was over the Rhine and headed for the Ruhr, he did not see how Eisenhower could halt his drive. The Supreme Commander would have little choice, he reasoned, but to let him continue toward Berlin—thus ending the war, as Montgomery put it, "reasonably quickly." Confidently, Montgomery set Sunday, September 17, as D Day for

Operation Market-Garden. The brilliant scheme he had devised was to become the greatest airborne operation of the entire war.

Not everyone shared Montgomery's certainty about Market-Garden. At least one of his senior officers had reason to be worried. General Miles Dempsey, commander of the British Second Army, unlike the Field Marshal, did not dispute the authenticity of Dutch resistance reports. From these, Dempsey's intelligence staff had put together a picture indicating rapidly increasing German strength between Eindhoven and Arnhem, in the very area of the planned airborne drop. There was even a Dutch report that "battered panzer formations have been sent to Holland to refit," and these too were said to be in the Market-Garden area. Dempsey sent along this news to Browning's British I Airborne Corps, but the information lacked any back-up endorsement by Montgomery or his staff. The ominous note was not even included in intelligence summaries. In fact, in the mood of optimism prevailing at 21st Army Group headquarters, the report was completely discounted.

❈ 7 ❈

FIELD MARSHAL GERD VON RUNDSTEDT's high-risk gamble to rescue the remains of General Von Zangen's encircled Fifteenth Army in the Pas de Calais was paying off. Under cover of darkness, ever since September 6, a hastily assembled fleet consisting of two ancient Dutch freighters, several Rhine barges and some small boats and rafts had been plying back and forth across the three-mile mouth of the Schelde estuary ferrying men, artillery, vehicles and even horses.

Although powerful coastal guns on Walcheren Island protected against attack from the sea, the Germans were surprised that Allied naval forces made no effort to interfere. Major General Walter Poppe expected the convoy carrying his splintered 59th Infantry Division to be "blown out of the water." To him the one-hour trip between Breskens and Flushing "in completely darkened ships, exposed and defenseless, was a most unpleasant experience." The Allies, the Germans suspected, completely underestimated the size of the evacuation. Certainly they knew about it. Because both Von Rundstedt and Army Group B's commander, Field Marshal Walter Model, desperately in need of reinforcements, were demanding speed, some daylight trips had been made. Immediately, fighters pounced on the small convoys. Darkness, however unpleasant, was much safer.

The most hazardous part of the journey was on the Schelde's northern bank. There, under the constant threat of Allied air attack, Von Zangen's forces had to follow a single main road, running east from Walcheren Island, across the Beveland peninsula and into Holland. Part of the escape route, at the narrow neck joining the mainland, was only a few miles from Antwerp and British lines on the Albert Canal. Inexplicably the British even now made no serious effort to attack north, spring the trap, and cut the base of the isthmus. The escape route remained open. Although hammered by incessant Allied air attacks Von Zangen's Fifteenth Army would eventually reach Holland—at a most crucial moment for Montgomery's Market-Garden operation.

While the Fifteenth Army had been extricated more by calculated design than by luck, now the opposite occurred: fate, the unexpected and unpredictable, took a hand. Some eighty miles away the battered armored units of Lieutenant General Wilhelm Bittrich's elite, veteran II SS Panzer Corps reached bivouac areas in the vicinity of Arnhem. As directed by Field Marshal Model on September 4, Bittrich had slowly disengaged the 9th and 10th SS

Panzer divisions for "refitting and rehabilitation." Model had chosen the Arnhem area. The two reduced, but still tough, divisions were fanned out to the north, east and south of the town. Bittrich assigned the 9th SS to a huge rectangular sector north and northeast of Arnhem, where most of the division's men and vehicles were on high ground and conveniently hidden in a densely wooded national park. The 10th was encamped in a semicircle to the northeast, east and southeast. Thus, camouflaged and hidden in nearby woods, villages and towns—Beekbergen, Apeldoorn, Zutphen, Ruurlo and Doetinchem—both divisions were within striking distance of Arnhem; some units were within a mile or two of the suburbs. As Bittrich was later to recall, "there was no particular significance in Model choosing the Arnhem vicinity—except that it was a peaceful sector where nothing was happening."

The possibility that this remote backwater might have any strategic value to the Allies was obviously discounted. On the morning of September 11, a small group of Model's staff officers was dispatched in search of a new site for Army Group B's headquarters—in Arnhem.

One of Model's aides, his general headquarters administration and transportation officer, thirty-five-year-old Lieutenant Gustav Sedelhauser, later remembered that "we visited the 9th and 10th SS division headquarters at Beekbergen and Ruurlo and General Bittrich's command post at Doetinchem. Then we inspected Arnhem itself. It had everything we wanted: a fine road net and excellent accommodations. But it was not until we drove west to the outlying district of Oosterbeek that we found what we were looking for." In the wealthy, residential village just two and a half miles from the center of Arnhem was a group of hotels, among them the gracious, white Hartenstein, with its broad expanse of crescent-shaped lawn, stretching back into parklike surroundings where deer roamed undisturbed, and the smaller, two-story, tree-shaded Tafelberg with its glassed-in veranda and paneled rooms. Impressed by the facilities and, as Sedelhauser recalled, "especially the accommodations," the group promptly recommended

Oosterbeek to the chief of staff, Lieutenant General Hans Krebs, as "perfect for Army Group B's headquarters." Model approved the decision. Part of the staff, he decided, would live at the Hartenstein, while he would occupy the more secluded, less ostentatious Tafelberg. Lieutenant Sedelhauser was delighted. Since his tenure the headquarters had never remained anywhere for more than a few days, and now Sedelhauser "was looking forward to some peace and a chance to get my laundry done." By September 15, Model directed, Army Group B's headquarters was to be fully operational in Oosterbeek—approximately three miles from the broad expanse of heaths and pastureland where the British 1st Airborne Division was due to land on September 17.

Part Two

✺

THE PLAN

✺

☆ 1 ☆

IN THE EARLY EVENING of September 10, within hours of General Browning's meeting with Field Marshal Montgomery, Lieutenant General Lewis H. Brereton held the first basic planning conference on Operation Market. At his Sunninghill Park headquarters near the fashionable Ascot racecourse thirty-five miles from London, twenty-seven senior officers crowded into Brereton's large map-lined office. After General Browning briefed the group on Montgomery's plan, Brereton told them that, because there was so little time, "major decisions arrived at now must stand—and these have to be made immediately."

The task was monumental, and there were few guidelines. Never before had there been an attempt to send a mammoth airborne force, complete with vehicles, artillery and equipment, capable of fighting on its own, deep behind enemy front lines. In comparison with Market, previous airborne attacks had been small; yet months had gone into their planning. Now, to prepare for the greatest paratroop and glider-borne infantry operation ever conceived, Brereton and his planners had barely seven days.

Brereton's greatest concern was not the deadline, but the possibility that this operation, like its predecessors, might be canceled. His long-idle airborne troops were impatient for action, and a serious morale problem had developed as a consequence. For weeks his elite, highly trained divisions had stood down while ground forces on the Continent swept victoriously across France and Belgium. There was a widespread feeling that victory was so near that the war might end before the First Allied Airborne Army got into battle.

The General harbored no doubts about the ability of his staff to meet the tight, one-week Market schedule. There had been so many "dry runs" in developing previous airborne schemes that his headquarters and division staffs had reached a stage of high-speed efficiency. Additionally, much of the planning that had gone into Comet and other canceled operations could be readily adapted to Market. In preparing for the aborted Comet mission, for example, the British 1st Airborne Division and the Polish Brigade, charged with that operation, had made a thorough study of the Arnhem area. Still, most of the Market concept meant vastly expanded planning—and all of it was time-consuming.

General Brereton was outwardly confident and calm, but members of his staff noted that he smoked one cigarette after another. On his desk was a framed quotation which the General often pointed out to his staff. It read: "Where is the Prince who can afford so to cover his country with troops for its defense, as that 10,000 men descending from the clouds, might not, in many places, do an infinite deal of mischief before a force could be brought together to repel them?" It had been written in 1784 by Benjamin Franklin.

Brereton was fascinated by the vision of the eighteenth-century statesman and scientist. "Even after a hundred sixty years," he had told his staff, "the idea remains the same." But Franklin would have been bewildered by the complexities and size of Operation Market. To invade Holland from the sky, Brereton planned to land almost 35,000 men—nearly twice the number of paratroops and glider-borne infantry used in the invasion of Normandy.

To "grab the bridges with thunderclap surprise," as Brereton put it, and hold open the narrow, one-highway advance corridor for the British Garden ground forces—from their attack line near the Dutch-Belgian border to Arnhem sixty-four miles north— three and one half airborne divisions were to be used. Two would be American. Almost directly ahead of General Horrocks' XXX Corps tanks, Major General Maxwell D. Taylor's 101st Airborne Division was to capture canal and river crossings over a fifteen-mile stretch between Eindhoven and Veghel. North of them, Brigadier General James M. Gavin's veteran 82nd Division was charged with the area between Grave and the city of Nijmegen, approximately a ten-mile stretch. They were to seize crossings over the great Maas and Waal rivers, in particular the huge multispan bridge at Nijmegen, which, with its approaches, was almost a half-mile long. The single most important objective of Operation Market-Garden was Arnhem and its vital crossing over the 400-yard-wide Lower Rhine. The great concrete-and-steel, three-span highway bridge, together with its concrete ramps, was almost 2,000 feet long. Its capture was assigned to the British and Poles—Major General Robert "Roy" E. Urquhart's 1st Airborne Division and, under his command, Major General Stanislaw Sosabowski's Polish 1st Parachute Brigade. Arnhem, lying farthest away from the Garden forces, was the prize. Without the Rhine crossing, Montgomery's bold stroke to liberate Holland, outflank the Siegfried Line and springboard into Germany's industrial Ruhr would fail.

To carry the huge force to targets three hundred miles away, an intricate air plan had to be designed. Three distinct operations were required: transportation, protection and resupply. No fewer than twenty-four different airfields would be needed for takeoff. Brereton planned to use every operable glider in his command—an immense fleet of more than 2,500. Besides hauling heavy equipment such as jeeps and artillery, the gliders were to ferry more than a third of the 35,000-man force; the rest would drop by parachute. All the craft had to be checked out, loading space allotted, heavy equipment and cargo stowed, and troop complements prepared.

Gliders posed only a single problem in the air planning. Transports to carry paratroops and tow planes to pull the gliders must be diverted from their normal task of supplying the advancing armies and grounded in order to be readied for Market. The crews of bomber squadrons had to be alerted and briefed for missions in the Market-Garden area prior to, and during, the attack. Swarms of fighter squadrons from all over England—more than 1,500 planes—would be needed to escort the airborne force. Intricate aerial traffic patterns were of prime importance. Routes between England and Holland had to be laid out to avoid heavy enemy antiaircraft fire and the equally dangerous possibility of air collision. Air-sea rescue operations, resupply missions, even a dummy parachute drop in another area of Holland to deceive the enemy, were also planned. In all, it was estimated that almost 5,000 aircraft of all types would be involved in Market. To develop plans and ready this vast air armada would take a minimum of seventy-two hours.

The most pressing question of the conference, in Brereton's opinion, was whether the operation should be undertaken by day or by night. Previous major airborne operations had taken place in moonlight. But semidarkness had led to confusion in finding landing zones, lack of troop concentration and unnecessary casualties. The General decreed that the huge airborne assault would take place in broad daylight. It was an unprecedented decision. In the history of airborne operations, a daylight drop of such proportions had never before been made.

Brereton had other reasons than the desire to avoid confusion. The week scheduled for Operation Market was a no-moon period and night landings on a large scale were therefore impossible. Apart from that, Brereton chose a daylight attack because, for the first time in the war, it was feasible. Allied fighters held such overwhelming superiority over the battlefields that now interference from the Luftwaffe was practically nonexistent. But the Germans did have night fighters. In a night drop, against columns of slow-moving troop-carrying planes and gliders, they might prove devastatingly effective. German antiaircraft strength was another consideration: flak maps of the approaches to the Market drop areas were dotted with antiaircraft positions. The charts, based on photo-reconnaissance flights and the experience of bomber crews flying over Holland en route to Germany, looked formidable—particularly so because gliders were without protective armor, except in the cockpits, and C-47 troop-carriers and tow planes had no self-sealing gas tanks. Nevertheless, Brereton believed that enemy antiaircraft positions could be neutralized by concentrated bomber and fighter attacks preceding and during the assault. In any event, most antiaircraft was radar-directed, and therefore was as effective after dark as it was during the day. Either way, losses were to be expected. Still, unless bad weather and high winds intervened, the airborne force, by attacking in daylight, could be dropped with almost pinpoint accuracy on the landing zones, thus guaranteeing a quick concentration of troops in the corridor. "The advantages," Brereton told his commanders, "far outweigh the risks."

Brereton made his final announcement. To command the giant operation he appointed his deputy, the fastidious forty-seven-year-old Lieutenant General Frederick "Boy" Browning, head of the British I Airborne Corps. It was an excellent choice, though disappointing to Lieutenant General Matthew B. Ridgway, commander of the other corps in the airborne army—the XVIII Airborne Corps. Still, Browning had been slated to command the aborted Operation Comet, which, though smaller and utilizing only British and Polish airborne troops, was similar in concept to Market-Garden. Now, under the enlarged and innovative plan Montgomery had devised, American paratroops would serve under a British airborne commander for the first time.

To the assembled airborne commanders Browning delivered an optimistic summation. He ended his talk with the kind of picturesque confidence that had always made him a heroic figure to his men. As his chief of staff, Brigadier Gordon Walch, remembers, "General Browning was in high spirits, delighted that at last we were going. 'The object,' he told us, 'is to lay a carpet of airborne troops down over which our ground forces can pass.' He believed this single operation held the key to the duration of the war."

Browning's enthusiasm was catching. As the large meeting broke up, to be replaced by smaller staff conferences which would last throughout the night, few officers were aware that an underlying friction existed between Brereton and Browning. Originally, when the First Allied Airborne Army was formed, British hopes ran high that Browning, Britain's senior airborne authority and one of the pioneers in the use of paratroops, would be named commander. Because of the preponderance of American troops and equipment within the newly organized army, the coveted post went to an American, General Brereton.

In rank, Browning was six months Brereton's senior; and although the American was a distinguished tactical air force officer, he had never before commanded airborne forces. Additionally, there were wide personality differences between the two men. Brereton had been a World War I flyer and had served brilliantly in World War II, first in the Far and Middle East and later as commanding general of the U.S. Ninth Air Force in England. He was tenacious and single-minded, but his zeal to achieve was cloaked by a quiet, stolid demeanor. Now Brereton proceeded on the awesome assignment he had been handed with the determination and bulldozing tactics that characterized many of his fellow American career officers.

Browning, a Grenadier Guards officer, was also a perfectionist, equally determined to prove the worth of paratroops. But he had never commanded an airborne corps before. In contrast to Brereton, "Boy" Browning was a somewhat glamorous figure, elegant and impeccably groomed, with an air of easy assurance often misunderstood for arrogance, not only by Americans but by some of his own commanders. Though he was temperamental and sometimes overly impatient, his reputation as an airborne theorist was legendary among his admirers. Still, he lacked the battle experience of some other officers, such as General Richard Gale of the British 6th Airborne Division and the veteran American commanders, Generals Gavin and Taylor. And, Browning had yet to prove that he possessed the administrative genius of the most experienced of all airborne commanders, General Ridgway.

Only days before, an incident had occurred that pointed up the differences between Brereton and Browning. On September 3, Browning had protested to Brereton the dangers of trying to launch an airborne assault on just thirty-six hours' notice. Since D Day on June 6, seventeen airborne operations had been prepared and canceled. In the thirty-three days of Brereton's command, in his eagerness to get into action, plans had been processed at the rate of almost one a week. None reached the launching stage. Browning, watching the mass production of airborne schemes, was deeply concerned about the haste and the risks being run. When Operation Linnet I—a drop before the British army in Belgium—was canceled on September 2, Brereton quickly found new objectives ahead of the speeding armies and proposed Operation Linnet II, as a substitute attack to take place on the morning of September 4.

As Brereton later recalled the incident, "Browning was quite agitated about Operation Linnet II in which there was a serious shortage of information, photographs and, in particular, maps. As a result, 'Boy' claimed his troops could not be briefed properly." Airborne operations, Browning contended, "should not be attempted on such short notice." In principle Brereton had agreed, but he had told his deputy that "the disorganization of the enemy demands that chances be taken." The disagreement between the two men had ended with Browning stiffly stating that he intended to submit his protest in writing. A few hours later his letter had arrived. Because "of our sharp differences of opinion," Browning wrote, he could no longer "continue as Deputy Commander of the First Allied Airborne Army." Brereton, unintimidated, had begun at once to consider the problem of Browning's replacement. He had alerted General Ridgway to "stand by to take over." The delicate problem was solved when Operation Linnet II was canceled; the following day Brereton had persuaded Browning to withdraw his letter of resignation.

Now, their differences set aside, both men faced the huge, complex task of preparing Market. Whatever reservations Browning entertained were now secondary to the job ahead.

There was one decision Brereton could not make at the initial meeting: exactly how the airborne troops comprising the carpet were to be carried to the targets. The airborne commanders could not make detailed plans until this greatest of all problems was solved. The fact was that the airborne army was only as mobile as the planes that would carry it. Apart from gliders, Brereton had no transports of his own. To achieve complete surprise, the ideal plan called for the three and one-half divisions in Market to be delivered to landing zones on the same day at the same hour. But the immense size of the operation ruled out this possibility. There was an acute shortage of both aircraft and gliders; the planes would have to make more than one trip. Other factors also forced a different approach. Each division had separate combat requirements. For example, it was essential that the transport for General Taylor's 101st Airborne carry more men than equipment when the attack began so that the division could carry out its assigned task of achieving a link-up with the Garden forces within the first few hours. Also, Taylor's men had to join quickly with the 82nd Airborne on the corridor north of them. There, General Gavin's troops not only had to secure the formidable bridges across the Maas and the Waal but also hold the Groesbeek ridge to the southeast, terrain which had to be denied the Germans because it dominated the countryside. Gavin's special assignment also imposed special requirements. Because the 82nd Airborne would have to fight longer than the 101st before the link-up occurred, Gavin needed not only troops but artillery.

Farther north, the problems of the British 1st Airborne under General Urquhart were different still. The British 1st was to hold the Arnhem bridge until relieved. With luck, German reaction would be sluggish enough so that ground forces could reach the lightly armed British troopers before any real enemy strength developed. But until Horrocks' tanks arrived, Urquhart's men would have to hang on. Urquhart could not dissipate his strength by sending units south to link up with Gavin. Lying at the farthest end of the airborne carpet, the British 1st Airborne would have to hold longer than anyone else. For this reason, Urquhart's force was the largest, his division bolstered by the addition of Polish paratroops, plus the 52nd Lowland Division, which was to be flown in as soon as air strips could be located and prepared in the Arnhem area.

On the morning of the eleventh, after a hectic night of assessing and analyzing aircraft availability for the attack, Major General Paul L. Williams, commander of the U.S. IX Troop Carrier Command, and in charge of all Market air operations, gave his estimate to Brereton. There was such a shortage of gliders and planes, he reported, that even with an all-out effort, at best only half the troop strength of Browning's total force could be flown in on D Day. Essential items such as artillery, jeeps and other heavy cargo scheduled for the gliders could be included only on a strict priority basis. Brereton urged his air commander to explore the possibility of two D-Day airlifts but the suggestion was found impractical. "Owing to the reduced hours of daylight and the distances involved, it would not be possible to consider more than one lift per day," General Williams said. It was too risky. There would be no time for maintenance or battle-damage repair, he pointed out, and almost certainly "casualties would result from pilot and crew fatigue."

Hamstrung by the shortage of aircraft and the time limit, Brereton made some general assessments. A full day would be required to take aerial-reconnaissance photographs of the Dutch bridges and terrain; two days must go into the preparation and distribution of maps of the areas; intelligence had to be gathered and analyzed; detailed battle plans must be prepared. The most crucial decision of all: Brereton was forced to tailor the Market plan to suit the existing airlift capability. He must transport his force in installments, flying the three and one half divisions to their targets over a period of three days. The risks were great: German reinforcements might reach the Market-Garden area faster than anyone anticipated; antiaircraft fire could intensify; and there was always the possibility of bad weather. Fog, high winds, a sudden storm—all likely at this time of the year—could cause disaster.

Worse, once on the ground, the paratroopers and glider-borne infantry, arriving without heavy artillery or tanks, would be highly vulnerable. General Horrocks' XXX Corps tank columns, using one narrow highway, could not make the 64-mile dash to Arnhem and beyond unless Brereton's men seized the bridges and held open the advance route. Conversely, the airborne army had to be relieved at top speed. Cut off far behind enemy lines and dependent on supplies by air, the airborne forces could expect German reinforcements to increase with each passing day. At best the beleaguered troopers might hold out in their "airheads" for only a few days. If the British armored drive was held up or failed to move fast enough, the airborne troops would inevitably be overrun and destroyed.

More could go wrong. If General Taylor's "Screaming Eagles" failed to secure the bridges directly ahead of the British Second Army's tank spearheads, it would make little difference whether or not the men under General Gavin's or General Urquhart's command secured their objectives in Nijmegen and Arnhem. Their forces would be isolated.

Certain classic airborne risks had to be accepted: divisions might be dropped or landed by gliders in the wrong areas; crossings might be destroyed by the enemy even as the attack began; bad weather could make air resupply impossible; and even if all the bridges were seized, the corridor might be cut at any point. These were but a few of the imponderables. The planners were gambling on speed, boldness, accuracy and surprise—all deriving from a precise synchronized land-and-airborne plan that, in its turn, gambled on German disorganization and inadequate strength. Each link in Market-Garden was interlocked with the next. If one gave way, disaster might result for all.

In Brereton's opinion, such risks had to be accepted. The opportunity might never arise again. Additionally, on the basis of the latest information of enemy strength, from Montgomery's 21st Army Group, Allied Airborne headquarters still felt that Brereton's forces would meet an "ill-organized enemy of varying standards." It was not expected that "any mobile force larger than a brigade group [about 3,000 men] with very few tanks and guns could be concentrated against the airborne troops before relief by the ground forces." It was expected "that the flight and landings would be hazardous, that the capture intact of the bridge objectives was more a matter of surprise and confusion than hard fighting." There was nothing here that the planners had not already taken under consideration. The last words of the intelligence summation seemed almost superfluous—"the advance of the ground forces would be very swift if the airborne operations were successful."

Major Brian Urquhart was deeply disturbed by the optimism permeating General Browning's British I Airborne Corps headquarters. The twenty-five-year-old intelligence chief felt that he was probably the only one on the staff with any doubts about Market-Garden. Urquhart (no relation to the British 1st Airborne Division commander, Major General Robert Urquhart) did not believe the optimistic estimates on enemy strength which arrived almost daily from Montgomery's 21st Army command. By the morning of Tuesday, September 12, with D Day only five days away, his doubts about Market-Garden amounted to near-panic.

His feeling had been triggered by a cautious message from General Dempsey's British Second Army headquarters. Quoting a Dutch report, Dempsey's intelligence staff warned of an increase in German strength in the Market-Garden area and spoke of the presence of "battered panzer formations believed to be in Holland to refit." Admittedly, the information was vague. Lacking any kind of confirmation, Dempsey's report was not included in the latest intelligence summaries of either Montgomery's or Eisenhower's headquarters. Urquhart could not understand why. He had been receiving similar disquieting news from Dutch liaison officers at Corps headquarters itself. And, like General Dempsey's staff, he believed them. Adding his own information to that received from Dempsey's command, Major Urquhart felt reasonably certain that elements of at least two panzer divisions were somewhere in the Arnhem area. The evidence was thin. The units were unidentified, with strength unknown, and he could not tell whether they were actually being refitted or merely passing through Arnhem. Nevertheless, Urquhart, as he later recalled, "was really very shook up."

Ever since the inception of Operation Comet and its evolution into Market-Garden, Major Urquhart's fears had been growing. Repeatedly, he had voiced his objections to the operation to "anybody who would listen on the staff." He was "quite frankly horrified by Market-Garden, because its weakness seemed to be the assumption that the Germans would put up no effective resistance." Urquhart himself was convinced that the Germans were rapidly recovering and might well have more men and equipment in Holland than anyone realized. Yet the whole essence of the scheme, as he saw it, "depended on the unbelievable notion that once the bridges were captured, XXX Corps's tanks could drive up this abominably narrow corridor—which was little more than a causeway, allowing no maneuverability—and then walk into Germany like a bride into a church. I simply did not believe that the Germans were going to roll over and surrender."

At planning conferences, Major Urquhart became increasingly alarmed at what he saw as "the desperate desire on everybody's part to get the airborne into action." There were constant comparisons between the current situation and the collapse of the Germans in 1918. Urquhart remembers that General Browning, perhaps reflecting Montgomery's views and those of "several other British commanders, was thinking about another great breakthrough." It seemed to the worried intelligence officer that everyone around him thought the war would be over by winter and "the Arnhem attack might be the airborne's last chance of getting into action." Urquhart was appalled at the lighthearted metaphor—"it was described as a 'party'"—used in reference to Market-Garden. And, in particular, he was upset by General Browning's statement that the object of the airborne attack was to "lay a carpet of airborne troops down over which our ground forces can pass." He believed that "that single cliché had the psychological effect of lulling many commanders into a passive and absolutely unimaginative state of mind in which no reaction to German resistance, apart from dogged gallantry, was envisaged." He considered the atmosphere at headquarters so unrealistic that, at one of the planning conferences, he asked "whether the 'carpet' was to consist of live airborne troops or dead ones."

"It was absolutely impossible," he said later, "to get them to face the realities of the situation; their personal longing to get into the campaign before it ended completely blinded them." But young Urquhart was convinced that General Dempsey's warning was accurate. He believed there was German armor in the vicinity of Arnhem, but he needed to substantiate the report by getting more evidence. A Spitfire fighter squadron equipped with special cameras for taking oblique pictures was stationed, Urquhart knew, at nearby Benson in Oxfordshire. The squadron was currently searching out rocket sites along the Dutch coast.

On the afternoon of September 12, Major Urquhart requested low-level R.A.F. reconnaissance sweeps of the Arnhem area. To avoid detection, enemy tanks would be hidden in forests or beneath camouflaged netting and might well escape high-altitude photographic flights. Urquhart's request was acknowledged; low-level missions would be flown over the Arnhem area, and he would get the results as fast as possible. Photographs of the tanks, if they were there, might prove to all concerned that Major Urquhart's fears were justified.

There was too little time now for airborne division commanders to check out intelligence reports firsthand. They were dependent on Corps or First Allied Airborne headquarters for the latest estimates. From experience, each commander knew that even this information would be several days old by the time he received it. Still, in the general view, there was little reason to anticipate any powerful enemy resistance. The risks involved in Market-Garden were, as a result, considered acceptable.

Once Generals Brereton and Browning had outlined the plan, determined the objectives and decided on airlift capability, each commander developed his own combat plans. The choice of drop zones and landing sites had priority. From previous operations, veteran airborne commanders knew that the best chance of success depended on how close to their objectives assaulting troops could be dropped. Ideally, they should be landed almost on their targets or within quick marching distance, especially if they were expected to seize a bridge. With the meager ground transport available, the pinpointing of these sites was vital.

Major General Maxwell D. Taylor was all too aware that his sites must be chosen for maximum effect. While Taylor would have the majority of his Screaming Eagle paratroops on D Day, his engineering units, artillery and most of the 101st transport would not arrive until D plus 1 and 2. Studying the southernmost part of the corridor where the 101st Airborne Division was to hold between Eindhoven and Veghel, Taylor quickly noted that over the fifteen-mile stretch of highway, his troops must capture two major canal crossings and no less than nine highway and railroad bridges. At Veghel, over the river Aa and the Willems Canal, there were four bridges, one a major canal crossing. Five miles south in St. Oedenrode, a bridge over the Lower Dommel had to be seized; four miles from there was the second major canal crossing, over the Wilhelmina Canal near the village of Son, and to the west a bridge near the hamlet of Best. Five miles farther south in Eindhoven, four bridges over the Upper Dommel had to be taken.

After studying the flat terrain between Eindhoven and Veghel, with its veining waterways, dikes, ditches and tree-lined roads, Taylor decided to pinpoint his major landing site almost in the center of his assault area, by the edge of a forest barely one and one half miles from Son and roughly equidistant between Eindhoven and Veghel. He would land two of his regiments, the 502nd and the 506th, on this zone. The 502nd was charged with objectives in St. Oedenrode and Best; the 506th with those in Son and Eindhoven. The third regiment, the 501st, was to land in two areas north and west of Veghel, within a few hundred yards of the vital four bridges. It was a formidable assignment for his men to accomplish on D Day without their back-up auxiliary units, but Taylor believed that "with luck, we can make it."

The task of the 82nd Airborne was more intricate. Its ten-mile sector was wider than that of the 101st. In this central segment of the corridor, the huge, nine-span, 1,500-foot-long bridge over the Maas river at Grave and at least one of four smaller railroad and highway crossings over the Maas-Waal Canal must be seized. The great bridge over the Waal river at Nijmegen, almost in the center of this city of 90,000, was also a prime objective. None of these could be called "secured" unless the Groesbeek Heights, dominating the area two miles southwest of Nijmegen, were held. Also, to the east was the great belt of forest along the German border—the Reichswald—where the Germans might assemble for attack. When General Gavin explained to his headquarters' officers what was expected of them, his chief of staff, Colonel Robert H. Wienecke, protested, "We'll need two divisions to do all that." Gavin was terse. "There it is, and we're going to do it with one."

Remembering the 82nd Airborne's attacks in Sicily and Italy, when his troops were scattered sometimes as far as thirty-five miles from their drop zone (the standard division joke was that "we always use blind pilots"), Gavin was determined to land his men this time almost on their targets. In order of priority, he decided that his objectives were: first, the Groesbeek Heights; second, the bridge at Grave; third, the crossings on the Maas-Waal Canal; and fourth, the Waal bridge at Nijmegen. "Because of probable quick enemy reaction," Gavin later recalled, "I decided to drop the largest part of my paratroops between the Groesbeek Heights and the Reichswald." He chose two landing zones in the Groesbeek vicinity less than a mile and a half from the ridge itself and three to four miles southwest of Nijmegen. There, his 508th and 505th regiments, plus the headquarters staff, would land. The third regiment, the 504th, was to drop on the western side of the Groesbeek Heights in the triangle between the

Maas river and the Maas-Waal Canal, a mile from the eastern end of the Grave bridge and two miles west of the Maas-Waal Canal bridges. To insure the capture of the vital Grave bridge, which might be prepared for demolition, an additional phase of his plan was developed in which a company of the 504th was to be dropped a half mile from the western end of the bridge. Before the enemy could retaliate, the 504th would rush the bridge from both ends.

Obviously, the great Nijmegen bridge was the most important of all his objectives and crucial to the entire Market-Garden operation. Yet Gavin was well aware that, without holding the other objectives, the Waal river crossing by itself would be useless. General Browning agreed with him. If the first bridges were not taken or if the enemy held the Groesbeek Heights, the corridor for the Garden forces would never be opened. Therefore, Browning specifically directed, Gavin was not to attempt an attack on the Nijmegen bridge until the primary objectives were secured.

Although he was concerned about the wide dispersal of his troops, Gavin was satisfied with the plan. One aspect bothered him, as it had bothered Taylor. His entire division would not be organically complete until supporting units arrived on D plus 1 and 2, and he wondered how his men—who knew nothing about Market-Garden as yet—would react. Still, in the experienced 82nd, morale was high as always; many of his men had made three combat jumps already. "Jumping Jim" Gavin, at thirty-seven the youngest brigadier general in the U.S. Army, had no doubts that his "fugitives from the law of averages," as they called themselves, would do their job.

The most difficult and dangerous assignment, by far, had been given to a modest, reticent career officer, Major General Robert "Roy" Urquhart, forty-two-year-old commander of the British 1st Airborne Division and the attached Polish Brigade.

Unlike General Browning and his American colleagues, Urquhart, a highly professional soldier who had fought with great distinction in North Africa, Sicily and Italy, had no airborne warfare experience. He would be commanding an airborne division in battle for the first time. Browning had chosen him because he was "hot from battle," but Urquhart had been surprised at his appointment. He had always considered airborne units "tightly knit organizations, closed family affairs and quite exclusive." Yet Urquhart had confidence in his ability to lead the elite unit. Once the force was on the ground the basic fighting rules remained the same, and he viewed his airborne division as "very highly trained infantry troops."

Despite his long combat experience, Urquhart was bothered about one thing: he had never parachuted or been in a glider. "I was even prone to airsickness," he was later to remark. On taking command in January, 1944, nine months before, Urquhart had suggested to General Browning that perhaps, as the new division commander, he ought to have some parachute training. Browning, who impressed Urquhart as a "lithe, immaculately turned-out man who gave the appearance of a restless hawk," answered that Urquhart's job was to get his division ready for an invasion of the Continent. Looking over the six-foot, 200-pound Scotsman, Browning added, "Leave the parachuting to younger chaps. Not only are you too large, but you're getting on."[*]

Throughout the long months of training, Urquhart "often felt like an outsider, a kind of military landlubber." He was aware of "being watched closely; not with hostility, though some airborne officers had reservations and a few did not bother to conceal them. I was on trial; my actions were being judged. It was an unenviable position, but one I accepted." Slowly, Urquhart's confident, assured handling of the division won over his officers. And among the troopers, Urquhart was far more popular than he knew. Private James W. Sims, of the 1st Airborne Division's 1st Parachute Brigade, remembers "the General's supreme confidence and his calmness." Sergeant John Rate, of Division headquarters, had the impression that "General Urquhart did whatever job had

---

[*] At their first interview Urquhart was still wearing his Brigadier's badges and tight-fitting Tartan trousers (trews) and spats of the Highland Division. As the meeting broke up, Browning, pointing to Urquhart's pants, said, "You might also get yourself properly dressed and get rid of those trews."

to be done. He didn't just ask someone else to do it. The General didn't stand on ceremony." Signalman Kenneth John Pearce called him "a big wonderful fellow. He called us 'son' or used our first names if he knew them." And from Sergeant Roy Ernest Hatch, of the Glider Pilot Regiment, Urquhart earned the supreme compliment. "He was," Hatch asserted, "a bloody general who didn't mind doin' the job of a sergeant."

To Urquhart's frustration, his division had not been chosen for the Normandy invasion, and "the summer passed interminably, planning one operation after another, only to see each canceled." Now, his "Red Devils" were "hungering for a fight." They had almost given up. "We were calling ourselves 'The Stillborn Division,'" recalls Major Geoffrey S. Powell of the 4th Parachute Brigade. "We figured we were being kept in reserve for use in the victory parade." As Urquhart saw it, "there was a dangerous mixture of ennui and cynicism slowly creeping into our lives. We were trained to a fine edge and I knew that if we didn't get into battle soon, we would lose it. We were ready and willing to accept anything, with all the 'ifs.'"

Urquhart's principal target—the prize of Operation Market-Garden—was Arnhem's concrete-and-steel highway bridge over the Lower Rhine. Additionally, Urquhart's men had two secondary objectives: a nearby floating pontoon bridge and a double-track railway crossing upriver, two and a half miles west of the town.

Urquhart's assignment presented a series of problems. Two were particularly worrisome. Reports of heavy antiaircraft defenses in the area indicated that some enemy units were massing in the vicinity of the Arnhem bridge itself. And Urquhart was uneasy about the three days it would take to airlift his entire force of British and Polish paratroops to their objectives. Both these problems had a direct bearing on Urquhart's choice of landing sites. Unlike the 82nd and 101st Airborne Divisions, he could not pick zones almost on or even close to the principal target. Ideally, he should land his forces near the Arnhem bridge on both sides of the river; but Urquhart's terrain was by no means ideal.

The northern exit of the crossing ran directly into the densely populated, built-up center of Arnhem itself. Near the southern exit, low-level polder land was, according to reports, too marshy for men or gliders. "Many of my own commanders," Urquhart remembers, "were quite willing to land on the southern side, even though it was marshy. Indeed, some were ready to risk injury by parachuting on the northern side—on the town itself."

In the previous week, bomber crews returning from other missions had reported a 30 percent increase in antiaircraft fire near the Arnhem crossing and from Deelen airfield seven miles to the north. Consequently, R.A.F. commanders whose pilots were scheduled to tow Urquhart's glider-borne troops raised strong objections to landing zones close to the Arnhem bridge. If sites were located near the southern exit, tug aircraft wheeling north after releasing gliders would run into heavy flak over the airfield. Turning south was almost as bad; planes might risk collision with aircraft dropping the 82nd Airborne near Nijmegen, eleven miles away. Urquhart was confronted with a dilemma: he could insist that the R.A.F. place his troops in proximity to the bridge, or he could choose drop zones much farther away, outside Arnhem itself, with all the dangers that choice entailed—delay, loss of surprise, possible German opposition. The risks were multiplied because on D Day Urquhart would have only a part of his division. "My problem was to get enough men down on the first lift," Urquhart recalled, "not only to seize the main bridge in the town itself, but also to guard and defend the drop zones and landing areas for the succeeding lifts. To seize the main bridge on the first day my strength was reduced to just one parachute brigade."

Faced with these restrictions, Urquhart appealed to Browning for extra planes. It seemed to him, he told the Corps commander, "that the Americans are getting all they need." Browning disagreed. The allocation of aircraft, he assured Urquhart, was "entirely due to priorities and not to any high-level American pressure." The entire operation, he explained, had to be planned from south to north, "bottom to top"; objectives in the southern and central sections of the corridor must be "seized first to get the ground forces through. Otherwise, the 1st Airborne would be wiped out."

In his command caravan on the Moor Park golf course near the clubhouse that General Browning used as headquarters, Urquhart pored over his maps and pondered the situation. Some open sectors existed north of Arnhem in a national park, but these were too small and the terrain was unsuitable. At best, these spots might accommodate a small parachute force but no gliders. The only alternative was to land in some broad expanses of open heaths and pasture land bordered by pine woods, 250 feet above sea level, lying west and northwest of Arnhem. The heathlands were firm and flat, perfect for gliders and parachutists. They were ideal in every way—except one: the areas lay between six and eight miles from the Arnhem bridge. Faced with the R.A.F.'s continued opposition to a drop in the immediate vicinity of the bridge, Urquhart reluctantly decided on the distant sites. "There was nothing else to do," he recalled, "but to accept the risks and plan for them. I was left with no choice."*

By September 12, Urquhart had his plan ready. Outlined on the map were five landing and drop zones straddling the Arnhem-Amsterdam railroad in the vicinity of Wolfheze, approximately four miles northwest of Arnhem. Three sites lay north of Wolfheze and two south, the southern zones together making up an irregular box-shaped tract more than a mile square. All were at least six miles away from the bridge at Arnhem; the farthest, northwest of Wolfheze, was eight.

On D Day two brigades would go in—Brigadier Philip "Pip" Hicks's 1st Airlanding Brigade, scheduled to hold the drop zones, and Brigadier Gerald Lathbury's 1st Parachute Brigade, which would make a dash for Arnhem and its highway, railroad and pontoon bridges. Leading the way would be a motorized reconnaissance squadron of jeeps and motorcycles. Urquhart was

---

* Colonel George S. Chatterton, commanding the Glider Pilot Regiment, recalls that he wanted a *coup de main*, "a force of five or six gliders to land near the bridge and take it. I saw no reason why we could not do it, but apparently nobody else saw the need for it, and I distinctly remember being called a bloody murderer and assassin for suggesting it."

counting on Major C. F. H. "Freddie" Gough's highly specialized force of some 275 men in four troops—the only unit of its kind in the British army—to reach the highway bridge and hold it until the main body of the brigade arrived.

The next day, D plus 1, Brigadier John "Shan" Hackett's 4th Parachute Brigade was due to arrive, together with the remainder of the Airlanding Brigade; and on the third day, Major General Stanislaw Sosabowski's Polish 1st Parachute Brigade was to be landed. Urquhart had marked in a sixth drop zone for the Poles. Because it was anticipated that, by D plus 2, the bridge would be captured and the flak batteries knocked out, the Poles were to drop on the southern bank of the Lower Rhine near the village of Elden about one mile south of the Arnhem crossing.

Despite the risks he must accept, Urquhart felt confident. He believed he had "a reasonable operation and a good plan." Casualties, he thought, might be "somewhere in the neighborhood of 30 percent"; considering the intricate nature of the attack, he did not think the cost was too high. In the early evening of September 12, he briefed his commanders on the operation and, Urquhart remembers, "everybody seemed quite content with the plan."

One commander, however, had grave misgivings. Major General Stanislaw Sosabowski, the trim, fifty-two-year-old leader of the Polish 1st Parachute Brigade, was quite sure that "we were in for a bitter struggle." The former Polish War Academy professor had already stated his position to Generals Urquhart and Browning when he first heard about Operation Comet. At that time he had demanded that Urquhart give him his orders in writing so that "I would not be held responsible for the disaster." With Urquhart he had visited Browning and told him "this mission cannot possibly succeed." Browning asked why. As Sosabowski remembered, "I told him it would be suicide to attempt it with the forces we had and Browning answered, 'But, my dear Sosabowski, the Red Devils and the gallant Poles can do anything!'"

Now, one week later, as he listened to Urquhart, Sosabowski thought, "the British are not only grossly underestimating German strength in the Arnhem area, but they seem ignorant of the significance Arnhem has for the Fatherland." Sosabowski believed that to the Germans Arnhem represented "the gateway to Germany, and I did not expect the Germans to leave it open." He did not believe that "troops in the area were of very low caliber, with only a few battered tanks sitting around." He was appalled when Urquhart told the assembled brigade commanders that the 1st Airborne was to be dropped "at least six miles from the objective." To reach the bridge the main body of troops would have "a five-hour march; so how could surprise be achieved? Any fool of a German would immediately know our plans."

There was another part of the plan Sosabowski did not like. Heavy equipment and ammunition for his brigade was to go in by glider on an earlier lift. Thus, his stores would be on a northern landing zone when his troops landed on the southern bank. What would happen if the bridge was not taken by the time the Poles landed? As Urquhart spelled out the plan, Sosabowski learned to his astonishment that, if the bridge was still in German hands by that time, his Polish troops would be expected to take it.

Despite Sosabowski's anxieties, at the September 12 briefing he remained silent. "I remember Urquhart asking for questions and nobody raised any," he recalled. "Everyone sat nonchalantly, legs crossed, looking bored. I wanted to say something about this impossible plan, but I just couldn't. I was unpopular as it was, and anyway who would have listened?"

Later, when the entire airborne operation was reviewed for all commanders at General Browning's headquarters, others had grave misgivings about the British part of the plan but they too remained silent. Brigadier General James M. Gavin, commander of the American 82nd Airborne, was so astonished when he heard of Urquhart's choice of landing sites that he said to his operations chief, Lieutenant Colonel John Norton, "My God, he can't mean it." Norton was equally appalled. "He does," he said grimly, "but I wouldn't care to try it." In Gavin's view, it was far better to take "10 percent initial casualties by dropping either on or close to the bridge than to run the risk of landing on distant drop zones." He was "surprised that General Browning did not question Urquhart's plan." Still, Gavin said nothing "for I assumed that the British, with their extensive combat experience, knew exactly what they were doing."

❖ 2 ❖

SS Sturmbannführer (Major) Sepp Krafft did not intend to move again if he could avoid it. In the past few weeks his under-strength SS Panzer Grenadier Training and Reserve Battalion had been ordered back and forth across Holland. Now, after only five days, the unit was being ordered out of the village of Oosterbeek—and not by a superior of Krafft's, but by a Wehrmacht major.

Krafft protested vehemently. The main body of his three companies of men was billeted in the village, with the rest in Arnhem, and another 1,000 SS recruits were due to arrive momentarily for training. The Wehrmacht major was adamant. "I don't care about that," he told Krafft bluntly, "you've got to get out." Krafft fought back. The ambitious thirty-seven-year-old officer took orders only from his SS superiors. "I refuse," he said. The Wehrmacht officer was not intimidated. "Let me make things clear to you," he said. "You're moving out of Oosterbeek because Model's headquarters is moving in."

Krafft quickly calmed down. He had no wish to run afoul of Field Marshal Walter Model. Still, the order rankled. Krafft moved, but not very far. He decided to bivouac his troops in the woods and farms northwest of Oosterbeek, not far from the village of Wolfheze. The spot he happened to choose was alongside the Wolfheze road, almost between the zones marked on maps in England for the men of the British 1st Airborne Division to land, and blocking the route into Arnhem itself.

☆ 3 ☆

Henri Knap, Arnhem's underground intelligence chief, felt safe in his new role. To protect his wife and two daughters from complicity in his activities, he had left home four months earlier and moved a few blocks away. His headquarters were now in the offices of a general practitioner, Dr. Leo C. Breebaart. The white-coated Knap was now the doctor's "assistant," and certain "patients" were messengers and couriers belonging to his intelligence network: forty men and women and a few teen-agers.

Knap's was a time-consuming and frustrating job. He had to evaluate the information he received and then pass it along by phone. Arnhem's resistance chief, Pieter Kruyff, had given Knap three telephone numbers, each with twelve to fifteen digits, and told him to commit them to memory. Knap never knew where or to whom he was calling. His instructions were to dial each number in turn until contact was made.°

Gathering intelligence was even more complicated. Knap's requests were passed down through the network chain, and he never knew what agent procured the information. If a report seemed dubious, Knap investigated on his own. At the moment he

---

° Knap has never learned who his contacts were except that his reports were passed on to a top-secret unit known as the "Albrecht Group." He knew the calls he made were long distance. At the time, Dutch telephone numbers consisted of four digits. A brilliant telephone technician named Nicolaas Tjalling de Bode devised a method for underground members under which, by using certain telephone numbers, they could bypass local switchboards and automatically call all over Holland.

was intrigued and puzzled by several reports that had reached him about enemy activity in Oosterbeek.

A German officer wearing staff insignia, Major Horst Smöckel, had visited a number of stores in Renkum, Oosterbeek and Arnhem and ordered a variety of supplies to be delivered to Oosterbeek's Tafelberg Hotel. What Knap found curious were the requisitions; among them were hard-to-find foods and other specialty items which the Dutch population rarely saw anymore, such as *Genever* gin.

Additionally, German signalmen had been busy laying a welter of telephone cables to a number of hotels in the suburbs, including the Tafelberg. The conclusion, Knap felt, was obvious: a high-ranking headquarters was moving into Oosterbeek. But which one? Who was the general? And had he arrived?

It was even more important for Knap to keep abreast of the enemy strength in and around the Arnhem region. He knew there were other intelligence men sending back information in each town and that he was "only a small cog in a vast collection system." As a result, there was probably "much duplication of effort." Nevertheless, everything was important, for "what one cell might miss, we might pick up."

Two weeks before, as he later recalled, "there was almost no German strength in the Arnhem region." Since then, the military picture had changed dramatically. Now, Knap was alarmed at the German buildup. From his network sources, over the previous seven days, Knap had reported that "the remains of several divisions, including panzer units, were in the process of reorganizing in and around Arnhem or were moving into Germany." By now, more specific news had come. His sources reported the presence of tanks north and northeast of Arnhem. Knap believed that "parts of at least one or even two panzer divisions" were in the area, but their identity and exact location were, so far, not known.

Knap wanted details quickly. Urgently, he passed the word to his network. He demanded more exact information on the panzer activity and he wanted to know immediately the identity of the "new occupant" in the Tafelberg Hotel.

Twenty-five-year-old Wouter van de Kraats had never heard of Henri Knap. His contact in the underground was a man he knew only as "Jansen" who lived somewhere in Arnhem. Jansen had a new assignment for him—the Tafelberg Hotel. A high-ranking German officer had arrived, he was told, and Van de Kraats was to see if any of the staff cars outside "carried an identifying pennant or flag." If so, he was to report the colors and symbols on the standard.

Van de Kraats had noticed an influx of German activity around the hotel. German military police and sentries had moved into the area. His problem was how to get through the sentries along the road—the Pietersbergweg—running past the Tafelberg. He decided to bluff his way through.

As he made for the hotel, he was immediately stopped by a sentry. "But I must get through," Van de Kraats told the German. "I work at the petrol station up the street." The German let him pass. Three other sentries gave him only a cursory glance. Then, as Van de Kraats passed the Tafelberg, he quickly looked at the entrance and the driveway. None of the parked cars had any identifying markings, but near the front door of the hotel stood a checkerboard black, red and white metal pennant—the insignia of a German army group commander.

On the afternoon of Thursday, September 14, Henri Knap heard from his network. Several sources reported large formations of panzer troops, tanks and armored vehicles encamped in a semi-circle to the north of Arnhem. There were units at Beekbergen, Epse and along the Ijssel River. There was even a startling report of "20 to 30 Tiger tanks." Exactly how many units were involved, he was unable to ascertain. He was able to clearly identify only one, and that by a fluke. One of his agents noted "strange markings—reverse *F*'s with a ball at the foot of them"—on some tanks. Checking through a special German manual, Knap was able to identify the unit. He immediately called his telephone contact and reported the presence of the 9th SS Panzer Division Hohenstaufen. From the agent's report, Knap located its position as lying approximately to the north between Arnhem and Apeldoorn and from there, eastward to Zutphen.

Shortly afterward he received word about the Tafelberg Hotel. He passed this report on, too. The significant black, red and white checkerboard pennant told its own story. There was only one German army group commander in this part of the western front. Although Knap reported the news as hearsay, it seemed to him the officer had to be Field Marshal Walter Model.

�֎ 4 ✷

TWENTY-FIVE MILES EAST of Oosterbeek at his II SS Panzer Corps headquarters in a small castle on the outskirts of Doetinchem, General Wilhelm Bittrich held a meeting with his two remaining division commanders. Bittrich was in a bad mood, barely able to contain his temper. The outlook for his battered panzer corps was now far worse than it had been a week earlier. Impatiently Bittrich had awaited replacements in men, armor and equipment. None had arrived. On the contrary, his force had been whittled down even more. He had been ordered to send two combat groups to the front. One was with the German Seventh Army trying to hold the Americans near Aachen; the other was dispatched to bolster General Kurt Student's First Parachute Army after British tanks successfully breached the Albert Canal line,

147

crossed the Meuse-Escaut Canal and grabbed a bridgehead at Neerpelt almost on the Dutch border. Now, at a time when the British were massing to renew their offensive—an attack that the intelligence chief at Army Group B called "imminent"—Bittrich had received through Field Marshal Model a "crazy directive from the fools in Berlin." One of his shattered divisions was to be cannibalized and pulled back into Germany.

A once-ardent Nazi, Bittrich denounced the order acridly. He "was sick and tired of Berlin's orders and the sycophants around Hitler who were indulging in all kinds of gimmickry." Courageous and able, Bittrich had spent most of his adult life in uniform. In World War I, he had served as a lieutenant in the German air force and had been twice wounded. Later, for a few years, he worked in a stockbroker's office. Then, rejoining the armed forces, Bittrich became a member of a secret German airforce team and for eight years taught flying to the Russians. When Hitler came to power, Bittrich joined the newly formed Luftwaffe but in the mid-thirties he switched to the Waffen SS, where promotion was faster.°

In Normandy, Bittrich's faith in Hitler's leadership began to waver. He sided with Field Marshal Rommel against Hitler's "insane fight-to-the-last-man" philosophy. Once he confided to Rommel that "we are being so badly led from above that I can no longer carry out senseless orders. I have never been a robot and don't intend to become one." After the July 20 plot, when he learned that his former commander Colonel General Eric Hoepner, as a conspirator, had been condemned to death by hanging, Bittrich raged to his staff that "this is the blackest day for the German army." Bittrich's outspoken criticism of Hitler's military leadership soon reached Berlin. As Bittrich later recalled, "my

° As a suspected war criminal, Bittrich spent eight years in prison after World War II; on June 22, 1953, he was found innocent and released. Waffen SS commanders are difficult to locate and interview, but Bittrich and his officers were extremely helpful to me in setting the record straight on many hitherto unknown events in the Arnhem battle. Bittrich wanted me to clarify one minor matter relating to his personal life. In various British accounts "I have been described as a musician who hoped to be a conductor," he told me. "But the authors have confused me with my brother, Dr. Gerhard Bittrich, an extremely talented pianist and conductor."

remarks were reported to the chief of the SS, Reichsführer Heinrich Himmler, and the name Bittrich was no longer mentioned around Hitler's headquarters." Only the near-collapse of the German front in the west, a situation demanding Bittrich's kind of expertise, and the attitude of sympathetic commanders had saved him from being recalled. Even so, Himmler was still "eager for me to return to Germany for a little talk." Bittrich had no illusions about Himmler's invitation. Nor had Model; he was determined to keep Bittrich in the west and flatly refused to entertain Himmler's repeated requests to send Bittrich home.

Now the outraged Bittrich outlined Berlin's latest plan to the commanders of his divisions—SS Brigadeführer (Brigadier General) Heinz Harmel of the 10th Frundsberg Division and SS Obersturmbannführer (Lieutenant Colonel) Walter Harzer of the 9th Hohenstaufen Division. Bittrich told Harzer—who had already learned something about the plan from Model's chief of staff, Lieutenant General Hans Krebs—that his 9th Hohenstaufen Division was to entrain immediately for Germany, where it would be located near Siegen, northeast of Koblenz. Harmel's 10th Division was to remain in Holland. It would be refitted and brought up to strength in its present location east and southeast of Arnhem, ready to be committed again.

The thirty-eight-year-old Harmel, whose bluff heartiness had earned him the affectionate nickname of *"der alte Frundsberg"* from his men, was not pleased with the decision. It seemed to him that "Bittrich was, as usual, showing preference for the Hohenstaufen Division, perhaps because it had been his own before he became corps commander and perhaps, too, because Harzer had been his chief of staff." Although he did not think "Bittrich was consciously unfair, it always seemed to work out that the Hohenstaufen got the cushy jobs."

His younger counterpart, thirty-two-year-old Walter Harzer, was elated at the news, even though he thought "the likelihood of getting Berlin leave seemed doubtful." Ideally, after refitting he expected to have a "brand-new Hohenstaufen Division." Privately, too, the tough Harzer, his face marked by a saber scar, had high hopes now of achieving his ambition: to be promoted to the rank befitting an SS division commander—brigadier general. Still, as Bittrich outlined the entire plan, one segment was not to Harzer's liking.

Although badly depleted, his division was still stronger than Harmel's. Instead of the usual 9,000 men, the Hohenstaufen had barely 6,000, the Frundsberg about 3,500. Harzer had close to twenty Mark V Panther tanks, but not all were serviceable. He did, however, have a considerable number of armored vehicles: self-propelled guns, armored cars and forty armored personnel carriers, all with heavy machine guns, some mounted with artillery pieces. Harmel's Frundsberg Division had almost no tanks and was desperately short of all kinds of armored vehicles. Both divisions still had formidable artillery, mortar and antiaircraft units. To build up the Frundsberg Division, which would remain behind, Bittrich said, Harzer was to transfer as much of his transportation and equipment as he could to Harmel. Harzer was skeptical. "In my heart," Harzer later recalled, "I knew damn well that if I gave over my few tanks or the armored personnel carriers to Harmel, they'd never be replaced." Harzer did not protest the decision, but he had no intention of giving up all his vehicles.

Harzer had long ago learned to husband his division's resources. He had more vehicles than even Bittrich realized—including American jeeps he had captured during the long retreat from France. He decided to ignore the order by "some paper maneuvering." By removing caterpillar tracks, wheels or guns from his vehicles, he could make them temporarily unserviceable until he reached Germany. In the meantime they would be listed on his armored strength returns as disabled.

Even with the extra men and vehicles from Harzer's cannibalized division, Bittrich continued, the Frundsberg would still be understrength. There was only one way to stress the urgency of the situation to Berlin: by presenting the facts directly to SS operational headquarters. Maybe then, replacements and reinforcements would be forthcoming. But Bittrich had no intention of visiting Berlin; Harmel was made the emissary, to his surprise.

"I don't know why he chose me rather than Harzer," Harmel remembers. "But we urgently needed men and armor, and perhaps Bittrich thought a general might carry more weight. The whole matter was to be kept secret from Field Marshal Model. So, as we were not expecting any trouble in the Arnhem area, it was decided that I would leave for Berlin on the evening of September 16."

The exchange of equipment between Harzer and Harmel and the move of the cannibalized Hohenstaufen Division to Germany, Bittrich ordered, was to begin immediately. While the operation was in process, he added, Field Marshal Model wanted small mobile attack groups to be readied as *Alarmeinheiten* ("alarm units") which could be committed in case of emergency. As a result, Harzer privately decided that his "best units would be entrained last." Bittrich expected the entire equipment transfer and move completed by September 22. Because six trains a day left for Germany, Harzer thought the task could be completed much earlier. He believed his last and best units could leave for the Fatherland in just three more days—probably on the afternoon of September 17.

A demoralizing rumor was making the rounds. By September 14, several senior German officers in Holland were saying that an airborne drop would take place.

The talk originated from a conversation between Hitler's operations chief, Colonel General Alfred Jodl, and the Commander in Chief, West, Field Marshal von Rundstedt. Jodl was concerned that the Allies might invade Holland from the sea. If Eisenhower followed his usual tactics, Jodl said, airborne troops would be dropped as a prelude to the seaborne attack. Von Rundstedt, though skeptical of the suggestion (he, by contrast, was convinced that paratroopers would be dropped in conjunction with an attack on the Ruhr), passed the information on to Army Group B's commander, Field Marshal Model. Model's view was the same as Von Rundstedt's. Nevertheless, he could not ignore Jodl's warning. He ordered the German armed forces commander in Holland, the jittery Luftwaffe general, Friedrich Christiansen, to dispatch units of his meager grab bag of army, navy, Luftwaffe and Dutch Waffen SS personnel to the coast.

Since Jodl's call on September 11, the scare had traveled down the various echelons of command, particularly through Luftwaffe channels. Although the invasion had so far failed to materialize, the fear of an airborne drop was still mounting. Everyone was speculating on possible sites. From their maps, some Luftwaffe commanders saw the large open areas between the north coast and Arnhem as possible landing zones. Others, nervously awaiting the renewal of the British offensive into Holland from the bridgehead over the Meuse-Escaut Canal at Neerpelt, wondered if paratroopers might be used in conjunction with that attack and dropped into the area of Nijmegen.

On September 13, Luftwaffe Colonel General Otto Dessloch, commander of the 3rd Air Fleet, heard about Berlin's fears at Von Rundstedt's headquarters in Koblenz. Dessloch was so concerned that he telephoned Field Marshal Model the following day. Model, he recalls, thought Berlin's invasion scare was "nonsense." The Field Marshal was so unconcerned "that he invited me to dinner at his new headquarters in the Tafelberg Hotel in Oosterbeek." Dessloch refused. "I have no intention of being made a prisoner," he told Model. Just before he hung up, Dessloch added: "If I were you, I would get out of that area." Model, Dessloch remembers, merely laughed.

At Deelen airfield north of Arnhem word of a possible airborne attack reached Luftwaffe fighter commander Major General Walter Grabmann. He drove to Oosterbeek for a conference with Model's chief of staff, Lieutenant General Hans Krebs. When Grabmann expressed the Luftwaffe's fears, Krebs said, "For God's sake, don't talk about such things. Anyway, where would they land?" Grabmann went to a map and, pointing to areas west of Arnhem, said, "Anywhere here. The heath is perfect for paratroopers." Krebs, Grabmann later recalled, "laughed and warned me that if I continued to talk this way, I'd make myself look ridiculous."

Holland's notorious police chief, SS Lieutenant General Hanns Albin Rauter, heard the rumor too, possibly from his superior General Christiansen. Rauter was convinced that anything was possible, including an airborne attack. Rauter, chief architect of Nazi terror in the Netherlands, expected the Dutch underground to attack and the population to rise at any moment. He was determined to stamp out any kind of insurrection by the simple expedient of executing three Dutch nationals for each Nazi killed. Rauter had declared an "emergency" immediately after the German retreat and the stampede of Dutch Nazis to Germany two weeks before. His police had taken bitter revenge against anyone even remotely involved with the Dutch resistance. Men and women were arrested, shot or sent off into concentration camps. Ordinary citizens fared little better. All travel between provinces was forbidden. More restrictive rules were imposed. Anyone found on the streets during curfew risked being fired on without warning. All over southern Holland, in anticipation of the British offensive, the Dutch were pressed into service as laborers digging trenches for the Wehrmacht. In Nijmegen, Rauter filled his workforce quota by threatening to throw entire families into concentration camps. Gatherings of any kind were forbidden. "Where more than five persons are seen together," one of Rauter's posters warned, "they will be fired on by the Wehrmacht, SS or police troops."

Now, with the British attack from the south imminent and Berlin's warning of a possible air and sea attack in the north, Rauter's world was beginning to come apart. He was terrified.°

° In the safety of his prison cell after the war, Rauter admitted to Dutch interrogators that "at the time I was very nervous. . . . I had to paralyze the resistance." Rauter was found guilty by a Dutch court on January 12, 1949, of a wide range of offenses, including "persecution of the Jews, deportation of inhabitants for slave labor, pillage, confiscation of property, illegal arrests, detentions . . . and the kill-

Learning that Model was in Holland, Rauter decided to seek reassurance and set out for the Tafelberg Hotel. On the evening of September 14, Rauter met with Model and his chief of staff, General Krebs. He was "convinced," Rauter told them, "that the Allies would now use airborne forces in southern Holland." He felt that it was the right psychological moment. Model and Krebs disagreed. Elite airborne formations, Model said, were too "precious, their training too costly" for indiscriminate use. The Field Marshal did indeed expect Montgomery to attack into Holland from Neerpelt, but the situation was not critical enough to justify the use of airborne troops. Also, since assault forces would be separated by three broad rivers to the south, he did not think that a British attack toward Arnhem was possible. Both Nijmegen and Arnhem were too far from the British forces. Besides, Model continued, Montgomery was "tactically a very cautious man. He would never use airborne forces in a reckless adventure."

By the time the prisoner reached Major Friedrich Kieswetter's headquarters in the village of Driebergen, west of Oosterbeek, on September 15, the deputy chief of Wehrmacht counterintelligence in Holland knew a great deal about him. There was an ample file on slow-witted, twenty-eight-year-old Christiaan Antonius Lindemans, better known, because of his huge size (6'3", 260 lbs.), as "King Kong." Lindemans had been captured by a patrol near the Dutch-Belgian border, in the no man's land between the British and German lines. At first, because of his British battle dress, Lindemans was taken for a soldier but, at the battalion command post near Valkenswaard, to the amazement of his interrogators, he demanded to see Lieutenant Colonel Hermann Giskes—German spy chief in Holland and Kieswetter's superior. After a series of phone calls, Lindemans' captors were

ings of innocent civilians as reprisals for offenses . . . against the occupying authorities." He was executed on March 25, 1949.

even more astonished to receive orders to drive the prisoner immediately to Driebergen. Lindemans alone displayed no surprise. Some of his compatriots thought him to be a stanch member of the Dutch underground; but the Germans knew him in another capacity—as a spy. King Kong was a double agent.

Lindemans had turned traitor in 1943. At that time he offered to work for Giskes in return for the release of his current mistress and younger brother, Henk, arrested by the Gestapo as a member of the underground and said to be awaiting execution. Giskes had readily agreed; and ever since, Lindemans had served the Germans well. His perfidy had resulted in the penetration of many underground cells and the arrest and execution of numerous Dutch and Belgian patriots. Although he was crude and boastful, given to wild, drunken excesses and possessed of an insatiable appetite for women, Lindemans had so far miraculously escaped exposure. However, many resistance leaders considered him a dangerous risk, unlike certain Allied officers in Brussels who were so impressed by King Kong that Lindemans now worked for a British intelligence unit under the command of a Canadian captain.

In Giskes' absence, Kieswetter dealt with Lindemans for the first time. He found the towering braggart, who introduced himself to everyone in the office as the "great King Kong," disgusting. Lindemans told the major of his latest mission. The Canadian intelligence officer had sent him to warn underground leaders in Eindhoven that downed Allied pilots were no longer to be sent through the "escape line" into Belgium. Because the British were due to break out from the Neerpelt bridgehead toward Eindhoven, the pilots were to be kept hidden. Lindemans, who had spent five days coming through the lines, was able to give Kieswetter some details on the British buildup. The attack, he said flatly, would take place on September 17.

The imminence of the British move was hardly news. Kieswetter, like everyone else, had been expecting it momentarily. Lindemans also informed Kieswetter of another development: coincidental with the British attack, he reported, a paratroop drop was planned beyond Eindhoven to help capture the town.° The revelation made no sense to Kieswetter. Why use paratroopers when the British army could easily reach Eindhoven by itself? Perhaps because Lindemans' information seemed unrealistic or more likely because of his antipathy toward King Kong, Kieswetter told Lindemans to continue on with his mission and then return to the British lines. Kieswetter took no immediate action. He thought so little of Lindemans' information that he did not pass it on directly to Wehrmacht headquarters. He sent it, instead, through the Sicherheitsdienst (SS security and intelligence service). He also dictated a brief memorandum of his conversation with Lindemans for Giskes, at the moment away on another assignment. Giskes, who had always considered King Kong reliable, would not receive it until the afternoon of September 17.

° After the war, some British newspapers charged that it was because Lindemans pinpointed Arnhem as the main airborne objective that the panzer divisions were waiting. Obviously this is not so. Bittrich's corps reached its positions before Eisenhower and Montgomery met on September 10 and decided on Market-Garden. Neither could Lindemans have known anything about the Arnhem attack or the massive dimensions of the operation. Again, Allied decisions on dates, placement of drop zones, etc. were made long after Lindemans left Brussels to cross the German lines. A second often-repeated story is that Lindemans was taken to Colonel General Kurt Student's headquarters at Vught for questioning, and it has been suggested that the airborne expert correctly evaluated the report and gave the alert. Student flatly denies this allegation. "It is a large fat lie," he told me. "I never met Lindemans. Indeed, I first heard of the whole affair in a prison camp after the war." Student adds, "The truth is, nobody in the German command knew anything about the attack until it happened." Shortly after Market-Garden, suspicion fell on Lindemans and he was arrested by the Dutch. King Kong, the great Lothario, lived up to his reputation to the very end. In July, 1946, forty-eight hours before his trial, Lindemans, in a prison hospital, was found unconscious with a prison nurse nearby. Both of them, in a bizarre "love pact," had taken overdoses of sleeping pills. Lindemans died, the girl survived.

☆ 5 ☆

OPERATION MARKET-GARDEN was now less than forty-eight hours away. In his office Lieutenant General Walter Bedell Smith, Eisenhower's chief of staff, listened to SHAEF's intelligence chief, British Major General Kenneth W. Strong, disclose his latest news with growing alarm. Beyond doubt, Strong said, there was German armor in the Market-Garden area.

For days, Strong and his staff had been sifting and assessing every intelligence report in an effort to determine the whereabouts of the 9th and 10th SS Panzer divisions. Since the first week in September there had been no contact with the units. Both were badly cut up, but it was considered unlikely that they had been completely destroyed. One theory held that the units might have been ordered back into Germany. Now Dutch underground messages told a different story. The lost divisions had been spotted.

The 9th and, presumably, the 10th SS Panzer divisions were in Holland, Strong reported to Smith, "in all probability to be refitted with tanks." Exactly what remained of the units or their fighting capability no one could say, but there was no longer any doubt about their location, Strong reported. They were definitely in the vicinity of Arnhem.

Deeply concerned about Market-Garden and, in his own words, "alarmed over the possibility of failure," Smith immediately conferred with the Supreme Commander. The British 1st Airborne Division, due to land at Arnhem, "could not hold out against two armored divisions," Smith told Eisenhower. To be sure, there was a question—a big question—about the strength of the units, but to be on the safe side Smith thought that Market-Garden should be reinforced. He believed two airborne divisions would be required in the Arnhem area. (Presumably, Smith had in mind as the additional unit the veteran British 6th Airborne Division, commanded by Major General Richard Gale, which had been used successfully during the Normandy invasion, but was not included in Market-Garden.) Otherwise, Smith told Eisenhower, the plan must be revised. "My feeling," he later said, "was that if we could not drop the equivalent of another division in the area, then we should shift one of the American airborne divisions, which were to form the 'carpet' further north, to reinforce the British."

Eisenhower considered the problem and its risks. On the basis of this intelligence report and almost on the eve of the attack, he was being urged to override Monty's plan—one that Eisenhower himself had approved. It meant challenging Montgomery's generalship and upsetting an already delicate command situation. As Supreme Commander, he had another option open: Market-Garden could be canceled; but the only grounds for such a decision would be this single piece of intelligence. Eisenhower had obviously to assume that Montgomery was the best judge of enemy strength before him and that he would plan accordingly. As Eisenhower explained to Smith, "I cannot tell Monty how to dispose of his troops," nor could he "call off the operation, since I have already given Monty the green light." If changes were to be made, Montgomery would have to make them. Still, Eisenhower was prepared to let Smith "fly to 21st Army Group headquarters and argue it out with Montgomery."

Bedell Smith set out immediately for Brussels. He found Montgomery confident and enthusiastic. Smith explained his fears about the panzer units in the Arnhem area and strongly suggested that the plan might need revision. Montgomery "ridiculed the idea. Monty felt the greatest opposition would come more from terrain difficulties than from the Germans. All would go well, he kept repeating, if we at SHAEF would help him surmount his logistical difficulties. He was not worried about the German armor. He thought Market-Garden would go all right as set." The conference was fruitless. "At least I tried to stop him," Smith said, "but I got nowhere. Montgomery simply waved my objections airily aside."[°]

Even as Montgomery and Smith conferred, across the Channel startling evidence reached British I Airborne Corps headquarters. Earlier in the day, fighters of the R.A.F.'s specially equipped photo-reconnaissance squadron returning from The Hague had made a low-level sweep over the Arnhem area. Now, in his office, intelligence officer Major Brian Urquhart took up a magnifying glass and examined five oblique-angle pictures—an "end of the run" strip from one of the fighters. Hundreds of aerial photographs of the Market-Garden area had been taken and evaluated in the previous seventy-two hours, but only these five shots showed what Urquhart had long feared—the unmistakable presence of German armor. "It was the straw that broke the camel's back," Urquhart later recalled. "There, in the photos, I could clearly see tanks—if not on the very Arnhem landing and drop zones, then certainly close to them."

Major Urquhart rushed to General Browning's office with the photographic confirmation. Browning saw him immediately. Placing the pictures on the desk before Browning, Urquhart said, "Take a look at these." The General studied them one by one. Although Urquhart no longer remembers the exact wording, to the best of his recollection, Browning said, "I wouldn't trouble myself about these if I were you." Then, referring to the tanks in the photos, he continued, "They're probably not serviceable at any rate." Urquhart was stunned. Helplessly he pointed out that the armor, "whether serviceable or not, were still tanks and they

---

[°] I have based this entire section on information supplied to me by General S. L. A. Marshall, Chief Historian for the European Theatre of Operations during World War II, who kindly allowed me to see his various monographs on Market-Garden and also his 1945 interview with General Bedell Smith on the meeting with Eisenhower and later Montgomery.

had guns." Looking back, Urquhart feels that "perhaps because of information I knew nothing about, General Browning was not prepared to accept my evaluation of the photos. My feeling remained the same—that everyone was so *gung-ho* to go that nothing could stop them."

Urquhart was unaware that some members of Browning's staff considered the young intelligence officer almost too zealous. The show was about to begin, and most officers were anxious and eager to get on with it. Urquhart's pessimistic warnings irritated them. As one senior staff officer put it, "His views were colored by nervous exhaustion. He was inclined to be a bit hysterical, no doubt brought on by overwork."

Shortly after his meeting with Browning, Urquhart was visited by the corps medical officer. "I was told," Urquhart recalls, "that I was exhausted—who wasn't?—and that perhaps I should take a rest and go on leave. I was out. I had become such a pain around headquarters that on the very eve of the attack I was being removed from the scene. I was told to go home. There was nothing I could say. Although I disagreed with the plan and feared the worst, still, this was going to be the big show and, curiously, I did not want to be left behind."

✢6✢

BY NOON ON SATURDAY, September 16, the German proclamation was plastered on bulletin boards all over Arnhem.

By order of the Security Police, the following is announced:

During the night an attack with explosives was made on the railroad viaduct at Schaapsdrift.

The population is called upon to cooperate in tracing the culprits of this attack.

If they have not been found before 12 o'clock noon on Sunday, September 17, 1944, a number of hostages will be shot.

I appeal to the cooperation of all of you in order that needless victims be spared.

The acting Burgomaster,

LIERA

In a cellar, leading members of the Arnhem underground met in an emergency meeting. The sabotage of the railroad viaduct had been badly botched. Henri Knap, the Arnhem intelligence chief, had not been happy about the mission from its inception. He felt that, "at best, we are all rank amateurs when it comes to sabotage." In his view, "it is far better to concentrate on feeding intelligence to the Allies and to leave demolition jobs to men who know what they are doing." The chief of the Arnhem underground, thirty-eight-year-old Pieter Kruyff, asked for the others' opinions. Nicolaas Tjalling de Bode voted that the members give themselves up. Knap remembers thinking "this was a very steep price to pay—the lives of the hostages, innocent people—for a small hole in a bridge." Gijsbert Jan Numan was conscience-stricken. He had been involved along with Harry Montfroy, Albert Deuss, Toon van Daalen and others in procuring the materials for the explosives and in planning the sabotage, and no one wanted innocent men to suffer. Yet what was to be done? Kruyff heard everyone out, then he made his decision. "The organization must stay intact even though innocent people may be shot," he decreed. Looking around at the assembled leaders, as Nicolaas de Bode remembers, Kruyff told them, "No one will give himself up to the Germans. That's my order." Henri Knap had a feeling of dread. He knew that if the Germans followed their usual procedure, ten or twelve leading citizens—doctors, lawyers and teachers among them—would be publicly executed in an Arnhem square at noon on Sunday.

☆ 7 ☆

ALL DOWN THE ALLIED LINE of command the evaluation of intelligence on the panzers in the Arnhem area was magnificently bungled. SHAEF's Intelligence Summary No. 26 issued on September 16, the eve of Market-Garden—containing the ominous warning that had caused General Bedell Smith's alarm—was disregarded. In part, it read, "9th SS Panzer Division, and presumably the 10th, has been reported withdrawing to the Arnhem area in Holland; there, they will probably collect new tanks from a depot reported in the area of Cleves."

The information, already discredited by Montgomery at his meeting with Smith, was now discounted by General Dempsey's British Second Army headquarters—the same headquarters that had originally noted the presence in Holland of "battered panzer formations" on September 10. In the most serious blunder of all, Dempsey's intelligence staff, on September 14, described the Germans in the Market-Garden area as "weak, demoralized and likely to collapse entirely if confronted with a large airborne attack." Now, in a complete reversal of their original position, they dismissed the presence of the panzers, *because Dempsey's staff officers were unable to spot enemy armor on any reconnaissance photos.*

At First Allied Airborne Army headquarters, General Brereton's chief intelligence officer, British Lieutenant Colonel Anthony Tasker, was not prepared to accept SHAEF's report either. Reviewing all the information available, he decided there was no direct evidence that the Arnhem area contained "much more than the considerable flak defenses already known to exist."

Everyone, it seemed, accepted the optimistic outlook of Montgomery's headquarters. As the British I Airborne Corps's chief of staff, Brigadier Gordon Walch, remembers, "21st Army Group headquarters was the principal source of our intelligence, and we took what they gave us to be true." General Urquhart, commander of the British 1st Airborne Division, put it another way. "Nothing," he said, "was allowed to mar the optimism prevailing across the Channel."

Yet, besides SHAEF's report on the "missing" panzers, there was other evidence of German buildup, again almost cursorily noted. At the front, ahead of General Horrocks' XXX Corps Garden forces, it was plain that an increasing number of German units were moving into the line. Now the strategic error at Antwerp ten days before was beginning to build and threaten the grand design of Operation Market-Garden. The German troops filling out General Student's front were none other than units of the splintered divisions that had escaped across the mouth of the Schelde—the battered men of Von Zangen's Fifteenth Army, the army the Allies had practically written off. Intelligence officers did note that, though the Germans had increased in number, the new units in the line were "believed to be in no fit state to resist any determined advance." Any British Tommy along the Belgium-Dutch frontier could have told them otherwise.[*]

The cobblestone streets of the dingy mining town of Leopoldsburg in northern Belgium, barely ten miles from the front, were

---

[*] British Major General Hubert Essame (retired) in his excellent book *The Battle for Germany* (p. 13), writes: "In misappreciation of the actual situation at the end of August and the first half of September, Allied intelligence staffs sank to a level only reached by Brigadier John Charteris, Haig's Chief Intelligence Officer at the time of the Passchendaele Battles in 1917." At that time the wartime Prime Minister David Lloyd George alleged that Charteris "selected only those figures and facts which suited his fancy and then issued hopeful reports accordingly." At various times during the 1917 Flanders campaign Charteris reported the enemy as "cracking," "mangled," "with few reserves," and even "on the run." In the dreadful battles that ensued around Passchendaele between July 31 and November 12, casualties, according to the official British history, totaled a staggering 244,897.

choked with jeeps and scout cars. All roads seemed to lead to a cinema opposite the railway station—and never before had the nondescript theater held such an audience. Officers of Lieutenant General Horrocks' XXX Corps—the Garden forces that would drive north through Holland to link up with the paratroopers—crowded the street and milled around the entrance as their credentials were inspected by red-capped military police. It was a colorful, exuberant group and it reminded Brigadier Hubert Essame, commanding officer of the 214th Brigade, 43rd Wessex Infantry Division, of "an army assembly at a point-to-point race or a demonstration on Salisbury Plain in time of peace." He was fascinated by the colorful dress of the commanders. There was a striking variety of headgear. No one had a steel helmet, but berets of many colors bore the proud badges of famous regiments, among them the Irish, Grenadier, Coldstream, Scotch, Welsh and Royal Horse Guards, the Royal Army Service Corps and Royal Artillery. There was a regal casualness about everyone's attire. Essame noted that most commanders were dressed in "sniper's smocks, parachutists' jackets and jeep coats over brightly colored slacks, corduroys, riding britches or even jodhpurs." Instead of ties many sported ascots or "scarves of various colors."*

The renowned Lieutenant Colonel J.O.E. ("Joe") Vandeleur, the solidly built, ruddy-faced, six-foot commander of the Irish Guards Armored Group, personified the kind of devil-may-care elegance of the Guards' officers. The forty-one-year-old Vandeleur was wearing his usual combat garb: black beret, a multi-colored camouflaged parachutist's jacket, and corduroy trousers above high rubber boots. Additionally, Vandeleur wore, as always, a .45 Colt automatic strapped to his hip and, tucked into his jacket, what had become a symbol for his tankers, a flamboyant emerald-green scarf. The fastidious General "Boy" Browning, back in England, would have winced. Even Horrocks had

* In his history of *The 43rd Wessex Division at War* (p. 115), Essame writes: "Sartorial disciplinarians of the future" might remember "that when the morale of the British Army was as high as at any time in its history, officers wore the clothing they found most suitable to the conditions under which they had to live and fight."

once dryly admonished Vandeleur. "If the Germans ever get you, Joe," he said, "they'll think they've captured a peasant." But on this September 16 even Horrocks lacked the usual elegance of the impeccably dressed British staff officer. Instead of a shirt he wore a ribbed polo sweater and, over his battle dress, a sleeveless leather jerkin reminiscent of a British yeoman's dress.

As the popular Horrocks made his way down the aisle of the crowded theater he was greeted on all sides. The meeting he had called had sparked high excitement. Men were eager to get going again. From the Seine to Antwerp, Horrocks' tanks had often averaged fifty miles in a single day, but ever since the disastrous three-day halt on September 4 to "refit, refuel and rest," the going had been rough. With the British momentum gone, the enemy had quickly recovered. In the two vital weeks since, the British advance had been reduced to a crawl. It had taken four days for the Guards Armored Division—led by Joe Vandeleur's Irish Guards Group—to advance ten miles and capture the vital bridge over the Meuse-Escaut Canal near Neerpelt, from which the attack into Holland would begin the next day. Horrocks had no illusions about the German opposition, but he was confident that his forces could break through the enemy crust.

At precisely 11 A.M. Horrocks stepped onto the stage. All those assembled knew that the British offensive was about to be renewed, but so great was the security surrounding Montgomery's plan that only a few general officers present knew the details. With D Day for Operation Market-Garden barely twenty-four hours away, the Field Marshal's commanders now learned of the attack for the first time.

Attached to the cinema screen was a huge map of Holland. Colored tape snaked north along a single highway, crossing the great river obstacles and passing through the towns of Valkenswaard, Eindhoven, Veghel, Uden, Nijmegen and thence to Arnhem, a distance of some sixty-four miles. From there the tape continued for another thirty-odd miles to the Zuider Zee. Horrocks took a long pointer and began the briefing. "This is a tale you will tell your grandchildren," he told his audience. Then he paused and, much to the delight of the assembled officers, added: "And mightily bored they'll be."

In the audience, Lieutenant Colonel Curtis D. Renfro, liaison officer from the 101st Airborne Division and one of the few Americans present, was impressed by the Corps commander's enthusiasm and confidence. He talked for an hour, Curtis recorded, "with only an occasional reference to notes."

Step by step Horrocks explained the complexities of Market-Garden. The airborne army would go in first, he said. Its objectives: to capture the bridges in front of XXX Corps. Horrocks would give the word for the attack to begin. Depending on the weather, zero hour for the ground forces was expected to be 2 P.M. At that moment 350 guns would open fire and lay down a massive artillery barrage that would last thirty-five minutes. Then, at 2:35 P.M., led by waves of rocket-firing Typhoons, XXX Corps tanks would break out of their bridgehead and "blast down the main road." The Guards Armored Division would have the honor of leading the attack. They would be followed by the 43rd Wessex and 50th Northumberland divisions, and then by the 8th Armored Brigade and the Dutch Princess Irene Brigade.

There was to be "no pause, no stop," Horrocks emphasized. The Guards Armored was "to keep going like hell" all the way to Arnhem. The breakout from the bridgehead, Horrocks believed, would be "almost immediate." He expected the first Guards tanks to be in Eindhoven within two or three hours. If the enemy reacted fast enough to blow all the bridges before the airborne troops could secure them, then the 43rd Wessex Infantry Division engineers, coming up behind, would rush forward with men and bridging equipment. This massive engineering operation, should it be required, Horrocks explained, could involve 9,000 engineers and some 2,277 vehicles already in the Leopoldsburg area. The entire XXX Corps armored column was to be fed up the main road with the vehicles two abreast, thirty-five vehicles per mile. Traffic would be one way, and Horrocks expected "to pass 20,000 vehicles over the highway to Arnhem in sixty hours."

General Allan Adair, the forty-six-year-old commander of the famed Guards Armored Division, listening to Horrocks, thought Market-Garden was a bold plan, but he also believed "it might be tricky." He expected the worst moment to be the breakout from the Meuse-Escaut Canal bridgehead. Once through that, although he fully expected German resistance, he thought the going would "not be difficult." Besides, he had every faith in the unit that would lead off the attack—Lieutenant Colonel Joe Vandeleur's Irish Guards Group.

Joe Vandeleur, as he learned that his tanks would spearhead the breakout, remembers thinking to himself, "Oh, Christ! Not us again." Vandeleur was proud that his veteran unit had been chosen, yet he knew his troops were tired and his units under-strength. Since the breakout from Normandy he had received very few replacements in either men or tanks; furthermore, "they weren't allowing a hell of a lot of time for planning." But then he thought, how much time do you really need to plan for a straight bash through the German lines? Next to him, his cousin, thirty-three-year-old Lieutenant Colonel Giles Vandeleur, who commanded the 2nd Battalion under Joe, was "struck with horror at the plan to blast through the German resistance on a one-tank front." To him, it was not proper armored warfare. But he recalls "swallowing whatever misgivings I had and succumbing to a strange, tense excitement, like being at the pole at the start of a horse race."

To three men in the theater, the announcement produced deep personal feelings. The senior officers of the Dutch Princess Irene Brigade had led their men in battle all the way from Normandy. First they had fought alongside the Canadians; then, after the fall of Brussels, they were transferred to the British Second Army. Now they would be coming home. Much as they looked forward to the liberation of Holland, the commander, Colonel Albert "Steve" de Ruyter van Steveninck; his second in command, Lieutenant Colonel Charles Pahud de Mortanges; and the chief of staff, Major Jonkheer Jan Beelaerts van Blokland, had grave misgivings about the manner in which it was to be accomplished.

Steveninck considered the entire plan risky. Mortanges' impression was that the British were more offhand about what lay ahead than the facts justified. As he put it, "It was made to seem quite elementary. First, we'll take this bridge; then that one and hop this river. . . . The terrain ahead with its rivers, marshes, dikes and lowlands, was extremely difficult—as the British well knew from our many presentations." The thirty-three-year-old chief of staff, Beelaerts van Blokland, could not help thinking of past military history. "We seemed to be violating Napoleon's maxim about never fighting unless you are at least 75 percent sure of success. Then, the other 25 percent can be left to chance. The British were reversing the process; we were leaving 75 percent to chance. We had only forty-eight hours to get to Arnhem, and if the slightest thing went wrong—a bridge blown, stiffer German resistance than anticipated—we'd be off schedule." Blokland had a private worry, too. His parents lived in the village of Oosterbeek, just two and a half miles from the Arnhem bridge.

One of the few officers below the rank of brigade major who heard the briefing was twenty-one-year-old Lieutenant John Gorman of the Irish Guards. He was stimulated by the whole affair and thought Horrocks was "at his finest." The Corps commander, Gorman later recalled, "called into play all his wit and humor, interspersing the more dramatic or technical points with humorous little asides. He really was quite a showman." Gorman was particularly pleased with Operation Garden because "the Guards were to lead out and obviously their role would be tremendously dramatic."

When the meeting had ended and commanders headed out to brief their troops, young Gorman felt his first "private doubts about the chances of success." Lingering in front of a map, he remembers thinking that Market-Garden was "a feasible operation—but only just feasible." There were simply "too many bridges." Nor was he enthusiastic about the terrain itself. He thought it was poor tank country and advancing on "a one-tank front, we would be very vulnerable." But the promise of support from rocket-firing Typhoons was reassuring. So was another promise of sorts. Gorman remembered the day, months before, when he had received the Military Cross for bravery from Montgomery himself.[*] At the investiture, Monty had said, "If I were a betting man I should say it would be an even bet that the war will be over by Christmas." And Horrocks, Gorman recalls, had "told us that this attack could end the war." The only alternative Gorman could find to "going north seemed to be a long dreary winter camped on or near the Escaut Canal." Monty's plan, he believed, "had just the right amount of dash and daring to work. If there was a chance to win the war by Christmas, then I was for pushing on."

Now, in the flat, gray Belgian countryside with its coal fields and slag heaps which reminded so many of Wales, the men who would lead the way for General Dempsey's British Second Army heard of the plan and the promise of Arnhem. Along side roads, in bivouac areas and in encampments, soldiers gathered around their officers to learn the part they would play in Operation Market-Garden. When Lieutenant Colonel Giles Vandeleur told his officers that the Irish would be leading out, twenty-nine-year-old Major Edward G. Tyler remembers that a "half moan" went up from the assembled officers. "We figured," he recalls, "that we deserved a bit of a break after taking the bridge over the Escaut Canal, which we named 'Joe's bridge' after Joe Vandeleur. But our commanding officer told us that it was a great honor for us to be chosen." Despite his desire for a reprieve, Tyler thought so too. "We were used to one-tank fronts," he remembers, "and in this case we were trusting to speed and support. No one seemed worried."

But Lieutenant Barry Quinan, who had just turned twenty-one, was "filled with trepidation." He was going into action for the first time with the lead Guards Armored tank squadron under Captain Mick O'Cock. Quinan's infantry would travel on the backs of the tanks, Russian-style. To him, "the number of rivers ahead seemed

---

[*] Gorman won his Military Cross during the fighting at Caen, Normandy. Leading a trio of Sherman tanks, he was suddenly confronted by four German tanks, one a 60-ton Tiger. His men dispatched the German armor and Gorman rammed the huge Tiger tank, destroyed its gun and killed its crew as they tried to escape.

ominous. We were not amphibious." Yet Quinan felt proud that his men would be "leading the entire British Second Army."

Lieutenant Rupert Mahaffey, also twenty-one, vividly remembers being told that "if the operation was a success the wives and children at home would be relieved from the threat of the Germans' V-2 rockets." Mahaffey's mother lived in London, which by that time was under intense bombardment. Although he was excited at the prospect of the attack, the single road leading all the way up to Arnhem was, he thought, "an awfully long way to go."

Captain Roland S. Langton, twenty-three, just returned from five days in a field hospital after receiving shrapnel wounds, learned that he was no longer adjutant of the 2nd Irish Guards Battalion. Instead, he was assigned as second in command of Captain Mick O'Cock's breakout squadron. He was jubilant about the assignment. The breakout seemed to Langton a straightforward thing. Garden could not be anything but a success. It was "obvious to all that the Germans were disorganized and shaken, lacking cohesion, and capable only of fighting in small pockets."

Not everyone was so confident. As Lieutenant A. G. C. "Tony" Jones, twenty-one, of the Royal Engineers, listened to the plan, he thought it was "clearly going to be very difficult." The bridges were the key to the entire operation and, as one officer remarked, "The drive of the XXX Corps will be like threading seven needles with one piece of cotton and we only have to miss one to be in trouble." To veteran Guardsman Tim Smith, twenty-four, the attack was "just another battle." On this day his greatest concern was the famed St. Leger race at Newmarket. He had a tip that a horse called Tehran, to be ridden by the famous jockey Gordon Richards, was "a sure thing." He placed every penny he had on Tehran with a lance corporal at battalion headquarters. If Market-Garden was the operation that would win the war, this was just the day to win the St. Leger. To his amazement, Tehran won. He was quite sure now that Market-Garden would succeed.

One man was "decidedly uncomfortable." Flight Lieutenant Donald Love, twenty-eight, an R.A.F. fighter-reconnaissance pilot, felt completely out of place among the officers of the Guards Armored. He was part of the air liaison team which would call in the rocket-firing Typhoon fighters from the ground when the breakout began. His lightly armored vehicle (code-named "Winecup"), with its canvas roof and its maze of communications equipment, would be up front close to Lieutenant Colonel Joe Vandeleur's command car. Love felt naked and defenseless: the only weapons the R.A.F. team possessed were revolvers. As he listened to Vandeleur talking about "a rolling barrage that would move forward at a speed of 200 yards per minute" and heard the burly Irishman describe Love's little scout car as an "armored signal tender for direct communication with pilots in the sky," Love's concern mounted. "I got the distinct impression that I would be the one responsible for calling in the 'cab rank' of Typhoons overhead." The thought was not reassuring. Love knew very little about the radio setup, and he had never before acted as a ground-to-air tactical officer. Then, to his acute relief, he learned that an expert, Squadron Leader Max Sutherland, would join him the following day to handle the communications for the initial breakout. Thereafter, Love would be in charge. Love began to wonder whether he should have volunteered in the first place. He had only taken the job "because I thought it might be a nice change of pace."

A change of a different sort bothered the commander of the Irish Guards. During the capture of the bridgehead over the Escaut Canal, Joe Vandeleur had lost "a close and distinguished friend." His broadcasting van, with its huge trumpetlike loudspeaker on the roof, had been destroyed by a German shell. All through training back in England and in the great advance from Normandy, Joe had used the van to broadcast to his troops and after each session, being a lover of classical music, he had always put on a record or two—selections that didn't always please the Guardsmen. The van had been blown to pieces and shards of the classical records—along with Vandeleur's favorite popular tune—had showered down over the countryside. Joe was saddened by his loss; not so, his Irish Guardsmen. They thought the drive to

Arnhem would be arduous enough without having to listen to Joe's loudspeaker blaring out his current theme song, "Praise the Lord and Pass the Ammunition."

Meanwhile, in England the paratroopers and glider-borne infantry of the First Allied Airborne Army were even now in marshaling areas, ready for the moment of takeoff. Over the previous forty-eight hours, using maps, photographs and scale models, officers had briefed and rebriefed their men. The preparations were immense and meticulous. At twenty-four air bases (8 British, 16 American), vast fleets of troop-carrying aircraft, tow planes and gliders were checked out, fueled and loaded with equipment ranging from artillery to jeeps. Some ninety miles north of London, Brigadier General James M. Gavin's "All-American" 82nd Airborne Division was already shut off from the outside world at a cluster of airfields around Grantham in Lincolnshire. So were part of General Roy Urquhart's Red Devils, the British 1st Airborne Division, and Major General Stanislaw Sosabowski's Polish 1st Parachute Brigade. To the south around Newbury, roughly eighty miles west of London, Major General Maxwell D. Taylor's Screaming Eagles, the 101st Airborne Division, were also "sealed in." In the same area, and stretching as far down as Dorsetshire, was the remainder of Urquhart's division. The majority of his units would not move to the airfields until the morning of the seventeenth, but in hamlets, villages and bivouac areas close to the departure points, they too made ready. Everywhere now, the airborne forces of Market-Garden waited out the time until takeoff and the historic invasion of Holland from the sky.

Some men felt more concern at being sealed in than about the mission itself. At an airfield near the village of Ramsbury, the security precautions made Corporal Hansford Vest, of the 101st Division's 502nd Regiment, distinctly uneasy. Aircraft and gliders "were parked for miles all over the countryside and there were guards everywhere." He noted that the airfield was surrounded by a barbed-wire fence with "British guards on the outside and our own guards on the inside." Vest had the "feeling that our freedom was gone." Private James Allardyce of the 508th Regiment, in his crowded tent city, tried to ignore the barbed wire and guards. He checked and rechecked his equipment "until it was almost worn out." Allardyce could not shake off the feeling that "we were like condemned men waiting to be led off."

Other men worried principally about their chances of going on the mission. So many previous operations had been canceled that one new recruit, nineteen-year-old Private Melvin Isenekev, of the 506th Regiment (he had arrived from the States on June 6, the day the 101st had jumped into Normandy), still didn't believe they would go when they reached the marshaling area. Isenekev felt he had trained "long and hard for this and I didn't want to be held back." Yet he almost was. Trying to light a makeshift oil burner used for heating water, he threw a lighted match into an oil drum. When nothing happened, Isenekev "put my head over it to look in and it exploded." Temporarily blinded, he instantly thought, "Now I've done it. They won't let me go." However within a few minutes his eyes stopped burning and he could see again. But he believes he was the only member of the 101st jumping into Holland with no eyebrows.

First Sergeant Daniel Zapalski, twenty-four, of the 502nd, "sweated out the jump; hoping the chute was packed right; hoping the field was soft; and hoping I didn't land in a tree." He was eager to go. Although he had not fully recovered from a Normandy leg wound, Zapalski believed his injury "was not serious enough to keep me from doing my normal duty." His battalion commander, the popular Lieutenant Colonel Robert G. Cole, disagreed. He had turned down Zapalski's pleas. Undeterred, Zapalski had bypassed Cole and obtained a written release certifying his combat readiness from the regimental surgeon. Though Zapalski and Cole had fought together in Normandy, the sergeant now got a "typical Cole chewing out. He called me 'a fatheaded Polack, impractical, burdensome and unreasonable.'" But he let Zapalski go.

Captain Raymond S. Hall, the 502nd's regimental chaplain, had a somewhat similar problem. He was "most anxious to return to action and to be with my men." But he too had been wounded in Normandy. Now the doctors would not let him jump. He was finally told that he could go in by glider. The chaplain was horrified. A veteran paratrooper, he considered gliders distinctly unsafe.

Fear of death or of failure to perform well disturbed others. Captain LeGrand Johnson, twenty-two-year-old company commander, remembering "the horrors and narrow escapes" during the 101st's night airborne attack preceding the Normandy invasion, was fatalistically "resigned." He was convinced that he would not return from this mission. Still, the young officer "fully intended to raise as much hell as I could." Johnson was not sure he liked the idea of a daylight drop. It might produce more casualties. On the other hand, this time "we would be able to see the enemy." To hide his nervousness, Johnson made bets with his fellow troopers on who would get the first Dutch beer. One of Johnson's staff sergeants, Charles Dohun, was "almost numb" with worry. He did "not know how to compare this daylight jump with Normandy or what to expect." Within forty-eight hours, his numbness forgotten, Staff Sergeant Dohun would heroically save the life of the fatalistic Captain Johnson.

Technical Sergeant Marshall Copas, twenty-two, had perhaps more reason than most for anxiety. He was one of the "pathfinders" who would jump first to mark the drop zones for the 101st. In the Normandy drop, Copas recalled, "we had forty-five minutes before the main body of troopers began jumping—now we had only twelve minutes." Copas and his friend Sergeant John Rudolph Brandt, twenty-nine, had one concern in common: both would have felt better "had General Patton's Third Army been on the ground below us, rather than the British. We had never fought with the Tommies before."

In the Grantham area, Private John Garzia, a veteran of three combat jumps with the 82nd Airborne Division, was stunned. To him, Market-Garden "was sheer insanity." He thought "Ike had transferred to the German side."

Now that Operation Market-Garden was actually on, Lieutenant Colonel Louis Mendez, battalion commander of the 82nd's 508th Regiment, had no hesitation in speaking out on one particular subject. With the nighttime experiences of his regiment in Normandy still painfully clear in his mind, Colonel Mendez delivered a scathing warning to the pilots who would carry his battalion into action the next day. "Gentlemen," Mendez said coldly, "my officers know this map of Holland and the drop zones by heart and we're ready to go. When I brought my battalion to the briefing prior to Normandy, I had the finest combat-ready force of its size that will ever be known. By the time I gathered them together in Normandy, half were gone. I charge you: put us down in Holland or put us down in hell, but put us all down together in one place."

Private First Class John Allen, twenty-four, a three-jump veteran and still recovering from wounds sustained in Normandy, was philosophical about the operation: "They never got me in a night jump," he solemnly told his buddies, "so now they'll be able to see me and get off a good shot." Staff Sergeant Russell O'Neal, with three night combat jumps behind him, was convinced that his "Irish luck was about to run out." When he heard the 82nd was to jump in daylight, he composed a letter he never sent— "You can hang a gold star in your window tonight, Mother. The Germans have a good chance to hit us before we even land." To lighten the atmosphere—though in doing so he may have made it worse—Private Philip H. Nadler, of the 504th Regiment, spread a few rumors. The one he liked best was that a large German camp of SS men were bivouacked on one of the 82nd drop zones.

Nadler had not been overly impressed by the briefing of the platoon. One of the 504th's objectives was the bridge at Grave. Gathering the men around him, the briefing lieutenant threw back the cover on a sandtable model and said, "Men, this is your destination." He rested a pointer on the bridge which bore the single word "Grave." Nadler was the first to comment. "Yeah, we know that, Lieutenant," he said, "but what country are we droppin' on?"

Major Edward Wellems, of the 504th's 2nd Battalion, thought

the name of the bridge was rather ominous, too, despite the fact that the officers who briefed his group suddenly began to change the pronunciation, referring to it as the "gravey bridge."

The briefings caused mixed reactions. Nineteen-year-old Corporal Jack Bommer thought that "six or eight weeks would see us home and then they'd send us on to the Pacific." Private Leo Hart, twenty-one, did not believe they were going at all. He had heard—probably as a result of Private Nadler's rumor—that there were 4,000 SS troops in the general jump area.

Major Edwin Bedell, thirty-eight, remembers that one private's sole concern was the safety of a live hare that he had won in a local village raffle. The private was fearful that his pet, which was so tame that it followed him everywhere, would not survive the jump, and that if it did it might still wind up in a stew pot.

Near Spanhoe airfield in the Grantham area, Lieutenant "Pat" Glover of the British 1st Airborne Division's 4th Parachute Brigade worried about Myrtle, a reddish-brown chicken that had been Glover's special pet since early summer. With parachute wings fastened to an elastic band around her neck, Myrtle "the parachick" had made six training jumps. At first she rode in a small zippered canvas bag attached to Glover's left shoulder. Later, he released her at fifty feet above the ground. By now Myrtle was an expert, and Glover could free her at three hundred feet. With a frenzied flutter of wings and raucous squawking, Myrtle gracelessly floated down to earth. There, Glover recalls, "this rather gentle pet would wait patiently on the ground for me to land and collect her." Myrtle the parachick was going to Arnhem. It would be her first combat jump. But Glover did not intend to tempt fate. He planned to keep Myrtle in her bag until he hit the ground in Holland.

Lance Corporal Sydney Nunn, twenty-three, of the 1st Airlanding Brigade, based in the south near Keevil, was only too glad to get away from his "pet." He thought the camp was "a nightmare." Nunn couldn't wait to get to Arnhem or anyplace else, so long as it was far enough away from the persistent mole who kept burrowing into his mattress.

For the men of the British 1st Airborne Division, now standing by in bases stretching from the Midlands south to Dorsetshire, the prevailing mood was one of relief that, at last, they were going into action. Besides, briefing officers stressed the fact that Market-Garden could shorten the war. For the British, fighting since 1939, the news was heady. Sergeant Ron Kent, of the 21st Independent Parachute Company, heard that "the success of the operation might even give us Berlin" and that ground opposition in Arnhem "would consist mainly of Hitler Youth and old men on bicycles." Sergeant Walter Inglis, of the 1st Parachute Brigade, was equally confident. The attack, he thought, would be "a piece of cake." All the Red Devils had to do was "hang on to the Arnhem bridge for forty-eight hours until XXX Corps tanks arrived; then the war would be practically over." Inglis expected to be back home in England in a week. Lance Corporal Gordon Spicer, of the 1st Parachute Brigade, offhandedly considered the operation "a fairly simple affair with a few backstage Germans recoiling in horror at our approach"; while Lance Bombardier Percy Parkes, of the 1st Airlanding Brigade, felt, after his briefing, that "all we would encounter at Arnhem was a mixed bag of Jerry cooks and clerks." The presence of tanks, Parkes says, was "mentioned only in passing, and we were told our air cover would be so strong that it would darken the sky above us." Confidence was such that Medic Geoffrey Stanners expected only "a couple of hernia battalions" and Signalman Victor Read was "looking forward to seeing German WAAF's who," he thought, "would be the only Germans defending Arnhem."

Some men who could legitimately remain behind were eager to go. Sergeant Alfred Roullier, of the 1st Airlanding Brigade's Artillery, was one of these. The thirty-one-year-old trooper discovered that he was not slated for the Arnhem operation. Although Roullier had been trained as an artilleryman, he was currently the acting mess sergeant at his battalion headquarters. Because of his culinary expertise, it appeared that he might spend the remainder of the war in the job. Twice, Alf Roullier had appealed to Sergeant Major John Siely to be included in the attack, but each time he was turned down. For the third time Alf pressed his case. "I know this operation can shorten the war," he told Siely. "I've got a wife and two children, but if this attack will get me home quicker and guarantee them a better future, then I want to go." Siely pulled a few strings. Alf Roullier's name was added to the list of those who would go to Arnhem—where, within the next week, the assistant mess sergeant would become something of a legend.

In the prevailing high mood before the onset of Market-Garden, there were undercurrents of doubt among some officers and enlisted men. They were troubled for a variety of reasons, although most took care to hide their feelings. Corporal Daniel Morgans, of the 1st Parachute Brigade, considered "Market a snorter of an operation." Still, "to drop six or seven miles from the objective and then to fight through a city to get there, was really asking for trouble." Regimental Sergeant Major J. C. Lord, with a lifetime in the army behind him, thought so, too. "The plan was a bit dicey," he felt. Nor did Lord give much credence to the talk of an understrength, worn-out enemy. He knew that "the German is no fool and a mighty warrior." Still, J. C. Lord, whose demeanor could intimidate even the veterans in his charge (almost in awe, some called him "Jesus Christ" behind his back), did not reveal his uneasiness, because "it would have been catastrophic to morale."

Captain Eric Mackay, whose engineers were, among other tasks, to race to the main road bridge in Arnhem and remove expected German charges, was suspicious of the entire operation. He thought the division "might just as well be dropped a hundred miles away from the objective as eight." The advantage of surprise and "a quick lightning stroke" would surely be lost. Mackay quietly ordered his men to double the amount of ammunition and grenades each would carry and personally briefed everyone in the troop on escape techniques.*

---

* One of the most accurate accounts of the First British Airborne's activities on the Arnhem bridge is to be found in "The Battle of Arnhem Bridge" by Eric Mackay, *Blackwood's* Magazine, October 1945.

Major Anthony Deane-Drummond, twenty-seven, second in command of 1st Airborne Division Signals, was particularly concerned about his communications. Apart from the main command units, he was worried about the smaller "22" sets that would be used between Urquhart and the various brigades during the Arnhem attack. The "22's" could best transmit and receive within a diameter of three to five miles. With drop zones seven to eight miles from the objective, performance was expected to be erratic. Worse, the sets must also contact General Browning's Airborne Corps headquarters, planned for Nijmegen, from the drop zones approximately fifteen miles to the south. Adding to the problem was the terrain. Between the main road bridge at Arnhem and the landing areas was the town itself, plus heavily wooded sections and suburban developments. On the other hand, an independent fact-gathering liaison unit, called "Phantom"—organized to collect and pass on intelligence estimates and immediate reports to each commander in the field, in this case General Browning of Airborne Corps—was not worried about the range of its own "22's." Twenty-five-year-old Lieutenant Neville Hay, in charge of the Phantom team's highly trained specialists, was even a "little disdainful of the Royal Corps of Signals," whom his group was inclined to treat "as poor cousins." By using a special kind of antenna, Hay and his operators had been able to transmit at distances of over one hundred miles on a "22."

Even with Hay's success and although various forms of communications* would be used in the event of emergency, Deane-Drummond was uneasy. He mentioned to his superior, Lieutenant Colonel Tom Stephenson, that "the likelihood of the sets working satisfactorily in the initial phases of the operation is very doubtful." Stephenson agreed. Still, it would hardly matter. In the surprise assault, troops were expected to close up on the Arnhem bridge very quickly. Therefore, it was believed that units would not be out of touch with headquarters for more than one or

---

* Included in the communications setup were 82 pigeons provided from R.A.F. sources. The lofts for these birds were situated in the London area—meaning that the birds, if they survived the airborne landing and the Germans, would have to fly approximately 240 miles to deliver a message.

two hours, by which time, Deane-Drummond heard, "things would have sorted themselves out and Urquhart's command post would be with the 1st Parachute Brigade on the bridge itself." Although not entirely reassured, Deane-Drummond recalled that, "like almost everyone else, I was swept along with the prevailing attitude: 'Don't be negative; and for God's sake, don't rock the boat; let's get on with the attack.'"

Now the final word depended not on men but on the weather. From Supreme Command headquarters down, senior officers anxiously awaited meteorological reports. Given less than seven days to meet Montgomery's deadline, Market-Garden was as ready as it would ever be, but a minimum forecast of three full days of fair weather was needed. In the early evening of September 16, the weather experts issued their findings: apart from some early morning fog, the weather for the next three days would be fair, with little cloud and virtually no winds. At First Allied Airborne Army headquarters Lieutenant General Brereton quickly made his decision. The coded teleprinter message that went out to his commanders at 7:45 P.M. read, "CONFIRM MARKET SUNDAY 17TH. ACKNOWLEDGE." In his diary, Brereton recorded, "At last we are going into action." He thought he would sleep well this night for, as he told his staff, "Now that I've made the decision, I've quit worrying."

In crowded hangars, cities of tents and Nissen huts, the waiting men were given the news. On a large mirror over the fireplace in the sergeants' mess of the British 1st Airborne Division Signals near Grantham, someone chalked up "14 hours to go . . . no cancellation." Sergeant Horace "Hocker" Spivey noted that, as each hour passed, the number was rechalked. To Spivey, tired of being briefed for operations that never came off, the ever-diminishing number on the mirror was the best proof yet that this time "we were definitely going."

On all their bases the men of the First Allied Airborne Army made last-minute preparations. They had been fully briefed, their weapons had been checked and their currency exchanged for Dutch guilders, and there was little now for the isolated troopers to do but wait. Some spent the time writing letters, "celebrating" their departure the following morning, packing personal belongings, sleeping or participating in marathon card games ranging from blackjack and poker to bridge. Twenty-year-old Sergeant Francis Moncur, of the 1st Parachute Brigade's 2nd Battalion, played blackjack hour after hour. To his surprise, he won steadily. Looking at the ever-growing pile of guilders before him, Moncur felt like a millionaire. He expected to have a "whale of a time in Arnhem after the battle," which, in his opinion, would "last only forty-eight hours." That would be long enough for the sergeant to settle a score with the Germans. Seventy-two hours earlier, Moncur's brother, a seventeen-year-old R.A.F. flight sergeant, had been killed in an attempt to jump from his disabled bomber at 200 feet. His parachute had failed to open completely.

South of Grantham at a base in Cottesmore, Sergeant "Joe" Sunley of the 4th Parachute Brigade was on security patrol, making sure that "no paratroopers had slipped off base into the village." Returning to the airdrome, Sunley saw Sergeant "Ginger" Green, a physical-training instructor and a "gentle giant of a man," tossing a deflated football up in the air. Green deftly caught the ball and threw it to Sunley. "What the hell are you doing with this?" Sunley asked. Ginger explained that he was taking the deflated ball to Arnhem, "so we can have a little game on the drop zone after we're finished."

At Manston, Kent, Staff Sergeant George Baylis of the Glider Pilot Regiment was also looking forward to some recreation. He had heard that the Dutch liked to dance; so George carefully packed his dancing pumps. Signalman Stanley G. Copley of the 1st Parachute Brigade Signals bought extra film for his camera. As little opposition was expected he thought it was "a perfect chance to get some pictures of the Dutch countryside and towns."

One man was taking presents that he had bought in London a few days earlier. When the Netherlands was overrun, thirty-two-year-old Lieutenant Commander Arnoldus Wolters of the Dutch navy had escaped in his minesweeper and sailed to England. Since that time, he had been attached to the Netherlands government in exile, holding a variety of desk jobs dealing with information and intelligence. A few days earlier, Wolters had been asked to go to Holland as part of the military government and civil affairs team attached to General Urquhart's headquarters. It was proposed that Wolters become military commissioner of the Netherlands territories to be liberated by the airborne forces. "It was a startling suggestion—going from a desk chair to a glider," he recalled. He was attached to a unit under Colonel Hilary Barlow, second in command of the 1st Airlanding Brigade, who was designated to become the town commandant in Arnhem after its capture. Wolters would be his assistant. Now, excited about the prospect of returning to Holland, Wolters "was struck by the optimism, and I believed everything I was told. I really did not expect the operation to be very difficult. It seemed that the war was virtually over and the attack dead easy. I expected to land on Sunday and be home on Tuesday with my wife and child at Hilversum." For his wife, Maria, Wolters had bought a watch, and for his daughter, whom he had last seen as a baby four years before, he had a two-foot Teddy bear. He hoped nobody would mind if he took it in the glider.

Lieutenant Colonel John Frost, thirty-one, who was to lead the battalion assigned to capture the Arnhem bridge, packed his copper fox-hunting horn with the rest of his battle gear. It had been presented to him by the members of the Royal Exodus Hunt, of which he was Master in 1939–40. During training, Frost had used the horn to rally his men. He would do so on this operation. Frost had no qualms about a daylight jump. From the information given at briefings, "we were made to feel that the Germans were weak and demoralized and German troops in the area were of a decidedly low category and badly equipped." Frost did have misgivings about the drop zones. He had been told that the "polder on the southern side of the bridge was unsuitable for parachutists and gliders." Why then, he wondered, were the Poles to drop on the southern side of the bridge "if it was so unsuitable?"

Though he was anxious to get into action, Frost "hated to leave for Holland." Secretly, he hoped for a last-minute cancellation or postponement. He had enjoyed the area of Stoke Rochford in Lincolnshire and wished for "perhaps another day or two just doing all the pleasant things I had done in the past." But with these thoughts were others, "telling me that we had been here long enough and it was time to get away." Frost slept soundly on September 16. Although he wasn't naïve enough to think the battle of Arnhem would be "much of a lark," he did tell his batman, Wicks, to pack his gun, cartridges, golf clubs and dinner jacket in the staff car that would follow.

On the mirror above the fireplace in the sergeants' mess, now empty, there was one last notation, scrawled before men became too busy to bother. It read: "2 hours to go . . . no cancellation."

Part Three

✷

THE ATTACK

✷

☼ 1 ☼

THE THUNDER OF THE HUGE FORMATIONS was earsplitting. Around British glider bases in Oxfordshire and Gloucestershire, horses and cattle panicked and bolted in the fields. In southern and eastern England thousands of people watched in amazement. In some villages and towns road traffic jammed and came to a halt. Passengers in speeding trains crowded one another to stare out of windows. Everywhere people gaped, dumfounded, at a spectacle no one had ever seen before. The mightiest airborne force in history was off the ground and heading for its targets.

By coincidence on this bright Sunday morning, September 17, 1944, special services were being held all over England to commemorate "the valiant few," the handful of R.A.F. pilots who had boldly challenged Hitler's Luftwaffe four years before and fought them to a standstill. As worshipers knelt in prayer, the steady, overpowering drone of propellers completely drowned out some services. In London's great Westminster Cathedral the soaring organ tones of the solemn Magnificat could not be heard. In twos and threes, people left their pews to join the crowds already gathered in the streets. There, Londoners stared upward, overwhelmed by the din as formation after formation of aircraft passed overhead at low altitude. In north London, a Salvation Army band overpowered by the noise gave up, but the bass drummer, his eyes on the sky, thumped out a symbolic beat: three dots and a dash—in Morse code, V for *victory*.

To the onlookers, the nature of the attack was clearly revealed by the great streams of planes towing gliders. But it would be six more hours before the British people learned that they had witnessed the opening phase of the most momentous airborne offensive ever conceived. A Red Cross worker, Angela Hawkings, may have best summed up the reactions of those who saw the vast armada pass. From the window of a train, she stared up, astonished, as wave after wave of planes flew over like "droves of starlings." She was convinced that "this attack, wherever bound, must surely bring about the end of the war."

The men of the First Allied Airborne Army were as unprepared as the civilians on the ground for the awesome spectacle of their own departure. The paratroopers, glider-borne infantry and pilots who set out for Holland were staggered by the size and majesty of the air fleets. Captain Arie D. Bestebreurtje, a Dutch officer attached to the 82nd Airborne, thought the sight was "unbelievable. Every plane the Allies possessed must have been engaged in this single scheme." In fact, some 4,700 aircraft were involved—the greatest number ever used on a single airborne mission.

The operation had begun in the predawn hours and continued on throughout the morning. First, more than 1,400 Allied bombers had taken off from British airfields and had pounded German antiaircraft positions and troop concentrations in the Market-Garden area. Then, at 9:45 A.M. and for two and one quarter hours more, 2,023 troop-carrying planes, gliders and their tugs swarmed into the air from twenty-four U.S. and British bases.* C-47's carrying paratroopers flew in long 45-plane formations. More C-47's and British bombers—Halifaxes, Stirlings and Albemarles—pulled 478 gliders. In seemingly endless sky trains, these huge equipment- and troop-carrying gliders bounced behind their tow planes at the end of 300-foot-long ropes. Swaying among the smaller Horsa and Waco gliders were massive slab-

---

* Many official accounts give 10:25 A.M. as the time when the first Market aircraft left the ground. Perhaps they had in mind the departure of the pathfinders, who arrived first. From an examination of log books and air controllers' time schedules, it is clear that the airlift began at 9:45 A.M.

sided Hamilcars, each with a cargo capacity of eight tons; they could hold a small tank or two 3-ton trucks with artillery or ammunition. Above, below and on the flanks, protecting these huge formations, were almost 1,500 Allied fighters and fighter-bombers—British Spitfires, rocket-firing Typhoons, Tempests and Mosquitoes; U.S. Thunderbolts, Lightnings, Mustangs and low-level dive bombers. There were so many planes in the air that Captain Neil Sweeney of the 101st Airborne Division remembered that "it looked like we could get out on the wings and walk all the way to Holland."

The British glider forces were the first to take off. Farther north on the Market-Garden corridor than the Americans and with different requirements, General Urquhart needed the maximum in men, equipment and artillery—especially antitank guns—in the first lift, to capture and hold his objectives until the land forces could link up. Therefore, the bulk of his division was glider-borne; 320 gliders carried the men, transport and artillery of Brigadier Philip "Pips" Hicks's 1st Airlanding Brigade. They would reach landing zones west of Arnhem a little after 1 P.M. Thirty minutes later, Brigadier Gerald Lathbury's 1st Parachute Brigade, in 145 troop-carrying planes, would begin dropping. Because the unwieldy gliders and tugs were slower—120 miles per hour versus 140 for the paratroop-carrier planes—these immense "sky trains"—or serials, as the airborne called them—had to be launched first. From eight bases in Gloucestershire and Oxfordshire, gliders and tugs rolled down runways and rose in the air at a launch rate never before attempted: one combination per minute. Forming up was especially intricate and dangerous. Climbing slowly to altitude, the planes headed west over the Bristol Channel. Then, speeds synchronized, the tugs and gliders echeloned to the right in pairs, turned back, flew over the takeoff bases and headed for a marshaling point above the town of Hatfield, north of London.

Even as the first British glider serials were forming up above the Bristol Channel, twelve British Stirling bombers and six U.S.

C-47's began taking off at 10:25 A.M. for Holland. In them were U.S. and British pathfinders—the men who would land first to mark landing and drop zones for the Market forces.

Simultaneously, the men of the U.S. 82nd Airborne and the paratroop elements of the British First Division took off from bases around Grantham, Lincolnshire, in 625 troop-carrier planes and 50 C-47's towing gliders. With astonishing precision, the planes of the IX Troop Carrier Command left the ground at five- to twenty-second intervals. In wave after wave they rendezvoused above the town of March, Cambridgeshire, and from there set out in three parallel streams to cross the coast at Aldeburgh.

At the same time, from southern airfields around Greenham Common, the 101st Airborne took to the air, in 424 C-47's plus 70 gliders and tugs. Forming up, they too passed over the traffic control point at Hatfield and flew east to cross the coast at Bradwell Bay.

In immense triple columns, together at least ten miles across and approximately a hundred miles long, the vast armada swept over the English countryside. The 82nd Airborne and British 1st Division, enroute to Nijmegen and Arnhem, flew along the northern track. A special serial of 38 gliders carrying General Browning's Corps headquarters, bound for Nijmegen, traveled with them. On the southern route, passing over Bradwell Bay, the 101st Airborne headed for its drop zones slightly north of Eindhoven. By 11:55 A.M., the entire force—more than 20,000 troops, 511 vehicles, 330 artillery pieces and 590 tons of equipment—was off the ground. First Lieutenant James J. Coyle of the 82nd Airborne, looking down on the English countryside from an altitude of only 1,500 feet, saw nuns waving from the courtyard of a convent. He thought "the beautiful day and the nuns made a picture that had the quality of an oil painting." Waving back, he wondered "if they could possibly know who we were and where we were going."

For the majority of the airborne troops, the mood of the initial part of the journey, across England, was lighthearted. To Private Roy Edwards of the 1st Parachute Brigade, "everything was so serene it was like going on a bus outing to the seaside." Private A. G. Warrender remembers that "this was a perfect Sunday; a morning for a walk down a country lane and a pint at the local."

The commanding officer of the Glider Pilot Regiment, Colonel George S. Chatterton, piloting the glider carrying General Browning, described the Sunday as "an extremely fine day. It did not seem possible that we were taking off for one of the greatest battles in history." Chatterton was struck by Browning's entourage and equipment. With the General were his batman, headquarters' medical officer, cook, as well as his tent and personal jeep. Browning sat on an empty Worthington Beer crate between the pilot and copilot, and Chatterton noted that he was "immaculately dressed in a Barathea battle dress, with a highly polished Sam Browne belt, knife-edge-creased trousers, leather holster gleaming like glass, a swagger stick and spotless gray kid gloves." The General, says Chatterton, "was in tremendous form, because he realized he had reached one of the climaxes of his career. There was an air of immense gaiety."

In another glider serial, the quiet Scot with the most difficult Market-Garden assignment, the 1st Airborne Division's General Roy Urquhart, thought it was "difficult not to feel excited that we were off at last." Yet the popular officer's mind, as always, was on his men and the job that lay ahead. Like Browning, he had an entourage. Now, looking down the length of the Horsa glider—which was carrying his aide Roberts, batman Hancock, the Reverend G. A. Pare, padre of the Glider Pilot Regiment, a signaler, two military police, their motorcycles and the General's jeep—Urquhart felt a pang of conscience. He thought of his paratroopers, laden down with packs, guns and equipment, crowded into heavy transport planes. Urquhart carried only a small shoulder pack, two hand grenades, a map case and a notebook. He was bothered by his own comfort.

Almost up to the moment of takeoff Urquhart had been called

on to make difficult decisions. Some hours before leaving, his chief of staff, Colonel Charles Mackenzie, had received a telephone call from a senior American air force officer. Was the mental asylum at Wolfheze to be bombed? The American, Mackenzie had reported, "wanted a personal assurance from Urquhart that there were Germans in it and not lunatics; otherwise the Americans could not accept responsibility." The asylum was dangerously close to the division's assembly point, and Urquhart's staff believed it to be held by the Germans. Mackenzie had accepted responsibility. "On your head be it," the American had replied. Urquhart had approved his chief of staff's action. "I meant to be as prepared as possible and that's all there was to it," he remembered.

As Mackenzie was about to leave for his own glider, Urquhart had taken him privately aside. "Look, Charles," he had told Mackenzie, "if anything happens to me the succession of command should be as follows: first, Lathbury, then Hicks and Hackett in that order." Urquhart's choice was based on experience. "Everyone knew that Lathbury was my deputy," he later recalled. "Hackett was senior in rank to Hicks, but he was much younger and I was quite convinced that Hicks had more experience in handling infantry. My decision was no reflection on Hackett's ability to command." Perhaps, Urquhart reflected, he should have informed each of his brigadiers of his decision earlier, but he had "frankly considered the whole question quite academic." The chance of the division losing both Urquhart and Lathbury was remote.

Now, all decisions made, Urquhart idly watched "squadrons of fighters flashing past the glider trains." This was his first operational trip in a glider, and earlier he had taken a couple of airsickness pills. His throat was dry and he had difficulty swallowing. He was conscious, too, that "Hancock, my batman, was watching me, a look of concern on his face. Like everyone else, he expected me to be airsick." Urquhart did not oblige. "We were in a huge stream of aircraft and I concentrated on impressions. We were committed. We had made a good plan. I still wished we

could have gotten closer to the bridge, but I did not brood on it."

In spite of the operational efficiency displayed in launching the giant armada, mishaps occurred almost immediately. Just before takeoff, the port wing of one glider was chewed off by the propeller of a Stirling bomber. No one was hurt. As the glider carrying Lieutenant Alan Harvey Cox of the Airlanding Brigade lumbered into the air, it ran into trouble. Low clouds obstructed the glider pilot's view and he was unable to line up with the tail of his tug. The glider went in one direction, the plane in another, the tow rope threatening to loop the glider's wing and overturn it. Unable to realign with his tug, the glider pilot grabbed for the red-topped release lever and cast off. Cox's glider landed without damage in a hay field at Sandford-on-Thames. A more bizarre incident occurred in a C-47 carrying the men of the 82nd Airborne, who sat facing each other on opposite sides of the plane. Five minutes after takeoff, Corporal Jack Bommer saw "the cargo hatch directly behind the men facing me spring open." The force of air almost sucked the men through the hatchway into space. As they desperately hung on, recalls Bommer, "the pilot did a beautiful tail flip and the hatch slammed shut."

Lance Corporal Sydney Nunn, who was so anxious to leave his base near Keevil and the activities of the mole in his mattress, now felt lucky to be alive. After more than an hour of uneventful flight, his glider ran into cloud. Emerging from the cloud bank, the glider pilot saw that the tow rope had twisted itself around the port wing. Over the intercom to his tug, Nunn heard the glider pilot say, "I'm in trouble! I'm in trouble!" The next instant, he cast off. "We seemed to come to a dead stop in the air," Nunn remembers. "Then the glider's nose dropped and we careened earthward with the tow rope streaming alongside like a broken kite string." Nunn sat "petrified," listening to the wind screaming along the fuselage, "hoping that the chains holding a jeep in the glider would take the strain." Then he heard the pilot warn them to "Brace up, blokes. Here we come." The glider hit the ground, bounced, hit once more, and came slowly to a stop. In the sudden silence, Nunn heard the pilot ask, "Are you blokes all right?" Everyone was, and the men were returned to Keevil to fly out in the second lift on September 18.

Others were not so fortunate. Tragedy struck one glider serial over Wiltshire. R.A.F. Sergeant Walter Simpson, sitting in the plexiglass turret of a Stirling bomber, was watching the Horsa glider trailing along behind. Suddenly, "The glider just seemed to part in the middle; it looked as if the back end just dropped off the front." Horrified, Simpson shouted to the captain, "My God, the glider's coming apart!" The tow rope broke and the front of the glider sank "like a rock falling to earth." The Stirling left formation, gradually lost height, and turned back to locate the wreckage. The front half was spotted in a field. The tail was nowhere to be seen. Marking the spot, the crew returned to Keevil and drove by jeep to the crash location. There, Simpson saw what appeared "like a match box that had been stepped on." The bodies of the men had remained inside. Simpson had no way of estimating how many dead there were—"it was just a mass of arms, legs and bodies."

By the time the last serials reached the English coast—the northern streams passing over the checkpoint at Aldeburgh, the southern columns flying over Bradwell Bay—thirty troop- and equipment-carrying gliders were down. Tug engine failure, broken tow ropes, and, in places, heavy clouds had caused the abortions. Although by military standards the operation had begun with eminent success—casualties were light, and many of the men and most of the downed cargo would be flown in on later lifts—the losses were sure to hurt. On this vital day when every man, vehicle and piece of equipment was important to General Urquhart, twenty-three of his glider loads were already lost. Not until the Arnhem force reached its drop and landing zones would commanders discover just how crucial these losses would be.

Now, as the long sky trains swarmed out over the English Channel and the land fell behind, a new kind of expectancy began to permeate the armada. The "Sunday outing" mood was fast disappearing. As American serials passed over the seaside resort of Margate, Private Melvin Isenekev of the 101st Airborne saw the white cliffs of Dover off to the right. From the distance, they looked like the wintry hillsides of the Adirondacks near his home in upper New York State. Corporal D. Thomas of the 1st British Airborne, staring out through an open plane door until his country's coastline disappeared, felt his eyes fill with tears.

From the marshaling points at March and Hatfield, the airborne columns had been aided by various navigational devices: radar beacons, special hooded lights and radio direction-finding signals. Now, beacons on ships in the North Sea began to guide the planes. Additionally, strings of launches—17 along the northern route; 10 below the southern flight path—stretched away across the water. To Flight Sergeant William Tompson, at the controls of a plane towing a four-ton Horsa glider, "there wasn't much navigating to do. The launches below us were set out like stepping stones across the Channel." But these fast naval vessels were much more than directional aids. They were part of a vast air-sea rescue operation, and they were already busy.

In the thirty-minute trip across the North Sea, men saw gliders bobbing on the gray waters as low-flying amphibious planes circled to mark their positions until rescue launches could reach the spot. Lieutenant Neville Hay, of the Phantom fact-gathering liaison unit, watched "with complete detachment two downed gliders and another ditching." He tapped his corporal on the shoulder. "Have a look down there, Hobkirk," Hay shouted. The corporal glanced down and, as Hay remembers, "I could almost see him turn green." Hay hurriedly reassured the man. "There's nothing to worry about. Look at the boats already picking them up."

Staff Sergeant Joseph Kitchener, piloting a glider, was equally impressed by the speed of the air-sea rescue launch that came alongside a floating glider he had spotted. "They picked up the men so fast I don't even think they got their feet wet," he recalls. Men in a glider piloted by Staff Sergeant Cyril Line were less fortunate—but lucky to be alive. In an aerial train of swaying black Horsas, Line observed one combination drop slowly out of position. Mesmerized, he watched the Horsa cut loose and descend almost leisurely toward the sea. A ring of white foam appeared as it hit the water. He wondered "who the poor devils were." At that moment, the starboard propellers on the Stirling pulling his glider slowed, and stopped. As the plane's speed was reduced Line found himself "in the embarrassing position of overtaking my own tug." He immediately released the tow line and his copilot called out, "Stand by for ditching!" From behind in the cabin, they could hear rifle butts crashing against the side of the glider's plywood fuselage as the frantic passengers tried to open up an escape route. Rapidly losing altitude, Line looked back and was horrified to see that the desperate troopers had "cut through the top of the glider and the sides were just beginning to go." Line screamed out, "Stop that! Strap yourselves in!" Then, with a heavy thud, the glider hit the water. When Line surfaced, he saw the wreckage floating some thirty feet away. There was no sign whatever of the cabin, but every one of his passengers was accounted for. Within minutes, all were picked up.

In all, eight gliders ditched safely during this first lift; once they were on the water, the air-sea rescue service, in a spectacular performance, saved nearly all crews and passengers. Once again, however, it was Urquhart's force that was whittled down. Of the eight gliders, five were Arnhem-bound.

Apart from some long-range inaccurate shelling of a downed glider, there was no serious enemy opposition during the Channel crossing. The 101st Airborne Division, following the southern route, which would bring it over Allied-held Belgium, was experiencing an almost perfect flight. But as the Dutch coastline appeared in the distance, the 82nd and the British troopers in the northern columns began to see the ominous telltale gray and black puffs of flak—German antiaircraft fire. As they flew on, at an altitude of only 1,500 feet, enemy guns firing from the outer Dutch isles of Walcheren, North Beveland and Schouwen were clearly visible. So were flak ships and barges around the mouth of the Schelde.

Escorting fighters began peeling out of formation, engaging the gun positions. In the planes men could hear spent shrapnel scraping against the metal sides of the C-47's. Veteran paratrooper Private Leo Hart of the 82nd heard a rookie aboard his plane ask, "Are these bucket seats bullet proof?" Hart just glowered at him; the light metal seats wouldn't have offered protection against a well-thrown stone. Private Harold Brockley, in another C-47, remembers one replacement wondering, "Hey, what are all those little black and gray puffs below?" Before anyone could answer, a piece of shrapnel came through the bottom of the ship and pinged harmlessly against a mess kit.

Veteran troopers hid their fears in different ways. When Staff Sergeant Paul Nunan saw the "familiar golf balls of red tracer bullets weaving up toward us" he pretended to doze off. Tracers barely missed Private Kenneth Truax's plane. "No one said anything," he recalls. "There was only a weak smile or two." Sergeant Bill Tucker, who had gone through antiaircraft fire in Normandy, was haunted by a "horrible fear of getting hit from underneath." He felt "less naked" sitting on three air-force flak jackets. And Private Rudolph Kos remembers that he felt "like sitting on my helmet, but I knew I would need it on my head."

One man was more concerned with the danger within than that without. Copilot Sergeant Bill Oakes, struggling to hold his Horsa glider steady in the air, looked back to see how his passengers were faring. To his horror, three troopers were "calmly sitting on the floor brewing up a mess tin of tea over a small cooker. Five others were standing around with their mugs, waiting to be served." Oakes was galvanized into action. He handed the controls over to the pilot and hurried aft, expecting the glider's plywood floor to catch fire at any minute. "Or, worse still, the mortar bombs in the trailer we were carrying could explode. The heat from that little field stove was terrific." He was livid with anger. "We're just having a little brew up," one of the troopers told him soothingly. Oakes hurried back to the cockpit and reported the matter to the pilot, Staff Sergeant Bert Watkins. The pilot smiled. "Tell 'em not to forget us when the tea's ready," he said. Oakes sank into his seat and buried his head in his hands.

Although the escort fighters silenced most of the coastal flak positions, some planes were damaged and one tug, its glider and a troop-carrier C-47 were shot down over Schouwen Island. The tug crash-landed, and its crew was killed. The glider, an 82nd Airborne Waco, broke up in mid-air and may have been seen by Major Dennis Munford, flying in a British column nearby. He watched, aghast, as the Waco disintegrated and "men and equipment spilt out of it like toys from a Christmas cracker." Others saw the troop-carrier go down. Equipment bundles attached beneath the C-47 were set on fire by tracer bullets. "Yellow and red streamers of flame appeared in the black smoke," recalls Captain Arthur Ferguson, who was flying in a nearby plane. Within minutes the C-47 was blazing. First Lieutenant Virgil Carmichael, standing in the door of his plane, watched as paratroopers jumped from the stricken aircraft. "As our men were using camouflaged chutes, I was able to count them as they left and saw that all had escaped safely."

The pilot, although the aircraft was engulfed in flames, somehow kept the plane steady until the paratroopers jumped. Then Carmichael saw one more figure leave. "The Air Corps used white parachutes, so I figured he had to be the crew chief." He was the last man out. Almost immediately the blazing plane nosedived and, at full throttle, plowed into a flooded area of Schouwen Island below. Carmichael remembers that, "on impact, a white chute billowed out in front of the plane, probably ejected by the force of the crash." To First Lieutenant James Megellas the sight of the downed C-47 had a "terrible effect." As jumpmaster in his plane, he had previously told his men that he would give the command "to stand up and hook up five minutes before reaching the drop zone." Now, he immediately gave the order. In many other planes, jumpmasters reacted as Megellas had and gave similar commands. To them, the battle was already joined—and, in fact, the drop and landing zones for the airborne men were now only thirty to forty minutes away.

☆ 2 ☆

INCREDIBLY, DESPITE THE NIGHT's widespread bombing, and now the aerial attacks against Arnhem, Nijmegen and Eindhoven, the Germans failed to realize what was happening. Throughout the chain of command, attention was focused on a single threat: the renewal of the British Second Army's offensive from its bridgehead over the Meuse-Escaut Canal.

"Commanders and troops, myself and my staff in particular, were so overtaxed and under such severe strain in the face of our difficulties that we thought only in terms of ground operations," recalls Colonel General Kurt Student. Germany's illustrious airborne expert was at his headquarters in a cottage near Vught, approximately twenty-one miles northwest of Eindhoven, working on "red tape—a mountain of papers that followed me even into the battlefield." Student walked out onto a balcony, watched the bombers for a few moments, then, unconcerned, returned to his paper work.

Lieutenant Colonel Walter Harzer, commanding officer of the 9th SS Panzer Division Hohenstaufen, had by now transferred as much equipment as he intended to his rival, General Heinz Harmel of the 10th SS Panzer Division Frundsberg. Harmel, on Bittrich's orders and without Model's knowledge, was by now in Berlin. The last flatcars containing Harzer's "disabled" armored personnel carriers were ready to leave on a 2 P.M. train for Germany. Having been bombed repeatedly from Normandy onward, Harzer "paid little attention to planes." He saw nothing unusual about the huge bomber formations over Holland. He and his veteran tankers knew "it was routine to see bombers traveling east to Germany and returning several times a day. My men and I were numb from constant shelling and bombing." With Major Egon Skalka, the 9th Panzer's chief medical officer, Harzer set out from his headquarters at Beekbergen for the Hoenderloo barracks, about eight miles north of Arnhem. In a ceremony before the 600-man reconnaissance battalion of the division, he would decorate its commander, Captain Paul Gräbner, with the Knight's Cross. Afterward there would be champagne and a special luncheon.

At II SS Panzer Corps headquarters at Doetinchem, Lieutenant General Wilhelm Bittrich was equally unconcerned about the air attacks. To him, "it was routine fare." Field Marshal Walter Model, in his headquarters at the Tafelberg Hotel in Oosterbeek, had been watching the bomber formations for some time. The view at headquarters was unanimous: the squadrons of Flying Fortresses were returning from their nightly bombing of Germany, and as usual, other streams of Fortresses in the neverending bombing of Germany were enroute east heading for other targets. As for the local bombing, it was not uncommon for bombers to jettison any unused bombs over the Ruhr and often, as a result, into Holland itself. Model and his chief of staff, Lieutenant General Hans Krebs, believed the bombardment and low-level strafing were "softening-up operations"—a prelude to the opening of the British ground offensive.

One officer was mildly concerned by the increased aerial activity over Holland. At the headquarters of OB West in Aremberg near Koblenz, approximately 120 miles away, Field Marshal Gerd von Rundstedt—although he still believed that airborne forces would be used only in an attack against the Ruhr—wanted more information. In Annex 2227 of the morning report for September 17, his operations chief recorded that Von Rundstedt had asked Model to investigate the possibility that a combined sea and airborne invasion was underway against northern Holland. The notation read, "The general situation and notable increase of enemy reconnaissance activities . . . has caused the Commander in Chief, West, to again examine the possibilities of ship assault and air landing operations. . . . Results of the survey are to be reported to OKW [Hitler]."

The message reached Model's headquarters at about the time the first planes of the armada crossed the coast.

Over Arnhem at 11:30 A.M. columns of black smoke rose in the sky as fires burned throughout the city in the aftermath of a three-hour near-saturation bombing. In Wolfheze, Oosterbeek, Nijmegen and Eindhoven, whole buildings were leveled, streets were cratered and littered with debris and glass, and casualties were mounting minute by minute. Even now, low-level fighters were strafing machine-gun and antiaircraft positions all over the area. The mood of the Dutch, huddling in churches, homes, cellars and shelters or, with foolhardy courage, cycling the streets or staring from rooftops, alternated between terror and exultation. No one knew what to believe or what would happen next. To the south, eighty-three miles from Nijmegen, Maastricht, the first Dutch city to be liberated, had been entered by the U.S. First Army on September 14. Many Dutch expected American infantry to arrive at any moment in their own towns and villages. Radio Orange, broadcasting from London, fed this impression in a flurry of bulletins: "The time is nearly here. What we have been waiting for is about to happen at last. . . . Owing to the rapid advance of the Allied armies . . . it is possible that the troops will not carry Dutch money yet. If our Allies offer French or Belgian notes . . . cooperate and accept this money in payment. . . . Farmers should finish off and deliver their harvest. . . ." Prince Bernhard, in a radio message, urged the Dutch "not to show joy by offering flowers or fruit when Allied troops liberate Netherlands territory . . . in the past the enemy has concealed explosives among offerings presented to the liberators." Uppermost in the minds of most Dutchmen was the certainty that these intensive bombings were the prelude to Allied invasion—the opening of the ground offensive. Like their German conquerors, the Dutch had no inkling of the impending airborne attack.

Jan and Bertha Voskuil, taking shelter in the home of Voskuil's father-in-law in Oosterbeek, thought the bombers in their area were aiming for Model's headquarters in the Tafelberg Hotel. The bright day, Voskuil remembers, "was perfect bombing weather." Yet he found it hard to "reconcile the war that was coming with the smell of ripe beetroots and sight of hundreds of sunflowers, their stems bent under the weight of their great heads. It did not seem possible that men were dying and buildings burning." Voskuil felt strangely calm. From his father-in-law's front veranda, he watched fighters flashing overhead and was sure they were strafing the hotel. Suddenly, a German soldier appeared in the garden without helmet or rifle and dressed only in a shirt and trousers. Politely he asked Voskuil, "May I take shelter here?" Voskuil stared at the man. "Why?" he asked. "You have your trenches." The German smiled. "I know," he answered, "but they are full." The soldier came up on the porch. "It is a very heavy bombing," he told Voskuil, "but I don't think Oosterbeek is the target. They seem to be concentrating more to the east and west of the village."

From inside the house, Voskuil heard voices. A friend of the family had just arrived from the Wolfheze area. It had been heavily hit, she told them, and many people were dead. "I am afraid," she said, tremblingly, "it is our Last Supper." Voskuil looked at the German. "Perhaps they're bombing the Tafelberg because of Model," he said mildly. The German's face was impassive. "No," he told Voskuil, "I don't think so. No bombs fell there." Later, after the soldier had gone, Voskuil went out to survey the damage. Rumors abounded. He heard that Arnhem had been heavily hit and that Wolfheze was almost leveled. Surely, he thought, the Allies were now under march and would arrive at any hour. He was both elated and saddened. Caen, in Normandy, he remembered, had been reduced to rubble during the invasion. He was convinced that Oosterbeek, where he and his family had found shelter, would become a ruined village.

Around Wolfheze, German ammunition caches in the woods were exploding, and the famed mental institute had received direct hits. Four pavilions surrounding the administration building were leveled, forty-five patients were dead (the toll would increase to over eighty), and countless more were wounded. Sixty terrified inmates, mostly women, were wandering about in the adjoining woods. The electricity had failed, and Dr. Marius van der Beek, the deputy medical superintendent, could not summon help. Impatiently he awaited the arrival of doctors from Oosterbeek and Arnhem, who, he knew, would surely hear the news and come. He needed to set up two operating theaters with surgical teams as quickly as possible.

One of the "inmates," Hendrik Wijburg, was in reality a member of the underground hiding out in the asylum. "The Germans," he recalls, "were not actually inside the institute at the moment, although they did have positions nearby and artillery and ammunition stored in the woods." During the bombings when the dump was hit, Wijburg, on the veranda of one building, was knocked to the floor. "There was a huge explosion," he remembers, "and shells from the dump began whizzing into the hospital, killing and injuring many." Wijburg hastily scrambled to his feet and helped nurses, at the height of the strafing attacks, to lay out white sheets forming a huge cross on the grass. The entire area had been so badly hit that it looked to him as if "the place would soon be filled to the rafters with the dead and dying."

In Arnhem, fire brigades fought desperately to bring the spreading flames under control. Dirk Hiddink, in charge of a fifteen-man outdated fire-fighting unit (his men pushed two carts—one loaded with coiled hoses, the other with ladders), was ordered to the German-occupied Willems Barracks, which had received direct hits from low-flying Mosquitoes. Although the barracks were blazing, Hiddink's instructions from the Arnhem Fire Brigade Headquarters were unusual: let them burn down, he was told, but protect the surrounding houses. When his unit arrived, Hiddink saw that it would have been impossible to save the barracks in any case. The fires were too far advanced.

From his father's apartment at Willemsplein 28, Gerhardus Gysbers saw everything around him engulfed in flames. Not only the barracks, but the nearby high school and the Royal Restaurant, opposite, were burning. The heat was so intense that Gysbers remembers "the glass in our windows suddenly became wavy and then melted completely." The family evacuated the building immediately, scrambling over bricks and lumber into the square. Gysbers saw Germans stumbling from the blasted rubble of the barracks with blood pouring from their noses and ears. Streetcar driver Hendrik Karel reached the Willemsplein unintentionally. With the electric power cut by the bombing, Karel's pale-yellow streetcar coasted down a slight incline to reach a stop at the square. There he found a jumble of other streetcars which, like his own, had coasted into the square and were unable to leave. Through the smoke, crowds and debris, Karel saw waiters from the Royal Restaurant make their escape from the burning building. Abandoning the few diners who were heading for the doors, the waiters jumped right through the windows.

At the Municipal Gas Works just southeast of the great Arnhem bridge, technician Nicolaas Unck admired the skill of the bombardiers. Looking across the Rhine, he saw that twelve anti-aircraft positions had been knocked out. Only one gun was left but its barrels were twisted and bent. Now that the city was without electricity, Unck was faced with his own problems. The technicians could no longer make gas. After the fuel remaining in the three huge gasometers was exhausted, there would be no more. Aside from coal and firewood, Arnhem was now without electricity, heating or cooking fuels.

Thousands of people remained cloistered in their churches. In the huge Dutch Reformed "Grote Kerk" Church alone, there were 1,200 people, Sexton Jan Mijnhart remembers. "Even though we had clearly heard the bombs exploding outside," he says, "the Reverend Johan Gerritsen had calmly continued his sermon. When the power was cut off, the organ stopped. Some one of the congregation came forward and began pumping the bellows manually." Then, against a background of sirens, explosions and thundering planes, the organ pealed out and the entire congregation stood up to sing the "Wilhelmus," the Dutch national anthem.

In the nearby Calvinist church, near the Arnhem railroad station, Gijsbert Numan of the resistance listened to a sermon delivered by Dominee Both. Numan felt that even the intense bombing would not deter the Germans from carrying out their threat to execute civilian hostages sometime during the day in reprisal for the resistance's attack on the viaduct. His conscience bothered him as he listened to Dominee Both's sermon on "the responsibility for your acts toward God and your fellow man," and he decided that once the service had ended, he would give himself up to the Germans. Leaving the church, Numan made his way through the littered streets to a telephone. There, he called Pieter Kruyff and told the regional commander his decision. Kruyff was blunt and to the point. "Rejected," he told Numan. "Carry on with your work." But Kruyff's was not to be the final decision. Market-Garden would save the hostages.

In Nijmegen, eleven miles to the south, bombers had hit German antiaircraft positions with such accuracy that only one was still firing. The great, towering PGEM power station, supplying electricity for the entire province of Gelderland, had received only superficial damage, but high-tension wires were severed, cutting off power throughout the area. A rayon factory near the PGEM station was badly damaged and ablaze. Houses in many parts of the city had received direct hits. Bombs had fallen on a girls' school and a large Catholic social center. Across the Waal in the village of Lent, a factory was destroyed and ammunition dumps exploded.

In the city's air-raid command post, the staff worked by candlelight. The air-raid workers were more and more puzzled by the stream of reports piling in. Working at his desk in semidarkness, Albertus Uijen registered the incoming reports and found himself growing more confused by the moment. The widespread bombings gave no clear picture of what was happening, except that all German positions on Nijmegen's perimeter had been attacked.

The principal approaches to the city—Waalbrug, St. Annastraat and Groesbeekseweg—were now blocked off. It almost seemed that an effort had been made to isolate the city.

As in Arnhem, most people in Nijmegen sought shelter from the fighters continually strafing the streets, but Elias Broekkamp, whose house was not far from the Waal bridge, had climbed to the roof for a better look. To Broekkamp's astonishment, so had the personnel of the German Town Major's office, five houses from Broekkamp's. The Germans, Broekkamp remembers, "looked very anxious. I looked, obviously, full of delight. I even remarked that the weather was lovely."

Nurse Johanna Breman watched Germans panic during the strafing. From a second-floor window of an apartment building south of the Waal bridge, Nurse Breman looked down at "wounded German soldiers helping each other along. Some were limping quite badly and I could see many with bandages. Their tunics were open and most had not even bothered to put their helmets on. On their heels came German infantrymen. As they headed toward the bridge, they fired into the windows whenever they saw Dutch peering out." When the Germans reached the bridge approaches, they began digging foxholes. "They dug everywhere," Miss Breman remembers, "next to the street leading up to the bridge, in grassy areas nearby and beneath trees. I was sure the invasion was coming and I remember thinking, 'What a beautiful view of the battle we shall have from here.' I had a feeling of expectancy." Nurse Breman's expectations did not include her marriage some months later to Master Sergeant Charles Mason of the 82nd, who would land in Glider 13 near the Groesbeek Heights, two miles southwest of her apartment.

Some towns and villages on the edges of the major Market-Garden objectives suffered damage as severe as the principal targets and had little, if any, rescue services. Close by the hamlet of Zeelst, approximately five miles west of Eindhoven, Gerardus de Wit had taken shelter in a beet field during the bombings. There had been no air raid alarm. He had seen planes high in the sky, and suddenly bombs rained down. De Wit, on a visit to his brother in the village of Veldhoven, four miles south, had turned around, pulled off the road and dived into a ditch adjoining the field. Now, he was frantic to get back to his wife and their eleven children.

Although planes were strafing, De Wit decided to risk the trip. Raising his head to look across the field, he saw that "even the leaves were scorched." Leaving his cycle behind, he climbed out of the ditch and ran across the open field. As he neared the village, he noted that bombs presumably intended for the Welschap airfield outside Eindhoven had fallen, instead, directly on little Zeelst. De Wit could see nothing but ruins. Several houses were burning, others had collapsed; and people stood about dazed and crying. One of De Wit's acquaintances, Mrs. Van Helmont, a widow, spotted him and begged him to come with her to cover a dead boy with a sheet. Tearfully, she explained that she could not do it herself. The child had been decapitated, but De Wit recognized the body as a neighbor's son. Quickly, he covered the corpse. "I didn't look at anything more," he remembers. "I just tried to get home as quickly as possible." As he neared his own house, a neighbor who lived opposite tried to detain him. "I'm bleeding to death," the man called out. "I've been hit by a bomb splinter."

At that moment, De Wit saw his wife, Adriana, standing in the street crying. She ran to him. "I thought you'd never get here," she told him. "Come quickly. Our Tiny has been hit." De Wit went past his injured neighbor. "I never thought of anything but my son. When I got to him I saw that the whole of his right side was open and his right leg was cut almost through. He was still fully conscious and asked for water. I saw that his right arm was missing. He asked me about his arm and, to comfort him, I said, 'You're lying on it.'" As De Wit knelt by the boy, a doctor arrived. "He told me not to hope anymore," De Wit remembers, "because our son was going to die." Cradling the boy, De Wit set out for the Duc George cigar factory, where a Red Cross post had been set up. Before he reached the factory, his fourteen-year-old son died in his arms.

In all the terror, confusion and hope, few of the Dutch saw the vanguard of the Allied Airborne Army. At approximately 12:40 P.M., twelve British Stirling bombers swept in over the Arnhem area. At 12:47, four U.S. C-47's appeared over the heaths north of Eindhoven, while two others flew across the open fields southwest of Nijmegen, close to the town of Overasselt. In the planes were British and American pathfinders.

Returning to his farm bordering Renkum heath, less than a mile from Wolfheze, Jan Pennings saw planes coming from the west, flying low. He thought they had returned to bomb the railway line. He watched them warily, ready to dive for cover if bombs dropped. As the planes came over Renkum heath, the astounded Pennings saw "bundles dropped, and then parachutists coming out. I knew that in Normandy the Allies had used parachutists and I was sure this was the beginning of *our* invasion."

Minutes later, cycling up to his farm, Jan shouted to his wife, "Come out! We're free!" Then, the first paratroopers he had ever seen walked into the farmyard. Dazed and awed, Pennings shook their hands. Within half an hour, they told him, "hundreds more of us will arrive."

Chauffeur Jan Peelen too saw the pathfinders land on Renkum heath. He recalls that "they came down almost silently. They were well-disciplined and immediately began to peg out the heath." Like other pathfinders north of the railway line, they were marking out the landing and dropping zones.

Fifteen miles south, near the town of Overasselt, nineteen-year-old Theodorus Roelofs, in hiding from the Germans, was suddenly liberated by 82nd Airborne pathfinders who landed in the vicinity of the family farm. The Americans, he remembers, were "scouts, and my big fear was that this small group of braves could easily be done away with." The pathfinders wasted little time. Discovering that the young Dutchman spoke English, they quickly enlisted Roelofs to help as guide and interpreter. Confirming positions on their maps and directing them to the designated landing sites, Roelofs watched with fascination as the troopers marked the area with "colored strips and smoke stoves." Within three minutes a yellow-paneled "O" and violet smoke clearly outlined the area.

The four C-47's carrying the 101st pathfinders to zones north of Eindhoven ran into heavy antiaircraft fire. One planeload was shot down in flames. There were only four survivors. The other three planes continued on, and the pathfinders dropped accurately on the 101st's two zones. By 12:54 P.M. dropping and landing zones throughout the entire Market-Garden area were located and marked. Incredibly, the Germans still had not raised an alarm.

At Hoenderloo barracks, Lieutenant Colonel Walter Harzer, commander of the Hohenstaufen Division, toasted newly decorated Captain Paul Gräbner. A few minutes before, Harzer had seen a few parachutes fall to the west of Arnhem. He was not surprised. He thought they were bailed-out bomber crews. In Oosterbeek, at the Tafelberg Hotel, Field Marshal Model was having a preluncheon aperitif—a glass of chilled Moselle—with his chief of staff, Lieutenant General Hans Krebs, the operations officer Colonel Hans von Tempelhof and the headquarters adjutant Colonel Leodegard Freyberg. As administrations officer Lieutenant Gustav Sedelhauser remembers, "Whenever he was at the headquarters, the Field Marshal was punctual to a fault. We always sat down to luncheon at precisely 1300 hours." That time was H Hour for the Market forces.

☆ 3 ☆

Now, IN TIGHT FORMATIONS, the great procession of C-47's carrying the 101st Airborne thundered across Allied-held Belgium. Some twenty-five miles beyond Brussels, the serials swung north heading for the Dutch border. Then, men in the planes looked down and, for the first time, saw their earthbound counterpart, the Garden forces whose ground attack was to be synchronized with the air assault. It was a spectacular, unforgettable sight. The vast panoply of General Horrocks' XXX Corps spread out over every field, trail and road. Massed columns of tanks, half-tracks, armored cars and personnel carriers and line after line of guns stood poised for the breakout. On tank antennas pennants fluttered in the wind, and thousands of Britishers standing on vehicles and crowding the fields waved up to the men of the airborne. Orange smoke billowing into the air marked the British front line. Beyond was the enemy.

Skimming the ground, fighter-bombers led the way to the drop zones, attempting to clear everything ahead of the formations. Even though the intense bombing that preceded the airborne assault had leveled many antiaircraft batteries, camouflaged nettings suddenly swung back to reveal hidden enemy positions. Some men remember seeing the tops of haystacks open to disclose nests of 88 and 20 mm. guns. Despite the thoroughness of the fighter-plane attacks, it was impossible to silence all enemy opposition. Just seven minutes away from their drop zones north of Eindhoven, the men of the 101st ran into intense flak.

Pfc. John Cipolla was dozing when he was suddenly awakto Nijmegen

AA R.

WILLEMS CANAL

**1ST BATTALION
501 REGT.**

Uden

MARSH

**501 REGT. LESS
1ST BATTALION**

Veghel

MARSH

Glider with Market-Garden plans
lands and is captured
near Student's Hq.

DOMMEL R.

WILLEMS CANAL

AA R.

St. Oedenrode

1ST BATTALION

502 REGT.

DIV. HQ., SIG. CO., MED. CO.,
RECON. PLAT. & TRANSP.
LANDED BY PARACHUTE & GLIDER

506 REGT.

CO. H

Best

FOREST

Son

WILHELMINA CANAL

BRIDGE BLOWN

N

ASSAULT AREA
U.S. 101st AIRBORNE DIV.

SEPT. 17, 1944

EINDHOVEN

palacios

DOMMEL R.

0   Miles   4

ened by "the sharp crack of antiaircraft guns, and shrapnel ripped through our plane." Like everyone else, Cipolla was so weighted down by equipment that he could hardly move. Besides his rifle, knapsack, raincoat and blanket, he had ammunition belts draping his shoulders, pockets full of hand grenades, rations and his main parachute plus reserve. In addition, in his plane, each man carried a land mine. As he recalls, " a C-47 on our left flank burst into flames, then another, and I thought 'My God, we are next! How will I ever get out of this plane!'"

His C-47 was shuddering and everyone seemed to be yelling at the same time, "Let's get out! We've been hit!" The jumpmaster gave the order to "Stand up and hook up." Then he calmly began an equipment check. Cipolla could hear the men as they called out, "One O.K. Two O.K. Three O.K." It seemed hours before Cipolla, the last man of the stick, was able to shout, "Twenty-one O.K." Then the green light went on and, in a rush, the men were out and falling, parachutes blossoming above them. Looking up to check his canopy, Cipolla saw that the C-47 he had just left was blazing. As he watched, the plane went down in flames.

Despite the bursting shells that engulfed the planes, the formations did not waver. The pilots of the IX Troop Carrier Command held to their courses without deviating. Second Lieutenant Robert O'Connell remembers that his formation flew so tight, "I thought our pilot was going to stick his wing into the ear of the pilot flying on our left." O'Connell's plane was on fire. The red prejump warning light was on, and "so much smoke was fogging the aisle that I could not see back to the end of my stick." Men were coughing and yelling to get out. O'Connell "braced himself against the door to keep them in." The pilots flew on steadily, without taking evasive action, and O'Connell saw that the formation was gradually losing altitude and slowing down, preparatory to the jump. O'Connell hoped that "if the pilot thought the ship was going down, he would give us the green in time for the troops to get out." Calmly, the pilot held his flaming plane on course until he was right over the drop zone. Then the green light went on and O'Connell and his men jumped safely. O'Connell learned later that the plane crash-landed but the crew survived.

In total disregard for their own safety, troop-carrier pilots brought their planes through the flak and over the drop zones. "Don't worry about me," Second Lieutenant Herbert E. Shulman, the pilot of one burning C-47, radioed his flight commander. "I'm going to drop these troops right on the DZ." He did. Paratroopers left the plane safely. Moments later, it crashed in flames. Staff Sergeant Charles A. Mitchell watched in horror as the plane to his left streamed flame from its port engine. As the pilot held it steady on course, Mitchell saw the entire stick of paratroopers jump right through the fire.

Tragedies did not end there. Pfc. Paul Johnson was forward next to the pilot's cabin when his plane was hit dead center and both fuel tanks caught fire. Of the sixteen paratroopers, pilot and copilot, only Johnson and two other troopers got out. They had to climb over the dead in the plane to make their jumps. Each survivor was badly burned and Johnson's hair was completely seared away. The three came down in a German tank-bivouac area. For half an hour they fought off the enemy from a ditch. Then, all three injured, they were overwhelmed and taken prisoner.

Just as the green light went on in another plane, the lead paratrooper, standing in the door, was killed. He fell back on Corporal John Altomare. His body was quickly moved aside and the rest of the group jumped. And, as another stick of troopers floated to the ground, a C-47 out of control hit two of them, its propellers chopping them to pieces.

Typically, the Americans found humor even in the terrifying approach to the drop zones. Just after Captain Cecil Lee stood to hook up, his plane was hit. Shrapnel ripped a hole through the seat he had just vacated. Nearby, a trooper shouted disgustedly, "*Now* they give us a latrine!" In another plane, Second Lieutenant Anthony Borrelli was sure he was paralyzed. The red light went on and everyone hooked up—except Borrelli, who couldn't move. An officer for only two weeks and on his first combat mission, Borrelli, who was Number 1 in the stick, was conscious of all eyes on him. To his embarrassment, he discovered he had hooked his belt to the seat. Private Robert Boyce made the trip despite the good intentions of the division dentist, who had marked him "L.O.B." (Left Out of Battle) because of his dental problems. With the intervention of his company commander, Boyce, a Normandy veteran, was permitted to go. Besides a bad tooth, he had other worries. Several new paratroop innovations—leg packs for machine guns, quick-release harness on some chutes and combat instead of jump boots—made him and many other men nervous. In particular, the troopers were concerned that their shroud lines might catch on the buckles of their new combat boots. As his plane flew low in its approach, Boyce saw Dutch civilians below holding up two fingers in the V-for-victory salute. That was all Boyce needed. "Hey, look," he called to the others, "they're giving us two to one we don't make it."

The odds against their ever reaching their drop zones seemed at least that high to many. Colonel Robert F. Sink, commander of the 506th Regiment, saw "a tremendous volume of flak coming up to greet us." As he was looking out the door, the plane shuddered violently and Sink saw a part of the wing tear and dangle. He turned to the men in his stick and said, "Well, there goes the wing." To Sink's relief, "nobody seemed to think much about it. They figured by this time we were practically in."

In plane Number 2, Sink's executive officer, Lieutenant Colonel Charles Chase, saw that their left wing was afire. Captain Thomas Mulvey remembers that Chase stared at it for a minute and then remarked mildly, "I guess they're catching up on us. We'd better go." As the green light went on in both planes, the men jumped safely. The plane in which Chase was traveling burned on the ground. Sink's plane, with its damaged wing, is thought to have made the journey back to England safely.

Similar intense flak engulfed the serials of the 502nd Regiment, and planes of two groups almost collided. One serial, slightly off course, strayed into the path of a second group, causing the latter to climb for altitude and its troopers to make a higher jump than had been planned. In the lead plane of one of the serials was the division commander, General Maxwell D. Taylor, and the 502nd's 1st Battalion commander, Lieutenant Colonel Patrick Cassidy. Standing in the doorway, Cassidy saw one of the planes in the group burst into flames. He counted only seven parachutes. Then fire broke out in another C-47 just off to the left. All the paratroopers jumped from it. Mesmerized by the blazing plane, Cassidy failed to notice that the green light was on. General Taylor, standing behind him, said quietly, "Cassidy, the light's on." Automatically Cassidy answered, "Yes, sir. I know it," and jumped. Taylor was right behind him.

To General Taylor, the 101st jump was "unusually successful; almost like an exercise." In the initial planning, Taylor's staff had anticipated casualties as high as 30 percent. Of the 6,695 paratroopers who enplaned in England, 6,669 actually jumped. Despite the intense flak, the bravery of the C-47 and fighter pilots gave the 101st an almost perfect jump. Although some units were dropped from one to three miles north of the drop zones, they landed so close together that assembly was quick. Only two planes failed to reach the drop zone, and the IX Troop Carrier Command took the brunt of all casualties by their heroic determination to get the troopers to their targets. Of the 424 C-47's carrying the 101st, every fourth plane was damaged, and sixteen went down, killing their crews.

Glider losses were heavy, too. Later, as these serials began to come in, only 53 of the original 70 would arrive without mishap on the landing zone near Son. Still, despite abortions, enemy flak and crash-landings, the gliders would eventually deliver nearly 80 percent of the men and 75 percent of the jeeps and trailers they carried.* Now, Taylor's Screaming Eagles began to move on their

---

* Because Market-Garden was considered an all-British operation, few American correspondents were accredited to cover the attack. None was at Arnhem. One of the Americans attached to the 101st was a United Press reporter named Walter Cronkite, who landed by glider. Cronkite recalls that "I thought the wheels of the glider were for landing. Imagine my surprise when we skidded along the ground and the wheels came up through the floor. I got another shock. Our helmets, which we all swore were hooked, came flying off on impact and seemed more dangerous than the incoming shells. After landing I grabbed the first helmet I saw, my trusty musette bag with the Olivetti typewriter inside and began crawling toward the canal which was the rendezvous point. When I looked back, I found a half dozen

objectives—the bridges and crossings over the vital fifteen-mile stretch of corridor ahead of the British ground forces.

<h1 style="text-align:center">✣ 4 ✣</h1>

COLONEL GENERAL KURT STUDENT and his chief of staff, Colonel Reinhard, stood on the balcony of the General's cottage near Vught and "simply stared, stunned, like fools." Student remembers clearly that "everywhere we looked, we saw chains of planes—fighters, troop carriers and cargo planes—flying over us. We climbed onto the roof of the house to get a better idea of just where these units were going." Streams of planes seemed to be heading in the direction of Grave and Nijmegen and, only a few miles to the south near Eindhoven and Son, he could clearly see troop carriers—one after the other—coming in and dropping paratroopers and equipment. Some aircraft flew so low that Student and Reinhard instinctively ducked. "On the grounds of the headquarters, our clerks, quartermasters, drivers and signalmen were out in the open, firing with all sorts of weapons. As usual, there was no sign of our own fighter planes." Student was completely baffled. "I could not tell what was happening or where these airborne units were going. In these moments, I never once thought of the danger of our own position." But Student, the paratroop expert, was filled with admiration and envy. "This mighty spectacle deeply impressed me. I thought with reflection and longing of our own airborne operations and I said to Reinhard, 'Oh, if ever I'd had such means at my disposal. Just once, to have this many planes!'" Rein-

---

guys crawling after me. It seems that I had grabbed the wrong helmet. The one I wore had two neat stripes down the back indicating that I was a lieutenant."

217

hard's feelings were very much in the present. "Herr General," he told Student, "we've got to *do* something!" They left the roof and went back to Student's office.

Only the previous evening, Student, in his daily report, had warned, "Heavy columns of traffic south of the Maas-Schelde Canal indicate an impending attack." The problem was: had it already begun? If so, then these airborne units were after the bridges around Eindhoven, Grave and Nijmegen. All the spans were prepared for demolition and protected by special engineer parties and security detachments. A bridge commander had been assigned to each crossing with strict orders to destroy the bridge in case of attack. "The obvious move for the Allies," it occurred to Student, "was to use airborne troops in this situation to seize the bridges before we could destroy them." At this time, Student did not even think of the importance of the Lower Rhine bridge at Arnhem. "Get me Model," he told Reinhard.

Reinhard picked up the phone to discover that the telephone lines were out. The headquarters was already cut off.

In Oosterbeek, some thirty-seven miles away, at the Tafelberg Hotel, Lieutenant Gustav Sedelhauser, Model's administration officer, was angry. "Are you hung over from last night?" he shouted into a field phone. Unteroffizier Youppinger, one of the 250-man company which, under Sedelhauser, was assigned to protect Model, repeated what he had said. At Wolfheze, "gliders are landing in our laps," he insisted. Sedelhauser slammed down the phone and rushed into the operations office, where he reported the message to a startled lieutenant colonel. Together, they hurried to the dining room, where Model and his chief of staff General Krebs were at lunch. "I've just had news that gliders are landing at Wolfheze," the colonel said. The operations officer, Colonel Tempelhof, stared; the monocle fell out of Krebs's eye. "Well, now we're for it," Tempelhof said.

Model jumped to his feet and issued a flurry of orders to evacuate the headquarters. As he headed out of the dining room to collect his own belongings, he shouted back over his shoulder, "They're after me and this headquarters!" Moments later, carrying only a small case, Model rushed through the Tafelberg's entrance. On the sidewalk he dropped the case, which flew open, spilling his linens and toilet articles.

Krebs followed Model outside in such haste that, Sedelhauser saw, "he had even forgotten his cap, pistol and belt." Tempelhof had not even had time to remove the war maps in the operations office. Colonel Freyberg, the headquarters adjutant, was equally rushed. As he passed Sedelhauser, he shouted, "Don't forget my cigars." At his car, Model told his driver, Frombeck, "Quick! Doetinchem! Bittrich's headquarters!"

Sedelhauser waited until the car drove off and then returned to the hotel. In the operations office, he saw the war maps—showing positions all the way from Holland to Switzerland—still on a table. He rolled them up and took them with him. Then he ordered the Hartenstein Hotel and the Tafelberg immediately evacuated; all transport, he said, "every car, truck and motorbike, is to leave here immediately." The last report he received before leaving for Doetinchem was that the British were less than two miles away. In all the confusion he completely forgot Freyberg's cigars.

�֏ 5 ֏

SURROUNDED BY GROUND HAZE and the smoke and fire of burning buildings, the mighty British glider fleet was landing. Already the areas marked by orange and crimson nylon strips were beginning

4TH PARACHUTE
BRIGADE
(HACKETT)
SEPT. 18

EDE-ARNHEM HIGHWAY

1ST
PARACHUTE
BRIGADE
(LATHBURY)
SEPT. 17

DOBIE'S 1ST BATTALION (LEOPARD)

URQUHART
1ST BRITISH
AIRBORNE DIV.
1ST AIR LANDING BRIGADE
(HICKS)
1ST PARACHUTE BRIGADE
(LATHBURY)
4TH PARACHUTE BRIGADE
(HACKETT)
1ST POLISH BRIGADE
(SOSABOWSKI)

SUPPLIES
DROP ZONE

WOLFHEZE

KRAFFT'S SS BATTALION

1ST. AIR LANDING
BRIGADE (HICKS)
"   "
1ST PARACHUTE
BRIGADE (LATHBURY)
SEPT. 17

FITCH'S 3RD BATTALION (TIGER)

HARTEN
HOTE

FROST'S 2ND BATTALION (LION)

RENKUM

HEELSUM

SECONDARY ROAD

FERRY

LOWER RHINE

DRIEL

palacios

ARNHEM
THE ATTACK
D DAY SEPT. 17, 1944

0   Miles   1

N

BITTRICH
II SS PANZER CORPS

SUPPLIES
DROP ZONE

9TH SS PANZER
"HOHENSTAUFEN" DIV.

HARZER

UTRECHT-ARNHEM
HIGHWAY

10 TH SS PANZER "FRUNDSBERG" DIV.

HARMEL

OSTERBEEK

PONTOON
BRIDGE

ARNHEM

4
SS PANZER
GRENADIERS

ARNHEM
BRIDGE

RAILWAY
BRIDGE

ELDEN

GRÄBNER'S
RECONNAISSANCE
UNIT

to Nijmegen

POLISH 1ST BRIGADE
(SOSABOWSKI)

to look like vast aircraft parking lots. Blue smoke eddied up from the two landing zones—"Reyers Camp Farm" to the north and "Renkum Heath" to the southwest—near Wolfheze. From these zones, in chain after chain, tugs and gliders stretched back almost twenty miles to their approach point near the town of s'Hertogenbosch, southwest of Nijmegen. Swarms of fighters protected these ponderous columns. Traffic was so dense that pilots were reminded of the rush-hour congestion around London's busy Piccadilly Circus.

The serials—each group separated from the next by a four-minute interval—flew slowly over the flat, water-veined Dutch countryside. The landmarks pilots had been briefed to recognize now began to pass beneath them: the great wide rivers Maas and Waal and up ahead, the Lower Rhine. Then, as each formation began its descent, men saw Arnhem off to the right and their vital objectives: the rail and highway bridges. Incredibly, despite the R.A.F. prediction of intense antiaircraft fire, the immense glider cavalcade encountered virtually no resistance. The preassault bombings had been far more effective around Arnhem than in the Eindhoven area. Not a single tug or glider was shot down in making the approach.

With clocklike precision, the skilled pilots of the R.A.F. and the Glider Pilot Regiment came over the zones. As gliders cast off, their tugs made climbing turns to free air space for the combinations coming up behind. These intricate maneuvers and the heavy traffic were causing problems of their own. Sergeant Pilot Bryan Tomblin remembers chaotic congestion over the landing zones. "There were gliders, tugs, ropes and all sorts of things in the sky," he recalls. "You had to be on the lookout all the time."

Staff Sergeant Victor Miller, piloting a Horsa, recalls coming in over the Lower Rhine and finding it "unbelievably calm." Beyond, he suddenly spotted his landing zone, with its "triangular-shaped woods and little farm nestling in the far corner." Seconds later, Miller heard the voice of his Stirling tug's navigator. "O.K. Number 2. When you're ready." Miller acknowledged. "Good luck, Number 2," the navigator told him. Miller immediately cast off. His tug disappeared, the tow rope flapping in its wake. It would be dropped, Miller knew, "on the enemy as a parting gift before the Stirling turned onto its homeward course."

The glider's air speed fell off and the field loomed nearer. Miller called for half-flaps and his copilot, Sergeant Tom Hollingsworth, instantly pushed a lever. For a moment the glider bucked, "as the great flaps descending from underneath each wing braked against our speed." The landing zone, Miller estimated, was now less than a mile away. "I reminded Tom to look out for gliders on his side. One slid across and above us less than fifty yards away," and, to Miller's amazement, "swung in on the same course. Another glider seemed to be drifting into us from starboard. I don't think the pilot even saw us, he was so intent on getting down in the field." To avoid collision, Miller deliberately dived under the incoming glider. "A great black shape flashed over our cockpit, too close for my liking. I was concentrating so hard to set down in one piece that I never wondered if the enemy was firing at us—not that we could have done much about it."

Miller continued his descent with "tree tops leaping toward our floor boards and past the wings. As the ground rushed up, another glider came alongside. I pulled back on the wheel, leveled, we hit once, bounced about three feet, and came down to stay. Tom had slammed on the brakes and we careened across the plowed field. Then the wheels sank into soft soil and we ground to a halt fifty yards short of a heavy-looking line of trees." In the silence, after the continuous deafening roar of the slip stream, Miller heard the distant crackle of small-arms fire, "but my one thought was to get out of the glider before another crashed or landed on us. I was the last man out. I didn't even pause, but jumped straight through the ramp door and hit the ground of Holland, four feet below, rather hard."

The glider in which Signalman Graham Marples was riding circled and came back over its landing zone because of the congestion. "But, by then, we had run out of wind," Marples remembers. "I saw trees coming through the glider floor. They just ripped the floor to pieces, and the next thing I knew, we nosed over and came down. I could hear everything breaking, like dry twigs snapping. We landed squarely on our nose but no one was hurt except for a few scratches and bruises." Later, the pilot told Marples he had pulled up to avoid collision with another glider.

Many gliders, having surmounted all the problems of the long trip, touched down to disaster. Staff Sergeant George Davis stood near his empty Horsa and watched other gliders come in. One of the first to land, Davis had brought in thirty-two men of the 1st Airlanding Brigade. He saw two gliders "almost side by side bump across the landing zone and into the trees. The wings of both were sheared off." Seconds later, another Horsa rumbled in. Its speed was such that Davis knew it would never be able to stop in time. The glider plowed into the trees. No one got out. With his copilot, Staff Sergeant Williams, Davis ran to the glider and looked into the plexiglass-covered cockpit. Everyone inside was dead. A 75 mm. howitzer had broken from its chain mooring, crushing the gun crew and decapitating the pilot and copilot.

Lieutenant Michael Dauncey had just landed his glider—carrying a jeep, trailer and six gunners from an artillery battery—when he saw a huge eight-ton Hamilcar touch down. "The field was soft," he recalls, "and I saw the nose of the Hamilcar digging up earth in front of it." Weight and ground speed drove it deeper until the huge tail rose up in the air and the Hamilcar flipped over on its back. Dauncey knew "it was useless to try to dig them out. A Horsa's flat on top but a Hamilcar's got a hump where the pilots sit, and we knew the pilots were finished."

Making his approach in another Hamilcar, Staff Sergeant Gordon Jenks saw the same crash and immediately deduced that the ground ahead was too soft. Instantly, he decided against landing in the field. "I reckoned if we went into a dive right then," he remembers, "we would have enough speed for me to hold her off the deck until we had cleared the fence and got safely into the next field." Jenks pushed the control column forward, dived, then leveled out a few feet above the ground. Easing the huge aircraft gently over the fence, Jenks "put her down in the far field as lightly as a feather."

All over the landing zones now the tails of gliders were being unbolted and swung back, and artillery pieces, equipment, stores, jeeps and trailers were being unloaded. The men in Lance Corporal Henry Brook's glider, like many others, found that the unloading maneuver was fine in theory but more difficult in practice. "There were eight pins with a protective wire holding the glider tail on," Brook explained. "Back in England in practice exercises, you could always get the tail off and jeep and trailer out in two minutes flat. In action, it was different. We cut the wire and got the pins out but the tail wouldn't budge." Brook and the other troopers finally chopped it off. Lance Bombardier J. W. Crook was similarly frustrated, but a nearby jeep came to the aid of his men and, with its hawser, yanked off the tail.

All over the two zones men were beginning to salvage cargo from wrecked gliders. The crash of two giant Hamilcars was a serious loss. They contained a pair of 17-pound artillery pieces plus three-ton trucks and ammunition trailers. But all of the fifteen 75 mm. pack howitzers of the 1st Airlanding Light Regiment artillery arrived safely.

Most men who came in by glider recall a strange, almost eerie silence immediately after landing. Then, from the assembly point, men heard the skirl of bagpipes playing "Blue Bonnets." At about the same time, soldiers on the edge of Renkum Heath saw Dutch civilians wandering aimlessly through the woods or hiding in fright. Lieutenant Neville Hay of the Phantom unit remembers that "it was a sobering sight. Some were in white hospital gowns and seemed to be herded along by attendants. Men and women capered about, waving, laughing and jabbering. They were obviously quite mad." Glider Pilot Victor Miller was startled by voices in the woods. Then, "groups of weird white-clothed men and women filed past." It was only later that the troopers learned the strangely behaved civilians were inmates from the bombed Wolfheze Psychiatric Institute.

General Urquhart had landed at Renkum Heath. He too was struck by the stillness. "It was," he recalls, "incredibly quiet. Unreal." While his chief of staff, Colonel Charles Mackenzie, set up the division's tactical headquarters at the edge of the woods, Urquhart headed for the parachute dropping zones, four hundred yards away. It was nearly time for Brigadier Lathbury's 1st Parachute Brigade to arrive. From the distance came the drone of approaching aircraft. The bustle and activity all over the glider zones paused as men looked up to see the long lines of C-47's. Small-arms and antiaircraft fire during the paratroop drop was as limited and spasmodic as during the glider landings. At exactly 1:53 P.M., and for the next fifteen minutes, the sky was filled with brilliant-colored parachutes as the 1st Brigade began jumping. Some 650 parapacks with bright-yellow, red and brown chutes—carrying guns, ammunition and equipment—fell rapidly through the streams of troopers. Other supply chutes, pushed out of the planes before the men jumped, floated down with a variety of cargo, including miniature foldable motorcycles. Many already overburdened paratroopers also jumped with large kitbags. In theory, these were to be lowered by a cord just before the men touched ground. Scores of the packs broke away from troopers and smashed on the zones. Several contained precious radio sets.

British Private Harry Wright jumped from an American C-47. As he fell through the air, he lost both his helmet and kitbag. He hit the ground very hard. Regimental Quartermaster Sergeant Robertson came running up. Wright's forehead was streaming blood. "Were you hit by flak?" Robertson asked. Wright slowly shook his head. "No, sarge," he said. "It was that bloody Yank. We were going too fast when we jumped." Robertson applied a dressing and then, to Wright's surprise, offered the injured man a pork pie from his haversack. "I nearly died right then of the shock," Wright recalls. "First, Robertson was a Scot, and then, as a quartermaster, he never offered anyone anything."

Odd things seemed to be happening all over the drop zones. The first person Sergeant Norman Swift saw when he landed was Sergeant Major Les Ellis, who was passing by holding a dead partridge. The amazed Swift asked where the bird had come from. "I landed on it," Ellis explained. "Who knows? It'll be a bit of all right later on, in case we're hungry."

Sapper Ronald Emery had just slipped out of his chute when an elderly Dutch lady scuttled across the field, grabbed it up and raced away, leaving the startled Emery staring after her. In another part of the field, Corporal Geoffrey Stanners, loaded down with equipment, landed on the top of a glider wing. Like a trampoline, the wing sprang up, flipping Stanners back into the air. He landed with both feet on the ground.

Dazed after a hard fall, Lieutenant Robin Vlasto lay still for a few moments, trying to orient himself. He was conscious of "an incredible number of bodies and containers coming down all around me and planes continued to pour out paratroopers." Vlasto decided to get off the drop zone quickly. As he struggled to get out of his harness, he heard a weird sound. Looking around, he saw Lieutenant Colonel John Frost, the 2nd Battalion's commander, walking past, blowing his copper hunting horn.

Frost was also observed by Private James W. Sims. Sims had already gone through quite a day even before he landed. Having always flown with the R.A.F.—whose attitude, Sims recalls, was: "Don't worry, lads, whatever it's like, we'll get you through"— Sims received quite a shock on seeing his American pilot. "He was a lieutenant colonel with one of those soft hats. His flying jacket was hanging open and he was smoking a big cigar. Our lieutenant saluted him quite smartly and asked if the men should move up to the front of the plane on takeoff." The American grinned. "Why, hell, no, lieutenant," Sims remembers him saying. "I'll get this goddam crate off the ground if I have to drag its ass halfway down the runway." Sims's officer was too startled to speak. Now, although he was fond of his colonel, Sims, watching Frost go by, had reached the limit of his patience. Surrounded by his equipment, he sat on the ground and muttered, "There goes old Johnny Frost, a .45 in one hand and that bloody horn in the other."

All over the drop and landing zones, where 5,191 men of the division had arrived safely, units were assembling, forming up and moving out. General Urquhart "couldn't have been more pleased. Everything appeared to be going splendidly." The same thought occurred to Sergeant Major John C. Lord. The veteran paratrooper recalls that "this was one of the best exercises I'd ever been on. Everyone was calm and businesslike." But the reservations he'd had before takeoff still bothered Lord. As he looked about, seeing the men assembling rapidly, with no enemy to contend with, he remembers thinking, "It's all too good to be true." Others had the same thought. As one group prepared to move off, Lieutenant Peter Stainforth heard Lieutenant Dennis Simpson say quietly, "Everything is going too well for my liking."

The man with the most urgent task on landing was forty-three-year-old Major Freddie Gough of the 1st Airborne Division reconnaissance unit. Leading a four-troop squadron in heavily armed jeeps, Gough was to make a dash for the bridge before Colonel John Frost's marching battalion reached it. Gough and his men parachuted in, and then sought their ground transport, which was being flown in by glider. Quickly Gough located his second in command, Captain David Allsop, on the landing zone and received some bad news. The entire transport for one of the four units—approximately twenty-two vehicles—had failed to arrive, Allsop reported. Thirty-six of the 320 gliders scheduled for Arnhem had been lost, and with them were lost the jeeps of Gough's A troop. Nevertheless, both Gough and Allsop believed that there were enough vehicles to race for the Arnhem bridge. Gough gave the order to move out. With his force whittled down, everything now depended on the reaction of the Germans.

☼6☼

I<small>N ALL THE PANIC</small> and confusion, the first German senior officer to raise the alert was General Wilhelm Bittrich, commander of the II SS Panzer Corps. At 1:30 P.M., Bittrich received his first report from the Luftwaffe communications net that airborne troops were landing in the Arnhem vicinity. A second report, arriving minutes later, gave the assault area as Arnhem and Nijmegen. Bittrich could not raise anybody at Field Marshal Model's headquarters at the Tafelberg in Oosterbeek. Nor was he able to contact either the town commander of Arnhem or General Student at his headquarters in Vught. Although the situation was obscure, Bittrich immediately thought of General Von Zangen's Fifteenth Army, most of which had escaped across the mouth of the Schelde and into Holland. "My first thought was that this airborne attack was designed to contain Von Zangen's army and prevent it from joining with the remainder of our forces. Then, probably, the objective would be a drive by the British Army across the Rhine and into Germany." If his reasoning was correct, Bittrich believed that the key to such an operation would be the Arnhem-Nijmegen bridges. Immediately he alerted the 9th Hohenstaufen and the 10th Frundsberg SS Panzer divisions.

Lieutenant Colonel Walter Harzer, commander of the Hohenstaufen, attending the luncheon following the decoration of Captain Paul Gräbner, was "in the middle of my soup" when Bittrich's call reached him. Tersely, Bittrich explained the situation and ordered Harzer to "reconnoiter in the direction of Arnhem and Nijmegen." The Hohenstaufen was to move out immediately, hold the Arnhem area and destroy airborne troops west of Arnhem near Oosterbeek. Bittrich warned Harzer that "quick action is imperative. The taking and securing of the Arnhem bridge is of decisive importance." At the same time, Bittrich ordered the Frundsberg Division—whose commander, General Harmel, was in Berlin—to move toward Nijmegen, "to take, hold and defend the city's bridges."

Harzer was now faced with the problem of unloading the last Hohenstaufen units, due to leave by train for Germany in less than an hour—including the "disabled" tanks, half-tracks and armored personnel carriers he had been determined to keep from Harmel. Harzer looked at Gräbner. "Now what are we going to do?" he asked. "The vehicles are dismantled and on the train." Of these, forty vehicles belonged to Gräbner's reconnaissance battalion. "How soon can you have the tracks and guns put back?" Harzer demanded. Gräbner immediately called his engineers. "We'll be ready to move within three to five hours," he told Harzer. "Get it done in three," Harzer snapped as he headed for his headquarters.

Although he had guessed right for the wrong reasons, General Bittrich had set in motion the panzer divisions that Montgomery's intelligence officers had totally dismissed.

The officer who had been ordered out of Oosterbeek to make way for Field Marshal Model's headquarters found himself and his men based almost on the British landing zones. SS Major Sepp Krafft, commander of the Panzer Grenadier Training and Reserve Battalion, was "sick to my stomach" with fright. His latest headquarters, in the Wolfheze Hotel, was less than one mile from Renkum Heath. Bivouacked nearby were two of his companies; a third was in reserve in Arnhem. From the hotel, Krafft could see the heath "jammed with gliders and troops, some only a few hundred yards away." He had always believed that it took hours for airborne troops to organize, but as he watched "the English were assembling everywhere and moving off ready to fight." He could not understand why such a force would land in this area. "The only military objective I could think of with any importance was the Arnhem bridge."

The terrified commander knew of no German infantry close by, other than his own understrength battalion. Until help could arrive, Krafft decided that "it was up to me to stop them from getting to the bridge—if that's where they were going." His companies were positioned in a rough triangle, its base—the Wolfheze road—almost bordering Renkum Heath. North of Krafft's headquarters was the main Ede–Arnhem road and the Amsterdam–Utrecht–Arnhem railway line; to the south, the Utrecht road ran via Renkum and Oosterbeek into Arnhem. Because he lacked the strength to maintain a line from one road to the other, Krafft decided to hold positions roughly from the railroad on the north to the Utrecht–Arnhem road to the south. Hurriedly, he ordered his reserve company out of Arnhem to join the rest of the battalion at Wolfheze. Machine-gun platoons were dispatched to hold each end of his line while the remainder of his troops fanned out in the woods.

Although lacking men, Krafft had a new experimental weapon at his disposal: a multibarreled, rocket-propelled launcher capable of throwing oversized mortar shells.° Several of these units had been left with him for training purposes. Now he planned to use them to confuse the British and give an impression of greater strength; at the same time, he ordered twenty-five-man attack groups to make sharp forays which might throw the paratroops off balance.

As Krafft was issuing his directions, a staff car roared up to his headquarters and Major General Kussin, Arnhem's town commander, hurried inside. Kussin had driven out of Arnhem at

° This weapon should not be confused with the smaller German mortar thrower, *Nebelwerfer*. Krafft maintains that there were only four of these experimental launchers in existence. I have not been able to check this fact, but I can find no record of a similar weapon on the western front. There is no doubt that it was used with devastating effect against the British. Countless witnesses describe the scream and impact of the oversized mortars, but, inexplicably, there is no discussion of the weapon in any of the British after-action reports.

breakneck speed to see at first-hand what was happening. On the way he had met Field Marshal Model heading east toward Doetinchem. Stopping briefly on the road, Model had instructed Kussin to raise the alert and to inform Berlin of the developments. Now, looking across the heath, Kussin was flabbergasted at the sight of the vast British drop. Almost desperately he told Krafft that somehow he would get reinforcements to the area by 6 P.M. As Kussin started out to make the drive back to Arnhem, Krafft warned him not to take the Utrecht–Arnhem road. Already he had received a report that British troopers were moving along it. "Take the side roads," Krafft told Kussin. "The main road may already be blocked." Kussin was grim-faced. "I'll get through all right," he answered. Krafft watched as the staff car raced off toward the highway.

He was convinced that Kussin's replacements would never reach him, and that it was only a matter of time before his small force would be overpowered. Even as he positioned his troops along the Wolfheze road, Krafft sent his driver, Private Wilhelm Rauh, to collect his personal possessions. "Pack them in the car and head for Germany," Krafft told Rauh. "I don't expect to get out of this alive."

At Bad Saarnow near Berlin, the commander of the 10th Frundsberg Division, General Heinz Harmel, conferred with the chief of Waffen SS Operations, Major General Hans Juttner, and outlined the plight of Bittrich's understrength II Panzer Corps. If the corps was to continue as an effective combat unit, Harmel insisted, "Bittrich's urgent request for men, armor, vehicles and guns must be honored." Juttner promised to do what he could, but he warned that "at this moment the strength of every combat unit is depleted." Everyone wanted priorities, and Juttner could not promise any immediate help. As the two men talked, Juttner's aide entered the office with a radio message. Juttner read it and wordlessly passed it to Harmel. The message read: "Airborne attack Arnhem. Return immediately. Bittrich." Harmel rushed out of the office and got into his car. Arnhem was an eleven-and-a-half-hour drive from Bad Saarnow. To his driver, Corporal Sepp Hinterholzer, Harmel said: "Back to Arnhem—and drive like the devil!"

❊ 7 ❊

MAJOR ANTHONY DEANE-DRUMMOND, second in command of the British 1st Airborne Division Signals, could not understand what was wrong. At one moment his radio sets were getting perfect reception from Brigadier Lathbury's brigade as it headed for its objectives, including the Arnhem bridge. But now, as Lathbury's battalions moved closer to Arnhem, radio signals were fading by the minute. From Deane-Drummond's signalmen came a constant stream of reports that disturbed and puzzled him. They were unable to contact some jeep-borne sets at all, and the signals they received from others were so weak as to be barely audible. Yet the various battalions of Lathbury's brigade and Major Freddie Gough's reconnaissance units could scarcely be more than two to three miles away.

Of particular concern to Deane-Drummond was Lathbury's messages. They were vital to General Urquhart in his direction of the battle. Deane-Drummond decided to send out a jeep with a radio and operator to pick up Lathbury's signals and relay them back to Division. He instructed the team to set up at a point midway between Division and Lathbury's mobile communications. A short time later, Deane-Drummond heard signals from the relay team. The range of their set seemed drastically reduced—at minimum, the "22's" should have operated efficiently at least up to five miles—and the signal was faint. Either the set was not functioning properly, he reasoned, or the operator was poorly located to send. Even as he listened, the signal faded completely. Deane-Drummond was unable to raise anybody. Nor could a special team of American communications operators with two radio jeeps. Hastily assembled and rushed to British Airborne Division headquarters only a few hours before takeoff on the seventeenth, the Americans were to operate ground-to-air "very high frequency" sets to call in fighters for close support. In the first few hours of the battle, these radio jeeps might have made all the difference. Instead, they were found to be useless. Neither jeep's set had been adjusted to the frequencies necessary to call in planes. At this moment, with the battle barely begun, British radio communications had totally broken down.°

☆ 8 ☆

A s if on signal, German guns opened up as the planes carrying the 82nd Airborne Division made their approach to the drop zones. Looking down, Brigadier General James M. Gavin saw ground fire spurting from a line of trenches paralleling the Maas-Waal

---

° In Christopher Hibbert's *The Battle of Arnhem*, p. 96, dealing specifically with the British at Arnhem and equally critical of British communications, he claims that "American air-support parties were insufficiently trained . . . the disastrous consequence was that not until the last day of the operation . . . was any effective close air support given to the airborne troops." There appears to be no information on who erred in the allocation of the frequencies, nor are the names of the Americans known. The two teams, who found themselves in the middle of the battle with the means of perhaps changing the entire course of history on that vital day, have never been found. Yet these two combat units are the only American ones known to have been in the Arnhem battle.

Canal. In wooded areas, enemy batteries that had remained silent and hidden until now also began to fire. Watching, Gavin wondered if his battle plan for the 82nd, which had been based on a calculated risk, might founder.

Charged with holding the middle sector of the Market-Garden corridor, the division had widespread objectives, running ten miles south-to-north and twelve miles west-to-east. Besides the drop of one paratroop company near the western end of the Grave bridge, which was to be seized by a surprise *coup de main* assault, Gavin had chosen three drop areas and one large landing zone. The latter would accommodate his fifty Waco gliders and the thirty-eight Horsas and Wacos of General Frederick Browning's British I Airborne Corps headquarters. But Gavin had ordered only one drop zone, north of Overasselt, to be marked by pathfinders. The other three, lying close to the Groesbeek ridge and the German border, were deliberately left unmarked. Gavin's paratroopers and gliders would land without identifying beacons or smoke in order to confuse the enemy as to their touchdown areas. Some thirteen minutes after the 82nd was down, Browning's Corps headquarters would land.

Because Gavin's primary concern was that enemy tanks might suddenly emerge from the Reichswald along the German border east of his largest glider and drop zone, he had given two unusual orders. To protect both his division and Browning's headquarters, he had instructed paratroopers to jump close to any antiaircraft batteries they were able to spot from the air and render them useless as quickly as possible. And, for the first time in airborne history, he was parachuting in a complete battalion of field artillery, dropping it onto the large zone directly facing the forest and approximately one and one-half miles from the German border itself. Now, looking at the intense antiaircraft fire and thinking of the possibility of enemy tanks in the Reichswald, Gavin knew that while he had planned for nearly all eventualities, the men of the 82nd faced a tough task.

Gavin's Normandy veterans had never forgotten the slaughter of their own in Ste. Mère Église. Dropped by accident on that village, men had been machine-gunned by the Germans as they came down; many were killed as they hung helpless in their parachutes, from telephone lines and trees around the village square. Not until Ste. Mère Église was finally secured by Lieutenant Colonel Ben Vandervoort were the dead troopers cut down and buried. Now, as the 82nd prepared to jump over Holland, some men called out to troopers still hooked up behind them: "Remember Ste. Mère Église." Although it was a risky procedure, many troopers jumped with their guns blazing.

Captain Briand Beaudin, coming down over his drop zone near the Groesbeek Ridge, saw that he was descending directly over a German antiaircraft emplacement with guns aiming at him. Beaudin began firing with his Colt .45. "Suddenly I realized," Beaudin remembers, "how futile it was, aiming my little peashooter while oscillating in the air above large-caliber guns." Landing close to the flak site, Beaudin took the entire crew prisoner. He thinks the Germans "were so startled they couldn't fire a single shot."

First Lieutenant James J. Coyle thought he was heading for a landing on a German tent hospital. Suddenly, enemy troops poured out of the tent and began running for 20 mm. antiaircraft guns around the perimeter. He, too, worked his .45 from its holster but his parachute began to oscillate and Coyle drifted away from the tent. One of the Germans started to run in Coyle's direction. "I couldn't get off a shot at the Kraut," Coyle recalls. "One second I'd be pointing the pistol at the ground; the next, I'd be aiming at the sky. I did have enough sense left to put the Colt back into the holster so I wouldn't drop it or shoot myself when I hit." On the ground, even before he tried to get out of his harness, Coyle drew his pistol once more. "The Kraut was now only a few feet away, but he was acting as though he didn't know I existed. Suddenly I realized that he wasn't running toward me; he was just running away." As the German hurried past Coyle he threw away his gun and helmet, and Coyle could see "he was only a kid, about eighteen years old. I just couldn't shoot an unarmed man. The last I saw of the boy he was running for the German border."

When tracer bullets began ripping through his canopy, Private Edwin C. Raub became so enraged that he deliberately sideslipped his chute so as to land next to the antiaircraft gun. Without removing his harness, and dragging his parachute behind him, Raub rushed the Germans with his Tommy gun. He killed one, captured the others and then, with plastic explosives, destroyed the flak-gun barrels.

Although enemy opposition to the 505th and 508th regiments in the Groesbeek area was officially considered negligible, a considerable amount of antiaircraft and small-arms fire came from the woods surrounding the zones. Without waiting to assemble, 82nd troopers, individually and in small groups, swarmed over these pockets of resistance, quickly subduing them and taking prisoners. Simultaneously, fighter planes skimmed over the tree tops, machine-gunning the enemy emplacements. The Germans scored heavily against these low-level attacks. Within a matter of minutes, three fighters were hit and crashed near the woods. Staff Sergeant Michael Vuletich saw one of them. It cartwheeled across the drop zone and when it finally stopped, only the plane's fuselage was intact. Moments later, the pilot emerged unscathed and stopped by the wreckage to light a cigarette. Vuletich remembers that the downed flier remained with the company as an infantryman.

From the ground, Staff Sergeant James Jones saw a P-47 aflame at about 1,500 feet. He expected the pilot to bail out but the plane came down, skidded across the drop zone and broke apart. The tail snapped off, the motor rolled away, and the cockpit came to rest on the field. Jones was sure the pilot was dead but, as he watched, the canopy slid back and "a little tow-headed guy with no hat on and a .45 under his arm ran toward us." Jones remembers asking, "Man, why in the devil didn't you jump?" The pilot grinned. "Hell, I was afraid to," he told Jones.

Just after landing and assembling his gear, Staff Sergeant Russell O'Neal watched a P-51 fighter dive and strafe a hidden German position near his field. After the plane had made two passes over the machine-gun nest, it was hit; but the pilot was able to circle and make a safe belly landing. According to O'Neal, "this guy jumped out and ran up to me, shouting, 'Give me a gun, quick! I know right where that Kraut s.o.b. is and I'm gonna get him.'" As O'Neal stared after him, the pilot grabbed a gun and raced off toward the woods.

Within eighteen minutes, 4,511 men of the 82nd's 505th and 508th regiments, along with engineers and seventy tons of equipment, were down on or near their drop zones straddling the town of Groesbeek on the eastern side of the wooded heights. As the men assembled, cleared the zones and struck out for objectives, special pathfinder teams marked the areas for the artillery drop, the 82nd's glider force, and the British Corps headquarters. So far, General Gavin's calculated risk was succeeding. Yet, although radio contact between the regiments was established almost immediately, it was still too early for Gavin, who had jumped with the 505th, to learn what was occurring eight miles west, where the 504th Regiment had dropped north of Overasselt. Nor did he know whether the special assault against the Grave bridge was proceeding according to plan.

Like the rest of the division's planes, the 137 C-47's carrying Colonel Reuben H. Tucker's 504th Regiment ran into spasmodic antiaircraft fire as they neared the Overasselt drop zone. As in the other areas, pilots held their courses, and at 1:15 P.M., some 2,016 men began to jump. Eleven planes swung slightly west and headed for a small drop site near the vital nine-span, 1,500-foot-long bridge over the Maas river near Grave. These C-47's carried Company E of Major Edward Wellems' 2nd Battalion to the most crucial of the 82nd's immediate objectives. Their job was to rush the bridges from the western approach; the remainder of Wellems' battalion would strike out from Overasselt and head for the eastern side. If the Grave bridge was not taken quickly and intact, the tight Market-Garden schedule could not be maintained. Loss of the bridge might mean failure for the entire operation.

As E Company's planes headed for the western assault site,

platoon leader Lieutenant John S. Thompson could clearly see the Maas river, the town of Grave, the mass jump of the 504th to his right near Overasselt and then, coming up, the ditch-lined fields where the company was to drop. As Thompson watched, other men from the company were already out of their planes and falling toward the Grave bridge zone; but in the lieutenant's C-47 the green light had not yet flashed on. When it did, Thompson saw that they were directly over some buildings. He waited for a few seconds, saw fields beyond and jumped with his platoon. By a fortuitous error, he and his men came down only some five or six hundred yards from the southwestern edge of the bridge.

Thompson could hear erratic firing from the direction of Grave itself, but around the bridge everything seemed quiet. He did not know whether he should wait until the remainder of the company came up or attack with the sixteen men in his platoon. "Since this was our primary mission, I decided to attack," Thompson says. Sending Corporal Hugh H. Perry back to the company commander, Thompson gave him a laconic message to deliver: "We are proceeding toward the bridge."

Firing from the town and nearby buildings was now more intense, and Thompson led the platoon to cover in nearby drainage ditches. Working their way toward the bridge, men waded in water up to their necks. They began to receive fire from a flak tower close to the bridge and Thompson noticed enemy soldiers with bags in their arms running to and from a building near the crossing. He thought it must be a maintenance or power plant. Fearful that the Germans were carrying demolition charges to the bridge in preparation for destroying it, Thompson quickly deployed his men, encircled the building and opened fire. "We raked the area with machine guns, overran the power plant, found four dead Germans and one wounded," Thompson recalls. "Apparently they had been carrying their personal equipment and blankets." Suddenly, two trucks came racing down the highway from Grave, heading toward the bridge. One of Thompson's men killed a driver whose truck careened off the road as its load of German soldiers scrambled to get out. The second vehicle stopped immediately and the soldiers in it jumped to the ground. Thompson's men opened up, but the Germans showed no desire to fight. Without returning fire, they ran away.

Fire was still coming from the flak tower, but by now it was passing over the heads of the platoon. "The gunners were unable to depress the 20 mm. flak gun sufficiently to get us," Thompson remembers. The platoon's bazooka man, Private Robert McGraw, crawled forward and, at a range of about seventy-five yards, fired three rounds, two of them into the top of the tower, and the gun ceased firing.

Although a twin 20 mm. gun in a tower across the river near the far end of the bridge was firing, Thompson and his men nonetheless destroyed electrical equipment and cables that they suspected were hooked up to demolitions. The platoon then set up a roadblock and placed land mines across the highway at the southwestern approach to the bridge. In the flak tower they had knocked out, they found the gunner dead but his 20 mm. weapon undamaged. Thompson's men promptly began firing it at the flak tower across the river. The platoon, he knew, would soon be reinforced by the rest of E Company coming up behind and, shortly after, by Major Wellems' battalion even now rushing from Overasselt to grab the northeastern end of the bridge. But, as far as Lieutenant Thompson was concerned, the prime objective was already taken.[*]

By now, the remaining battalions of Tucker's 504th Regiment were moving eastward, like spokes on a wheel, for the three road crossings and the railroad bridge over the Maas-Waal Canal. Rushing toward the bridge also were units of the 505th and 508th regiments, bent on seizing the crossings from the opposite ends. Not all these objectives were essential to the Market-Garden

[*] The 82nd's after-action report and that of the 504th commander, Colonel Tucker, state the bridge was "taken" at 2:30 P.M. But Major Wellems' account states that because the bridge was still under harassing fire, the first men to actually cross from the northeastern end went over at 3:35 P.M. Still, the E Company platoon under Lieutenant Thompson held the bridge and prevented its demolition from 1:45 P.M. until it was described as "secure" at 5 P.M.

advance. In the surprise of the assault and the ensuing confusion, Gavin hoped to seize them all; but one, in addition to the all-important Grave bridge, would suffice.

To keep the enemy off balance, defend his positions, protect General Browning's Corps headquarters and aid his paratroopers as they moved on their objectives, Gavin was depending heavily on his howitzers; and now the guns of the 376th Parachute Field Artillery were coming in. Small artillery units had been dropped in previous operations, but they had been badly scattered and slow to assemble and fire. The unit of 544 men now approaching was hand-picked, every soldier a veteran paratrooper. Among the forty-eight planes carrying the battalion was the artillery—twelve 75 mm. howitzers, each broken down into seven pieces. The howitzers would be dropped first, followed by some 700 rounds of ammunition. Lining up, the C-47's came in and, in quick succession, the guns rolled out. Ammunition and men followed, all making a near-perfect landing.

One accident caused scarcely a pause. Lieutenant Colonel Wilbur Griffith, commanding the 376th, broke his ankle on the jump but his men quickly liberated a Dutch wheelbarrow in which to carry him. "I shall never forget the Colonel being trundled from place to place," Major Augustin Hart recalls, "and barking out orders for everybody to get assembled at top speed." When the job was complete, Griffith was wheeled over to General Gavin. There he reported: "Guns in position, sir, and ready to fire on call." In just over an hour, in the most successful drop of its kind ever made, the entire battalion was assembled and ten of its howitzers were already firing.

Fourteen minutes after the 82nd's field artillery landed, Waco gliders carrying an airborne antitank battalion, engineers, elements of Division headquarters, guns, ammunition, trailers and jeeps began to come in. Of the original fifty gliders leaving England, all but four reached Holland. Not all, however, touched down on their landing zone. Some gliders ended up a mile or two away. One, copiloted by Captain Anthony Jedrziewski, cut loose late from its tug and Jedrziewski saw with horror that "we were heading straight for Germany on a one-glider invasion." The pilot made a 180-degree turn and began to look for a place to land. As they came in, Jedrziewski remembers, "we lost one wing on a haystack, the other on a fence and ended up with the glider nose in the ground. Seeing earth up to my knees, I wasn't sure if my feet were still a part of me. Then, we heard the unwelcome sound of an 88 and, in nothing flat, we had the jeep out and were racing back toward our own area."

They were luckier than Captain John Connelly, whose pilot was killed during the approach. Connelly, who had never flown a glider before, took the controls and landed the Waco just inside the German border, six to seven miles away, near the town of Wyler. Only Connelly and one other man escaped capture. They were to hide out until darkness and finally reached their units by midmorning of September 18.

Yet, in all, the 82nd Airborne had successfully brought in 7,467 paratroopers and glider-borne men. The last elements to touch down in the area were 35 Horsas and Wacos carrying General Frederick Browning's Corps headquarters. Three gliders had been lost en route to the drop zone, two before reaching the Continent; the third, south of Vught, had crash-landed in the vicinity of General Student's headquarters. Browning's headquarters landed almost on the German frontier. "There was little flak, if any, and almost no enemy opposition," Browning's chief of staff, Brigadier Gordon Walch, remembers. "We set down about a hundred yards west of the Reichswald Forest and my glider was roughly fifty yards away from Browning's."

Colonel George S. Chatterton, commanding the Glider Pilot Regiment, was at the controls of Browning's Horsa. After clipping off a front wheel on an electric cable, Chatterton slid into a cabbage patch. "We got out," Chatterton recalls, "and Browning, looking around, said, 'By God, we're here, George!'" Nearby, Brigadier Walch saw Browning run across the landing zone toward the Reichswald. When he returned a few minutes later, he explained to Walch, "I wanted to be the first British officer to pee in Germany."

While Browning's jeep was being unloaded, a few German shells exploded nearby. Colonel Chatterton promptly threw himself into the closest ditch. "I shall never forget Browning standing above me, looking like some sort of explorer, and asking, 'George, whatever in the world are you doing down there?'" Chatterton was frank. "I'm bloody well hiding, sir," he said. "Well, you can bloody well stop hiding," Browning told him. "It's time we were going." From a pocket in his tunic, Browning took out a parcel wrapped in tissue paper. Handing it to Chatterton, he said, "Put it on my jeep." Chatterton unfolded the tissue and saw that it contained a pennant bearing a light-blue Pegasus against a maroon background, the insignia of the British Airborne.° With the pennant fluttering from the jeep's fender, the commander of the Market forces drove away.

At Renkum Heath west of Arnhem, Lieutenant Neville Hay, the highly trained specialist in charge of the fact-gathering liaison unit "Phantom," was totally baffled. His team of experts had assembled their radio set with its special antenna and expected immediate contact with General Browning's Corps headquarters. Hay's first priority on landing was to get through to Corps and give his position. Earlier, he had learned that Division communications had broken down. While he might have anticipated that problems would arise among the less experienced Royal Signal Corps operators, he was not prepared to believe that the difficulties he was having stemmed from his own men. "We were set up on the landing zone and, although it was screened by pine woods, we had got through in considerably worse country than

° Some accounts have stated that Browning's pennant was made by his wife, the novelist Daphne du Maurier. "I am sorry," she writes, "to disappoint the mythmakers . . . but anyone who has seen my attempts to thread a needle would know this was beyond me. It is a delightful thought, however, and would have greatly amused my husband." Actually, the pennant was made by Hobson & Sons Ltd., London, under the supervision of Miss Claire Miller, who also, at Browning's direction, hand-sewed tiny compasses into 500 shirt collars and belts just prior to Market-Garden.

this," he remembers. "We kept trying and getting absolutely nothing." Until he could discover where the trouble lay, there was no way of informing General Browning of the progress of General Urquhart's division or of relaying Browning's orders to the British 1st Airborne. Ironically, the Dutch telephone system was in full operation, including a special network owned and operated by the PGEM power station authorities at Nijmegen and connected with the entire province. Had he known, all Hay had to do, with the aid of the Dutch resistance, was to pick up a telephone.

Fifteen miles away there was already anxiety at General Browning's headquarters, now set up on the edge of the Groes- beek ridge. Both of the 82nd Airborne's large communication sets had been damaged on landing. Browning's had come through safely, and one of these was allocated to the 82nd, insuring immediate communication with General Gavin. The Corps com- munications section had also made radio contact with General Dempsey's British 2nd Army and Airborne Corps rear head- quarters in England and Browning had radio contact with the 101st. But the signal section was unable to raise Urquhart's division. Brigadier Walch believes that Corps signals was to blame. "Before the operation was planned, we asked for a proper headquarters signals section," he says. "We were frightfully cog- nizant that our sets were inadequate and our headquarters signals staff weak and inexperienced." While Browning could direct and influence the movements of the 82nd, the 101st and Horrocks' XXX Corps, at this vital junction the all-important battle at Arnhem was beyond his control. As Walch says, "We had abso- lutely no idea what was happening in Arnhem."

A kind of creeping paralysis was already beginning to affect Montgomery's plan. But at this early stage no one knew it. Throughout the entire Market-Garden area, some 20,000 Allied soldiers were in Holland, heading out to secure the bridges and hold open the corridor for the massive Garden units whose lead tanks were expected to link up with 101st paratroopers by nightfall.

�֍ 9 ✧

From the flat roof of a large factory near the Meuse-Escaut Canal, General Brian Horrocks, commander of the British XXX Corps, watched the last of the huge airborne glider formations pass over his waiting tanks. He had been on the roof since 11 A.M., and as he put it, "I had plenty of time to think." The sight of the vast armada was "comforting, but I was under no illusion that this was going to be an easy battle," Horrocks remembers. Meticulously, he had covered every possible contingency, even to ordering his men to take as much food, gas and ammunition as they could carry, "since we were likely to be out in the blue on our own." There was one worry the General could not eliminate, but he had not discussed it with anyone—he did not like a Sunday attack. "No assault or attack in which I had taken part during the war which started on a Sunday had ever been completely successful." Bringing up his binoculars, he studied the white ribbon of road stretching away north toward Valkenswaard and Eindhoven. Satisfied that the airborne assault had now begun, Horrocks gave the order for the Garden forces to attack. At precisely 2:15 P.M., with a thunderous roar, some 350 guns opened fire.

The bombardment was devastating. Ton after ton of explosives flayed the enemy positions up ahead. The hurricane of fire, ranging five miles in depth and concentrated over a one-mile front, caused the earth to shake beneath the tanks of the Irish

Guards as they lumbered up to the start line. Behind the lead squadrons, hundreds of tanks and armored vehicles began to move slowly out of their parking positions, ready to fall into line as the first tanks moved off. And up above, a "cab rank" of rocket-firing Typhoon fighters circled endlessly, waiting on call for the commander of the Irish Guards Group, Lieutenant Colonel Joe Vandeleur, to direct them to targets up ahead. At 2:35 P.M., standing in the turret of the lead tank of No. 3 Squadron, Lieutenant Keith Heathcote shouted into his microphone, "Driver, advance!"

Slowly the tanks rumbled out of the bridgehead and moved up the road at eight miles an hour. Now, the curtain of artillery fire lifted to creep ahead of the armor at exactly the same speed. Tankers could see shells bursting barely one hundred yards in front of them. As the squadrons moved forward, engulfed in the dust of the barrage, men could not tell at times whether the tanks were safely back of their own fire.

Behind the lead squadrons came the scout cars of Lieutenant Colonel Joe Vandeleur and his cousin Giles. Standing in his car, Vandeleur could see, both in front of and behind him, infantry riding on the tanks, each tank marked with yellow streamers to identify it to the Typhoons above. "The din was unimaginable," Vandeleur remembers, "but everything was going according to plan." By now, the lead tanks had burst out of the bridgehead and were across the Dutch frontier. Captain "Mick" O'Cock, commanding No. 3 Squadron, radioed back, "Advance going well. Leading squadron has got through." Then, in seconds, the picture changed. As Vandeleur recalls, "The Germans really began to paste us."

Ensconced in well-hidden, fortified positions on both sides of the road, German gunners had not only survived the tremendous barrage but had waited until it passed over them. Holding their fire, the Germans let the first few tanks go through. Then, within two minutes three tanks of the lead squadron and six of the next were knocked out of action. Burning and disabled, they littered a half mile of road. "We had just crossed the border when we were ambushed," Lieutenant Cyril Russell recalls. "Suddenly the tanks in front either slewed across the road or burned where they stood. The awful realization dawned on me that the next one to go was the one I was sitting on. We jumped into the ditches by the roadside." As Russell went forward to see how the remainder of his platoon was faring, a machine gun opened up; he was hit in the arm and fell back into the ditch. For Russell, the war was over.

Lance Corporal James Doggart's tank was hit. "I don't remember seeing or hearing the explosion," he says. "I was suddenly flat on my back in a ditch with the tank leaning over me. I had a Bren gun across my chest and next to me was a young lad with his arm nearly severed. Nearby, another of our men was dead. The tank was on fire and I don't recall seeing any of the crew get out."

Lieutenant Barry Quinan, in the last tank of the lead squadron, remembers that his Sherman swung left into a ditch, and Quinan thought the driver was trying to bypass the burning tanks ahead. But the tank had been hit by a shell which killed both the driver and codriver. The Sherman began to burn and Quinan's gunner, "trying to scramble out of the hatch, half lifted me out of the turret before I realized we were 'brewing up.'" As the two men climbed out of the tank, Quinan saw others coming up behind. One after the other, the tanks were hit. "I actually saw the commander of one tank trying to shield his face from a sheet of flame that engulfed the entire machine."

The breakout had been stopped before it had really begun and nine disabled tanks now blocked the road. Squadrons coming up could not advance. Even if they could bypass the burning hulks, hidden German gunners would pick them off. To get the advance rolling again, Vandeleur called in the rocket-firing Typhoons and, aided by purple smoke shells fired from the tanks to indicate suspected German positions, the fighters screamed down. "It was the first time I had ever seen Typhoons in action," Vandeleur recalls, "and I was amazed at the guts of those pilots. They came in, one at a time, head to tail, flying right through our own barrage. One disintegrated right above me. It was incredible—

guns firing, the roar of planes, the shouts and curses of the men. In the middle of it all, Division asked how the battle was going. My second in command just held up the microphone and said, 'Listen.'"

As the planes swooped down on their targets, Vandeleur sent forward an armored bulldozer to push the burning tanks off the road. The bedlam of the battle now raged over several miles of highway, stretching back as far as Vandeleur's own car and the R.A.F. communications tender, which called the Typhoons down on demand. Flight Lieutenant Donald Love, the fighter reconnaissance pilot attached to the communications unit, was now convinced that he should never have volunteered for the job. While Squadron Leader Max Sutherland directed the Typhoons, Love got out to see what was happening. Black smoke billowed up from the road ahead and an antitank gun carrier, almost in front of the communications tender, was afire. As Love watched, a Bren gun carrier came back along the road carrying wounded. One man's shoulder was blown off, and his clothes were burned and charred. "I was sure we were surrounded," says Love. "I was horrified and I kept wondering why hadn't I stayed with the Air Force, where I belonged."

The waiting tankers farther back in the halted columns felt, as Captain Roland Langton describes it, "a strange sense of powerlessness. We could go neither forward nor backward." Langton watched infantry moving up to clean out the woods on either side of the road with two Bren gun carriers out in front. Langton thought the soldiers might be an advance party of the 43rd Infantry Division. "Suddenly I saw both carriers catapulted into the air," Langton remembers. "They had run over enemy land mines." When the smoke cleared, Langton saw "bodies in the trees. I don't know how many, it was impossible to tell. There were pieces of men hanging from every limb."

With the Typhoons firing only yards away from them, the British infantry men grimly began to dig out the Germans from their hidden trenches. Lance Corporal Doggart had escaped from the ditch where he landed when his tank was hit. He raced across the road and jumped into an empty enemy slit trench. "At the same moment, two Germans—one a young fellow without a jacket, the other a tough-looking bastard of about thirty—jumped in after me from the opposite direction," Doggart says. Without hesitating, Doggart kicked the older German in the face. The younger man, immediately cowed, surrendered. Covering both with his rifle, Doggart sent them marching back along the road "with streams of other Germans, all running with their hands behind their heads. Those that were too slow got a fast kick in the backside."

From the woods, in ditches, around haystacks and along the roadway, now being slowly cleared of the disabled tanks, came the stutter of Sten guns as the infantry mopped up. The Guardsmen showed no quarter, particularly toward snipers. Men remember that prisoners were made to double-time down the road, and when they slowed they were promptly prodded with bayonets. One prisoner in the now-growing lines tried to break away, but there was more than a company of infantry in the vicinity and several men recall that—in the words of one—"he was dead the second the thought entered his mind."

Joe Vandeleur watched the prisoners being marched past his scout car. As one German came along, Vandeleur caught a sudden movement. "The bastard had taken a grenade he'd concealed and lobbed it into one of our gun carriers. It went off with a tremendous explosion and I saw one of my sergeants lying in the road with his leg blown off. The German was cut down on all sides by machine guns."

At his command post, General Horrocks received word that the road was gradually being cleared and that the infantry, although suffering heavy casualties, had routed the Germans on the flanks. As he later put it, "The Micks were getting tired of being shot at, and as so often happens with these great fighters, they suddenly lost their tempers."

Perhaps no one was more enraged than Captain Eamon Fitzgerald, the 2nd Battalion's intelligence officer, who interrogated the captured crew of an antitank gun. According to Lieutenant

Colonel Giles Vandeleur, "Fitzgerald had an interesting way of extracting information. A huge giant of a man, he spoke German well, but with an atrocious accent. His normal custom was to produce his pistol, poke it into the German's belly and, standing as close as possible, shout questions in the man's face." The results, Vandeleur always thought, "were positively splendid. Within a few minutes after interrogating this crew, our tanks were picking off the German camouflaged antitank positions with creditable accuracy and the road was being sufficiently cleared to allow us to continue the advance."

Many Irish Guardsmen believe Sergeant Bertie Cowan turned the tide of the battle. Commanding a 17-pounder Sherman, Cowan had spotted a German antitank position and demolished it with a single shot. During the fight, Major Edward G. Tyler, in command of the squadron, was astonished to see that a German was standing on Cowan's tank directing operations. He saw the tank cross the road and open fire; then, busy himself, Tyler forgot the incident. Later, Tyler learned that Cowan had knocked out three German guns. "When I could take a moment, I went to congratulate him," Tyler says. "Cowan told me the Jerry on his tank had been a crew chief in the first position he'd overrun who had surrendered." He had been interrogated by Captain Fitzgerald and then returned to Cowan where he had proven "most cooperative."

The Irish Guards were on the way again, but constant fighting continued. The German crust was far tougher than anyone had anticipated. Among the prisoners were men of renowned parachute battalions and—to the complete surprise of the British—veteran infantrymen from the 9th and 10th SS Panzer divisions: elements of the combat groups General Wilhelm Bittrich had sent to bolster Student's First Parachute Army. To compound the surprise, some prisoners were discovered to belong to General von Zangen's Fifteenth Army. As the Irish Guards' war diary notes, "Our intelligence spent the day in a state of indignant surprise: one German regiment after another appeared which had no right to be there."

General Horrocks had expected that his lead tanks would drive the thirteen miles to Eindhoven "within two to three hours." Precious time had been lost, and the Irish Guards would cover only seven miles, reaching Valkenswaard by nightfall. Market-Garden was already ominously behind schedule.

In order to be as mobile as possible, General Maxwell D. Taylor's gliders had brought in mostly jeeps—no artillery. The fact that the British were late in reaching Eindhoven was a blow. Taylor had hoped for the support of the tankers' guns along the fifteen-mile stretch of corridor the Screaming Eagles must control. Taylor's Dutch liaison officers discovered the true situation—that the 101st would have to operate independently for longer than planned—almost immediately; with the aid of the resistance, they simply used the telephone to learn what was happening with the British.

With lightning speed Taylor's paratroopers took Veghel, the northernmost objective along the corridor, and its four crossings—the rail and highway bridges over the river Aa and the Willems Canal. Heavy fighting would ensue; nevertheless, these four objectives were seized within two hours. Farther south, midway between Veghel and Son, the town of St. Oedenrode and its highway crossing over the Dommel river were captured with relative ease. According to official Dutch telephone log books, Johanna Lathouwers, a loyal operator with the state telephone exchange, heard "an unmistakable American voice came on the Oed 1 (St. Oedenrode) line, at 1425 hours, asking for Valkenswaard, a connection that lasted forty minutes."*

The Americans quickly learned that the spearhead of the Garden forces had not as yet even reached Valkenswaard. It now seemed unlikely that Horrocks' tanks, already delayed, would reach Eindhoven at the southern end of the corridor before

---

* By Allied clocks it was actually 1525 hours; there was a one-hour difference between German and British times.

nightfall; and that would be too late to help the Americans seize and control their widespread targets. The men of the 101st had achieved spectacular success. Now, they ran into problems.

The most pressing of Taylor's objectives was the highway bridge over the Wilhelmina Canal at Son, approximately five miles north of Eindhoven. As a contingency plan in case this main traffic artery was blown, Taylor had decided to seize a bridge over the canal at Best, four miles to the west. Because the bridge was considered secondary, only a single company of the 502nd Regiment was detailed to Best, and it was thought that only a few Germans would be in the area. Taylor's intelligence was unaware that Colonel General Student's headquarters lay only ten miles northwest of the 101st drop zones and that recent arrivals of Von Zangen's Fifteenth Army were quartered at nearby Tilburg. Among these forces was Major General Walter Poppe's battered 59th Infantry Division plus a considerable amount of artillery.

Almost immediately upon approaching the bridge, H Company radioed that it had run into enemy roadblocks and was meeting strong resistance. The message signaled the beginning of a bloody battle that would last throughout the night and most of the following two days. What had begun as a single-company operation eventually involved more than an entire regiment. But already the heroic men of H Company, though taking heavy casualties, were blunting the first, unexpectedly strong, German blows.

While H Company was setting out for the bridge at Best, Colonel Robert F. Sink's 506th Regiment was going for the main highway bridge at Son. There was almost no opposition until troops reached the northern outskirts of the village. Then they were fired on by a German 88 artillery piece. In less than ten minutes, the advance party destroyed the gun emplacement with a bazooka and killed its crew. Fighting through the streets, the Americans were a bare fifty yards from the canal itself when the bridge was blown up, debris falling all around the paratroopers. For Colonel Sink, who was to take Eindhoven and its crossings by 8 P.M., the loss of the bridge was a bitter blow. Reacting quickly and still under fire, three men—Major James LaPrade, Second

Lieutenant Millford F. Weller and Sergeant John Dunning—dived into the canal and swam to the far side. Other members of the battalion followed their lead or went across in rowboats. On the southern bank, they subdued the German opposition and set up a bridgehead.

The central column of the bridge was still intact, and 101st engineers immediately began the construction of a temporary crossing. Help came from an unexpected source. Dutch civilians reported that a considerable amount of black-market lumber was being stored by a contractor in a nearby garage. Within one and a half hours the engineers, utilizing the bridge's center trestle and the liberated lumber, spanned the canal. As Colonel Sink recalled, "the bridge was unsatisfactory from every point of view, except that it did enable me to put the rest of the regiment across, single file." Until bridging equipment could be brought up, the Market-Garden corridor at Son was reduced to a single wooden footpath.

✲10✲

FIELD MARSHAL MODEL was still shaken when he reached General Bittrich's headquarters at Doetinchem. Normally, it would have taken him no longer than half an hour to cover the distance, but today, because he had made numerous stops along the way to alert area commanders to the airborne assault, the trip had lasted well over an hour. Although the Field Marshal seemed calm, Bittrich remembers "his first words to me were, 'They almost got me! They were after the headquarters. Imagine! They almost got me!'"

Bittrich immediately brought Model up to date on the latest

information received by II SS Panzer Corps. No clear picture of the Allied intent was emerging as yet, but Bittrich told Model his own theory: that the assault was aimed at containing the Fifteenth Army while the British Second Army drove for the Ruhr. That would require the Allies to capture the Nijmegen and Arnhem bridges. Model disagreed completely. The Arnhem bridge was not the objective, he said. These airborne troops would swerve and march northeast for the Ruhr. The situation, Model believed, was still too obscure for any final conclusions. He was puzzled as to why airborne forces had landed in the Nijmegen area. Nevertheless, he approved the measures Bittrich had already taken.

Bittrich still pressed the subject of the bridges. "Herr Field Marshal, I strongly urge that the bridges at Nijmegen and Arnhem be immediately destroyed," he said. Model looked at him in amazement. "They will not be destroyed," he told Bittrich firmly. "No matter what the English plan, these bridges can be defended. No. Absolutely not. The bridges are not to be blown." Then, dismissing the subject, Model said, "I'm looking for a new headquarters, Bittrich." Before Bittrich could answer, Model said again musingly, "You know, they almost got me."

At his headquarters at Vught, Colonel General Kurt Student faced a dilemma: his First Parachute Army had been split in two by the airborne assault. Without telephone communications and now solely dependent on radio, he was unable to direct his divided army. For the moment units were fighting on their own without any cohesive direction. Then, by a momentous and fantastic stroke of luck, an undamaged briefcase found in a downed Waco glider near his headquarters was rushed to him.

"It was incredible," Student says. "In the case was the complete enemy attack order for the operation." Student and his staff officers pored over the captured plans. "They showed us everything—the dropping zones, the corridor, the objectives, even the names of the divisions involved. Everything! Immediately we could see the strategic implications. They had to grab the bridges before we could destroy them. All I could think of was, 'This is retribution. Retribution! History is repeating itself.' During our airborne operation in Holland in 1940, one of my officers, against strict orders, had taken into battle papers that detailed our entire attack, and these had fallen into enemy hands. Now the wheel had turned full circle. I knew exactly what I had to do."[*]

Model, as yet, did not. Student had never felt so frustrated. Because of his communications breakdown, it would be nearly ten hours before he could place the secret of Market-Garden in Model's possession. The secret was that the Arnhem bridge was of crucial importance. The captured plans clearly showed that it was Montgomery's route into the Ruhr.

This was the kind of battle that Model liked best: one that demanded improvisation, daring and, above all, speed. From Bittrich's headquarters, Model telephoned OB West, Von Rundstedt. With characteristic abruptness, he described the situation and asked for immediate reinforcements. "The only way this airborne assault can be defeated is to strike hard within the first twenty-four hours," he told Von Rundstedt. Model asked for anti-aircraft units, self-propelled guns, tanks and infantry; and he wanted them on the move to Arnhem by nightfall. Von Rund-

[*] In the legend of Arnhem the story of the captured documents, like that of the spy Lindemans, is always included. Some accounts claim that the Market-Garden plan was found on the body of a dead American captain. I interviewed Student and examined all his documents. At no point does he confirm that the briefcase was carried by a captain. Nor is there any such mention in official British and American records. Perhaps, since Student says that the plans came from "a Waco freight glider," it was generally assumed that only American personnel were aboard. However, part of General Browning's Corps headquarters flew to Holland in Wacos; and one of these did crash-land near Student's headquarters. In any case, whether the personnel were British or American, I think it highly unlikely that the entire Market-Garden operational plan could have been in the possession of a captain. First, great care was taken in the distribution of the plan; and second, each copy was both numbered and restricted solely to officers of staff rank.

stedt told him that such reinforcements as were available would be on the way. Turning to Bittrich, Model said triumphantly, "Now, we'll get reinforcements!" Model had decided to operate from Doetinchem; but, although he was apparently recovered from the shock of his hasty departure from Oosterbeek, this time he was taking no chances of being caught unawares. He refused accommodations at the castle; he would direct the battle from the gardener's cottage on the grounds.

Bittrich's early foresight was already having its effect. Sections of Harzer's Hohenstaufen Division were heading swiftly toward the battle zone. Harmel's Frundsberg Division—Harmel himself was expected back from Germany during the night—were on the move, too. Bittrich had ordered Harzer to set up his headquarters in a high school in the northern Arnhem suburbs overlooking the city, and that transfer was underway. But Harzer was chafing with impatience. The armored vehicles that had been scheduled to leave for Germany in the early afternoon were still being refitted with tracks and guns. Harzer had already moved the units closest to the British landing and drop zones into blocking positions at points west of Arnhem. For the moment, he had only a few armored cars, several self-propelled guns, a few tanks and some infantry. Still, Harzer hoped that by employing hit-and-run tactics he could halt and confuse British troops until the bulk of his division was again battle-ready.

Curiously, Harzer did not even know that Major Sepp Krafft's SS Panzer Grenadier Training and Reserve Battalion was in the area and, at the moment, the only unit in the path of the British airborne forces. Harzer concentrated his own strength on the two major highways running into Arnhem: the Ede-Arnhem road and the Utrecht-Arnhem road. Certain that the paratroopers must use these main arteries, he placed his units in a semicircular screen across the two highways. By oversight, or perhaps because he lacked sufficient forces at the moment, Harzer failed to position any groups along a quiet secondary road running parallel to the northern bank of the Rhine. It was the single unprotected route the British could take to the Arnhem bridge.

�֍ 11 �֍

I N THEIR CAMOUFLAGE BATTLE SMOCKS and distinctive crash helmets, laden with weapons and ammunition, the men of Brigadier Lathbury's 1st Parachute Brigade were on the way to Arnhem. Interspersed among the columns of marching troopers were jeeps pulling artillery pieces and four-wheeled carts loaded with guns and stores. As General Roy Urquhart watched them pass, he remembered a compliment paid him some months before by General Horrocks. "Your men are killers," Horrocks had said admiringly. At the time, Urquhart had considered the remark an overstatement. On this Sunday, he was not so sure. As the 1st Brigade had moved off, Urquhart had felt a surge of pride.

The plan called for the three battalions of Lathbury's brigade to converge on Arnhem, each from a different direction. Lieutenant Colonel John Frost's 2nd Battalion was given the prime objective: marching along a secondary road running close to the north bank of the Rhine, Frost's men were to capture the main highway bridge. En route, they were to take the railway and pontoon bridges west of the great highway crossing. The 3rd Battalion, under Lieutenant Colonel J. A. C. Fitch, would move along the Utrecht-Arnhem road and approach the bridge from the north, reinforcing Frost. Once these two battalions had been successfully launched, Lieutenant Colonel D. Dobie's 1st Battalion was to advance along the main Ede-Arnhem highway—the most northerly route—and occupy the high ground north of the city. Lathbury had given each route a code name. Dobie's, farthest north, was designated "Leopard"; Fitch's, in the middle, was "Tiger"; and Frost's, the most crucial route, was "Lion." Speeding ahead of the entire brigade, the jeeps of Major Freddie Gough's reconnaissance squadron were expected to reach the bridge, seize it in a *coup de main,* and hold until Frost arrived.

So far, Urquhart thought, the initial phase was going well. He was not unduly alarmed by the breakdown of communications within the division at this time. He had experienced temporary signals disruption often in the North African desert campaigns. Since he could not raise Brigadier Hicks's 1st Airlanding Brigade, whose job it was to hold the landing and drop zones for the air lifts on the following two days, Urquhart drove to Hicks's headquarters. The Airlanding Brigade, he learned, was in position, and Hicks was for the moment away directing the disposition of his battalions. However, at Hicks's headquarters, Urquhart received news that one vital part of the plan to take the Arnhem bridge had gone wrong. He was told—erroneously—that most of Major Freddie Gough's reconnaissance vehicles had been lost in glider crashes; no one at Hicks's headquarters knew where Gough had gone. Without waiting for Hicks to return, Urquhart drove back to his own headquarters. He had to find Gough quickly and devise some alternative plan, but his greatest concern now was to warn Lathbury and, in particular, Frost, that the 2nd Battalion was on its own. Frost would have to take the main Arnhem bridge without the aid of Gough's planned surprise attack.

At Division, further bad news awaited Urquhart. "Not only was there no word of Gough," Urquhart recalls, "but apart from some short-range radio signals, headquarters communications had completely failed. The 1st Parachute Brigade and, indeed, the outside world, could not be contacted." Colonel Charles Mackenzie, Urquhart's chief of staff, watched the General pace up and down, "restive and anxious for news." Urquhart ordered his signals officer, Major Anthony Deane-Drummond, to investigate the "communications foul-up, see what had happened to the radio equipment and then set it right." Messengers were also sent out in search of Gough. As time passed without any new information, the worried Urquhart decided to wait no longer. Normally, he would have directed the battle from Division headquarters; but now, as each moment passed without communications, he was beginning to feel that this battle was anything but normal. Turning to Mackenzie, he said, "I think I'll go and have a look myself, Charles." Mackenzie did not try to stop him. "At the time," Mackenzie recalls, "since we were getting practically no information, it didn't seem a particularly bad thing to do." Taking only his driver and a signalman in his jeep, Urquhart set out after Lathbury. The time was 4:30 P.M.

Moving along the northern, Leopard route—the Ede-Arnhem road—Major Freddie Gough of the 1st Airlanding reconnaissance unit was making good time. Although the vehicles of A troop had failed to arrive, Gough had started off from the landing zone with the rest of the squadrons at 3:30 P.M. He was confident that he had sufficient jeeps for the *coup de main* attempt on the bridge. "In fact," he remembered, "I left several jeeps behind on the landing zone in reserve. We had more than enough to get to Arnhem." Gough had even detached twelve men from his unit to make their way south to join the 2nd Battalion, moving on the Lion route to the bridge. He was unaware that the loss of A troop's jeeps had raised a flurry of rumors and misinformation.[*]

From the beginning, Gough had had reservations about his recco unit's role in the Arnhem plan. Instead of a *coup de main*, Gough had urged that a screen of reconnaissance jeeps be sent ahead of each of the three battalions. "In that way," he says, "we would have quickly discovered the best and easiest way to reach the bridge." Failing that, he had asked that a troop of light tanks be brought in by glider to escort the *coup de main* force. Both requests had been turned down. Yet Gough had remained optimistic. "I wasn't the least bit concerned. There were supposed to

[*] Some accounts of the Arnhem battle claim that Gough's unit could not operate because so many of his vehicles failed to arrive by glider. "The failure, if it can be called that," Gough says, "was not due to a lack of jeeps, but to the fact that no one had warned us that the 9th and 10th SS Panzer divisions were in the area."

be only a few old, gray Germans in Arnhem and some ancient tanks and guns. I expected it to be a pushover."

Now, as they moved swiftly along Leopard, the lead jeeps of the unit were suddenly ambushed by German armored cars and 20 mm. guns. Gough's second in command, Captain David Allsop, happened to note the time. It was exactly 4 P.M. Gough pulled out to drive to the head of the column and investigate. "Just as I was on the point of going forward, I got a message saying that Urquhart wanted to see me immediately. I didn't know what the hell to do," Gough says. "I was under Lathbury, and I thought I should at least tell him I was going, but I had no idea where he was. The unit was now in a heavy fire fight and pinned down in defensive positions near the railroad tracks on the outskirts of Wolfheze. I reckoned they would be all right for a time, so I turned around and headed back to Division headquarters on the landing zone. That was at 4:30."

At the precise moment that General Urquhart set out to find Lathbury, Gough was speeding back to Division to report to Urquhart.

All along the three strategic lines of march, the men of the 1st Parachute Brigade were encountering jubilant, hysterical throngs of Dutch. Many civilians from farms and outlying hamlets had followed the paratroopers from the time they left the landing zones, and as the crowds grew, the welcome seemed almost to overwhelm the march itself. Captain Eric Mackay, traveling the southernmost, Lion route with Colonel Frost's 2nd Battalion, was disturbed by the holiday atmosphere. "We were hampered by Dutch civilians," he says. "Waving, cheering and clapping their hands, they offered us apples, pears, something to drink. But they interfered with our progress and filled me with dread that they would give our positions away." Lieutenant Robin Vlasto remembers that "the first part of our march was in the nature of a victory parade, and the civilians were quite delirious with joy. It all seemed so unbelievable that we almost expected to see Horrocks' XXX Corps tanks coming out of Arnhem to meet us. People lined the road and great trays of beer, milk and fruit were offered. We had the greatest difficulty forcing the men to keep alive to the possibility of a German attack."

Young Anje van Maanen, whose father was a doctor in Oosterbeek, recalls receiving an exuberant call from the Tromp family in Heelsum, just south of the British landing zone on Renkum Heath. "We are free. Free!" the Tromps told her. "The Tommies dropped behind our house and they are on their way to Oosterbeek. They are so nice! We are smoking Players and eating chocolate." Anje put the phone down, "crazy with joy. We all jumped and danced around. This is it! An invasion! Lovely!" Seventeen-year-old Anje could hardly wait for her father to come home. Dr. van Maanen was delivering a baby at a patient's home, and Anje thought it "very annoying, particularly now, because the husband of the woman was a Dutch Nazi." Mrs. Ida Clous, the wife of an Oosterbeek dentist and a friend of the Van Maanens, also heard that the airborne troops were on their way. She worked feverishly, hunting through boxes and sewing scraps to find every bit of orange cloth she possessed. When the British got to Oosterbeek, she intended to rush outside with her three small children and greet the deliverers with small handmade orange flags.

Jan Voskuil, hiding out in the home of his wife's parents in Oosterbeek, was torn between his own desire to head up the Utrecht road to greet the paratroopers and the need to prevent his father-in-law from coming with him. The elder man was adamant. "I'm seventy-eight years old and I've never been in a war before and I want to see it." Voskuil's father-in-law was finally persuaded to stay in the garden and Voskuil, joining streams of other civilians heading out to meet the British, was turned back by a policeman on the outskirts of Oosterbeek. "It's too dangerous," the officer told the crowds. "Go back." Voskuil walked slowly home. There he ran into the same German soldier who had asked for shelter when the bombing had begun during the morning. Now the soldier was in full uniform, with camouflage jacket, helmet and rifle. He offered Voskuil some chocolates and cigarettes. "I am going away now," he said. "The Tommies will come." Voskuil smiled. "Now, you will go back to Germany," he said. The soldier studied Voskuil for several seconds. Then he shook his head slowly. "No, sir," he told Voskuil. "We will fight." The Dutchman watched the German walk away. "It begins now," Voskuil thought, "but what can I do?" Impatiently he paced the yard. There was nothing to do but wait.

Unhampered by police restraints or warnings to stay indoors, Dutch farmers and their families lined each route of march in throngs. Sergeant Major Harry Callaghan, on the middle, Tiger route, remembers a farm woman breaking through the crowds and running toward him with a pitcher of milk. He thanked her and the woman smiled and said, "Good, Tommy. Good." But, like Eric Mackay on the lower road, Callaghan, a Dunkirk veteran, was bothered by the number of civilians surrounding the troops. "They ran along beside us wearing armbands, aprons, and little pieces of ribbon, all orange," he remembers. "Children, with little snippets of orange cloth pinned to their skirts or blouses, skipped along, shrieking with delight. Most of the men were reaching in their packs to hand them chocolate. It was such a different atmosphere that the men were behaving as if they were on an exercise. I began to be concerned about snipers."

As Callaghan had feared, the victory parade came to a sudden halt. "It all happened so quickly," he says. "One moment we were marching steadily toward Arnhem; the next, we were scattered in the ditches. Snipers had opened fire, and three dead airborne soldiers lay across the road." The veteran sergeant major wasted no time. He had spotted a burst of flame from trees about fifty yards ahead. As the Dutch scattered, Callaghan took a party of twelve men forward. He stopped short of one tree and looked up. Something flashed. Raising his Sten gun, he fired directly into the tree. A Schmeisser automatic pistol clattered to the ground and, as Callaghan sighted up along the trunk of the tree, he saw a German dangling limply from a rope.

Now, too, on the middle route, other men from Lieutenant Colonel Fitch's 3rd Battalion were suddenly engaged in an unexpected encounter. Private Frederick Bennett had just passed around some apples to other troopers when a German staff car came speeding down the road. Bennett opened up with his Sten gun. The car screeched to a stop and tried to back up. But it was too late. Everyone near Bennett began firing and the car came to an abrupt halt, riddled with bullets. As the troopers cautiously approached, they saw that the driver was hanging halfway out of the car. The body of a senior German officer had been thrown partly out another door. To Bennett "he looked like some high-ranking Jerry officer," as indeed he was. Major General Kussin, the Arnhem town commander, had disregarded the warning of SS Major Sepp Krafft to avoid the main Utrecht-Arnhem road.°

Many men recall that the first serious German opposition began after the first hour of march—around 4:30 P.M. Then two of the three battalions—Dobie's, on the northern route, and Fitch's, in the center—were unexpectedly engaged in fierce enemy hit-and-run attacks. Major Gough's reconnaissance unit, now commanded by Captain Allsop, was desperately trying to find a way to outflank the German forces and clear a path for Dobie's 1st Battalion. But, according to Allsop, "each movement we made was blunted by an enemy force in front of us." Trooper William Chandler of the reconnaissance unit remembers that as his C Troop explored the terrain, "German bullets came so close and so thick that they almost stung as they went by."

As the battalion approached Wolfheze, it was almost completely stopped. "We halted," Private Walter Boldock recalls. "Then we started off again. Then we halted and dug in. Next, we moved on again, changing direction. Our progress was dictated by the success of the lead companies. Mortar bombs and bullets

---

° Kussin, on Model's orders issued as the Field Marshal fled east that morning, had informed Hitler's headquarters of the landings and of Model's narrow escape. The Allied assault had caused Hitler hysterical concern. "If such a mess happens here," he conjectured, "here I sit with my own Supreme Command—Goering, Himmler, Ribbentrop. Well, then, this is a most worthwhile catch. That's obvious. I would not hesitate to risk two parachute divisions here if with one blow I could get my hands on the whole German command."

harassed us all the way." Beside a hedge, Boldock saw a sergeant he knew, lying seriously wounded. Farther ahead, he came upon the smoldering body of a lieutenant. He had been hit by a phosphorus bomb. To another soldier, Private Roy Edwards, "it just seemed we kept making a detour of the countryside and getting into running battles all afternoon."

The paratroopers were stunned by the ferociousness of the unanticipated enemy attacks. Private Andrew Milbourne, on the northern route, heard firing in the distance off to the south and was momentarily glad that the 1st Battalion had been given the assignment to hold the high ground north of Arnhem. Then, nearing Wolfheze, Milbourne realized that the column had swung south off the main road. He saw the railway station and, close to it, a tank. His first reaction was one of elation. "My God!" he thought, "Monty was right. The Second Army's here already!" Then, as the turret swung slowly around, Milbourne saw that a black cross was painted on the tank. Suddenly, he seemed to see Germans everywhere. He dived into a ditch and, raising his head cautiously, began looking for a good spot to position his Vickers machine gun.

Sergeant Reginald Isherwood saw the same tank. A jeep towing a light artillery piece drove up and started to turn around in order to engage it. "One of their sergeants yelled, 'We'd better fire before they do. Otherwise we've had it,'" Isherwood recalls. "The gun was swung around like lightning, but as our man yelled 'Fire!' I heard the German commander do the same. The Jerries must have got their shell off one tenth of a second sooner than us." The tank scored a direct hit. The jeep exploded and the gun crew were killed.

In the mounting confusion and the intense fire from all sides, it was now clear to Colonel Dobie that the opposition in front of him was heavier than anyone had expected. Nor did he believe it was still possible to occupy the high ground north of Arnhem. He was unable to raise Brigadier Lathbury by radio, and his casualties were mounting by the minute. Dobie decided to side-slip the battalion still farther south and attempt to join up with Frost going for the main Arnhem bridge.

The breakdown of communications and subsequent lack of direction was making it impossible for battalion commanders to know with any clarity what was happening now. In the unfamiliar countryside, with maps that often proved highly inaccurate, companies and platoons were frequently out of touch with one another. At a crossroads near the stretch of highway where men of Colonel Fitch's 3rd Battalion had killed General Kussin, the British caught the full brunt of SS Major Krafft's rocket-propelled mortars and machine guns. The marching columns broke as men scattered into the woods. The screeching mortars, exploding in air bursts above their heads, hurled deadly fragments in every direction.

Signalman Stanley Heyes remembers the intense enemy harassment vividly. He sprinted for some woods and dropped a spare radio transmitter; bending to recover it he was struck in the ankle. Heyes managed to crawl into the woods. As he sank down in the underbrush, he realized that the man alongside him was German. "He was young and as frightened as I was," Heyes says, "but he used my field dressing on my ankle. A short time later we both were wounded again by the mortar fire and we just lay there waiting for someone to pick us up." Heyes and the young German would remain together until well after dark, when British stretcher-bearers found and evacuated them.

Like the 1st Battalion, the 3rd too was pinned down. After two hours on the road, both battalions had covered a bare two and a half miles. Now, Colonel Fitch reached the same conclusion as Dobie on the upper road; he too would have to find an alternate route to the Arnhem bridge. Time was precious, and the bridge was still a good four miles away.

In the woods around Wolfheze SS Major Sepp Krafft was convinced he was surrounded. He estimated that the British outnumbered his understrength battalion by twenty to one. But, although he considered his defense "insane," he could hardly believe the success of his blocking action. The rocket-propelled mortars had created havoc among the British, and his men now reported that paratroopers moving along the Utrecht-Arnhem road were halted in some places, and at others appeared to be abandoning the main road entirely. Krafft still believed that his was the only German unit in the area, and he had no illusions about stopping the British for long. He was running out of mortar ammunition and suffering heavy casualties, and one of his lieutenants had deserted. Still, Krafft was ebullient about "the courageous impetuosity of my young lads." The ambitious Krafft, who would later write a fulsome self-serving report to Himmler on his Grenadier Training and Reserve Battalion's actions, had no idea that his "young lads" were now being bolstered by the tanks, artillery and armored cars of Lieutenant Colonel Walter Harzer's Hohenstaufen Division only a mile or two east of Krafft's own headquarters.

Major Freddie Gough was totally baffled. Urquhart's message summoning him back to Division had carried no hint of what the General had in mind. When he left the Leopard route of the 1st Battalion, Gough brought back with him four escort jeeps and troops of his reconnaissance unit. Now, at Division headquarters, Urquhart's chief of staff, Colonel Charles Mackenzie, could not enlighten him either. The General, Mackenzie said, had gone off in search of Brigadier Lathbury, whose headquarters was following Colonel Frost's battalion along the southern, Lion route. Taking his escort, Gough set out once more. Surely, someplace along the route, he would find either one officer or the other.

☆ 12 ☆

Gᴇɴᴇʀᴀʟ UʀQᴜʜᴀʀᴛ's ᴊᴇᴇᴘ sped down the Utrecht-Arnhem
highway and turned south off the main artery onto a side road
that led him to Frost's Lion route. Within a few minutes he caught
up with the rear elements of the 2nd Battalion. They were moving
single file, along both sides of the road. Urquhart could hear firing
in the distance, but it seemed to him "there was a lack of urgency.
Everyone appeared to be moving slowly." Driving swiftly along
the cobbled road, Urquhart reached Frost's headquarters company only to discover that Frost was up with the leading units,
which had run into German opposition. "I tried to impart a sense
of urgency that I hoped would be conveyed to Frost," Urquhart
writes, "and told them about the ill-fortune of the Recco Squadron." Learning that Lathbury had gone up to the middle road to
see how the 3rd Battalion was doing, Urquhart retraced his
route. Once again, he and Gough would miss each other by
minutes.

Reaching the rear elements of the 3rd Battalion on the Tiger
route, the General was told that Lathbury had gone forward. He
followed. At a crossroads on the Utrecht-Arnhem road, Urquhart
found the Brigadier. The area was under devastating mortar fire.
"Some of these bombs were falling with unsettling accuracy on
the crossroads and in the woodland where many of the Third
Battalion were under cover," Urquhart was later to write. "This
was the first real evidence to come my way of the speed and
determination of the German reaction."[*]

[*] Major General R. E. Urquhart, C.B., D.S.O. (with Wilfred Greatorex), *Arnhem*,
p. 40.

Taking cover in a slit trench, Urquhart and Lathbury discussed the situation. Both officers were worried about the slow progress of the brigade, and now the critical lack of communications was paralyzing their own efforts to command. Lathbury was completely out of touch with the 1st Battalion and had only intermittent communication with Frost. It was apparent that both were able to direct operations only in the area where they physically happened to be. For the moment, Lathbury's concern was to get the 3rd Battalion off the crossroads, out of the surrounding woods and on the move again. Urquhart decided to try to contact Division headquarters on his jeep's radio. As he neared the vehicle, he saw it had been struck by a mortar and his signalman was badly wounded. Although the radio set seemed undamaged, Urquhart could not raise Division. "I cursed the appalling communications," Urquhart later wrote. "Lathbury dissuaded me from attempting to go back to my own headquarters. The enemy was now thick between us and the landing zones . . . I decided he was right . . . and I stayed. But it was at this point that I realized I was losing control of the situation."

The men of the 1st and 3rd battalions were engaging in constant, bitter skirmishes. Hardened and desperate Waffen SS troopers, inferior in numbers but bolstered by half-tracks, artillery and tanks, were reducing the British advance on the two upper roads to a crawl. In the confusion, men were separated from their officers and from one another as companies scattered into the woods or fought along side roads and in the back gardens of houses. The Red Devils had recovered from the initial surprise of the German armored strength and, though taking heavy casualties, individually and in small groups they were striking back tenaciously. Still, there was little chance that the 1st and 3rd battalions could reach their Arnhem objectives as planned. Now everything depended upon Colonel John Frost's 2nd Battalion, moving steadily along the lower Rhine road, the secondary route that the Germans had largely dismissed.

Although Frost's battalion had been held up briefly several

times by enemy fire, he had refused to allow his men to scatter or deploy. His spearheading A Company, commanded by Major Digby Tatham-Warter, pressed forward, leaving stragglers to join the companies coming up behind. From prisoners taken by the advance parties, Frost learned that an SS company was believed to be covering the western approaches of Arnhem. Using some captured transport as well as their own jeeps to scout ahead and to the sides, the battalion moved steadily on. A little after 6 P.M., the first of Frost's objectives, the railway bridge over the Lower Rhine slightly southeast of Oosterbeek, came into view. According to plan, Major Victor Dover's C Company peeled off and headed for the river. The bridge looked empty and undefended as they approached. Lieutenant Peter Barry, twenty-one, was ordered to take his platoon across. "It was quiet when we started out," Barry recalls. "As we ran across the fields I noticed that there were dead cattle everywhere." Barry's platoon was within 300 yards of the bridge when he saw "a German run onto the bridge from the other side. He reached the middle, knelt down, and started doing something. Immediately, I told one section to open fire and a second section to rush the bridge. By this time, the German had disappeared."

Barry recalls that they "got onto the bridge and began racing across at full speed. Suddenly, there was a tremendous explosion and the bridge went up in our faces." Captain Eric Mackay of the Royal Engineers felt the ground shake under the impact. "A yellow-orange flame punched up and then black smoke rose over the bridge. I think the second span from the south bank was blown," Mackay says. On the bridge, under cover of smoke bombs, Lieutenant Barry ordered his men off the wreckage and back to the northern bank. As the platoon began to move, Germans hidden across the river opened fire. Barry was hit in the leg and arm and two other men were wounded. Watching the troopers return through the smoke and fire, Mackay, who had been uneasy about the operation from the beginning, remembers thinking, "Well, there goes number one." Colonel Frost was more philosophical. "I knew one of the three bridges was gone, but it was the least important. I didn't realize then what a disadvantage it would be." It was now 6:30 P.M. and there were two more bridges to go.

✵ 13 ✵

I T HAD TAKEN THE Hohenstaufen Division engineers five hours to reassemble all the tanks, half-tracks and armored personnel carriers that Harzer had planned to send back to Germany. Newly decorated Captain Paul Gräbner, his forty-vehicle reconnaissance battalion ready, now set out from Hoenderloo Barracks, north of Arnhem, and drove quickly south. Harzer had instructed him to make a sweep of the area between Arnhem and Nijmegen to assess the strength of the Allied airborne troops in that area. Gräbner raced swiftly through Arnhem and, by radio, informed Hohenstaufen headquarters that the city seemed almost deserted. There was no sign of enemy troops. A little before 7 P.M., Gräbner's unit crossed over the great Arnhem highway bridge. A mile past the southern end, Gräbner stopped his car to report, "No enemy. No paratroopers." Mile after mile, his light armored cars slowly patrolling both sides of the highway, Gräbner's radio messages conveyed the same information. At Nijmegen itself the news was unchanged. On orders of Hohenstaufen headquarters, Gräbner was then instructed to further patrol the outskirts of Nijmegen and then return to headquarters.

Gräbner's unit and the forward elements of Frost's 2nd Battalion had missed each other by approximately an hour. Even as Gräbner had driven out of Arnhem, Frost's men were in the city itself and were stealthily approaching their remaining objectives. Inexplicably, despite General Bittrich's explicit instructions, Harzer had completely failed to safeguard the Arnhem bridge.

14

I T WAS GROWING DARK as Colonel Frost quickened the battalion's pace toward the next objective, the pontoon crossing less than a mile west of the Arnhem bridge. Major Digby Tatham-Warter's A Company, still in the lead, was again momentarily held up on the high ground at the western outskirts of Arnhem. Enemy armored cars and machine guns had forced the company off the road and into the back gardens of nearby houses. Coming up behind, Frost found ten Germans guarded by a lone A Company man and, as he was later to write, surmised that "Digby's back-garden maneuver had been completely successful and that the company had rushed on again." Frost returned to the battalion. In the dusk, bursts of fire sporadically swept the road but as the men moved along, they passed damaged vehicles and a number of dead and wounded Germans—clear evidence, Frost thought, of "Digby's quite satisfactory progress."

Moving rapidly through the streets of Arnhem, the battalion reached the pontoon bridge and halted, faced with their second setback. The center section of the bridge had been removed and it was useless. As Captain Mackay stood looking at the dismantled crossing, he decided that "it was typical of the whole cocked-up operation. My one thought was, 'Now we've got to get that other bloody bridge.' " He stared off in the distance. Barely a mile away, the great concrete-and-steel span was silhouetted against the last light.

On the 3rd Battalion's Tiger route, moving haltingly toward Arnhem, General Urquhart knew with certainty that he was stranded. In the growing darkness, with enemy forays constantly harassing the march, there was no possibility of his returning to Division headquarters. His mood was bleak. "I wished with every step that I knew what was going on elsewhere." Just before nightfall, Urquhart learned that the 3rd's leading companies had reached the outskirts of Oosterbeek "near someplace called the Hartenstein Hotel. . . . We were making little progress," Urquhart was later to write, "and Lathbury, after a discussion with Fitch, the battalion commander, called a halt."

In a large house set well back from the road, Urquhart and Lathbury prepared to spend the night. The owner of the house, a tall, middle-aged Dutchman, brushed aside the General's apologies for inconveniencing him and his wife, and gave the two officers a downstairs front room overlooking the main road. Urquhart was restless and unable to relax. "I kept checking to see if any contact had been made with either Gough or Frost, but there was nothing from my headquarters or from anyone else."

The great bridge loomed ahead. The concrete ramps alone were immense complexes unto themselves with roads running beneath them and along the river bank from west to east. On either side the rooftops of houses and factory buildings came up to the level of the ramps. In the twilight, the massive approaches and the high-arched girders spanning the Rhine looked awesome and intimidating. Here finally was the main objective—the pivot of Montgomery's audacious plan—and to reach it Frost's men had fought on the march for nearly seven hours.

Now, as lead elements of the 2nd Battalion neared the bridge, Lieutenant Robin Vlasto, in command of one of A Company's platoons, was amazed by "its incredible great height." Vlasto noted "pillboxes at each end, and even in the general air of desertion, they looked threatening." In darkness A Company quietly took up positions beneath the huge supports at the northern end. From above them came the slow rumble of traffic.

Captain Eric Mackay of the Royal Engineers, approaching the bridge through a mosaic of streets, reached a small square leading to the ramp. He remembers that "the quietness as we went through the streets was oppressive, and all around us there seemed to be soft movement. Men were beginning to feel the strain, and I wanted to get that bridge as quickly as we could." Suddenly the darkness was ripped by German fire from a side street. One of the engineers' explosives trolleys went up in flames, and the men were clearly illuminated. Instantly, Mackay ordered his men with their equipment across the square. They dashed over, defying the German fire. Within a few minutes, without losing a man, they were at the bridge. Studying the terrain below the northern ramp, Mackay saw four houses on the east side. "One of them was a school and it was on the corner of a crossroads," he remembers. "I thought that whoever held these houses held the bridge." Mackay promptly ordered his engineers into the school.

Shortly after 8 P.M., Colonel Frost and the battalion headquarters arrived. Frost had sent Major Douglas Crawley's B Company to the high ground above the nearby railway embankment with antitank guns to protect the battalion's left flank, freeing A Company to dash for the bridge.° C Company, under Major Dover, was instructed to follow the forward elements into the city and seize the German commandant's headquarters. Now, at the bridge, Frost was unable to raise either company by radio. Quickly he dispatched messengers to determine their whereabouts.

Deciding not to wait, Frost ordered A Company platoons onto

° Frost recalls that "a map I had taken from a German prisoner . . . showed the routes of an enemy armored-car patrol unit and I realized that the German strength was to my left."

the bridge. As the men began to move across, the Germans came to life. Troopers were raked with fire from the pillbox at the northern end and by a lone armored car on the southern end of the bridge itself. A platoon, aided by Eric Mackay's sappers carrying flamethrowers, began to move through the top floors of houses whose roofs and attics were at eye level with the ramp. Simultaneously, Lieutenant Vlasto's platoon worked its way through basements and cellars, going from house to house until it reached Mackay's locations. In position, they attacked the pillbox. As the flamethrowers went into action, Frost recalls that "all hell seemed to be let loose. The sky lit up, and there was the noise of machine-gun fire, a succession of explosions, the crackling of burning ammunition and the thump of a cannon. A wooden building nearby was wreathed in flames, and there were screams of agony and fear."[*] Now, too, Frost could hear the crash of Vlasto's Piat[†] bombs smashing into the pillbox. Suddenly, the brief savage battle was over. The guns in the pillbox fell silent and through the fires, Frost saw German soldiers staggering toward his men. A Company had successfully cleared the north end of the bridge and it was theirs. But now, hampering fires and exploding ammunition made it suicidal to risk a second rush to grab the southern side. Only half an hour earlier, Frost could have succeeded.[‡] But now, on the south bank, a group of SS Panzer Grenadiers had taken up positions.

Frost attempted to contact Major Crawley once more. He wanted to locate boats or barges in which Crawley's company could cross the river and attack the Germans on the southern side. Again, radio communications were out. Worse, messengers could not even find the company; and, they reported, there were

[*] Several accounts state that the flamethrowers' aim was diverted and instead of hitting the pillbox, the fiery liquid hit several huts containing explosives.
[†] A short-range, spring-loaded British antitank gun weighing 33 pounds and capable of firing a projectile that could penetrate four inches of tempered armor plate.
[‡] According to Dutch Police Sergeant Johannes van Kuijk the bridge was deserted and without guards when he came on duty at 7:30 that evening. Earlier, according to Van Kuijk, when the airborne landings began, the bridge garrison of twenty-five World War I veterans deserted their post.

no boats to be seen. As for C Company, the patrol sent out to contact them were pinned down and heavily engaged near the German commandant's headquarters.

Grimly Frost's men looked across the Arnhem bridge. How strong were the Germans holding the southern end? Even now, A Company believed there was a chance of seizing the southern end by a surprise attack across the river, if only the men and boats could be found.

But that opportunity had passed. In one of the great ironies of the Arnhem battle, the Lower Rhine could have been crossed within the first hour of landing. Exactly seven miles west, at the village of Heveadorp—through which Frost's battalion had marched en route to their objectives—a large cable ferry, capable of carrying automobiles and passengers, had operated back and forth all day on its normal passage across the Lower Rhine between Heveadorp on the north bank and Driel on the south. Frost knew nothing about the ferry. Nor was it ever listed as one of Urquhart's objectives. In the meticulous planning of Market-Garden an important key to the taking of the Arnhem bridge—the ferry at Driel—had been totally overlooked.°

Major Freddie Gough had finally overtaken Lathbury's brigade headquarters, following Frost's battalion on the Lion route. Quickly he sought out Major Tony Hibbert, the second in com-

---

° In the official orders issued to Urquhart, no reference to the Driel ferry as an objective seems to exist. R.A.F. reconnaissance photographs, used at briefings, show it clearly and one must assume that at some stage of the planning it was discussed. However, General Urquhart, when I interviewed him on the subject, told me "I can't recall that the ferry ever came up." When Urquhart finally learned of the ferry's existence, it was too late to be of any use. Says Urquhart, "By that time I did not have enough men to put across the river." In oral orders, however, the engineers were warned that "the seizure of all ferries, barges and tugs becomes of paramount importance to assist the subsequent advance of XXX Corps." Obviously, however, in the last-minute stages of the planning these orders apparently carried lower priority, for they were never formally issued. "No one told us about the ferry at Driel," Colonel Frost told the author, "and it could have made all the difference."

mand. "Where's the General and the Brigadier?" Gough asked. Hibbert didn't know. "They're together someplace," he told Gough, "but they've both gone off." Gough was now totally confused. "I didn't know what to do," he recalls. "I tried to contact Division without success, so I just decided to keep on going after Frost." Leaving Hibbert, Gough set out once more.

It was dark when Gough and his troopers drove into Arnhem and found Frost and his men holding positions near the northern end of the bridge. Immediately Gough asked where Urquhart was. Like Hibbert, Frost had no idea. He assumed Urquhart was back with Division. Once more Gough tried his radio. Now adding to his anxiety was the absence of any news of his own reconnaissance forces near Wolfheze. But again he could make no contact with anyone. Ordering his tired men to a building close by the bridge, Gough climbed to the roof just in time to see the whole southern end of the bridge "go up in flames" as Frost's men made their first attempt to seize the far end. "I heard this tremendous explosion and the whole end of the bridge seemed to be on fire. I remember somebody saying 'We've come all this way just to have the damn bridge burn down.'" Gough himself was momentarily alarmed. Then, through the smoke he saw that only the pillbox and some ammunition shacks were destroyed. Concerned and weary, Gough turned in for a few hours' rest. He had traveled route after route all day in search of Urquhart. Now, at the bridge, at least one problem was solved. He was where he had set out to be and there he would stay.

There was little more that Lieutenant Colonel Frost could do this night, except to guard the northern end of the bridge from enemy attacks on the southern side. He still had no contact with his missing companies and now, in a house on a corner overlooking the bridge, Frost set up battalion headquarters. Lance Corporal Harold Back of the 2nd Battalion's cipher section remembers that from the front window of the house, the headquarters personnel could look out on the ramp. "The side window of the room gave us a direct view of the bridge itself," says Back. "Our signalers stuck their antennas through the roof and moved their sets constantly, but they couldn't make contact with anybody."

Shortly after, Brigade headquarters arrived and set up in the attic of a house near Frost's. After conferring with his officers, Frost thought it was now obvious that the 1st and 3rd battalions had either been held up on the Tiger and Leopard routes or were fighting north of the bridge somewhere in Arnhem. Without communications, it was impossible to tell what had happened. But if the two battalions did not reach Arnhem during the hours of darkness, the Germans would have the precious time necessary to close the area between Frost's men and the rest of the division. Additionally, Frost was worried that the great bridge might still be blown. In the opinion of the engineers, the heat from fires had already destroyed any fuses laid from the bridge to the town and all visible cables had already been cut by sappers. Still, no one knew exactly where other cables might be hidden. And, as Frost recalls, "the fires prevented even one man from being able to get on to the bridge to remove any charges that might still be there."

But the northern end of the Arnhem bridge was in Frost's hands and he and his courageous men had no intention of giving it up. Although he worried about his missing companies and the rest of the division, he did not show his concern. Visiting various sections now billeted in several houses near the ramp, he found his men "in great heart, as they had every reason to be." As Private James Sims recalls, "We felt quite pleased with ourselves, with the Colonel making jokes and inquiring about our comfort."

At battalion headquarters, Frost himself now settled down for the first time during the day. Sipping from a large mug of tea, he thought that, all in all, the situation was not too bad. "We had come eight miles through close, difficult country, to capture our objective within seven hours of landing in Holland . . . a very fine feat of arms indeed." Although restless, Frost, like his men, was optimistic. He now had a force numbering about five hundred men of various units, and he had every faith that his own

KADE

EUSEBIUS BINNEN SINGEL

EMBANKMENT

EUSEBIUS BUITEN SINGEL

WESTERVOOTSCHE DYK

NORTHERN RAMP

NIEUWE KADE

CAPT. ERIC MACKAY'S POSITION

GRENADIERS

N

missing companies would reach him at the bridge. In any case, he would only have to hold, at most, for another forty-eight hours—until the tanks of General Horrocks' XXX Corps arrived.

✻15✻

FROM BERLIN TO THE WESTERN FRONT, the German high command was stunned by the sudden Allied attack. Only in Arnhem, where the British 1st Airborne Division had dropped almost on top of General Bittrich's two panzer divisions, was the reaction both fierce and quick. Elsewhere, baffled and confused commanders tried to determine whether the startling events of September 17 were indeed the opening phase of an invasion of the Reich. A ground attack by the British out of Belgium had been anticipated. All available reserves, including General Von Zangen's Fifteenth Army, so worn down that men had little else but the rifles they carried, had been thrown into defense positions to hold against that threat. Trenches had been dug and strategic positions built in an all-out effort to force the British to fight for every foot of ground.

No one had foreseen that airborne forces would be used simultaneously with the British land advance. Were these airborne attacks the prelude to an invasion of Holland by sea, as Berlin feared? In the hours of darkness, while staff officers tried to analyze the situation, reports of additional airborne attacks further confused the picture. American paratroopers, their strength unknown and their units still unidentified, were in the Eindhoven-Nijmegen area; and the British 1st Airborne Division had clearly landed around Arnhem. But now new messages told of paratroopers in the vicinity of Utrecht, and a totally bewildering report claimed that airborne forces had landed in Warsaw, Poland.°

At Field Marshal Gerd von Rundstedt's headquarters in Koblenz, the general reaction was one of astonishment.† The crusty, aristocratic Von Rundstedt was not so much surprised at the nature of the attack as by the man who, he reasoned, must be directing it—Montgomery. Initially, Von Rundstedt doubted that these sudden and apparently combined land-and-air operations were the opening of Eisenhower's offensive to invade the Reich. The Field Marshal had long been certain that Patton and the American Third Army driving toward the Saar posed the real danger. To combat that threat, Von Rundstedt had committed his best troops to repulse Patton's racing tanks. Now Germany's most renowned soldier was caught temporarily off balance. Never had he expected Eisenhower's main offensive to be led by Montgomery, whom he had always considered "overly cautious, habit-ridden and systematic."

He was astounded by the boldness of Montgomery's move. The messages pouring in from Model's headquarters carried a note of hysteria attesting all the more to the surprise and gravity of the attack: "We must reckon with more airborne landings being made at night . . . the enemy obviously believes his attack to be of major importance and the British have achieved considerable initial success against Student and pushed forward to Valkenswaard . . . the position here is particularly critical . . . the lack of fast, strong reserves is increasing our difficulties . . . the general situation of Army Group B, stretched as it is to the limits, is critical . . . we require, as fast as possible, panzers, artillery, heavy mobile antitank weapons, antiaircraft units, and it is

---

° The R.A.F. did drop dummy paratroops over a wide area around Utrecht, diverting some German troops for days. No troops were dropped on Warsaw and the report may have been garbled in transmission or, more simply, may have been the result of unfounded rumor.

† "When we first informed Von Rundstedt's headquarters of the airborne attack," Colonel Hans von Tempelhof, Model's operations chief, told me, "OB West seemed hardly perturbed. In fact the reaction was almost callously normal. It quickly changed."

absolutely essential that we have fighters in the sky day and night . . ."

Model ended with these words: ". . . the main concentration of the Allies is on the northern wing of our front." It was one of the few times Von Rundstedt had ever respected the opinion of the officer he had caustically referred to as having the makings of a good sergeant major. In that fragment of his message, Model had stripped away Von Rundstedt's last doubts about who was responsible for the startling developments. The "northern wing" of Army Group B *was* Montgomery.

During the night hours it was impossible to estimate the strength of the Allied airborne forces in Holland, but Von Rundstedt was convinced that further landings could be expected. It would now be necessary not only to plug gaps all along the German front but to find reserves for Model's Army Group B at the same time. Once again, Von Rundstedt was forced to gamble. Messages went out from his headquarters transferring units from their positions facing the Americans at Aachen. The moves were risky but essential. These units would have to travel north immediately, and their commitment in the line might take forty-eight hours at minimum. Von Rundstedt issued further orders to defense areas along Germany's northwest frontier, calling for all available armor and antiaircraft units to proceed to the quiet backwater of Holland where, the Field Marshal was now convinced, imminent danger to the Third Reich lay. Even as he worked steadily on through the night to shore up his defenses, Germany's Iron Knight pondered the strangeness of the situation. He was still amazed that the officer in charge of this great Allied offensive was Montgomery.

It was late evening when the staff car carrying General Wilhelm Bittrich from his headquarters at Doetinchem arrived in the darkened streets of Arnhem. Bittrich was determined to see for himself what was happening. As he reconnoitered through the city, fires were still burning and debris littered the streets—the effect of the morning's bombing. Dead soldiers and smoldering vehicles in many areas attested, as Bittrich was later to say, to "the turbulent fighting that had taken place." Yet, he had no clear picture of what was happening. Returning to his own headquarters, Bittrich learned from reports received from two women telephone operators in the Arnhem Post headquarters—whom he was later to decorate with the Iron Cross—that the great highway bridge had been taken by British paratroopers. Bittrich was infuriated. His specific order to Harzer to hold the bridge had not been carried out. Now it was crucial that the Nijmegen bridge over the Waal river be secured before the Americans in the south could seize it. Bittrich's only chance of success was to crush the Allied assault along the corridor and squeeze the British to a standstill in the Arnhem area. The paratroopers now on the north end of the Arnhem bridge and the scattered battalions struggling to reach them must be totally destroyed.

The top-secret Market-Garden plan that had fallen into Colonel General Kurt Student's possession finally reached Field Marshal Model at his new headquarters. He had abandoned the gardener's cottage on the Doetinchem castle grounds and moved about five miles southeast near the small village of Terborg. It had taken Student the best part of ten hours to locate the Field Marshal and transmit the document by radio. Arriving in three parts and now decoded, Market-Garden lay revealed.

Model and his staff studied it intently. Before them was Montgomery's entire plan: the names of the airborne divisions employed, the successive air and resupply lifts ranging over a three-day period, the exact location of the landing and drop zones, the crucial bridge objectives—even the flight routes of the aircraft involved. Model, as Harzer was later to learn from the Field Marshal himself, called the plan "fantastic." It was so fantastic that in these critical hours Model refused to believe it.

The plans were too pat, too detailed for credibility. Model suggested to his staff that the very preciseness of the document argued against its authenticity. He stressed again his own firm conviction that the landings west of Arnhem were the spearhead of a large-scale airborne attack toward the Ruhr, via Bocholt and Münster, some forty miles east. Additional airborne landings should be expected, he warned, and once assembled would undoubtedly swerve north and then east. Model's reasoning was not without validity. As he told his staff, "If we are to believe these plans and are to assume that the Arnhem bridge is the true objective, why were not troops dropped directly on the bridge? Here, they arrive on vast open areas suitable for assembly, and moreover, eight miles to the west."

Model did not inform General Bittrich of the document. "I never realized until after the war," says Bittrich, "that the Market-Garden plans had fallen into our hands. I have no idea why Model did not tell me. In any case, the plans would simply have confirmed my own opinion that the important thing to do was prevent the link-up between the airborne troops and the British Second Army—and for that, they certainly needed the bridges."[*] One officer under Bittrich's command did learn of the document. Lieutenant Colonel Harzer seemed to be the only officer outside the Field Marshal's staff with whom Model talked about the plan. Harzer recalls that "Model was always prepared for the worst, so he did not discount it entirely. As he told me, he had no intention of being caught by the short hairs." Only time would tell the Germans whether the document was, in fact, genuine. Although the temperamental, erratic Field Marshal was not fully prepared to accept the evidence before him, most of his staff were impressed. With the Market-Garden plan in their hands, Model's headquarters alerted all antiaircraft units already on the move of the drops that the plan said would take place a few hours later.

One assumption, at least, was laid to rest. Lieutenant Gustav

[*] OB West was not informed of the captured Market-Garden plans either; nor is there any mention in Model's reports to Von Rundstedt of the documents. For some reason Model thought so little of the plans that he did not pass them on to higher headquarters.

Sedelhauser, the general-headquarters administrative officer, recalls that on the basis of the captured documents, Model was now of the opinion that he and his Oosterbeek headquarters had not been the objective of the airborne assault after all.

�֍16✗

At THE PRECISE TIME that Lieutenant Colonel John Frost secured the northern end of the Arnhem bridge, a cautious approach to another prime objective eleven miles away was only just beginning. The five-span highway bridge over the Waal river at Nijmegen in the 82nd Airborne's central sector of the corridor was the last crossing over which the tanks of General Horrocks' XXX Corps would pass on their drive to Arnhem.

With spectacular success, Brigadier General James M. Gavin's 504th paratroopers had grabbed the crucial Grave bridge eight miles southwest of Nijmegen; and, at about 7:30 P.M., units of the 504th and 505th regiments secured a crossing over the Maas-Waal Canal at the village of Heumen, less than five miles due east of Grave. Gavin's hope of capturing all three canal crossings and a railroad bridge was in vain. The bridges were blown or severely damaged by the Germans before the 82nd could grab them. Yet, within six hours of landing, Gavin's troopers had forged a route over which the British ground forces would travel. Additionally, patrols of the 505th Regiment probing the area between the 82nd's drop zones near the Groesbeek Heights and the Reichswald encountered only light resistance; and, by nightfall, other troopers of the 508th Regiment had secured a 3½-mile stretch of woods along the Holland-German border north of the Groesbeek

ASSAULT AREA
U.S. 82nd AIRBORNE DIV.
SEPT. 17, 1944

WAAL R.

HOLLAND

GERMANY

WAAL R.

Wyler

508 REGT.

505 REGT.

Groesbeek

505 REGT.

REICHSWALD

palacios

GROESBEEK HEIGHTS

to Arnhem

Lent

NIJMEGEN

RR. BRIDGE

WAAL R.

MAAS-WAAL CANAL

Mook

MAAS R.

504 REGT.

Overasselt

Grave

1 CO. OF 504 REGT.

N

0   Miles   3

drop zone and running to the southeastern outskirts of Nijmegen. Now, with three of the 82nd's four key objectives in hand, everything depended upon the capture of the 1,960-foot-long road bridge at Nijmegen.

Although General Browning had directed Gavin not to go for the Nijmegen crossing until the high ground around Groesbeek was secured, Gavin was confident that all the 82nd's objectives could be taken on this first day. Evaluating the situation some twenty-four hours before the jump, Gavin had called in the 508th's commander, Colonel Roy E. Lindquist, and directed him to send one battalion racing for the bridge. In the surprise and confusion of the airborne landings, Gavin reasoned, the gamble was well worth taking. "I cautioned Lindquist about the dangers of getting caught in streets," Gavin remembers, "and pointed out that the way to get the bridge was to approach from east of the city without going through built-up areas." Whether by misunderstanding or a desire to clean up his initial assignments, Lindquist's own recollection was that he was not to commit his troopers in an assault on the bridge until the regiment's other objectives had been achieved. To the 1st Battalion, commanded by Lieutenant Colonel Shields Warren, Jr., Lindquist assigned the task of holding protective positions along the Groesbeek-Nijmegen highway about a mile and a quarter southeast of the city. Warren was to defend the area and link up with the regiment's remaining two battalions to the west and east. Only when these missions were accomplished, Warren recalled, was he to prepare to go into Nijmegen. Thus, instead of driving for the bridge from the flat farming areas to the east, Warren's battalion found itself squarely in the center of those very built-up areas Gavin had sought to avoid.

It was nightfall before Warren achieved his other objectives. Now with precious time lost, lead companies began to move slowly through the quiet, almost deserted streets of Nijmegen. The main objective was to reach the traffic circle leading to the southern approaches of the bridge. There was a diversionary target as well. The Dutch underground reported that the detonating mechanism for destroying the great crossing was situated in the main post-office building. This vital information reached Warren's units only after they had begun moving toward the bridge. A platoon was hurriedly sent to the post office, where, after subduing the German guards, engineers cut wires and blew up what they believed to be the detonating controls. Whether this apparatus was, in fact, actually hooked up to explosives on the bridge, no one would ever know for certain, but now, at least, electrical circuits and switchboards were destroyed. When the platoon attempted to withdraw to rejoin the main force they found that the enemy had closed in behind them. They were cut off and for the next three days would be forced to hold out in the post office until help arrived.

Meanwhile, as the remainder of Warren's force approached a park that led toward the bridge, they came suddenly under intense machine-gun and armored-car fire. Captain Arie D. Bestebreurtje, the Dutch officer assigned to the 82nd, remembers that "guns suddenly opened up on us, and I could see the flashes of fire from the muzzles. They seemed to be all around us." Before he could raise his carbine to fire, Bestebreurtje was hit in the left hand and elbow and the right index finger.* To Corporal James R. Blue, the eerie battle raging in the blacked-out streets was like a nightmare. "Right away we were engaged in hand-to-hand combat," Blue remembers. He was moving through the streets with Private First Class Ray Johnson, both armed with M-1 rifles with fixed bayonets, when they came face to face with SS troops. As Johnson tried to get one of the Germans with his bayonet, Blue went after an officer with a trench knife. "Our orders were not to fire. If we came to close combat we were to use knives and bayonets. But," Blue recalls, "that trench knife seemed mighty short, so I used my Tommy gun. That closed that chapter, but almost immediately a self-propelled gun began to fire in our direction and we moved up to the park and tied in with other

* Several days later, Bestebreurtje was told by doctors that the finger must be amputated. "I told them absolutely not," Bestebreurtje says. "It was my finger and I was not going to have it amputated. Besides, it would have ruined my piano playing." He still has the finger.

platoons." Private James Allardyce remembers hearing a call for medics up front, but "bullets were whistling down the street and there was so much confusion in the darkness that men did not know where others were. We set up a perimeter defense around a modern brick schoolhouse. Out front we heard German voices and the moaning and cries of the wounded. We couldn't make it to the bridge. Finally it came through to us that the Jerries had stopped us."

As indeed they had. Captain Paul Gräbner's Reconnaissance Battalion, which had missed Frost at the Arnhem bridge, had arrived in Nijmegen well in advance of the late-starting Americans.

By midnight on this first day of the mightiest airborne assault in history, British and American paratroops were on, or fighting toward, their major objectives. Through long hours of march and savage encounters with an unexpectedly strong and tenacious enemy, they had gained most of the objectives that the planners had expected them to take swiftly and with ease. From the gallant men of Colonel John Frost's 2nd Battalion clinging to the north end of the Arnhem bridge, all along the corridor south to where Colonel Robert Sink's 101st troopers struggled to repair the bridge at Son, the mood was one of fierce determination; they must hold open the highway along which the British Second Army tanks and infantry would drive. On this midnight, troopers did not doubt that relief was on the way or that reinforcements and supplies, scheduled to arrive on the eighteenth, would further bolster their position. Despite heavy casualties, confusion, and communications setbacks, the men of the airborne army were completely optimistic. All in all, it had not been a bad Sunday outing.

✲17✲

THERE WAS A RED GLOW in the sky over Arnhem as the speeding car bringing Major General Heinz Harmel back from Berlin neared the city. Apprehensive and tired after the long trip, Harmel arrived at the Frundsberg Division headquarters in Ruurlo, only to find that his command post was now situated in Velp, approximately three miles northeast of Arnhem. There, he found his chief of staff, Lieutenant Colonel Paetsch, looking exhausted. "Thank God you're back!" Paetsch said. Quickly he briefed Harmel on the day's events and on the orders received from General Bittrich. "I was dumfounded," Harmel recalls. "Everything seemed confused and uncertain. I was very tired, yet the gravity of the situation was such that I called Bittrich and told him I was coming to see him."

Bittrich had not slept either. As Harmel was shown in, Bittrich began immediately to outline the situation. Angry and frustrated, he bent over his maps. "British paratroopers have landed here, west of Arnhem," he told Harmel. "We have no idea of their actual strength or intentions." Pointing to Nijmegen and Eindhoven, the corps commander said, "American airborne forces have secured lodgments in these two areas. Simultaneously, Montgomery's forces have attacked north from the Meuse-Escaut Canal. My belief is that the object is to split our forces. In my opinion, the objectives are the bridges. Once these are secured, Montgomery can drive directly up to the center of Holland and from there, into the Ruhr." Bittrich waved his hands. "Model disagrees. He still believes further airborne forces will be dropped north of the Rhine, east and west of Arnhem and march toward the Ruhr."

Harzer's Hohenstaufen Division, Bittrich went on to explain, had been ordered to mop up the British west and north of Arnhem. The armed forces commander in the Netherlands, General Christiansen, had been directed to send in his forces—a mixture of defense and training battalions—under command of Lieutenant General Hans von Tettau. Their mission was to aid the Hohenstaufen Division on the flanks in an effort to overrun the British landing and drop zones.

The Frundsberg Division, Bittrich continued, was charged with all activities to the east of Arnhem and south to Nijmegen. Stabbing the map with his finger, Bittrich told Harmel, "The Nijmegen bridge must be held at all costs. Additionally the Arnhem bridge and the area all the way south to Nijmegen is your responsibility." Bittrich paused and paced the room. "Your problems," he told Harmel, "have been made more difficult. Harzer failed to leave armored units at the north end of the Arnhem bridge. The British are now there."

As he listened, Harmel realized with growing alarm that with the Arnhem bridge in British hands, there was no way to get his armor quickly across the Rhine and down to Nijmegen. Nor was there another bridge crossing over the river east of the Arnhem bridge. His entire division would have to be taken over the Rhine at a ferry landing in the village of Pannerden, some eight miles southeast of Arnhem. Bittrich, anticipating the problem, had already ordered the ferry operations to begin. It would be a slow, tedious, roundabout way of reaching Nijmegen, and to ferry the division's trucks, armor and men would take all of Harmel's resources.

As he left Bittrich's headquarters, Harmel asked his commander, "Why not destroy the Nijmegen bridge before it's too late?" Bittrich's tone was ironic. "Model has flatly refused to consider the idea. We may need it to counterattack." Harmel stared in amazement. "With what?" he asked.

In the dark, Harmel set out once again, heading for Pannerden. His units were already on the move toward the ferry crossing and the roads were choked with troops and vehicles. In Pannerden itself, Harmel saw the reason for the chaotic conditions he had witnessed on the road. Vehicles congested the streets in one gigantic traffic jam. At the river's edge, makeshift ferries composed of rubber rafts were slowly floating trucks across the river. From his chief of staff, Harmel learned that one battalion had reached the far shore and was already en route to Nijmegen. Some trucks and smaller vehicles were also across. But as yet, heavier armored equipment had not even been loaded. In Paetsch's opinion, Harmel's Frundsberg units might not be in action in the Arnhem-Nijmegen area until September 24 if the slow, cumbersome ferrying could not be speeded up.

Harmel knew there was only one solution to the problem. He would have to retake the Arnhem bridge and open the highway route to Nijmegen. As this first day of Market-Garden, September 17, ended all the German frustrations now focused on a single obstinate man—Colonel John Frost at the Arnhem bridge.

Convinced that Holland was on the verge of liberation and completely oblivious to the dangers, the Dutch climbed on their roofs to watch the vast armada of troop carrier planes and gliders.

British troopers enplane for Holland [ABOVE], and an American Waco glider [BELOW] is loaded. · [OPPOSITE] Planes tow gliders of 101st Airborne over Eindhoven, and [NEXT PAGE] men of 82nd Airborne land over Groesbeek in mass jump.

Gliders and paratroopers of British 1st Airborne [ABOVE] land near Arnhem, and planes drop supplies [BELOW] in the face of heavy anti-aircraft fire.

A tow plane behind the Waco glider [ABOVE] crash-lands and explodes on Arnhem drop zone. Tail of the huge Horsa glider [BELOW] was quickly removed to unload the cargo.

In spite of warnings, Arnhem's German commander, General Kussin, took the wrong road and was killed by British troopers.

[ABOVE] *Artillery chief Lieutenant Colonel "Sheriff" Thompson (at left) unloads gear from Horsa glider.* · *A Guards Armored tank passes a knocked-out German armored vehicle* [BELOW]. *Terrain difficulties and narrow, one-tank-width roads hindered the advance of the armored drive.*

In the corridor [ABOVE] *a supply truck explodes after receiving direct hit. A German patrol* [BELOW] *moves up during first hours of battle.*

Flight Lieutenant David Lord [BELOW, AT RIGHT], in an unprecedented act of courage, witnessed by British paratroopers, circled his flaming Dakota again and again over the drop zone in a successful attempt to parachute precious supplies. The only survivor was Flying Officer Henry King [ABOVE LEFT]. · Typical of courageous glider pilots was Sergeant Victor Miller [ABOVE RIGHT], who successfully landed his huge, unwieldy craft. His one concern was that another glider might "crash-land on top of me."

Lieutenant Tony Jones [ABOVE LEFT], called by General Horrocks the "bravest of the brave," rushed across Nijmegen bridge in wake of tanks and cut the German detonating explosive wires. · *A badly wounded paratrooper [ABOVE RIGHT] is rushed to casualty station.* · *82nd Airborne troopers [BELOW] move through outskirts of Nijmegen.*

[ABOVE] British "Red Devils" move forward through the debris at Arnhem. [BELOW] Antoon Derksen's house at 14 Zwarteweg, where General Urquhart hid out when caught behind German lines.

101st Airborne troopers are greeted by Dutch [ABOVE] *as they pass through Eindhoven.* · *Terrain difficulties are clearly shown* [BELOW] *on one-tank front, where Guards Armored column has been halted on "island" dike-top road.*

On Arnhem bridge Colonel Frost's and Captain Mackay's men successfully repulsed a German armored attack, knocking out twelve lead vehicles. The German commander, Gräbner, was killed in the attack.

[BELOW, LEFT TO RIGHT] *Field Marshal Model; General Bittrich; the one-legged Major Knaust (also shown above left as he is today); and Major General Heinz Harmel confer during battle. Knaust's Tiger tanks stopped the last drive of British to relieve the Arnhem bridge defenders. · Major Egon Skalka* [ABOVE RIGHT], *Hohenstaufen Division medical officer, who cooperated in exchanging the wounded during the truce. The SS man, obviously worried about his future, requested a letter of commendation from a British medical officer.*

Dutch women who had collaborated with Germans [ABOVE] were quickly rounded up by the Resistance and had their heads shaved [BELOW].

[LEFT] *The Hartenstein Hotel in Oosterbeek, General Urquhart's headquarters during the battle.* [CENTER] *The Schoonoord Hotel and* [BOTTOM] *the Tafelberg Hotel, shown before and during the battle.*

Perhaps the finest journalistic coverage of the war came out of Arnhem. Sergeants Lewis and Walker, Army cameramen [ABOVE], share a meal with Dutch girl. · London Daily Express war correspondent Alan Wood [BELOW] electrified Britain with his brilliant dispatches from the field.

The build-up of the 35,000-man Allied Airborne Army was slowed by inclement weather. Parachutes of 101st Airborne troopers [ABOVE] dot countryside on second day of attack. · At Arnhem bridge, Major Digby Tatham-Warter (shown below as he is today and in 1944) bolstered the men's morale by his eccentric charges against the enemy under an open umbrella.

In Oosterbeek perimeter, cut off and without supplies, Medic "Taffy" Brace [RIGHT] used makeshift paper bandages to save the life of machine gunner Corporal Andrew Milbourne (shown above then and now), who lost an eye and both hands. · Another British hero was Sergeant Alfred Roullier (shown below then and now), who cooked and served hot stew in the midst of battle to the hungry troops.

A major British miscalculation was the failure to use the Dutch underground. The most frustrated of all were Dutch liaison officer Lieutenant Commander *Arnoldus Wolters* [ABOVE LEFT] *and Douw van der Krap* [ABOVE RIGHT], *whose efforts to form a fighting unit proved fruitless.*

In Oosterbeek, baker Dirk van Beek [LEFT] saw that "things are going bad," but vowed to continue "baking to the last." · Rare book seller Gerhardus Gysbers [ABOVE], whose shop was next to the German barracks, was one of the first to realize that the British Arnhem attack was doomed to failure.

In the pre-attack bombing, Resistance worker Albertus Uijen [BELOW LEFT] saw that Nijmegen was being isolated by bombers. · Telephone technician Nicolaas de Bode [BELOW RIGHT], using secret lines, was able to pass on vital information to the underground and Allies. · Johannus Penseel [ABOVE LEFT] took advantage of German confusion to move an arsenal of weapons "beneath Germans' noses." · Gysbert Numan [ABOVE RIGHT] wanted to surrender himself and others rather than allow twelve innocent men to be executed for the abortive sabotage of a viaduct on September 15th. Arnhem Resistance chief Kruyff refused the request.

The Germans systematically destroyed British strongholds. · [BELOW] A knocked-out German tank lies amidst the ruins, and [ABOVE] British troopers hold positions around the Hartenstein Hotel. In background is the tennis court where German prisoners were held. · [OPPOSITE] Church in lower Oosterbeek was almost totally destroyed.

"They are throwing us away," Colonel Tilly [ABOVE RIGHT] *confided to his second-in-command, Major Grafton* [ABOVE LEFT], *after he learned that his Dorset unit was to cross the Lower Rhine and make a last stand while the remnants of Urquhart's division were evacuated. Of 10,000 Britishers in the Arnhem attack, only 2,323 crossed the river to safety. Some of the survivors are shown below.*

A cipher code hidden in a .303 cartridge was supposed to be fired before evacuation. In the excitement of escape, Signaler James Cockrill forgot his instructions and later found the code and bullet in his battle dress pocket.

In the late sixties, during a photo-mapping of Holland by KLM Airlines, experts were mystified by what appeared to be aircraft on the heaths near Arnhem [OPPOSITE]. On careful examination cartographers discovered that the ghostly images were outlines of gliders. During and after the battle in 1944, wrecked gliders were burned, indelibly branding the heath. Confirmation of the silhouettes was made by Robert Voskuil, son of Jan and Bertha, who compared the wartime aerial photographs with KLM pictures and presented his findings in the Journal of the Royal Geographic Society.

The chief personalities of the airborne attack as they are today
General James M. Gavin of 82nd Airborne [ABOVE LEFT]; *General Maxwell D. Taylor of 101st Airborne* [ABOVE RIGHT]; [BELOW, LEFT TO RIGHT, IN 1966] *General Stanislaw Sosabowski; General John Hackett; General Roy Urquhart; Colonel C. F. Gough; General John Frost; and Brigadier Graeme Warrack.* · *Refusing to return to Communist-dominated Poland at war's end, Sosabowski worked for a time in Britain as a common laborer. He died as this book was being written.*

Part Four

✸

THE SIEGE

✸

✳ 1 ✳

Early morning mist rising from the Rhine swirled around the Arnhem bridge and the silent darkened houses surrounding it. A short distance from the northern ramp, the Eusebius Buiten Singel—a long, landscaped boulevard bordering the historic inner city—stretched back toward the outlying areas north and east and ended at the Musis Sacrum, Arnhem's popular concert hall. On this Monday, September 18, in the thin, indistinct light, the ancient capital of Gelderland appeared deserted. Nothing moved in the streets, gardens, squares or parks.

From their positions around the northern end of the bridge, Colonel Frost's men could begin to see for the first time the whole sprawl of the city with its houses and municipal buildings: the Court of Justice, Provincial Government House, State Archives buildings, the town hall, general post office and the railroad station less than a mile to the northwest. Nearer, the Church of St. Eusebius, with its 305-foot-high steeple, dominated the city. Few of Frost's men, looking warily out from shattered windows and freshly dug foxholes in a perimeter composed of eighteen houses, realized that the great church now had a sinister significance. German snipers had moved into the tower during the night. Carefully concealed, they, like the British, waited tensely for full light.

The battle for the bridge had raged all night. A midnight lull had been short-lived. When the fighting broke out again, it almost seemed that each man was engaged in individual contest. Twice during the night Frost's men had tried to rush the southern end of the bridge, only to be beaten back. Lieutenant John Grayburn, leading both charges, had been badly wounded in the face, but stayed on the bridge and oversaw the evacuation of all his men to safety.* Later, truckloads of German infantry tried to ram their way across the bridge, only to be met by the concentrated fire of the British troopers. With flamethrowers, Frost's men had set the vehicles on fire. Panzer Grenadiers were burned alive in the inferno and fell screaming to the Rhine one hundred feet below. The acrid smell of burning rubber and thick black smoke eddying up from the debris hampered rescue parties from both sides searching for their wounded among the bodies littering the bridge. Lance Corporal Harold Back, in one such party, was helping to carry wounded into the basement of one of the houses held by Frost's men. In the darkness of the cellar, he saw what he thought were a few candles burning. Injured troopers were laid out all over the floor and suddenly Back realized that what he saw were tiny fragments glowing on the bodies of some of the wounded. Hit by splinters from phosphorous shells, the men were glowing in the dark.

Inexplicably, in these first moments of daylight, the battle halted again. It was almost as though both sides were drawing a deep breath. Across the road from Frost's battalion headquarters, on a side street under the ramp itself, Captain Eric Mackay made a quiet reconnaissance of the houses that his little force of engineers and small groups of men from other units now controlled. During a vicious nighttime battle, Mackay had managed to hang on to two of the four houses in the area and set up a command post in one of them, a brick schoolhouse. The Germans, counterattacking, had crept through the landscaped grounds to toss hand grenades into the houses. Infiltrating the buildings, the Germans

---

* Grayburn was killed in the battle for Arnhem. On September 20 he stood in full view of an enemy tank and directed the withdrawal of his men to a main defense perimeter. For supreme courage, leadership and devotion to duty during the entire engagement, he was posthumously awarded Britain's highest military honor, the Victoria Cross.

fought a deadly, almost silent hand-to-hand battle with the British. Ranging through the cellars and from room to room, Mackay's men drove back swarms of the enemy with bayonets and knives. Then, taking a small group of men, Mackay went out into the bushes after the retreating Germans. Again, with bayonets and grenades, the British routed the enemy. Mackay was hit in the legs by shrapnel and a bullet punctured his helmet, grazing his scalp.

Now, checking his troopers, Mackay discovered casualties similar to his own. Adding to his problems, the supply situation was not good. There were six Bren guns, ammunition, grenades and some explosives. But Mackay had no antitank weapons, little food and no medical supplies except morphia and field dressings. Additionally, the Germans had cut off the water. Now, all that was available was what the men still had in their canteens.

Terrible as the nighttime fighting had been, Mackay maintained a fierce determination. "We were doing well and our casualties were comparatively light," he recalls. "Besides, now with the coming of daylight, we could see what we were doing and we were ready." Still, Mackay, like Frost, had few illusions. In this most deadly kind of fighting—street by street, house by house and room by room—he knew it was only a question of time before the British garrison at the bridge was overwhelmed. The Germans obviously hoped to crush Frost's small force, by sheer weight of numbers, within a matter of hours. Against such powerful and concentrated attacks, all that could save the courageous defenders at the bridge was the arrival of XXX Corps or the remaining battalions of the 1st Parachute Brigade still fighting their way into the city.

It had been a night of unceasing horror for the SS soldiers who fought near the bridge. Colonel Harzer, apparently satisfied that he had halted Urquhart's battalions, had underestimated both the number and the caliber of the men who had reached the northern end. Harzer did not even bother to order his few self-propelled guns to be brought up as support. Instead, squad after squad of SS were thrown against the British positions in the buildings around the ramp. These tough units met a foe most of them remember as the fiercest soldiers they had ever encountered.

SS Squad Leader Alfred Ringsdorf, twenty-one, an experienced soldier who had fought in Russia, was on a freight train heading toward Arnhem where, he was told, his group was to be refitted. There was utter confusion at the Arnhem station when Ringsdorf and his men arrived. Troops from a hodgepodge of units were milling about, being lined up and marched off. Ringsdorf's unit was told to report immediately to a command post in the city. There, a major attached them to a company of the 21st Panzer Grenadier Regiment. The squad had arrived without arms, but by late Sunday afternoon they were outfitted with machine guns, carbines, hand grenades and a few *Panzerfäuste*.° Questioning the limited amount of ammunition, they were told that supplies were en route. "At this time," says Ringsdorf, "I had no idea where we were going to fight, where the battle was, and I had never been in Arnhem before."

In the center of the city, there was evidence that heavy street fighting had already taken place. For the first time, Ringsdorf learned that British paratroopers had landed and were holding the northern end of the Arnhem bridge. No one seemed to know how large the force was. His squad was assembled in a church and given their orders. They were to infiltrate behind the buildings on either side of the bridge ramp and rout out the British. Ringsdorf knew how deadly this kind of fighting was. His experiences at the Russian front had taught him that. Yet, the men in his command were seasoned young veterans. They thought the battle would be brief.

All through the area leading to the bridge, the squad saw houses heavily damaged by bombing, and the men had to work their way through the rubble. As they neared the perimeter

° A German version of the American recoilless antitank bazooka capable of firing a 20-pound projectile with extreme accuracy.

326

positions the British had set up around the north end of the bridge, they came under intense machine-gun fire. Pinned down, the squad was unable to get within six hundred yards of the bridge approach. A lieutenant called for a volunteer to cross the square and toss a demolition charge into the house where the heaviest machine-gun fire seemed to be centered. Ringsdorf volunteered. Under covering fire, he dashed across the square. "I stopped behind a tree near a cellar window where the shooting was coming from and tossed the charge inside. Then I ran back to my men." Lying in rubble waiting for the explosion to go off, Ringsdorf looked back just as a tall house on a corner, where a number of German engineers were sheltering, was suddenly hit by shells. The entire front of the house crumbled, burying everybody. It struck Ringsdorf that had his own men been there, the entire squad would have been wiped out. At that moment, the demolition charge he had thrown into the cellar exploded on the street not far from where he lay. The British had tossed it back out the window.

At nightfall various squads began to infiltrate the buildings to dig the British out. Ringsdorf's objective was a big red building which, he was told, was a school. Heading toward it, his squad quickly encountered alert British marksmen who forced the Germans to take refuge in a nearby house. Smashing the windows, the SS men opened fire. The British immediately took cover in the house next door and a vicious fire fight began. "The British shooting was deadly," Ringsdorf recalls. "We could hardly show ourselves. They aimed for the head, and men began to fall beside me, each one with a small, neat hole through the forehead."

With losses mounting, the Germans fired a panzerfaust directly at the British-occupied house. As the shell crashed into the building, Ringsdorf's squad charged. "The fighting was cruel," he remembers. "We pushed them back room by room, yard by yard, suffering terrible losses." In the middle of the melee, the young squad leader was ordered to report to his battalion commander; the British, he was told, must be driven out at all costs. Back with his men, Ringsdorf ordered the squad to dash forward, lobbing showers of grenades to keep the English under constant attack. "Only in this way," says Ringsdorf, "were we able to gain ground and continue our advance. But I certainly had not expected when I came from Germany to find myself suddenly engaged in bitter fighting in a restricted area. This was a harder battle than any I had fought in Russia. It was constant, close-range, hand-to-hand fighting. The English were everywhere. The streets, for the most part, were narrow, sometimes not more than fifteen feet wide, and we fired at each other from only yards away. We fought to gain inches, cleaning out one room after the other. It was absolute hell!"

Advancing cautiously toward one house, Ringsdorf caught a glimpse of an English helmet with camouflage netting momentarily outlined in an open cellar doorway. As he raised his arm to throw a grenade, he heard a low voice and the sound of moaning. Ringsdorf did not lob the grenade. Silently he moved down the cellar steps, then yelled, "Hands up." The command was unnecessary. In Ringsdorf's words, "Before me was a frightening sight. The cellar was a charnel house full of wounded English soldiers." Ringsdorf spoke soothingly, knowing that the British would not understand his words, but might comprehend his meaning. "It's O.K.," he told the wounded men. "It's all right." He called for medics and, collecting his prisoners, ordered the British moved back of his own lines for attention.

As the troopers were brought out of the cellar, Ringsdorf began to search one of the walking wounded. To his astonishment, the man uttered a low moan and crumpled at Ringsdorf's feet, dead. "It was a bullet meant for me," Ringsdorf says. "The English were protecting their own. They couldn't know we were trying to save their wounded. But for one moment, I was paralyzed. Then I broke out in a cold sweat and ran."

As the British troopers hung on grimly around the school, Ringsdorf knew that even his elite unit was not strong enough to force a surrender. As dawn broke on Monday, he and the depleted squad retreated back up the Eusebius Buiten Singel. Encountering an artillery commander, Ringsdorf told him that "the only way to get the British out is to blast the buildings down, brick by brick. Believe me, these are real men. They won't give up that bridge until we carry them out feet first."

Master Sergeant Emil Petersen had good reason to reach the same conclusion. He was attached to the Reichsarbeitsdienst (Reich Work Service) and, as Germany's manpower shortage became increasingly acute, Petersen and his thirty-five-man platoon had been transferred to a heavy antiaircraft unit, then to an infantry outfit. They had retreated all the way from France.

On Sunday afternoon, waiting at the Arnhem station for transportation back to Germany where they were to be reorganized, Petersen's platoon had been mobilized and told by a lieutenant that they were to be committed against British airborne troops who had landed in the city. "The unit we joined consisted of 250 men," Petersen recalls. "No one had any weapons. Only I and four others had machine pistols."

Petersen's men were tired. They had been without food for twenty-four hours, and the sergeant remembers thinking that had the train been on time, the platoon would have been fed, would have missed the battle and would have reached home in Germany.

At an SS barracks, the group was issued weapons. "The situation was laughable," Petersen says. "First, none of us liked fighting with the Waffen SS. They had a reputation for being merciless. The arms they gave us were ancient carbines. To break open mine, I had to bang it against a table. The morale of my men was not exactly high when they saw these old weapons."

It took some time to make the guns serviceable and, as yet, the unit had not received any orders. Nobody seemed to know what was happening or where the men were to be committed.

Finally, at dusk, the group was marched off to the town commander's headquarters. Arriving, they found the building deserted. Again, they waited. "All we could think about was food," says Petersen. Eventually, an SS lieutenant arrived and announced that the men were to push through the center of the city to the Rhine bridge.

The unit marched in platoons down Markt Street toward the Rhine. In the dark they could see nothing; but, Petersen recalls, "we were conscious of movement all around us. Occasionally we heard shooting in the distance and the sound of vehicles. Once or twice I thought I saw the dull silhouette of a helmet."

Less than three hundred yards from the bridge, Petersen was aware that they were passing through lines of soldiers and he guessed the group he was with must be replacing these men. Then one of the soldiers said something that, to Petersen, was unintelligible. Instantly Petersen realized that the man had spoken English. "We were marching alongside a British unit heading, like us, for the bridge." The mistaken identity was suddenly apparent to everyone. An English voice yelled out, "They're Jerries!" Petersen remembers shouting, "Fire!"

Within seconds the street reverberated with machine-gun and rifle fire as the two forces fought face to face. A stream of bullets missed Petersen by inches, ripping through his knapsack. The force of the fire slammed him to the ground. Quickly, he took cover behind a dead comrade.

"Everywhere you looked, men were firing from scattered positions, often mistakenly at their own side," Petersen remembers. Slowly he began to crawl forward. He came to an iron fence enclosing a small park and climbed the fence. There, he found most of the other survivors of the German platoons sheltering among trees and shrubs. The British had drawn back to a group of houses on both sides of the park, and now in the little square the Germans were caught in a crossfire. "I could hear the screams of the wounded," Petersen says. "The British fired flares pinpointing our positions and cut our group to pieces. Fifteen men in my platoon were killed in less than five minutes."

Just at dawn the British stopped firing. The Germans also halted. In the early light, Petersen saw that of the 250 men who had set out for the bridge, more than half were either dead or wounded. "We never did get near the approaches to the bridge. We just lay there and suffered, without support from the vaunted SS or a single self-propelled gun. That," Petersen says, "was our introduction to the Arnhem battle. For us, it was nothing less than a massacre."

Hour by hour, men of the two missing battalions of the 1st British Airborne Division somehow reached the bridge. They had managed, by twos and threes, to fight through Colonel Harzer's defense ring to the north and west. Many were wounded, hungry and cold. They would add to the medical and supply problems of Colonel Frost's group. But in these hours, the stragglers were proud and in high spirits, despite their exhaustion and wounds. They had arrived where briefing officers back in England and their own commanders had told them to come. They streamed in from every unit that had started out so confidently for the Arnhem bridge the previous afternoon, and by dawn on the eighteenth Frost estimated that he now had between 600 and 700 men on the northern approach. But each hour that brought more troopers to the bridge brought, too, the increasing sounds of mechanized equipment as General Harmel's armored units entered the city and took up positions.

Even the German armor found Arnhem a hazardous and frightening place. Along various routes throughout the city, ordinary Dutch civilians had blocked the roads. Braving German and British bullets, men and women living in the fighting areas had begun to collect the dead—British, German, and their own countrymen. Sergeant Reginald Isherwood, of the 1st Battalion, finally found his way to the center of Arnhem at daybreak, after a hazardous night on the roads. There he saw "a sight that will live with me until the end of my days." The Dutch, emerging from basements, cellars, gardens and wrecked buildings, were collecting bodies. "They carried the wounded to makeshift dressing stations and shelters in the basements," Isherwood recalls, "but the bodies of the dead were stacked like sandbags in long rows, the heads and feet placed alternately." The proud, grieving citizens of Arnhem were laying the bodies of friend and foe alike across the streets in five-to-six-foot-high human roadblocks to prevent German tanks from reaching Frost at the bridge.

For the civilians in the inner city, dawn brought no release from the terror and confusion. Fires were out of control and spreading rapidly. Huddled in cellars and basements, few people had slept. The night had been punctuated by the crash of shells, the dull crump of mortars, the whine of snipers' bullets and the staccato burst of machine guns. Strangely, outside the older part of town, the citizens of Arnhem were untouched by what was happening, and they were totally confused. They telephoned friends in the inner city seeking information, only to learn from the frightened householders that a pitched battle was taking place on the northern end of the bridge, which the British were holding against repeated German attacks. It was obvious to the callers that German troops and vehicles were moving into the city from all directions. Yet the faith of the Dutch did not falter. They believed that liberation by the British and Americans was imminent. In these outer parts of the city, people prepared for work as usual. Bakeries opened, milkmen made their rounds, telephone operators, railroad employees, utility workers—all were on their jobs. Civil servants were planning to go to work, firemen still attempted to keep up with the ever-growing number of burning buildings and, a few miles north of Arnhem, Dr. Reinier van Hooff, director of Burgers Zoological Gardens, tended his nervous, skittish animals.* Perhaps the only Dutch who knew the extent of the battle were doctors and nurses who answered calls constantly throughout the night. Ambulances raced through the city, collecting casualties and rushing them to St. Elisabeth's Hospital on the northwestern outskirts and to smaller nursing

---

* In the zoo were 12,000 carrier pigeons which the Germans had collected from bird keepers throughout Arnhem. Fearing that the Dutch might use the pigeons to carry reports, the birds had been confiscated and housed in the zoo. German soldiers appeared daily to count the birds and even dead pigeons were ordered kept until the Germans could check their registration numbers.

homes within the city. No one in Arnhem realized as yet that the city was already a no man's land and that the situation would grow steadily worse. Arnhem, one of the most scenic spots in the Netherlands, would soon become a miniature Stalingrad.

The Dutch in the inner city were, however, aware almost from the beginning that liberation would not come easily. In the middle of the night at the government police station on Euse-biusplein, less than a quarter of a mile from the bridge, twenty-seven-year-old Sergeant Joannes van Kuijk heard a quiet tapping at the station door. Opening up, he saw British soldiers standing outside. Immediately Van Kuijk asked them in. "They wanted the answers to all sorts of questions bearing on the locations of buildings and landmarks," he remembers. "Then a number of them left and began digging themselves in across the road in the direction of the bridge—all of it done as silently as possible." In front of a doctor's house nearby, Van Kuijk watched as the British set up a mortar site and then positioned a 6-pounder antitank gun in a corner of the doctor's garden. By dawn, Van Kuijk saw that the British had formed a tight perimeter around the northern extremity of the bridge. To him, these soldiers acted less like liberators than like grim-faced defenders.

On the other side of Eusebius Buiten Singel, the winding, grass-stripped boulevard close by the bridge, Coenraad Hulleman, a labor mediator staying with his fiancée, Truid van der Sande, and her parents in their villa, had been up all night listening to the firing and explosions around the schoolhouse a street away, where Captain Mackay's men were fighting off the Germans. Because of the intensity of the battle, the Van der Sandes and Hulleman had taken refuge in a small, windowless cellar beneath the central portion of the house.

Now, at dawn, Hulleman and his future father-in-law stole cautiously upstairs to a second-floor room overlooking the boulevard. There, they stared down in amazement. A dead German lay in the middle of a patch of marigolds in the landscaped street, and all through the grass plots they saw Germans in one-man slit trenches. Glancing along the boulevard to his right, Hulleman saw several German armored vehicles parked beside a high brick wall, drawn up and waiting. Even as the two men watched, a new battle broke out. Machine guns on the tanks suddenly fired into the towers of the nearby Walburg Church, and Hulleman saw a fine red dust spew out. He could only assume that paratroopers were in lookout positions in the church. Almost immediately the tank fire was answered, and the Germans in slit trenches began to machine-gun the houses on the opposite side of the street. One of them was a costume shop and in its windows were knights in armor. As Hulleman looked on, the bullets shattered the show window and toppled the knights. Moved to tears, Hulleman turned away. He hoped the sight was not prophetic.

A few blocks north, in a house near the concert hall, Willem Onck was awakened shortly after dawn by the sound of troop movements in the street. Someone hammered on his door and a German voice ordered Onck and his family to stay inside and to draw the blinds. Onck did not immediately obey. Running to the front window, he saw Germans with machine guns at every corner of the street. In front of the Musis Sacrum was an 88 mm. battery, and to Onck's utter amazement, German soldiers were sitting next to it on the auditorium's chairs which they had carried into the street. Watching them chatting casually with one another, Onck thought they looked as if they were only waiting for the concert to begin.

The most frustrated and angry civilians in the area were the members of the Dutch underground. Several of them had contacted the British almost immediately at the bridge, but their help had been politely refused. Earlier, Arnhem's underground chief, Pieter Kruyff, had sent Toon van Daalen and Gijsbert Numan to Oosterbeek to establish contact with the British. They too had found that their assistance was not needed. Numan remembers warning the troopers of snipers in the area and advising them to avoid main roads. "One of them told me their orders were to proceed to the bridge only, and they would follow their indicated routes," Numan says. "I got the impression that they were in dread of provocateurs and simply did not trust us."

334

Now, at dawn, Johannus Penseel held a meeting in his cellar with his resistance workers. Penseel planned to take over a local radio station and broadcast a proclamation that the city was free. A telephone call from Numan changed his mind. "It goes badly," Numan reported. "The situation is critical, and I think everything is already lost." Penseel was stunned. "What do you mean?" he asked. Numan was now near St. Elisabeth's Hospital. The British were finding it impossible to get through the German lines and march to the bridge, he said. Penseel immediately telephoned Pieter Kruyff, who advised the group to hold back any planned activities—"a temporary nonintervention," as Henri Knap, who attended the meeting, recalls. But the long-term hopes of the resistance workers were crushed. "We were prepared to do any-thing," Penseel recalls, "even sacrifice our lives if necessary. Instead, we sat useless and unwanted. It was now increasingly clear that the British neither trusted us nor intended to use us."

Ironically, in these early hours of Monday, September 18, when neither SHAEF, Montgomery nor any Market-Garden com-mander had a clear picture of the situation, members of the Dutch underground passed a report through secret telephone lines to the 82nd Airborne's Dutch liaison officer, Captain Arie Bestebreurtje, that the British were being overwhelmed by panzer divisions at Arnhem. In the 82nd's message logs, the notation appears: "Dutch report Germans winning over British at Arnhem." In the absence of any direct communications from the Arnhem battle area, this message was actually the first indication that the Allied High Command received of the crisis that was overtaking the 1st British Airborne Division.

✿ 2 ✿

A<small>T THE FERRY LANDING STAGE</small> in the little village of Driel, seven miles southwest of the Arnhem bridge, Pieter, the ferryman, prepared for his first trip of the day across the Lower Rhine. The early-morning commuters, who worked in the towns and villages on the northern side of the river, huddled together in small groups, chilled by the morning mist. Pieter took no part in the talk of his passengers about the fighting going on west of Arnhem and in the city itself. His concern was with the operation of the ferry and the daily schedules he must maintain, as he had done for years.

A few cars, and farm carts filled with produce for stores and markets to the north, were loaded first. Then men and women pushing bicycles came aboard. At exactly 7 A.M. Pieter swung out into the river, the ferry running smoothly along its cable. The trip took only a few minutes. Edging up to the ramp below the village of Heveadorp on the northern bank, passengers and vehicles disembarked. Above them, the Westerbouwing, a hundred-foot-high hill, dominated the countryside. On the northern bank, most commuters set off on roads leading east to Oosterbeek, whose tenth-century church tower rose above groves of oaks and lupine-covered moors. Beyond was Arnhem.

Other passengers waited to cross back to Driel. There, once again, Pieter took on northbound travelers. One of them was young Cora Baltussen. Only two weeks earlier, on September 5, which would always be remembered by the Dutch as Mad Tuesday, she had watched the Germans' frantic retreat. In Driel, the conquerors had not returned. For the first time in months,

Cora had felt free. Now, once again, she was apprehensive. The joy of the news of the paratroop landings the day before had been diminished by rumors of the intense fighting in Arnhem. Still, Cora could not believe the Germans would ever defeat the powerful Allied forces that had come to liberate her country.

At the Heveadorp landing on the north side of the river, Cora pushed her bicycle off the ferry and pedaled to Oosterbeek and the local baker's shop. She had given her meager hoard of sugar rations to the pastry shop for a special occasion. On this Monday, September 18, the Baltussen preserves factory was observing its seventy-fifth year in business and Cora's mother was celebrating her sixty-second birthday. For the first time in months all of the family would be together. Cora had come to Oosterbeek early to pick up the birthday cake, which would mark both the company's anniversary and Mrs. Baltussen's birthday.

Friends had tried to dissuade Cora from making the trip. Cora refused to listen. "What can possibly happen?" she had asked one friend. "The British are in Oosterbeek and Arnhem. The war is almost over."

Her trip was uneventful. In these early hours Oosterbeek seemed peaceful. There were British troops in the streets, the shops were open, and a holiday mood prevailed. For the moment, although gunfire could be heard only a few miles away, Oosterbeek was tranquil, not yet touched by the battle. Although her order was ready, the baker was amazed that she had come. "The war is all but over," she told him. With her parcels, she cycled back to Heveadorp and waited until Pieter brought the ferry in again. On the southern bank she returned to the somnolent peace of little Driel, where, as usual, absolutely nothing was happening.

✳ 3 ✳

O N THE BRITISH LANDING and drop zones, the officer with perhaps the least glamorous job of all was going about it with his
usual capability. All through the night the men of Brigadier Philip
"Pip" Hicks's 1st Airlanding Brigade had staved off a series of
vicious enemy attacks, as the motley groups under Von Tettau's
command harassed the brigade. Hicks's men were dug in around
the perimeters to hold the zones for the expected 10 A.M. drop of
Brigadier Shan Hackett's 4th Parachute Brigade, and the resupply
missions that would follow. The zones under Hicks's protection
were also the supply dumps for the British airborne.

Neither Hicks nor his men had managed more than an hour or
two of sleep. The Germans, attacking from the woods, had set the
forest on fire in some areas in the hope of burning out the British
defenders. The Red Devils promptly responded. Slipping behind
the enemy, they charged with fixed bayonets and forced the
Germans into their own fire. Signalman Graham Marples remembers the bitter nighttime battles vividly. He and a few others
came upon a platoon of dead British troopers who had been overrun and completely wiped out. "No one said anything," Marples
remembers. "We just fixed bayonets and went right on into the
woods. We came out, but the Jerries didn't." Private Robert
Edwards, who had seen action in North Africa, Sicily and Italy,
recalls that "I had managed to come through all those actions
more or less unscathed, but in one day in Holland I had been in
more fire fights than all else put together."

The unending skirmishes had taken their toll. Several times

during the night Hicks had called upon Lieutenant Colonel
W. F. K. "Sheriff" Thompson for artillery support to force back the
persistent enemy attacks. His real fear was that German armor,
which he now knew was holding up the battalions going for the
bridge, would break through his meager defenses and drive him
off the landing and drop zones. "I went through some of the worst
few hours I have ever spent in my life," Hicks recalls. "Two
things were clear: although we did not know it at the time we
had landed virtually on top of two panzer divisions—which
weren't supposed to be there—and the Germans had reacted with
extraordinary speed." Under attack from Von Tettau's groups
from the west and Harzer's armor from the east, Hicks's lightly
armed paratroopers had no option but to hold until relieved, or
until reinforcements and supplies were safely down.

Colonel Charles Mackenzie, General Urquhart's chief of staff,
had spent the night on the Renkum Heath landing zone, about
three miles away from Hicks's command post. The intense fighting had caused Division to move out of the woods and back onto
the field. There the headquarters staff took shelter in gliders for
the rest of the night. Mackenzie was concerned about the absence
of any word from Urquhart. "For more than nine hours, we had
heard nothing whatsoever from the General," he recalls. "I assumed that he was with Lathbury's 1st Brigade, but communications were out and we had heard nothing from either officer. I
knew that a decision would soon have to be made about the
command of the division. There always existed the possibility
that Urquhart had been captured or killed."

Early Monday, still without news, Mackenzie decided to confer
with two senior staff officers, Lieutenant Colonel R. G. Loder-
Symonds and Lieutenant Colonel P. H. Preston. Mackenzie informed them of Urquhart's conversation with him prior to takeoff
in England: the succession of command, in case anything happened to Urquhart, should be Lathbury, Hicks, then Hackett.
Now, with Lathbury missing as well, Mackenzie felt that Briga-

dier Hicks should be contacted. The other officers agreed. Immediately they drove to Hicks's headquarters. There, in a house close by the Heelsum-Arnhem road, Mackenzie told Hicks what he knew. "We had a scanty report that Frost had taken the bridge, but that the First and Third battalions were caught up in street fighting and had not as yet been able to reinforce him," Mackenzie remembers.

The best course of action now, Mackenzie believed, was for Hicks to release one of his Airlanding battalions and send it to the bridge. It could be reinforced later by elements of Hackett's 4th Paratroop Brigade when it arrived later in the morning. At the same time, Hicks was asked to take command of the division immediately.

Hicks seemed stunned. His forces were already understrength and he did not have a full battalion to send to the bridge. Yet it appeared the British battle plan was faltering. If Frost failed to get help immediately, the bridge might be lost; and if the landing areas were overrun, Hackett's 4th Brigade could be destroyed before it was even assembled.

Additionally, there seemed to be a tacit acknowledgment that Hicks was being asked to assume command of a division already in the process of disintegration through a total breakdown of communications and the absence of the commanding officer. Reluctantly, Hicks released half of one battalion—all he could spare—for defense of the bridge.* Obviously, that decision was most urgent. The bridge had to be held. Then, as Mackenzie remembers, "We finally convinced Hicks that he must take command of the division."

Few men had ever been asked to accept battleground responsibility for an entire division under such a complexity of circumstances. Hicks quickly discovered how critically the communications breakdown was affecting all operations. The few messages from Frost at the bridge were being received via Lieutenant

---

* He ordered half of the South Staffords to start off for Arnhem. The other half of this battalion would not arrive until the second lift, when, supplementing the advance of Hackett's 11th Battalion, these units would also move out.

Colonel Sheriff Thompson, commanding the Airlanding Light Regiment artillery. From an observation post in the steeple of the Oosterbeek Laag church, two and one-half miles from the bridge, Thompson had established a radio link with Major D. S. Munford's artillery command post at Brigade headquarters in a waterworks building near the bridge. The Thompson-Munford link afforded the only dependable radio communications at Hicks's disposal.

Equally critical, Division had no communications with General Browning's Corps headquarters near Nijmegen, or with the special "Phantom Net" sets at Montgomery's headquarters. Of the few vital messages that did reach England, most were sent over a BBC set, which had been specially flown in for British war correspondents. Its signal was weak and distorted. A high-powered German station and the British set were operating on the same frequency. Ironically, Division could pick up signals from rear Corps headquarters back in England, but were unable to transmit messages back. What sparse communications did get through via the BBC set were picked up at Browning's rear Corps headquarters at Moor Park and then relayed to the Continent. The transmission took hours and when the messages arrived they were outdated and often virtually meaningless.

Frustrated and worried, Hicks had three immediate concerns: the weather over England; the inability to confirm the planned arrival time of the second lift; and his lack of a means of informing anyone of the true situation in the Arnhem area. Additionally he could not warn Hackett of the perilous hold the British had on the landing areas where the 4th Brigade would expect to drop in cleared and protected zones.

Less crucial, but nonetheless troublesome, was the forthcoming encounter with Brigadier Shan Hackett. The volatile Hackett, Mackenzie told Hicks, would be informed of Urquhart's decision regarding the chain of command the moment he landed. "I knew Hackett's temperament," Mackenzie recalls, "and I was not looking forward to the meeting. But telling him was my job and I was following General Urquhart's orders. I could no longer take the chance that something had not happened to both the General and Lathbury."

At least Hicks was relieved of that delicate confrontation. The new division commander had enough on his mind. "The situation was more than just confusing," he remembers. "It was a bloody mess."

✲ 4 ✲

IN THE WESTERN SUBURBS of Arnhem, the once tidy parks and clean-swept streets were scarred and pitted by the battle as the British 1st and 3rd battalions struggled to reach the bridge. Glass, debris and the broken boughs of copper beech trees littered the cobblestone streets. Rhododendron bushes and thick borders of bronze, orange and yellow marigolds lay torn and crushed, and vegetable gardens in back of the neat Dutch houses were in ruins. The snouts of British antitank guns protruded from the shattered windows of shops and stores, while German half-tracks, deliberately backed into houses and concealed by their rubble, menaced the streets. Black smoke spewed up from burning British and German vehicles and constant showers of debris rained down as shells slammed into strong points. The crumpled bodies of the wounded and dead lay everywhere. Many soldiers remember seeing Dutch men and women, wearing white helmets and overalls emblazoned with red crosses, dashing heedlessly through the fire from both sides, to drag the injured and dying to shelter.

This strange, deadly battle now devastating the outskirts of the city barely two miles from the Arnhem bridge seemed to have no plan or strategy. Like all street fighting, it had become one massive, fierce, man-to-man encounter in a checkerboard of streets.

The Red Devils were cold, unshaven, dirty and hungry. The fighting had been too constant to allow men more than an occasional "brew-up" of tea. Ammunition was running short and casualties were mounting; some companies had lost as much as 50 percent of their strength. Sleep had been impossible, except in brief snatches. Many men, weary and on the move for hours, had lost all sense of time. Few knew exactly where they were or how far away the bridge still was, but they were grimly determined to get there. Years later, men like Private Henry Bennett of Colonel Fitch's 3rd Battalion, on the middle, Tiger route, would remember that throughout the constant skirmishes, sniping and mortar fire, one command was constant: "Move! Move! Move!"

Yet to General Urquhart, now absent from Division headquarters for nearly sixteen hours and without radio contact, the progress of the attack was agonizingly slow. Since 3 A.M., when he had been roused at the villa where he had spent a restless few hours, Urquhart, along with Brigadier Lathbury, had been on the road continuously with the 3rd Battalion. "Sharp encounters, brief bursts of fire, kept bringing the entire column to a stop," Urquhart says. The psychological effectiveness of German snipers disturbed the General. He had anticipated that some of his men who had not been in action before would be "a bit bullet-shy initially," but would rally quickly. Instead, along some streets, sniper fire alone was slowing up the progress of the entire battalion. Yet, rather than interfere with Fitch's command, Urquhart remained silent. "As a divisional commander mixed up in a battalion encounter . . . I was in the worst possible position to intervene, but all the time I was conscious of each precious second that was being wasted." German snipers were dealt with effectively, but Urquhart was appalled at the time it took to dig them out.

So was Regimental Sergeant Major John C. Lord. Like the General, Lord was chafing at the delay. "German resistance was fierce and continuous, but at least a large part of our delay was caused by the Dutch as well. They were out in the streets early, waving, smiling, offering us ersatz coffee. Some of them had even

343

draped Union Jacks over their hedges. There they were, right in the midst of the fighting, and they didn't even seem to realize it was going on. They, with all their good intentions, were holding us up as much as the Germans."

Suddenly the intensive sniper fire was replaced by something far more serious: the piercing crack of the enemy's 88 mm. artillery and self-propelled guns. At this point the forward units of Fitch's battalion were close by the massive St. Elisabeth's Hospital, less than two miles northwest of the Arnhem bridge. The hospital lay almost at the confluence of the two main highways leading into Arnhem, along which the 1st and 3rd battalions were attempting to march to the bridge. Here, elements of the Hohenstaufen Division's armor had been positioned throughout the night. Both Colonel Dobie's 1st Battalion on the Ede-Arnhem road and Fitch's 3rd Battalion on the Utrecht road must pass on either side of the junction to get to the bridge. Dobie's battalion was the first to feel the force of Colonel Harzer's fanatical SS units.

From a horseshoe-shaped perimeter covering the northern and western approaches of the city, the Germans had forced Dobie's men off the upper road and into cover in the surrounding built-up areas. SS men, hidden on the rooftops, and snipers in attics had allowed forward units to pass unhindered before opening up with a murderous fire on troops coming up behind. In the confusion of the surprise attack, companies and platoons were dispersed in all directions.

Now, employing the same tactics, the Germans were concentrating on Fitch's 3rd Battalion. And, in a situation that could have disastrous consequences, four critical officers—the commanders of the 1st and 3rd battalions, the officer in charge of the 1st Parachute Brigade and the commander of the 1st British Airborne Division—all found themselves bottled up in the same small, heavily populated area. Ironically, as in the case of Model and his commanders at Oosterbeek, General Urquhart and Brigadier Lathbury were surrounded by an enemy oblivious to their presence.

Trapped by fire from ahead and behind, the British columns scattered. Some men headed for buildings along the Rhine, more took to the nearby woods and others—among them, Urquhart and Lathbury—ran for safety into narrow streets of identical brick houses.

Urquhart and his group had just reached a three-story house in a block of buildings near the main Utrecht-Arnhem road when the Germans shelled the building. The British were uninjured, but German armor, Urquhart was later to note, "moved through the streets with almost casual immunity." As one tank rumbled down the street, its commander standing in the open hatch looking for targets, Major Peter Waddy leaned out of an upper-floor window of a house next to Urquhart's and expertly dropped a plastic explosive into the open turret, blowing the tank to pieces.* Other men, following Waddy's example, demolished two more tanks. But, although the British fought fiercely, the lightly armed troopers were no match for the German armor.

Urquhart's own predicament was increasing by the minute. He was desperately anxious to get back to Division headquarters and gain control of the battle. Caught up in the fighting, he believed his only means of escape was to take to the streets and, in the confusion, try to get through the German positions. His officers, fearful for his safety, disagreed, but Urquhart was adamant. The intense fighting was, as he saw it, still only "company-size action" and, as the buildings the British occupied were not yet surrounded, he felt the group should get out quickly before German strength increased and the ring tightened.

During the hasty conference amid the noise of the battle, Urquhart and his officers were dumfounded to see a British Bren gun carrier clatter down the street, as though unaware of the German fire, and pull up outside the building. A Canadian lieutenant, Leo Heaps, who in Urquhart's words "seemed to have a charmed existence," leaped out of the driver's seat and raced for the building. Behind Heaps was Charles "Frenchie" Labouchère,

---

* A short time later, reconnoitering the British positions, Waddy was killed by a mortar blast.

of the Dutch resistance, who was acting as Heaps's guide. The carrier was loaded with supplies and ammunition which Heaps hoped to deliver to Colonel Frost on the bridge. With German armor everywhere, the small vehicle and its two occupants had miraculously survived enemy fire and en route had, by chance, discovered Urquhart's whereabouts. Now, for the first time in hours, Urquhart learned from Heaps what was happening. "The news was far from encouraging," Urquhart later recalled. "Communications were still out. Frost was on the northern end of the bridge under heavy attack, but holding, and I was reported missing or captured." After listening to Heaps, Urquhart told Lathbury that it was now imperative "before we're completely bottled up to take a chance and break out."

Turning to Heaps, Urquhart told the Canadian that if he reached Division headquarters after completing his mission at the bridge, he was to urge Mackenzie to "organize as much help as he could for Frost's battalion." At all costs, including his own safety, Urquhart was determined that Frost must get the supplies and men needed to hold until Horrocks' tanks reached Arnhem.

As Heaps and Labouchère left, Urquhart and Lathbury set about making their escape. The street outside was now being swept constantly by enemy fire and buildings were crumpling under the pounding of shells. Urquhart noted "a growing pile of dead around the houses we occupied," and concluded that any exit via the street would be impossible. The commanders, along with others, decided to leave from the rear of the building, where, under covering fire and smoke bombs, they might be able to get away. Then, taking advantage of plantings in the back gardens of the row houses, Urquhart and Lathbury hoped eventually to reach a quiet area and make their way back to headquarters.

The route was nightmarish. While paratroopers laid down a heavy smoke screen, Urquhart's group dashed out the back door, sprinted through a vegetable garden and climbed a fence separating the house from its neighbor. As they paused for a moment near the next enclosure, Lathbury's Sten gun went off accidentally, barely missing the General's right foot. As Urquhart was later to write, "I chided Lathbury about soldiers who could not keep their Stens under control. It was bad enough for a division commander to be jinking about . . . and it would have been too ironic for words to be laid low by a bullet fired by one of my own brigadiers."

Climbing fence after fence, and once a ten-foot-high brick wall, the men moved down the entire block of houses until, finally, they reached an intersecting cobbled street. Then, confused and weary, they made a drastic miscalculation. Instead of veering left, which might have given them a margin of safety, they turned right toward St. Elisabeth's Hospital, directly into the German fire.

Running ahead of Urquhart and Lathbury were two other officers, Captain William Taylor of the Brigade's headquarters staff and Captain James Cleminson of the 3rd Battalion. One of them called out suddenly but neither Urquhart nor Lathbury understood his words. Before Taylor and Cleminson could head them off, the two senior officers came upon a maze of intersecting streets where, it seemed to Urquhart, "a German machine gun was firing down each one." As the four men attempted to run past one of these narrow crossings, Lathbury was hit.

Quickly the others dragged him off the street and into a house. There, Urquhart saw that a bullet had entered the Brigadier's lower back and he appeared to be temporarily paralyzed. "All of us knew," Urquhart recalls, "that he could travel no farther." Lathbury urged the General to leave immediately without him. "You'll only get cut off if you stay, sir," he told Urquhart. As they talked, Urquhart saw a German soldier appear at the window. He raised his automatic and fired at point-blank range. The bloodied mass of the German's face disappeared. Now, with the Germans so near, there was no longer any question that Urquhart must leave quickly. Before going, he talked with the middle-aged couple who owned the house and spoke some English. They promised to get Lathbury to St. Elisabeth's Hospital as soon as there was a lull in the fighting. In order to save the owners from German reprisal, Urquhart and his party hid Lathbury in a cellar beneath a stairway until he could be removed to the hospital. Then, Urquhart remembers, "we left by the back door and into yet another maze of tiny, fenced gardens." The three men did not get far, but Urquhart's life may well have been saved by the prompt action of fifty-five-year-old Antoon Derksen, owner of a terrace house at Zwarteweg 14.

In the maelstrom of firing, Antoon, his wife Anna, their son Jan, and daughter Hermina were sheltering in the kitchen at the rear of the house. Glancing through a window, Derksen was amazed to see three British officers vault over the fence into his back garden and head for the kitchen door. Quickly, he let them in.

Unable to communicate—he didn't speak English and no one in Urquhart's party knew Dutch—Antoon, gesturing, tried to warn the Britishers that the area was surrounded. "There were Germans in the street," he later recalled, "and at the back, in the direction the officers had been going. At the end of the row of gardens there were Germans in position at the corner."

Derksen hastily ushered his visitors up a narrow staircase to a landing and from there into a bedroom. In the ceiling was a pull-down door with steps leading to the attic. Cautiously looking out the bedroom window the three men saw the reason for Derksen's wild pantomime. Only a few feet below them, in positions all along the street, were German troops. "We were so close to them," Urquhart remembers, "we could hear them talking."

Urquhart was unable to guess whether the Germans had spotted his group as they entered the rear of the house, or whether they might burst in at any moment. In spite of Derksen's warning that the area was surrounded, he pondered the twin risks of continuing through the chain of back gardens or making a dash down the front street, using hand grenades to clear the way. He was ready to take any chance to return to his command. His officers, fearful for him, were not. At the moment, the odds were simply too great. It was far better, they argued, to wait until British troops overran the sector than for the commanding general to risk capture or possible death.

The advice, Urquhart knew, was sound, and he did not want to compel his officers to take risks that might prove suicidal. Yet, "my long absence from Division headquarters was all I could think about, and anything seemed better to me than to stay out of the battle in this way."

The familiar creaking clack of caterpillar treads forced Urquhart to stay put. From the window the three officers saw a German self-propelled gun come slowly down the street. Directly outside the Derksen house, it came to a halt. The top of the armored vehicle was almost level with the bedroom window, and the crew, dismounting, now sat talking and smoking directly below. Obviously, they were not moving on and at any moment the Britishers expected them to enter the house.

Quickly Captain Taylor pulled down the attic steps and the three officers hurriedly climbed up. Crouched down and looking about him, the six-foot Urquhart saw that the attic was little more than a crawl space. He felt "idiotic, ridiculous, as ineffectual in the battle as a spectator."

The house was now silent. Antoon Derksen, as a loyal Dutchman, had sheltered the British. Now, fearing possible reprisal if Urquhart was found, he prudently evacuated his family to a neighboring house. In the nearly airless attic, and without food or water, Urquhart and his officers could only wait anxiously, hoping either for the Germans to pull back or for British troops to arrive. On this Monday, September 18, with Market-Garden only a day old, the Germans had almost brought the Arnhem battle to a halt and, compounding all the errors and miscalculations of the operation, Urquhart, the one man who might have brought cohesion to the British attack, was isolated in an attic, trapped within the German lines.

It had been a long, tedious mission for Captain Paul Gräbner and his 9th SS Panzer Reconnaissance Battalion. Allied paratroopers had not landed in the eleven-mile stretch between Arnhem and Nijmegen. Of that, Gräbner was quite certain. But enemy units were in Nijmegen. Immediately after a few of Gräbner's vehicles had crossed the great Waal river bridge, there had been a short, brisk small-arms encounter. In the darkness, the enemy had seemed to show no great inclination to continue the fight against his armored vehicles, and Gräbner had reported to headquarters that the Allies seemed to have little strength in the city as yet.

Now, his scouting mission completed, Gräbner ordered a few self-propelled guns from his forty-vehicle unit to guard the southern approaches to the Nijmegen bridge. With the rest of the patrol, he headed back north to Arnhem. He had seen neither paratroopers nor any enemy activity when crossing the Arnhem bridge the night before. However, from radio messages, he had learned that some British troops were on one side of the bridge. Harzer's headquarters had merely called them "advance units." Gräbner halted once more, this time at the town of Elst, approximately midway between Arnhem and Nijmegen. There again, to be within striking distance of either highway bridge, he left off part of his column. With the remaining twenty-two vehicles, he sped back toward the Arnhem bridge to clear it of whatever small enemy units were there. Against paratroopers armed with only rifles or machine guns, Gräbner expected little difficulty. His powerful armored units would simply smash through the lightly held British defenses and knock them out.

At precisely 9:30 A.M., Corporal Don Lumb, from his rooftop position near the bridge, yelled out excitedly, "Tanks! It's XXX Corps!" At Battalion headquarters nearby, Colonel John Frost heard his own spotter call out. Like Corporal Lumb, Frost felt a moment's heady exhilaration. "I remember thinking that we would have the honor of welcoming XXX Corps into Arnhem all by ourselves," he recalls. Other men were equally cheered. On the opposite side of the northern approach, the men under the ramp near Captain Eric Mackay's command post could already hear the sound of heavy vehicles reverberating on the bridge above.

Sergeant Charles Storey pounded up the stairs to Corporal Lumb's lookout. Peering toward the smoke still rising from the southern approach, Storey saw the column Lumb had spotted. His reaction was immediate. Racing back downstairs, the pre-Dunkirk veteran shouted, "They're Germans! Armored cars on the bridge!"

At top speed, the vanguard of Captain Paul Gräbner's assault force came on across the bridge. With extraordinary skill, German drivers, swerving left and right, not only avoided the smoldering wreckage cluttering the bridge, but drove straight through a mine field—a string of platelike Teller mines that the British had laid during the night. Only one of Gräbner's five lead vehicles touched off a mine—and only superficially damaged, kept on coming. On his side of the ramp, Captain Mackay stared with amazement as the first of the squat camouflaged cars, machine guns firing constantly, barreled off the ramp, smashed through the British perimeter defenses, and kept on going straight toward the center of Arnhem. Almost immediately, Mackay saw another go past. "We had no antitank guns on our side," Mackay says, "and I just watched helplessly as three more armored cars sped right past us and took off up the avenue."

Gräbner's daring plan to smash across the bridge by force and speed was underway. Out of the sight of the British, on the southern approach to the bridge, he had lined up his column. Now, half-tracks, more armored cars, personnel carriers and even a few truckloads of infantry, firing from behind heavy sacks of grain, began to advance. Crouching behind the half-tracks were other German soldiers, firing steadily.

The sudden surprise breakthrough of Gräbner's lead vehicles had stunned the British. They recovered quickly. Antitank guns from Frost's side of the bridge began to get the range. From the entire northern area a lethal fire enveloped the German column. From parapets, rooftops, windows and slit trenches, troopers opened fire with every weapon available, from machine guns to hand grenades. Sapper Ronald Emery, on Mackay's side of the ramp, shot the driver and codriver of the first half-track to cross.

As the second came into view, Emery shot its drivers, too. The half-track came to a dead halt just off the ramp, whereupon the remainder of its crew of six, abandoning the vehicle, were shot one by one.

Relentlessly, Gräbner's column pressed on. Two more half-tracks nosed across the bridge. Suddenly, chaos overtook the German assault. The driver of the third half-track was wounded. Panicked, he threw his vehicle into reverse, colliding with the half-track behind. The two vehicles, now inextricably tangled, slewed across the road, one bursting into flames. Doggedly the Germans coming up behind tried to force a passage. Accelerating their vehicles, frantic to gain the northern side, they rammed into one another and into the growing piles of debris tossed up by shells and mortar bursts. Out of control, some half-tracks hit the edge of the ramp with such force that they toppled over the edge and down into the streets below. Supporting German infantrymen following the half-tracks were mercilessly cut down. Unable to advance beyond the center of the bridge, the survivors raced back to the southern side. A storm of fire ricocheted against the girders of the bridge. Now, too, shells from Lieutenant Colonel Sheriff Thompson's artillery, situated in Oosterbeek, and called in by Major Dennis Munford from the attic of Brigade headquarters near Frost's own building, screamed into Gräbner's stricken vehicles. Through all the din came the yelling of the now-exuberant British paratroopers as they shouted the war cry, "Whoa Mohammed," which the Red Devils had first used in the dry hills of North Africa in 1942. *

The fierceness of the raging battle stunned the Dutch in the area. Lambert Schaap, who lived with his family on the Rijnkade —the street running east and west of the bridge—hurried his wife and nine children off to a shelter. Schaap himself remained in his

---

* In that campaign, paratroopers noted that the Arabs, shouting messages to one another, seemed to begin each communication with these two words. In Arnhem, the war cry was to take on special meaning. It enabled paratroopers on both sides of the northern ramp to determine who was friend or foe in the various buildings and positions, since the Germans seemed unable to pronounce the words. According to Hilary St. George Saunders in *By Air to Battle,* the war cry "seemed to rouse the men to their highest endeavours."

house until a hail of bullets came through the windows, pitting walls and smashing furniture. Under this intense barrage Schaap fled. To Police Sergeant Joannes van Kuijk, the battle seemed endless. "The firing was furious," he recalls, "and one building after another seemed to be hit or burning. Telephone calls from colleagues and friends were constant, asking for information about what was happening. We were having a hard time of it in our building, and neighboring premises were catching fire. The houses on Eusebius Buiten Singel were also alight."

On that wide boulevard near the northern approach, Coenraad Hulleman, in his fiancée's house only a few doors away from Captain Mackay's command post, now stayed with the rest of the Van der Sande family in their basement shelter. "There was a funny sound overriding all the other noise and someone said it was raining," Hulleman remembers. "I went up to the first floor, looked out, and saw that it was fire. Soldiers were running in every direction, and the entire block seemed to be in flames. The battle moved right up the boulevard, and suddenly it was our turn. Bullets smacked into the house, smashing windows, and upstairs we heard musical notes as the piano was hit. Then, amazingly, a sound like someone typing in Mr. Van der Sande's office. The bullets were simply chewing up the typewriter." Hulleman's fiancée, Truid, who had followed him up, saw that shots were hitting the tower of the massive Church of St. Eusibius. As she watched in amazement the gold hands of the huge clock on the church spun crazily as though, Truid remembers, "time was racing by."

To the bridge fighters, time had lost all meaning. The shock, speed and ferocity of the battle caused many men to think that the fight had gone on for many hours. Actually, Gräbner's attack had lasted less than two. Of the armored vehicles that Colonel Harzer had jealously guarded from General Harmel, twelve lay wrecked or burning on the northern side. The remainder disengaged from the carnage and moved back to Elst, minus their commander. In the bitter no-quarter fighting, Captain Paul Gräbner had been killed.

Now the British, in pride and triumph, began to assess the damage. Medics and stretcher-bearers, braving the unrelenting sniper fire, moved through the smoke and litter, carrying the wounded of both sides to shelter. The Red Devils on the bridge had repulsed and survived the horror of an armored attack and, almost as though they were being congratulated on their success, 2nd Battalion signalmen suddenly picked up a strong clear message from XXX Corps. The grimy, weary troopers imagined that their ordeal was all but over. Now, beyond any doubt, Horrocks' tanks must be a scant few hours away.

From airfields behind the German border, swarms of fighters took to the air. To amass and fuel the planes, the nearly depleted Luftwaffe had mounted an all-out effort. Now, after a frantic, sleepless night, during which fighters had been rushed in from all over Germany, some 190 planes gathered over Holland between 9 and 10 A.M. Their mission was to destroy the second lift of Market. Unlike the skeptical Field Marshal Model, the Luftwaffe generals believed the captured Market-Garden plans to be authentic. They saw a glittering opportunity to achieve a major success. From the plans, German air commanders knew the routes, landing zones and drop times of the Monday lift. Squadrons of German fighters patrolling the Dutch coast across the known Allied flight paths and drop zones waited to pounce on the airborne columns, due to begin their drops at 10 A.M. Zero hour passed with no sign of the Allied air fleet. The short-range fighters were ordered to land, refuel and take off again. But the sky remained empty. None of the anticipated targets materialized. Baffled and dismayed, the Luftwaffe high command could only wonder what had happened.

What had happened was simple. Unlike Holland, where the weather was clear, Britain was covered by fog. On the bases, British and American airborne troops, ready to go, waited impatiently by their planes and gliders. On this crucial morning, when every hour mattered, General Lewis H. Brereton, the First Allied Airborne Army commander, was, like the men of the second lift, at the mercy of the weather. After consultation with the meteorologists, Brereton was forced to reschedule zero hour. The men in and around Arnhem and the Americans down the corridor—all holding against the increasing German buildup—must now wait four long hours more. The second lift could not reach the drop zones before 2 P.M.

✲ 5 ✲

At Valkenswaard, fifty-seven miles south of Arnhem, ground fog had held up the planned 6:30 A.M. jump-off time for the tanks of XXX Corps. Scout cars, however, had set out on schedule. Patrolling ahead and to the east and west since daybreak, they were feeling out the German strength. To the east, heather-covered sand and small streams made the area barely negotiable even for reconnaissance vehicles. West of the village, wooden bridges over streams and rivers were considered too light to support tanks. As scout cars in the center moved along the narrow, one-tank-wide main road out of Valkenswaard, they suddenly encountered a German tank and two self-propelled guns, which drove off toward Eindhoven as the patrol approached. From all reports it seemed clear that the quickest route into Eindhoven was still the highway, despite the sighting of German armor and the expectation of running into more as the British approached the city. Now, three hours later, General Horrocks' tanks were only just beginning to roll again. As Colonel Frost's men engaged Captain Gräbner's units at the Arnhem bridge, the spearheading Irish Guards were finally on the move, heading up the main road toward Eindhoven.

Stiff German resistance had thwarted Horrocks' plan to smash out from the Meuse-Escaut Canal on Sunday and link up with General Taylor's 101st Airborne Division in Eindhoven in less than three hours. By nightfall on the seventeenth, Lieutenant Colonel Joe Vandeleur's tankers had come only seven miles to Valkenswaard, six miles short of the day's objective. There had seemed little reason to push on during the night. Brigadier Norman Gwatkin, chief of staff of the Guards Armored Division, had told Vandeleur that the Son bridge beyond Eindhoven was destroyed. Bridging equipment would have to be brought up before Vandeleur's tanks could cross. As Vandeleur remembers, Gwatkin said, "Push on to Eindhoven tomorrow, old boy, but take your time. We've lost a bridge."

Unaware of the setback, men were impatient at the delay. Lieutenant John Gorman, who had attended General Horrocks' briefing in Leopoldsburg prior to the break-out, had thought at the time that there were too many bridges to cross. Now Gorman, recipient of the Military Cross a few weeks earlier, was edgy and irritable. His original fears seemed justified. Anxious to be off, Gorman could not understand why the Guards Armored had spent the night in Valkenswaard. Habit, he noted, "seemed to dictate that one slept at night and worked by day," but now, Gorman felt, such behavior should not apply. "We must get on," he remembers saying. "We can't wait." Lieutenant Rupert Mahaffey was equally disturbed at the Guards' slow advance. "I began having the first faint traces of conscience," he says. "Our advance seemed slower than intended, and I knew that if we did not pick up the pace soon we weren't going to get to Arnhem on time."

Although the scouting patrols of the Household Cavalry had warned of waiting German armor and infantry, the tanks of the Irish Guards met little opposition until they reached the village of Aalst, halfway to Eindhoven. Then, from the pinewood forests flanking the highway, a hail of infantry fire engulfed the column, and a lone self-propelled gun engaged the leading tanks. It was quickly put out of action and Vandeleur's force rumbled on through the village. Two miles north, at a small bridge over the river Dommel, the Irish were held up again, this time by heavy artillery fire. Four 88 mm. guns covered the bridge. Infantry with heavy machine guns were hidden in nearby houses and behind concrete walls. Immediately the lead vehicles halted and British troops, jumping from the tanks, fought back.

To move on as quickly as possible, Vandeleur decided to call in the rocket-firing Typhoons that had aided the column so expertly during the previous day's advance. Flight Lieutenant Donald Love, now in complete charge of ground-to-air communication, put through the request. To his astonishment, he was turned down. In Belgium, the squadrons were weathered in by fog. Vandeleur, Love recalls, "was livid." Squinting into the bright weather over Holland, he asked Love sarcastically "if the R.A.F. is frightened by sunshine."

By now the entire column, stretching back almost to the Belgian border, was stalled by the well-sited enemy guns. Lead tanks tried to edge forward, and one gun, firing directly down the road, stopped them at point-blank range. As his tanks opened up against the Germans, Vandeleur called for heavy artillery and quickly ordered patrols to move out west along the river in search of a bridge or ford where his vehicles might cross, outflank the German battery and attack from the rear.

A barrage of steel whistled over the lead tanks as British batteries began to engage the enemy. Well positioned and fiercely determined, the Germans continued to fire. For two hours the battle went on. Fuming at the delay, Vandeleur was helpless. All he could do was wait.

But, barely four miles to the north, one of the reconnaissance units had met with unexpected success. After a circuitous cross-country trip through water-veined terrain and marshes, and across fragile wooden bridges, one troop of scout cars, skirting the German positions, came suddenly upon American paratroopers north of Eindhoven. Shortly before noon, Lieutenant John Palmer, commanding the Household Cavalry scout unit, was warmly greeted by Brigadier General Gerald Higgins, deputy commander of the 101st Screaming Eagles. By radio, Palmer jubilantly informed his headquarters that the "Stable Boys have contacted our Feathered Friends." The first of three vital link-ups along the corridor had been made, eighteen hours behind Market-Garden's schedule.

With contact finally established, discussion immediately turned to the Son bridge. Waiting British engineering units needed complete details in order to bring forward the materials and equipment needed to repair the damaged crossing. Sappers, moving up alongside Vandeleur's lead columns, prepared to rush to the bridge the moment the advance picked up again. Information could have been passed by radio, but the Americans had already discovered a simpler method. The surprised British were radioed to ask their engineers to telephone "Son 244." The call went immediately through the German-controlled automatic telephone exchange, and within minutes the Americans at the Son bridge had given British engineers the vital information they needed to bring up the proper bridging equipment.

In the village of Aalst, Vandeleur's tankers were startled by a sudden abrupt end to the German fire which had kept them immobilized so long on the main road. One of their own squadrons had opened the way. Working slowly down the western bank of the Dommel river, a British reconnaissance force came upon a crossing a mile north of Aalst and behind the German positions. The squadron charged the German guns from the rear, overran their positions and ended the battle.

Unaware of the move, the stalled tankers at Aalst thought the sudden silence was a lull in the fighting. Major Edward Tyler, in charge of the lead Number 2 Squadron, was debating whether he should take advantage of the cessation and order his tanks to smash on, when he spotted a man cycling down the main road toward the column. Stopping on the far bank, the man jumped off the bicycle and, waving frantically, ran across the bridge. The astounded Tyler heard him say: "Your General! Your General! The Boche have gone!"

Breathlessly, the Dutchman introduced himself. Cornelis Los, forty-one, was an engineer employed in Eindhoven but living in Aalst. "The road," Los told Tyler, "is open and you have put out of action the only German tank at the village entrance." Then, Tyler recalls, "he produced a detailed sketch of all the German positions between Aalst and Eindhoven."

Immediately, Tyler gave the order to advance. The tanks moved over the bridge and up the road, passing the now ruined and deserted German artillery positions. Within the hour, Tyler saw the sprawl of Eindhoven up ahead and what appeared to be thousands of Dutch thronging the road, cheering and waving flags. "The only obstruction holding us up now are the Dutch crowds," Major E. Fisher-Rowe radioed back down the column. In the heady carnival atmosphere, the cumbersome tanks of XXX Corps would take more than four hours to move through the city. Not until shortly after 7 P.M. did advance units reach the Son bridge, where Colonel Robert F. Sink's weary engineers were working, as they had been ever since it was destroyed, to repair the vital span.

From the outset, the synchronized Market-Garden schedule had allowed little margin for error. Now, like the thwarted advance of the British battalions into Arnhem, the damage to the bridge at Son was a major setback that threatened the entire operation. Twenty-eight miles of the corridor—from the Belgian border north to Veghel—were now controlled by the Anglo-Americans. With extraordinary speed, the 101st Division had covered its fifteen-mile stretch of highway, capturing the principal towns of Eindhoven, St. Oedenrode and Veghel, and all but two of eleven crossings. Yet Horrocks' 20,000-vehicle relief column could advance no farther until the Son crossing was repaired. British engineers and equipment, moving up with the lead tanks, must work against time to repair the bridge and move XXX Corps over the Wilhelmina Canal, for there was no longer an alternative route that Horrocks' tanks could take.

In the planning stages General Maxwell Taylor, knowing that the Son bridge was vital to a straight dash up the corridor, had included a secondary target as well. To counteract just such a setback as had occurred at Son, Taylor had ordered a one-hundred-foot-long concrete road bridge over the canal at the village of Best to be taken as well. Four miles west of the main road, the bridge could still be used in an emergency. Since intelligence sources believed that the area held few German troops, a lone company had been assigned to grab the bridge and a nearby railway crossing.

Best was to become a tragic misnomer for the American troopers sent to secure it. Lieutenant Edward L. Wierzbowski's reinforced company had been greatly reduced during ferocious night fighting on the seventeenth. Infiltrating along dikes and canal banks, and through marshes, the dogged troopers under Wierzbowski's command pressed on against overwhelming German forces; once they were within fifteen feet of the bridge before being stopped by a barrage of fire. At various times during the night, word filtered back that the bridge had been taken. Other reports claimed that Wierzbowski's company had been wiped out. Reinforcements, like the original company, became quickly engulfed in the desperate, unequal struggle. At 101st headquarters, it was soon clear that German forces were heavily concentrated at Best. Far from being lightly held, the village contained upwards of one thousand troops—units of the forgotten German Fifteenth Army. And like a sponge, Best was drawing more and more American forces. As fighting raged throughout the area, Wierzbowski and the few survivors of his company were almost in the dead center of the battle. So surrounded that their own reinforcements did not know they were there, they continued to fight for the bridge.

Around noon, as advance parties of British and Americans linked up in Eindhoven, the bridge at Best was blown by the Germans. So close were Wierzbowski and his men that falling debris added to the wounds they had already sustained. Elsewhere in the area, casualties were also heavy. One of the most colorful and acerbic of the 101st commanders, Lieutenant Colonel Robert Cole, who held the Congressional Medal of Honor, was killed. The medal also would be awarded posthumously to another soldier. Private Joe E. Mann, so badly wounded at the bridge that both arms were bandaged and tied to his sides, saw a German grenade land among the men he was with. Unable to free his arms, Mann fell on the grenade, saving the others around him. As Wierzbowski reached him, Mann spoke just once. "My back is gone," he told the lieutenant. Then he was dead.

With the Best bridge gone, the success of Market-Garden now hinged more critically than ever on the speed with which engineers could repair the Son crossing. In the interlocking phases of the plan—each link dependent on the next—the road beyond Son was empty of the tanks that should have moved along it hours before. Montgomery's daring attack was moving into ever-deepening trouble.

The farther up the corridor, the more compounded the problems became. Isolated in the center from General Taylor's Screaming Eagles to the south and the Red Devils in Arnhem, General Gavin's 82nd Airborne were holding firmly to the 1,500-foot-long bridge at Grave and the smaller one near Heumen. To the southwest, after a brisk fight, platoons of the 504th and 508th, attacking simultaneously from opposite sides of the Maas-Waal Canal, seized another bridge over the Grave-Nijmegen highway at the village of Honinghutie, opening an alternate route into Nijmegen for Horrocks' tanks. But just as the damaged Son bridge was holding up the British advance into the middle sector of the corridor, so the inability of the 82nd to seize the Nijmegen crossing quickly had created its own problems. There, SS troops were now dug in at the southern approaches. Well protected and concealed, they repeatedly repulsed attacks by a company of the 508th. As each hour passed, German strength was building, and Gavin could not spare more men in an all-out effort to get the bridge; for throughout the 82nd's vast lodgment—an area ranging ten miles north to south and twelve miles east to west—a series of wild, apparently uncoordinated enemy attacks threatened disaster.

Patrols along the Grave-Nijmegen highway were being constantly attacked by infiltrating enemy troops. Corporal Earl Oldfather, on the lookout for snipers, saw three men in a field the 504th was occupying. "One was bailing water out of his hole, the other two were digging," Oldfather recalls. "I waved and saw one of them pick up his rifle. They were Jerries who had gotten right into our field and were firing at us from our own foxholes."

Farther east, the two vital landing zones between the Groesbeek Heights and the German frontier quickly became battlefields as waves of low-caliber German infantry were thrown against the troopers. Among them were naval and Luftwaffe personnel, communications troops, soldiers on furlough, hospital orderlies, and even recently discharged convalescents. Corporal Frank Ruppe remembers that the first Germans he saw wore a bewildering variety of uniforms and rank insignia. The attack began so suddenly, he recalls, that "we were ambushed practically next to our own outposts." Units appeared as though from nowhere. In the first few minutes Lieutenant Harold Gensemer captured an overconfident German colonel who boasted that "my men will soon kick you right off this hill." They almost did.

Swarming across the German border from the town of Wyler and out of the Reichswald in overwhelming numbers, the Germans burst through the 82nd's perimeter defenses and quickly overran the zones, capturing supply and ammunition dumps. For a time the fighting was chaotic. The 82nd defenders held their positions as long as they could, then slowly pulled back. All over the area troops were alerted to rush to the scene. Men on the edge of Nijmegen force-marched all the way to the drop zones to give additional support.

A kind of panic seemed to set in among the Dutch also. Private Pat O'Hagan observed that as his platoon withdrew from the

Nijmegen outskirts, the Dutch flags he had seen in profusion on the march into the city were being hurriedly taken down. Private Arthur "Dutch" Schultz,° a Normandy veteran and a Browning automatic gunner for his platoon, noticed that "everyone was nervous, and all I could hear was the chant 'BAR front and center.'" Everywhere he looked he saw Germans. "They were all around us and determined to rush us off our zones." It was clear to everyone that until German armor and seasoned reinforcements arrived, the enemy units, estimated at being close to two battalions, had been sent on a suicide mission: to wipe out the 82nd at any cost and hold the drop zones—the division's lifeline for reinforcements and supplies. If the Germans succeeded they might annihilate the second lift even as it landed.

At this time, General Gavin believed that the scheduled lift had already left England. There was no way of stopping or diverting them in time. Thus, Gavin had barely two hours to clear the areas and he needed every available trooper. Besides those already engaged, the only readily available reserves were two companies of engineers. Immediately Gavin threw them into the battle.

Bolstered by mortar and artillery fire, the troopers, outnumbered sometimes five to one, fought all through the morning to clear the zones.† Then with fixed bayonets many men went after the Germans down the slopes. It was only at the height of the battle that Gavin learned that the second lift would not arrive until 2 P.M. The woods remained infested with a hodgepodge of German infantry and it was obvious that these enemy forays heralded more concentrated and determined attacks. By juggling his troops from one area to another, Gavin was confident of holding, but he was only too well aware that for the moment the 82nd's situation was precarious. And now with information that the Son bridge was out and being repaired, he could not expect a

° See Cornelius Ryan, *The Longest Day*, pp. 63, 300.
† In the wild, chaotic fighting that ensued over a period of four hours on the zones, one of the most beloved officers in the 82nd, the heavyweight champion of the division, Captain Anthony Stefanich, was killed. "We've come a long way together," he told his men. "Tell the boys to do a good job." Then he died.

British link-up before D plus 2. Impatiently and with growing concern, Gavin waited for the second lift, which would bring him desperately needed artillery, ammunition and men.

❈ 6 ❈

Fʀᴏᴍ ᴛʜᴇ sᴍᴏᴋɪɴɢ ʀᴜɪɴs ᴏꜰ Aʀɴʜᴇᴍ to the damaged crossing at Son, in foxholes, forests, alongside dikes, in the rubble of demolished buildings, on tanks and near the approaches of vital bridges, the men of Market-Garden and the Germans they fought heard the low rumble come out of the west. In column after column, darkening the sky, the planes and gliders of the second lift were approaching. The steady, mounting drone of motors caused a buoyant renewal of vigor and hope in the Anglo-Americans and the Dutch people. For most Germans, the sound was like a forerunner of doom. Combatants and civilians alike stared skyward, waiting. The time was a little before 2 P.M. Monday, September 18th.

The armada was gigantic, dwarfing even the spectacle of the day before. On the seventeenth, flights had followed two distinct northern and southern paths. Now, bad weather and the hope of effecting greater protection from the Luftwaffe had caused the entire second lift to be routed along the northern path to Holland. Condensed into one immense column covering mile after mile of sky, almost four thousand aircraft were layered at altitudes from 1,000 to 2,500 feet.

Flying wing tip to wing tip, 1,336 American C-47's and 340 British Stirling bombers made up the bulk of the sky train. Some of the planes carried troops. Others towed a staggering number of gliders—1,205 Horsas, Wacos and mammoth Hamilcars. Positioned at the rear of the 100-mile-long convoy, 252 four-engined Liberator bombers were ferrying cargo. Protecting the formations above and on the flanks, 867 fighters—ranging from squadrons of British Spitfires and rocket-firing Typhoons to American Thunderbolts and Lightnings—flew escort. In all, at time of takeoff, the second lift carried 6,674 airborne troops, 681 vehicles plus loaded trailers, 60 artillery pieces with ammunition and nearly 600 tons of supplies, including two bulldozers.°

Wreathed by flak bursts, the huge armada made landfall over the Dutch coast at Schouwen Island, then headed inland due east to a traffic-control point south of the town of s'Hertogenbosch. There, with fighters leading the way, the column split into three sections. With timed precision, executing difficult and dangerous maneuvers, the American contingents swung south and east for the zones of the 101st and 82nd as British formations headed due north for Arnhem.

As on the previous day, there were problems, although they were somewhat diminished. Confusion, abortions and fatal mishaps struck the glider fleets in particular. Long before the second lift reached the drop zones, 54 gliders were downed by structural or human error. Some 26 machines aborted over England and the Channel; two were seen to disintegrate during flight, and 26 more were prematurely released on the 80-mile flight over enemy territory, landing far from their zones in Belgium and Holland and behind the German frontier. In one bizarre incident a distraught trooper rushed to the cockpit and yanked the release lever separating the glider from its tow plane. But troop casualties over-all were low. The greatest loss, as on the previous day, was in precious cargo. Once again Urquhart's men seemed

---

° In the compilation of plane figures there are some discrepancies. American sources give a total of 3,807 aircraft; British figures list 4,000. The count used above comes from General Browning's after-action Corps report, indicating that the difference in figures seems to lie in the number of fighter planes. According to U.S. sources, 674 England-based fighters flew escort for the second lift, but not included in that number were 193 Belgium-based planes, which brings the over-all total of fighters to 867. By far the best account of the air action in Market-Garden, particularly as it pertains to the troop carriers, is the official U.S.A.F. Historical Division's Study No. 97, by Dr. John C. Warren, entitled *Airborne Operations in World War II, European Theater."*

plagued by fate—more than half of the lost cargo gliders were bound for Arnhem.

Fate had ruled the Luftwaffe too. At 10 A.M., with no sign of the expected Allied fleet, German air commanders pulled back more than half the 190-plane force to their bases, while the remainder patrolled the skies over northern and southern Holland. Half of these squadrons were caught in the wrong sector or were being refueled as the second lift came in. As a result, fewer than a hundred Messerschmitts and FW-190's rushed to battle in the Arnhem and Eindhoven areas. Not a single enemy plane was able to penetrate the massive Allied fighter screen protecting the troop carrier columns. After the mission Allied pilots claimed 29 Messerschmitts destroyed against a loss of only five American fighters.

Intense ground fire began to envelop the air fleet as it neared the landing zones. Approaching the 101st's drop areas north of Son, slow-moving glider trains encountered low ground haze and rain, cloaking them to some extent from German gunners. But sustained and deadly flak fire from the Best region ripped into the oncoming columns. One glider, probably carrying ammunition, caught a full antiaircraft burst, exploded, and completely disappeared. Releasing their gliders, four tow planes were hit, one after the other. Two immediately caught fire; one crashed, the other made a safe landing. Three gliders riddled with bullets crash-landed on the zones with their occupants miraculously untouched. In all, of the 450 gliders destined for General Taylor's 101st, 428 reached the zones with 2,656 troopers, their vehicles and trailers.

Fifteen miles to the north, General Gavin's second lift was threatened by the battles still raging on the drop zones as the gliders began to come in. Losses to the 82nd were higher than in the 101st area. Planes and gliders ran into a hail of antiaircraft fire. Although less accurate than on the day before, German gunners managed to shoot down six tow planes as they turned steeply away after releasing their gliders. The wing of one was blasted off, three others crashed in flames, another came down in

Germany. The desperate fire fight for possession of the zones forced many gliders to land elsewhere. Some came down three to five miles from their targets; others ended up in Germany; still more decided to put down fast on their assigned landing zones. Pitted by shells and mortar, crisscrossed by machine-gun fire, each zone was a no man's land. Coming in quickly to hard landings, many gliders smashed undercarriages or nosed over completely. Yet the pilots' drastic maneuvers worked. Troops and cargo alike sustained surprisingly few casualties. Not a man was reported hurt in landing accidents, and only forty-five men were killed or wounded by enemy fire in flight or on the zones. Of 454 gliders, 385 arrived in the 82nd's area, bringing 1,782 artillerymen, 177 jeeps and 60 guns. Initially, more than a hundred paratroopers were thought to have been lost, but later more than half the number made their way to the 82nd's lines after distant landings. The grimly determined glider pilots sustained the heaviest casualties; fifty-four were killed or listed as missing.

Although the Germans failed to seriously impede the arrival of the second lift, they scored heavily against the bomber resupply missions arriving after the troop-carrier and glider trains. By the time the first of the 252 huge four-engined B-24 Liberators approached the 101st and 82nd zones, antiaircraft gunners had found the range. Swooping down ahead of the supply planes, fighters attempted to neutralize the flak guns. But, just as German batteries had done when Horrocks' tanks began their break-out on the seventeenth, so now the enemy forces held their fire until the fighters passed over. Then, suddenly they opened up. Within minutes, some 21 escort planes were shot down.

Following the fighters, bomber formations came in at altitudes varying from 800 to 50 feet. Fire and haze over the zones hid the identifying smoke and ground markers, so that even experienced dropmasters aboard the planes could not locate the proper fields. From the bays of the B-24s, each carrying approximately two tons of cargo, supplies began to fall haphazardly, scattering over a wide area. Racing back and forth throughout their drop zones, 82nd troopers managed to recover 80 percent of their supplies, almost in the faces of the Germans. The 101st was not so fortunate. Many of their equipment bundles landed almost directly among the Germans in the Best area. Less than 50 percent of their resupply was recovered. For General Taylor's men in the lower part of the corridor, the loss was serious, since more than a hundred tons of cargo intended for them consisted of gasoline, ammunition and food. So devastating was the German assault that about 130 bombers were damaged by ground fire, seven were shot down, and four others crash-landed. The day that had begun with so much hope for the beleaguered Americans along the corridor was rapidly becoming a grim fight for survival.

Lieutenant Pat Glover of Brigadier Shan Hackett's 4th Parachute Brigade was out of the plane and falling toward the drop zone south of the Ede-Arnhem road. He felt the jerk as his chute opened, and instinctively reached across and patted the zippered canvas bag attached to the harness over his left shoulder. Inside the bag, Myrtle the parachick squawked and Glover was reassured. Just as he had planned it back in England, Myrtle was making her first combat jump.

As Glover looked down it seemed to him that the entire heath below was on fire. He could see shells and mortars bursting all over the landing zone. Smoke and flames billowed up, and some paratroopers, unable to correct their descent, were landing in the inferno. Off in the distance where gliders were bringing in the remainder of Brigadier Pip Hicks's Airlanding Brigade, Glover could see wreckage and men running in all directions. Something had gone terribly wrong. According to the briefings, Glover knew that Arnhem was supposed to be lightly held and the drop zones, by now, should certainly be cleared and quiet. There had been no indication before the second lift left from England that anything was wrong. Yet it seemed to Glover that a full-scale battle was going on right beneath him. He wondered if by some mistake they were jumping in the wrong place.

As he neared the ground the stutter of machine guns and the dull thud of mortar bursts seemed to engulf him. He hit ground, careful to roll onto his right shoulder to protect Myrtle, and quickly shucked off his harness. Nearby, Glover's batman, Private Joe Scott, had just set down. Glover handed him Myrtle's bag. "Take good care of her," he told Scott. Through the haze covering the field, Glover spotted yellow smoke which marked the rendezvous point. "Let's go," he yelled to Scott. Weaving and crouching, the two men started out. Everywhere Glover looked there was utter confusion. His heart sank. It was obvious that the situation was going badly.

As Major J. L. Waddy came down, he too heard the ominous sound of machine-gun fire that seemed to be flaying the area on all sides. "I couldn't understand it," he recalls. "We had been given the impression that the Germans were in flight, that there was disorder in their ranks." Swinging down in his parachute, Waddy found that the drop zone was almost obscured by smoke from raging fires. At the southern end of the field where he landed, Waddy set out for the battalion's rendezvous area. "Mortars were bursting everywhere, and I saw countless casualties as I went along." When he neared the assembly point, Waddy was confronted by an irate captain from Battalion headquarters who had jumped into Holland the previous day. "You're bloody late," Waddy recalls the man shouting. "Do you realize we've been waiting here for four hours?" Agitatedly, the officer immediately began to brief Waddy. "I was shocked as I listened," Waddy remembers. "It was the first news we had that things weren't going as well as had been planned. We immediately got organized, and as I looked around, it seemed to me that the whole sky up ahead was a mass of flames."

On both landing zones west of the Wolfheze railway station— at Ginkel Heath and Reyers-Camp—paratroopers and glider-borne infantrymen were dropping into what appeared to be a raging battle. From the captured Market-Garden documents the Germans had known the location of the landing areas. And through enemy radar installations in the still-occupied Channel ports such as Dunkirk, they, unlike the British on the ground, could calculate with accuracy the time the second lift was due to arrive. SS units and antiaircraft, hurriedly disengaged in Arnhem, were rushed to the zones. Twenty Luftwaffe fighters, vectored in, continuously strafed the sectors. Ground fighting was equally intense. To clear parts of the heath of the encroaching enemy, the British, as they had during the night and early morning, charged with fixed bayonets.

Mortar bursts, hitting gliders that had landed the day before, turned them into flaming masses that in turn ignited the heath. Infiltrating enemy units used some gliders as cover for their attacks and the British set the machines on fire themselves, rather than let them fall into enemy hands. Nearly fifty gliders blazed in a vast inferno on one section of the field. Yet Brigadier Pip Hicks's Airlanding Brigade—minus the half battalion that had been sent into Arnhem—was managing with dogged courage to hold the zones. The paratroop and glider landings, bringing in 2,119 men, were far more successful than the men in the air or on the ground could believe. Even with the battle underway, 90 percent of the lift was landing—and in the right places.

Flight Sergeant Ronald Bedford, a rear gunner in a four-engined Stirling, found Monday's mission far different from the one he had flown on Sunday. Then, the nineteen-year-old Bedford had been frankly bored with the routineness of the flight. Now, as they neared the landing zone, firing was continuous and intense. Spotting an antiaircraft battery mounted on a truck at the edge of the field, Bedford tried desperately to turn his guns on it. He could see his tracers curving down, and then the battery stopped firing. Bedford was exuberant. "I got him!" he shouted. "Listen, I got him!" As the Stirling held steady on its course, Bedford noticed that gliders all around seemed to be breaking away from their tugs prematurely. He could only assume that the heavy fire had caused many glider pilots to release and try to get down as fast as possible. Then he saw the tow rope attached to their own Horsa falling away. Watching the glider swoop down, Bedford was sure it would collide with others before it could land. "The entire scene was chaotic," he recalls. "The gliders seemed to be going into very steep dives, leveling off, and coasting down, often, it looked, right into each other. I wondered how any of them would make it."

Sergeant Roy Hatch, copiloting a Horsa carrying a jeep, two trailers filled with mortar ammunition, and three men, wondered how they were going to get down when he saw the antiaircraft fire ahead of them on the run-in. As Staff Sergeant Alec Young, the pilot, put the glider into a steep dive and leveled off, Hatch noticed to his amazement that everyone seemed to be heading toward the same touch-down point—including a cow which was frantically running just in front of them. Somehow Young put the glider down safely. Immediately the men jumped out and began unbolting the tail section. Nearby, Hatch noticed three gliders lying on their backs. Suddenly, with a tearing, rasping sound, another Horsa crash-landed on top of them. The glider came straight in, sliced off the nose of Hatch's glider, including the canopy and the cockpit where Hatch and Young had been sitting only moments before, then slid forward, coming to a halt directly in front of them.

Other gliders missed the zones altogether, some crash-landing as far as three miles away. Two came down on the southern bank of the Rhine, one near the village of Driel. Leaving casualties in the care of Dutch civilians, the men rejoined their units by crossing the Rhine on the forgotten but still active Driel ferry.°

Several C-47's were hit and set afire as they made their approach to the zones. About ten minutes from landing, Sergeant Francis Fitzpatrick noticed that flak was coming up thick. A young trooper, Private Ginger MacFadden, jerked and cried out, his hands reaching for his right leg. "I'm hit," MacFadden mumbled. Fitzpatrick examined him quickly and gave him a shot of morphia. Then the sergeant noticed that the plane seemed to be

° The story is probably apocryphal but the Dutch like to tell it. According to Mrs. Ter Horst of Oosterbeek, when the British troopers and their equipment, including an antitank gun, boarded the Driel ferry, Pieter was faced with a dilemma: whether or not to charge them for the trip. By the time they reached the northern bank, Pieter had decided to give them the ride free.

laboring. As he bent to look out the window, the door to the pilot's compartment opened and the dispatcher came out, his face tense. "Stand by for a quick red and green," he said. Fitzpatrick looked down the line of paratroopers, now hooked up and ready to go. He could see smoke pouring from the port engine. Leading the way, Fitzpatrick jumped. As his chute opened, the plane went into a racing dive. Before Fitzpatrick hit the ground he saw the C-47 plow into a field off to his right and nose over. He was sure the crew and Ginger MacFadden had not escaped.

In another C-47 the American crew chief jokingly told Captain Frank D. King, "You'll soon be down there and I'll be heading home for bacon and eggs." The American sat down opposite King. Minutes later the green light went on. King glanced over at the crew chief. He seemed to have fallen asleep, slumped back with his chin on his chest, his hands in his lap. King had a feeling something was not quite right. He shook the American by the shoulder and the man fell sideways. He was dead. Behind him, King saw a large hole in the fuselage which looked as though it had been made by a .50-caliber machine-gun bullet. Standing in the doorway ready to jump, King saw that flames were streaming from the port wing. "We're on fire," he shouted to Sergeant Major George Gatland, "Check with the pilot." Gatland went forward. As he opened the cockpit door a sheet of flame shot out, sweeping the entire length of the plane. Gatland slammed the door shut and King ordered the men to jump. He believed they were now pilotless.

As the troopers went out the door, Gatland estimated the plane was between two and three hundred feet off the ground. He landed with a jar and began a head count. Four men were missing. One man had been killed by gun fire in the doorway before he had a chance to leave the plane. Another had jumped but his chute had caught fire; and a third, Gatland and King learned, had landed a short distance away. Then the fourth man arrived still in his parachute. He had come down with the plane. The crew, he told them, had somehow crash-landed the plane and they had miraculously walked away from it. Now, fifteen miles from

Oosterbeek and far from the British lines, King's group set out to make their way back. As they moved out, the C-47, blazing a quarter of a mile away, blew up.

In some areas paratroopers jumped safely only to find themselves falling through waves of incendiary fire. Tugging desperately at parachute lines to avoid the tracers, many men landed on the edges of the zones in dense forests. Some, as they struggled to shed their chutes, were shot by snipers. Others landed far away from their zones. In one area, part of a battalion came down behind the Germans, then marched for the rendezvous point bringing eighty prisoners with them.

Under fire on the zones, troopers, discarding their chutes, ran swiftly for cover. Small clusters of badly wounded men lay everywhere. Private Reginald Bryant was caught by the blast of a mortar shell and so severely concussed that he was temporarily paralyzed. Aware of what was happening around him, he could not move a muscle. He stared helplessly as the men from his plane, believing Bryant dead, picked up his rifle and ammunition and hurriedly struck out for the assembly point.

Many men, surprised by the unexpected and unremitting machine-gun and sniper fire that swept the zones, sprinted for cover in the woods. In minutes the areas were deserted except for the dead and wounded. Sergeant Ginger Green, the physical-training instructor who had optimistically brought along a football to have a game on the zone after the expected easy action, jumped and hit the ground so hard that he broke two ribs. How long he lay there, Green does not know. When he regained consciousness, he was alone except for casualties. Painfully he sat up and almost immediately a sniper fired at him. Green got to his feet and began to dart and weave his way toward the woods. Bullets pinged all around him. Again and again, the pain in his ribs forced Green to the ground. He was certain that he would be hit. In the billowing smoke rolling across the heath, his strange duel with the sniper went on for what seemed like hours. "I could only make five or six yards at a time," he remembers, "and I figured I was up against either a sadistic bastard or a damned bad shot." Finally, hugging his injured ribs, Green made one last dash for the woods. Reaching them, he threw himself into the undergrowth and rolled against a tree just as a last bullet smacked harmlessly into the branches above his head. He had gained vital yardage under the most desperate circumstances of his life. Spent and aching, Green slowly removed the deflated football from inside his camouflage smock and painfully threw it away.

Many men would remember the first terrible moments after they jumped. Running for their lives from bullets and burning brush on Ginkel Heath at least a dozen troopers recall a young twenty-year-old lieutenant who lay in the gorse badly wounded. He had been shot in the legs and chest by incendiary bullets as he swung helplessly in his parachute. Lieutenant Pat Glover saw the young officer as he moved off the zone. "He was in horrible pain," Glover remembers, "and he just couldn't be moved. I gave him a shot of morphia and promised to send back a medic as soon as I could." Private Reginald Bryant, after recovering from his paralysis on the drop zone, came across the officer as he was heading for the assembly area. "When I got to him, smoke was coming from wounds in his chest. His agony was awful. A few of us had come upon him at the same time and he begged us to kill him." Someone, Bryant does not remember who, slowly reached down and gave the lieutenant his own pistol, cocked. As the men hurried off, the fire on the heath was slowly moving toward the area where the stricken officer lay. Later, rescue parties came across the body. It was concluded that the lieutenant had committed suicide.°

With characteristic precision Brigadier Shan Hackett, commander of the 4th Parachute Brigade, landed within three hundred yards of the spot he had chosen for his headquarters. In

---

° Although numerous witnesses confirm the story, I have withheld the officer's name. There is still doubt that he shot himself. He was both popular and brave. He may, indeed, have used his pistol, or he may have been killed by a sniper.

spite of enemy fire, the Brigadier's first concern was to find his walking stick, which he had dropped on the way down. As he was searching for it, he came across a group of Germans. "I was more scared than they were," he recalled, "but they seemed eager to surrender." Hackett, who spoke German fluently, brusquely told them to wait; then, recovering his stick, the trim, neatly mustached Brigadier calmly marched his prisoners off.

Impatient, prickly and temperamental at best of times, Hackett did not like what he saw. He, too, had expected the zones to be secure and organized. Now, surrounded by his officers, he prepared to move out his brigade. At this moment, Colonel Charles Mackenzie, General Urquhart's chief of staff, drove up to perform his painful duty. Taking Hackett aside, Mackenzie—in his own words—"told him what had been decided and concluded with the touchy matter of command." Brigadier Pip Hicks had been placed in charge of the division in Urquhart's and Lathbury's absence. Mackenzie went on to explain that Urquhart had made the decision back in England that Hicks was to take over in the event both he and Lathbury should be missing or killed.

Hackett was none too happy, Mackenzie recalls. "Now look here, Charles, I'm senior to Hicks," he told Mackenzie. "I should therefore command this division." Mackenzie was firm. "I quite understand, sir, but the General did give me the order of succession and we must stick to it. Further, Brigadier Hicks has been here twenty-four hours and is now much more familiar with the situation." Hackett, Mackenzie said, might only make matters worse if he "upset the works and tried to do something about it."

But it was obvious to Mackenzie that the matter would not end there. A delicate rift had always existed between Urquhart and Hackett. Although the volatile Brigadier was eminently fit for command, in Urquhart's opinion he lacked the older Hicks's infantry experience. Additionally, Hackett was a cavalryman, and Urquhart was known to hold a lesser opinion of cavalry brigadiers than of the infantrymen with whom he had long been associated. He had once jestingly referred to Hackett in public as "that broken-down cavalryman"—a remark that Hackett had not found amusing.

Mackenzie told Hackett that his 11th Battalion was to be detached from the brigade. It would move out immediately for Arnhem and the bridge. To Hackett, this was the final insult. His pride in the brigade stemmed, in part, from its qualities as a highly trained integrated unit that fought as an independent team. He was appalled that it was being separated and broken into parts. "I do not like being told to give up a battalion without being consulted," he told Mackenzie hotly. Then, on reflection, he added, "Of course, if any battalion should go, it is the 11th. It has been dropped in the southeastern corner of the zone and is closest to Arnhem and the bridge." But he requested another battalion in exchange and Mackenzie replied that he thought Hicks would give him one. And there the matter ended for the moment. The brilliant, explosive and dynamic Hackett bowed to inevitability. For the time, Hicks could run the battle, but Hackett was determined to run his own brigade.

For the British it was a grim and bloody afternoon. With a problem-ridden second lift, the fate of General Urquhart and Brigadier Lathbury still unknown, with Colonel Frost's small force precariously clinging to the north end of the Arnhem bridge, and with a swelling clash of personalities developing between two brigadiers, one more unforeseen disaster had taken place.

Depleted in numbers, worn out by constant fighting, the troopers of Hicks's Airlanding Brigade watched in despair as thirty-five Stirling bomber-cargo planes dropped supplies everywhere but on the zones. Of the eighty-seven tons of ammunition, food and supplies destined for the men of Arnhem, only twelve tons reached the troops. The remainder, widely scattered to the southwest, fell among the Germans.

In Antoon Derksen's house less than five miles away, General Urquhart was still surrounded by Germans. The self-propelled gun and crew on the street below were so close that Urquhart and the two officers with him had not dared risk talk or movement. Apart from some chocolate and hard candy, the men were without food. The water had been cut off and there were no sanitary arrangements. Urquhart felt a sense of desperation. Unable to rest or sleep, he brooded about the progress of the battle and the arrival of the second lift, unaware of its delayed start. He wondered how far Horrocks' tanks had advanced and if Frost still held at the bridge. "Had I known the situation at that moment," he later recalled, "I would have disregarded the concern of my officers and made a break for it, Germans or no Germans." Silent and withdrawn, Urquhart found himself staring fixedly at Captain James Cleminson's mustache. "The enormity in hirsute handlebars had earlier been lost on me," he wrote, "but now there was little else to look at." The mustache irritated him. It looked "damned silly."

With all his preoccupation, Urquhart had never thought of the decision he had made regarding chain of command within the division, a last-minute instruction that was fast building toward a complex confrontation between Hicks and Hackett. By now, at 4 P.M. on Monday, September 18, Urquhart had been absent from his headquarters for almost one full day.

General Wilhelm Bittrich, commander of the II SS Panzer Corps, was shocked by the enormous size of the second lift. Badgered by Field Marshal Model to quickly capture the Arnhem bridge and pressed by Colonel Harzer and General Harmel for reinforcements, Bittrich found his problems growing increasingly acute. As he grimly watched the skies west of Arnhem blossom with hundreds of multicolored parachutes, then fill with an apparently unceasing stream of gliders, he despaired. From the Luftwaffe communications net, he learned that two other massive drops had taken place. Trying to guess the Allied strength, Bittrich greatly overestimated the number of Anglo-Americans now in Holland. He believed that maybe another division had landed, enough to tilt the balance in favor of the attackers.

To Bittrich, the buildup of Allied strength versus the arrival of German reinforcements had become a deadly race. So far only a trickle of men and matériel had reached him. By comparison, the Allies seemed to have inexhaustible resources. He feared that they might mount yet another airborne drop the following day. In the narrow confines of Holland, with its difficult terrain, bridges, and proximity to the undefended frontiers of Germany, a force that size could mean catastrophe.

There was little coordination between Bittrich's forces and Colonel General Student's First Parachute Army to the south. Although Student's men were being constantly reinforced by the remnants of Von Zangen's Fifteenth Army, that shattered force was desperately short of transport, guns and ammunition. Days, perhaps weeks, would be needed to re-equip them. Meanwhile, the entire responsibility for halting Montgomery's attack lay with Bittrich, and his most pressing problems remained the crossing at Nijmegen and the unbelievable defense by the British at the northern approach of the Arnhem bridge.

So long as the Allied troopers held out there, Bittrich was prevented from moving his own forces down the highway to Nijmegen. Harmel's Frundsberg Division, trying to get across the Rhine, was dependent entirely on the ferry at Pannerden—a slow, tedious method of crossing. Ironically, while the British at Arnhem were experiencing their first tentative doubts of their ability to hang on, Bittrich was gravely concerned about the outcome of the battle. He saw the Reich as dangerously close to invasion. The next twenty-four hours might tell the story.

Bittrich's superiors had problems of wider scope. All along Army Group B's vast front, Field Marshal Model was juggling forces, trying to stem the relentless attacks of the American First and Third Armies. Although the reinstatement of the illustrious Von Rundstedt to his old command had brought a renewal of order and cohesion, he was scraping the bottom of the nation's manpower barrel for reinforcements. Locating gasoline to move units from one area to another was also becoming an increasingly critical problem, and there was little help from Hitler's headquarters. Berlin seemed more preoccupied with the Russian menace from the east than with the Allied drive from the west.

Despite his other worries, Model seemed confident of overcoming the threat in Holland. He remained convinced that the country's marshes, dikes and water barriers could work for him in providing time to halt and defeat Montgomery's attack. Bittrich had no such optimism. He urged Model to take several important steps before the situation worsened. In Bittrich's view, the destruction of the Nijmegen and Arnhem bridges was necessary immediately, but that proposal irritated Model every time Bittrich suggested it. "Pragmatic, always demanding the impossible, Model visited me every day," Bittrich was to recall. "On the spot, he would issue a stream of orders referring to immediate situations, but he never stayed long enough at any conference to hear out or approve long-range plans." Model, Bittrich feared, did not grasp the appalling eventualities that could ensue for Germany if an Allied breakthrough occurred. Instead, he seemed obsessed with details; he was particularly concerned about the German failure to recapture the Arnhem bridge. Stung by the implied criticism, Bittrich told the Field Marshal, "In all my years as a soldier, I have never seen men fight so hard." Model was unimpressed. "I want that bridge," he said coldly.

On the afternoon of the eighteenth Bittrich tried again to explain his view of the over-all situation to an impatient Model. The Nijmegen bridge was the key to the entire operation, he argued. Destroy it and the head of the Allied attack would be severed from its body. "Herr Field Marshal, we should demolish the Waal crossing before it is too late," Bittrich said. Model was adamant. "No!" he said. "The answer is no!" Not only did Model insist that the bridge could be defended; he demanded that Student's army and the Frundsberg Division halt the Anglo-Americans before they ever reached it. Bittrich said bluntly that he was far from sure the Allies could be contained. As yet there was almost no German armor in the area and, he told Model, there was grave danger that Montgomery's overwhelming tank strength would achieve a breakthrough. Then Bittrich expressed his fears that further airborne drops could be expected. "If the Allies succeed in their drive from the south and if they drop one more airborne division in the Arnhem area, we're finished," he said. "The route to the Ruhr and Germany will be open." Model would not be swayed. "My orders stand," he said. "The Nijmegen bridge is not to be destroyed, and I want the Arnhem bridge captured within twenty-four hours."

Others knew the difficulty of carrying out Model's commands. Lieutenant Colonel Harzer, commander of the Hohenstaufen Division, had run out of men. All his forces were fully engaged. No additional reinforcements had arrived, and the size of the second lift posed grave doubts as to the ability of his soldiers to halt and contain the enemy. Like Bittrich, Harzer was convinced that "the Allies had dropped no more than an airborne spearhead. I was sure that more would follow and then they would drive for the Reich." With limited armor, Harzer did not know whether he could stop the enemy. He had, however, succeeded in making one place secure—the grounds of his own headquarters. There, with cynical disregard for the rights of prisoners, he had ordered several hundred British troopers to be held under guard in wire enclosures. "I was quite sure," he was to recall, "that the R.A.F. would not bomb their own troops."

Harzer, a self-professed Anglophile ("I had a real weakness for the English"), had once studied as an exchange student in Great Britain. He enjoyed sauntering among the prisoners trying to engage in conversation to practice his English and, hopefully, to elicit information. He was struck by the British morale. "They were contemptuous and self-assured, as only veteran soldiers can be," he recalled. The caliber of his prisoners convinced Harzer that the battle was far from won. To keep Urquhart's forces off balance and to prevent any kind of cohesive attack, he ordered his Hohenstaufen Division on the evening of the eighteenth "to attack unceasingly at whatever cost throughout the night."

The commander of the Frundsberg Division, General Harmel,

was "too busy to worry about what might happen next. I had my hands full fighting the Lower Rhine." Charged with the capture of the Arnhem bridge and the defense of the Waal crossing and the area in between, Harmel's problems were far more acute than Harzer's. The move of his division by ferry across the river was proceeding at a snail's pace. Troops, equipment and tanks were loaded on makeshift rubber or log rafts. Roads leading down to the water's edge had become quagmires. Tanks and vehicles had slid off rafts, and some had even been swept away. Worse, because of constant strafing by Allied planes, nearly all ferrying and convoying operations had to take place during darkness. In twenty-four hours Harmel's engineers had succeeded in moving only two battalions with their vehicles and equipment into the Arnhem-Nijmegen area. To speed up operations, truck shuttles carrying troops ran back and forth between the south bank landing stage and Nijmegen. But the movement was far too slow. To be sure, Harmel's men were now in the center of Nijmegen and on the southern side of the highway bridge, but he doubted that they could stop a determined attack by the Anglo-Americans. Although he had been ordered not to destroy it, Harmel was prepared for the eventuality. His engineers had already laid charges and set up detonating apparatus in a roadside bunker near the village of Lent on the northern bank. He hoped Bittrich would approve the blowing of the highway and railroad bridges if they could not be held. But if he did not, Harmel's decision was already made. If British tanks broke through and started across, he would defy his superiors and destroy the bridges.

⁂ 7 ⁂

THE PROSPEROUS VILLAGE OF OOSTERBEEK seemed infused with a strange mixture of gaiety and uneasiness. Like an island in the middle of the battle, the village was assaulted by the noise of fighting on three sides. From the drop zones to the west came the nearly constant thunder of guns. To the northwest the chattering of machine guns and the steady cough of mortars could be clearly heard in the flower-lined streets, and to the east, two and a half miles away in Arnhem, black smoke hung over the horizon, a somber backdrop to the unceasing timpani of heavy artillery.

The bombing and strafing preceding the troop and glider landings on the previous day had produced casualties among the villagers and some damage to shops and houses, as had infiltrating snipers and ill-directed mortar bursts, but the war had not so far made serious inroads into Oosterbeek. The neat resort hotels, landscaped villas and tree-lined streets were still largely untouched. Yet it was becoming obvious with every hour that the fighting was coming closer. Here and there, concussion from distant explosions splintered panes of glass with startling suddenness. Charred particles of paper, cloth and wood, carried like confetti by the wind, rained down into the streets, and the air was acrid with the smell of cordite.

On Sunday Oosterbeek had been filled with troops as the British arrived almost on the heels of a frantic German departure. No one had slept during the night. A nervous excitement, heightened by the low whine of jeeps, the clatter of Bren gun carriers and the tramp of marching men, made rest impossible. Throughout most of the eighteenth the movement had continued. The villagers, joyous and yet apprehensive, had decked the streets and houses with Dutch flags and plied their liberators with food, fruit and drink as the British Tommies hurried through. To almost everyone the war seemed all but over. Now, subtly, the atmosphere was changing. Some British units were apparently firmly established in the village, and Lieutenant Colonel Sheriff Thompson's artillery spotters occupied the tower of the tenth-century Dutch Reformed church near the Rhine in lower Oosterbeek, but troop movement had noticeably slowed. By late afternoon most thoroughfares were disquietingly empty, and the Dutch noted that antitank and Bren gun positions were now sited at strategic points on the main road. Seeing them, villagers had a sense of foreboding.

As he walked through Oosterbeek trying to discover exactly what was happening, Jan Voskuil recalls seeing a British officer ordering civilians to take in their flags. "This is war," he heard the officer tell one villager, "and you are in the middle of it." Throughout his walk, Voskuil noted that the mood of the people was changing. From Jaap Koning, a local baker, Voskuil learned that many Dutch were pessimistic. There were rumors, Koning said, that "things are not going well." Apprehension was replacing the heady sense of liberation. "The British," Koning said, "are being pushed back everywhere." Voskuil was profoundly concerned. Koning was always well informed, and although his was the first bad news Voskuil had heard, it confirmed his own fears. As each hour passed, Voskuil thought that the canopy of shells screaming over the town toward Arnhem was growing heavier. Remembering anew the terrible destruction of the Normandy villages, Voskuil could not rid himself of an overwhelming feeling of hopelessness.

A second tradesman, baker Dirk van Beek, was as depressed as Koning and Voskuil. The news he had heard on his delivery rounds had dampened his first excited reaction to the Allied drop. "What if the war comes here—what will we do?" he asked his wife, Riek. But he already knew the answer: he would remain in Oosterbeek and keep on baking. "People have to eat," he told Riek. "Anyway, where would we go if we left the shop?" Absorbing himself in work, Van Beek tried to reassure himself that everything would work out for the best. He had received his monthly allotment of wheat and yeast a few days earlier. Now, determined to stay and to keep his shop open, he remembered that an old baker had once told him of a method of making bread that required less than half the usual amount of yeast. He decided to stretch his supplies to the limit. He would continue to bake until everything was gone.

At the Tafelberg, Schoonoord and Vreewijk Hotels it was obvious that the battle had taken a serious turn: the airy, comfortable resorts were being turned into casualty stations. At the Schoonoord British medics and Dutch civilians began a full-scale house cleaning to make ready to receive the wounded. Jan Eijkelhoff, of the underground, saw that the Germans, in their hasty departure, had left the hotel "looking like a pig pen. Food was all over the place. Tables had been overturned, plates broken, clothing and equipment were scattered around. Papers and rubbish littered every room." From surrounding houses extra mattresses were brought in and placed on the ground floor. Rows of beds were set up in the main reception rooms and stretchers were placed along the glassed-in veranda. Every room, including the cellars, would be needed by nightfall, the Dutch were told. Eijkelhoff learned that St. Elisabeth's Hospital in Arnhem was already filled to capacity. Yet the British medics with whom he worked remained optimistic. "Don't worry," one of them told him, "Monty will be here soon."

At the Tafelberg Hotel, where Dr. Gerrit van Maanen was setting up a hospital, seventeen-year-old Anje van Maanen, who had come to help her father, noted the startling change in other volunteers. "We are afraid," she wrote in her diary, "but we don't know why. We have a queer feeling that weeks have passed between yesterday and today." As at the Schoonoord, there were rumors at the Tafelberg that Montgomery's forces were on the way. On the lookout for their quick arrival, Anje wrote, "We stare constantly out of the upstairs windows. The shooting is stronger. There are lights and fires, but the great army is not here yet."

A few blocks away, the ornate twelve-room Hartenstein Hotel, sited amid its parklike surroundings, wore a gaunt, deserted look. In Daliesque disarray, tables and chairs were scattered across the fine green lawn and among them, the result of a sharp fire fight the day before, lay the crumpled bodies of several Germans.

As he cycled up to the building, twenty-seven-year-old William Giebing was sickened by the appearance of the once elegant hotel. A few months after he took possession of the building, leasing it from the town of Oosterbeek in 1942, the Germans had moved into the village and requisitioned the hotel. From that time on, Giebing and his wife, Truus, were relegated to the position of servants. The Germans allowed them to clean the Hartenstein and to oversee the cuisine, but the management of the hotel was in German hands. Finally, on September 6, Giebing was summarily ordered to leave, but his wife and two maids were allowed to return each day to keep the place clean.

On the seventeenth, "crazy with joy at the landings," Giebing jumped on a bicycle and set out for the Hartenstein from Wester-bouwing, where his father-in-law, Johan van Kalkschoten, operated the hilltop restaurant overlooking the Heveadorp-Driel ferry. He was just in time to see the last of the Germans departing. Running into the building, he felt for the first time that "the hotel was finally mine." But the air of desertion was unnerving. In the dining room two long tables covered with white damask tablecloths were set for twenty. There were soup bowls, silver, napkins and wine glasses and, in the center of each table, a large tureen of vermicelli soup. Touching it, Giebing found it still warm. In silver servers on the sideboard was the main course: fried sole.

Giebing wandered from room to room looking at the rich, gold-covered damask walls, the ornate plaster angels and garlands, the bridal suite where gold stars speckled the sky-blue ceiling. The Germans, he was relieved to find, had not looted the hotel. Not a spoon was missing and the refrigerators were still full of food. Making the rounds, Giebing heard voices coming from the veranda. Rushing out he found several British soldiers drinking his sherry. Eight empty bottles lay on the floor. Unaccountably, after all the days of occupation, Giebing lost his temper. The Germans had, at least, left his beloved hotel clean. "So this is the first thing you do," he yelled at the troopers. "Break open my cellar and steal my sherry." The British were embarrassed and apologetic, and Giebing was mollified, but once again he was told he could not remain. However, the British assured him that his property would be respected.

Now, a day later, hoping that the British had passed through and left his hotel, Giebing returned. His heart sank as he approached the building. Jeeps were parked in the rear of the building and, behind the wire netting of the tennis courts, he saw German prisoners. Slit trenches and gun positions had been dug in around the perimeter of the grounds and staff officers seemed to be everywhere. Disheartened, Giebing returned to Wester-bouwing. In the afternoon his wife visited the Hartenstein and explained who she was. "I was treated very politely," she recalls, "but we were not permitted to move back. The British, like the Germans, had requisitioned the hotel." There was one consolation, she thought: the war would soon be over and then the Giebings could truly operate what they considered the best hotel in Oosterbeek. The courteous English officers with whom she talked did not inform her that the Hartenstein, as of 5 p.m. on September 18, was now the headquarters of the 1st British Airborne Division.

In the strange mixture of anxiety and joy that permeated Oosterbeek, one incident terrified many of the inhabitants more than the thought of the encroaching battle. During the day prisoners had been released from the Arnhem jail. Many were resistance fighters, but others were dangerous convicts. In their striped prison garb, they flooded out of Arnhem, and more than fifty ended up in Oosterbeek. "They added a final touch of madness," recalls Jan ter Horst, a former Dutch army artillery captain, a lawyer and a leading member of the Oosterbeek resistance. "We rounded the convicts up and put them temporarily in the concert hall. But the question was, what to do with them? They seemed harmless enough at the moment, but many of these felons had been imprisoned for years. We feared the worst—especially for our women folk—when they finally realized that they were free."

Talking with the convicts Ter Horst found that they wanted only to get out of the immediate combat zone. The sole route across the Rhine was by the Heveadorp-Driel ferry. Pieter, the ferryman, flatly refused to cooperate. He did not want fifty convicts running loose on the southern bank. Further, the ferry was now moored on the north side and Pieter wanted it to remain there. After several hours of testy negotiations, Ter Horst was finally able to get Pieter to take the prisoners across. "We were glad to see them go," he remembers. "The women were more scared of the convicts than they had been of the Germans." Prudently Ter Horst insisted that the ferry be returned to the northern bank, where it could be used by the British.

As a former army officer, Ter Horst was puzzled as to why the Heveadorp-Driel ferry had not been immediately seized by the British. When the troopers entered Oosterbeek he had questioned them about the ferry. To his amazement, he discovered they knew nothing about it. A former artilleryman, he was astounded that the British had not occupied nearby Westerbouwing, the only high ground overlooking the Rhine. Whoever held these heights with artillery controlled the ferry. Further, the choice of the Hartenstein as British headquarters disturbed him. Surely, he thought, the restaurant and its buildings on the heights at Westerbouwing were a far preferable site. "Hold the ferry and Westerbouwing," he urged several British staff officers. They were polite, but uninterested. One officer told Ter Horst, "We don't intend to stay here. With the bridge in our hands and the arrival of Horrocks' tanks, we don't need the ferry." Ter Horst hoped the man was right. If the Germans reached Westerbouwing, less than two miles away, their guns not only could command the ferry but could totally demolish British headquarters at the Hartenstein. The British now knew about the ferry and they had been briefed about Westerbouwing. There was little else Ter Horst could do. The former Dutch officer had, in fact, pointed out one of the most crucial oversights in the entire operation—the failure of the British to realize the strategic importance of the ferry and the Westerbouwing heights. Had General Urquhart stayed at his headquarters and in control of the battle the situation might have been rectified in time.°

Brigadier Hicks, commanding the division in Urquhart's absence, was facing almost hourly the bewildering problem of orienting himself to the complex, constantly shifting moves of the hard-pressed airborne unit. With the breakdown of radio communications between headquarters and the battalions, there was little precise information about what was happening, nor could Hicks gauge the strength and potential of the enemy forces opposing him. What scant news reached him was brought by spent, dirt-streaked messengers, who risked their lives to bring him information, which was often hopelessly out of date by the time they arrived at headquarters, or by the various members of the Dutch underground, whose reports were often disregarded or viewed as suspect. Hicks found himself depending strongly on one slender channel of communication—the tenuous Thompson-to-Munford artillery radio link existing between Oosterbeek and Frost's forces at the bridge.

Mauled and battered, the 2nd Battalion and the valiant stragglers who had reached it were still holding, but Frost's situation

---

° The same point is made in several monographs written by the eminent Dutch military historian, Lieutenant Colonel Theodor A. Boeree. "Had Urquhart been there," he writes, "he might well have abandoned the defense of the bridge, recalled Frost's battalion, if possible, concentrated his six original batallions and the three of the 4th Parachute Brigade that had just landed, and established a firm bridgehead somewhere else on the northern side of Lower Rhine . . . with the high ground at Westerbouwing . . . as the center of the bridgehead. There they could have awaited the arrival of the British Second Army."

had been desperate for hours and was deteriorating rapidly. "We were getting constant messages from the bridge asking for relief and ammunition," Hicks recalled. "Enemy pressure and the steadily increasing strength of German armor was building everywhere, and there was absolutely no contact with Urquhart, Lathbury, Dobie or Fitch. We could not raise Browning at Corps headquarters to explain the gravity of the situation, and we were desperate for help." From prisoner interrogations Hicks now knew that the troopers were up against battle-hardened SS men of the 9th Hohenstaufen and 10th Frundsberg divisions. No one had been able to tell him how strong these units were or to estimate the number of tanks that were being thrown against him. Worse, Hicks did not know whether the original preattack plan could withstand the present German pressure. If the enemy was heavily reinforced the entire mission might founder.

Help, he knew, was coming. On the nineteenth, Major General Stanislaw Sosabowski's Polish Brigade would arrive in the third lift. Horrocks' tanks should also be arriving and were, indeed, already late. How close were they to Arnhem and could they arrive in time to relieve and balance the situation? "In spite of everything," Hicks recalls, "I believed Frost would hold the northern end of the bridge until Monty's tanks got to it. The bridge was still our objective, after all, and my decisions and actions were centered solely on seizing and holding that objective." Balancing all the factors, Hicks felt he must stick to the original plan, and so did Brigadier Hackett at this time.

The original task of Hackett's 4th Parachute Brigade was to occupy the high ground north of Arnhem to prevent German reinforcements from reaching the bridge. But at the time that plan was conceived it was thought that enemy strength would prove negligible and, at worst, manageable. In fact, enemy reaction had been so fast, concentrated and effective that Hicks could not assess the true situation. Bittrich's corps held the north of Arnhem; his troops had bottled up Frost at the bridge and successfully prevented Dobie and Fitch's battalions from relieving them. The advance of these two units was now virtually sheared off. In the built-up areas around St. Elisabeth's Hospital barely a mile or so from the bridge, the battalions were stopped in their tracks. The South Staffordshires, already en route to help, and the 11th Battalion from Hackett's brigade were faring no better. "We now came to the wide-open, exposed riverside stretch of road in front of St. Elisabeth's Hospital, and then everything suddenly let loose," remembers Private Robert C. Edwards of the South Staffordshires. "We must have looked like targets in a shooting gallery. All Jerry had to do was line up his guns and mortars on this one gap—about a quarter of a mile wide—and fire. He couldn't miss." Edwards saw Captain Edward Weiss, second in command of his company, running tirelessly up and down the column "totally ignoring all the metal flying about him, his voice growing ever hoarser as he yelled out 'On, on, on, D Company, on.'"

Weiss seemed to be everywhere. Men were falling all around. If troopers halted or hesitated, Weiss was "immediately beside them urging them on. You just couldn't crawl and watch him stand upright. You had to follow his lead through that hell of fire." Edwards threw some smoke bombs to try to hide their advance and "then put my head down and ran like a hare." He stumbled over "heaps of dead, slithered in pools of blood, until I reached the partial shelter afforded by houses and buildings on the far side of the road." There he discovered that Captain Weiss had been hit as he ran across. "Major Phillips had been badly wounded. No one seemed to have much idea of what was going on or what we should do next." As for D Company, when a count was made, "only 20 percent remained, and quite obviously we couldn't continue against such overwhelming German strength. Hopefully we waited for the dawn."

It was as if a solid wall had been built between the division and Frost's pitiful few at the bridge.

In exchange for his 11th Battalion, Hackett had been given the 7th Battalion of the King's Own Scottish Borderers (KOSB's). They had guarded the drop zones since landing on the seventeenth. Now they moved out with Hackett's 10th and 156th battalions via Wolfheze northwest of Oosterbeek. In that area the KOSB's would guard Johannahoeve Farm, a landing zone where transport and artillery of the Polish Brigade were due to arrive by glider in the third lift.

After the initial fighting on the zones, Hackett's brigade moved off without incident, and by nightfall the KOSB's had taken up positions around Johannahoeve Farm. There, suddenly, the battalions ran into heavy German opposition from strongly held machine-gun positions. A pitched battle began. In the growing darkness, commands went out to hold positions and then attempt to rout the enemy at dawn. It was vitally important to secure the area. Sosabowski's paratroopers were scheduled to land on the nineteenth on the southern side of the Arnhem bridge, in the polder land that Urquhart and the R.A.F. had deemed unsuitable—because of antiaircraft considerations—for the large-scale initial landings. By the time the Poles were to arrive, it had been expected that the bridge would be in British hands. If it was not, the Poles had been assigned to take it. At Browning's rear Corps headquarters in England, where no one was aware of the compounding setbacks developing at Arnhem, the Polish drop was still scheduled to take place as planned. If Frost could hold out and the Polish drop was successful, there was still a chance even now that Market-Garden could succeed.

Everywhere men were still struggling toward the bridge. On the lower road that Frost had taken on what now seemed to many a long-ago day, Private Andrew Milbourne and a small group of stragglers from other battalions passed stealthily near the ruins of the railway bridge that Frost's men had tried to capture on their march to the prime objective. In fields to his left, Milbourne saw white mounds gleaming in the darkness. "They were dozens of dead bodies, and the Dutch were moving quietly around the area, covering our comrades with white sheets," he recalls. Up ahead, fires reddened the sky and an occasional flash of guns outlined the great bridge. All afternoon the little band had been held up by superior German forces. Now, once more, they were pinned down. As they took refuge in a boathouse on the edge of the river, Milbourne began to despair of ever reaching the bridge. A lone signalman in the group began to work his radio set and, as the men gathered around, he suddenly picked up the BBC from London. Milbourne listened as the clear, precise voice of the announcer recounted the day's happenings on the western front. "British troops in Holland," he reported, "are meeting only slight opposition." In the gloomy boathouse someone laughed derisively. "Bloody liar," Milbourne said.

Now, as the courageous men of the 1st British Airborne Division fought for their very existence, two of His Majesty's brigadiers chose to have a heated argument over which of them should command the division. The dispute was triggered by a smolderingly angry Brigadier Shan Hackett who, by evening of the eighteenth, saw the situation as not only disquieting but "grossly untidy." The enemy seemed to have the upper hand everywhere. British battalions were scattered and fighting uncohesively, without knowledge of one another's whereabouts. Lacking communications, pinned down in built-up areas, many units came upon one another quite by chance. It appeared to Hackett that there was no over-all command or coordination of effort. Late in the evening, still smarting over the startling announcement by Mackenzie concerning the command of the division, the temperamental Hackett drove to the Hartenstein Hotel in Oosterbeek to have it out with Hicks. "He arrived about midnight," Hicks recalls. "I was in the operations room, and from the very beginning it was perfectly clear that, as he was senior in grade to me, he was less than happy that I had been given command. He was young, with firm ideas and rather argumentative."

Initially, Hackett's displeasure focused on the fact that Hicks had detached the 11th Battalion from him. He demanded to know what orders it had been given and who was in command of the sector. "He thought," recalls Hicks, "that the situation was too

fluid, and obviously disagreed with the decisions I had made."
Patiently the older Hicks explained that because of strong German resistance, the present battle situation had been totally
unforeseen. Each battalion, therefore, was now fighting individually to reach the bridge and, although instructed to follow
specific routes, battalions had been warned that due to the
unusual conditions some overlapping might occur. Two or more
units might well find themselves forced into the same vicinity.
Hackett brusquely commented that "the command setup was
clearly unsatisfactory."

Hicks agreed, but the object, he told Hackett, "was to help
Frost at the bridge in whatever way we can and as fast as
possible." While agreeing that Frost had to be reinforced quickly,
Hackett sarcastically suggested that this might be done in a
"more coordinated manner with more drive and cohesion." There
was much to be said for Hackett's argument: a coordinated drive
might indeed succeed in breaking through the German ring and
reaching Frost; but, lacking communications and kept off balance
by constant German attacks, Hicks had had little time to organize
such an all-out attack.

The two men then turned to the role that Hackett's brigade
would play the next day. In Hicks's view, Hackett should not
attempt to occupy the high ground north of Arnhem. "I felt he
could aid Frost better by driving into Arnhem and helping to
hold the northern end of the bridge." Hackett objected strongly.
He wanted a definite objective, and he appeared to know what it
should be. He would take the high ground east of Johannahoeve
first, he announced, and then "see what I can do to assist the
operations in Arnhem." In the quiet, understated but bitter verbal
fencing, Hackett insisted that he be given a time schedule so that
he could relate "my actions to everyone else." He wanted "a
sensible plan." Otherwise, Hackett said, he would be compelled
"to raise the question of command of the division."

Lieutenant Colonel P. H. Preston, the headquarters administrative officer, was present at what Hicks has since tactfully called
"our discussion." Preston remembers that Hicks, "his face tightly

drawn," turned to him and said, "Brigadier Hackett thinks he ought to be in command of the division." Hackett protested the choice of words. Preston, sensing that the conversation was becoming overly tense, immediately left the room and sent the duty officer, Gordon Grieve, in search of the chief of staff, Colonel Mackenzie.

In a room upstairs Mackenzie was resting, unable to sleep. "I had been there about half an hour when Gordon Grieve came in. He told me that I should come downstairs immediately, that the two Brigadiers, Hicks and Hackett, 'were having a flaming row.' I was already dressed. On the way down I tried to think quickly. I knew what the row was about and that it might be necessary for me to take decisive action. I had no intention of going into the operations room and exchanging pleasantries. I felt at this point that General Urquhart's orders were being questioned and I intended to back Hicks in everything."

As Mackenzie entered the room the conversation between the two brigadiers abruptly ceased. "Both men had begun to compose themselves," recalls Mackenzie, "and it was immediately clear that the worst was over." Hicks, glancing up at Mackenzie, was almost casual. "Oh, hello, Charles," Mackenzie remembers him saying, "Brigadier Hackett and I have had a bit of a row, but it is all right now." Hicks was certain that "things had settled back to normal. I was rather firm with Hackett and when he left I knew he would follow my orders." However much he may have appeared to accept Hicks's new role, Hackett's view was largely unchanged. "I intended to take orders from Pip if they made sense," he remembers. "What I was told to do was far from that. Therefore, I was inclined to assert my position as senior brigadier of the two and issue the sort of orders for my brigade's operation which did make sense."*

---

* I believe the row was far more heated than related above, but understandably Hicks and Hackett, good friends, are reluctant to discuss the matter in greater detail. There are at least four different versions of what transpired, and none of them may be entirely accurate. My reconstruction is based on interviews with Hackett, Hicks and Mackenzie, and on accounts in Urquhart's *Arnhem*, pp. 77–90, and Hibbert's *The Battle of Arnhem*, pp. 101–3.

Under any other circumstances, the confrontation between the brigadiers would have been merely an historical footnote. Two courageous, dedicated men, under intense strain and with identical aims, lost their tempers for a moment. In the balance sheet of Market-Garden when the plan was in such jeopardy and every soldier was needed if a coordinated effort to seize the Arnhem bridge was to succeed, cooperation among commanders and cohesion in the ranks were vital. Particularly so, since the fate of the First Allied Airborne Army had taken yet another turn: throughout the Market-Garden area, Field Marshal Von Rundstedt's promised reinforcements were arriving from all over the western front in a steady, unceasing flow.

Nicolaas de Bode, the highly skilled technician who had made the first secret telephone connection for the underground between north and south Holland, had remained in his room all day. On instructions from the regional resistance chief Pieter Kruyff, De Bode sat by a small side window which looked out on the Velper Weg, the wide street leading from the eastern side of Arnhem to Zutphen in the north. Although he had not strayed from his post, calls had reached him from outlying areas to the west and had deeply disturbed him. In the Wolfheze and Oosterbeek areas, underground members reported trouble. The excited talk of liberation had stopped. For some hours now, all he had heard was that the situation was worsening. De Bode was asked to keep a constant watch for any sign of heavy German movement from the north and east. So far he had seen nothing. His messages, phoned to underground headquarters hourly, contained the same terse information. "The road is empty," he had reported again and again.

In the late evening, some twenty minutes before his next call, he heard "the sound of armored cars running on rubber tires and the clanking of armor." Wearily he walked to the window, and gazed up the Velper Weg. The road seemed empty as before. Then in the distance, visible in the fiery glow that hung over the city, he saw two massive tanks coming into view. Moving side by side along the wide street, they were heading straight down the road leading into the old part of the city. As De Bode watched wide-eyed, besides the tanks he saw trucks "carrying clean-looking soldiers, sitting straight up on the seats with their rifles in front of them. Then, more tanks and more soldiers in rows on trucks." Promptly he called Kruyff and said, "It looks like an entire German army complete with tanks and other weapons is heading straight into Arnhem."

The man who had warned London on September 14 about the presence of Bittrich's II SS Panzer Corps, Henri Knap, Arnhem's underground intelligence chief, was now receiving a steady stream of reports of German reinforcements from his network. Knap abandoned caution. He telephoned British headquarters at the Hartenstein directly and spoke to a duty officer. Without preamble Knap told him that "a column of tanks, among them some Tigers, is moving into Arnhem and some are heading toward Oosterbeek." The officer politely asked Knap to hold on. A few minutes later he came back on the line. Thanking Knap, he explained that "the Captain is doubtful about the report. After all, he's heard a lot of fairy tales." But the skepticism at British headquarters quickly disappeared when Pieter Kruyff confirmed through Lieutenant Commander Arnoldus Wolters, of the Royal Dutch Navy, acting as an intelligence liaison officer for the division, that at least "fifty tanks are heading into Arnhem from the northeast."

The stench of battle permeated the inner city. On the bridge, wreckage jutted high above the concrete shoulders and littered streets along the Rhine. Heavy smoke smeared buildings and yards with a greasy film. All along the waterfront hundreds of fires burned unattended, and men remember that the ground shook constantly from the concussion of heavy explosives as the Germans, in the final hours of this second day of battle, battered

British strongholds along the northern ramp in the bitter contest for possession of Montgomery's prime objective.

Around midnight Lieutenant Colonel John Frost left his headquarters on the western side of the ramp and made his way around the perimeter, checking his men. Although the battle had continued almost without letup since Gräbner's armored attack during the morning, morale was still high. Frost was proud of his tired, dirty troopers. All day long they had doggedly repelled attack after attack. Not a single German or vehicle had reached the north end of the bridge.

During the afternoon the Germans had changed their tactics. With phosphorous ammunition, they attempted to burn the British out of their strong points. A long-barreled 150 mm. gun hurled 100-pound shells directly against Frost's headquarters building, forcing the men to the cellar. Then British mortars got the range and scored a direct hit, killing the gun crew. As the troopers cheered and hooted derisively, other Germans rushed out under fire and towed the gun away. Houses around the perimeter were burning fiercely, but the British held out in them until the very last minute before moving to other positions. Damage was awesome. Burning trucks and vehicles, wrecked halftracks and smoking piles of debris cluttered every street. Sergeant Robert H. Jones remembers the sight as "a Sargasso sea of blazing collapsed buildings, half-tracks, trucks and jeeps." The battle had become an endurance contest, one that Frost knew his men could not win without help.

Cellars and basements were filled with wounded. One of the battalion chaplains, the Reverend Father Bernard Egan, and the battalion medical officer, Captain James Logan—who had been friends since the North African campaign—tended the casualties from a rapidly dwindling stock of medical supplies. There was almost no morphia left and even field dressings were almost gone. The men had set out for the bridge with only enough light rations for forty-eight hours. Now, these were almost exhausted, and the Germans had cut off the water. Forced to scrounge for food, the troopers were existing on apples and a few pears stored in the cellars and basements of the houses they occupied. Private G. W. Jukes remembers his sergeant telling the men, "You don't need water if you eat lots of apples." Jukes had a vision of "being eventually relieved, standing back-to-back defiantly in blood-stained bandages, surrounded by dead Germans, spent cartridge cases and apple cores."

Hour after hour Frost waited vainly for Dobie's or Fitch's relieving battalions to break through the German ring and reach the bridge. Although sounds of battle came from the direction of western Arnhem, there was no sign of large-scale troop movements. All through the day Frost had expected some further word from Horrocks' XXX Corps. Nothing had been heard from them since the single strong radio signal picked up during the morning. Stragglers from the 3rd Battalion who had managed to get through to Frost brought news that Horrocks' tanks were still far down the corridor. Some had even heard from Dutch underground sources that the column had not reached Nijmegen as yet. Worried and uncertain, Frost decided to keep this information to himself. He had already begun to believe that the men of his proud 2nd Battalion, which he had commanded since its inception, would be alone far longer than he believed it possible to hold.

In the last hours of Monday, Frost's hopes hinged on the third lift and the expected arrival of Major General Stanislaw Sosabowski's 1st Polish Parachute Brigade. "They were to drop south of the bridge," Frost later wrote, "and I dreaded the reception they would have . . . but it was important that they find a handful of friends to meet them." To prepare for the Poles' arrival, Frost organized a "mobile storming party." Using two of Major Freddie Gough's armored reconnaissance jeeps and a Bren-gun carrier, Frost hoped to rush across the bridge and, in the surprise and confusion of the assault, open a passage and bring the Poles through. Major Gough, who was to lead the group, was "thoroughly miserable and quite unenthusiastic about the idea." He had celebrated his forty-third birthday on September 16. If

Frost's plan was carried out, Gough felt quite certain he would not see his forty-fourth.[*]

The Poles were not expected to land before 10 A.M., on the nineteenth. Now, making his rounds of men in slit trenches, machine-gun emplacements, basements and cellars, Frost warned them to save precious ammunition. They were to fire only at close quarters, to make every shot count. Signalman James Haysom was sighting his rifle on a German when the Colonel's order was passed along. "Stand still, you sod," Haysom shouted. "These bullets cost money."

While Frost knew that reducing the rate of fire would help the enemy improve his positions, he also believed that the Germans would be misled into thinking the British had lost heart as well as numbers. This attitude, Frost was certain, would cost the Germans dearly.

On the opposite side of the ramp, the little band of men with Captain Eric Mackay was already proving Frost's theory.

In the scarred and pitted schoolhouse under the ramp, Mackay had compressed his small force into two rooms and posted a handful of men in the hall outside to ward off any enemy attempt at infiltration. Mackay had barely positioned his men when the Germans launched a murderous machine-gun and mortar attack. Lance Corporal Arthur Hendy remembers the firing was so intense that bullets "whizzed through the shattered windows, chopped up the floorboards and we dodged as many flying splinters as we did actual bullets."

As men ducked for cover, Mackay discovered that the Germans had brought up a flamethrower, and within minutes a demolished half-track near the school was set afire. Then, Mackay recalls, "the Germans set fire to the house to our north and it burned

---

[*] After the war Gough learned that General Horrocks had been thinking about a similar idea. Remembering how a fast reconnaissance unit had gone ahead of the British column and linked up with the 101st, he thought that a similar fast patrol might well take its chances and reach the Arnhem bridge. "Colonel Vincent Dunkerly was alerted to lead the group," Gough says, "and, like me, he admitted that he spent the entire day peeing in his knickers at the thought."

merrily, sending down showers of sparks on our wooden roof which promptly caught fire." In the pandemonium, men sprinted for the roof, where for over three hours, using fire extinguishers from the school and their own camouflage smocks, they worked frantically to extinguish the flames. To Lance Corporal Hendy the stench was "like burning cheese and burning flesh. The whole area was lit up. The heat in the attic was intense and all the time the Germans were sniping away at us. Finally the fire was put out."

As the exhausted troopers collected once again in the two rooms, Mackay ordered his soldiers to bind their feet with their smocks and shirts. "The stone floors were thick with glass, plaster and metal fragments and the stairs were slippery with blood. Everything scrunched under our feet and made a terrific racket." As Mackay was about to go to the cellar to check on his wounded, he remembers "a blinding flash and a terrific explosion. The next thing I knew, someone was slapping my face." During the fire the Germans had brought up antitank Panzerfäuste in an effort to demolish the little force once and for all. With dazed disbelief Mackay saw that the entire southwest corner of the school and part of the still-smoldering roof had been blown away. Worse, the classrooms now resembled a charnel house with dead and wounded everywhere. "Only a few minutes later," Mackay recalls, "someone came over and said he thought we were surrounded. I looked out one of the windows. Down below was a mass of Germans. Funnily enough, they weren't doing anything, just standing around on the grass. They were on all sides of us except the west. They must have thought the Panzerfäuste had finished us off, because we had stopped firing."

Making his way carefully around the bodies on the floor, Mackay ordered his men to take up grenades. "When I yell 'Fire!' open up with everything you have," he said. Back at the southeast window, Mackay gave the order. "The boys dropped grenades on the heads below and we instantly followed up with all we had left: six Brens and fourteen Sten guns, firing at maximum rate." In the din, paratroopers stood silhouetted in the windows, firing their machine guns from the hip and yelling their war cry, "Whoa Mohammed." Within minutes the counterattack was over. As Mackay recalls, "when I looked out again, all I could see below was a carpet of gray. We must have wiped out between thirty and fifty Germans."

Now his men went about collecting the dead and wounded. One man was dying with fifteen bullets in the chest. Five other men were critically injured and almost all the troopers had sustained burns trying to save the blazing roof. Mackay had also been hit again by shrapnel and he discovered that his foot was pinned to his boot. Neither Mackay nor Sapper Pinky White, the acting medical orderly, could remove the metal and Mackay laced his boot tighter to keep the swelling down. Out of fifty men, Mackay now had only twenty-one in good shape; four were dead, and twenty-five wounded. Although he had no food and only a little water, he had collected a plentiful supply of morphia and was able to ease the pains of the injured. "Almost everybody was suffering from shock and fatigue," he remembers, "but we had gotten ourselves another temporary breathing space. I just didn't think things looked too bright, but we'd heard the BBC and they told us that everything was going according to plan. I got on the wireless to the Colonel, gave in our strength return and said we were all happy and holding our own."

As Lance Corporal Hendy tried to catch a few minutes' sleep he heard a church bell off in the distance. At first he thought that it was ringing to announce the approach of Horrocks' tanks, but the sound was not measured and consistent. Hendy realized that bullets or shell fragments must be hitting the bell. He thought of the men around Colonel Frost's headquarters on the other side of the ramp and wondered if they were holding safe. He heard the bell again and felt himself shivering. He could not rid himself of an eerie, doomed feeling.

The help that Frost so urgently needed was agonizingly close—barely more than a mile away. Four battalions spread between St. Elisabeth's Hospital and the Rhine were desperately trying to reach him. Lieutenant Colonel J. A. C. Fitch's 3rd Battalion had been attempting to force its way along the Lion route—the Rhine river road that Frost had used in reaching the bridge two days before. In darkness, without communications, Fitch was unaware that three other battalions were also on the move—Lieutenant Colonel David Dobie's 1st, Lieutenant Colonel G. H. Lea's 11th, and Lieutenant Colonel W. D. H. McCardie's 2nd South Staffordshires; Dobie's men were separated from him by only a few hundred yards.

At 4 A.M. on Tuesday, September 19, the 11th Battalion and the 2nd South Staffs began to move through the heavily built-up area between St. Elisabeth's Hospital and the Arnhem Town Museum. South of them, on the Lion route, where Fitch had already encountered devastating opposition, the 1st Battalion was now attempting to push its way through. Initially the three battalions, coordinating their movements, gained ground. Then, with dawn, their cover disappeared. German opposition, uneven throughout the night, was suddenly fiercely concentrated. The advance ground to a halt as the battalions found themselves in a tight net, trapped on three sides by an enemy who seemed almost to have waited for them to arrive at a preplanned position. And the Germans were prepared for a massacre.

Forward elements were hit and stopped in their tracks by German tanks and half-tracks blocking the streets ahead. From the windows of houses on the high escarpment of the railway marshaling yards to the north, waiting machine-gun crews opened up. And from the brickworks across the Rhine multibarreled flak guns, firing horizontally, ripped into Dobie's battalion and flayed Fitch's men as they tried to move along the lower Rhine road. Fitch's battalion, already badly mauled in the fighting since landing two days before, was now so cut to pieces by the unremitting flak fire that it could no longer exist as an effective unit. Men broke in confusion. They could go neither forward nor back. With virtually no protection on the open road, they were methodically mowed down. "It was painfully obvious," says Captain Ernest Seccombe, "that the Jerries had much more ammunition than we did. We tried to move in spurts, from cover to cover. I had just begun one dash when I was caught in a murderous crossfire. I fell like a sack of potatoes. I couldn't even crawl." Seccombe, who had been hit in both legs, watched helplessly as two Germans approached him. The British captain, who spoke fluent German, asked them to look at his legs. They bent down and examined his wounds. Then one of the Germans straightened up. "I'm sorry, Herr Hauptmann," he told Seccombe. "I'm afraid for you the war is over." The Germans called their own medics and Seccombe was taken to St. Elisabeth's Hospital.*

By chance one of Fitch's officers discovered the presence of Dobie's forces on the lower road, and the men of the 1st Battalion, despite their own heavy casualties, hurried forward, toward the pitiable remnants of Fitch's group. Dobie was now hell bent on reaching the bridge, but the odds were enormous. As he moved up into the intense fire and leapfrogged over Fitch's men, Dobie himself was wounded and captured (he later succeeded in making his escape); by the end of the day it was estimated that only forty men of his battalion remained. Private Walter Boldock was one of them. "We kept trying to make it, but it was a disaster. We were constantly mortared, and German tanks whirled right up to us. I tried to get one with my Bren gun and then we seemed to be going backwards. I passed a broken water main. A dead civilian in blue overalls lay in the gutter, the water lapping gently around his body. As we left the outskirts of Arnhem, I knew somehow we wouldn't be going back."

---

* Throughout most of the Arnhem battle, the hospital was used by both British and German doctors and medics to care for their wounded. Seccombe, as a German prisoner, was moved to the small Dutch town of Enschede, about five miles from the German border. During his stay there, both legs were amputated. He was liberated in April, 1945.

Fitch's men, attempting to follow Dobie's battalion, were shredded once again. The march had lost all meaning; after-action reports indicate the total confusion within the battalion at this point. "Progress was satisfactory until we reached the area of the dismantled pontoon bridge," reads the 3rd Battalion's report. "Then casualties from the 1st Battalion began passing through us. Heavy machine guns, 20 mm. and intense mortar fire began . . . casualties were being suffered at an ever-increasing rate, and the wounded were being rushed back in small groups every minute."

With his force in danger of total destruction, Fitch ordered his men back to the Rhine Pavilion, a large restaurant-building complex on the bank of the river, where the remnants of the battalion could regroup and take up positions. "Every officer and man must make his way back as best he can," Fitch told his troopers. "The whole area seems covered by fire, and the only hope of getting out safely is individually." Private Robert Edwards remembers a sergeant "whose boots were squelching blood from his wounds, telling us to get out and make our way back to the first organized unit we came to." Colonel Fitch did not reach the Rhine Pavilion. On the deadly road back, he was killed by mortar fire.

By an odd set of circumstances, two men who should never have been there actually made their way into Arnhem. Major Anthony Deane-Drummond, the second in command of Division signals, had become so alarmed over the breakdown of communications that, with his batman-driver, Lance Corporal Arthur Turner, he had gone forward to discover the trouble. Deane-Drummond and Turner had been on the road since early Monday. First they had located Dobie's battalion, where they had learned that Frost was on the bridge and Dobie was preparing an attack to get through to him. Setting off on the river road, Deane-Drummond caught up with elements of the 3rd Battalion struggling toward Arnhem and traveled with them. Heavy fire engulfed the group and in the fighting that ensued Deane-Drummond found himself leading the remnants of a company whose officer had been killed.

Under constant small-arms fire and so surrounded that Deane-Drummond remembers the Germans were tossing stick grenades at the men, he led the group along the road to some houses near a small inlet. Ahead, he could see the bridge. "The last couple of hundred yards to the houses I had decided on, the men were literally dropping like flies," he recalls. "We were down to about twenty men, and I realized the rest of the battalion was now far to the rear and not likely to reach us." Dividing the men into three parties, Deane-Drummond decided to wait until darkness, move down to the river, swim across it, then try to recross and join Division to the west. In a small corner house with the Germans all around, he settled down to wait. A banging began on the front door. Deane-Drummond and the three men with him raced to the back of the house and locked themselves in a small lavatory. From the noise from outside the little room, it was clear that the Germans were busy converting the house into a strong point. Deane-Drummond was trapped. He and the others would remain in the tiny room for the better part of three more days.[*]

Meanwhile, the 11th Battalion and the South Staffordshires, after several hours of relentless street fighting, had also come to a standstill. Counterattacking German tanks hammered the battalions, forcing them to pull slowly back.

Private Maurice Faulkner remembers that elements of the battalions reached the museum with heavy casualties, only to encounter the tanks. "I saw one man jump out of a window on top of a tank and try to put a grenade in," Faulkner recalls. "He was killed by a sniper, but I think he was probably trapped anyway, and he may have figured that was the only way out." Private

---

[*] Deane-Drummond was captured on Friday, September 22, shortly after he left the house near the Arnhem bridge. In an old villa near Velp, used as a P.O.W. compound, he discovered a wall cupboard in which to hide. In these cramped confines, he remained for thirteen days, rationing himself to a few sips of water and a small amount of bread. On October 5 he escaped, contacted the Dutch underground and on the night of October 22, was taken to the 1st Airborne Casualty Clearing Station at Nijmegen. One of the three men with him in Arnhem, Deane-Drummond's batman, Lance Corporal Arthur Turner, was also captured and taken to the Velp house. Eventually he was shipped to a P.O.W. camp in Germany and was liberated in April, 1945. Deane-Drummond's own story is told most effectively in his own book, *Return Ticket*.

William O'Brien says that the situation was "suddenly chaotic. Nobody knew what to do. The Germans had brought up those *Nebelwerfer* mortar throwers and we were scared out of our minds at the screaming sound. It began to seem to me that the generals had gotten us into something they had no business doing. I kept wondering where the hell was the goddam Second Army."

Private Andrew Milbourne, near the church at Oosterbeek, heard the call go out for machine-gunners. Milbourne stepped forward and was told to take his gun and a crew to the juncture of the road near St. Elisabeth's Hospital to help cover and protect the two battalions as they disengaged. Putting his Vickers machine gun in a jeep, Milbourne set off with three others. Milbourne positioned his gun in the garden of a house at the crossroads. Almost immediately he seemed to be engulfed in his own private battle. Mortar bursts and shells appeared to be aimed directly at him. As troopers began to fall back around him, Milbourne sent a constant arc of bullets out in front of them. He remembers hearing a rushing sound, like wind, and then a flash. Seconds later he knew that something was wrong with his eyes and hands. He remembers someone saying, "Lord, he's copped it."

Private Thomas Pritchard heard the voice and ran to where men were now standing over Milbourne. "He was lying over the twisted Vickers with both hands hanging by a thread of skin and an eye out of its socket. We started yelling for a medic." Not far away Milbourne's best friend, Corporal Terry "Taffy" Brace of the 16th Field Ambulance, heard someone shout. Leaving a shrapnel case he had treated, Brace sprinted forward. "Quick," a man called out to him, "the Vickers has caught it." As he ran, Brace remembers, he could hear an almost steady sound of machine-gun fire, and shells and mortars seemed to be dropping everywhere. Approaching a cluster of men, he pushed his way through and, to his horror, saw Milbourne lying on the ground. Working frantically, Brace wrapped Milbourne's arms and put a dressing just below the injured man's cheekbone to cushion his left eye. Brace remembers talking constantly as he worked. "It's just a scratch, Andy," he kept saying. "It's just a scratch." Picking up his friend, Brace carried Milbourne to a nearby dressing station where a Dutch doctor immediately set to work. Then he went back to battle.*

Brace passed what seemed to be hundreds of men lying in the fields and along the road. "I stopped at every one," he recalls. "The only thing I could do for most of them was take off their smocks and cover their faces." Brace treated one injured sergeant as best he could and then as he prepared to set out again, the man reached out to him. "I'm not going to make it," he told Brace. "Please hold my hand." Brace sat down and cupped the sergeant's hand in both of his. He thought of Milbourne, his best friend, and of the many men who had come streaming back through the lines this day. A few minutes later, Brace felt a slight pull. Looking down, he saw that the sergeant was dead.

By now the British were in confusion, without antitank guns, out of Piat ammunition and suffering heavy casualties. The attack had become a shambles. The two battalions could not drive beyond the built-up areas around St. Elisabeth's Hospital. But in that maze of streets one action was both positive and successful. The attack had overrun a terrace house at Zwarteweg 14, the building from which General Roy Urquhart had been unable to escape.

"We heard the wheeze of the self-propelled gun outside and the rattle of its track," Urquhart later wrote. "It was moving off." Antoon Derksen then appeared and "announced excitedly that the British were at the end of the road. We ran down the street and I thanked God we had made contact again."

Urquhart, learning from an officer of the South Staffordshires that his headquarters was now in a hotel called the Hartenstein in Oosterbeek, commandeered a jeep and, driving at full speed through a constant hail of sniper fire, at last reached Division.

---

* Milbourne was later captured in the cellar of the Ter Horst house in Oosterbeek. He lost his left eye and both hands were amputated by a German surgeon in Apeldoorn. He spent the rest of the war in a prisoner-of-war camp in Germany.

The time was 7:25 A.M. He had been absent and lacking control of the battle in its most crucial period, for almost thirty-nine hours.

At the Hartenstein, one of the first men to see Urquhart was Chaplain G. A. Pare. "The news had not been so good," he recalls. "The General had been reported a prisoner and there was no sign of the Second Army." As Pare came down the steps of the hotel "who should be ascending but the General. Several of us saw him, but nobody said a word. We just stared—completely taken aback." Dirty and with "two days' beard on my face I must have been something to see," Urquhart says. At that moment Colonel Charles Mackenzie, the chief of staff, came rushing out. Staring at Urquhart, Mackenzie told him, "We had assumed, sir, that you had gone for good."

Quickly Mackenzie briefed the anxious Urquhart on the events that had occurred during his absence and gave him the situation—as Division knew it—at the moment. The picture was appalling. Bitterly, Urquhart saw that his proud division was being scattered and cut to ribbons. He thought of all the setbacks that had dogged his Market forces: the distance from the drop zones to the bridge; the near-total breakdown of communications; the weather delay of Hackett's 4th Brigade plus the loss of precious resupply cargo; and the slow progress of Horrocks' tanks. Urquhart was stunned to learn that XXX Corps was not reported to have reached even Nijmegen as yet. The command dispute between Hackett and Hicks was upsetting, particularly as it stemmed from Urquhart's and Lathbury's own unforeseeable absence in the crucial hours when precise direction was required in the battle. Above all, Urquhart rued the incredible overoptimism of the initial planning stages that had failed to give due importance to the presence of Bittrich's Panzer Corps.

All these factors, one compounding another, had brought the division close to catastrophe. Only superb discipline and unbelievable courage were holding the battered Red Devils together. Urquhart was determined to somehow instill new hope, to coordinate the efforts of his men down even to company level. In doing so, he knew that he must demand more of his weary and wounded men than any airborne commander ever had demanded. He had no choices. With the steady inflow of German reinforcements, the dedicated, soft-spoken Scotsman saw that unless he acted immediately "my division would be utterly destroyed." Even now, it might be too late to save his beloved command from annihilation.

A look at the map told its own desperate story. Quite simply, there was no front line. Now that all his troopers but the Polish Brigade had arrived, the main dropping zones to the west had been abandoned and, apart from resupply areas, the lines around them held by Hicks's men had been shortened and pulled in. Hackett was going for the high ground northeast of Wolfheze and Johannahoeve Farm, he saw. The 11th Battalion and the South Staffordshires were fighting near St. Elisabeth's Hospital. There was no news of the progress of the 1st and 3rd battalions on the lower Rhine road. Yet Frost, Urquhart learned with pride, still held at the bridge. Everywhere on the situation map red arrows indicated newly reported concentrations of enemy tanks and troops; some actually appeared to be positioned *behind* the British units. Urquhart did not know if there was time enough remaining to reorganize and coordinate the advance of his dwindling forces and send them toward the bridge in one last desperate drive. Ignorant for now of the cruel damage done to the 1st and 3rd battalions, Urquhart believed there might still be a chance.

"The thing that hit me was this," he remembers. "Who was running the battle in the town? Who was coordinating it? Lathbury was wounded and no longer there. No one had been nominated to make a plan." As he began to work on the problem Brigadier Hicks arrived. He was extremely happy to see Urquhart and to return the division to his care. "I told him," Urquhart says, "that we would have to get somebody into town immediately. A senior officer, to coordinate Lea and McCardie's attack. I realized that they had been only a few hundred yards away from me, and it would have been better if I had remained in town to direct. Now, I sent Colonel Hilary Barlow, Hicks's deputy. He was the man for the job. I told him to get into town and tie up the loose ends. I explained exactly where Lea and McCardie were and sent him off with a jeep and wireless set and ordered him to produce a properly coordinated attack."

Barlow never reached the battalions. Somewhere en route he was killed. "He simply vanished," Urquhart recalls, and the body was never found.

The arrival of the Poles in the third lift was of almost equal urgency. They would now land directly on a prepared enemy on the southern approaches of the bridge, as Frost knew only too well; and by now, Urquhart reasoned, the Germans were obviously reinforced by armor. The drop could be a slaughter. In an effort to stop them and even though communications were uncertain—no one knew whether messages were getting through—Urquhart sent a warning message and requested a new drop zone. At rear Corps headquarters the signal was never received. But it was irrelevant. In yet another setback, fog covered many of the airfields in England where the planes and gliders of the vital third lift were readying to go.

The corridor through which Horrocks' tanks had to drive was open once again. At Son, forty-six miles south of Arnhem, engineers watched the first British armor thud across the temporary Bailey bridge they had erected. The Guards Armored Division was once more on its way, the drive now led by the Grenadiers. Now, at 6:45 A.M. on September 19, the Garden forces were behind schedule by thirty-six hours.

No one in this sector of the corridor could guess as yet what that time loss would mean in the final reckoning—and worse was to come. The great Waal bridge at Nijmegen, thirty-five miles north, was still in German hands. If it was not taken intact and soon, airborne commanders feared the Germans would blow it up.

That fear gave urgency to the armored drive. To General Gavin, General Browning, the Corps commander, and to Horrocks, the Nijmegen bridge was now the most critical piece in the

plan. As yet the commanders did not know the true plight of the
1st British Airborne Division. German propaganda broadcasts
had boasted that General Urquhart was dead° and his division
smashed, but there had been no news at all from Division itself.
In the tank columns men believed that Market-Garden was going
well. So did General Taylor's Screaming Eagles. "To the individual 101st trooper, the sound of the tanks, the sight of their
guns was both an assurance and a promise," General S. L. A.
Marshall was later to write—"an assurance that there was a plan
and a promise that the plan might work."

As the tanks rumbled by, the watching troopers of General
Taylor's 101st took just pride in their own achievements. Against
unexpectedly strong resistance they had taken and held the
fifteen-mile stretch of road from Eindhoven up to Veghel. Along
the route men waved and cheered as armored cars of the Household Cavalry, the tanks of the Grenadiers and the mighty mass of
XXX Corps swept by. In minutes the column moved from Son to
Veghel. Then, with the kind of dash that Montgomery had
envisioned for the entire drive, the armored spearhead, flanked by
cheering, flag-waving Dutch crowds, sped on, reaching its first
destination at Grave at 8:30 A.M. There, the tanks linked up with
Gavin's 82nd. "I knew we had reached them," recalls Corporal
William Chennell, who was in one of the lead armored cars,
"because the Americans, taking no chances, halted us with warning fire."

Moving quickly on, the first tanks reached the Nijmegen suburbs at midday. Now two thirds of the vital Market-Garden corridor had been traversed. The single road, jammed with vehicles, could have been severed at any time had it not been for the
vigilant, tenacious paratroopers who had fought and died to keep
it open. If Montgomery's bold strategy was to succeed, the
corridor was the lifeline which alone could sustain it. Men felt the
heady excitement of success. According to official pronounce-

---

° According to Bittrich the Germans learned from P.O.W.'s that Urquhart was
either dead or missing and also, he claims, "we were monitoring radio messages and
listening to phone calls."

ments, including those from Eisenhower's headquarters, everything was going according to plan. There was not even a hint of the dire predicament that was slowly engulfing the men at Arnhem.

Yet, General Frederick Browning was uneasy. During the afternoon of the eighteenth he met with General Gavin. The Corps commander had received no news from Arnhem. Other than scant Dutch underground information, Browning's communications men had not received a single situation report. Despite official announcements that the operation was proceeding satisfactorily, messages relayed to Browning from his own rear headquarters and from General Dempsey's Second Army had roused in him a gnawing concern. Browning could not rid himself of the feeling that Urquhart might be in grievous trouble.

Two reports in particular fed his anxiety. German strength and reaction in Arnhem had unquestionably proved heavier and faster than the planners had ever anticipated. And R.A.F. photo-reconnaissance information indicated that only the northern end of the Arnhem bridge was held by the British. But even now, Browning was unaware that two panzer divisions were in Urquhart's sector. Disturbed by the lack of communications and nagged by his suspicions, Browning warned Gavin that the "Nijmegen bridge must be taken today. At the latest, tomorrow." From the moment he had first learned of Market-Garden, the bridge at Arnhem had worried Browning. Montgomery had confidently expected Horrocks to reach it within forty-eight hours. At the time, Browning's view was that Urquhart's paratroopers could hold for four days. Now, on D plus two—one day short of Browning's estimate of the division's ability to function alone—although unaware of the grave condition of the 1st British Airborne Division, Browning told Gavin, "we must get to Arnhem as quickly as possible."[*]

---

[*] Many British accounts of Arnhem, including Chester Wilmot's excellent *Struggle for Europe*, imply that Browning knew more about Urquhart's situation at this time than he actually did. A careful check of the scattered and inconclusive information passed on to Corps headquarters shows that the first direct message from the Arnhem sector reached Browning at 8:25 A.M. on the nineteenth. Two others arrived during the course of the day and dealt with the bridge, troop locations and a re-

Immediately after the link-up in the 82nd's sector, Browning called a conference. The Guards' lead armored cars were sent back to pick up the XXX Corps commander, General Horrocks, and the commander of the Guards Armored Division, General Allan Adair. With Browning, the two officers drove to a site northeast of Nijmegen, overlooking the river. From there Corporal William Chennell, whose vehicle had picked up one of the two officers, stood with the little group observing the bridge. "To my amazement," Chennell remembers, "we could see German troops and vehicles moving back and forth across it, apparently completely unconcerned. Not a shot was fired, yet we were hardly more than a few hundred yards away."

Back at Browning's headquarters, Horrocks and Adair learned for the first time of the fierce German opposition in the 82nd's area. "I was surprised to discover upon arrival that we did not have the Nijmegen bridge," Adair says. "I assumed it would be in airborne hands by the time we reached it and we'd simply sweep on through." Gavin's troopers, the generals now learned, had been so hard-pressed to hold the airhead that companies had been recalled from Nijmegen to protect the landing zones from massed enemy assaults. Elements of the 508th Battalion had been unable to make any headway against the strong SS units holding the bridge approaches. The only way to take the bridge quickly, Browning believed, was by a combined tank and infantry assault. "We're going to have to winkle these Germans out with more than airborne troops," Browning told Adair.

The Nijmegen bridge was the last crucial link in the Market-Garden plan. With the time limit that Browning had placed on the British paratroopers' ability to hold out about to expire, the pace of the operation must be accelerated. Eleven miles of corridor remained to be forced open. The Nijmegen bridge, Browning stressed, had to be captured in record time.

---

quest for air support. Although many messages giving the true picture had been sent, they had not been received, and these three gave no indication that Urquhart's division was being methodically destroyed. In some quarters, Montgomery and Browning have been unjustly criticized for not taking more immediate and positive steps. At this time they knew virtually nothing of Urquhart's critical problems.

Major General Heinz Harmel, the Frundsberg Division commander, was irritable and more than a little frustrated. Despite constant pressure from General Bittrich, he had still been unable to bludgeon Frost and his men from the Arnhem bridge. "I was beginning to feel damn foolish," Harmel recalls.

By now he knew that the paratroopers were nearing the end of their supplies and ammunition. Also their casualties, if his own were an example, were extremely high. "I had determined to bring tanks and artillery fire to bear and level every single building they held," Harmel says, "but in view of the fight they were putting up, I felt I should first ask for their surrender." Harmel ordered his staff to arrange for a temporary truce. They were to pick a British prisoner of war to go to Frost with Harmel's ultimatum. The soldier selected was a newly captured engineer, twenty-five-year-old Sergeant Stanley Halliwell, one of Captain Mackay's sappers.

Halliwell was told to enter the British perimeter under a flag of truce. There he was to tell Frost that a German officer would arrive to confer with him about surrender terms. If Frost agreed, Halliwell would once more return to the bridge to stand unarmed with Frost until the German officer joined them. "As a P.O.W. I was supposed to return to the Jerries as soon as I delivered the message and got the Colonel's answer and I didn't like that part of the business at all," Halliwell says. The Germans brought Halliwell close to the British perimeter, where, carrying the truce flag, he crossed into the British-held sector and arrived at Frost's headquarters. Nervously, Halliwell explained the situation to Frost. The Germans, he said, believed it pointless for the fight to continue. The British were surrounded with no hope of relief. They had no choice but to die or surrender. Questioning Halliwell, Frost learned that "the enemy seemed to be most disheartened at their own losses." His own spirits lifted momentarily at the news, and he remembers thinking that "if only more ammunition would arrive, we would soon have our SS opponents in the bag." As to the German request for negotiations, Frost's answer to Halliwell was explicit. "Tell them to go to hell," he said.

Halliwell was in full agreement. As a P.O.W. he was expected to return, but he did not relish the idea of repeating the Colonel's exact words and, he pointed out to Frost, it might prove difficult to return through the lines. "It is up to you to make that decision," Frost said. Halliwell had already done so. "If it's all the same with you, Colonel," he told Frost, "I'll stay. Jerry will get the message sooner or later."

On the far side of the ramp Captain Eric Mackay had just received a similar invitation, but he chose to misinterpret it. "I looked out and saw a Jerry standing with a not-very-white hanky tied to a rifle. He shouted 'Surrender!' I promptly assumed that they wanted to surrender, but perhaps they meant us." In the now nearly demolished schoolhouse in which his small force was holding out, Mackay, still thinking the German was making a surrender offer, thought the whole idea impractical. "We only had two rooms," he says. "We would have been a bit cramped with prisoners."

Waving his arms at the German, Mackay shouted, "Get the hell out of here. We're taking no prisoners." The medical orderly, Pinky White, joined Mackay at the window. "*Raus!*" he shouted. "Beat it!" Amid a series of hoots and catcalls, other troopers took up the cry. "Bugger off! Go back and fight it out, you bastard." The German seemed to get the point. As Mackay recalls, he turned around and walked quickly back to his own building, "still waving his dirty hanky."

Harmel's attempt to seek a surrender from the spirited, beleaguered men on the bridge had failed. The battle began again in all its fury.

�֍ 8 ✣

At fog-covered bases near Grantham, England, the 1st Polish Parachute Brigade was waiting to take off. Zero hour for the drop had been scheduled for 10 A.M., but weather had forced a five-hour postponement. The brigade was now due to come in at 3 P.M. Major General Stanislaw Sosabowski, the Poles' fiercely independent, mercurial commander, had kept his men by their planes during the wait. It seemed to the fifty-two-year-old Sosabowski that England was fogged in every morning. If the weather cleared more quickly than expected, orders might change and Sosabowski intended to be ready to go on short notice. He felt that every hour mattered now. Urquhart, Sosabowski believed, was in trouble.

Apart from instinct, there was no specific reason for Sosabowski's feeling. But the Market-Garden concept had not appealed to him from the outset. He was certain that the drop zones were too far from the bridge to effect surprise. Further, no one in England appeared to know what was happening in Arnhem, and Sosabowski had been alarmed to discover at headquarters that communications with the 1st British Airborne Division had broken down. All that was known was that the north end of the Arnhem bridge was in British hands. Since there had been no change in the plan, Sosabowski's men, dropping to the south near the village of Elden, would take the other end.

But the General was worried about the lack of information. He could not be sure that Urquhart's men were still on the bridge. Liaison officers from Browning's rear headquarters, on whom Sosabowski was dependent for news, seemed to know little about what was actually happening. He had thought of going to First Allied Airborne Army Headquarters at Ascot to talk directly with General Lewis Brereton, the commanding officer. Protocol dictated otherwise. His troops were under General Browning's command, and Sosabowski was reluctant to bypass military channels. Any alterations in the plan should come only from Browning, and none had been received. Yet, Sosabowski felt that something had gone wrong. If the British were holding only the north end of the bridge, the enemy had to be in strength to the south and the Poles might well have the fight of their lives. Sosabowski's transport and artillery, due to leave in forty-six gliders from the southern Down Ampney and Torrant Rushton bases, were still scheduled for a midday takeoff. Since that part of the plan remained unchanged, Sosabowski tried to convince himself that all would go well.

Lieutenant Albert Smaczny was equally uneasy. He was to lead his company across the Arnhem bridge and occupy some buildings in the eastern part of the city. If the bridge had not been captured, he wondered how he would put his men across the Rhine. Smaczny had been assured that the crossing would be in British hands, but ever since his escape from the Germans in 1939 (his sixteen-year-old brother had been shot by the Gestapo in reprisal) Smaczny had schooled himself "to expect the unexpected."

Hour after hour the Poles waited, while the fog in the Midlands persisted. Corporal Wladijslaw Korob "was beginning to get nervous. I wanted to go," he remembers. "Standing around the airdrome wasn't my idea of the best way to kill Germans." Looking at the assemblage of planes on the field, Lieutenant Stefan Kaczmarek felt "a joy that almost hurt." He, too, was getting tired of standing around idle. The operation, he told his men, "is the second-best alternative to liberating Warsaw. If we succeed, we'll walk into Germany right through the kitchen."

But the Poles were to be disappointed. At noon Sosabowski received fresh orders. Although planes were operating from the southern fields, in the Midlands the bases remained weathered in.

The jump was canceled for the day. "It's no good, General," the chief liaison officer, Lieutenant Colonel George Stevens, told the protesting Sosabowski. "We can't get you out." The assault was postponed until the following morning, Wednesday, September 20. "We'll try it then at 10 A.M.," he was told. There was no time to transfer troop loads to bases in the south. To Sosabowski's chagrin, he learned that his glider supply lift had already left and was on the way to Holland. The General fumed with impatience. Each hour that passed meant greater enemy resistance, and the following day might bring an infinitely harder fight—unless his nagging fears were completely unjustified.

They were not. Sosabowski's glider supply lift with men, artillery and transport was heading for near annihilation. The third air lift would be a disaster.

Low-scudding clouds blanketed the southern route all the way across the Channel. The third lift, heading for the 101st, 82nd and British drop zones, encountered trouble right from the beginning. Clear weather had been predicted by afternoon. Instead, conditions were deteriorating even as the formations took to the air. Squadrons of fighters, caught in cloud and unable to see ground targets, were forced to turn back. In zero visibility, unable to see their tow planes, many gliders cut loose to make emergency landings in England or in the Channel and whole serials were forced to abort and return to base.

Of the 655 troop carriers and 431 gliders that did take off, little more than half reached the drop and landing zones, although most of the plane-glider combinations carrying troops were able to land safely back in England or elsewhere. But over the Continent intense enemy ground fire and Luftwaffe attacks, combined with the poor weather, caused the loss of some 112 gliders and 40 transports. Only 1,341 out of 2,310 troops and only 40 out of 68 artillery pieces bound for the 101st Airborne Division got through. So hard-pressed were General Taylor's men that the 40 guns went into action almost as soon as they landed.

General Gavin's 82nd Airborne fared even worse. At this time, when every trooper was needed for the attack on the critical Nijmegen bridges, Gavin's 325th Glider Infantry Regiment did not arrive at all. Like the Polish paratroops, the 325th's planes and gliders, also based in the Grantham area, were unable to leave the ground. Worse, out of 265 tons of stores and ammunition destined for the 82nd, only about 40 tons were recovered.

In the British sector, where Urquhart was expecting not only the Poles but a full-cargo resupply mission, tragedy struck. The supply dropping zones had been overrun by the enemy, and although intensive efforts were made to divert the 163-plane mission to a new area south of the Hartenstein Hotel, the effort failed. Desperately short of everything, particularly ammunition, Urquhart's men saw the formations approach through a blizzard of antiaircraft fire. Then enemy fighters appeared, firing on the formations and strafing the new supply dropping zones.

At about 4 P.M., the Reverend G. A. Pare, chaplain of the Glider Pilot Regiment, heard the cry, "Third lift coming!" Suddenly, the chaplain remembers, "there was the most awful crescendo of sound and the very air vibrated to a tremendous barrage of guns. All we could do was gaze in stupefaction at our friends going to inevitable death."

Pare watched "in agony, for these bombers, used to flying at 15,000 feet at night, were coming in at 1,500 feet in daylight. We saw more than one machine blazing, yet carrying on its course until every container was dropped. It now became obvious to us that we had terrible opposition. A signal had been sent asking that supplies be dropped near our headquarters, but hardly anything did."

Without fighter escort and doggedly holding course, the unwavering formations released supplies on the old dropping zones. Men on the ground tried desperately to attract attention by firing flares, igniting smoke bombs, waving parachutes and even setting parts of the heath on fire—and as they did they were strafed by diving enemy Messerschmitts.

Many soldiers recall one British Dakota, its starboard wing on fire, coming in over the drop zone now held by the Germans. Sergeant Victor Miller, one of the glider pilots who had landed in the first lift on Sunday, was "sick at heart to see flames envelop almost the whole of the lower half of the fuselage." Watching for the crew to bail out, Miller found himself muttering, "Jump! Jump!" As the plane flew low, Miller saw the dispatcher standing in the door, pushing out containers. Mesmerized, he watched the flaming Dakota turn and make another run in, and through the smoke he saw more containers tumbling out. Sergeant Douglas Atwell, another glider pilot, remembers that men climbed out of their trenches staring silently at the sky. "We were dead tired, and we had little to eat or drink, but I couldn't think of anything but that plane at the moment. It was as if it was the only one in the sky. Men were just riveted where they stood—and all the time that dispatcher kept on pushing out bundles." The pilot held his burning plane steady, making a second slow pass. Major Geoffrey Powell "was awestruck that he would do this. I couldn't take my eyes off the craft. Suddenly it wasn't a plane any more, just a big orange ball of fire." As the burning plane plunged to the ground, its pilot, thirty-one-year-old Flight Lieutenant David Lord, still at the controls, Miller saw beyond the trees "only an oily column of smoke to mark the resting place of a brave crew who died that we might have the chance to live."

But Sergeant Miller was wrong. One member of the crew of the ill-fated Dakota did survive. Flying Officer Henry Arthur King, the navigator on that flight, remembers that just a few minutes before 4 P.M. as the plane was approaching the drop zone, flak set the starboard engine afire. Over the intercom Lord said, "Everyone O.K.? How far to the drop zone, Harry?" King called back, "Three minutes' flying time." The plane was listing heavily to the right and King saw that they were losing altitude rapidly. Flames had begun to spread along the wing toward the main fuel tank. "They need the stuff down there," he heard Lord say. "We'll go in and bail out afterwards. Everyone get your chutes on."

King spotted the drop zone and informed Lord. "O.K., Harry, I can see it," the pilot said. "Go back and give them a hand with the baskets." King made his way back to the open door. Flak had hit the rollers used to move the heavy supply bundles, and the dispatcher, Corporal Philip Nixon, and three soldiers from the Royal Army Service Corps were already manhandling eight heavy panniers of ammunition to the door. The men had taken off their parachutes in order to tug the baskets forward. Together the five men had pushed out six baskets when the red light, indicating that the plane was now off the drop zone, came on. King went on the intercom. "Dave," he called to Lord, "we've got two left." Lord put the plane in a tight left turn. "We'll come round again," he answered. "Hang on."

King saw they were then at about 500 feet and Lord "was handling that ship like a fighter plane. I was trying to help the R.A.S.C. boys get their chutes back on. The green light flashed and we pushed out our bundles. The next thing I remember is Lord shouting, 'Bail out! Bail out! For God's sake, bail out!' There was a tremendous explosion and I found myself hurtling through the air. I don't remember pulling the ripcord but I must have done it instinctively. I landed flat and hard on my back. I remember looking at my watch and seeing it was only nine minutes since we took the flak. My uniform was badly scorched and I couldn't find my shoes."

Nearly an hour later, King stumbled across a company of the 10th Battalion. Someone gave him tea and a bar of chocolate. "That's all we've got," the trooper told him. King stared at him. "What do you mean, that's all you've got? We just dropped supplies to you." The soldier shook his head. "You dropped our tins of sardines all right, but the Jerries got them. We got nothing." King was speechless. He thought of Flight Lieutenant Lord, and the crew and men who had shed their chutes in a desperate effort to get precious ammunition bundles out to the anxious troops below. Of all these men, only King was alive. And now he had just learned that the sacrifice of his crew had been for nothing.*

---

* Flight Lieutenant David Lord, holder of the Distinguished Flying Cross, was posthumously awarded the Victoria Cross. The bodies of the three R.A.F. officers and the four Army dispatchers—Pilot Officer R. E. H. Medhurst, Flying Officer

Planes crash-landed throughout the area, mainly around Wageningen and Renkum. Some ended up on the southern side of the Rhine. Sergeant Walter Simpson remembers hearing his pilot shout over the intercom, "My God, we've been hit!" Looking out, Simpson saw that the port engine was on fire. He heard the engines being throttled back and then the plane went into a dive. The frightened Simpson remembers that the plane "dragged its tail across the north bank of the river, lifted slightly, then catapulted across the water and came down on the southern side."

On impact Simpson was hurtled forward and thrown to one side of the fuselage. The wireless operator, Sergeant Runsdale, crashed into him and lay huddled across Simpson's body. The interior of the plane was a shambles, fuel was burning, and Simpson could hear the crackling of flames. As he tried to ease his legs from under the wireless operator, Runsdale screamed and fainted. His back was broken. Simpson staggered up and carried the sergeant out through the escape hatch. Four crew members, dazed and in shock, were already there. Simpson went back for the others still inside. He found the bombardier unconscious. "His shoe had been blown off, part of his heel was missing and both arms were broken," he recalls. Simpson picked up this man, too, and carried him out. Although the plane was now burning fiercely, Simpson went back a third time for the engineer, whose leg was broken. He, too, was brought to safety.

In the village of Driel, young Cora Baltussen, her sister Reat and their brother Albert saw Simpson's plane come down. The three immediately set out for the site of the crash. "It was horrible," Cora recalls. "There were eight men and some of them were terribly injured. We dragged them away from the burning plane just as it exploded. I knew that the Germans would be looking for the crew. I told the pilot, Flight Officer Jeffrey Liggens, who was unharmed, that we'd have to hide him out while we took the injured men to the small surgery in the village.

A. Ballantyne, Corporal Nixon, Drivers James Ricketts, Leonard Sidney Harper and Arthur Rowbotham—were all identified and are buried in the British Military Cemetery at Arnhem.

We hid him and two others in a nearby brickworks and told them we'd return at dark." That evening Cora assisted the lone physician in the village, a woman, Dr. Sanderbobrorg, as she amputated the bombardier's foot. The war had finally reached both Cora and little Driel.

In all, out of 100 bombers and 63 Dakotas, 97 were damaged and 13 were shot down—and, in spite of the heroism of pilots and crews, Urquhart's stricken division had not been bolstered. Of 390 tons of stores and ammunition dropped, nearly all fell into German hands. Only an estimated 21 tons was retrieved.

Worse problems were to engulf the Polish transport and artillery lift. Before leaving England in the Polish lift, Sergeant Pilot Kenneth Travis-Davison, copilot of a Horsa glider, was struck by the almost complete absence of information relating to conditions at their destination. Routes were laid out on maps, and the drop zones for the Poles' artillery and transport were marked; but, says Travis-Davison, "we were told that the situation was unknown." The only landing instruction was that "gliders should land on the area marked by purple smoke." In Travis-Davison's opinion, "the briefing was ludicrous."

Yet, despite the inadequacy of information, R.A.F. planes correctly located the drop zone near Johannahoeve Farm and 31 out of 46 gliders reached the zone. As they came in, the air erupted with fire. A squadron of Messerschmitts hit many of the machines, riddling the thin canvas-and-plywood hulls, puncturing the gas tanks of jeeps and setting some afire. Antiaircraft bursts caught others. Those that made it to the ground landed in the midst of a battlefield. Troopers of Hackett's 4th Brigade, struggling to disengage from an enemy that threatened to overrun them, were unable to reach the high ground and the drop zone beyond in time to protect the area. As the British and Germans fought fiercely, the Poles landed directly in the middle of the cataclysmic battle. In the terror and confusion the Poles were fired on from both sides. Gliders, many already on fire, crash-landed on the field or plowed into nearby trees. Polish artillerymen, caught in the crossfire and unable to tell friend from foe, fired back at both the Germans and British. Then, hastily unloading the usable jeeps and artillery, the dazed men ran a gauntlet of fire as they left the landing zone. Surprisingly, ground casualties were light, but many of the men, bewildered and shocked, were taken prisoner. Most of the jeeps and supplies were destroyed and of eight desperately needed six-pounder antitank guns, only three came through undamaged. General Stanislaw Sosabowski's fears were more than justified. And the ordeal of the 1st Polish Parachute Brigade was only just beginning.

Some forty miles south along the highway, General Maxwell Taylor's 101st troopers were now fighting hard to keep the corridor open. But the German Fifteenth Army's fierce defense at Best was draining Taylor's forces. More and more men were being caught up in the bitter engagement that one division intelligence officer wryly termed "a minor error in estimate." Pressure was building all along Taylor's 15-mile sector, which the Screaming Eagles had newly named "Hell's Highway." It was now obvious that the enemy's intent was to cut off Horrocks' tank spearhead, using Best as the base.

The jammed columns of vehicles massing the highway were easy targets for artillery fire. Bulldozers and tanks roamed constantly up and down the road, pushing wreckage out of the convoys to keep the columns rolling. Since Sunday, Best, the minor secondary objective, had grown to such proportions that it threatened to overpower all other action along Taylor's stretch of road. Now, the 101st commander was determined to crush the enemy at Best completely.

Early Tuesday afternoon, with the support of British tanks, Taylor threw almost the entire 502nd Regiment against Von Zangen's men at Best. The mammoth attack caught the enemy by surprise. Bolstered by the recently arrived 327th Glider Infantry Regiment and by British armor on the highway, the 2nd and 3rd battalions relentlessly swept the forested areas east of Best.

Caught in a giant ring and forced back toward the Wilhelmina Canal, the Germans suddenly broke. With the commitment of fresh forces, the battle that had continued without letup for close to forty-six hours was suddenly over in two. Taylor's men had achieved the first major victory of Market-Garden. More than three hundred of the enemy were killed and over a thousand captured, along with fifteen 88 mm. artillery pieces. "By late afternoon," reads the official history, "as hundreds of Germans gave up, the word went out to send all Military Police available." Lieutenant Edward Wierzbowski, the platoon leader who had come closest to seizing the Best bridge before it was blown, brought in his own prisoners after having first been captured himself. Out of grenades and ammunition, with his casualties all about him—only three men of his valiant platoon had not been wounded—Wierzbowski had finally surrendered. Now, dead tired and begrimed, Wierzbowski and his men, including some of the wounded, disarmed the doctors and orderlies in the German field hospital to which the men had been taken and marched back to Division, bringing their prisoners with them.

Successful as the engagement had been, General Taylor's difficulties were far from over. Even as the battle at Best ended, German armor struck out for the newly installed bridge at Son in yet another attempt to sever the corridor. Taylor himself, leading his headquarters troops—his only available reinforcements—rushed to the scene. With bazooka fire and a single antitank gun, a German Panther tank was knocked out almost as it reached the bridge. Similarly, several other tanks were quickly dispatched. The German attack collapsed, and traffic continued to move. But the vigilance of the Screaming Eagles could not be relaxed. "Our situation," Taylor later noted, "reminded me of the early American West, where small garrisons had to contend with sudden Indian attacks at any point along great stretches of vital railroad."

The Germans' hard, fast, hit-and-run tactics were taking their toll. Almost 300 men of the 101st had been killed or wounded or were missing in ground actions. Men in slit trenches holding positions on either side of the highway or in the fields around

Best were in constant danger of being overrun from the flanks, and each night brought its own particular fear. In darkness, with the Germans infiltrating the 101st's perimeter, no one knew whether the man in the next foxhole would be alive by the following morning. In the confusion and surprise of these sharp enemy actions men suddenly disappeared, and when the fire fights were over their friends searched for them among the dead and wounded on the battle ground and at aid stations and field hospitals.

As the Best battle ended and the long lines of prisoners were being herded back to Division, thirty-one-year-old Staff Sergeant Charles Dohun set out to find his officer, Captain LeGrand Johnson. Back in England prior to the jump, Dohun had been almost "numb with worry." The twenty-two-year-old Johnson had felt much the same. He was "resigned to never coming back." The morning of the nineteenth Johnson had thrown his company into an attack near Best. "It was that or be slaughtered," he recalls. In the fierce battle, which Johnson remembers as "the worst I have ever seen or heard," he was shot in the left shoulder. With his company reduced from 180 to 38 and surrounded in a field of burning haystacks, Johnson held off the Germans until relieving companies, driving back the enemy, could reach and evacuate the survivors. As Johnson was being helped back to an aid station he was shot once again, this time through the head. At the battalion aid station his body was placed among other fatally wounded men in what the medics called the "dead pile." There, after a long search, Sergeant Dohun found him. Kneeling down, Dohun was convinced there was a flicker of life.

Picking up the inert officer, Dohun laid Johnson and four other casualties from his company in a jeep and set out for the field hospital at Son. Cut off by Germans, Dohun drove the jeep into the woods and hid. When the German patrol moved on, he set out again. Arriving at the hospital, he found long lines of casualties waiting for treatment. Dohun, certain that Johnson might die at any minute, passed down the lines of wounded until he came to a surgeon who was checking the casualties to determine who was in need of immediate aid. "Major," Dohun told the doctor, "my captain needs attention right away." The major shook his head. "I'm sorry, sergeant," he told Dohun. "We'll get to him. He'll have to wait his turn." Dohun tried again. "Major, he'll die if you don't look at him quick." The doctor was firm. "We've got a lot of injured men here," he said. "Your captain will be attended to as soon as we can get to him." Dohun pulled out his .45 and cocked the trigger. "It's not soon enough," he said calmly. "Major, I'll kill you right where you stand if you don't look at him right now." Astonished, the surgeon stared at Dohun. "Bring him in," he said.

In the operating theater Dohun stood by, his .45 in hand as the doctor and a medical team worked on Johnson. As the sergeant watched, Johnson was given a blood transfusion, his wounds cleaned and a bullet was removed from his skull and another from his left shoulder. When the operation was completed and Johnson was bandaged, Dohun moved. Stepping up to the doctor, he handed over his .45. "O.K.," he said, "thanks. Now you can turn me in."

Dohun was sent back to the 2nd Battalion of the 502nd. There, he was brought before the commanding officer. Dohun snapped to attention. He was asked if he was aware of exactly what he had done and that his action constituted a court-martial offense. Dohun replied, "Yes, sir, I do." Pacing up and down, the commander suddenly stopped. "Sergeant," he said, "I'm placing you under arrest"—he paused and looked at his watch—"for exactly one minute." The two men waited in silence. Then the officer looked at Dohun. "Dismissed," he said. "Now get back to your unit." Dohun saluted smartly. "Yes, sir," he said, and left.*

---

* I am indebted to Mrs. Johnson for this story. She first learned of it from the adjutant of the 502nd, Captain Hugh Roberts. Although Captain Roberts did not mention the commanding officer's name, I must assume that it was Lieutenant Colonel Steve Chappuis of the 2nd Battalion. Captain Johnson remembers only that he "woke up in England six weeks later—blind, deaf, dumb, forty pounds lighter and with a big plate in my head." Except for partial blindness, he recovered. Sergeant Dohun, in his correspondence and interview for this book, made little mention of the role he played in saving Captain Johnson's life. But he acknowledges that it happened. "I don't know to this day," he wrote, "if I would have shot that medic or not."

Now, in General Gavin's sector of the corridor, as Horrocks' tanks rolled forward toward Nijmegen, the quick capture of the city's crossings assumed critical importance. On the seventeenth the Germans had had only a few soldiers guarding the approaches to the Waal river bridge. By afternoon of the nineteenth Gavin estimated that he was opposed by more than five hundred SS Grenadiers, well-positioned and supported by artillery and armor. The main body of the Guards Armored Division was still en route to the city. Only the spearhead of the British column—elements of the 1st Battalion of the Grenadier Guards under the command of Lieutenant Colonel Edward H. Goulburn—was available for an attack and Gavin's 82nd troopers in their ten-mile stretch of corridor were widely dispersed by their efforts to fight off a constantly encroaching enemy. Since Gavin's Glider Infantry Regiment, based in the fogbound Midlands of England, had been unable to take off, he could afford to release only one battalion for a combined attack with the British spearhead tanks. Gavin chose the 2nd Battalion of the 505th under the command of Lieutenant Colonel Ben Vandervoort. There was a chance that the attack, based on speed and surprise, might succeed. If anyone could help effect it, Gavin believed it was the reserved, soft-spoken Vandervoort.° Still, the operation carried heavy risks. Gavin thought the British appeared to underestimate the German strength, as indeed they did. The Grenadier Guards' after-action report noted that "It was thought that a display in the shape of tanks would probably cause the enemy to withdraw."

At 3:30 P.M. the combined attack began. The force quickly penetrated the center of the city without encountering serious opposition. There, approximately forty British tanks and armored vehicles split into two columns, with American troops riding on the tanks and following behind them. On top of lead tanks and in

° In Normandy, Vandervoort had fought for forty days with a broken ankle. See *The Longest Day*, pp. 143, 181.

reconnaissance cars were twelve specially chosen Dutch underground scouts guiding the way—among them a twenty-two-year-
old university student named Jan van Hoof, whose later actions
would become a subject of sharp dispute. "I was reluctant to use
him," recalls the 82nd's Dutch liaison officer, Captain Arie D.
Bestebreurtje. "He seemed highly excited, but another underground member vouched for his record. He went in with a British
scout car and that was the last I ever saw of him." As the force
divided, one column headed for the railroad bridge and the
second, with Goulburn and Vandervoort, approached the main
highway crossing over the Waal.

At both objectives the Germans were waiting in strength. Staff
Sergeant Paul Nunan remembers that as his platoon approached
an underpass near the railroad bridge, "we began receiving sniper
fire. With a thousand places for snipers to hide, it was hard to tell
where fire was coming from." Men dived for cover and slowly
began to pull back. British armor fared no better. As tanks began
to roll toward the bridge, 88's, firing down the street at almost
point-blank range, knocked them out. A wide street, the Kraijen-
hoff Laan, led to a triangular park west of the crossing. There, in
buildings facing the park on three sides, the paratroopers re-
grouped for another attack. But again the Germans held them off.
Snipers on roofs and machine guns firing from a railroad overpass
kept the men pinned down.

Some troopers remember Lieutenant Russ Parker, a cigar
clenched in his teeth, moving into the open and spraying the
rooftops to keep snipers' heads down. A call went out for tanks,
and Nunan remembers that "at that instant the entire park
seemed filled with tracer slugs coming from a fast-firing automatic weapon sited to our left across the street." Nunan turned to
Herbert Buffalo Boy, a Sioux Indian and a veteran 82nd trooper.
"I think they're sending a German tank," he said. Buffalo Boy
grinned. "Well, if they've got infantry with them, it could get to
be a very tough day," he told Nunan. The German tank did not
materialize, but a 20 mm. antiaircraft gun opened up. With
grenades, machine guns and bazookas, the troopers fought on

until word was passed for forward platoons to pull back and consolidate for the night. As men moved out, the Germans set buildings along the river's edge on fire, making it impossible for Vandervoort's men to infiltrate, overrun artillery positions and clear out pockets of resistance. The railroad bridge attack had ground to a halt.

Under cover of heavy American artillery fire, the second column had made for Huner Park, the ornamental gardens leading to the approaches of the highway bridge. Here, in a traffic circle, all roads leading to the bridge converged and an ancient ruin with a sixteen-sided chapel—the Valkhof—once the palace of Charlemagne and later rebuilt by Barbarossa, commanded the area. In this citadel the enemy was concentrated. It almost seemed to Colonel Goulburn that "the Boche had some sort of an idea of what we were trying to do." As indeed they had.

Captain Karl Heinz Euling's battalion of SS Panzer Grenadiers was one of the first units to cross the Rhine at Pannerden. Acting on General Harmel's orders to protect the bridge at all costs, Euling had ringed the Huner Park area with self-propelled guns and had positioned men in the chapel of the old ruin. As British tanks rattled around the corners of the streets leading to the park, they came under Euling's guns. Meeting a punishing artillery barrage, the tanks pulled back. Colonel Vandervoort immediately took to the street, and getting a mortar crew into action with covering fire, he moved one company forward. As the company's lead platoon, under First Lieutenant James J. Coyle, sprinted for a row of attached houses facing the park, they came under small-arms and mortar fire. Lieutenant William J. Meddaugh, second in command, saw that this was "observed fire. The guns and snipers were being directed by radio. British tanks covered our front as Lieutenant Coyle moved into a block of buildings overlooking the entire enemy position. Other platoons were stopped, unable to move, and the situation looked rotten."

Covered by British smoke bombs Meddaugh succeeded in bringing the rest of the company forward, and the commander,

Lieutenant J. J. Smith, consolidated his men in houses around Coyle. As Meddaugh recalls, "Coyle's platoon now had a perfect view of the enemy, but as we started to move tanks up, some high-velocity guns opened up that had not done any firing as yet. Two tanks were knocked out, and the others retired." As Coyle's men replied with machine guns, they immediately drew antitank gun fire from across the streets. When darkness closed in, Euling's SS men attempted to infiltrate the American positions. One group got to within a few feet of Coyle's platoon before they were spotted and a fierce fire fight broke out. Coyle's men suffered casualties, and three of the Germans were killed before the attack was driven back. Later, Euling sent medics to pick up his wounded, and Coyle's paratroopers waited until the injured Germans were evacuated before resuming the fight. In the middle of the action, Private First Class John Keller heard a low pounding noise. Going to a window, he was amazed to see a Dutchman on a stepladder calmly replacing the shingles on the house next door as though nothing was happening.

In late evening, with small-arms fire continuing, any further attempt to advance was postponed until daylight. The Anglo-American assault had been abruptly stopped barely 400 yards from the Waal river bridge—the last water obstacle on the road to Arnhem.

To the Allied commanders it was now clear that the Germans were in complete control of the bridges. Browning, worried that the crossings might be destroyed at any moment, called another conference late on the nineteenth. A way must be found to cross the 400-yard-wide Waal river. General Gavin had devised a plan which he had mentioned to Browning at the time of the link-up. Then the Corps commander had turned down the scheme. At this second conference Gavin proposed it again. "There's only one way to take this bridge," he told the assembled officers. "We've got to get it simultaneously—from both ends." Gavin urged that "any boats in Horrocks' engineering columns should be rushed forward immediately, because we're going to need them." The

British looked at him in bewilderment. What the 82nd commander had in mind was an assault crossing of the river—by paratroops.

Gavin went on to explain. In nearly three days of fighting, his casualties were high—upwards of 200 dead and nearly 700 injured. Several hundred more men were cut off or scattered and were listed as missing. His losses, Gavin reasoned, would grow progressively worse if blunt head-on attacks continued. What was needed was a means of capturing the bridge quickly and cheaply. Gavin's plan was to throw a force in boats across the river a mile downstream while the attack continued for possession of the southern approaches. Under a barrage of tank fire the troopers were to storm the enemy defenses on the northern side before the Germans fully realized what was happening.

Yet total surprise was out of the question. The river was too wide to enable boatloads of men to escape detection, and the bank on the far side was so exposed that troopers, once across the river, would have to negotiate 200 yards of flat ground. Beyond was an embankment from which German gunners could fire down upon the invading paratroopers. That defense position would have to be overrun too. Although heavy casualties could be expected initially, in Gavin's opinion they would still be less than if the assault were continued against the southern approaches alone. "The attempt has to be made," he told Browning, "if Market-Garden is to succeed."

· Colonel George S. Chatterton, commander of the British Glider Pilot Regiment, remembers that, besides Browning and Horrocks, commanders of the Irish, Scots, and Grenadier Guards were present at the conference. So was cigar-chewing Colonel Reuben Tucker, commander of the 82nd's 504th Regiment, whose men Gavin had picked to make the river assault if his plan won approval. Although intent on Gavin's words, Chatterton could not help noting the differences in the men assembled. "One brigadier wore suede shoes and sat on a shooting stick," he recalls. "Three Guards' commanders had on rather worn corduroy trousers, chukka boots and old school scarves." Chatterton thought "they seemed relaxed, as though they were discussing an exercise, and I couldn't help contrast them to the Americans present, especially Colonel Tucker, who was wearing a helmet that almost covered his face. His pistol was in a holster under his left arm, and he had a knife strapped to his thigh." To Chatterton's great amusement, "Tucker occasionally removed his cigar long enough to spit and every time he did faint looks of surprise flickered over the faces of the Guards' officers."

But the daring of Gavin's plan provided the real surprise. "I knew it sounded outlandish," Gavin recalls, "but speed was essential. There was no time even for a reconnaissance. As I continued to talk, Tucker was the only man in the room who seemed unfazed. He had made the landing at Anzio and knew what to expect. To him the crossing was like the kind of exercise the 504th had practiced at Fort Bragg." Still, for paratroopers, it was unorthodox and Browning's chief of staff, Brigadier Gordon Walch, recalls that the Corps commander was "by now filled with admiration at the daring of the idea." This time Browning gave his approval.

The immediate problem was to find boats. Checking with his engineers, Horrocks learned they carried some twenty-eight small canvas and plywood craft. These would be rushed to Nijmegen during the night. If the planning could be completed in time, Gavin's miniature Normandy-like amphibious assault of the Waal would take place at 1 P.M. the next day, on the twentieth. Never before had paratroopers attempted such a combat operation. But Gavin's plan seemed to offer the best hope of grabbing the Nijmegen bridge intact; and then, as everyone still believed, another quick dash up the corridor would unite them with the men at Arnhem.

In the grassy expanse of the Eusebius Buiten Singel, General Heinz Harmel personally directed the opening of the bombardment against Frost's men at the bridge. His attempt to persuade

Frost to surrender had failed. Now, to the assembled tank and artillery commanders his instructions were specific: they were to level every building held by the paratroopers. "Since the British won't come out of their holes, we'll blast them out," Harmel said. He told gunners to "aim right under the gables and shoot meter by meter, floor by floor, until each house collapses." Harmel was determined that the siege would end, and since everything else had failed this was the only course. "By the time we're finished," Harmel added, "there'll be nothing left but a pile of bricks." Lying flat on the ground between two artillery pieces, Harmel trained his binoculars on the British strongholds and directed the fire. As the opening salvos zeroed in he stood up, satisfied, and handed over to his officers. "I would have liked to stay," he recalls. "It was a new experience in fighting for me. But with the Anglo-Americans attacking the bridges at Nijmegen I had to rush down there." As Harmel left, his gunners, with methodical, scythelike precision, began the job of reducing Frost's remaining positions to rubble.

Of the eighteen buildings that the 2nd Battalion had initially occupied, Frost's men now held only about ten. While tanks hit positions from the east and west, artillery slammed shells into those facing north. The barrage was merciless. "It was the best, most effective fire I have ever seen," remembers SS Grenadier Private Horst Weber. "Starting from the rooftops, buildings collapsed like doll houses. I did not see how anyone could live through this inferno. I felt truly sorry for the British."

Weber watched three Tiger tanks rumble slowly down the Groote Markt, and while machine guns sprayed every window in a block of buildings opposite the northern approaches to the bridge, the tanks "pumped shell after shell into each house, one after the other." He remembers a corner building where "the roof fell in, the two top stories began to crumble and then, like the skin peeling off a skeleton, the whole front wall fell into the street revealing each floor on which the British were scrambling like mad." Dust and debris, Weber remembers, "soon made it impossible to see anything more. The din was awful but even so, above it all we could hear the wounded screaming."

In relays, tanks smashed houses along the Rhine waterfront and under the bridge itself. Often, as the British darted out, tanks rammed the ruins like bulldozers, completely leveling the sites. At Captain Mackay's headquarters under the ramp in the nearly destroyed schoolhouse, Lieutenant Peter Stainforth estimated that "high-explosive shells came through the southern face of the building at the rate of one every ten seconds." It became "rather hot," he recalls, "and everyone had some sort of wound or other." Yet the troopers obstinately hung on, evacuating each room in its turn "as ceilings collapsed, cracks appeared in the walls, and rooms became untenable." In the rubble, making every shot count, the Red Devils, Stainforth recalls proudly, "survived like moles. Jerry just couldn't dig us out." But elsewhere men were finding their positions almost unendurable. "The Germans had decided to shell us out of existence," Private James W. Sims explains. "It seemed impossible for the shelling and mortaring to get any heavier, but it did. Burst after burst, shell after shell rained down, the separate explosions merging into one continuous rolling detonation." With each salvo Sims repeated a desperate litany, "Hold on! Hold on! It can't last much longer." As he crouched alone in his slit trench the thought struck Sims that he was "lying in a freshly dug grave just waiting to be buried alive." He remembers thinking that "unless XXX Corps hurries, we have had it."

Colonel Frost realized that disaster had finally overtaken the 2nd Battalion. The relieving battalions had not broken through, and Frost was sure they were no longer able to come to his aid. The Polish drop had failed to materialize. Ammunition was all but gone. Casualties were now so high that every available cellar was full, and the men had been fighting without letup for over fifty hours. Frost knew they could not endure this punishment much longer. All about his defensive perimeter, houses were in flames, buildings had collapsed, and positions were being overrun. He did not know how much longer he could hold out. His beloved 2nd Battalion was being buried in the ruins of the buildings around him. Yet Frost was not ready to oblige his enemy. Beyond hope, he was determined to deny the Germans the Arnhem bridge to the last.

He was not alone in his emotions. Their ordeal seemed to affect his men much as it did Frost. Troopers shared their ammunition and took what little they could find from their wounded, preparing for the doom that was engulfing them. There was little evidence of fear. In their exhaustion, hunger and pain, the men seemed to develop a sense of humor about themselves and their situation which grew even as their sacrifice became increasingly apparent.

Father Egan remembers meeting Frost coming out of a toilet. "The Colonel's face—tired, grimy, and wearing a stubble of beard—lit up with a smile," Egan recalls. " 'Father,' he told me, 'the window is shattered, there's a hole in the wall, and the roof's gone. But it has a chain and it works.' "

Later, Egan was trying to make his way across one street to visit wounded in the cellars. The area was being heavily mortared and the chaplain was taking cover wherever he could. "Outside, strolling unconcernedly up the street was Major Digby Tatham-Warter, whose company had taken the bridge initially," he recalls. "The major saw me cowering down and walked over. In his hand was an umbrella." As Egan recalls, Tatham-Warter "opened the umbrella and held it over my head. With mortar shells raining down everywhere, he said, 'Come along, Padre.' " When Egan showed reluctance, Tatham-Warter reassured him. "Don't worry," he said, "I've got an umbrella." Lieutenant Patrick Barnett encountered the redoubtable major soon afterward. Barnett was sprinting across the street to a new defense area Frost had ordered him to hold. Tatham-Warter, returning from escorting Father Egan, was out visiting his men in the shrinking perimeter defenses and holding the umbrella over his head. Barnett was so surprised that he stopped in his tracks. "That thing won't do you much good," he told the major. Tatham-Warter looked at him in mock surprise. "Oh, my goodness, Pat," he said. "What if it rains?"

During the afternoon, as the bombardment continued, Major Freddie Gough saw Tatham-Warter leading his company, umbrella in hand. Tanks were thundering down the streets firing at everything. "I almost fainted when I saw those huge Mark IV's firing at us at almost point-blank range," recalls Gough. Then the tension was suddenly relieved. "There, out in the street leading his men in a bayonet charge against some Germans who had managed to infiltrate, was Tatham-Warter," Gough recalls. "He had found an old bowler someplace and he was rushing along, twirling that battered umbrella, looking for all the world like Charlie Chaplin."

There were other moments of humor equally memorable. As the afternoon wore on, battalion headquarters was heavily bombarded and caught fire. Father Egan went down to the cellar to see the wounded. "Well, Padre," said Sergeant Jack Spratt, who was regarded as the battalion comic, "they're throwing everything at us but the kitchen stove." He had barely said the words when the building suffered another direct hit. "The ceiling fell in, showering us with dirt and plaster. When we picked ourselves up, there right in front of us was a kitchen stove." Spratt looked at it and shook his head. "I knew the bastards were close," he said, "but I didn't believe they could hear us talking."

Toward evening it began to rain, and the German attack seemed to intensify. Captain Mackay, on the opposite side of the bridge, contacted Frost. "I told the Colonel I could not hold out another night if the attack continued on the same scale," Mackay wrote. "He said he could not help me, but I was to hold on at all costs."

Mackay could see the Germans were slowly compressing Frost's force. He saw British troopers scurrying from burning houses along the riverbank toward a couple almost opposite him, which were still standing. "They were beginning to hem us in," he noted, "and it was obvious that if we didn't get help soon, they'd winkle us out. I went up to the attic and tuned into the 6 o'clock

BBC news. To my utter amazement the newscaster said that British armor had reached the airborne troops."*

Almost immediately Mackay heard a cry from the floor below, "Tiger tanks are heading for the bridge." (It was exactly 7 P.M. German time; 6 P.M. British time.) Two of the huge 60-ton tanks were heading in from the north. On his side of the bridge Frost saw them, too. "They looked incredibly sinister in the half light," he noted. "Like some prehistoric monsters, as their great guns swung from side to side breathing flame. Their shells burst through the walls. The dust and slowly settling debris following their explosions filled the passages and rooms."

One complete side of Mackay's building was hit. "Some of the shells must have been armor-piercing," Lieutenant Peter Stainforth says, "because they went through the school from end to end, knocking a four-foot hole in every room." Ceilings came down, walls cracked and "the whole structure rocked." Staring at the two tanks on the ramp, Mackay thought the end had come. "A couple more rounds like that and we'll be finished," he said. Still, with the stubborn and fearless resistance that the fighters at the bridge had shown since their arrival, Mackay thought that he might "be able to take a party out and blow them up. But just then the two tanks reversed and pulled back. We were still alive."

At Frost's headquarters, Father Egan had been hit. Caught on a stairway when shells began coming in, he fell two flights to the first floor. When he recovered consciousness, the priest was alone except for one man. Crawling to him, Egan saw that the trooper was near death. At that moment another barrage hit the building and Egan again lost consciousness. He awoke to find that the room and his clothes were on fire. Desperately he rolled along the floor, beating the flames out with his hands. The injured man he had seen earlier was dead. Now Egan could not use his legs. Slowly, in excruciating pain, he hauled himself toward a window. Someone called his name, and the intelligence officer, Lieutenant Bucky Buchanan, helped him through the window and dropped

---

* Mackay thought the report referred to Arnhem; in fact, it related to the link-up of Horrocks' tanks with the 82nd Airborne in Nijmegen.

him into the arms of Sergeant Jack Spratt. In the cellar, where Dr. James Logan was at work, the priest was put on the floor with other wounded. His right leg was broken and his back and hands were peppered with shrapnel splinters. "I was pretty well out of it," Egan recalls. "I couldn't do much now but lie there on my stomach." Nearby, slightly wounded, was the incredible Tatham-Warter, still trying to keep men's spirits up, and still hanging on to his umbrella.

Occasionally there was a pause in the terrible pounding, and Captain Mackay believed the Germans were stocking up with more ammunition. As darkness set in during one of these intervals, Mackay issued benzedrine tablets to his tired force, two pills per man. The effect on the exhausted, weary men was unexpected and acute. Some troopers became irritable and argumentative. Others suffered double vision and for a time could not aim straight. Among the shocked and wounded, men became euphoric and some began to hallucinate. Corporal Arthur Hendy remembers being grabbed by one trooper, who pulled him to a window. "Look," he commanded Hendy in a whisper. "It's the Second Army. On the far bank. Look. Do you see them?" Sadly, Hendy shook his head. The man became enraged. "They're right over there," he shouted, "plain as anything."

Mackay wondered if his small force would see out the night. Fatigue and wounds were taking their toll. "I was thinking clearly," Mackay remembers, "but we had had nothing to eat and no sleep. We were limited to one cup of water daily, and everyone was wounded." With his ammunition nearly gone, Mackay set his men to making homemade bombs from the small stock of explosives still remaining. He intended to be ready when the German tanks returned. Taking a head count, Mackay now reported to Frost that he had only thirteen men left capable of fighting.

From his position on the far side of the bridge, as the night of Tuesday, September 19, closed in, Frost saw that the entire city appeared to be burning. The spires of two great churches were flaming fiercely and as Frost watched, "the cross which hung between two lovely towers was silhouetted against the clouds rising far into the sky." He noted that "the crackle of burning wood and the strange echoes of falling buildings seemed unearthly." Upstairs, Signalman Stanley Copley, sitting at his radio set, had abandoned sending in Morse code. Now he was broadcasting in the clear. Continually he kept repeating, "This is the 1st Para Brigade calling Second Army. . . . Come in Second Army. . . . Come in Second Army."

At his headquarters in Oosterbeek's Hartenstein Hotel, General Urquhart tried desperately to save what remained of his division. Frost was cut off. Every attempt to reach him at the bridge had been mercilessly beaten back. German reinforcements were pouring in. From the west, north and east, Bittrich's forces were steadily chopping the gallant 1st British Airborne to pieces. Cold, wet, worn out, but still uncomplaining, the Red Devils were trying to hold out—fighting off tanks with rifles and Sten guns. The situation was heartbreaking for Urquhart. Only quick action could save his heroic men. By Wednesday morning, September 20, Urquhart had developed a plan to salvage the remnants of his command and perhaps turn the tide in his favor.

September 19—"a dark and fateful day," in Urquhart's words— had been the turning point. The cohesion and drive that he had hoped to instill had come too late. Everything had failed: the Polish forces had not arrived; the cargo drops had been disastrous; and battalions had been devastated in their attempts to reach Frost. The division was being pushed closer and closer to destruction. The tally of Urquhart's remaining men told a frightful story. All through the night of the nineteenth, battalion units still in contact with division headquarters reported their strength. Inconclusive and inaccurate as the figures were, they presented a grim accounting: Urquhart's division was on the verge of disappearing.

Of Lathbury's 1st Parachute Brigade, only Frost's force was

fighting as a coordinated unit, but Urquhart had no idea how many men were left in the 2nd Battalion. Fitch's 3rd Battalion listed some 50 men, and its commander was dead. Dobie's 1st totaled 116, and Dobie had been wounded and captured. The 11th Battalion's strength was down to 150, the 2nd South Staffordshires to 100. The commanders of both units, Lea and McCardie, were wounded. In Hackett's 10th Battalion there were now 250 men, and his 156th reported 270. Although Urquhart's total division strength was more—the figures did not include other units such as a battalion of the Border Regiment, the 7th KOSB's engineers, reconnaissance and service troops, glider pilots and others—his attack battalions had almost ceased to exist. The men of these proud units were now dispersed in small groups, dazed, shocked and often leaderless.

The fighting had been so bloody and so terrible that even battle-hardened veterans had broken. Urquhart and his chief of staff had sensed an atmosphere of panic seeping through headquarters as small groups of stragglers ran across the lawn yelling, "The Germans are coming." Often, they were young soldiers, "whose self-control had momentarily deserted them," Urquhart later wrote. "Mackenzie and I had to intervene physically." But others fought on against formidable odds. Captain L. E. Queripel, wounded in the face and arms, led an attack on a German twin machine-gun nest and killed the crews. As other Germans, throwing grenades, began to close in on Queripel and his party, Queripel hurled the "potato mashers" back. Ordering his men to leave him, the officer covered their retreat, throwing grenades until he was killed.[*]

Now, what remained of Urquhart's shattered and bloodied division was being squeezed and driven back upon itself. All roads seemed to end in the Oosterbeek area, with the main body of troops centered around the Hartenstein in a few square miles running between Heveadorp and Wolfheze on the west, and from Oosterbeek to Johannahoeve Farm on the east. Within that rough corridor, ending on the Rhine at Heveadorp, Urquhart planned to

[*] Queripel was posthumously awarded the Victoria Cross.

make a stand. By pulling in his troops, he hoped to husband his strength and hang on until Horrocks' armor reached him.

All through the night of the nineteenth orders went out for troops to pull back into the Oosterbeek perimeter, and in the early hours of the twentieth, Hackett was told to abandon his planned attack toward the Arnhem bridge with his 10th and 156th battalions and disengage them too. "It was a terrible decision to make," Urquhart said later. "It meant abandoning the 2nd Battalion at the bridge, but I knew I had no more chance of reaching them than I had of getting to Berlin." In his view, the only hope "was to consolidate, form a defensive box and try to hold on to a small bridgehead north of the river so that XXX Corps could cross to us."

The discovery of the ferry operating between Heveadorp and Driel had been an important factor in Urquhart's decision. It was vital to his plan for survival; for on it, theoretically, help could arrive from the southern bank. Additionally, at the ferry's landing stages on either bank, there were ramps that would help the engineers to throw a Bailey bridge across the Rhine. Admittedly the odds were great. But if the Nijmegen bridge could be taken swiftly and if Horrocks moved fast and if Urquhart's men could hold out long enough in their perimeter for engineers to span the river—a great many *if*s—there was still a chance that Montgomery might get his bridgehead across the Rhine and drive for the Ruhr, even though Frost might be overrun at Arnhem.

All through the nineteenth, messages had been sent from Urquhart's headquarters requesting a new drop zone for the Poles. Communications, though still erratic, were slightly improved. Lieutenant Neville Hay of the Phantom net was passing some messages to British Second Army headquarters, who in turn relayed them to Browning. At 3 A.M. on the twentieth, Urquhart received a message from Corps asking for the General's suggestions regarding the Poles' drop zone. As Urquhart saw it, only one possible area remained. In view of his new plan he requested the 1,500-man brigade be landed near the southern terminal of the ferry in the vicinity of the little village of Driel.

Abandoning Frost and his men was the most bitter part of the plan. At 8 A.M. on Wednesday, Urquhart had an opportunity to explain the position to Frost and Gough at the bridge. Using the Munford-Thompson radio link, Gough called division headquarters and got through to Urquhart. It was the first contact Gough had had with the General since the seventeenth, when he had been ordered back to Division only to discover that Urquhart was somewhere along the line of march. "My goodness," Urquhart said, "I thought you were dead." Gough sketched in the situation at the bridge. "Morale is still high," he recalls saying, "but we're short of everything. Despite that, we'll continue to hold out." Then, as Urquhart remembers, "Gough asked if they could expect reinforcements."

Answering was not easy. "I told him," Urquhart recalls, "that I was not certain if it was a case of me coming for them or they coming for us. I'm afraid you can only hope for relief from the south." Frost then came on the line. "It was very cheering to hear the General," Frost wrote, "but he could not tell me anything really encouraging. . . . they were obviously having great difficulties themselves." Urquhart requested that his "personal congratulations on a fine effort be passed on to everyone concerned and I wished them the best of luck." There was nothing more to be said.

Twenty minutes later, Urquhart received a message from Lieutenant Neville Hay's Phantom net. It read:

200820 (From 2nd Army). Attack at Nijmegen held up by strongpoint south of town. 5 Guards Brigade halfway in town. Bridge intact but held by enemy. Intention attack at 1300 hours today.

Urquhart immediately told his staff to inform all units. It was the first good news he had had this day.

Tragically, Urquhart had an outstanding force at his disposal whose contributions, had they been accepted, might well have altered the grim situation of the British 1st Airborne Division.

The Dutch resistance ranked among the most dedicated and disciplined underground units in all of occupied Europe. In the 101st and 82nd sectors Dutchmen were fighting alongside the American paratroopers. One of the first orders Generals Taylor and Gavin had given on landing was that arms and explosives be issued to the underground groups. But in Arnhem the British virtually ignored the presence of these spirited, brave civilians. Armed and poised to give immediate help to Frost at the bridge, the Arnhem groups were largely unheeded, and their assistance was politely rejected. By a strange series of events only one man had held the power to coordinate and weld the resistance into the British assault, and he was dead. Lieutenant Colonel Hilary Barlow, the officer Urquhart had sent to coordinate the faltering attacks of the battalions in the western suburbs, was killed before he could put his own mission into full effect.

In the original plan, Barlow was to have assumed the role of Arnhem's town major and military-government chief once the battle ended. His assistant and the Dutch representative for the Gelderland province had also been named. He was Lieutenant Commander Arnoldus Wolters of the Dutch Navy. Prior to Market-Garden, an Anglo-Dutch intelligence committee had given Barlow top-secret lists of Dutch underground personnel who were known to be completely trustworthy. "From these lists," recalls Wolters, "Barlow and I were to screen the groups and use them in their various capabilities: intelligence, sabotage, combat and the like. Barlow was the only other man who knew what our mission really was. When he disappeared, the plan collapsed." At division headquarters, Wolters was thought to be either a civil-affairs or an intelligence officer. When he produced the secret lists and made recommendations, he was looked on with suspicion. "Barlow trusted me completely," Wolters says. "I regret to say that others at headquarters did not."

With Barlow's death, Wolters' hands were tied. "The British wondered why a Dutch Navy type should be with them at all," he remembers. Gradually he won limited acceptance and although some members of the resistance were put to work, they were too few and their help was too late. "We hadn't time any longer to check everybody out to the satisfaction of headquarters," Wolters says, "and the attitude there was simply: 'Who can we trust?'" The opportunity to effectively organize and collate the underground forces in the Arnhem area had been lost.*

In England, a little before 7 A.M. on the twentieth, Major General Stanislaw Sosabowski learned that his drop zone had been changed. The Polish Brigade would now land in an area a few miles west of the original site, near the village of Driel. Sosabowski was stunned by the news his liaison officer, Lieutenant Colonel George Stevens, had brought. The brigade was already on the airfield and scheduled to leave for Holland in three hours. Within that time Sosabowski had to completely redesign his attack for an area that had not even been studied. Days had gone into the planning for the drop near Elden on the southern approaches of the Arnhem bridge. Now, he was to recall, "I was given the bare bones of a scheme, with only a few hours to develop a plan."

There was still very little news of Arnhem, but, as Stevens

---

* The British had long been wary of the Dutch underground. In 1942, Major Herman Giskes, Nazi spy chief in Holland, succeeded in infiltrating Dutch intelligence networks. Agents sent from England were captured and forced to work for him. For twenty months, in perhaps the most spectacular counterintelligence operation of World War II, nearly every agent parachuted into Holland was intercepted by the Germans. As a security check, monitors in England were instructed to listen for deliberate errors in Morse code radio transmissions. Yet messages from these "double agents" were accepted without question by British intelligence. It was not until two agents escaped that Giskes' Operation North Pole came to an end. Having hoodwinked the Allies for so long, Giskes could not resist boasting of his coup. In a plain-text message to the British on November 23, 1943, he wired: "To Messrs. Hunt, Bingham & Co., Successors Ltd., London. We understand you have been endeavoring for some time to do business in Holland without our assistance. We regret this . . . since we have acted for so long as your sole representative in this country. Nevertheless . . . should you be thinking of paying us a visit on the Continent on an extensive scale we shall give your emissaries the same attention as we have hitherto. . . ." As a result, although intelligence networks were purged and completely revamped—and although Dutch resistance groups were separate from these covert activities—nevertheless, many British senior officers were warned before Operation Market-Garden against placing too much trust in the underground.

briefed him on the new plan to ferry his troops across the Rhine from Driel to Heveadorp, it was obvious to Sosabowski that Urquhart's situation had taken a turn for the worse. He foresaw countless problems, but he noted that "nobody else seemed unduly alarmed. All Stevens had learned was that the picture was pretty confusing." Quickly informing his staff of the new developments, Sosabowski postponed the 10 A.M. takeoff until 1:00 P.M. He would need that time to reorient his troopers and to devise new attack plans, and the three-hour delay might enable Stevens to get more up-to-date information on Arnhem. Sosabowski doubted that his force could have been flown out at 10 A.M. in any case. Fog again covered the Midlands, and the forecast was not reassuring. "That and the paucity of information we received made me most anxious," Sosabowski recalled. "I did not think that Urquhart's operation was going well. I began to believe that we might be dropping into Holland to reinforce defeat."

☼ 9 ☼

At the Arnhem bridge the massive defiance by the valiant few was nearly over. At dawn the Germans had renewed their terrifying bombardment. In the morning light the stark pitted wrecks that had once been houses and office buildings were again subjected to punishing fire. On each side of the bridge and along the churned, mangled ruins of the Eusebius Buiten Singel, the few strongholds that still remained were being systematically blown apart. The semicircular defense line that had protected the northern approaches had almost ceased to exist. Yet, ringed by flames and sheltering behind rubble, small groups of obstinate men continued to fight on, denying the Germans the bridge.

Only the rawest kind of courage had sustained Frost's men up to now, but it had been fierce enough and constant enough to hold off the Germans for three nights and two days. The 2nd Battalion and the men from other units who had come by twos and threes to join it (a force that by Frost's highest estimate never totaled more than six or seven hundred men) had been welded together in their ordeal. Pride and common purpose had fused them. Alone they had reached the objective of an entire airborne division—and held out longer than the division was meant to do. In the desperate, anxious hours, awaiting help that never came, their common frame of mind was perhaps best summed up in the thoughts of Lance Corporal Gordon Spicer, who wrote, "Who's failing in their job? Not us!"

But now the time of their endurance had nearly run its course. Holed up in ruins and slit trenches, struggling to protect themselves and cellars full of wounded, shocked and concussed by nearly unceasing enemy fire, and wearing their filthy blood-stained bandages and impudent manners like badges of honor, the Red Devils knew, finally, that they could no longer hold.

The discovery produced a curious calmness, totally devoid of panic. It was as if men decided privately that they would fight until they dropped—if only to provoke the Germans more. Despite their knowledge that the fight was all but over, men invented still new ways to keep it going. Troopers of mortar platoons fired their last few bombs without tripods or base plates by standing the barrel up and holding it with ropes. Others, discovering there were no more detonators for the spring-loaded, Piat missile-throwers, tried instead to detonate the bombs with fuses made from boxes of matches. All about them friends lay dead or dying, and still they found the will to resist and, in doing so, often amused one another. Men remember an Irish trooper knocked unconscious by a shell burst opening his eyes at last to say, "I'm dead." Then, thinking it over, he remarked, "I can't be. I'm talking."

To Colonel John Frost, whose hunting horn had called them to him on the sunny Sunday that was to be the opening of their victory march, they would always remain unbeaten. Yet now, on this dark and tragic Wednesday, he knew there was "practically no possibility for relief."

The number of men still capable of fighting was, at best, between 150 and 200, concentrated mainly about the damaged headquarters buildings on the western side of the ramp. Over 300 British and German wounded filled the cellars. "They were crowded almost on top of each other," Frost noted, "making it difficult for doctors and orderlies to get around and attend them." Soon he would have to make a decision about these casualties. If the headquarters building was hit again, as it was almost certain to be, Frost told Major Freddie Gough, he "did not see how I can fight it out to the last minute, then go, and have our wounded be roasted." Measures would have to be taken to get out casualties before the building was demolished or overrun. Frost did not know how much time was left. He still believed he could control the approaches for a time, perhaps even another twenty-four hours, but his perimeter defenses were now so weak that he knew "a determined rush by the enemy could carry them into our midst."

On Captain Mackay's side of the ramp, the pulverized school-house looked, he thought, "like a sieve." As Mackay later recalled, "We were alone. All the houses on the eastern side had been burned down, except for one to the south, which was held by the Germans." And in the schoolhouse, horror had piled on horror. "The men were exhausted and filthy," Mackay wrote, "and I was sick to my stomach every time I looked at them. Haggard, with bloodshot and red-rimmed eyes, almost everyone had some sort of dirty field dressing and blood was everywhere." As wounded were carried down the stairway to the cellar, Mackay noted that "on each landing blood had formed in pools and ran in small rivulets down the stairs." His remaining thirteen men were huddled "in twos and threes, manning positions that required twice that number. The only things that were clean were the men's weapons." In the shell of the schoolhouse Mackay and his men

Colonel Frost's position around northern approaches of Arnhem bridge, from afteraction report.

fought off three enemy attacks in two hours, leaving around four times their number in enemy dead.

As morning wore on, the fighting continued. Then, around noon, the man who had so stubbornly defied the Germans was wounded. As Frost met with Major Douglas Crawley to discuss a fighting patrol to clear the area, he remembers "a tremendous explosion" that lifted him off his feet and threw him face downward several yards away. A mortar bomb had exploded almost between the two men. Miraculously both were alive, but shrapnel had torn into Frost's left ankle and right shinbone and Crawley was hit in both legs and his right arm. Frost, barely conscious, felt ashamed that he could not "resist the groans that seemed to force themselves out of me, more particularly as Doug never made a sound." Wicks, Frost's batman, helped drag the two officers to cover and stretcher-bearers carried them to the cellar with the other wounded.

In the crowded basement Father Egan tried to orient himself. In the dim recesses of the chilly room, Lieutenant Bucky Buchanan, the intelligence officer who had earlier helped to rescue Egan, appeared to have propped himself up wearily against the wall. But Buchanan was dead. A bomb blast had killed him outright without leaving a mark. Then, dazed and still in shock, Egan saw Frost being carried in. "I remember his face," Egan says. "He looked dead-tired and dejected." Other wounded in the cellar saw their battalion commander, too. To Lieutenant John Blunt, a friend of the dead Buchanan, the sight of the Colonel on a stretcher was a crushing blow. "We subalterns had always considered him irrepressible," Blunt wrote. "It hurt to see him carried in like that. He had never given in to anything."

Across the room Private James Sims, who also had a shrapnel wound, remembers somebody anxiously calling out to Frost, "Sir, can we still hold out?"

In England, Major General Sosabowski watched his brigade board the long lines of troop-carrier Dakotas. Ever since Sunday he had felt the tension build as his Poles waited to go. They had made the trip from their billets to the airfield on Tuesday only to have the operation canceled. This Wednesday morning, learning of the change in his drop zone, Sosabowski himself had postponed the flight by three hours in order to work out new plans. Now, a little before 1 P.M., as the heavily laden paratroopers moved toward the planes, the atmosphere of impatience was gone. The men were on the way at last, and Sosabowski noted "an almost lighthearted attitude among them."

His frame of mind was far different. In the few short hours since the switch in plans he had tried to learn everything he could about Urquhart's situation and the new drop zone. He had briefed his three-battalion brigade down to platoon level but the information he could give them was sparse. Sosabowski felt that they were ill-prepared, almost "jumping into the unknown."

Now, as propellers ticked over, his battalions began to climb aboard the 114 Dakotas that would take them to Holland. Satisfied with the loading, Sosabowski hoisted himself into the lead plane. With engines revving, the Dakota moved out, rolled slowly down the runway, turned and made ready for takeoff. Then it paused. To Sosabowski's dismay, the engines were throttled back. Minutes passed, and his anxiety grew. He wondered what was delaying takeoff.

Suddenly the door opened and an R.A.F. officer climbed in. Making his way up the aisle to the General, he informed Sosabowski that control had just received word to halt the takeoff. The situation was a repeat of Tuesday: the southern fields were open and bomber resupply planes were taking off, but in the Grantham area a heavy overcast was settling in. Sosabowski was incredulous. He could hear the curses of his officers and men as the news was relayed. The flight was canceled for twenty-four hours more—until 1 P.M. Thursday, September 21.

General Gavin's Glider Infantry Regiment too was grounded once again. On this day of the vital Waal river assault at Nijmegen, Gavin's sorely needed 3,400 men, with their guns and equipment, could not get out. The Driel-Heveadorp ferry was still in operation. On this crucial Wednesday, D plus 3, when the Polish Brigade might have been ferried across the Rhine to strengthen Urquhart's flagging troopers, the weather had struck again at Market-Garden.

Field Marshal Walter Model was finally ready to open his counteroffensive against the British and Americans in Holland. On this critical Wednesday, September 20, the entire corridor erupted in one German attack after another.

Model, his reinforcements steadily arriving, was certain that his forces were now strong enough to wipe out Montgomery's attack. He planned to pinch off the Allied corridor at Son, Veghel and Nijmegen. The Arnhem bridge, he knew, was almost in his hands. And Von Zangen's Fifteenth Army—the army that had been forgotten at Antwerp by Montgomery—was now slowly renewing its strength. Staffs were being newly organized, ammunition and supplies were arriving daily. Within forty-eight hours, in Army Group B's war diary, Annex 2342, Model would report Von Zangen's status to Von Rundstedt in these terms: "The total number of personnel and equipment ferried across the Schelde by the Fifteenth Army totals 82,000 men; 530 guns; 4,600 vehicles; over 4,000 horses and a large amount of valuable material. . . ."*

Model was now so confident of Von Zangen's ability to take over that within seventy-two hours he planned to completely reorganize his own command structure. Von Zangen would command all Army Group B forces west of the Allied corridor; General Student's First Parachute Army, now being systematically reinforced, would be assigned the eastern side. The moment had come for Model to begin his offensive with sharp probing attacks.

---

* Although these are the exact figures quoted from Army Group B's diary, they seem excessive particularly in the number of guns, vehicles and horses. The evacuation of the Fifteenth Army across the Schelde and around Antwerp was directed by General Eugene Felix Schwalbe. In 1946 he gave the following estimate: 65,000 men, 225 guns, 750 trucks and wagons and 1,000 horses (see Milton Shulman, *Defeat in the West*, p. 180). I cannot explain the discrepancy, but Schwalbe's figures seem much more realistic.

At the Son bridge on the morning of the twentieth, panzer forces, striking into the 101st's area, almost succeeded in taking the bridge. Only quick action by General Taylor's men and British tanks held off the attack. Simultaneously, as Horrocks' columns sped toward Nijmegen, the entire stretch of Taylor's sector came under pressure.

At 11 A.M. in General Gavin's area, German troops, preceded by a heavy bombardment, advanced out of the Reichswald and attacked the 82nd's eastern flank. Within a few hours a full-scale drive was in progress in the Mook area, threatening the Heumen bridge. Rushing to the scene from Nijmegen, where his men were preparing to assault the Waal, Gavin saw that "the only bridge we owned that would take armor" was in serious jeopardy. "It was essential to the survival of the British and Americans crowded into Nijmegen," he recalls. His problem was acute; every available 82nd unit was already committed. Hurriedly Gavin asked for help from the Coldstream Guards. Then, with Gavin personally leading the counterattack, a bitter, unrelenting battle began that was to last all day. Shifting his forces back and forth like chess men, Gavin held out and eventually forced the Germans to withdraw. He had always feared attack from the Reichswald. Now Gavin and the Corps commander, General Browning, knew that a new and more terrible phase of the fighting had begun. Among the prisoners taken were men from General Mendl's tough II Parachute Corps. Model's intention was now obvious: key bridges were to be grabbed, the corridor was to be squeezed and Horrocks' columns crushed.

For his part, Model was convinced that the Allies would never cross at Nijmegen and drive the last eleven miles to Arnhem. Within the week, he confidently told General Bittrich, he expected the battle to be over. Bittrich was less assured. He would feel happier, he told Model, if the Nijmegen bridges were destroyed. Model looked at him and angrily shouted, "No!"

Major General Heinz Harmel was annoyed by the attitude of his superior, General Wilhelm Bittrich. The II SS Panzer Corps commander had adopted too far-sighted a view of the battle, Harmel felt. Bittrich "seemed to have closed his mind completely to the ferrying problems at Pannerden." Those problems had hampered Harmel from the beginning, yet it appeared to him that Bittrich never remained long enough at the site "to see for himself the almost impossible task of getting twenty tanks across the river—and three of them were Royal Tigers." It had taken Harmel's engineers nearly three days to build a ferry capable of carrying an estimated 40-ton load across the Rhine. Although Harmel believed the operation could now be accelerated, only three platoons of tanks (twelve Panthers) had so far reached the vicinity of Nijmegen. The remainder, including his Tiger tanks, were fighting at the Arnhem bridge under the veteran eastern front commander, Major Hans Peter Knaust.

The thirty-eight-year-old Knaust had lost a leg in battle near Moscow in 1941. As Harmel recalls, "he stomped about with a wooden one and, although he was always in pain, he never once complained." Yet, Knaust too was the target for much of Harmel's displeasure.

To reinforce the Frundsberg Division, the "Knaust *Kampfgruppe*" had been rushed to Holland with thirty-five tanks, five armored personnel carriers and one self-propelled gun. But Knaust's veterans were of low caliber. Almost all of them had been badly wounded at one time or another; in Harmel's view they were "close to being invalids." Under normal conditions the men would not have been in active service. Additionally, Knaust's replacements were young, and many had had only eight weeks' training. The Arnhem bridge battle had gone on so long that Harmel was now fearful of the situation at Nijmegen. In case the British broke through, he would need Knaust's tanks to hold the bridge and defense positions between Nijmegen and Arnhem. More armored reinforcements were on the way, including fifteen to twenty Tiger tanks and another twenty Panthers. But Harmel had no idea when they would arrive or whether the Arnhem bridge would be open to speed their drive south. Even after its capture, Harmel envisioned a full day to clear the wreckage and get vehicles moving.

To oversee all operations, Harmel had set up an advance command post near the village of Doornenburg, two miles west of Pannerden and six miles northeast of Nijmegen. From there he drove west to roughly the mid-point of the Nijmegen-Arnhem highway to study the terrain, automatically fixing in his mind defense positions that might be used if a breakthrough occurred. His reconnaissance produced one clear impression: it seemed impossible for either British or German tanks to leave the highway. Only light vehicles could travel the thinly surfaced, brick-paved, secondary roads. His own tanks, moving to Nijmegen after crossing at Pannerden, had bogged down on just such roads, their weight crumbling the pavement. The main Nijmegen-Arnhem highway was, in places, a dike road, nine to twelve feet above soft polder on either side. Tanks moving along these high stretches would be completely exposed, silhouetted against the sky. Well-sited artillery could easily pick them off. At the moment, Harmel had almost no artillery covering the highway; thus it was imperative that Knaust's tanks and guns get across the Rhine and in position before a British breakthrough could occur at Nijmegen.

Returning to his headquarters at Doornenburg, Harmel heard the latest reports from his chief of staff, Colonel Paetsch. There was good news from Arnhem: more prisoners were being taken, and the fighting at the bridge was beginning to break up. Knaust now believed he might have the crossing by late afternoon. Fighting continued in Nijmegen, but Captain Karl Heinz Euling, although taking heavy casualties, was containing all efforts to seize the railway and road bridges there. The Americans and British had been stopped at both approaches. In the center of the city British forces had been held up too, but that situation was more precarious.

Euling's report reflected an optimism that Harmel did not share. Eventually, by sheer weight of numbers, British armor would surely overrun the German line. Lighting a cigar, Harmel told Paetsch that he "expected the full weight of the Anglo-American attack to be thrown at the highway bridge within forty-eight hours." If Knaust's tanks and artillerymen secured the Arnhem bridge quickly, they might halt the British armored drive. Should the panzers be slow in forcing the little band of British from the Arnhem bridge and clearing it of wreckage, Harmel knew that, against all orders, he must blow the Nijmegen highway bridge.

For all his careful consideration, he did not envision a most preposterous scheme: that the American paratroopers might try to ford the river in a major amphibious assault.

�֍ 10 ✦

WAITING PARATROOPERS CROWDED THE AREA not far from the crossing site, one mile downstream from the Nijmegen railway bridge. Throughout Tuesday night and well into Wednesday morning, as the Anglo-American forces under Lieutenant Colonel Goulburn and Lieutenant Colonel Vandervoort continued the battle for the railroad and highway bridges to the east, American and British soldiers labored to widen the area leading to the river bank so that the tanks and heavy artillery of the Guards Armored Division could take up firing positions to support the assault. Typhoons were scheduled to fly low over the northern bank thirty minutes before H Hour, spraying the entire area with rocket and machine-gun fire. On the ground, tanks and artillery would pound the site for another fifteen minutes. Then, under a smoke screen laid down by tanks, the first wave of men led by twenty-seven-year-old Major Julian Cook were to set out in one of the most daring river crossings ever made.

The plan was as thorough as commanders working throughout the night could make it. But the boats in which Cook's troopers would cross the 400-yard-wide river had not arrived. H Hour, originally set for 1 P.M., was postponed until 3 P.M.

In small groups the Americans waited as Cook paced up and down. "Where are the damned boats?" he wondered. Ever since he had been told by General Gavin and the 504th regimental commander, Colonel Tucker, that his 3rd Battalion would make the Waal assault crossing, Cook had been "shocked and dumfounded." It seemed to the young West Pointer that "we were being asked to make an Omaha beach landing all by ourselves." Many of his men had never even been in a small boat.

Cook was not the only one anxiously awaiting the arrival of the boats. Before noon General Frederick Browning had received the first clear indication of the seriousness of Urquhart's situation. Received via British Second Army communications, the Phantom message read in part:

(201105) . . . senior formation still in vicinity north end of main bridge but not in touch and unable resupply . . . Arnhem entirely in enemy hands. Request all possible steps expedite relief. Fighting intense and opposition extremely strong. Position not too good.

Browning was deeply disturbed. Every hour now mattered and the quick seizure of the Nijmegen bridges was vital to the survival of Urquhart's men. The relief of the Arnhem defenders was, at this moment, almost solely up to Cook and the 3rd Battalion—a fact of which Cook was unaware.

In any event, the boats were not at hand, and no one even knew what they were like. All through the night General Horrocks and his staff had been trying to speed their arrival. Far back in the engineering convoys three trucks carrying the craft had been inching their way up the jam-packed road. Back in Eindhoven they had been held up by a fierce Luftwaffe bombing attack. The whole center of the city was devastated. Scores of supply trucks had been destroyed and an entire ammunition convoy had been ignited, adding to the carnage. Now, at the Waal crossing less than one hour before H hour, there was still no sign of the trucks and the vital boats.

The assault site lay to the east of the massive PGEM electrical power plant, and originally it was believed that the crossing could be made from the plant itself. There, at the river's edge, a small inlet afforded protection for the loading, unobserved by the Germans. Colonel Tucker had rejected the site; it was too close to the enemy-held railway bridge. As the troopers emerged from the dock area, the Germans could sweep each assault wave with machine-gun fire. Here, too, at the mouth of the inlet, the 8- to 10-mile-an-hour current swirled stronger. Shifting farther west, Tucker planned to have the men rush the boats at double time down to the river's edge, launch them and paddle across. That, too, worried Cook. From the little he had learned, each craft weighed about 200 pounds; when they were loaded with the men's equipment and ammunition, that figure would probably double.

Once launched, each boat would carry thirteen paratroopers and a crew of three engineers to row the men across. The operation would be continuous. In wave after wave the assault craft were to cross back and forth until the whole of Cook's battalion and part of another, under Captain John Harrison, were across. Major Edward G. Tyler of the Irish Guards, whose tanks were to give fire support, was appalled by the whole concept. "It put the fear of God in me," Tyler recalls. He asked the cigar-chewing Colonel Tucker if his men had ever practiced this kind of operation before. "No," Tucker replied laconically. "They're getting on-the-job training."

From the ninth floor of the power plant, Cook and Lieutenant Colonel Giles Vandeleur, commanding the Irish Guards' 2nd Battalion, observed the north shore through binoculars. Directly across from where they stood, flat ground ran inland from the river's edge for 200 to 800 yards. Cook's men would have to cross this unprotected stretch after they landed. Beyond the level shore, a sloping dike embankment rose some 15 to 20 feet high, and topping it was a 20-foot-wide road running west to east. A squat building, called Fort Hof Van Holland, stood about 800 yards beyond the road. Cook and Vandeleur could clearly see enemy troops in position along the top of the embankment, and they were almost sure that observation and artillery posts were positioned inside the fort. "Somebody," Cook remembers thinking, "has come up with a real nightmare." Yet, effective H-Hour air and artillery support could soften the German resistance and enable the troopers to command the northern bank quickly. Cook was counting heavily on that support.

Vandeleur thought the crossing might prove "ghastly, with heavy casualties." But he intended his tanks to support the Americans to the utmost. He planned to use about thirty Sherman tanks—two squadrons under command of Major Edward G. Tyler and Major Desmond FitzGerald. At 2:30 P.M., the tanks were to move toward the river and mount the embankment, "track-to-track," their 75 mm. guns lined up to pound the far shore. This British bombardment would be reinforced by the 82nd's mortar and artillery fire. In all, 100 guns would batter the northern bank.

Cook's men, who had not seen the actual assault area as yet, had taken the briefing in their stride. But the width of the river shocked everyone. "At first when we were briefed, we thought they were joking," recalls Second Lieutenant John Holabird. "It all sounded too fantastic." Sergeant Theodore Finkbeiner, scheduled for the first wave, was sure that "our chances were pretty good because of the smoke screen." But Captain T. Moffatt Burriss, commander of I Company, believed the plan was nothing short of a suicide mission.

So did the 504th's Protestant chaplain, Captain Delbert Kuehl. Normally Kuehl would not have gone in with assault troops. Now he requested permission to be with Cook's men. "It was the hardest decision I ever made," he recalls, "because I was going on my own volition. The plan seemed absolutely impossible, and I felt if ever the men needed me, it would be on this operation."

Captain Henry Baldwin Keep, who was known as the battalion's millionaire because he was a member of the Philadelphia Biddle family, considered that "the odds were very much against us. In eighteen months of almost steady combat we had done everything from parachute jumps to establishing bridgeheads to acting as mountain troops and as regular infantry. But a river crossing was something else! It sounded impossible."

Cook, according to Lieutenant Virgil Carmichael, tried to lighten the atmosphere by announcing that he would imitate George Washington by "standing erect in the boat and, with clenched right fist pushed forward, shout, 'Onward, men! Onward!'" Captain Carl W. Kappel, commander of H Company, who had heard that the Arnhem attack was in trouble, was deeply concerned. He wanted "to get in the damn boat and get the hell across." He had a good friend in the British 1st Airborne, and he felt if anyone was on the Arnhem bridge it was "Frosty"—Colonel John Frost.

By 2 P.M. there was still no sign of the assault craft, and now it was too late to recall the approaching squadrons of Typhoons. Back of the jump-off site, hidden behind the river embankment, Cook's men and Vandeleur's tanks waited. At precisely 2:30 P.M. the Typhoon strike began. Flashing overhead, the planes peeled off and screamed down, one after another, shooting rockets and machine-gun fire at the enemy positions. Ten minutes later, as Vandeleur's tanks began taking up positions on the embankment, the three trucks carrying the assault craft arrived. With only twenty minutes to go, Cook's men saw, for the first time, the flimsy collapsible green boats.

Each boat was nineteen feet long with a flat, reinforced plywood bottom. The canvas sides, held in place by wooden pegs, measured thirty inches from floor to gunwales. Eight paddles, four feet long, were supposed to accompany each boat, but in many there were only two. Men would have to use their rifle butts to paddle.

Quickly engineers began assembling the boats. As each was put together, the paratroopers assigned to the craft loaded their equipment on board and got ready to dash for the bank. Against the deafening din of the barrage now lashing the far shore, the twenty-six boats were finally assembled. "Somebody yelled, 'Go!' " First Lieutenant Patrick Mulloy recalls, "and everybody grabbed the gunwales and started to lug the boats down to the river." From the rear, shells screamed over the men's heads; tank guns barked from the embankment ahead of them, and white smoke, "looking fairly thick" to Mulloy, drifted over the width of the river. The assault was on.

As the first wave of some 260 men—two companies, H and I, plus headquarters staff and engineers—got to the water the launching immediately began to assume the proportions of a disaster. Boats put into too-shallow water bogged down in the mud and would not budge. Struggling and thrashing in the shallows, men carried them to deeper parts, pushed them out and then climbed in. As some troopers tried to hoist themselves aboard, their boats overturned. Other boats, overloaded, were caught by the current and began circling out of control. Some sank under their heavy loads. Paddles were lost; men fell overboard. Captain Carl Kappel saw the scene as one "of mass confusion." His boat began to founder. "Private Legacie was in the water and starting to go down," Kappel remembers. Diving in after him, Kappel was surprised at the swiftness of the current. He was able to grab Legacie and pull him to safety "but by the time I got him to the bank I was an old man and worn out." Jumping into another boat Kappel started out again. First Lieutenant Tom MacLeod's craft was almost awash, and he thought they were sinking. "Paddles were flaying like mad," he remembers, and all he could hear above the din was Cook's voice, from a nearby boat, yelling, "Keep going! Keep going!"

The Major, a devout Catholic, was also praying out loud. Lieutenant Virgil Carmichael noticed that he had developed a kind of cadence with each line. "Hail Mary—full of Grace—Hail Mary—full of Grace," Cook chanted with every stroke of the paddle.° Then, in the midst of the confusion, the Germans opened up.

The fire was so intense and concentrated that it reminded Lieutenant Mulloy of "the worst we ever took at Anzio. They were blazing away with heavy machine guns and mortars, most of it coming from the embankment and the railroad bridge. I felt like a sitting duck." Chaplain Kuehl was sick with horror. The head of the man sitting next to him was blown off. Over and over Kuehl kept repeating "Lord, Thy will be done."

From his command post in the PGEM building, Lieutenant Colonel Vandeleur, along with General Browning and General Horrocks, watched in grim silence. "It was a horrible, horrible sight," Vandeleur remembers. "Boats were literally blown out of the water. Huge geysers shot up as shells hit and small-arms fire from the northern bank made the river look like a seething cauldron." Instinctively men began to crouch in the boats. Lieutenant Holabird, staring at the fragile canvas sides, felt "totally exposed and defenseless." Even his helmet "seemed about as small as a beanie."

Shrapnel ripped through the little fleet. The boat carrying half of First Lieutenant James Megellas' platoon sank without a trace. There were no survivors. First Lieutenant Allen McLain saw two craft blown apart and troopers thrown into the water. Around Captain T. Moffatt Burriss' boat fire was coming down "like a hailstorm," and finally the engineer steering the boat said, "Take the rudder. I'm hit." His wrist was shattered. As Burriss leaned over to help, the engineer was hit again, this time in the head. Shell fragments caught Burriss in the side. As the engineer fell overboard, his foot caught the gunwale, causing his body to act like a rudder and swinging the boat around. Burriss had to heave the dead man into the water. By then two more troopers sitting in front had also been killed.

Under a brisk wind the smoke screen had been blown to tatters.

° " 'The Lord is with Thee' was too long," Cook says, "so I kept repeating, 'Hail Mary' (one stroke), 'Full of Grace' (second stroke)." Captain Keep tried to remember his crewing days at Princeton but he found himself nervously counting "7-6-7-7-7-8-9."

Now German gunners raked each boat individually. Sergeant Clark Fuller saw that some men, in their haste to get across quickly, and desperately trying to avoid the fire, "rowed against each other, causing their boats to swing around in circles." The Germans picked them off easily. Fuller was "so scared that he felt paralyzed." Halfway across, Private Leonard G. Tremble was suddenly slammed into the bottom of the boat. His craft had taken a direct hit. Wounded in the face, shoulder, right arm and left leg, Tremble was sure he was bleeding to death. Taking water, the boat swung crazily in circles, then drifted slowly back to the southern shore, everyone in it dead but Tremble.

In the command post Vandeleur saw that "huge gaps had begun to appear in the smoke screen." His tankers had fired smoke shells for more than ten minutes, but now the Guardsmen were running low on every kind of ammunition. "The Germans had switched ammunition and were beginning to use big stuff, and I remember almost trying to will the Americans to go faster. It was obvious that these young paratroopers were inexperienced in handling assault boats, which are not the easiest things to maneuver. They were zigzagging all over the water."

Then the first wave reached the northern bank. Men struggled out of the boats, guns firing, and started across the exposed flat land. Sergeant Clark Fuller, who a few minutes before had been paralyzed with fear, was so happy to be alive that he felt "exhilarated. My fear had been replaced by a surge of recklessness. I felt I could lick the whole German army." Vandeleur, watching the landing, "saw one or two boats hit the beach, followed immediately by three or four others. Nobody paused. Men got out and began running toward the embankment. My God, what a courageous sight it was! They just moved steadily across that open ground. I never saw a single man lie down until he was hit. I didn't think more than half the fleet made it across." Then, to Vandeleur's amazement, "the boats turned around and started back for the second wave." Turning to Horrocks, General Browning said, "I have never seen a more gallant action."

As Julian Cook's assault craft neared the beach he jumped out and pulled the boat, eager to get ashore. Suddenly to his right he saw a bubbling commotion in the gray water. "It looked like a large air bubble, steadily approaching the bank," he remembers. "I thought I was seeing things when the top of a helmet broke the surface and continued on moving. Then a face appeared under the helmet. It was the little machine-gunner, Private Joseph Jedlicka. He had bandoliers of 30-caliber machine-gun bullets draped around his shoulders and a box in either hand." Jedlicka had fallen overboard in eight feet of water and, holding his breath, had calmly walked across the river bottom until he emerged.

Medics were already working on the beach and as First Lieutenant Tom MacLeod prepared to return across the Waal for another boatload of troopers, he saw that rifles had been stuck in the ground next to the fallen.

Shortly after 4 P.M., General Heinz Harmel received an alarming message at his headquarters in Doornenburg. It was reported that "a white smoke screen has been thrown across the river opposite Fort Hof Van Holland." Harmel, with some of his staff, rushed by car to the village of Lent, on the northern bank of the Waal, a mile from the Nijmegen highway bridge. The smoke could mean only one thing: the Anglo-Americans were trying to cross the Waal by boat. Still, Harmel could not believe his own analysis. The width of the river, the forces manning the northern bank, Euling's optimistic report of the morning, and his own estimate of the British and American forces in Nijmegen—all argued against the operation. But Harmel decided to see for himself. He remembers that "I had no intention of being arrested and shot by Berlin for letting the bridges fall into enemy hands—no matter how Model felt about it."

Major Julian Cook knew his losses were appalling, but he had
no time to assess them now. His companies had landed everywhere along the exposed stretch of beach. Units were inextricably
mixed up and, for the time, without organization. The Germans
were flaying the beach with machine-gun fire, yet his stubborn
troopers refused to be pinned down. Individually and in twos and
threes they headed for the embankment. "It was either stay and
get riddled or move," Cook remembers. Struggling forward, the
men, armed with machine guns, grenades and fixed bayonets,
charged the embankment and viciously dug the Germans out.
Sergeant Theodore Finkbeiner believes he was one of the first to
reach the high dike roadway. "I stuck my head over the top, and
stared right into the muzzle of a machine gun," he recalls. He
ducked, but "the muzzle blast blew my helmet off." Finkbeiner
tossed a grenade into the German emplacement, heard the explosion and the sound of men screaming. Then he quickly hoisted
himself up onto the embankment road and headed for the next
machine-gun nest.

Captain Moffatt Burriss had no time to think about the shrapnel wound in his side. When he landed he was "so happy to be
alive that I vomited." He ran straight for the dike, yelling to his
men to get "one machine gun firing on the left flank, another on
the right." They did. Burriss saw several houses back of the dike.
Kicking the door of one open, he surprised "several Germans who
had been sleeping, apparently unaware of what was happening."
Reaching quickly for a hand grenade, Burriss pulled the pin,
threw it into the room and slammed the door.

In the smoke, noise and confusion, some men in the first wave
did not remember how they got off the beach. Corporal Jack
Bommer, a communications man laden down with equipment,
simply ran forward. He "had only one thing in mind: to survive if
possible." He knew he had to get to the embankment and wait for
further instructions. On reaching the crest he saw "dead bodies
everywhere, and Germans—some no more than fifteen years old,
others in their sixties—who a few minutes before had been
slaughtering us in the boats were now begging for mercy, trying

to surrender." Men were too shocked by their ordeal and too angry at the death of friends to take many prisoners. Bommer recalls that some Germans "were shot out of hand at point-blank range."

Sickened and exhausted by the crossing, their dead and wounded lying on the beach, the men of the first wave subdued the German defenders on the dike road in less than thirty minutes. Not all the enemy positions had been overrun, but now troopers hunched down in former German machine-gun nests to protect the arrival of succeeding waves. Two more craft were lost in the second crossing. And, still under heavy shellfire, exhausted engineers in the eleven remaining craft made five more trips to bring all the Americans across the bloodstained Waal. Speed was all that mattered now. Cook's men had to grab the northern ends of the crossings before the Germans fully realized what was happening—and before they blew the bridges.

By now the embankment defense line had been overrun, and the Germans were pulling back to secondary positions. Cook's troopers gave them no quarter. Captain Henry Keep comments that "what remained of the battalion seemed driven to fever pitch and, rendered crazy by rage, men temporarily forgot the meaning of fear. I have never witnessed this human metamorphosis so acutely displayed as on this day. It was an awe-inspiring sight but not a pretty one."

Individually and in small groups, men who had sat helpless in the boats as friends died all around them took on four and five times their number with grenades, submachine guns and bayonets. With brutal efficiency they dug the Germans out and, without stopping to rest or regroup, continued their rampaging assault. They fought through fields, orchards and houses back of the embankment under the fire of machine guns and antiaircraft batteries hammering at them from Fort Hof Van Holland directly ahead. As some groups headed due east along the sunken dike road for the bridges, others stormed the fort, almost oblivious to the German guns. Some troopers, laden with grenades, swam the moat surrounding the fortress and began climbing the walls.

Sergeant Leroy Richmond, swimming underwater, took the enemy soldier guarding the causeway by surprise, then waved his men across. According to First Lieutenant Virgil F. Carmichael, troopers "somehow climbed to the top of the fort, then others below tossed up hand grenades which were promptly dropped into the turret portholes, one after the other." The German defenders quickly surrendered.

Meanwhile, units from two companies—Captain Burriss' I Company and Captain Kappel's H Company—were sprinting for the bridges. At the railroad bridge, H Company found the German defense so fierce that it looked as though the American attack might stall.° Then the continuing pressure from the British and American forces at the southern end and in Nijmegen itself caused the enemy suddenly to crack. To Kappel's amazement the Germans began to retreat across the bridge "in wholesale numbers"—right into the American guns. From his tank near the PGEM factory, Lieutenant John Gorman "could see what looked like hundreds of Germans, confused and panic-stricken, running across the bridge right toward the Americans." On the northern bank First Lieutenant Richard La Riviere and Lieutenant E. J. Sims also saw them coming. In disbelief, they watched as the Germans abandoned their guns and hurried toward the northern exit. "They were coming across in a mass," recalls La Riviere, "and we let them come—two thirds of the way." Then the Americans opened fire.

A hail of bullets ripped into the defenders. Germans fell everywhere—some into the girders under the bridge; others to the water below. More than 260 lay dead, many were wounded, and scores more were taken prisoner before the firing ceased. Within two hours of the Waal river assault, the first of the bridges had fallen. Major Edward G. Tyler of the Irish Guards saw "someone waving. I had been concentrating so long on that railroad bridge that, for me, it was the only one in existence. I got on the wireless

---

° According to Charles B. MacDonald, in *The Siegfried Line Campaign*, p. 181, the Germans on the bridge had a formidable array of armament which included 34 machine guns, two 20 mm. antiaircraft guns and one 88 mm. dual-purpose gun.

and radioed Battalion, 'They're on the bridge! They've got the bridge!'" The time was 5 P.M. Captain Tony Heywood of the Grenadier Guards received Major Tyler's message and found it "utterly confusing." Which bridge did the message refer to? The Grenadiers under Lieutenant Colonel Goulburn were still fighting alongside Colonel Vandervoort's troopers near the Valkhof, where Euling's SS forces continued to deny them the highway bridge. If the message meant that the highway bridge had been taken, Heywood remembers, "I couldn't figure how they had gotten across."

The railroad bridge was intact and physically in Anglo-American hands, but Germans—either prepared to fight to the last or too frightened to leave their positions—were still on it. The Americans had made a quick search for demolition charges at the northern end. Although they had found nothing, there was still a chance that the bridge was wired and ready to be destroyed. Captain Kappel now radioed Major Cook, urging him to get British tanks across as quickly is possible. With these as support, he and Captain Burriss of I Company believed, they could grab the big prize, the Nijmegen highway bridge, slightly less than a mile east. Then, recalls Kappel, Colonel Tucker arrived. The request, Tucker said, "had been relayed, but the Germans might blow both bridges at any moment." Without hesitation Cook's troopers pushed on for the highway bridge.

General Harmel could not make out what was happening. Binoculars to his eyes, he stood on the roof of a bunker near the village of Lent. From this position on the northern bank of the Waal barely a mile from the main Nijmegen highway bridge, he could see smoke and haze off to his right and hear the crash of battle. But no one seemed to know exactly what was taking place, except that an attempt had been made to cross the river near the railroad bridge. He could see the highway bridge quite clearly; there was nothing on it. Then, as Harmel recalls, "the wounded started to arrive, and I began to get conflicting reports." Americans, he learned, had crossed the river, "but everything was exaggerated. I could not tell if they had come across in ten boats or a hundred." His mind "working furiously trying to decide what to do next," Harmel checked with his engineers. "I was informed that both bridges were ready to go," he remembers. "The local commander was instructed to destroy the railroad bridge. The detonator for the highway bridge was hidden in a garden near the bunker at Lent, and a man was stationed there awaiting orders to press the plunger." Then Harmel received his first clear report: only a few boats had crossed the river, and the battle was still in progress. Looking through his binoculars again, he saw that the highway bridge was still clear and free of movement. Although his "instinct was to get this troublesome bridge weighing on my shoulders destroyed, I had no intention of doing anything until I was absolutely sure that it was lost." If he was forced to blow the highway bridge, Harmel decided, he would make sure that "it was crowded with British tanks and let them go up in the blast, too."

In Huner Park and in the Valkhof close by the southern approaches to the highway bridge, Captain Karl Euling's SS Panzer Grenadiers were fighting for their lives. The Anglo-American attack by Lieutenant Colonel Edward Goulburn's Grenadier Guards and Lieutenant Colonel Ben Vandervoort's 2nd Battalion of the 82nd's 505th Regiment was methodical and relentless. Vandervoort's mortars and artillery pounded the German defense line as his men sprinted from house to house. Closing the gap between themselves and Euling's steadily shrinking defenses, Goulburn's tanks moved up the converging streets, driving the Germans before them, their 17-pounders and machine guns blasting.

The Germans fought back hard. "It was the heaviest volume of fire I ever encountered," recalls Sergeant Spencer Wurst, then a nineteen-year-old veteran who had been with the 82nd since North Africa. "I had the feeling I could reach up and grab bullets with each hand." From his vantage point on the ledge of a house some twenty-five yards from the Valkhof, Wurst could look down into the German positions. "There were foxholes all over the park," he remembers, "and all the action seemed to be centered from these and from a medieval tower. I watched our men break out from right and left and charge right up to the traffic circle. We were so anxious to get that bridge that I saw some men crawl over to the foxholes and literally drag the Germans out." Wurst's own rifle barrel was so hot that cosmoline began to ooze from the wood stock.

As the murderous fire fight continued Wurst was astounded to see Colonel Vandervoort "stroll across the street, smoking a cigarette. He stopped in front of the house I was in, looked up and said, 'Sergeant, I think you better go see if you can get that tank moving.'" Vandervoort pointed to the entrance to the park where a British tank was sitting, its turret closed. Clambering off the roof, Wurst ran to the tank and rapped on its side with his helmet. The turret opened. "Colonel wants you to move it," Wurst said. "Come on. I'll show you where to fire." Advancing beside the tank in full view of the Germans, Wurst pointed out targets. As the intense fire coming from Vandervoort's men and Goulburn's tanks increased, the enemy defense ring began to collapse. The formidable line of antitank guns that had stopped each previous attack was obliterated. Finally only four self-propelled guns dug into the center of the traffic circle remained firing. Then, a little after 4 P.M., in an all-out tank and infantry assault, these too were overrun. As Vandervoort's troopers charged with bayonets and grenades, Goulburn lined his tanks up four abreast and sent them charging into the park. In panic the Germans broke. As they retreated, some tried to take cover in the girders of the bridge; others, farther away, raced through the American and British fire toward the medieval fort. As the Germans passed, scores of troopers lobbed grenades into their midst. The assault was over. "They had given us a real tough time," Wurst says. "We watched them charging right past us, up over the road leading onto the bridge and some went off to the east. We felt pretty good."

General Allan Adair, commander of the Guards Armored Division, directing operations in a nearby building, remembers "gritting my teeth, dreading the sound of an explosion that would tell me the Germans had blown the bridge." He heard nothing. The approaches to the great Waal bridge lay open, the span itself apparently intact.

Sergeant Peter Robinson's troop of four tanks had been waiting for just this moment. Now they moved out for the bridge.* The twenty-nine-year-old Dunkirk veteran had been alerted a few hours earlier by his squadron leader, Major John Trotter, "to stand ready to go for the bridge." Germans were still on the crossing, and Trotter now warned Robinson, "We don't know what to expect when you cross, but the bridge has to be taken. Don't stop for anything." Shaking hands with the sergeant, Trotter added jokingly, "Don't worry. I know where your wife lives and if anything happens, I'll let her know." Robinson was not amused. "You're bloody cheerful, aren't you, sir?" he. asked Trotter. Climbing onto his tank, Robinson led off for the bridge.

The troop of four tanks came into Huner Park by the right of the roundabout. To Robinson it appeared that "the whole town was burning. Buildings to my left and right were on fire." Wreathed in smoke, the great crossing looked "damned big." As Robinson's tank rumbled forward he reported constantly by radio to division headquarters. "Everyone else had been ordered off the air," he recalls. Clanking onto the approaches, Robinson remembers, "We came under heavy fire. There was an explosion. One of the idler wheels carrying the track on one side of the tank had been hit." The tank was still running, although "the wireless was dead and I had lost touch with headquarters." Shouting to his

---

* It has been said that an American flag was raised on the north end of the railroad bridge and, in the smoke and confusion, British tankers thought it was flying on the far end of the highway bridge—signaling the American seizure of that end. The story may be true, but in scores of interviews I have not found a single participant who confirmed it. I have walked over the entire area and it seems inconceivable that anyone looking across the highway bridge could mistake a flag flying a mile to the west as the terminus of this crossing.

driver to reverse, Robinson backed his tank to the side of the road. Quickly the sergeant jumped out, ran to the tank behind him and told its commander, Sergeant Billingham, to get out. Billingham began to argue. Robinson shouted that he was giving "a direct order. Get out of that tank damned quick and follow along in mine." The third tank in line, commanded by Sergeant Charles W. Pacey, had pulled out and was leading the way onto the bridge. Jumping aboard Billingham's tank, Robinson ordered the others to follow. As the four tanks advanced, Robinson recalls, they came under fire from a "big 88 parked on the other side of the river, near some burning houses and from what appeared to be a self-propelled gun in the far distance."

Colonel Vandervoort, watching the tanks, saw the 88 begin to fire. "It was pretty spectacular," he recalls. "The 88 was sandbagged into the side of the highway about one hundred yards from the north end of the bridge. One tank and the 88 exchanged about four rounds apiece with the tank spitting 30-caliber tracers all the while. In the gathering dusk it was quite a show." Then Robinson's gunner, Guardsman Leslie Johnson, got the 88 with another shot. Germans with grenades, rifles and machine guns clung to the girders of the bridge, Robinson remembers. The tank machine guns began "to knock them off like ninepins." And Johnson, answering the heavy enemy artillery fire, "pumped shells through his gun as fast as the loader could run them through." In a hail of fire Robinson's troop rattled forward, now approaching the halfway mark on the highway bridge.

In the twilight, billowing smoke clogged the distant Waal highway bridge. At his forward position near Lent, General Heinz Harmel stared through his binoculars. Guns were banging all around him, and troops were moving back through the village to take up new positions. Harmel's worst fear had now been realized. The Americans, against all expectations, had succeeded in making a bold, successful crossing of the Waal. In Nijmegen itself the optimism of Captain Karl Euling had proved unfounded. The last message received from him had been terse: Euling said he was encircled with only sixty men left. Now Harmel knew beyond doubt that the bridges were lost. He did not know whether the railroad bridge had been destroyed, but if he was to demolish the highway bridge, it must be done immediately.

"Everything seemed to pass through my mind all at once," he recalled. "What must be done first? What is the most urgent, most important action to take? It all came down to the bridges." He had not contacted Bittrich "beforehand to warn him that I might have to demolish the highway crossing. I presumed that it was Bittrich who had ordered the bridges readied for demolition." So, Harmel reasoned, in spite of Model's order, "if Bittrich had been in my shoes, he would have blown the main bridge. In my opinion, Model's order was now automatically canceled anyway." At any moment he expected tanks to appear on the highway bridge.

Standing next to the engineer by the detonator box, Harmel scanned the crossing. At first he could detect no movement. Then suddenly he saw "a single tank reach the center, then a second behind and to its right." To the engineer he said, "Get ready." Two more tanks appeared in view, and Harmel waited for the line to reach the exact middle before giving the order. He shouted, "Let it blow!" The engineer jammed the plunger down. Nothing happened. The British tanks continued to advance. Harmel yelled, "Again!" Once more the engineer slammed down the detonator handle, but again the huge explosions that Harmel had expected failed to occur. "I was waiting to see the bridge collapse and the tanks plunge into the river," he recalled. "Instead, they moved forward relentlessly, getting bigger and bigger, closer and closer." He yelled to his anxious staff, "My God, they'll be here in two minutes!"

Rapping out orders to his officers, Harmel told them "to block the roads between Elst and Lent with every available antitank gun and artillery piece because if we don't, they'll roll straight through to Arnhem." Then, to his dismay he learned that the railroad bridge was also still standing. Hurrying to a radio unit in one of the nearby command posts, he contacted his advance headquarters and spoke with his operations officer. "Stolley," Harmel said, "tell Bittrich. They're over the Waal."*

Sergeant Peter Robinson's four tanks pressed on across the bridge. A second 88 had stopped firing, and Robinson "reckoned we had put it out of operation, too." Looming ahead was a road-block of heavy concrete cubes with a gap of approximately ten feet in the middle. Robinson saw Sergeant Pacey's tank make it through and stop on the far side. Then Robinson got past and, as Pacey covered the three tanks, took the lead once more. Robinson remembers that "visibility was terrible. I was shouting like hell, trying to direct the gunner, the driver, and inform headquarters all at the same time. The noise was unbelievable, with all sorts of fire clanging off the girders." Three to four hundred yards ahead on the right, alongside the roadbed, Robinson saw another 88. He shouted to the gunner: "Traverse right 400 yards and fire." Guardsman Johnson blew the gun to pieces. As infantry around it began to run, Johnson opened up with his machine gun. "It was a massacre," he recalled. "I didn't even have to bother looking through the periscope. There were so many of them that I just

* This is the first account of the German attempt to destroy the Nijmegen highway bridge. General Harmel had never before given an interview to anyone on the subject. The failure of the demolition charge remains a mystery to this day. Many Dutch believe that the main crossing was saved by a young underground worker, Jan van Hoof, who had been sent into Nijmegen on the nineteenth by the 82nd's Dutch liaison officer, Captain Arie Bestebreurtje, as a guide to the paratroopers. Van Hoof is thought to have succeeded in penetrating the German lines and to have reached the bridge, where he cut cables leading to the explosives. He may well have done so. In 1949 a Dutch commission investigating the story was satisfied that Van Hoof had cut some lines, but could not confirm that these alone actually saved the bridge. The charges and transmission lines were on the Lent side of the Waal and Van Hoof's detractors maintain that it would have been impossible for him to have reached them without being detected. The controversy still rages. Although the evidence is against him, personally I would like to believe that the young Dutch-man, who was shot by the Germans for his role in the underground during the battle, was indeed responsible.

pulled the trigger." He could feel the tank "bumping over the bodies lying in the road."

From the turret Robinson saw that his three tanks were still coming on unharmed. He radioed to them to "close up and get a move on!" The troop was now nearing the northern end of the bridge. Within seconds a self-propelled gun began to fire. "There were two big bangs in front of us," Robinson recalls. "My tin hat was blown off, but I wasn't hit." Johnson fired off three or four shells. The gun and a nearby house "burst into flame and the whole area was lit up like day." Before he realized it, Robinson's tanks were across the bridge.

He ordered the gunners to cease fire, and as the dust cleared, he caught sight of some figures in the ditch. At first he thought they were German. Then "from the shape of their helmets I knew they were Yanks. Suddenly there were Americans swarming all over the tank, hugging and kissing me, even kissing the tank." Captain T. Moffatt Burriss, his clothes still damp and blood-soaked from the shrapnel wound he had received during the Waal crossing, grinned up at Johnson. "You guys are the most beautiful sight I've seen in years," he said. The huge, multi-spanned Nijmegen crossing, together with its approaches almost a half mile long, had fallen intact. Of the Market-Garden bridges, the last but one was now in Allied hands. The time was 7:15 P.M., September 20. Arnhem lay only eleven miles away.

Lieutenant Tony Jones of the Royal Engineers—a man whom General Horrocks was later to describe as "the bravest of the brave"—had followed Robinson's troop across the bridge. Searching carefully for demolitions, Jones worked so intently that he was unaware that Germans, still on the girders, were shooting at him. In fact, he recalls, "I don't ever remember seeing any." Near the roadblock in the center of the bridge he found "six or eight wires coming over the railing and lying on the footpath." Jones promptly cut the wires. Nearby he found a dozen Teller mines neatly stacked in a slit trench. He reasoned that "they were presumably to be used to close the ten-foot gap in the roadblock, but the Germans hadn't had the time to do it." Jones removed the detonators and threw them into the river. At the bridge's northern end he found the main explosive charges in one of the piers. He was "staggered by the preparations for the German demolition job." The tin demolition boxes, painted green to match the color of the bridge, "were manufactured precisely to fit the girders they were attached to. Each had a matching serial number, and altogether they were packed with about five hundred pounds of TNT." The explosives were designed to be fired electrically and the detonators were still in place and attached to the wires Jones had just cut on the bridge. He could not understand why the Germans had not destroyed the bridge unless the sudden smashing Anglo-American drive had given them no time. With the detonators now removed and all wires cut, the bridge was safe for vehicles and tanks.

But the British armored task force that the Americans had expected would move out immediately for Arnhem did not appear.

The link-up with the British 1st Airborne at the farthest end of the corridor weighed heavily on the minds of the Americans. Paratroopers themselves, they felt a strong kinship with the men still fighting up ahead. Cook's battalion had suffered brutally in crossing the Waal. He had lost more than half of his two companies—134 men had been killed, wounded or were missing—but the mission to capture the Nijmegen bridges from both ends and open the road north had been accomplished. Now, Cook's officers quickly pushed their units out into a perimeter defense about the northern end of the highway bridge and waited, expecting to see tanks race past them to relieve the British paratroopers up ahead. But there was no further movement over the bridge. Cook could not understand what was happening. He had expected the tanks to "go like hell" toward Arnhem before light failed.

Captain Carl Kappel, commander of H Company, whose friend Colonel John Frost was "somewhere up there," was on edge. His men had also found and cut wires on the northern end. He was certain that the bridge was safe. As he and Lieutenant La Riviere continued to watch the empty bridge, Kappel said impatiently, "Perhaps we should take a patrol and lead them over by the hand."

Second Lieutenant Ernest Murphy of Cook's battalion ran up to Sergeant Peter Robinson, whose troops had crossed the bridge, and reported to him that "we've cleared the area ahead for about a quarter of a mile. Now it's up to you guys to carry on the attack to Arnhem." Robinson wanted to go, but he had been told to "hold the road and the end of the bridge at all costs." He had no orders to move out.

Colonel Tucker, the 504th regimental commander, was fuming at the British delay. Tucker had supposed that a special task force would make a dash up the road the moment the bridge was taken and cleared of demolitions. The time to do it, he believed, "was right then, before the Germans could recover their balance." As he later wrote, "We had killed ourselves crossing the Waal to grab the north end of the bridge. We just stood there, seething, as the British settled in for the night, failing to take advantage of the situation. We couldn't understand it. It simply wasn't the way we did things in the American army—especially if it had been our guys hanging by their fingernails eleven miles away. We'd have been going, rolling without stop. That's what Georgie Patton would have done, whether it was daylight or dark."

Lieutenant A. D. Demetras overheard Tucker arguing with a major from the Guards Armored Division. "I think a most incredible decision was being made right there on the spot," he recalls. From inside a small bungalow being used as a command post, Demetras heard Tucker say angrily, "Your boys are hurting up there at Arnhem. You'd better go. It's only eleven miles." The major "told the Colonel that British armor could not proceed until infantry came up," Demetras recalls. "They were fighting the war by the book," Colonel Tucker said. "They had 'harbored' for the night. As usual, they stopped for tea."

Although his men were at less than half strength and almost

out of ammunition, Tucker thought of sending the 82nd troopers north toward Arnhem on their own. Yet, he knew that General Gavin would never have approved his action. The 82nd, strung out along its section of the corridor, could not afford the manpower. But Gavin's sympathies were with his men: the British should have driven ahead. As he was later to put it, "there was no better soldier than the Corps commander, General Browning. Still, he was a theorist. Had Ridgway been in command at that moment, we would have been ordered up the road in spite of all our difficulties, to save the men at Arnhem."°

Despite their apparent casualness, the British officers—Browning, Horrocks, Dempsey and Adair—were well aware of the urgency of moving on. Yet, the problems were immense. Horrocks' corps was short of gasoline and ammunition. He saw indications that his columns might be pinched off south of Nijmegen at any moment. Fighting was still going on in the center of the city, and Major General G. I. Thomas' 43rd Wessex Division, far back in the column, had not even reached the bridge at Grave, eight miles to the south. Cautious and methodical, Thomas had not been able to keep pace with the British columns. The Germans had cut the road at several points and Thomas' men had battled fiercely to resecure it and drive back attacks. Although worried by the viciousness of the German attacks that were now pressing on both sides of the narrow corridor running to Nijmegen, General Browning believed that Thomas could have moved faster. Horrocks was not so sure. Concerned by the massive traffic jams along the road, he told General Gavin, "Jim, never try to supply a corps up just one road."

Terrain—the difficulty Montgomery had foreseen and Model had counted on—greatly influenced the tactical considerations

---

° Says General Gavin, "I cannot tell you the anger and bitterness of my men. I found Tucker at dawn so irate that he was almost unable to speak. There is no soldier in the world that I admire more than the British, but British infantry leaders somehow did not understand the camaraderie of airborne troops. To our men there was only one objective: to save their brother paratroopers in Arnhem. It was tragic. I knew Tucker wanted to go, but I could never have allowed it. I had my hands full. Besides, Tucker and my other line officers did not appreciate some of the problems that the British had at that moment."

involved in moving on from the Nijmegen bridge. It was clear to General Adair, commanding the Guards Armored Division, that the tanks had reached the worst part of the Market-Garden corridor. The dead-straight high-dike road ahead between Nijmegen and Arnhem looked like an "island." "When I saw that island my heart sank," Adair later recalled. "You can't imagine anything more unsuitable for tanks: steep banks with ditches on each side that could be easily covered by German guns." In spite of his misgivings Adair knew they would "have to have a shot at it," but he had virtually no infantry and "to get along that road was obviously first a job for infantry." Horrocks had reached the same conclusion. The tanks would have to wait until infantry could move up and pass through the Guards Armored columns. It would be almost eighteen hours before a tank attack toward Arnhem could begin.

Yet the Corps commander, like the Americans, had held out hope for a quick move up the corridor. Immediately upon the capture of the Nijmegen crossing, believing that the northern end of the Arnhem bridge was still in British hands, General Browning had informed Urquhart that tanks were across. At two minutes to midnight, still optimistic about an early start, Browning sent the following message:

202358 . . . intention Guards Armored Division . . . at first light to go all-out for bridges at Arnhem . . .

Some forty-five minutes later, learning of the delay in bringing up infantry, Browning sent Urquhart a third message:

210045 . . . tomorrow attack 1st Airborne Division will be first priority but do not expect another advance possibly before 1200 hours.

In Arnhem the "first priority" was far too late. The men of Colonel John Frost's 2nd Battalion had already been enveloped by their tragic fate. Three hours before Sergeant Robinson's troop had rattled across the great Nijmegen span, the first three tanks under Major Hans Peter Knaust's command had at last bludgeoned their way onto the Arnhem bridge.

✤ 11 ✤

IN THE AFTERNOON, as the first wave of Major Cook's paratroopers began to cross the Waal, Captain Eric Mackay gave the order to evacuate the Arnhem schoolhouse his men had held for more than sixty hours—since evening on September 17. From seventy yards away a Tiger tank fired shell after shell into the southern face of the building. "The house was burning now," Mackay remembers, "and I heard my little stock of explosives, which we had left upstairs, blow up." Of the thirteen men still able to move about, each was down to just one clip of ammunition. Hobbling about the cellar, Mackay decided that his troopers would break out, fighting to the end.

He had no intention of leaving his wounded behind. With Lieutenant Dennis Simpson leading the way, Mackay and two men acted as rear guard as the paratroopers brought their casualties up from the cellar. While Simpson covered them, the injured were moved into a side garden. "Then just as Simpson moved toward the next house a mortar bombardment began and I heard him shout, 'Six more wounded.' I knew," Mackay recalls, "that we would be massacred—or the wounded would, at any rate—if we tried to escape with them. I yelled to Simpson to surrender."

Collecting the remaining five men, each armed with a Bren gun, Mackay headed east—the one direction, he believed, the Germans would not expect him to take. His plan was to "lay low for the night and try to make our way back west to join the main force." Mackay led his men across the road, through ruined houses on the opposite side and onto the next street. There, they came face to face with two tanks accompanied by fifty or sixty soldiers. Quickly moving line abreast, the six paratroopers riddled the mass of startled Germans. "We had time for only a single magazine apiece," Mackay recalls. "It was all over in two or three seconds. The Germans just dropped like half-filled sacks of grain." As Mackay shouted to his group to head for a nearby house, another man was killed and a second wounded. Reaching temporary shelter, Mackay told the three remaining men, "This fight is over." He suggested the troopers move out individually. "With luck," he said, "we might all meet together again by the bridge tonight."

One by one the men left. Ducking into a garden, Mackay crawled under a rose bush. There he took off his badges of rank and threw them away. "I figured I would sleep a bit," he recalls. "I had just shut my eyes and reached that drowsy stage when I heard German voices. I tried to breathe more softly and, with my charred and bloody clothes, I thought I might look convincingly dead." Suddenly he received "a terrific kick in the ribs." He took it limply, "like a newly dead corpse." Then he "felt a bayonet go into my buttocks and lodge with a jar against my pelvis." Strangely, Mackay recalls, "it didn't hurt, just shocked me a bit when it hit the pelvis. It was when the bayonet came out that I felt the pain." It triggered Mackay's anger. Pulling himself to his feet, he drew his Colt. "What the bloody hell do you mean stabbing a bayonet into a British officer?" he yelled. Unprepared for Mackay's outburst, the Germans drew back and Mackay realized that he could have "shot some of them if I had had any bullets. They couldn't shoot back," he remembers, "because they were ringed all around me. They would have hit one of their own. Their situation was so funny I laughed." As the Germans stared at him, Mackay contemptuously threw his Colt over a garden wall "so they couldn't get it as a souvenir."

Forcing Mackay to lean against a wall, the Germans began to search him. His watch and an empty silver flask that had been his father's were taken from him, but an escape map in his breast pocket was overlooked. An officer returned the flask. When

Mackay asked about his watch he was told, "You won't need it where you're going, and we're rather short on watches." Hands above his head, he was marched off to a building where other British prisoners of war were being held. Going from group to group Mackay reminded the men that it was their duty to escape. Suddenly Mackay, the only officer present, was taken into another room for interrogation. "I decided to go on the offensive," he recalls. "There was a German lieutenant who spoke perfect English, and I told him, firmly but politely, that it was all over for the Germans and I was quite prepared to take their surrender." The lieutenant stared at him in amazement but, Mackay remembers, "that was the end of the interrogation."

Shortly before dusk the prisoners were herded out to trucks, which took them east toward Germany. "They got a guard on the back, which made it harder to try to get away," Mackay says, "but I told the lads to scrunch up and crowd him so he couldn't use his gun." As the truck in which he was riding slowed down at a bend in the road, Mackay jumped off and tried to make his escape. "Unfortunately I had chosen the worst possible place," he recalls. "I dropped within three feet of a sentry. I jumped him and was trying to break his neck. Others arrived just then and they beat me senseless." When he came to, Mackay found himself crowded with other prisoners into a room in a small Dutch inn. He managed to drag himself up to a sitting position against a wall and then, for the first time in ninety hours, the young officer fell sound asleep. °

In the dusk around Colonel Frost's headquarters' building and alongside the ramp, nearly a hundred men in small groups were still fighting fiercely to hang on. The headquarters roof was burning and nearly every man was down to his last few rounds of ammunition. Yet the troopers seemed spirited as ever. Major

---

° The following day Mackay and three others escaped from the German town of Emmerich. One of the men with him was Lieutenant Dennis Simpson, who had led the breakout of the little group from the schoolhouse. The four men made their way across country and reached the Rhine. In a stolen boat they paddled all the way down to the Allied lines at Nijmegen.

Freddie Gough believed that "even now, if we could just hold out a few hours longer, we would be relieved."

At around 7 P.M. the 2nd Battalion's wounded commander awoke, annoyed to find that he had slept at all. Frost heard "the gibbering of some shell-shock cases" in the darkness of the cellar. The Germans were still pounding the building and Frost became aware that the heat in the cellar, now filled with over two hundred casualties, was intense. Attempting to move, he felt a shock of pain run through his legs. He asked that Gough be sent to him. "You'll have to take over," Frost told the major, "but don't make any crucial decisions without first referring them to me." By now Frost was becoming aware that what he had most feared had begun to happen: the building was burning down and the wounded were in danger "of being roasted alive." All over the dark room men were coughing from the acrid smoke. Dr. James Logan, the battalion's chief medical officer, knelt down beside Frost. The time had come, Logan said, to get the casualties out. "We've got to arrange a truce with the Germans, sir," Logan insisted. "We can't wait any longer." Turning to Gough, Frost ordered him to make the arrangements, "but to get the fighting soldiers to other buildings and carry on. I felt that even though the bridge was lost we could still control the approach for a time, perhaps enough time for our tanks to come."

Gough and Logan left to make arrangements for the truce. Logan proposed to unbolt the heavy front doors of the building and go out under a Red Cross flag. Gough was skeptical of the idea. He did not trust the SS; they might well open fire in spite of the flag. Going back to Frost, Logan received permission to proceed. As the doctor headed toward the doors, Frost removed his badges of rank. He hoped to "fade into the ranks and possibly get away later." Wicks, his batman, went in search of a stretcher.

Nearby, Private James Sims, one of the wounded, glumly heard the evacuation plans being made. Logically he knew there was no alternative. "Our position was obviously hopeless," he recalls. "Ammunition was all but exhausted, nearly all the officers and

NCO's were dead or wounded, and the building was well alight; the smoke was nearly choking everyone." He heard Frost tell the able-bodied and the walking wounded "to get out and make a run for it." Sims knew it was "the only sensible course, but the news that we were to be left behind was not well received."

Upstairs Doctor Logan unlocked the front door. Accompanied by two orderlies and carrying a Red Cross flag, Logan walked out to meet the Germans. The noise of battle halted. "I saw some Germans run around to the back where we had our jeeps and carriers parked," Gough remembers. "They needed them to move the wounded, and I mentally waved goodby to our remaining transport forever."

In the cellar men heard German voices in the passageways and Sims noticed "the heavy thud of German jackboots on the stairway." The cellar was suddenly quiet. Looking up Sims saw a German officer appear in the doorway. To his horror, "a badly wounded paratrooper brought up his Sten gun, but he was quickly overpowered. The officer," Sims remembers, "took stock of the situation and rapped out some orders. German soldiers filed in and began carrying the wounded upstairs." They were almost too late. As Sims was being moved, "a huge piece of burning timber nearly fell on top of us." He was acutely aware that the Germans were "nervous, decidedly trigger-happy, and a lot of them were armed with British rifles and Sten guns."

With the help of a shell-shocked paratrooper, Frost was carried up and laid on the embankment beside the bridge he had so desperately tried to hold. All about him he saw buildings burning fiercely. He watched as Germans and British together "worked at top speed to get us out, while the whole scene was brilliantly lit by the flames." Only minutes after the last casualty was carried up, there was a sudden roar and the building collapsed into a heap of fiery rubble. Turning to Major Douglas Crawley, lying on a stretcher beside him, Frost said tiredly, "Well, Doug, we didn't get away with it this time, did we?" Crawley shook his head. "No, sir," he said, "but we gave them a damn good run for their money."

As the British wounded watched in wary surprise, the Germans moved among them with extraordinary camaraderie, handing out cigarettes, chocolate and brandy. Bitterly, the paratroopers noticed that most of the supplies were their own, obviously collected from resupply drops that had fallen into German hands. As the hungry, thirsty men began to eat, German soldiers knelt beside them, congratulating them on the battle. Private Sims stared at a line of Mark IV tanks stretching back along the road. Seeing his expression a German nodded. "Yes, Tommy," he told Sims, "those were for you in the morning if you had not surrendered."

But Frost's stubborn able-bodied men had not given up. As the last wounded man was brought out of the cellar the battle began again, as intensely as an hour before. "It was a nightmare," Gough recalls. "Everywhere you turned there were Germans—in front, in back and on the sides. They had managed to infiltrate a large force into the area during the truce. They now held practically every house. We were literally overrun."

Gough ordered troopers to disperse and hide out for the night. At dawn he hoped to concentrate the force in a group of half-gutted buildings by the river bank. Even now he expected relief by morning, and "I thought that somehow we could hold till then." As the men moved off into the darkness, Gough crouched down beside his radio. Bringing the microphone close to his mouth, he said, "This is the First Para Brigade. We cannot hold out much longer. Our position is desperate. Please hurry. Please hurry."

The Germans knew the fight was over. All that now remained was a mopping-up operation. Ironically, although there were tanks on the bridge, they could not cross. As General Harmel had predicted, the massed wreckage would take hours to remove. Not until early Thursday, September 21, would a single pathway be finally cleared and movement across the bridge begin.

At first light on Thursday Gough and the scattered men remaining in the perimeter emerged from their hiding places. Relief had not come. Systematically the Germans overran positions, forcing men now out of ammunition to surrender. By ones and twos, survivors, undetected, scattered to attempt to make their escape. Slowly, defiantly, the last British resistance came to an end.

Major Gough had headed for the waterworks, hoping to hide and rest for a time and then attempt to make his way west toward the main body of troops under Urquhart's command. Just outside the waterworks building he heard German voices. Sprinting for a pile of wood, Gough tried to burrow under it. The heel of his boot protruded and a German grasped it and pulled Gough out. "I was so damn tired I just looked up at them and laughed," Gough says. Hands over his head, he was led away.

In a roomful of other prisoners a German major sent for Gough. He gave the British officer a Hitler salute. "I understand you are in command," the German said. Gough looked at him warily. "Yes," he said. "I wish to congratulate you and your men," the German told him. "You are gallant soldiers. I fought at Stalingrad and it is obvious that you British have had a great deal of experience in street fighting." Gough stared at the enemy officer. "No," he said. "This was our first effort. We'll be much better next time."

At some moment during these last hours one final message was radioed from someone near the bridge. It was not picked up by either Urquhart's headquarters or by the British Second Army, but at the 9th SS Hohenstaufen headquarters Lieutenant Colonel Harzer's listening monitors heard it clearly. Years later Harzer could not recall the complete message, but he was struck by the last two sentences: "Out of ammunition. God Save the King."

A few miles to the north near Apeldoorn, Private James Sims lay on the grass outside a German military hospital, surrounded by other wounded paratroopers awaiting processing and treatment. The men were quiet, drawn into themselves. "The thought that we had fought for nothing was a natural one," Sims wrote, "but I couldn't help but think about the main army, so strong, and yet unable to make those last few miles to us. The hardest thing to bear was the feeling that we had just been written off."

☼12☼

At exactly 10:40 a.m. on Thursday, September 21, Captain Roland Langton of the Irish Guards was told that his Number 1 Squadron was to dash out of the newly acquired Nijmegen bridgehead and make for Arnhem. H Hour, he was informed by Lieutenant Colonel Joe Vandeleur, would be 11 a.m. Langton was incredulous. He thought Vandeleur must be joking. He was being given just twenty minutes to brief his squadron and prepare them for a major attack. Langton, himself, was quickly briefed on a captured map. "The only other one we had was a road map devoid of details," he says. Information about enemy gun positions was contained in a single reconnaissance photo showing an antiaircraft site between the villages of Lent and Elst, and "the supposition was that it might no longer be there."

In Langton's view, everything about the plan was wrong—in particular, the fact that "they were actually going to launch this thing in twenty minutes." His squadron was to strike out with a second unit coming up behind. Two tanks would carry infantry; and more troops, Langton was told, would follow. Yet he could expect little artillery support, and the Typhoon "cab rank" air cover, used so successfully in the initial breakout, would not be immediately available: in Belgium the Typhoons were grounded by weather. Nevertheless, Langton was instructed "to go like hell and get on up to Arnhem."

Although he did not betray his feelings to Langton, Joe Vandeleur was pessimistic about the outcome of the attack. Earlier, he and others, including his cousin Lieutenant Colonel Giles Vandeleur, had crossed the Nijmegen bridge to study the elevated "island" highway running due north to Arnhem. To these officers the road seemed ominous. Joe Vandeleur's second in command, Major Desmond FitzGerald, was the first to speak. "Sir," he said, "we're not going to get a yard up this bloody road." Giles Vandeleur agreed. "It's a ridiculous place to try to operate tanks." Up to this point in the corridor advance, although vehicles had moved on a one-tank front, it had always been possible when necessary to maneuver off the main road. "Here," Giles Vandeleur recalls, "there was no possibility of getting off the road. A dike embankment with a highway running along its top is excellent for defense but it's hardly the place for tanks." Turning to the others, Giles said, "I can just imagine the Germans sitting there, rubbing their hands with glee, as they see us coming." Joe Vandeleur stared silently at the scene. Then he said, "Nevertheless, we've got to try. We've got to chance that bloody road." As Giles remembers, "Our advance was based on a time program. We were to proceed at a speed of fifteen miles in two hours." Brigadier Gwatkin, the Guards Armored chief of staff, had told them tersely, "Simply get through."

At exactly 11 A.M., Captain Langton picked up the microphone in his scout car and radioed: "Go! Go! Go! Don't stop for anything!" His tanks rumbled past the Lent post office and up the main road. Fatalistically, Langton thought, It is now or never. After fifteen or twenty minutes, he began to breathe easier. There was no enemy action, and Langton felt "a little ashamed for being so upset earlier. I began to wonder what I was going to do when I reached the Arnhem bridge. I hadn't really thought about it before."

Behind the lead tanks came the Vandeleurs in their scout car and, back of them, Flight Lieutenant Donald Love in his R.A.F. ground-to-air communications tender. With him once more was Squadron Leader Max Sutherland, quiet and anxious. As he climbed aboard the white armored scout car, Sutherland—who had directed the Typhoon strike at the breakout from the Meuse-Escaut Canal—told Love that "the airborne boys in Arnhem are in deep trouble and desperate for help." Love scanned the skies looking for the Typhoons. He was sure they would need them. Remembering the horrors of the breakout, Love "wasn't at all anxious to find himself in a similar position to the one I had been in the previous Sunday, when the Germans had stopped us cold."

The tanks of the Irish Guards moved steadily forward, passing the village of Oosterhout off to the left and the hamlets of Ressen and Bemmel on the right. From his scout car Captain Langton could hear Lieutenant Tony Samuelson, troop commander of the lead tanks, announce the locations. Samuelson called out that the first tank was approaching the outskirts of Elst. The Irish were approximately halfway to Arnhem. As he listened Langton realized that "we were out on our own." But tension was relaxing throughout the column. Flight Lieutenant Love heard a droning in the sky and saw the first Typhoons appear. The weather had cleared in Belgium, and now the squadrons came into view, one at a time. As they began to circle overhead, Love and Sutherland settled back relieved.

In his scout car, Captain Langton was examining his map. The entire column had passed the secondary Bemmel turning, off to the right. At that moment, Langton heard a violent explosion. Looking up, he saw "a Sherman sprocket wheel lift lazily into the air over some trees up ahead." He knew immediately that one of the lead tanks had been hit. Lieutenant Samuelson, much farther up the road, quickly confirmed the fact.

In the distance guns began to bark and black smoke boiled up into the sky. Far down the line Lieutenant Rupert Mahaffey knew that something had gone wrong. Abruptly the column halted. There was confusion as to what had happened, and voices on the radio became distorted and jumbled as the battle was joined. "There seemed to be a great deal of shouting," Giles Vandeleur remembers, "and I told Joe I had better go forward and see what the hell was happening." The commander of the Irish Guards agreed. "Let me know as quickly as you can," he told Giles.

Captain Langton was already on his way forward. Inching by the standing armor Langton came to a bend in the road. Ahead he saw that all four lead tanks, including Samuelson's, had been knocked out and some were ablaze. The shells were coming from a self-propelled gun in the woods to the left, near Elst. Langton ordered his driver to pull into a yard of a house near the bend. A few minutes later Giles Vandeleur joined him. Immediately machine-gun fire forced the men to take cover. Vandeleur was unable to get back to his armored car and report to his cousin Joe. Each time he called out to his driver, Corporal Goldman, to back up the vehicle—a Humber with a top hatch and a door at the side—"Goldman would lift the lid and the Germans would pour a burst of fire over his head, causing him to slam it shut again." Finally, exasperated, Giles crawled back along a ditch to Joe's command car.

Joe Vandeleur was already rapping out orders. Over the radio he called for artillery support; then, seeing the Typhoons overhead, he ordered Love to call them in. In the R.A.F. car Sutherland picked up the microphone. "This is Winecup . . . Winecup . . ." he said. "Come in please." The Typhoons continued to circle overhead. Desperate, Sutherland called again. "This is Winecup . . . Winecup . . . Come in." There was no response. Sutherland and Love stared at each other. "The set was dead," Love says. "We were getting no signal whatsoever. The Typhoons were milling around above us and, on the ground, shelling was going on. It was the most hopeless, frustrating thing I have ever lived through, watching them up there and not being able to do a damn thing about it." Love knew the pilots of the slowly wheeling Typhoons "had instructions not to attack anything on speculation." By now Giles Vandeleur had reached his cousin. "Joe," he said, "if we send any more tanks up along this road it's going to be a bloody murder." Together the two men set out for Captain Langton's position.

Now the infantry of the Irish Guards were off their tanks and moving up into orchards on both sides of the road. Langton had taken over one of the tanks. Unable to find cover or move off the road, he was maneuvering backward and forward, trying to fire at the self-propelled gun in the woods. Each time he fired a round, "the gun responded with five of its own."

The infantry captain, whose troops were also after the same target but were now huddling in a ditch, was livid with rage. "What the bloody hell do you think you're doing?" he yelled at Langton. The young officer stayed calm. "I'm trying to knock out a gun so we can get to Arnhem," he said.

As the Vandeleurs appeared, Langton, unsuccessful in his attempts to knock out the gun, climbed out to meet them. "It was a mess up there," Joe Vandeleur remembers. "We tried everything. There was no way to move the tanks off the road and down the steep sides of that damn dike. The only artillery support I could get was from one field battery, and it was too slow registering on its targets." His lone infantry company was pinned down and he was unable to call in the Typhoons. "Surely we can get support somewhere," Langton said. Vandeleur slowly shook his head, "I'm afraid not." Langton persisted. "We could get there," he pleaded. "We can go if we get support." Vandeleur shook his head again. "I'm sorry," he said. "You stay where you are until you get further orders."

To Vandeleur it was clear that the attack could not be resumed until the infantry of Major General G. I. Thomas' 43rd Wessex Division could reach the Irish Guards. Until then, Vandeleur's tanks were stranded alone on the high exposed road. A single self-propelled gun trained on the elevated highway had effectively stopped the entire relief column almost exactly six miles from Arnhem.

Farther back in the line of tanks, opposite a greenhouse near Elst, whose windows had miraculously remained almost wholly intact, Lieutenant John Gorman stared angrily up the road. Ever since the column had been halted at Valkenswaard far down the corridor, Gorman had felt driven to move faster. "We had come all the way from Normandy, taken Brussels, fought halfway through Holland and crossed the Nijmegen bridge," he said. "Arnhem and those paratroopers were just up ahead and, almost within sight of that last bloody bridge, we were stopped. I never felt such morbid despair."

Part Five

✵

DER HEXENKESSEL

[The Witches' Cauldron]

✵

☼ 1 ☼

MONTY'S TANKS ARE ON THE WAY!" All along the shrunken Oosterbeek perimeter—from slit trenches, houses now turned into strong points, crossroads positions, and in woods and fields—grimy, ashen-faced men cheered and passed the news along. To them, it seemed the long, isolated ordeal was coming to its end. General Urquhart's Rhine bridgehead had become a fingertip-shaped spot on the map. Now in an area barely two miles long, one and a half miles wide at its center, and one mile along its base on the Rhine, the Red Devils were surrounded and were being attacked and slowly annihilated from three sides. Water, medical supplies, food and ammunition were lacking or dwindling away. As a division the British 1st Airborne had virtually ceased to exist. Now men were once again heartened by the hope of relief. Now, too, a storm of fire roared overhead as British medium and heavy guns eleven miles south across the Rhine lashed the Germans only a few hundred yards from Urquhart's front lines.

By signal, General Browning had promised Urquhart that the batteries of XXX Corps's 64th Medium Regiment would be in range by Thursday and regiment artillery officers had asked for targets in order of priority. Without regard for their own safety, Urquhart's steely veterans had quickly complied. In good radio contact for the first time, via the 64th's communications net, the Red Devils savagely called down artillery fire almost on top of their own positions. The accuracy of the fire was heartening, its effect on the Germans unnerving. Again and again British guns

495

broke up heavy tank attacks that threatened to swamp the bearded, tattered paratroopers.

Even with this welcome relief, Urquhart knew that a massed coordinated German attack could wipe out his minuscule force. Yet now the men believed there was a modicum of hope—a chance to snatch victory at the eleventh hour. On this Thursday, the outlook was slightly brighter. Urquhart had limited communications and a link by way of the 64th's artillery support. The Nijmegen bridge was safe and open; the tanks of the Guards Armored were on the way; and, if the weather held, 1,500 fresh paratroopers of General Sosabowski's Polish 1st Brigade would land by late afternoon. If the Poles could be ferried quickly across the Rhine between Driel and Heveadorp, the bleak picture could well change.

Yet, if Urquhart was to hold, supplies were as urgent as the arrival of Sosabowski's men. On the previous day, out of a total of 300 tons, R.A.F. bombers had delivered only 41 to the Hartenstein zone. Until antitank guns and artillery arrived in number, close-in air support was critically important. Lacking ground-to-air communications—the special American ultra-high-frequency equipment, rushed to the British only hours before takeoff on D Day, the seventeenth, had been set to the wrong wavelength and was useless—division officers were forced to acknowledge that the R.A.F. seemed unprepared to abandon caution and make the kind of daring forays the airborne men knew to be essential and were prepared to risk. Urquhart had sent a continual stream of messages to Browning, urging fighters and fighter-bombers to attack "targets of opportunity" without regard to the Red Devils' own positions. It was the airborne way of operating; it was not the R.A.F.'s. Even at this critical stage, pilots insisted that enemy targets be pinpointed with near-cartographic accuracy—an utter impossibility for the beleagured paratroopers pinned down in their diminishing airhead. Not a single low-level air attack had been made, yet every road, field and woods around the perimeter and spreading east to Arnhem held enemy vehicles or positions.

Lacking the air strikes they so desperately urged, hemmed into the perimeter, suffering almost constant mortar bombardment and, in places, fighting hand-to-hand, the Red Devils placed their hopes on the Guards' columns, which they believed were rolling toward them. Urquhart was less optimistic. Outnumbered at least four to one, pounded by artillery and tanks, and with steadily mounting casualties, Urquhart knew that only a mammoth, all-out effort could save his fragmented division. Keenly aware that the Germans could steam-roller his pathetically small force, the dogged, courageous Scot kept his own lonely counsel even as he told his staff, "We must hold the bridgehead at all costs."

The perimeter defenses were now divided into two commands. Brigadier Pip Hicks held the western side; Brigadier Shan Hackett was to the east. Hicks's western arm was manned by soldiers from the Glider Pilot Regiment, Royal Engineers, remnants of the Border Regiment, some Poles and a polyglot collection of other troopers from various units. To the east were the survivors of Hackett's 10th and 156th battalions, more glider pilots and the 1st Airlanding Light Regiment, R.A. Curving up from these prime defenses the northern shoulders (close to the Wolfheze railroad line) were held by men of Major Boy Wilson's 21st Independent Parachute Company—the pathfinders who had led the way—and by Lieutenant Colonel R. Payton-Reid's 7th King's Own Scottish Borderers. Along the southern base, stretching roughly from east of the medieval church in lower Oosterbeek to the heights at Westerbouwing on the west, Hackett commanded additional elements of the Border Regiment and a miscellaneous group composed of the remains of the South Staffordshires, the 1st, 3rd and 11th battalions and a variety of service troops under the twice-wounded Major Dickie Lonsdale—the "Lonsdale Force." In the heart of that area was Lieutenant Colonel Sheriff Thompson's main force, the hard-pressed artillerymen whose batteries sought continually to serve the tight defense line and whose precious supply of ammunition was dwindling fast.*

* The consolidation of the southeastern end of the perimeter owed much to the quick thinking of Colonel Sheriff Thompson who, in the confusion of battle when men retreating from Arnhem on September 19 found themselves leaderless, quickly organized them in defense of the last piece of high ground before his gun posi-

On neat after-action report maps, each unit has its carefully inked-in place; but survivors would recall years later that there was really no perimeter, no front line, no distinction between units, no fighting as integrated groups. There were only shocked, bandaged, bloodstained men, running to fill gaps wherever and whenever they occurred. As Brigadier Hicks visited his exhausted men, tenaciously defending their sectors of the bridgehead, he knew "it was the beginning of the end, and I think we were all aware of it, although we tried to keep a reasonable face."

Unaware that Frost's gallant stand at the bridge had ended—although Lieutenant Colonel Sheriff Thompson suspected it had when his artillery radio link with Major Dennis Munford abruptly closed down—Urquhart could only place his hope in the Guards tanks' reaching the remnants of the 2nd Battalion in time.° That single bridge spanning the Rhine—the Reich's last natural defense line—had been the principal objective all along, Montgomery's springboard to a quick ending of the war. Without it, the 1st Airborne's predicament and, in particular, the suffering of Frost's brave men, would be for nothing. As Urquhart had told Frost and Gough, there was nothing more that he could do for them. Their help must come from the speed and armored strength of XXX Corps.

For Urquhart now the immediate priority was to get Sosabow-ski's Poles across the river and into the perimeter as quickly as

---

tions. These forces, together with others who had earlier become separated from their units—some 150 glider pilots and his own artillery men, about 800 in all—were known as the "Thompson Force." Subsequently augmented, they were placed under the command of Major Lonsdale. They withdrew late on September 20 and were deployed by Thompson about his gun positions. Owing to command changes and the general situation, some confusion has continued to exist regarding these events, but immediately before Thompson was wounded on September 21 all infantry in the gun area came under the command of what was later to be known as the "Lonsdale Force." The glider pilots remained under the command of the 1st Airlanding Brigade.

° Munford destroyed his wireless set shortly after dawn on Thursday as the Germans began rounding up the few men still attempting to hang on. "Enemy tanks and infantry were right up to the bridge," Munford recalls. "I helped carry some more wounded to a collecting point and then I bashed in the set. There was nothing more that Colonel Thompson could do for us and everybody who could wanted to get back to the division at Oosterbeek." Munford was captured on the outskirts of Arnhem as he tried to reach the British lines.

they landed. The cable ferry was particularly suited to the operation. Urquhart's engineers had signaled Corps headquarters that it was "a class-24 type and capable of carrying three tanks." Although Urquhart was worried about the heights of Westerbouwing and the possibility of German artillery controlling the ferry crossing from there, as yet no enemy troops had reached the area. With so few men to hold the perimeter, only a single platoon of the 1st Borderers had been detached to defend the position. In fact, the heights were unguarded by either side. Major Charles Osborne's D Company of the Border Regiment had been given the assignment soon after landing on Sunday but, Osborne says, "we never did hold Westerbouwing. I was sent on a reconnaissance patrol to lay out battalion positions. However, by the time I'd done this and returned to headquarters, plans had changed." By Thursday, Osborne's men "were moved rather piecemeal into a position near the Hartenstein Hotel." No one was on the vital heights.

On Wednesday engineers had sent reconnaissance patrols down to the Rhine to report back on the ferry, the depth, condition of the banks and speed of the current. Sapper Tom Hicks thought the survey was to "aid the Second Army when it tried bridging the river." Along with three other sappers and a Dutch guide, Hicks had crossed the Rhine on the ferry. Pieter, he saw, "operated it with a cable that the old man wound in by hand and it seemed that the current helped work it across." Tying a grenade to a length of parachute rigging and knotting the cord every foot along its length, Hicks took soundings and measured the current. On Wednesday night, after the Poles' drop zone had been changed to Driel, another patrol was sent to the ferry site. "It was a volunteer job," recalls Private Robert Edwards of the South Staffordshires. "We were to go down to the river at Heveadorp, find the ferry and stay there to protect it."

In darkness a sergeant, a corporal, six privates and four glider pilots set out. "Mortar bombs and shells were falling heavily as we plunged into the thickly wooded country between us and Heveadorp," says Edwards. Several times the group was fired on, and a glider pilot was wounded. Reaching the riverbank at the site marked on their maps, the patrol found no sign of the ferry. It had completely disappeared. Although the possibility remained that the craft was moored on the southern bank, the patrol had been told they would find it on their own side. Immediately the men spread out, searching along a quarter-mile strip on either side of the ferry's northern landing stage. The hunt was fruitless. Pieter's ferry could not be found. As Edwards remembers, the sergeant in charge of the patrol reached the conclusion that the boat had either been sunk or simply never existed. At first light the men gave up the search and began their dangerous journey back.

Only minutes later heavy machine-gun fire wounded three more of the patrol and the group was pulled back to the river. There the sergeant decided the men would have a better chance of getting back by splitting up. Edwards left with the corporal and two of the glider pilots. After "minor encounters and brushes with the Germans," his group reached the church in lower Oosterbeek just as a mortar burst landed. Edwards was thrown to the ground, both legs filled with "tiny pieces of shrapnel and my boots full of blood." In the house next to the church an orderly dressed his wounds and told the injured private to take a rest. "He didn't say where, though," Edwards recalls, "and every inch of space in the house was packed with badly wounded. The stench of wounds and death was something awful." He decided to leave and head for company headquarters, located in a laundry, "in order to find somebody to make my report to. I told an officer about the ferry and then I got into a weapons' pit with a glider pilot. I don't know if the others made it back or what happened to the men who got to the church with me."

Sometime later General Urquhart, still ignorant of Frost's fate, signaled Browning:

Enemy attacking main bridge in strength. Situation critical for slender force. Enemy attacking east from Heelsum and west from Arnhem.

Situation serious but am forming close perimeter around Hartenstein with remainder of division. Relief essential both areas earliest possible. Still maintain control ferry point at Heveadorp.

Even as the message was being sent via the 64th Medium Regiment's communications net, Division headquarters learned that the ferry had not been found. Urquhart's officers believed the Germans had sunk it. But Pieter's ferry was still afloat. Presumably artillery fire had cut its moorings. Far too late to be of use, it was eventually found by Dutch civilians near the demolished railroad bridge about a mile away, washed up but still intact. "If we had been able to search a few hundred yards closer to Oosterbeek, we would have found it," Edwards says.

As Urquhart returned to his headquarters on Thursday morning after an inspection of the Hartenstein defenses, he heard the crushing news. With the Poles' drop only hours away, his only quick way of reinforcing the perimeter with Sosabowski's men was gone.*

Looking down from a window in the lead Dakota, as the long columns of planes carrying the Polish 1st Parachute Brigade headed for the drop zone at Driel, Major General Stanislaw Sosabowski "learned the real truth, and what I had suspected all along." From Eindhoven, where the formations turned north, he saw "hundreds of vehicles below in chaotic traffic jams all along the corridor." Smoke churned up from the road. At various points along the highway enemy shells were landing, trucks and vehicles were ablaze, and "everywhere wreckage was piled up on the

---

* The true account of the ferry appears here for the first time. Even official histories state that it was sunk. Other versions imply that, to prevent its use, the Germans either destroyed the ferry with artillery fire or moved it to another location under their control. There is no reference in any German war diary, log, or afteraction report to sustain these conjectures. Interviewing German officers—such as Bittrich, Harzer, Harmel and Krafft—I found that none of them could recall ordering any such action. Assuming that the Germans wanted to seize the ferry, I believe they would have encountered the same difficulties in locating it that Edwards reported. In any case, no German officer remembers ordering the cable cut in order to prevent the British from using it.

sides." Yet, somehow, the convoys were still moving. Then, beyond Nijmegen, movement stopped. Through low clouds off to his right, Sosabowski could see the "island" road and the clogged, halted tanks on it. Enemy fire was falling on the head of the column. Moments later, as the planes banked toward Driel, the Arnhem bridge loomed into view. Tanks were crossing over it, driving north to south, and Sosabowski realized they were German. Shocked and stunned, he knew now that the British had lost the bridge.

On Wednesday night, agitated by the lack of information regarding Urquhart's situation, and "as I had visions of being court-martialed by my own government," Sosabowski had thrown caution to the winds. He demanded to see General Brereton, the First Allied Airborne Army commander. To Colonel George Stevens, the liaison officer with the Polish Brigade, Sosabowski had emotionally insisted that unless he was "given Urquhart's exact situation around Arnhem, the Polish Parachute Brigade will not take off." Startled, Stevens had rushed off to First Allied Airborne headquarters with Sosabowski's ultimatum. At 7 A.M. on Thursday morning, he returned with news from Brereton. There was confusion, Stevens admitted, but the attack was going as planned; the drop zone at Driel had not been changed and "the Heveadorp ferry was in British hands." Sosabowski was mollified. Now, looking down on the panorama of battle, he realized he "knew more than Brereton." Enraged as he saw what was obviously German armor about Oosterbeek and ahead a hail of antiaircraft fire coming up to greet his men, Sosabowski believed his brigade was "being sacrificed in a complete British disaster." Moments later he was out the door, falling through weaving curtains of antiaircraft fire. The time, the precise fifty-year-old general noted, was exactly 5:08 P.M.

As Sosabowski had feared, the Poles jumped into a holocaust. As before, the Germans were waiting. They had tracked and timed the formations from Dunkirk on and now, with far more reinforcements than before, the area bristled with antiaircraft guns. As the transports approached, twenty-five Messerschmitts suddenly appeared and, diving out of the clouds, raked the approaching planes.

As he fell through the air Sosabowski saw one Dakota, both engines flaming, fall toward the ground. Corporal Alexander Kochalski saw another go down. Only a dozen paratroopers escaped before it crashed and burned. First Lieutenant Stefan Kaczmarek prayed as he hung below his chute. He saw so many tracer bullets that "every gun on the ground seemed to be aimed at me." Corporal Wladijslaw Korob, his parachute full of holes, landed alongside a fellow Pole who had been decapitated.

In the Oosterbeek perimeter the Polish drop, barely two and one-half miles away, caused a momentary halt in the battle. Every German gun seemed to be concentrating on the swaying, defenseless men. "It was as if all the enemy guns lifted together and let fly simultaneously," Gunner Robert Christie noted. The reprieve from the constant shelling was too precious to waste: men quickly took the opportunity to move jeeps and equipment, dig new gun pits, bring up spare ammunition, rearrange camouflage nets and toss empty shell cases out of crowded slit trenches.

Six miles away on the elevated "island" road, Captain Roland Langton, whose lead tank squadron had been halted en route to Arnhem some six hours previously, watched the drop in agony. It was the most horrible sight he had ever seen. German planes dived at the defenseless Polish transports, "blasting them out of the air." Parachutists tried to get out of burning aircraft, "some of which had nosed over and were diving to the ground." Bodies of men "tumbled through the air, inert forms drifting slowly down, dead before they hit the ground." Langton was close to tears. "Where the hell is the air support?" he wondered. "We were told in the afternoon we couldn't have any for our attack toward Arnhem, because all available air effort had to go for the Poles. Where was it now? The weather? Nonsense. The Germans flew; why couldn't we?" Langton had never felt so frustrated. With all his heart, he knew that with air support his tanks "could have got through to those poor bastards at Arnhem." In anxiety and desperation he suddenly found himself violently sick.

Though they were shocked by the savagery of the combined air and antiaircraft assault, most of the Polish Brigade miraculously made the drop zone. Even as they landed, flak and high-explosive mortar shells—fired from tanks and antiaircraft guns along the Nijmegen-Arnhem elevated highway and by batteries north of Driel—burst among them, and Sosabowski saw that even machine guns seemed to be ranged in on the entire area. Hammered in the air and caught in a deadly crossfire on the ground, the men now had to fight their way off the drop zones. Sosabowski landed near a canal. As he ran for cover he came across the body of one trooper. "He lay on the grass, stretched out as if on a cross," Sosabowski later wrote. "A bullet or piece of shrapnel had neatly sliced off the top of his head. I wondered how many more of my men would I see like this before the battle was over and whether their sacrifice would be worthwhile."[*]

Aghast at the fierce German reception, the entire population of Driel was engulfed by the paratroop drop. Polish troopers came down all about the hamlet, landing in orchards, irrigation canals, on the top of the dikes, on the polder and in the village itself. Some men fell into the Rhine and, unable to shed their parachutes, were swept away and drowned. Disregarding the shell and machine-gun fire all about them, the Dutch ran to help the ill-fated Poles. Among them, as a member of a Red Cross team, was Cora Baltussen.

The landing, centered on drop zones less than two miles south of Driel, had come as a complete surprise to the villagers. No pathfinders had been used, and the Dutch underground was ignorant of the plan. Riding a bicycle with wooden tires, Cora Baltussen headed south on a narrow dike road toward a place known as Honingsveld, where many of the paratroopers appeared to have landed. Shocked and terrified, she did not see how anyone could have lived through the German fire. She expected enormous numbers of casualties. To her surprise, Cora saw men, under attack, forming up and running in groups toward the safety of dike embankments. She could hardly believe so many were still

[*] Stanislaw Sosabowski, *Freely I Served*, p. 124.

alive but "at last," she thought, "the Tommies have arrived in
Driel."

She had not spoken English in years, but Cora was the only
inhabitant of Driel familiar with the language. While her services
as a trained Red Cross nurse would be required, Cora also hoped
to act as an interpreter. Hurrying forward, she saw men waving
wildly at her, obviously "warning me to get off the road because
of the fire." But in her "excitement and foolishness," Cora was
unaware of the fusillade of enemy steel storming all about her.
Shouting "Hello Tommies" to the first group she encountered, she
was nonplused by their reply. These men spoke another language—not English. For a moment she listened. A number of
Poles, impressed into the German Army, had been stationed in
Driel some years before. Almost immediately she recognized the
language as Polish. This puzzled her still more.

After years of living under enemy occupation, Cora was wary.
Hiding in the Baltussen factory at this moment were several
British troopers and the crew of a downed plane. The Poles
seemed equally suspicious, as they eyed her carefully. They spoke
no Dutch, but some men ventured guarded questions in broken
English or German. Where, they asked, had she come from? How
many people were in Driel? Were there any Germans in the
village? Where was Baarskamp farm? The mention of Baarskamp
brought a torrent of words in both German and English from
Cora. The farm lay slightly east of the village and, although Cora
was not a member of the tiny underground force in Driel, she had
heard her brother, Josephus, an active member, refer to the
owner of the farm as a Dutch Nazi. She knew there were some
German troops around Baarskamp, along the Rhine dike road,
and manning antiaircraft gun sites in the brickworks along the
riverbank. "Don't go there," she pleaded. "German troops are all
about the place." The Poles seemed unconvinced. "They were not
sure whether to trust me or not," Cora recalls. "I did not know
what to do. Yet I was desperately afraid these men would set out
for Baarskamp and into some sort of a trap." Among the group
around her was General Sosabowski. "As he wore no distinctive

markings and looked like all the others," Cora remembers, "it was not until the next day that I learned that the short, wiry little man was the general." Sosabowski, she remembers, was calmly eating an apple. He was intensely interested in her information about Baarskamp farm; by sheer accident it had been chosen as the main rendezvous point for his brigade. Although Cora thought that no one in the group believed her, Sosabowski's officers now immediately sent off runners to inform other groups about Baarskamp. The compact little man with the apple now asked, "Where is the ferry site?"

One of the officers produced a map, and Cora pointed out the location. "But," she informed them, "it is not running." The people of Driel had not seen the tender since Wednesday. They had learned from Pieter that the cable had been cut, and they presumed that the ferry had been destroyed.

Sosabowski listened with dismay. On landing, he had sent out a reconnaissance patrol to locate the site. Now his fear had been confirmed. "I still waited for the patrol's report," he recalled, "but this young woman's information seemed accurate. I thanked her warmly."[*] A formidable task now lay before him. To send help quickly to Urquhart's beleaguered men in the perimeter, Sosabowski would have to put his force across the 400-yard-wide Rhine by boat or raft—and in darkness. He did not know whether Urquhart's engineers had found boats, or where he might find enough himself. His radiomen, Sosabowski learned, were unable to raise British 1st Airborne headquarters. He was ignorant of any new plans that might have been formulated.

Now, as Cora and her team set out to help the wounded, Sosabowski watched his men move up under the cover of smoke bombs, overrunning what little opposition there was in the area. So far, the only major resistance his brigade had encountered came from artillery shells and mortars. As yet no armor had

---

[*] Some accounts claim that Cora was a member of the underground and was sent to inform Sosabowski that the ferry was in German hands. "Nothing could be further from the truth," says Cora. "I was never a member of the resistance, though my brothers were involved. The British did not trust the underground and certainly we in Driel knew nothing about the drop until the Poles were right on us."

appeared. The soft polder seemed inadequate for tanks. Perplexed and grim, Sosabowski set up brigade headquarters in a farmhouse and waited for news from Urquhart. His mood was not improved when he learned that of his 1,500-man brigade, 500 troops had failed to arrive. Bad weather had forced the planes carrying almost one entire battalion to abort and return to their bases in England. In casualties, his remaining force had already paid a cruel price: although he did not have the exact figures, by nightfall only about 750 men had been assembled, among them scores of wounded.

At 9 P.M. news arrived, rather dramatically, from Urquhart. Unable to raise Sosabowski by radio, the Polish liaison officer at Urquhart's headquarters, Captain Zwolanski, swam across the Rhine. "I was working on a map," Sosabowski remembered, "and suddenly this incredible figure, dripping with water and covered with mud, clad in undershorts and camouflaged netting, came in."

Zwolanski told the General that Uruquhart "wanted us to cross that night and he would have rafts ready to ferry us over." Sosabowski immediately ordered some of his men up to the river line to wait. They remained there most of the night, but the rafts did not come. "At 3 A.M.," says Sosabowski, "I knew the scheme, for some reason, had failed. I pulled my men back into a defensive perimeter." By dawn he expected "German infantry attacks and heavy artillery fire." Any chance of getting across the Rhine "under cover of darkness this night was gone."

At the Hartenstein Hotel across the river, Urquhart had earlier sent an urgent message to Browning. It read:

(212144) No knowledge of elements of division in Arnhem for 24 hours. Balance of division in very tight perimeter. Heavy mortaring and machine-gun fire followed by local attacks. Main nuisance self-propelled guns. Our casualties heavy. Resources stretched to utmost. Relief within 24 hours vital.

At his small post in Brussels, near Montgomery's 21st Army Group headquarters, Prince Bernhard, Commander in Chief of the Netherlands Forces, followed each harrowing new development with anguish. Holland, which might have been liberated with ease in the first days of September, was being turned into a vast battlefield. Bernhard blamed no one. American and British fighting men were giving their lives to rid the Netherlands of a cruel oppressor. Still, Bernhard had rapidly become disenchanted with Montgomery and his staff. By Friday, September 22, when Bernhard learned that the Guards Armored tanks had been stopped at Elst and the Poles dropped near Driel rather than on the southern side of the Arnhem bridge, the thirty-three-year-old Prince lost his temper. "Why?" he angrily demanded of his chief of staff, Major General "Pete" Doorman. "Why wouldn't the British listen to us? Why?"

Senior Dutch military advisers had been excluded from the planning for Market-Garden; their counsel might have been invaluable. "For example," Bernhard recalls, "if we had known in time about the choice of drop zones and the distance between them and the Arnhem bridge, my people would certainly have said something." Because of "Montgomery's vast experience," Bernhard and his staff "had questioned nothing and accepted everything." But, from the moment Dutch generals learned of the route that Horrocks' XXX Corps columns proposed to take, they had anxiously tried to dissuade anyone who would listen, warning of the dangers of using exposed dike roads. "In our military staff colleges," Bernhard says, "we had run countless studies on the problem. We knew tanks simply could not operate along these roads without infantry." Again and again Dutch officers had told Montgomery's staff that the Market-Garden schedule could not be maintained unless infantry accompanied the tanks. General Doorman described how he had "personally held trials with armor in that precise area before the war."

The British, Bernhard says, "were simply not impressed by our negative attitude." Although everyone was "exceptionally polite, the British preferred to do their own planning, and our views were turned down. The prevailing attitude was, 'Don't worry, old boy, we'll get this thing cracking.'" Even now, Bernhard noted, "everything was being blamed on the weather. The general impression among my staff was that the British considered us a bunch of idiots for daring to question their military tactics." With the exception of a few senior officers, Bernhard knew that he was "not particularly loved at Montgomery's headquarters, because I was saying things that now unfortunately were turning out to be true—and the average Englishman doesn't like being told by a bloody foreigner that he's wrong."*

From his Brussels headquarters Bernhard had kept the sixty-four-year-old Queen Wilhelmina and the Dutch government in exile in London fully informed of events. "They could not have influenced British military decisions either," Bernhard says. "It would have done no good for the Queen or our government to take the matter up with Churchill. He would never have interfered with a military operation in the field. Monty's reputation was too big. There wasn't anything we could really do."

Queen Wilhelmina followed the battle anxiously. Like her son-in-law, she had expected a quick liberation of the Netherlands. Now, if Market-Garden failed, the royal family feared "the terrible reprisals the Germans would exact from our people. The Queen expected no sympathy from the Germans, whom she hated with a passion."

In the early progress of the operation, Bernhard had informed Wilhelmina that "soon we will be overrunning some of the royal castles and estates." The Queen replied, "Burn them all." Startled, Bernhard stammered, "I beg your pardon?" Wilhelmina said, "I will never again set foot in a place where the Germans have been

---

* Lieutenant Rupert Mahaffey of the Irish Guards remembers that an officer of the Dutch Princess Irene Brigade came to the Guards' mess for dinner shortly after the tanks were stopped at Elst. Looking around the table, the Dutch officer said, "You would have failed the examination." He explained that one of the problems in the Dutch Staff College examination dealt solely with the correct way to attack Arnhem from Nijmegen. There were two choices: a) attack up the main road; or b) drive up it for 1–2 miles, turn left, effect a crossing of the Rhine and come around in a flanking movement. "Those who chose to go straight up the road failed the examination," the officer said. "Those who turned left and then moved up to the river, passed."

sitting in my chairs, in my rooms. Never!" Bernhard attempted to mollify her. "Mother, you are exaggerating things a bit. After all, they are quite useful buildings. We can steam them out, use DDT." The Queen was adamant. "Burn the palaces down," she commanded. "I will never set foot in one of them." The Prince refused. "The Queen was angry because I occupied the palace with my staff (without destroying it) and not asking her first. She didn't talk to me for weeks, except on official matters."

Now Bernhard and his staff could only "wait and hope. We were bitter and frustrated at the turn of events. It had never entered our minds that costly mistakes could be made at the top." The fate of Holland itself made Bernhard even more apprehensive. "If the British were driven back at Arnhem, I knew the repercussions against the Dutch people in the winter ahead would be frightful."

❊ 2 ❊

OOSTERBEEK, THE QUIET ISLAND in the midst of the war, was now the very center of the fighting. In less than seventy-two hours —from Wednesday on—the village had been pounded to a shambles. Artillery and mortar fire had reduced it to one vast junk heap. The serene order of the town was gone. In its place was a ravaged raw landscape, pitted with shell craters, scarred by slit trenches, littered with splinters of wood and steel, and thick with red brick dust and ashes. From fire-blackened trees, fragments of cloth and curtains blew eerily in the wind. Spent brass cartridge cases glinted in the ankle-high dust along the streets. Roads were barricaded with burned-out jeeps and vehicles, trees, doors, sandbags, furniture—even bathtubs and pianos. Behind half-demolished houses and sheds, by the sides of streets and in ruined gardens lay the bodies of soldiers and civilians, side by side. Resort hotels, now turned into hospitals, stood among lawns littered with furniture, paintings and smashed lamps; and the gaily striped canopies, which had shaded the wide verandas, hung down in soiled, ragged strips. Nearly every house had been hit; some had burned down; and there were few windows left in the town. In this sea of devastation, which the Germans were now calling *Der Hexenkessel* (the witches' cauldron), the Dutch—some eight to ten thousand men, women and children—struggled to survive. Crowded into cellars, without gas, water or electricity and, like the troops in many sectors, almost without food, the civilians nursed their wounded, the British defenders and, when the occasion arose, their German conquerors.

In the Schoonoord Hotel, now one of the main casualty stations sitting squarely on the front line, Hendrika van der Vlist, the daughter of the owner, noted in her diary:

We are no longer afraid; we are past all that. There are wounded lying all around us—some of them are dying. Why shouldn't we do the same if this is asked of us? In this short time we have become detached from everything we have always clung to before. Our belongings are gone. Our hotel has been damaged on all sides. We don't even give it a thought. We have no time for that. If this strife is to claim us as well as the British, we shall give ourselves.

Along lanes, in fields and on rooftops, behind barricaded windows in the ruins of houses, near the church in lower Oosterbeek, in the deer park about the wrecked Hartenstein, tense, hollow-eyed paratroopers manned positions. The noise of the bombardment was now almost continuous. Soldiers and civilians alike were deafened by it. In Oosterbeek the British and Dutch were shocked into a kind of numbness. Time had little meaning, and events had become blurred. Yet soldiers and civilians helped to comfort each other, hoping for rescue, but almost too exhausted to worry about survival. Lieutenant Colonel R. Payton-Reid, commander of the 7th KOSB's, noted: "Lack of sleep is the most difficult of all hardships to combat. Men reached the stage when the only important thing in life seemed to be sleep." As Captain Benjamin Clegg of the 10th Parachute Battalion put it, "I remember more than anything the tiredness—almost to the point that being killed would be worth it." And Sergeant Lawrence Goldthorpe, a glider pilot, was so worn out that "I sometimes wished I could get wounded in order to lie down and get some rest." But there was no rest for anyone.

All about the perimeter—from the white Dreyeroord Hotel (known to the troops as the "White House") in the northern extremity of the fingertip-shaped salient, down to the tenth-century church in lower Oosterbeek—men fought a fiercely confused kind of battle in which the equipment and forces of defender and attacker were crazily intermingled. British troopers often found themselves using captured German ammunition and weapons. German tanks were being destroyed by their own mines. The Germans were driving British jeeps and were bolstered by the captured supplies intended for the airborne. "It was the cheapest battle we ever fought," Colonel Harzer, the Hohenstaufen commander, recalls. "We had free food, cigarettes and ammunition." Both sides captured and recaptured each other's positions so often that few men knew with certainty from hour to hour who occupied the site next to them. For the Dutch sheltering in cellars along the perimeter, the constant switching was terrifying.

Jan Voskuil, the chemical engineer, moved his entire family—his parents-in-law, his wife, Bertha, and their nine-year-old son, Henri—to the home of Dr. Onderwater, because the doctor's reinforced sand-bagged cellar seemed safer. At the height of one period of incessant shooting, a British antitank team fought from the floor above them. Minutes later the cellar door burst open and an SS officer, accompanied by several of his men, demanded to know if the group was hiding any British. Young Henri was playing with a shell case from a British fighter's wing gun. The German officer held up the casing. "This is from a British gun," he shouted. "Everyone upstairs!" Voskuil was quite sure that the cellar's occupants would all be shot. Quickly he intervened. "Look," he told the officer, "this is a shell from an English plane. My son found it and has simply been playing with it." Abruptly the German motioned to his men and the group moved to the upper floor, leaving the Dutch unharmed. Some time later, the cellar door burst open again. To everyone's relief, British paratroopers entered, looking, Voskuil thought, "unearthly, with their camouflage jackets and helmets still sprouting twigs. Like St. Nicholas they handed around chocolates and cigarettes which they had just captured from a German supply truck."

Private Alfred Jones, of Major Boy Wilson's pathfinders, was also caught up in the confusion of battle. Holding positions in a house at the crossroads near the Schoonoord Hotel, Jones and other members of a platoon saw a German staff car approach. The bewildered troopers stared as the car pulled up at the house next to them. "We watched openmouthed," Jones remembers, "as the driver opened the door for the officer and gave the Hitler salute and the officer made for the house." Then, Jones recalls, "we all woke up, the platoon opened fire, and we got them both."

Some brushes with the enemy were less impersonal. Leading a fighting patrol through dense undergrowth on the northern shoulder of the perimeter near the Dennenkamp crossroads, Lieutenant Michael Long of the Glider Pilot Regiment came face to face with a young German. He was carrying a Schmeisser submachine gun; Long had a revolver. Yelling to his men to scatter, the lieutenant opened fire, but the German was faster "by a split second." Long was hit in the thigh and fell to the ground; the German was "only nicked in the right ear." To Long's horror the German tossed a grenade "which landed about eighteen inches from me." Frantically Long kicked the "potato masher" away. It exploded harmlessly. "He searched me," Long remembers, "took two grenades from my pockets and threw them into the woods after my men. Then he calmly sat on my chest and opened fire with the Schmeisser." As the German sprayed the undergrowth, the hot shell cases dropped down into the open neck of Long's battle dress. Irate, Long nudged the German and, pointing at the shell cases, yelled, "*Sehr warm.*" Still firing, the German said, "Oh, *ja!*" and shifted his position so that the spent ammunition fell on the ground. After a few moments the German ceased firing and again searched Long. He was about to throw away the lieutenant's first-aid kit, when Long pointed to his thigh. The German pointed to his ear which Long's bullet had grazed. In the undergrowth, with firing going on all around them, the two men bandaged each other's wounds. Then Long was led away into captivity.

Slowly but surely the perimeter was being squeezed as men were killed, wounded or taken prisoner. Staff Sergeant George Baylis, the glider pilot who had brought his dancing pumps to Holland because he believed the Dutch loved to dance, was "winkled out" of a camouflaged slit trench in a garden by German soldiers. Lined up against a wall, Baylis was searched and interrogated. Ignoring his questioner, Baylis calmly took out a hand mirror and examining his grimy, unshaven face, asked the German, "You don't happen to know if there's a dance in town tonight, do you?" He was marched off.

Other paratroopers actually did hear dance music. From German loudspeakers came one of World War II's popular songs, Glenn Miller's "In the Mood." In trenches and fortified positions, haggard troopers listened silently. As the record ended, a voice speaking English told them, "Men of the First Airborne Division, you are surrounded. Surrender or die!" Sergeant Leonard Overton of the Glider Pilot Regiment "fully expected now not to leave Holland alive anyway." Overton and everyone nearby answered with machine-gun fire. Sergeant Lawrence Goldthorpe heard the loudspeaker, too. A few hours earlier he had risked his life to retrieve a resupply pannier—only to discover that it contained, not food or ammunition, but red berets. Now, when he heard the call to "Give yourselves up, while you still have time," he yelled: "Bugger off, you silly bastards!" As he lifted his rifle he heard other men in woods and trenches take up the cry. There was a blaze of machine-gun and rifle fire as enraged troopers trained their guns in the direction of the loudspeaker. Abruptly the voice stopped.

To the Germans, surrender seemed the only sensible course left to the British—as Major Richard Stewart of the 1st Airlanding Brigade discovered. Stewart, captured and found to speak German fluently, was taken to a large headquarters. He remembers the commanding officer vividly. General Bittrich "was a tall, slender man, probably in his early or middle forties, wearing a long black leather coat and cap," Stewart recalls. Bittrich did not interrogate him. "He simply told me that he wanted me to go to my division commander and persuade him to surrender to save the division from annihilation." Stewart politely refused. The General went into "a long dissertation. He told me it was in my power to save the 'flowering manhood of the nation.'" Again, Stewart said, "I cannot do it." Bittrich urged him once more. Stewart asked, "Sir, if our places were reversed, what would your answer be?" The German commander slowly shook his head. "My answer would be No." Stewart said, "That's mine too."

Although Bittrich "had never seen men fight as hard as the British at Oosterbeek and Arnhem," he continued to underestimate the determination of Urquhart's troopers, and he wrongly interpreted the Polish drop at Driel. While he considered the arrival of the Poles "a morale booster" for the embattled 1st British Airborne, Bittrich believed Sosabowski's principal task was to attack the German rear and prevent Harmel's Frundsberg Division, now using the Arnhem bridge, from reaching the Nijmegen area. He considered the Polish threat so serious that he "intervened in the operations against Oosterbeek" and ordered Major Hans Peter Knaust to rush his armored battalion south. The powerful Knaust *Kampfgruppe,* now reinforced with twenty-five 60-ton Tiger tanks and twenty Panthers, was to defend Elst and prevent the Poles from reaching the southern end of the Arnhem bridge and Horrocks' tanks from linking up with them. Harmel's Frundsberg Division, after it reformed, was ordered "to throw the Anglo-Americans in the Nijmegen area back across the Waal." To Bittrich, the British drive from Nijmegen was of utmost importance. Urquhart's division, Bittrich believed, was contained and finished. He had never considered that the Poles' objective was to reinforce Urquhart's bridgehead. Nevertheless, Bittrich's strategy—developed for the wrong reasons—would seal the fate of the 1st Airborne Division.

Early in the morning of Friday, September 22, as the last of Knaust's tanks arrived at Elst, General Urquhart heard from Horrocks, the XXX Corps commander. In two Phantom messages sent during the night Urquhart had informed British Second Army headquarters that the ferry was no longer held. Horrocks apparently had not been informed. The Corps commander's message read: "43rd Division ordered to take all risks to effect relief today and are directed on ferry. If situation warrants you should withdraw to or cross ferry." Urquhart replied, "We shall be glad to see you."

In the wine cellar of the wrecked Hartenstein Hotel—"the only place remaining that was relatively safe," Urquhart recalls—the General conferred with his chief of staff, Colonel Charles Mackenzie. "The last thing we wanted to be was alarmist," Urquhart remembers, "but I felt I had to do something to effect relief—and effect it immediately."

Outside, the "morning hate," as the troopers called the usual dawn mortaring, had begun. The shattered Hartenstein shook and reverberated from the concussion of near hits, and the harried Urquhart wondered how long they could hold. Of the 10,005 airborne troops—8,905 from the division and 1,100 glider pilots and copilots—that had landed on the Arnhem drop zones, Urquhart now estimated that he had fewer than 3,000 men. In slightly less than five days he had lost more than two thirds of his division. Although he now had communication with Horrocks and Browning, Urquhart did not believe they understood what was happening. "I was convinced," Urquhart says, "that Horrocks was not fully aware of our predicament, and I had to do something to acquaint them with the urgency and desperateness of the situation." He decided to send Colonel Mackenzie and Lieutenant Colonel Eddie Myers, the chief engineer, "who would handle the special arrangements for ferrying across men and supplies," to Nijmegen to see Browning and Horrocks. "I was told," Mackenzie says, "that it was absolutely vital to impress Horrocks and Browning with the fact that the division as such had ceased to exist— that we were merely a collection of individuals hanging on." The limit of endurance had been reached, Urquhart believed, and Mackenzie was to impress on them "that if we don't get men and supplies over by tonight, it may be too late."

Urquhart stood by as Mackenzie and Myers prepared to leave. He knew that the trip would be dangerous, perhaps impossible, yet it seemed reasonable to assume—if Horrocks' messages were to be believed and the 43rd Wessex attack was launched on schedule—that some kind of route would be open to Nijmegen by the time Mackenzie and Myers crossed the river. As the men left Urquhart had "one final word for Charles. I told him to try and make them realize what a fix we were in. Charles said he would do his best, and I knew he would." Taking a rubber boat, Myers and Mackenzie set out by jeep for lower Oosterbeek and the Rhine.

Ten miles away, in the Nijmegen area north of the Waal, twenty-six-year-old Captain Lord Richard Wrottesley, commanding a troop of the 2nd Household Cavalry, sat in an armored car ready to give the command to move out. During the night his reconnaissance unit had been ordered to lead the squadron ahead of the attacking 43rd Wessex Division and make contact with the airborne forces. Since the day before, when the Irish Guards had been stopped, Wrottesley had been "fully aware of the German strength north of Nijmegen." No news had been received from either the Poles at Driel or the 1st Airborne, "so somebody had to find out what was happening." The squadron's role, young Wrottesley remembers, was to "find a way past the enemy defenses by bashing through." By avoiding the main Nijmegen-Arnhem highway and traveling the gridiron of secondary roads to the west, Wrottesley believed, there was a good chance of sprinting through the enemy defenses under cover of an early morning mist "which could contribute to our luck." At first light Wrottesley gave the order to move out. Quickly his two armored cars and two scout cars disappeared into the fog. Following behind him came a second troop under Lieutenant Arthur Young. Traveling fast, the force swung west of the village of Oosterhout, following the Waal riverbank for about six miles. Then, looping back, they headed due north for Driel. "At one point we saw several Germans," Wrottesley remembers, "but they seemed to be more startled than we were." Two and a half hours later, at 8 A.M., Friday, September 22, the first link between the Market-Garden ground forces and the 1st British Airborne was made. The forty-eight hours that Montgomery had envisioned before the link-up had been stretched out to four days and eighteen hours. Wrottesley and Lieutenant Young, surpassing the attempt of the Guards Armored tanks on Thursday, had reached Driel and the Rhine without firing a shot.

Lieutenant H. S. Hopkinson's third troop, coming up behind them, ran into trouble. The morning mist suddenly lifted and as the unit was sighted, enemy armor opened up. "Driver Read in the first car was immediately killed," Hopkinson says. "I went forward to help, but the scout car was blazing and enemy tanks continued to fire on us. We were forced to retire." For the moment, the Germans once more had closed off a relief route to Urquhart's 1st Airborne Division.

The strange, crippling paralysis that had steadily invaded the Market-Garden plan from its very beginning was intensifying. At dawn on Friday, September 22, General Thomas' long-awaited 43rd Wessex Division was to break out from Nijmegen to aid the Guards Armored column still stalled at Elst. The plan called for one brigade—the 129th—to advance along each side of the elevated highway, through Elst and on to Arnhem; simultaneously, a second brigade, the 214th, was to attack farther west through the town of Oosterhout and strike for Driel and the ferry site. Incredibly, it had taken the Wessexes almost three days to travel from the Escaut Canal—a distance of a little more than sixty miles. In part this was due to the constant enemy attacks against the corridor; but some would later charge that it was also due to the excessive cautiousness of the methodical Thomas. His division might have covered the distance more quickly on foot.°

Now, mishap overtook the 43rd Wessex again. To the bitter disappointment of General Essame, commander of the 214th Brigade, one of his lead battalions, the 7th Somersets, had lost its way and had failed to cross the Waal during the night of the twenty-first. "Where the hell have you been?" Essame heatedly demanded of its commander when the force finally arrived. The Somersets had been held up by crowds and roadblocks in Nijmegen; several companies were separated in the confusion and directed over the wrong bridge. Essame's plan to take advantage of the dawn mist and drive toward Driel was lost. The two-pronged attack did not jump off until 8:30 A.M. In full light the enemy, alerted by the Household Cavalry's reconnaissance unit, was prepared. By 9:30 a resourceful German commander at Oosterhout, skillfully using tanks and artillery, had successfully pinned down the 214th Brigade; and the 129th, heading toward Elst and trying to support Colonel Vandeleur's Irish Guards, came under fire from Major Knaust's massed tanks, which General Bittrich had ordered south to crush the Anglo-American drive. On this critical Friday, when, in Urquhart's opinion, the fate of the British 1st Airborne was dependent on immediate relief, it would be late afternoon before the 43rd Wessex would capture Oosterhout—too late to move troops in mass to help the surrounded men in Oosterbeek.

Like Essame, others were angered by the sluggish progress of the attack. Lieutenant Colonel George Taylor, commanding the 5th Duke of Cornwall's Light Infantry,† could not understand "what was holding everything up." He knew the Garden forces were already three days behind schedule in reaching the 1st

---

° Chester Wilmot, *The Struggle for Europe*, p. 516.

† The names of the famous British regiments involved always caused confusion for Americans—especially when they were abbreviated. At First Allied Airborne headquarters a message concerning the Duke of Cornwall's Light Infantry arrived, reading, "5DCLI are to make contact with 1 Airborne Division . . ." The puzzled duty officer finally decoded the message. He reported "Five Duck Craft Landing Infantry" were on their way to Urquhart.

Airborne. He was uncomfortably aware that higher command headquarters was worried, too. On Thursday he had met General Horrocks, the Corps commander, who had asked him, "George, what would you do?" Without hesitation, Taylor had suggested rushing a special task force to the Rhine on Thursday night carrying 2½-ton amphibious vehicles (DUKWs) filled with supplies. "My idea was a shot in the dark," Taylor recalls. "Horrocks looked slightly startled and, as people do sometimes when they consider a suggestion impractical, he quickly changed the conversation."

Taylor now waited impatiently for orders to move his battalion across the Waal river. It was not until midday Friday that a major, a staff officer from XXX Corps, arrived to tell him that his battalion would be given two DUKWs loaded with supplies and ammunition to take up to Driel. Additionally, Taylor would have a squadron of tanks of the Dragoon Guards. "The situation at Arnhem is desperate," the major said. "The DUKWs must be moved across the river tonight." Looking at the heavily laden DUKWs that arrived in the assembly area at 3:00 P.M. on Friday afternoon, Taylor wondered if they carried enough supplies. "Surely," he remarked to his intelligence officer, Lieutenant David Wilcox, "we've got to get more than this across to them."

Even as the infantry was moving out of the Nijmegen bridge-head, Colonel Mackenzie and Lieutenant Colonel Myers had reached Sosabowski and the Poles at Driel. Their crossing of the Rhine had been surprisingly uneventful. "Only a few shots were fired at us," Mackenzie says, "and they went over our heads." On the southern side a full-scale battle was in progress and the Poles were hard pressed, holding off enemy infantry attacks from the direction of Elst and Arnhem. For some time Mackenzie and Myers had waited on the Rhine's southern bank for the Poles. "They had been told by radio to watch out for us," Mackenzie says. "But there was quite a battle going on, and Sosabowski had his hands full." Finally, riding bicycles, they were escorted to Sosabowski's headquarters.

Mackenzie was heartened to discover the Household Cavalry units. But his hopes of reaching General Browning at Nijmegen quickly were dashed. To Lord Wrottesley and Lieutenant Arthur Young, the failure of Hopkinson's third troop of reconnaissance vehicles to reach Driel meant that the Germans had closed in behind them; nor had the attack of the 43rd Wessex yet broken through. Mackenzie and Myers would have to wait until a route was opened.

Wrottesley recalls that "Mackenzie immediately asked to use my radio to contact Corps headquarters." He began to relay a long message via Wrottesley's squadron commander for Horrocks and Browning. Urquhart's chief of staff made no effort to encode his signal. Standing beside him, Wrottesley heard Mackenzie "in the clear" say, " 'We are short of food, ammunition and medical supplies. We cannot hold out for more than twenty-four hours. All we can do is wait and pray.' " For the first time Wrottesley realized "that Urquhart's division must be in a very bad way."

Mackenzie and Myers then conferred with Sosabowski about the urgency of getting the Poles across. "Even a few men now can make a difference," Mackenzie told him. Sosabowski agreed, but asked where the boats and rafts were to come from. Hopefully DUKWs, which had been requested, would arrive by night. Meanwhile, Myers thought, several two-man rubber dinghies, which the airborne had, could be used. Linked by hawser they could be pulled back and forth across the river. Sosabowski was "delighted with the idea." It would be painfully slow, he said, but "if unopposed, perhaps two hundred men might be shipped across during the night." By radio, Myers quickly contacted the Hartenstein to make arrangements for the dinghies. The pathetic and desperate operation, it was decided, would begin at nightfall.

In the bridgehead across the river, Urquhart's men continued to fight with extraordinary courage and resolution. Yet, at places about the perimeter, even the most resolute were voicing worry about relief. Here and there a looming sense of isolation was growing, infecting the Dutch as well.

Douw van der Krap, a former Dutch naval officer, had earlier been placed in command of a twenty-five-man Dutch underground unit which was to fight alongside the British. The group had been organized at the instigation of Lieutenant Commander Arnoldus Wolters, the Dutch liaison officer at Urquhart's headquarters. Jan Eijkelhoff, who had helped make ready the Schoonoord Hotel for casualties on Monday, was charged with finding German weapons for the group. The British could give each man only five rounds of ammunition—if weapons could be found. Driving as far as Wolfheze, Eijkelhoff found only three or four rifles. At first the newly appointed commander of the unit, Van der Krap, was elated at the idea, but his hopes dimmed. His men would be instantly executed if captured while fighting with the paratroopers. "Without relief and supplies for themselves, it was obvious the British couldn't last," Van der Krap recalls. "They couldn't arm us and they couldn't feed us and I decided to disband the group." Van der Krap, however, remained with the paratroopers. "I wanted to fight," he says, "but I didn't think we had a chance."

Young Anje van Maanen, who had been so excited by the paratroopers' arrival and the daily expectation of seeing "Monty's tanks," was now terrified by the continuous shelling and constantly changing battle lines. "The noise and the hell go on," she wrote in her diary. "I can't bear it any longer. I'm so scared and I can't think of anything but shells and death." Anje's father, Dr. Gerritt van Maanen, working alongside British doctors at the Tafelberg Hotel, brought news to his family whenever he could, but to Anje the battle had assumed unrealistic proportions. "I don't understand," she wrote. "One side of a street is British, the other German, and people kill each other from both sides. There are house, floor and room fights." On Friday, Anje wrote, "the British say Monty will be here at any moment. I don't believe that. Monty can go to hell! He will never come."

In the Schoonoord Hotel, where British and German wounded crowded the wide veranda and lay in the reception rooms, passageways and bedrooms, Hendrika van der Vlist could hardly believe it was Friday. The hospital was constantly changing hands. On Wednesday the hotel had been taken by the Germans, on Thursday by the British; and by Friday morning it had been recaptured by the Germans. Control of the Schoonoord was less important than the need to prevent it being fired on. A large Red Cross flag flew on the roof, and numerous smaller ones were spotted around the grounds, but the dust and flying debris often obscured the pennants. Orderlies, nurses and doctors worked on, seemingly oblivious to anything but the constant flow of wounded men.

Hendrika had slept in her clothes for only a few hours each night, getting up to assist doctors and orderlies as fresh casualties were carried in. Fluent in English and German, she had originally noted a pessimism among the Germans in contrast to the patient cheerfulness of the British. Now many of the severely wounded Red Devils seemed stoically prepared to accept their fate. As she brought one trooper the minuscule portion of soup and a biscuit that constituted the only meal the hospital could provide, he pointed to a newly arrived casualty. "Give it to him," he told Hendrika. Pulling down the man's blanket, she saw he wore a German uniform. "German, eh?" the trooper asked. Hendrika nodded. "Give him the food anyway," the Britisher said, "I ate yesterday." Hendrika stared at him. "Why is there a war on, really?" she asked. Tiredly, he shook his head. In her diary she put down her private fears: "Has our village become one of the bloodiest battlefields? What is holding up the main army? It cannot go on like this any longer."

In Dr. Onderwater's cellar, where the Voskuil family was sheltering along with some twenty others, both Dutch and British, Mrs. Voskuil noticed for the first time that the floor was slippery with blood. During the night two wounded officers, Major Peter Warr and Lieutenant Colonel Ken Smyth, had been brought in by British troopers. Both men were seriously wounded, Warr in the thigh and Smyth in the stomach. Shortly after the injured men were laid on the floor, the Germans burst in. One of them threw a grenade. Lance Corporal George Wyllie of

Colonel Smyth's 10th Battalion remembers "a flash of light and then a deafening explosion." Mrs. Voskuil, sitting behind Major Warr, felt "red hot pain" in her legs. In the now-dark cellar she heard someone shouting, "Kill them! Kill them!" She felt a man's body fall heavily across her. It was Private Albert Willingham, who had apparently jumped in front of Mrs. Voskuil to protect her. Corporal Wyllie saw a gaping wound open in Willingham's back. He remembers the woman sitting on a chair with a child beside her, the dead paratrooper across her lap. The child seemed covered with blood. "My God!" Wyllie thought as he lost consciousness, "we've killed a child." Suddenly the fierce battle was over. Someone shone a torch. "Do you still live?" Mrs. Voskuil called out to her husband. Then she reached for her son, Henri. The child did not respond to her cries. She was sure he was dead. "Suddenly I didn't care what happened," she says. "It just didn't matter any more."

She saw that soldiers and civilians alike were terribly wounded and screaming. In front of her, Major Warr's tunic was "bloody and gaping open." Everyone was shouting or sobbing. "Silence," Mrs. Voskuil yelled in English. "Silence!" The heavy burden across her body was pulled away and then she saw Wyllie nearby. "The English boy got up, shaking visibly. He had his rifle butt on the floor and the bayonet, almost level with my eyes, jerked back and forth as he tried to steady himself. Low animal-like sounds— almost like a dog or a wolf—were coming from him."

Corporal Wyllie's head began to clear. Someone had now lit a candle in the cellar, and a German officer gave him a sip of brandy. Wyllie noticed the bottle bore a Red Cross insignia, and underneath the words, "His Majesty's Forces." As he was led out Wyllie looked back at the lady "whose child was dead." He wanted to say something to her but "couldn't find the words."[*]

The German officer asked Mrs. Voskuil to tell the British "they have fought gallantly and behaved like gentlemen, but now they must surrender. Tell them it is over." As the paratroopers were

---

[*] Wyllie never again saw the Voskuils, nor did he know their names. For years he worried about the woman in the cellar and the child he believed dead. Today young Henri Voskuil is a doctor.

taken out, a German medical orderly examined Henri. "He is in a coma," he told Mrs. Voskuil. "He is grazed along the stomach and his eyes are discolored and swollen, but he will be all right." Mutely she nodded her head.

On the floor Major Warr, his shoulder bones protruding through the skin from the explosion, shouted, cursed and then fell unconscious again. Leaning over, Mrs. Voskuil moistened her handkerchief and wiped the blood from his lips. A short distance away Colonel Smyth mumbled something. A German guard turned, questioningly, toward Mrs. Voskuil. "He wants a doctor," she said softly. The soldier left the cellar and returned a few minutes later with a German doctor. Examining Smyth, the physician said, "Tell the officer I am sorry to have to hurt him but I must look at his wound. Tell him to grit his teeth." As he began pulling away the clothing, Smyth fainted.

At daylight the civilians were ordered to leave. Two SS men carried Mrs. Voskuil and Henri out into the street, and a Dutch Red Cross worker directed them to the cellar of a dentist, Dr. Phillip Clous. Voskuil's parents-in-law did not go. They preferred to take their chances at home. In the Clous house, the dentist warmly welcomed the family. "Don't worry," he told Voskuil. "It's going to be all right. The British will win." Voskuil, standing beside his wounded wife and child, his mind still filled with the night's horrors, stared at the man. "No," he said quietly, "they will not."

Though they were unwilling to recognize that their endurance had nearly run its course, many paratroopers knew that they could not hold on alone much longer. Staff Sergeant Dudley Pearson was tired "of being pushed around by the Germans." On the northern edge of the perimeter, he and his men had been chased by tanks, pinned down in woods and forced to fight off the Germans with bayonets. Finally, on Thursday night, as the perimeter tightened, Pearson's group was ordered to pull back. He was told to cover the withdrawal with a smoke grenade. Nearby he heard a lone Bren gun firing. Scrambling through underbrush he discovered a corporal hidden in a deep hollow in the woods. "Get out," Pearson told him. "I'm the last one here."

The corporal shook his head. "Not me, sergeant," he said. "I'm staying. I won't let those bastards by." As Pearson made his way back he could hear the Bren-gunner firing. He thought the situation was hopeless. He began to wonder if it wouldn't be better to surrender.

In a slit trench near the tennis courts at the Hartenstein—where the earth was now crisscrossed with foxholes that the German prisoners had been allowed to dig for their own protection—Glider Pilot Victor Miller stared at the body of another pilot, who lay sprawled a few yards away. Firing had been so intense that men had not been able to remove the dead. Miller saw that since the last mortaring the body was half buried by leaves and shattered branches. He kept staring at the corpse, wondering if anyone would come to pick it up. He was frightened that the features of his dead friend would change, and he was certain there was a "strong smell of death." He felt sick. He remembers thinking wildly that "if something isn't done soon, we'll all be corpses. The shells will eliminate us one by one, until this will be only a park of the dead."

Other men felt they were being exhorted to keep up courage without access to the facts. Private William O'Brien, near the church in lower Oosterbeek, remembers that "every night an officer came around and told us to hang on, the Second Army would arrive the next day. There was a helluva lot of apathy. Everyone was asking what the hell they were there for and where the hell was the goddam army. We'd had it." Sergeant Edward Mitchell, a glider pilot, in a position opposite the church, remembers one man locked himself in a nearby shed. "He would let no one near. Every now and again he'd shout, 'Come on, you bastards,' and empty a magazine all around the shed." For hours, the lone trooper alternately shouted and fired, then lapsed into periods of silence. As Mitchell and others debated how to get him out, there was another sharp burst of fire and then silence. Reaching the shed, they found the paratrooper dead.

Here and there shell-shocked, concussed, battle-fatigued men roamed the Hartenstein area, finally oblivious to the battle. Medic Taffy Brace, who on Tuesday had tended the mangled body of his friend, Andy Milbourne, was encountering these tragic, pathetic men as he treated the wounded. By now Brace had run out of morphia, and he was using paper bandages. He could not bring himself to reveal that he had no medication. "What would you be wanting morphia for?" he asked one critically wounded trooper. "Morphia's for people who are really hurt. You're doing fine."

As Brace bandaged the man, he was aware of a strange hooting sound behind him. Turning he saw a totally naked paratrooper, pumping his arms up and down and "sounding like a locomotive." As Brace caught his eye, the soldier began to curse. "Blast this fireman," the trooper said, "he was never any good." In one house near the perimeter Brace, arriving with a casualty, heard a man softly singing "The White Cliffs of Dover." Thinking the trooper was soothing the other injured, Brace smiled at him and nodded encouragement. The soldier lunged at Brace and tried to choke him. "I'll kill you," he yelled. "What do you know about Dover?" Brace loosened the fingers at his throat. "It's all right," he said gently, "I've been there." The man stepped back. "Oh," he said, "that's all right then." Minutes later he began to sing again. Others remember a shell-shocked trooper who walked among them at night. Bending over the huddled forms of men trying to sleep he would shake them roughly awake, stare into their eyes and ask them all the same question: "Have you got faith?"

Despite those pitiable, shocked and desperate men whose faith was gone, hundreds of others were bolstered by the actions of eccentric, undaunted soldiers who seemed utterly fearless and who refused to give in to wounds or hardships. Major Dickie Lonsdale, commander of the "Lonsdale Force," holding positions about the church in lower Oosterbeek, seemed to be everywhere. "His was a figure that would inspire terror," recalls Sergeant Dudley Pearson. "He had one arm in a bloodstained sling, an equally bloody wrapping around his head and a giant bandage on one leg." Hobbling about exhorting his men, Lonsdale led attack after attack.

Sergeant Major Harry Callaghan, who had added extra touches to his uniform—he had found a tall black hat in a hearse and wore it everywhere, explaining to the men that he had been named "the Airborne representative to Hitler's funeral"—remembers the awesome-looking Lonsdale deliver a ringing, defiant speech to men in the church. Officers and noncoms had rounded up troopers and sent them to the ancient ruined building. "The roof was gone," Callaghan remembers, "and each new explosion sent plaster cascading down." As soldiers leaned listlessly against walls and broken pews—smoking, lounging, half-asleep—Lonsdale climbed into the pulpit. Men stared upward at the fierce-looking, bloodstained figure. "We've fought the Germans in North Africa, Sicily and Italy," Callaghan remembers Lonsdale saying. "They weren't good enough for us then! They're bloody well not good enough for us now!" Captain Michael Corrie of the Glider Pilot Regiment had been struck as he entered the church "by the weariness I saw. But Lonsdale's speech was stirring. I felt stunned by his words, and proud. The men went in looking beaten, but as they came out, they had new spirit. You could read it on their faces."

Some men seemed to have overcome even the paralyzing fear that the brute force of enemy armored attacks instilled. With few antitank guns, troopers were helpless against tanks and self-propelled guns that roamed the perimeter, pulverizing position after position. Yet, somehow the foot soldiers were fighting back. Even 60-ton Tigers were destroyed—often by men who had never before fired an antitank gun. Lance Corporal Sydney Nunn, who had eagerly looked forward to Arnhem as an escape from the "nightmare" of his camp in England and the mole which had invaded his mattress, now faced a far more dreadful nightmare with outward calm. He and another paratrooper, Private Nobby Clarke, had become friendly with a glider pilot in an adjoining slit trench. During a lull in the mortaring, the pilot called over to Nunn, "I don't know whether you know it, old lad, but there's a whopping great tank out in front to our right. One of the Tiger family." Clarke looked at Nunn. "What are we supposed to do?" he asked. "Go drill holes in it?"

Cautiously Nunn looked over the edge of the trench. The tank was "enormous." Nearby in the bushes an antitank gun was concealed, but its crew had been killed, and no one in Nunn's group knew how to load or fire the weapon. Nunn and the glider pilot decided to crawl to it. As the men climbed out they were spotted and the tank's gun began firing. "We dug grooves in the soil with our noses, we were that low," Nunn recalls. "Our little woods began to look like a logging camp as trees came down all around us." The two men reached the gun just as the Tiger "began to give us personal attention with its machine gun." The pilot sighted down the barrel of the gun and shouted happily. "Our gun was pointed directly at the tank. If we'd known how to do it, we couldn't have aimed it better." Looking at Nunn, the glider pilot said, "I hope this thing works." He pulled the trigger. In the heavy explosion that followed, both men were thrown on their backs. "When our ears stopped ringing, I heard other men around us begin to laugh and cheer," Nunn says. As he stared disbelievingly, he saw the Tiger engulfed in flames, its ammunition exploding. Turning to Nunn, the glider pilot solemnly shook hands. "Our game, I think," he said.

Many men remember Major Robert Cain of the 2nd South Staffordshires as the real expert against tanks and self-propelled guns. It seemed to Cain that he and his men had been pursued and threatened by Tigers ever since they had arrived. Now, with his small force positioned at the church in lower Oosterbeek, in houses and gardens across the road, and in a laundry owned by a family named Van Dolderen, Cain was determined to knock out every piece of armor he saw. Searching for the best site from which to operate, Cain picked the Van Dolderen house. The laundry owner was unwilling to leave. Surveying the back garden, Cain said, "Well, be that as it may, I'm going to dig in out there. I'm using your place for my ammo dump."

Cain was using the bazookalike antitank weapon known as a

Piat to hunt down armor. On Friday, as the street battles grew in intensity, Cain's eardrums burst from his constant firing. Stuffing pieces of field dressing into his ears he continued lobbing bombs.

Suddenly someone called out to Cain that two tanks were coming up the road. At the corner of a building, Cain loaded the Piat and aimed it. Staff Sergeant Richard Long, a glider pilot, looked on aghast. "He was the bravest man I've ever seen," Long says. "He was only about a hundred yards away when he started to fire." The tank fired back before Cain could reload, and the shell hit the building in back of him. In the thick swirl of dust and debris, Cain fired again and then again. He saw the crew of the first tank bail out, spraying the street with machine-gun bullets. Immediately around Cain, paratroopers opened up with Bren guns and, Cain remembers, "the Germans were just cut off their feet." Reloading again, he fired, and Sergeant Long saw "a tremendous flash. The bomb had gone off inside the Piat. Major Cain threw his hands in the air and fell backward. When we got to him, his face was black. His first words were, 'I think I'm blind.'" Staff Sergeant Walton Ashworth, one of the Bren-gunners who had shot up the German tank crew, stared stonily as Cain was taken away. "All I could think was 'that poor bloody bastard.'"

Within half an hour Cain's sight had returned, but his face was imbedded with bits of metal. He refused morphia and, deciding that he "wasn't wounded enough to stay where he was," went back to the battle—as Captain W. A. Taylor described it, "to add to his bag of enemy tanks." By Friday afternoon, the thirty-five-year-old Cain had a bagful. Since landing on the eighteenth he had put out of action or driven off a total of six tanks, plus a number of self-propelled guns.

Ferocious men throughout the airhead were making heroic stands, unmindful of their own safety. By dusk on Friday Corporal Leonard Formoy, one of the survivors of Colonel Fitch's 3rd Battalion, who had made the desperate march to reach Frost's men at the Arnhem bridge, occupied a position on the western outskirts not far from Division headquarters at the Hartenstein

"We were being hit from practically all sides," Formoy remembers. Suddenly a Tiger tank, coming from the direction of Arnhem, rumbled toward the cluster of men around Formoy. In the twilight Formoy saw the turret swivel. Sergeant "Cab" Calloway picked up a Piat and rushed forward. "You're going where I'm going!" Formoy heard him yell. Approximately fifty yards away from the tank, Calloway fired. The bomb exploded against the tracks and the tank stopped, but Calloway was killed at almost the same moment by its guns. "It was an act of desperation," Formoy remembers. "He was just ripped in half, but he saved our lives."

Private James Jones remembers an unknown major who asked Jones and three others to go with him outside the perimeter on a search for guns and ammunition. The small party came suddenly upon some Germans in a machine-gun nest. Leaping up, the major fired, yelling, "There's some more of those bastards who won't live!" As the Germans opened up, the group scattered and Jones was trapped behind a disabled jeep. "I said a prayer, waited for another burst from the gun, and got back to the lines," Jones recalls. He never saw the major again.

Senior officers, often unaware of the impression they made, set examples their men would never forget. Brigadier Pip Hicks refused to wear a helmet throughout the battle. Trooper William Chandler, one of Major Freddie Gough's Reconnaissance Squadron men whose group had been cut off on the northern, Leopard route on Sunday and had been moved back to a crossroads at Oosterbeek, remembers Hicks's red beret standing out among groups of helmeted men. "Hey, Brigadier," someone called out, "put your bloody helmet on." Hicks just smiled and waved. "I wasn't trying to be debonair," Hicks explains. "I just couldn't stand the damn thing bouncing around on my head." His activities might have had something to do with that. Some men recall Hicks's frequent daily trips to Urquhart's headquarters. He started each journey at a jog and ended up sprinting a step ahead of German shellfire. "I felt fully my age when I finished those mad dashes," Hicks confesses.

Brigadier Shan Hackett, who had brought his battered 10th and 156th battalions back to the Oosterbeek area after their brave but futile attempt to break through the German defenses to the north and east and get to Arnhem, visited his men constantly, offering them quiet words of praise. Major Geoffrey Powell was commanding two platoons of the 156th in perimeter positions to the north. "We were short on food, ammunition and water," Powell remembers, "and we had few medical supplies." On Friday Hackett suddenly appeared at Powell's command post, where, says Powell, "we were literally poking right into the enemy's lines." Hackett explained that he had not had time to visit Powell until now, "but you've been holding so well, Geoffrey, I wasn't worried about you." Powell was pleased. "The only real mistake I've made so far, sir," he said, "is putting the headquarters in a chicken run. We're all alive with fleas." To Staff Sergeant Dudley Pearson, chief clerk of the 4th Brigade, Hackett earned respect because "he shared with us as though he had no rank. If we ate, he did, and if we went hungry, so did he. He didn't seem to have a mess kit. On Friday he sat down with us and ate a little piece of food with his fingers." Pearson went to find a knife and fork. On the way back he was wounded in the heel; but, he says, "I thought the Brigadier rather deserved something better than the way he was living among us."

And Signalman Kenneth Pearce, attached to Command Artillery Signals at Division headquarters, will always remember the man who came to his aid. Pearce was in charge of the heavy storage batteries, called "Dags"—each weighing approximately twenty-five pounds and encased in a wooden box with cast-iron handles—that powered the signal sets. In the late evening Pearce was struggling to move a fresh Dag from the deep trench in which they were stored. Above him, he heard someone say, "Here, let me help you." Pearce directed the man to grab one handle and pull up the set. Together the two dragged the cumbersome box to the command-post trench. "There's one more," Pearce said. "Let's go get it." The men made the second trip and, back at the command post, Pearce jumped into the trench as the other man hoisted the boxes down to him. As they walked away Pearce suddenly noticed that the man wore red staff officer's tabs. Stopping dead, he stammered, "Thank you very much, sir." General Urquhart nodded. "That's all right, son," he said.

Step by terrible step the crisis was mounting; nothing went right on this day, which General Horrocks was to call "Black Friday." Weather conditions in both England and Holland again grounded Allied planes, preventing resupply missions. In answer to Urquhart's plea for fighter strikes, the R.A.F. replied: ". . . After most careful examination regret owing to storm unable to accept . . ." And, at this moment, when Horrocks needed every man, tank and ton of supplies to retain Montgomery's bridgehead over the Rhine and break through to the Red Devils, Field Marshal Model's counteroffensive finally succeeded in cutting the corridor. Thirty minutes after receiving Mackenzie's message that Urquhart might be overrun in twenty-four hours, General Horrocks received another message: in the 101st Airborne's sector, powerful German armored forces had cut the corridor north of Veghel.

Model could hardly have chosen a more vital spot or timed his attack better. British infantry forces of the XII and VIII Corps, advancing on either side of the highway, had only now reached Son, barely five miles into the 101st's area. Fighting against stiff resistance, they had made agonizingly slow progress. The 101st's commander, General Taylor, had expected the British to reach his sector of "Hell's Highway" long before. After more than five days of continuous fighting without support, Taylor's hard-pressed troopers were thinly spread and vulnerable. Along some stretches the highway was unguarded except by the British armor and infantry moving along it on the way north. Elsewhere, the "front" was literally the sides of the road. Field Marshal Model had chosen to counterattack at Veghel for a particular reason: throughout the entire length of the Market-Garden corridor the

Veghel area contained the greatest cluster of bridges—no fewer than four, of which one was a major canal crossing. With one stroke Model hoped to strangle the Allied lifeline. He almost did. He might have succeeded, but for the Dutch underground.

During the night and early morning, in villages and hamlets east of Veghel, the Dutch spotted the German buildup; they promptly phoned liaison officers with the 101st. The warning came not a moment too soon. Massed German armor almost overwhelmed Taylor's men. Twice in four hours, in a wild melee that ranged over a five-mile stretch of the corridor, German tanks tried to push through to the bridges. Desperately, Taylor's men, aided by British artillery and armor on the road, threw back the attacks. But four miles to the north, at Uden, the Germans succeeded in cutting the corridor. Now, with the battle still raging and the forces in the rear cut off and isolated, Horrocks was forced to make a fateful decision: he would have to send armored units—urgently needed in his efforts to reach Urquhart—back south down the corridor to help General Taylor, whose need was now even more urgent. The 32nd Guards Brigade was sent rushing south to support the 101st in reopening the highway. The gallant 101st would hang on to the bridges, but even with the help of the Guards, not a man, tank or supply vehicle would move north along the corridor for the next twenty-four hours. Model's counteroffensive, though unsuccessful for the moment, had still paid enormous dividends. In the end, the battle for the corridor would decide the fate of Arnhem.

By 4 P.M. on Friday, September 22, in the Nijmegen-Arnhem area—six and one-half hours after they had first been pinned down by German tanks and artillery—British infantrymen finally bludgeoned their way through Oosterhout. The village was in flames, and SS prisoners were being rounded up. The relief route west of the "island" highway, the low-lying secondary roads used by the enterprising Household Cavalry in their race to Driel at dawn, was now believed to be free or, at worst, only lightly held by the enemy. The 5th Duke of Cornwall's Light Infantry, supported by a squadron of Dragoon Guards' tanks and carrying the precious two amphibious vehicles loaded with supplies, was ready to slam through whatever opposition remained and dash for the Rhine. Lieutenant Colonel George Taylor, commanding the force, was so eager to get to Urquhart that he "felt a mad desire to sweep my infantry onto the tanks with my hands and get moving."

In a small wood north of Oosterhout, his loaded vehicles waited to move out. Suddenly, off in the distance, Taylor spotted two Tiger tanks. Quietly he warned Lieutenant David Wilcox, his intelligence officer, "Don't say anything. I don't want anyone to know about those tanks. We can't stop now." Taylor waved the relief column up the road. "If we had waited five minutes more," he says, "I knew the route would have been closed again."

At full speed—his infantry mounted on tanks, carriers and trucks—Taylor's column rolled through Dutch hamlets and villages. Everywhere they were met by surprised, cheering villagers, but there was no slowdown. Taylor's only concern was to get to the Rhine. "I felt a sense of great urgency," he says. "Any time lost would give the enemy an opportunity to move up a blocking force." The convoy met no opposition, and for Taylor, "it was an exhilarating feeling as the light faded rapidly and the head of the column reached Driel." They had covered the ten-mile journey in just thirty minutes. At 5:30 P.M. the first tanks of the Dragoon Guards reached the Rhine and, skirting northeast along its banks, moved into the outskirts of the village. Taylor heard an explosion and guessed immediately what it was: on the cautious Sosabowski's defense perimeter, one of the tanks had run over a Polish mine.

It was dark when Taylor reached Sosabowski's headquarters. The information he had about Urquhart's division was vague. "I had no idea where they were in Arnhem or if they still held one end of the bridge." But Taylor planned to send his infantry and tanks immediately toward the southern end. He knew the DUKWs must get "across as soon as possible and if the bridge was still held it would be obviously quicker to drive them across than to float them over." At Sosabowski's headquarters, Taylor was astonished to find Colonel Charles Mackenzie and Lieutenant Colonel Myers. Quickly they dissuaded him from heading out for the Arnhem bridge. Nothing had been heard from Frost, Mackenzie explained, since Wednesday night and it was presumed at headquarters that "it was all over at the bridge."

Reluctantly Taylor gave up his plan and ordered out a reconnaissance group to scout along the riverbank for a site from which the DUKWs might be launched. Sosabowski's engineers were not optimistic; the awkward amphibious vehicles would prove cumbersome to manhandle across ditches and banks down to the river, especially in the dark. A short while later Taylor's reconnaissance group confirmed the Poles' opinion. The river could be approached, they thought, only by one narrow ditch-lined road. In spite of the serious obstacles, Taylor's men believed they could get the DUKWs down to the Rhine. Colonel Mackenzie, still unable to continue on to Nijmegen, would oversee the launching. The DUKWs would cross the river at 2 A.M. on Saturday, the twenty-third. First priority, however, was to get men into the bridgehead: Sosabowski's Poles had to be ferried over in the little string of rubber boats.

At 9 P.M. on Friday night that operation began. Silently crouching along the riverbank, the Polish soldiers waited. On both sides of the river engineers, under the direction of Lieutenant Colonel Myers, stood ready to pull the hawser attaching the rubber dinghies back and forth. In just four boats—two 2-man and two 1-man dinghies—only six men could cross the 400-yard-wide Rhine at a time. Supplementing the craft were several wooden rafts that the Polish engineers had constructed to carry small supplies and stores. On Sosabowski's order the first six men got into the boats and moved out. Within a few minutes the men were across. Behind them came a string of rafts. As fast as men landed on the northern bank the boats and rafts were hauled back. "It was a slow, laborious process," Sosabowski noted, "but so far the Germans seemed to suspect nothing."

Then, from a point to the west of the landing site across the river a light shot up into the sky, and almost immediately the whole area was brilliantly lit by a magnesium parachute flare. Instantly Spandau machine guns began raking the river, "stirring up small waves and making the water boil with hot steel," Sosabowski recalls. Simultaneously, mortar shells began to fall among the waiting Poles. Within minutes two rubber boats were riddled, their occupants heaved into the river. On the southern bank, men scattered, firing at the parachute flare. In the wild melee, Sosabowski halted the operation. Men moved back and took up new positions, trying to avoid the bursting mortar shells. The moment the flare dimmed and burned out, they ran to the boats and rafts, climbed in, and the crossings began again. Another flare burst in the sky. In this cruel game of hide-and-seek the Poles, suffering terrible casualties, continued to cross the river all night in the remaining boats. At the schoolhouse in Driel which had been temporarily turned into a casualty station, Cora Baltussen tended the injured as they were brought in. "We can't get across," a Pole told her. "It's a slaughter up there—and we can't even fire back."

At 2 A.M., Taylor's amphibious DUKWs began moving down to the river. Because of heavy rain during the day, the low, narrow, ditch-lined road was inches thick in mud. And, as the DUKWs, surrounded by sixty men, slowly approached the river, a heavy ground mist formed. Men could not see either the road or the river. Again and again, struggling soldiers labored to straighten the vehicles as they slid off the road. Supplies were unloaded to lighten the DUKWs, but even this was not enough. Finally, despite strenuous efforts to hold them back, the cumbersome vehicles slid into the ditch only yards from the Rhine. "It's no good," the despairing Mackenzie told Taylor. "It's just hopeless." At 3 A.M., the entire operation came to a halt. Only fifty men and almost no supplies had been ferried across the river into Urquhart's bridgehead.

�֍ 3 �֍

B Y THE TIME COLONEL CHARLES MACKENZIE finally reached General Browning's headquarters in Nijmegen on Saturday morning, September 23, he was "dead tired, frozen stiff, and his teeth were chattering," Brigadier Gordon Walch, the chief of staff, remembers. In spite of his determination to see Browning immediately, Mackenzie was promptly "put in a bath to thaw out."

British forces using the relief route west of, and parallel to, the "island" highway were now moving steadily up to Driel, but the roads were far from clear of the enemy. Still, Lord Wrottesley had decided to try to get Mackenzie and Lieutenant Colonel Myers back to Nijmegen. The brief trip, in a small convoy of reconnaissance vehicles, was hair-raising. As the party approached a crossroads, they found a partly destroyed German half-track lying slewed across it. Wrottesley got out to guide his vehicles, and at that point, a Tiger tank appeared farther down the road. To avoid an encounter, the armored car carrying Mackenzie began backing away, when suddenly the road collapsed beneath it and the car turned over. Mackenzie and the crew were forced to hide out from German infantry in a field as Wrottesley, yelling to the driver of his scout car "to go like hell," headed up the road toward Nijmegen to find British troops. Organizing a relief force, Wrottesley sped back down the road to find Mackenzie. When the little force arrived the German tank was gone and Mackenzie and the crew of the armored car came up to meet them from the field where they had taken cover. In the confusion Myers, following in a second armored car, became separated from the troop.

538

General Browning greeted Mackenzie anxiously. According to his staff, "the week had been a series of agonizing and tragic setbacks." More than anything else the lack of full communications with Urquhart had contributed to Browning's concern. Even now, although messages were passing between the British 1st Airborne Division and Corps, Browning's picture of Urquhart's situation was apparently very vague. In the original Market-Garden plan the 52nd Lowland Division was to have been flown into the Arnhem area once Urquhart's men had found a suitable landing site—ideally by Thursday, September 21. When Urquhart's desperate situation became known, the 52nd's commanding officer, Major General Edmund Hakewill Smith, promptly offered to risk taking in part of his unit by glider, to land as close as possible to the beleaguered 1st Airborne. On Friday morning Browning had rejected the proposal, radioing: "Thanks for your message but offer not repeat not required as situation better than you think . . . 2nd Army definitely . . . intend fly you in to Deelen airfield as soon as situation allows." Later General Brereton, First Allied Airborne Army commander, noting the message in his diary, commented, "General Browning was over-optimistic and apparently then did not fully appreciate the plight of the Red Devils." At the time, Brereton seemed no better informed than Browning. In a report to Eisenhower, which was sent on to General Marshall in Washington on Friday night, Brereton said of the Nijmegen-Arnhem area: "the situation in this sector is showing great improvement."

Within hours the optimism of Brereton and Browning had faded. Friday's futile efforts to reach Urquhart seemed to have been the turning point for the Corps commander. According to his staff, "he was disgusted with General Thomas and the 43rd Wessex Division." He felt they had not moved fast enough. Thomas, he told them, had been "too anxious to tidy things up as he went along." Additionally, Browning's authority extended only so far: the moment British ground troops entered the Nijmegen area, administrative control passed over to General Horrocks, the XXX Corps commander; decisions would be made by Horrocks and by his chief, the British Second Army's General Miles C. Dempsey. There was little that Browning could do.

Sitting with the somewhat revived Mackenzie, Browning now learned for the first time the details of Urquhart's appalling predicament. Mackenzie, sparing nothing, recounted everything that had happened. Brigadier Walch remembers Mackenzie telling Browning that "the division is in a very tight perimeter and low in everything—food, ammunition and medical supplies." While the situation was acute, Mackenzie said, "if there is a chance of the Second Army getting to us, we can hold—but not for long." Walch recollects Mackenzie's grim summation. "There isn't much left," he said. Browning listened in silence. Then he assured Mackenzie that he had not given up hope. Plans were now afoot to get men and supplies into the bridgehead during Saturday night. But, Brigadier Walch says, "I do remember Browning telling Charles that there did not seem to be much chance of getting a good party across."

As Mackenzie set out for Driel once more, he was struck by the ambivalence of the thinking at Corps headquarters—and by the dilemma that created for him. Obviously the fate of the British 1st Airborne still hung in the balance. No one had as yet made any definite decisions. But what should he tell Urquhart? "After seeing the situation on both sides of the river," he says, "I was convinced a crossing from the south would not be successful and I could tell him that. Or, I could report, as I was told, that everyone was doing his best, that there would be a crossing and we should hold on. Which was better? Tell him that in my opinion there wasn't a chance in hell of anyone getting over? Or that help was on the way?" Mackenzie decided on the latter, for he felt it would help Urquhart "to keep people going if I put it that way."

Like Browning, the Allied high command was only now learning the true facts of the 1st Airborne's plight. In off-the-record briefings at Eisenhower's, at Brereton's and at Montgomery's headquarters, war correspondents were told that the "situation is serious, but every measure is being taken to relieve Urquhart." That minor note of concern represented a radical change in attitude. Since its inception, Market-Garden had been painted in public reports as an overwhelming success. On Thursday, September 21, under a headline announcing that a "tank paradise lies ahead," one British newspaper's lead story stated: "Hitler's northern flank is crumbling. Field Marshal Montgomery, with the brilliant aid of the First Airborne Army, has paved the way into the Ruhr—and to the end of the war." Even the staid London *Times* on Friday had such headlines as "On the Road to Arnhem; Tanks Across the Rhine"; only the subhead hinted of possible trouble ahead: "Coming Fight for Arnhem; Airborne Forces' Hard Time." Correspondents could hardly be blamed. Lack of communications, overenthusiasm on the part of Allied commanders and strict censorship prevented accurate reporting. Then, overnight, the picture changed. On Saturday, the twenty-third, the *Times*'s headline read: "2nd Army Meets Tough Opposition; Airborne Forces' Grim Fight," and the London *Daily Express* was calling Arnhem a "Patch of Hell."°

Yet hopes remained high. On this Saturday, the seventh day of Market-Garden, the weather over England cleared and Allied planes took to the air again.† The last of the great fleet of gliders, grounded in the Grantham area since Tuesday, set out finally for Gavin's 82nd with 3,385 troops—his long-awaited 325th Glider Infantry Regiment—and Taylor's hard-pressed 101st Division was brought up to full strength by nearly 3,000 more men. But

---

° Some of the war's finest reporting came out of Arnhem. The ten-man press team attached to the 1st Airborne Division included Major Roy Oliver, a public information officer; censors Flight Lieutenant Billy Williams and Captain Peter Brett; army photographers Sergeants Lewis and Walker; and correspondents Alan Wood, London *Daily Express;* Stanley Maxted and Guy Byam, BBC; Jack Smythe, Reuter's, and Marek Swiecicki, a Polish correspondent attached to Sosabowski's brigade. Although limited by sparse communications to bulletins of only a few hundred words per day, these men, in the finest tradition of war reporting, portrayed the agonies of Urquhart's men. I have been unable to locate a single correspondent of the original team. Presumably, all are dead.

† Inexplicably, some official and semiofficial British accounts contend that bad weather prevented aerial activity on Saturday, September 23. Meteorological, Corps and Allied Air Force after-action reports all record Saturday's weather as fair, with more missions flown than on any day since Tuesday, the nineteenth. In the semiofficial *Struggle for Europe,* Chester Wilmot erred in stating that on Saturday "aerial resupply had been thwarted by bad weather." The phrase altered his chronology of the battle thereafter. Other accounts, using Wilmot as a guide, have compounded the inaccuracies.

Sosabowski, under heavy attack at Driel, could not be reinforced with the remainder of his brigade. Browning was forced to direct the rest of the Poles to drop zones in the 82nd's area. Because of weather Brereton's three-day air plan to deliver some 35,000 men in the greatest airborne operation ever conceived had taken more than double the planned time.

Once again, although resupply missions were successful elsewhere, Urquhart's men, in their rapidly diminishing pocket about Oosterbeek, watched cargo fall into enemy hands. Unable to locate the Hartenstein drop zone, and flying through savage antiaircraft fire, the supply planes were in constant trouble; 6 of the 123 planes were shot down and 63 damaged. In a message to Browning, Urquhart reported:

231605 . . . Resupply by air; very small quantity picked up. Snipers now severely curtailing movement and therefore collection. Also roads so blocked by falling trees, branches and houses that movement in jeeps virtually impossible. Jeeps in any case practically out of action.

Close-in fighter support was inadequate, too. In the Arnhem area the weather had been bad throughout the morning, clearing only by midday. As a result only a few flights of R.A.F. Spitfires and Typhoons attacked targets about the perimeter. Urquhart was baffled. "In view of our complete aerial superiority," he later recollected, "I was bitterly disappointed by the lack of fighter support." But to his men, who had not seen a fighter since D Day, the previous Sunday, the attacks were heartening. By now, too, most of them had learned that British troops had finally reached the southern bank of the Rhine at Driel. Relief, they believed, was close at hand.

In spite of all the setbacks, now that General Thomas' troops were moving up the side roads to Driel, General Horrocks believed that Urquhart's worsening situation could be alleviated. Brilliant, imaginative and determined, Horrocks was opposed to throwing away all that had been gained. Yet he must find some way to move troops and supplies into the bridgehead. "I am certain," he later put it, "that these were about the blackest moments in my life." He was so distressed at "the picture of the airborne troops fighting their desperate battle on the other side of the river" that he could not sleep; and the severing of the corridor north of Veghel, cut since Friday afternoon, threatened the life of the entire operation.

Now every hour was vital. Like Horrocks, General Thomas was determined to get men across the river. His 43rd Wessex was going all-out in a two-phase operation: attacking to seize Elst and driving toward Driel. Although by now no one had any illusions that the Arnhem bridge could be captured—from aerial reconnaissance photos it was clear the enemy held it in strength—Thomas' right flank, terminating at Elst, had to be protected if any operations were to be conducted across the Rhine from Driel. And Horrocks had hopes that, in addition to the Poles, some British infantry might cross into the bridgehead on Saturday night.

His optimism was premature. On the low-lying secondary roads west of the main Nijmegen-Arnhem highway a giant bottleneck developed as Thomas' two brigades, each totaling about 3,000 men—one brigade attacking northeast toward Elst, the other driving north for Driel—attempted to move through the same crossroads. Enemy shelling added to the crowding and confusion. Thus, it was dark by the time the bulk of Thomas' 130th Brigade began to reach Driel—too late to join the Poles in an organized attempt to cross the river.

Shortly after midnight, Sosabowski's men, heavily supported by artillery, began crossing, this time in sixteen boats left from the 82nd's assault across the Waal. They came under intense fire and suffered heavy losses. Only 250 Poles made it to the northern bank, and of these only 200 reached the Hartenstein perimeter.

On this grim day Horrocks and Thomas received just one piece of good news: at 4 P.M. the corridor north of Veghel was reopened and traffic began flowing again. In the engineering columns were more assault craft, and the stubborn Horrocks was hopeful that they could be rushed forward in time to pour infantry across the river on Sunday night.

But could the division hang on another twenty-four hours? Urquhart's plight was rapidly growing worse. In his situation report to Browning on Saturday night, Urquhart had said:

232015: Many attacks during day by small parties infantry, SP guns, tanks including flame thrower tanks. Each attack accompanied by very heavy mortaring and shelling within Div perimeter. After many alarms and excursions the latter remains substantially unchanged, although very thinly held. Physical contact not yet made with those on south bank of river. Resupply a flop, small quantities of ammo only gathered in. Still no food and all ranks extremely dirty owing to shortage of water. Morale still adequate, but continued heavy mortaring and shelling is having obvious effects. We shall hold but at the same time hope for a brighter 24 hours ahead.

The afternoon's giant Allied glider lift had caught Field Marshal Walter Model by surprise. At this late date in the battle he had not anticipated any further Allied airborne landings. These new reinforcements, coming just as his counteroffensive was gaining momentum, could change the tide of battle—and even more might be on the way. For the first time since the beginning of the Allied attack he began to have doubts about the outcome.

Driving to Doetinchem he conferred with General Bittrich, demanding, as the II SS Panzer Corps commander remembers, "a quick finish to the British at Oosterbeek." Model needed every man and tank. Too great a force was being tied down in a battle that "should have been brought to an end days before." Model was "very excited," Bittrich says, "and kept repeating, 'When will things finally be over here?' "

Bittrich insisted that "we are fighting as we have never fought before." At Elst, Major Hans Peter Knaust was staving off British tank and infantry columns trying to proceed up the main highway to Arnhem. But Knaust could not hold at Elst and also attack west against the Poles and British at Driel. The moment his heavy

Tigers moved onto the polder they bogged down. The assault toward Driel was a task for infantry and lighter vehicles, Bittrich explained. "Model was never interested in excuses," Bittrich says, "but he understood me. Still, he gave me only twenty-four hours to finish the British off."

Bittrich drove to Elst to see Knaust. The major was worried. All day the forces against him had appeared to be growing stronger. While he knew British tanks could not leave the main highway, the possibility of attacks from the west concerned him. "A British breakthrough must be halted at all costs," Bittrich warned. "Can you hold for another twenty-four hours, while we clean up Oosterbeek?" Knaust assured Bittrich that he could. Leaving Knaust, the Panzer Corps commander immediately ordered Colonel Harzer of the Hohenstaufen Division to "intensify all attacks against the airborne tomorrow. I want the whole affair ended."

Harzer's problems were also difficult. Although Oosterbeek was completely encircled, its narrow streets were proving almost impossible for maneuvering tanks—especially for the 60-ton Tigers, "which tore up the road foundations, making them look like plowed fields, and ripped off the pavement when they turned." Additionally, Harzer told Bittrich, "everytime we compress the airborne pocket and shrink it even tighter, the British seem to fight harder." Bittrich advised that "strong attacks should be thrown from east and west at the base of the perimeter to cut the British off from the Rhine."

The Frundsberg Division commander, General Harmel, charged with holding and driving back the Allied forces in the Nijmegen-Arnhem area, heard from Bittrich, too. The assembling of his whole division delayed by the wreckage on the Arnhem bridge, Harmel had not been able to form a blocking front on both sides of the elevated "island" highway. The British attack at Oosterbeek had split his forces. Only part of his division had been in position on the western side when the British attacked. Now, what remained of his men and equipment was east of the highway. Elst would be held, Harmel assured Bittrich. The British could not advance up the main road. But he was powerless to halt the drive to Driel. "I cannot prevent them going up or coming back," he told Bittrich. The II SS Panzer Corps leader was firm. The next twenty-four hours would be critical, he warned Harmel. "The British will try everything to reinforce their bridgehead and also drive for Arnhem." Harzer's attacks against the Oosterbeek perimeter would succeed—provided that Harmel held. As Bittrich put it, "We'll get the nail. You must amputate the finger."

The guns of the 43rd were thundering, and in the southwest corner of the Oosterbeek perimeter a big gasometer blazed, throwing an eerie, flickering, yellowish light over the Rhine. As he climbed out of a boat on the northern bank, Colonel Charles Mackenzie could see why he had been warned by radio to wait for a guide. The shoreline was unrecognizable; boat wreckage, fallen trees, and shell craters had buried the road running back into the bridgehead. If he had tried to set out by himself he would certainly have become lost. Now, following an engineer, he was guided to the Hartenstein.

Mackenzie had not changed his mind about the report he would make to Urquhart. Once again, while waiting to be rowed over to the division perimeter, he had thought about his options. In spite of all the preparations that he had seen in Driel and on the southern bank, he remained skeptical that help would ever reach the division in time. He felt guilty about the report he had decided to make. Yet, there was still the chance that his own view was far too pessimistic.

In the cellar of the shattered Hartenstein, Urquhart was waiting. Mackenzie gave the Airborne commander the official view: "Help is on the way. We should hang on." Urquhart, Mackenzie remembers, "listened impassively, neither disheartened nor gladdened by the news." The unspoken question for both men remained the same: How much *longer* must they hold? At this time, in the first hours of Sunday, September 24, after eight days of battle, Urquhart's estimated strength was down to fewer than 2,500 men. And for all of them there was only one question: When will Monty's forces arrive? They had thought about it in the loneliness of trenches, gunpits and outposts, in the wrecks of houses and shops, and in the hospitals and dressing stations, where anxious uncomplaining men lay wounded on pallets, mattresses and bare floors.

With infantry on the south bank of the river, the paratroopers did not doubt that the Second Army would eventually cross. They wondered only if any of them would be alive to see the relief for which they had waited so long. In these last tragic hours annihilation was their constant fear, and to allay this dread, men tried to raise one another's morale by any means they could. Jokes made the rounds. Wounded men, still holding at their posts, disregarded their injuries, and examples of extraordinary daring were becoming commonplace. Above all, Urquhart's men were proud. They shared a spirit in those days that was stronger, they said later, than they would ever know again.

From his kit Lance Bombardier James Jones of an artillery troop took out the single nonmilitary item he had brought along —the flute he had used as a boy. "I just wanted to play it again," he remembers. "It was raining mortar bombs for three or four days straight and I was frightened to death. I got out the flute and began to play." Nearby, Lieutenant James Woods, the gun-position officer, had an idea. With Jones leading, Lieutenant Woods and two other gunners climbed out of their trenches and began to march around the gun positions. As they proceeded single file, Lieutenant Woods began to sing. Behind him the two troopers removed their helmets and drummed on them with sticks. Battered men heard the strains of "British Grenadiers" and "Scotland the Brave" filtering softly through the area. Faintly at first, other men began to sing and then, with Woods "going at the top of his voice," the artillery positions erupted in song.

In the Schoonoord Hotel on the Utrecht-Arnhem road, approximately midway along the eastern side of the perimeter, Dutch volunteers and British medics cared for hundreds of wounded under the watchful eyes of German guards. Hendrika van der Vlist wrote in her diary:

Sunday, September 24. This is the day of the Lord. War rages outside. The building is shaking. That is why the doctors cannot operate or fix casts. We cannot wash the wounded because nobody can venture out to find water under these conditions. The army chaplain scribbles in his notebook. I ask him what time the service will be held.

Padre G. A. Pare finished his notes. With Hendrika he made the rounds of all the rooms in the hotel. The shelling seemed "particularly noisy," he recalls, "and I could hardly hear my own voice above the battle outside." Yet, "looking into the faces of men stretched out all over the floor," Chaplain Pare "felt inspired to fight the noise outside with God's peace inside." Quoting from St. Matthew, Pare said, " 'Take no thought for the morrow. What ye shall eat or what ye shall drink, or where withal ye shall be clothed.' " Then he, like the men in the artillery positions, began to sing. As he began "Abide With Me," men just listened. Then they began to hum and sing softly themselves. Against the thunderous barrage outside the Schoonoord, hundreds of wounded and dying men took up the words, " 'When other helpers fail and comforts flee, God of the helpless, O abide with me.' "

Across the street from the church in lower Oosterbeek, Kate ter Horst left her five children and the eleven other civilians sheltering in the ten-by-six-foot cellar of her house and made her way past the wounded on the upper floor. The fourteen-room, 200-year-old house, a former vicarage, was totally unrecognizable. The windows were gone and "every foot of space in the main hall, dining room, study, garden room, bedrooms, corridors, kitchen, boiler room and attic was crowded with wounded," Mrs. ter Horst recalls. They lay, too, in the garage and even under the stairs. In all, more than three hundred injured men crowded the house and grounds, and others were being brought in by the minute. Outdoors on this Sunday morning Kate ter Horst saw that a haze hung over the battlefield. "The sky is yellow," she wrote, "and there are dark clouds hanging down like wet rags.

The earth has been torn open." On the grounds she saw "the dead, our dead, wet through from rain, and stiff. Lying on their faces, just as they were yesterday and the day before—the man with the tousled beard and the one with the black face and many, many others." Eventually, fifty-seven men would be buried in the garden, "one of them a mere boy," Mrs. ter Horst wrote, "who died inside the house for lack of space." The lone doctor among the medical teams in the house, Captain Randall Martin, had told Mrs. ter Horst that the boy "had simply banged his head against a radiator until he was gone."

Picking her way gingerly about the rooms, Kate ter Horst thought of her husband, Jan, who had left on Tuesday night by bicycle to scout the area and bring back information about German positions to an artillery officer. The perimeter had been formed while he was gone and, in the heavy fighting, Jan was unable to get back home. They would not see each other for two more weeks. Working with Dr. Martin and the orderlies ever since Wednesday, Mrs. ter Horst had hardly slept. Going from room to room, she prayed with the wounded and read to them from the 91st Psalm, "Thou shalt not be afraid for the terror by night, nor for the arrow that flieth by day."

Now, all this morning, snipers, infiltrating into the perimeter during the night, were firing "shamelessly into a house from which never a shot was fired," she wrote. "Bullets whizzed through rooms and corridors crowded with helpless people." Carrying a stretcher past a window, two orderlies were shot. Then, what everyone feared most might happen occurred: Dr. Martin was wounded. "It's only my ankle," he told Mrs. ter Horst. "In the afternoon I'll go hopping around again."

Outside the sniping gave way to shelling. The thunder and crash of mortar bursts "defies description," Kate ter Horst recorded. To Private Michael Growe, "the lady seemed terribly calm and unflustered." Growe, already wounded in the thigh from shrapnel, was now hit again in the left foot by a shell burst. Hastily medics moved Growe and other newly injured men away from a line of French windows.

Corporal Daniel Morgans, hit in the head and right knee as he was holding a position near the Oosterbeek church, was carried to the Ter Horst house just as a German tank came up the road. As an orderly was explaining to Morgans that "they were practically out of dressings and had no anesthetics or food, and only a little water," the tank sent a shell crashing against the house. In an upstairs room, Private Walter Boldock, with bullet wounds in the side and back, stared in horror as the tank "ground and wheeled. I could hear the gibberish chatter of machine guns and then a shell tore through the wall above my back. Plaster and debris began falling everywhere and many of the wounded were killed." Downstairs Bombardier E. C. Bolden, a medical orderly, was in a white-hot rage. Grabbing a Red Cross flag, he rushed out of the house and straight for the tank. Corporal Morgans heard him clearly. "What the hell are you doing?" Bolden screamed at the German tank commander. "This house is clearly marked with a Red Cross flag. Get the hell away from here!" As the anxious wounded listened, they heard the sound of the tank backing off. Bolden returned to the house, "almost as angry," Morgans remembers, "as when he left. We asked him what happened." Bolden replied tersely: "The German apologized but he also got the hell out."

Although the house was not shelled again, there was no letup in the fire about them. Kate ter Horst wrote: "All around these men are dying. Must they breathe their last in such a hurricane? Oh, God! Give us a moment's silence. Give us quiet, if only for a short moment, so that they at least can die. Grant them a moment's holy silence while they pass on to Eternity."

All about the perimeter, tanks crashed through defenses as weary, groggy troopers reached the limits of exhaustion. There were horrors everywhere—particularly from flamethrowers. In one incident of SS brutality, a jeep carrying wounded under a Red Cross flag was stopped by four Germans. One of the medics tried to explain that he was carrying wounded to a casualty station. The Germans turned a flamethrower on him, then walked away. But throughout the battle, both at the Arnhem bridge and in the perimeter, there were singular examples of chivalry.

On Brigadier Hackett's eastern perimeter defenses a German officer drove up to the British positions under a white flag and asked to see the commander. Hackett met him and learned that the Germans "were about to attack, first laying down mortar and artillery fire on my forward positions." As the Germans knew that one of the casualty stations was in the line of attack, Hackett was requested to move his forward positions back 600 yards. "We do not want to put down a barrage that will hit the wounded," the German explained. Hackett knew he could not comply. "If the line had been moved back the distance demanded by the Germans," General Urquhart later wrote, "it would have put Divisional headquarters 200 yards behind the German lines." Despite his inability to move, Hackett noted that when the attack finally came the barrage was carefully laid down to the south of the casualty station.

At the Tafelberg, another doctor, Major Guy Rigby-Jones, who had been operating on a billiard table in the game room of the hotel, lost all his equipment when an 88 shell came through the roof of the building. He had not been able to operate since Thursday, although one of the field ambulance teams had set up a theater in the Petersburg Hotel. "We had 1,200 to 1,300 casualties and neither the nursing facilities nor the staff to properly treat them," he remembers. "All we had was morphia to kill the pain. Our main problem was food and water. We had already drained the central heating system to get water, but now, having ceased operating, I became more or less a quartermaster, trying to feed the wounded." One of them, Major John Waddy of the 156th Battalion, shot in the groin by a sniper on Tuesday, had been wounded again. A mortar shell landing on the window sill of a large bay window exploded and a shell fragment embedded itself in Waddy's left foot. Then the room took a direct hit. Waddy's right shoulder, face and chin were lacerated by falling bricks and wood splinters. Dr. Graeme Warrack, the division's chief medical officer, whose headquarters were at the Tafelberg, rushed outside. Waddy hauled himself up to see Warrack standing in the street shouting at the Germans: "You bloody bastards! Can't anybody recognize a Red Cross?"

The Van Maanen family—Anje, her brother Paul and her aunt—were working around the clock in the Tafelberg, under direction of Dr. van Maanen. Paul, who was a medical student, remembers that "Sunday was terrible. We seemed to be hit all the time. I remembered that we mustn't show fear in front of the patients, but I was ready to jump out of the room and scream. I didn't, because the wounded stayed so calm." As injured men were carried from one damaged room to another, Paul remembers that "we began to sing. We sang for the British, for the Germans, for ourselves. Then everyone seemed to be doing it and with all the emotion people would stop because they were crying, but they would start up again."

For young Anje van Maanen, the romantic dream of liberation by the bright stalwart young men who had dropped from the skies was ending in despair. Many Dutch civilians brought to the Tafelberg had died of their wounds; two, Anje noted in her diary, were "lovely girls and good skaters, as old as I am, just seventeen. Now I will never see them again." To Anje the hotel now seemed to be constantly hit by shells. In the cellar she began to cry. "I am afraid to die," she wrote. "The explosions are enormous and every shell kills. How can God allow this hell?"

By 9:30 A.M. on Sunday morning Dr. Warrack decided to do something about the hell. The nine casualty stations and hospitals in the area were so jammed with wounded from both sides that he began to feel that "the battle could no longer continue in this fashion." Medical teams "were working under impossible conditions, some without surgical instruments." And under the intensified German attacks, casualties were steadily mounting—among them now the courageous Brigadier Shan Hackett, who suffered severe leg and stomach wounds from a mortar-shell burst shortly before 8 A.M.

Warrack had determined on a plan which needed General

Urquhart's consent, and he set out for the Hartenstein. "I told the General," Warrack says, "that despite Red Cross flags, all the hospitals were being shelled. One had taken six hits and was set afire, forcing us to quickly evacuate a hundred fifty injured." The wounded, he said, were being "badly knocked about, and the time had come to make some sort of arrangement with the Germans." As it was quite impossible to evacuate wounded across the Rhine, Warrack believed that many lives would be saved "if casualties were handed over to the Germans for treatment in their hospitals in Arnhem."

Urquhart, Warrack recalls, "seemed resigned." He agreed to the plan. But under no circumstances, he warned Warrack, "must the enemy be allowed to think that this was the beginning of a crack in the formation's position." Warrack was to make clear to the Germans that the step was being taken solely on humane grounds. Negotiations could take place, Urquhart said, "on condition that the Germans understand you are a doctor representing your patients, not an official emissary from the division." Warrack was permitted to ask for a truce period during the afternoon so that the battlefield could be cleared of wounded before "both sides got on with the fight."

Warrack hurried off to find Lieutenant Commander Arnnoldus Wolters, the Dutch liaison officer, and Dr. Gerritt van Maanen, both of whom he asked to help in the negotiations. Because Wolters, who would act as interpreter, was in the Dutch military and "might run a great risk going to a German headquarters," Warrack gave him the pseudonym "Johnson." The three men quickly headed for the Schoonoord Hotel to contact the German division medical officer.

By coincidence, that officer, twenty-nine-year-old Major Egon Skalka, claims he had reached the same conclusion as Warrack. As Skalka recalls that Sunday morning, he felt "something had to be done not only for our wounded but the British in *der Hexenkessel*. In the Schoonoord Hotel "casualties lay everywhere—even on the floor." According to Skalka, he had come to see "the British chief medical officer to suggest a battlefield clearing" before

Warrack arrived. Whoever first had the idea, they did meet. Warrack's impression of the young German doctor was that "he was effeminate in appearance, but sympathetic and apparently quite anxious to ingratiate himself with the British—just in case." Confronting the slender, dapper officer, handsome in his finely cut uniform, Warrack, with "Johnson" interpreting, made his proposal. As they talked, Skalka studied Warrack, "a tall, lanky, dark-haired fellow, phlegmatic like all Englishmen. He seemed terribly tired but otherwise not in bad shape." Skalka was prepared to agree to the evacuation plan, but, he told Warrack, "first we will have to go to my headquarters to make sure there are no objections from my General." Skalka refused to take Dr. van Maanen with them. In a captured British jeep, Skalka, Warrack and "Johnson" set out for Arnhem with Skalka driving. Skalka recalls that he "drove very fast, zigzagging back and forth. I did not want Warrack to orient himself and he would have had a tough time of it the way I drove. We went very fast, part of the time under fire, and twisted and turned into the city."

To Wolters, the short drive into Arnhem was "sad and miserable." Wreckage lay everywhere. Houses were still smoking or in ruins. Some of the roads they followed, chewed up by tank tracks and cratered by shellfire, "looked like plowed fields." Wrecked guns, overturned jeeps, charred armored vehicles and "the crumpled bodies of the dead" lay like a trail all the way into Arnhem. Skalka had not blindfolded the two men, nor did Wolters feel he made any attempt to conceal the route he took. It struck him that the elegant SS medical officer seemed "eager for us to see the German strength." Through the still-smoking, debris-strewn streets of Arnhem, Skalka drove northeast and pulled up outside Lieutenant Colonel Harzer's headquarters, the high school on Hezelbergherweg.

Although the arrival of Warrack and Wolters created surprise among the staff officers, Harzer, alerted by phone, was waiting for them. Skalka, leaving the two officers in an outer room, reported to his commander. Harzer was angry. "I was amazed," he says, "that Skalka had not blindfolded them. Now they knew the exact location of my headquarters." Skalka had laughed. "The way I drove I would be very surprised if they could find their way anywhere," he assured Harzer.

The two Germans sat down with the British emissaries. "The medical officer proposed that his British wounded be evacuated from the perimeter since they no longer had the room or supplies to care for them," Harzer says. "It meant calling a truce for a couple of hours. I told him I was sorry our countries were fighting. Why should we fight, after all? I agreed to his proposal."

Wolters—"a Canadian soldier named Johnson," as Warrack introduced him—remembers the conference in a completely different context. "At first the German SS colonel refused to even consider a truce," he says. "There were several other staff officers in the room, including the acting chief of staff, Captain Schwarz, who finally turned to Harzer and said that the whole matter would have to be taken up with the General." The Germans left the room. "As we waited," Wolters says, "we were offered sandwiches and brandy. Warrack warned me not to drink on an empty stomach. Whatever kind of filling was in the sandwiches was covered with sliced onions."

As the Germans reentered the room, "everyone snapped to attention and there was much 'Heil Hitlering.'" General Bittrich, hatless, in his long black leather coat, came in. "He stayed only a moment," Wolters remembers. Studying the two men, Bittrich said, *Ich bedauere sehr diesen Krieg zwischen unseren Vaterländern"* (I regret this war between our two nations). The General listened quietly to Warrack's evacuation plan and gave his consent. "I agreed," Bittrich says, "because a man cannot—provided, of course, that he has such feelings to start with—lose all humanity, even during the most bitter fight." Then Bittrich handed Warrack a bottle of brandy. "This is for your General," he told Warrack, and he withdrew.

By 10:30 A.M. Sunday, agreement on the partial truce was reached, although Wolters recollects "that the Germans seemed worried. Both the Tafelberg and the Schoonoord hotels were sitting on the front lines and the Germans could not guarantee to stop mortaring and shelling." Harzer was mainly concerned about the long-range shelling of the British south of the Rhine and whether it could be controlled during the casualty evacuation. Skalka says that after assurances had been given on this point, he received a radio message from British Second Army headquarters. "It was simply addressed to the medical officer, 9th SS Panzer Division, thanking me and asking if a cease-fire could extend long enough for the British to bring up medical supplies, drugs and bandages from across the Rhine." Skalka radioed back, "We do not need your help but request only that your air force refrain from bombing our Red Cross trucks continually." He was answered immediately: "Unfortunately, such attacks occur on both sides." Skalka thought the message "ridiculous." Angrily he replied, "Sorry, but I have not seen our air force in two years." Back came the British message: "Just stick to the agreement." Skalka was now enraged, so much so, he claims, that he radioed back, "Lick my —— "*

The arrangement, as finally worked out, called for a two-hour truce beginning at 3 P.M. The wounded would leave the perimeter by a designated route near the Tafelberg Hotel. Every effort was to be made "to slacken fire or stop completely." Troops on both sides holding front-line positions were warned to hold their fire. As Skalka began to order "every available ambulance and jeep to assemble behind the front lines," Warrack and Wolters, about to head back to their own lines, were allowed to fill their pockets with morphia and medical supplies. Wolters "was glad to get out of there, especially from the moment Schwarz said to me, 'You don't speak German like a Britisher.'"

En route back to the perimeter, a Red Cross flag flying from their jeep and escorted by another German medical officer, Warrack and Wolters were permitted to stop at St. Elisabeth's Hospi-

---

* Skalka's account that some exchange of messages took place is probably true. Yet the wording of the messages is certainly questionable, especially his answer regarding the Luftwaffe, which was in the air during the week, harassing the British drops. Further, it is a belittlement of forces of his own country. Such a contemptuous assessment of one's own side to an enemy was certainly uncommon among the SS.

tal to inspect conditions and visit the British wounded—among them Brigadier Lathbury, who, with badges of rank removed, was now "Lance Corporal" Lathbury. They were greeted by the chief British medical officer, Captain Lipmann Kessel; the head of the surgical team, Major Cedric Longland; and the senior Dutch surgeon, Dr. van Hengel—all of whom, Warrack remembers, "were desperately anxious for news." Heavy fighting had taken place about the hospital. At one point there had even been a pitched battle in the building with Germans firing over the heads of patients in the wards, Kessel reported. But since Thursday the area had been quiet and Warrack discovered that, in contrast to the harrowing ordeal of the wounded in the perimeter, in St. Elisabeth's "British casualties were in beds with blankets and sheets, and well cared for by Dutch nuns and doctors." Warning Kessel to be prepared for a heavy flow of casualties, the two men returned to Oosterbeek, just in time, Warrack recalls, "to step into a packet of mortaring near the Tafelberg."

At 3 P.M. the partial truce began. The firing suddenly diminished and then stopped altogether. Lance Bombardier Percy Parkes, for whom the "overwhelming noise had become normal, found the silence so unreal that for a second I thought I was dead." With British and German medical officers and orderlies supervising the moves, ambulances and jeeps from both sides began loading casualties. Sergeant Dudley R. Pearson, the 4th Parachute Brigade's chief clerk, was put beside his Brigadier's stretcher on a jeep. "So you got it too, Pearson," said Hackett. Pearson was wearing only his boots and trousers. His right shoulder was heavily bandaged "where shrapnel had torn a huge hole." Hackett was gray-faced and obviously in great pain from his stomach wound. As they moved off toward Arnhem, Hackett said, "Pearson, I hope you won't think I'm pulling rank, but I think I'm a bit worse off than you are. At the hospital do you mind if they get to me first?"*

* Both Lathbury and Hackett became "lance corporals" in the hospital. Sergeant Dave Morris, who gave blood to Hackett before his operation, was cautioned that the Brigadier's identity was not to be revealed. Lathbury, in the hospital since the nineteenth, got his first news of the division when the Oosterbeek wounded arrived

Lieutenant Pat Glover, who had jumped with Myrtle the "parachick," was moved to St. Elisabeth's in agony. A bullet had severed two veins in his right hand and on the way to the Schoonoord dressing station he was hit again by shrapnel in the right calf. There was so little morphia that he was told he could not be given a shot unless he deemed it absolutely necessary. Glover did not ask for any. Now, sleeping fitfully, he found himself thinking of Myrtle. He could not remember what day she had been killed. During the fighting he and his batman, Private Joe Scott, had traded Myrtle's satchel back and forth. Then, in a slit trench under fire, Glover suddenly realized that Myrtle's bag was not there. "Where's Myrtle?" he had yelled to Scott. "She's up there, sir." Scott pointed to the top of Glover's trench. Inside her bag, Myrtle lay on her back, feet in the air. During the night Glover and Scott buried the chicken in a shallow little grave near a hedge. As Scott brushed earth over the spot, he looked at Glover and said, "Well, Myrtle was game to the last, sir." Glover remembered he had not taken off Myrtle's parachute wings. Now, in a haze of pain, he was glad that he had buried her with honor and properly—with her badge of rank—as befitted those who died in action.

At the Schoonoord, Hendrika van der Vlist watched as German orderlies began to move casualties out. Suddenly firing began. One of the Germans yelled, "If it does not stop we will open fire and not a casualty, a doctor or a nurse will come out alive." Hendrika paid no attention. "It is always the youngest soldiers

—including the information that Urquhart had been able to rejoin the division and that Frost's men had held the Arnhem bridge for almost four days. Both brigadiers later escaped from the hospital with the help of the Dutch and hid out. Lathbury eventually joined the irrepressible Major Digby Tatham-Warter, who, dressed in civilian clothes and working with the Dutch underground, "went about quite openly and on one occasion helped to push a German staff car out of a ditch." With a group of approximately 120 troopers, medics and pilots who had been hidden by the Dutch, and led by a Dutch guide, Lathbury reached American troops south of the Rhine on the evening of October 22. The incredible Tatham-Warter helped about 150 British soldiers to escape. Incidentally, it took the author seven years to discover his whereabouts—then by accident. My British publisher met him in Kenya where he has been living since the end of the war. Tatham-Warter says that he "carried the umbrella in battle more for identification purposes than for anything else, because I was always forgetting the password."

who yell the loudest," she noted, "and we're used to the German threats by now." The firing ceased and the loading continued.

Several times again firing broke out as the long lines of walking wounded and convoys of jeeps, ambulances and trucks moved out toward Arnhem. "Inevitably," General Urquhart recalled, "there were misunderstandings. It is not easy to still a battle temporarily." Doctors at the Tafelberg had "some uneasy moments as they cleared combative Germans off the premises." And nearly everyone remembers that the recently arrived Poles could not understand the necessity for the partial cease-fire. "They had many old scores to settle," says Urquhart, "and saw no legitimate reason for holding their fire." Ultimately, they were "prevailed upon to curb their eagerness until the evacuation was completed."

Major Skalka, along with Dr. Warrack, kept the convoys moving throughout the afternoon. Some 200 walking wounded were led out and more than 250 men were carried in the medical convoys. "I have never seen anything like the conditions at Oosterbeek," Skalka says. "It was nothing but death and wreckage."

At St. Elisabeth's, Lieutenant Peter Stainforth, recovering from a chest wound received in Arnhem, heard the first walking wounded coming in. "I felt a shiver of excitement run up my spine," he says. "I have never been so proud. They came in and the rest of us were horror-stricken. Every man had a week's growth of beard. Their battle dress was torn and stained; and filthy, blood-soaked bandages poked out from all of them. The most compelling thing was their eyes—red-rimmed, deep-sunk, peering out from drawn, mud-caked faces made haggard by lack of sleep, and yet they walked in undefeated. They looked fierce enough to take over the place right then and there."

As the last convoy left Oosterbeek, Warrack thanked the SS medical officer for his help. "Skalka looked me in the eye and said, 'Can I have that in writing?' " Warrack ignored the remark. At 5 P.M. the battle began again as though it had never stopped.

At Lance Bombardier Percy Parkes's gun position near the Dolderen laundry, "all hell broke loose again. The Jerries threw

559

everything at us." After the relative quiet during the evacuation of the wounded, Parkes felt a sense of relief. "Everything had returned to normal, and I could orient to that. I was back in business again." Germans, taking advantage of the temporary truce, had infiltrated many areas. Men heard screaming and firing from all directions as Germans and British chased one another through streets and gardens. From his trench Parkes saw a tank coming across a cabbage patch toward battery headquarters. Two artillerymen sprinted for a 6-pounder on the road. As the troopers began to fire, Parkes looked up in amazement as cabbages began to sail over his trench. "The force of the gun was sucking up the cabbages, pulling them right out of the ground and hurling them through the air. Then there was a tremendous bang and we saw a shell hit the tank."

Major Robert Cain heard someone yell, "Tigers!" and he raced for the small antitank gun set up alongside a building in his block. A gunner ran up the street to help him. Together the two men rolled the gun into position. "Fire!" Cain shouted. He saw that the shell had hit the tank, disabling it. "Let's have another go to be sure," he yelled. The gunner looked at Cain and shook his head. "Can't, sir," he said. "She's finished. The recoil mechanism's gone."

Inside the Ter Horst house the noise was so loud that everyone was numbed and deafened. Suddenly Kate ter Horst felt "a tremendous shock. There was a thunder of bricks. Timbers cracked and there were stifled cries from all sides." The force of the explosion had jammed the cellar door. In the choking dust that swirled through the little room, she heard "men working with spades and tools . . . sawing and the breaking of timbers . . . footsteps crunching through bricks and mortar . . . and heavy things dragged back and forth." The cellar door was broken open and fresh air poured in. Upstairs Kate saw that part of the corridor and the garden room were open to the outdoors and a section of one wall had been blown in. Men lay everywhere, tossed about by the explosion. Dr. Martin had been hit again and was unable to get about at all. A soldier who had been brought in several days earlier suffering from shell shock roamed through the carnage in the house. Staring at Kate ter Horst, he said, "I think I've seen you someplace before." Gently she led him to the cellar and found room for him on the stone floor. Almost immediately he fell asleep. Wakening later, he moved over to Mrs. ter Horst. "We can be taken at any moment now," he said quietly. He went to sleep again. Leaning tiredly against a wall, her five children beside her, Kate waited, as "the ghastly hours stretched slowly."

In a trench not far from Major Cain's position, Sergeant Alf Roullier saw another tank appear in the street. He and a gunner dashed to the only antitank gun that seemed to be left in the artillery troop he was with. The two men reached the gun just as the tank turned toward them. They fired and saw a flash as the tank was hit. At that moment a machine gun opened up. The gunner with Roullier gasped and sagged against him. As Roullier turned to ease the man down, a bullet tore into his left hand. It began to shake uncontrollably and Roullier assumed the bullet had hit a nerve. Easing the gunner over his back, Roullier made it to his trench. "I'll go get help," he told the bloodstained trooper. At the Ter Horst house Roullier stopped, unwilling to go in. He heard men screaming and babbling, begging for water, crying out the names of relatives. "Oh, God!" Roullier said. "What have I come here for?" Bombardier E. C. Bolden appeared at that moment. "Blimey, mate," Bolden said, looking at Roullier's shaking hand, "you been out typewriting?" Roullier explained that he had come for help for the wounded gunner. "All right," Bolden said, bandaging Roullier's hand, "I'll get there." Returning to his position, Roullier passed the Ter Horst garden and stopped, staring in horror. He had never seen so many dead in one place before. Some had smocks over their faces but others were uncovered and "their eyes stared off in all directions." There were piles of dead, so many that a man could not step between them.

At the trench Roullier waited until Bolden arrived with two stretcher-bearers. "Don't worry," Bolden told Roullier. He raised his thumb. "Everything will be O.K." Roullier didn't think so. Back in England, the thirty-one-year-old trooper had pleaded to go on the mission. His age was against it, and although Roullier was an artilleryman, he had become acting mess sergeant. But he had won out, and finally had been allowed to go. Now, staring at the tired, thirsty, hungry troopers around him, he remembers that "something clicked in my mind. I just forgot the battle. I was obsessed with getting us something to eat." He does not know how long he crawled through torn-up gardens and half-demolished houses in the area, ransacking shelves and searching cellars for bits and pieces of food. Someplace he found an undamaged galvanized tub. Into it he threw everything he found—a few withered carrots, some onions, a bag of potatoes, salt and some bouillon cubes. Near the house he found a chicken coop. Only one bird was still alive. Roullier took it along.

On the stone floor of a ruined house he built a circle of bricks to hold the tub. Tearing strips of wallpaper off walls and using pieces of wood, he built a fire. He does not remember the battle still raging in the streets as he made one more trip outside to find water—but he staggered back with the tub partly filled. He killed and plucked the chicken, and dropped it into the tub. Just at dusk when he decided the stew was finished he pulled a pair of curtains off a window frame to wrap the hot handles of the pot and, with the help of another trooper, set out for the trenches. For the first time in hours he was aware of mortars coming in. The two men moved at intervals, stopping at each near burst, then going on again. At the artillery position, Roullier yelled out, "Come and get it!" Amazed, bleary troopers appeared in cautious groups with battered ration cans and mess kits. Dazedly mumbling their thanks, they dipped into the hot tub and disappeared into the growing darkness. In ten minutes the stew was gone. Peering into the bottom of the tub, Alf Roullier could just make out a few small chunks of potatoes. He picked them out and, for the first time that day, ate some food. He had never felt happier.

On the grounds of the Hartenstein Hotel in a five-man trench, Sergeant Leonard Overton, the glider pilot, stared out into the growing dusk. The four men who shared his trench had disappeared. Suddenly Overton saw dark shapes approaching. "It's only us," someone said quietly. As the four soldiers dropped into the trench, Overton saw that they carried a gas cape bundled together. Carefully the men opened the cape and, holding a can at one edge, emptied almost a pint of rain water into the container. One man produced a cube of tea and began to stir the liquid. Overton looked on, dazed. "We had had nothing to eat or drink that day and only two hard biscuits which we had shared on Saturday," he says. Then, to Overton's surprise, the troopers offered the tin can to him. He took a sip and passed it on. "Many happy returns," each man told him softly. Overton had forgotten that Sunday, September 24, was his twenty-third birthday.

In the Schoonoord the critical cases and the walking wounded were gone, but shell-shocked men still lingered in the big hotel. As Chaplain Pare walked through a half-deserted room, he heard a thin shaking voice somewhere in the echoing building singing "Just a song at twilight." Climbing to an upstairs room, Pare knelt beside a badly shocked young trooper. "Padre," the boy said, "will you tuck me in? I get so frightened with all the noise." Pare had no blanket but he pretended to cover the trooper. "That feels fine, Padre. I feel very well now. Will you do me one more favor?" Pare nodded. "Say the Lord's Prayer with me." Pare did. He soothed back the young man's hair. "Now close your eyes," Pare told him. "Sleep well. God bless you." The trooper smiled. "Good night, Padre. God bless you." Two hours later a medic came for Pare. "You know that lad you said the prayers with?" Pare asked, "What's wrong?" The medic shook his head. "He died just now. He said to tell you he couldn't stand the noise outside."

As evening set in, Colonel R. Payton-Reid in the KOSB's area of the perimeter was not unhappy to see "the twenty-fourth grow to its melancholy close. The high hopes of early support by the ground forces was a subject now, by mutual consent, taboo."

Late Sunday night Lieutenant Neville Hay, the Phantom Net operator, was called into General Urquhart's room in the cellar of the Hartenstein. "He handed me a long message," Hay says, "and told me when I had finished encoding it to return it to him. I remember him saying that perhaps by that time he wouldn't have to send it." Hay was stunned as he read the message. "What it really meant was that they had to come and get us or we would be wiped out." Hay encoded the signal and returned it to Urquhart. "I hoped he wouldn't have to send it, either," Hay says. As sent out, the message read:

Urquhart to Browning. Must warn you unless physical contact is made with us early 25 Sept. consider it unlikely we can hold out long enough. All ranks now exhausted. Lack of rations, water, ammunition and weapons with high officer casualty rate. Even slight enemy offensive action may cause complete disintegration. If this happens all will be ordered to break toward bridgehead if anything rather than surrender. Any movement at present in face of enemy impossible. Have attempted our best and will do so as long as possible.°

Over two consecutive nights, attempts to move men and supplies into Urquhart's lodgment had failed. Yet the stubborn XXX Corps commander, General Horrocks, refused to abandon the effort. If the bridgehead was to be saved and the relief of Urquhart's men effected, it must take place this Sunday night. Once again the weather was unfavorable; no help could be expected from England-based planes flying supply or support missions. But troops were now in strength in the Driel-Nijmegen area, and Horrocks—achieving the near-impossible by driving his entire corps up the narrow, one-tank-wide corridor to his spearpoint on the Rhine—was obsessed by the 400 yards of river that separated him from the airborne forces. Success was tantalizingly close. He ordered General Thomas' 43rd Wessex to make one last push: with the remaining Poles, troops of Lieutenant Colonel Gerald Tilly's 4th Dorsets would assault the river and try to cross into the bridgehead beginning at 10 P.M.

Tilly's move would be a first step in a wider plan. "If things

° Several versions of this message have appeared in other accounts of the battle. The one above is the original. Lieutenant Neville Hay retained his timed Phantom message logs and made them available to me. I am extremely grateful for his co-operation.

51.   From Phantom   Source G Ops 1330 hrs. Enemy continues to
      1 Airborne Div   attack in small parties with SP guns in support.
                                 Small numbers of Pz Kw IV area 694788. Mortar
                                 fire continues. Poles who crossed last night
                                 now fighting area 698782.

                                 TOO 241330   THI 241945

52.   From Phantom   Source G Ops 0845 hrs. Only 300 Polish over
      1 Airborne Div   last night. Water and food and ammunition short.
                                 Shelling and mortaring continues and intense.

                                 TOO 241630   THI 241805

53.   From Phantom   Perimeter very weak and casualties mounting.
      1 Airborne Div   Essential relieving troops make contact
                                 immediately on crossing. Enemy attacks
                                 made with SP guns or tanks and following
                                 infantry were NOT formidable. Heavy shelling
                                 and mortaring continues.

                                 TOO 242205   THI 242330

54.   From Phantom   URQUHART TO BROWNING. MUST WARN YOU UNLESS
      1 Airborne Div   PHYSICAL CONTACT IS MADE WITH US EARLY 25
                                 SEP CONSIDER IT UNLIKELY WE CAN HOLD OUT LONG
                                 ENOUGH, ALL RANKS NOW EXHAUSTED. LACK OF
                                 RATIONS, WATER, AMMUNITION AND WEAPONS WITH
                                 HIGH OFFICER CASUALTY RATE. EVEN SLIGHT
                                 ENEMY OFFENSIVE ACTION MAY CAUSE COMPLETE
                                 DISINTEGRATION. IF THIS HAPPENS, ALL WILL
                                 BE ORDERED TO BREAK TOWARD BRIDGEHEAD IF
                                 ANYTHING RATHER THAN SURRENDER. ANY MOVEMENT
                                 AT PRESENT IN FACE OF ENEMY IMPOSSIBLE.
                                 HAVE ATTEMPTED OUR BEST AND WILL DO SO AS
                                 LONG AS POSSIBLE.

                                 TOO 250830   THI 251040

55.   From Phantom   Source G2 Ops 1330 hrs. Perimeter still
      1 Airborne Div   holding though situation so fluid impossible
                                 state exact locations.

                                 TOO 251345   THI 252035

Extract from Lieutenant Hay's "Phantom" log, showing memorable Urquhart message to Browning.

went well," Horrocks later wrote, "I hoped to side-slip the 43rd Division across the Rhine farther to the west and carry out a left hook against the German force attacking the airborne perimeter." The alternative was withdrawal. On this eighth day of Market-Garden, Horrocks obstinately refused to face that choice. Others, however, were now seriously planning how it might be done.

According to his chief of staff, Brigadier Gordon Walch, the First Airborne Corps commander, General Browning, now spoke "quite openly about withdrawing." While the 43rd Wessex was moving up to Driel the decision had been in the balance, but "as soon as they became stuck, Browning became convinced we would have to get Urquhart's men out." The British Second Army commander, General Miles C. Dempsey, had reached the same conclusion. He had not met with Horrocks since the beginning of the attack. Now, as time ran out, Dempsey ordered Horrocks to a meeting down the corridor at St. Oedenrode. In line of command, Dempsey, on authority from Montgomery, would have the last word. The agonizing decision would be forced on them by one man—Field Marshal Model.

As Horrocks drove south to St. Oedenrode, Lieutenant Colonel Tilly of the 4th Dorsets prepared for the night's river crossing. His battalion was rushing up to the assembly area in Driel, and assault craft, now that the corridor was open again, were on the way. Tilly's instructions were clear. Briefed personally by his brigade commander, Brigadier Ben Walton, Tilly was told to "broaden the base of the perimeter." The crossing was to be made at the old ferry site, about a mile west of Oosterbeek. Once across, the Dorsets were "to hang on until reinforced." They would travel light, carrying only enough food and ammunition to last three or four days. As the thirty-five-year-old Tilly saw it, his men "were a task force leading the way for the whole of Dempsey's Second Army." He was acutely conscious of the urgent necessity of reaching Urquhart's men quickly. From all he had learned, the division was dying by the hour.

On Sunday Tilly had climbed to the spire of a damaged Driel church three times to observe the area where his troops would

land on the Rhine's northern bank. As the afternoon wore on, at his orchard headquarters south of Driel, he impatiently awaited the full arrival of his battalion from the village of Homoet, a few miles southwest of Driel, and the assault boats being brought up from the corridor.

Shortly after 6 P.M. Brigadier Ben Walton sent for Tilly. At Walton's headquarters in a house south of Driel, Tilly expected the brigade commander to review once more the details of the night's operation. Instead, Walton told him there had been a change in plan. Word had been received, Walton said, that "the whole operation—the large-scale crossing—was off." Tilly's battalion would still cross, but for a different purpose. Tilly listened with increasing dismay. His men were to hold the base of the perimeter while Urquhart's 1st Airborne Division was withdrawn! He was to take as few men as possible—"only enough to do the job"; approximately 400 infantry and 20 officers. Tilly did not need to go; he could detail his second in command, Major James Grafton, to take his place. Although Tilly replied that he would "think about it," he had already decided to lead his men over. As he left Walton's headquarters, Tilly felt that his men were being sacrificed. Walton had said nothing about getting them back. Yet he knew that Walton too was helpless to alter the situation. What puzzled him was what had happened; why had the plan been changed?

The decision to withdraw Urquhart's force—subject to confirmation by Montgomery, who was not to finally approve the order until 9:30 A.M. Monday, September 25—was reached by General Dempsey at the St. Oedenrode conference with Horrocks and General Browning on Sunday afternoon. After considering his Corps commander's plan for a full-scale crossing of the Rhine, Dempsey turned it down. Unlike Horrocks, Dempsey did not believe the assault could succeed. "No," he said to Horrocks. "Get them out." Turning to Browning, Dempsey asked, "Is that all right with you?" Silent and subdued, Browning nodded. Immediately Dempsey notified General Thomas in Driel. Even as the St. Oedenrode conference was taking place, the Germans, once again, severed the corridor north of Veghel. Cut off, Horrocks used an armored carrier and broke through the German lines to return to his headquarters at Nijmegen. Field Marshal Model's latest attacks would keep the corridor closed for more than forty hours.

In Driel, most of Lieutenant Colonel Tilly's battalion had now arrived. He walked among his troops picking the men he would take. Tapping soldiers on the shoulder, Tilly said, "You go" . . . "You're not going." The real purpose of the assault was secret. He could not tell protesting men why they were being left behind. Tilly "picked those veterans who were absolutely sure—essential—leaving the others behind."

The decision was bitter. Looking at the officers and men who, he believed, "were going to certain death," Tilly called over Major Grafton. "Jimmy," Grafton remembers Tilly saying, "I've got to tell you something, because someone other than me has to know the real purpose of the crossing." Outlining the change in plan, Tilly added quietly, "I'm afraid we're being chucked away."

Stunned, Grafton stared at Tilly. It was vital, Tilly added, that no one else have the information. "It would be too risky," he explained.

Grafton knew what Tilly meant. It would be a terrible blow to morale if the truth was known. As Grafton prepared to leave, Tilly said, "Jimmy, I hope you can swim." Grafton smiled. "I hope so, too," he said.

By 9:30 P.M., as Tilly's men moved down to the river, there was still no sign of the assault craft. "How the hell do they expect me to cross without boats?" Tilly asked his engineering officer, Lieutenant Colonel Charles Henniker. Rations for his men had not arrived either. Testy and burdened by his knowledge of the true reason for the mission, Tilly spoke with Lieutenant Colonel Aubrey Coad, commander of the 5th Dorsets. "Nothing's right," Tilly told him. "The boats haven't come and we haven't been issued rations. If something isn't done soon, I'm not prepared to go." Coad ordered his battalion to turn over rations to Tilly's men.

For three long hours, in a cold, drizzling rain, Tilly's force waited for the assault craft. At midnight word arrived that the boats were now in Driel. But only nine had come through. In the darkness, some trucks had taken a wrong turn and driven into enemy lines; two others, skidding off a muddy dike road, had been lost. At the rendezvous point the boats were carried on the shoulders of the infantry for 600 yards through a swampy marsh to the launching point. Stumbling and slithering over the mud of the polder, the men took more than an hour to wrestle the boats to the river. Not until after 2 A.M. on Monday, September 25, was the assembly complete.

As the men prepared to launch, Tilly handed Major Grafton two messages for General Urquhart: one was a letter from General Browning; the other, a coded message from General Thomas outlining the withdrawal plan. There were two sets of these letters. Lieutenant Colonel Eddie Myers, Urquhart's engineering officer, had returned from Nijmegen and his meeting with Browning. Now Myers, bearing the same letters, was waiting to cross. "Your job," Tilly told Grafton, "is to get through to Urquhart with these messages in case the engineering officer doesn't make it." The paper containing the withdrawal plan was "absolutely vital," Tilly stressed.

At the river it was clear that the Germans were completely prepared for another crossing. Only some fifteen British assault craft—including three DUKWs and the remnants of the little fleet used on the previous night—remained. At the very last minute, because of the boat shortage, it was decided to halt a diversionary crossing scheduled by the Poles to the east of the Dorsets' launching area—and put Tilly's men over in five three-boat waves. As the preparations went on, mortar shells exploded on the southern bank, and heavy machine guns, apparently now carefully lined up along both edges of the perimeter base, swept the water. Lieutenant Colonel Tilly stepped into a boat. The first wave began to cross.

Although every available British gun on the southern side hammered away, sending a canopy of shells above the Dorsets, the crossing was brutally assaulted. The canvas-and-plywood craft were raked, holed and swept away. Some, like Major Grafton's, caught fire before leaving the south bank. Quickly Grafton set out in another. Halfway over he discovered his was the only remaining boat in the wave. In fifteen minutes, feeling "lucky to be alive," Grafton was across.

In the rain and darkness, hemmed in by well-sited machine-gun fire, each of the five waves sustained heavy losses. But the worst enemy by far was the current. Unused to the boats and the unexpected current, which increased in speed after midnight, the helpless Dorsets were swept past the perimeter base and into the hands of the enemy. Scattered for miles, those who survived were quickly cut off and surrounded. Of the 420 officers and men who set out for the perimeter, only 239 reached the northern bank. Lieutenant Colonel Tilly, who upon landing was met by an avalanche of grenades rolled like bowling balls down a hill, was heard leading his men out of the inferno, yelling "Get them with the bayonet!"*

The Dorsets were unable to link up as an effective unit with Urquhart's men. Only a few reached the Hartenstein perimeter, among them Major Grafton, who, with the withdrawal plan intact, came in through Major Dickie Lonsdale's positions near the lower Oosterbeek church. Lieutenant Colonel Myers had already arrived at Urquhart's headquarters with the documents he was carrying. Neither man knew the contents of Thomas' coded message, or its cruelly ironic name. When Montgomery had originally pressed Eisenhower for "a powerful and full-blooded thrust toward Berlin . . . to thus end the war," his single-thrust suggestion had been turned down. "Operation Market-Garden" had been the compromise. Now the withdrawal plan for Urquhart's bloodied men had been officially designated. The remnants of the British 1st Airborne Division were to be evacuated under the code name "Operation Berlin."

---

* One of the bouncing grenades actually hit Tilly's head and exploded. Incredibly he was only slightly wounded and survived as a prisoner of war until the end of hostilities.

⁘ 4 ⁘

Now MARKET-GARDEN, the operation Montgomery hoped would end the war quickly, proceeded inexorably toward its doom. For sixty terrible miles men hung on to bridges and fought for a single road, the corridor. In General Maxwell Taylor's sector north of Eindhoven, troopers bolstered by British armor and infantry repelled one fierce attack after another while trying to reopen the empty stretch of highway severed at Uden; in General Gavin's 82nd area the great Waal bridge was under constant bombardment and the enemy continued to press in from the Reichswald in steadily growing strength. Gone was the attitude of a week before, that the war was almost over. Enemy units were being encountered that had long been written off. The Nazi war machine, thought to be reeling and on the verge of collapse in the first week of September, had miraculously produced sixty Tiger tanks, which were delivered to Model on the morning of September 24.[*] Market-Garden was strangling, and now the principal objective of the plan, the foothold across the Rhine, the springboard to the Ruhr, was to be abandoned. At 6:05 A.M., Monday, September 25, General Urquhart received the order to withdraw.

In the planning of the Arnhem operation Urquhart had been promised relief within forty-eight hours. General Browning had expected the 1st Airborne Division to hold out alone for no longer than four days at maximum. In an unprecedented feat of arms for

[*] "The tanks arrived in the early hours of the morning," notes General Harmel in Annex No. 6 of his war diary, September 24th, adding that "II Panzer Corps headquarters allocated the bulk of this detachment, 45 tiger tanks, to the 10th SS Frundsberg Division."

an airborne division, outnumbered and outgunned, Urquhart's men had hung on for more than twice that long. To the courageous Scot, commanding an airborne division for the first time, withdrawal was bitter; yet Urquhart knew it was the only course. By now his strength was fewer than 2,500 men, and he could ask no more of these uncompromising troopers. Galling as it was to know that relieving British forces sat barely one mile away, separated from the division only by the width of the Rhine, Urquhart reluctantly agreed with his superiors' decision. The time had come to get the valiant men of Arnhem out.

At the Hartenstein, a weary Lieutenant Colonel Eddie Myers delivered the two letters—Browning's and the withdrawal order from General Thomas—to Urquhart. Browning's congratulatory and encouraging message, written more than twenty-four hours earlier, was outdated. In part it read, ". . . the army is pouring to your assistance, but . . . very late in the day," and "I naturally feel, not so tired and frustrated as you do, but probably almost worse about the whole thing than you do . . ."

The withdrawal order—especially coming from Thomas, whose slowness Urquhart, like Browning, could not forgive—was by far the more depressing. The 43rd Wessex was now beginning to feel the weight of increasing German pressure, Thomas' message said. All hope of developing a major bridgehead across the Rhine must be abandoned; and the withdrawal of the 1st Airborne would take place, by mutual agreement between Urquhart and Thomas, at a designated date and time.

Urquhart pondered his decision. As he listened to the continuing mortar and artillery bombardment outside, he had no doubts about the date and time. If any of his men were to survive, the withdrawal would have to be soon and, obviously, under cover of darkness. At 8:08 A.M. Urquhart contacted General Thomas by radio: "Operation Berlin," he told him, "must be tonight."

Some twenty minutes later Urquhart released the message prepared for Browning that he had given Lieutenant Neville Hay to encode the night before. It was still pertinent, particularly the

HARZER

9TH SS PANZER "HOHENSTAUFEN" DIVISION

VON TETTAU

HARTENSTEIN HOTEL

OOSTERBEEK

URQUHART
BRITISH 1ST AIRBORNE DIV.

KRAFFT

ARTILLERY

HEVEADORP

SITE OF FERRY

EVACUATION
ACROSS RHINE
NIGHT OF SEPT. 26,
OF 10,005 TROOPS
ONLY 2,163
CROSSED RHINE

DESTROYED
RAILWAY
BRIDGE

TO NIJMEGEN

DRIEL

SOSABOWSKI
POLISH 1ST
PARACHUTE BRIG.

THOMAS
43RD WESSEX INF. DIV.

TO NIJMEGEN

BITTRICH
II SS PANZER CORPS

ARNHEM

LOWER RHINE

DESTROYED
PONTOON
BRIDGE

ARNHEM
BRIDGE

THE END
EVACUATION OF THE OOSTERBEEK
PERIMETER, SEPT. 26, 1944

0   1   Kilometers   2   3

0   Miles   1

to Elst and Nijmegen

R "FRUNDSBERG" DIVISION

HARMEL

palacios

warning sentence, "Even slight enemy offensive action may cause complete disintegration." For at this moment Urquhart's situation was so desperate that he did not know whether his men could hold until darkness. Then the agonized general began to plan the most difficult maneuver of all: the withdrawal. There was only one way out—across the terrible 400 yards of the Rhine to Driel.

Urquhart's plan was designed along the lines of another classic British withdrawal—Gallipoli, in 1916. There, after months of fighting, troops had finally been pulled out under deceptive cover. Thinned-out lines cloaking the retreat had continued to fire as the main bulk of the force was safely withdrawn. Urquhart planned a similar maneuver. Along the perimeter small groups of men would keep up a fusillade to deceive the enemy while the larger body of troops slipped away. Gradually units along the northern face of the perimeter would move down along its sides to the river, to be evacuated. Then the last forces, closest to the Rhine, would follow. "In effect," Urquhart said later, "I planned the withdrawal like the collapse of a paper bag. I wanted small parties stationed at strategic places to give the impression we were still there, all the while pulling downward and along each flank."

Urquhart hoped to contrive other indications of "normality"— the usual pattern of radio transmissions would continue; Sheriff Thompson's artillery was to fire to the last; and military police in and about the German prisoner-of-war compound on the Harten-stein's tennis courts were to continue their patrols. They would be among the very last to leave. Obviously, besides a rear guard, other men would have to stay behind—doctors, medical orderlies and serious casualties. Wounded men unable to walk but capable of occupying defensive positions would stay and continue firing.

To reach the river, Urquhart's men would follow one route down each side of the perimeter. Glider pilots, acting as guides, would steer them along the escape path, marked in some areas with white tape. Troopers, their boots muffled by strips of cloth, were to make their way to the water's edge. There, beachmasters would load them into a small evacuation fleet: fourteen powered

storm boats—managed by two companies of Canadian engineers
—each capable of carrying fourteen men, and a variety of smaller
craft. Their number was indeterminate. No one, including the
beachmasters, would remember how many, but among them were
several DUKWs and a few canvas-and-plywood assault craft
remaining from previous crossings.

Urquhart was gambling that the Germans observing the boat
traffic would assume men were trying to move into the perimeter
rather than out of it. Apart from the dreadful possibility of his
troops being detected other hazardous difficulties could occur as
more than two thousand men tried to escape. If a rigid time
schedule was not maintained, Urquhart could foresee, an appalling bottleneck would develop at the narrow base of the perimeter, now barely 650 yards wide. If they were jammed into the
embarkation area, his men might be mercilessly annihilated. After
the futile experience of the Poles and the Dorsets in trying to
enter the perimeter, Urquhart did not expect the evacuation to go
unchallenged. Although every gun that XXX Corps could bring to
bear would be in action to protect his men, Urquhart still expected the Germans to inflict heavy casualties. Time was an
enemy, for it would take hours to complete the evacuation. There
was also the problem of keeping the plan secret. Because men
might be captured and interrogated during the day, no one, apart
from senior officers and those given specific tasks, was to be told
of the evacuation until the last minute.

After conferring with General Thomas by radio and obtaining
agreement on the major points in his withdrawal plan, Urquhart
called a meeting of the few senior officers left: Brigadier Pip
Hicks; Lieutenant Colonel Iain Murray of the Glider Pilot Regiment, now in charge of the wounded Hackett's command; Lieutenant Colonel R. G. Loder-Symonds, the division's artillery
chief; Colonel Mackenzie, the chief of staff; and Lieutenant
Colonel Eddie Myers, the engineering officer who would be in
charge of the evacuation. Just before the conference began,
Colonel Graeme Warrack, the chief medical officer, arrived to see
Urquhart and became the first man to learn of the plan. Warrack

was "downcast and unhappy. Not because I had to stay—I had an obligation to the wounded—but because up to this moment I had expected the division to be relieved in a very short time."

In the Hartenstein cellar, surrounded by his officers, Urquhart broke the news. "We're getting out tonight," he told them. Step by step he outlined his plan. The success of the withdrawal would depend on meticulous timing. Any concentration of troops or traffic jams could cause disaster. Men were to be kept moving, without stopping to fight. "While they should take evasive action if fired upon, they should only fire back if it is a matter of life or death." As his despondent officers prepared to leave, Urquhart cautioned them that the evacuation must be kept secret as long as possible. Only those with a need to know were to be told.

The news carried little surprise for Urquhart's senior officers. For hours it had been obvious that the position was hopeless. Still, like Warrack, they were bitter that relief had never arrived. In their minds, too, was the fear that their men might endure an even greater ordeal during the withdrawal than they had in the perimeter. By accident Signalman James Cockrill, attached to division headquarters, heard the terse message: "Operation Berlin is tonight." He puzzled over its meaning. Withdrawal did not even occur to him. Cockrill believed the division "would fight to the last man and the last bullet." He thought that "Operation Berlin" might mean an all-out attempt to break through for the Arnhem bridge "in some kind of heroic 'Charge of the Light Brigade' or something." Another man knew all too clearly what it meant. At the headquarters of the 1st Airlanding Brigade, Colonel Payton-Reid of the KOSB's, helping to arrange details of the evacuation of the western edge of the perimeter, heard Brigadier Pip Hicks mutter something about "another Dunkirk."

All through this day, in a frenzy of attacks, the Germans tried to overrun positions, but still the Red Devils held. Then, men would recall, shortly after 8 P.M. the news of the withdrawal began filtering down. To Major Geoffrey Powell of Hackett's 156th Battalion, at the top of the perimeter, the news was "an appalling blow. I thought of all the men who had died, and then I thought the whole effort had been a waste." Because his men were among those who had the farthest to come, Powell started them off in single file at 8:15 P.M.

Private Robert Downing of the 10th Parachute Battalion was told to leave his slit trench and go to the Hartenstein Hotel. There, he was met by a sergeant. "There's an old plastic razor over there," the sergeant told him. "You get yourself a dry shave." Downing stared at him. "Hurry up," the sergeant told him. "We're crossing the river and by God we're going back looking like British soldiers."

In a cellar near his position Major Robert Cain borrowed another razor. Someone had found water, and Cain scraped the razor over a week's growth of beard and then dried his face carefully on the inside of his smoke-blackened, bloodstained smock. Coming out he stood for a minute in lashing rain looking at the church in lower Oosterbeek. There was a gold cock on the weather vane. Cain had checked it at intervals during the battle. For him, it was a good luck symbol. As long as the gold cock remained, so would the division. He felt an overpowering sadness. He wondered if the weather vane would still be there tomorrow.

Like other men, Major Thomas Toler of the Glider Pilot Regiment had been told by Colonel Iain Murray to clean up a little. Toler couldn't have cared less. He was so tired that just "thinking about cleaning up was an effort." Murray handed over his own razor. "We're getting out. We don't want the army to think we're a bunch of tramps." With a small dab of lather that Murray had left, Toler too shaved his beard. "It was amazing how much better I felt, mentally and physically," he recalls. In Murray's command post was the Pegasus flag Hackett's men had planned to fly as the Second Army arrived. Toler stared at it for a moment. Then he carefully rolled it up and put it away.

In artillery positions where troopers now would fire at will to help disguise the evacuation, Gunner Robert Christie listened as the troop's signalman, Willie Speedie, called in to the battery. Speedie gave a new station as control and then said simply, "I am closing down now. Out."

579

Sergeant Stanley Sullivan, one of the pathfinders who had led the way nine days before, was furious when the news reached him. "I had already figured we'd had it anyway and we might as well go down fighting." Sullivan's outpost was in a school "where youngsters had been trying to learn. I was afraid for all those children if we pulled out. I had to let them know, and the Germans too, just how we felt." On the blackboard in the room he had been defending, Sullivan printed large block letters and underlined them several times. The message read: "We'll Be Back!!!"°

At precisely 9 P.M., the night sky was ripped by the flash of XXX Corps's massed guns, and fires broke out all along the edge of the perimeter as a torrent of shells rained down on the German positions. Forty-five minutes later, Urquhart's men started to pull out. The bad weather that had prevented the prompt arrival of troops and supplies during the week now worked for the Red Devils; the withdrawal began in near-gale-like conditions which —with the din of the bombardment—helped cover up the British escape.

In driving wind and rain the 1st Airborne survivors, faces blackened, equipment tied down and boots muffled against sound, climbed stiffly out of positions and lined up for the dangerous trek down to the river. The darkness and the weather made it impossible for men to see more than a few feet in front of them. The troopers formed a living chain, holding hands or clinging to the camouflage smock of the man ahead.

Sergeant William Tompson, a glider pilot, hunched his body against the pouring rain. Charged with helping to direct troopers to the riverbank, he was prepared for a long wet night. As he watched men file past he was struck by the fact that "few men but us had ever known what it was like to live in a mile-square abattoir."

To Signalman James Cockrill the meaning of "Operation

° The children would never see it. On September 27, in a brutal reprisal against the Dutch, the Germans ordered the entire Arnhem area evacuated. Arnhem and the surrounding villages were to remain uninhabited until the very last days of the war, when Canadian troops arrived on April 14, 1945.

Berlin" was now only too clear. He had been detailed to stay behind and operate his set as the troops withdrew. His instructions were "to stay on the air and keep the set functioning to make the Germans think everything is normal." Cockrill sat alone in darkness under the veranda of the Hartenstein, "bashing away on the key. I could hear a lot of movement around me, but I had no other instructions than to keep the set on the air." Cockrill was certain that he would be a prisoner before morning. His rifle was propped up beside him, but it was useless. One bullet was a dummy, containing the cypher code used to contact Second Army. It was the only one he had left.

On the Rhine's southern bank, doctors, medical orderlies and Dutch Red Cross nursing personnel stood ready in reception areas and at the collection point. In Driel convoys of ambulances and vehicles waited to move Urquhart's survivors back to Nijmegen. Although preparations for the arrival of the men were going on all about her, Cora Baltussen, after three days and nights tending the wounded, was so exhausted she thought the bombardment and the activities on the southern bank marked the prelude to yet another crossing attempt. In the concentrated shelling of Driel, Cora had been wounded by shrapnel in the head, left shoulder and side. Although the injuries were painful, Cora considered them superficial. She was more concerned about her bloody dress. She cycled home to change before returning to help tend the fresh flow of casualties she was certain would shortly arrive. On the way Cora rode into enemy shellfire. Thrown from her bicycle, she lay unhurt for some time in a muddy ditch, then she set off again. At home exhaustion overcame her. In the cellar she lay down for a short nap. She slept all through the night, unaware that "Operation Berlin" was taking place.

Along the river at the base of the perimeter the evacuation fleet, manned by Canadian and British engineers, lay waiting. So far the enemy's suspicions had not been aroused. In fact, it was clear that the Germans did not know what was happening. Their guns were firing at the remaining Dorsets, who had begun a diversionary attack west of the perimeter. Still farther west, Germans were firing as British artillery laid down a barrage to give the appearance of a river assault in that area. Urquhart's deception plan appeared to be working.

In the drenching rain, lines of men snaked slowly down both sides of the perimeter to the river. Some men were so exhausted that they lost their way and fell into enemy hands; others, unable to go on by themselves, had to be helped. In the inky darkness nobody stopped. To halt invited noise, confusion—and death.

In the ruddy glow of fires and burning buildings, Sergeant Ron Kent, of Major Boy Wilson's pathfinder group, led his platoon to a cabbage patch designated as the company rendezvous point. There they waited until the remainder of the company assembled before moving toward the river. "Although we knew the Rhine lay due south," Kent says, "we didn't know what point they were evacuating us from." Suddenly the men spotted lines of red tracers coming from the south and taking these as a guide, they moved on. Soon they came to white tape and the shadowy figures of glider pilots who directed them along. Kent's group heard machine-gun fire and grenade explosions off to their left. Major Wilson and another group of men had run into Germans. In the fierce skirmish that followed, with safety only a mile away, two soldiers were killed.

Men were to remember the evacuation by small details—poignant, frightening and sometimes humorous. As Private Henry Blyton of the 1st Battalion moved down to the river, he heard someone crying. Ahead, the line stopped. Troopers made for the side of the path. There, lying on the sodden ground, was a wounded soldier crying for his mother. The men were ordered to keep on moving. No one was to stop for the wounded. Yet many did. Before troopers in Major Dickie Lonsdale's force left their positions, they went to the Ter Horst house and took as many of the walking wounded as they could.

Lance Corporal Sydney Nunn, who with a glider pilot had knocked out a Tiger tank earlier in the week, thought he would never make it to the river. By the church where artillery positions had been overrun during the day, Nunn and a group of KOSB's had a sharp, brief skirmish with the Germans. In the rain and darkness most of the men got away. Lying on the ground Nunn received the first injury he had had in nine days of fighting. Shrapnel hit some stones and one of Nunn's front teeth was chipped by a pebble.

Sergeant Thomas Bentley of the 10th Battalion was following the Phantom operator, Lieutenant Neville Hay. "We were sniped at continually," he remembers. "I saw two glider pilots walk out from the shadows and deliberately draw the German fire, apparently so we could see where it was coming from." Both guides were killed.

In the Hartenstein, General Urquhart and his staff prepared to leave. The war diary was closed; papers were burned and then Hancock, the General's batman, wrapped Urquhart's boots with strips of curtain. Everybody knelt as a chaplain said the Lord's Prayer. Urquhart remembered the bottle of whiskey his batman had put in his pack on D Day. "I handed it around," Urquhart says, "and everyone had a nip." Finally Urquhart went down to the cellars to see the wounded "in their bloody bandages and crude splints" and said goodbye to those aware of what was happening. Others, drowsy with morphia, were mercifully unaware of the withdrawal. One haggard soldier, propping himself up against the cellar wall, told Urquhart, "I hope you make it, sir."

Lieutenant Commander Arnoldus Wolters, the Dutch liaison officer at Division headquarters, moving behind the General's group, observed absolute silence. "With my accent had I opened my mouth I might have been taken for a German," he says. At some point Wolters lost his grip on the man in front of him. "I didn't know what to do. I simply kept going, praying that I was heading in the right direction." Wolters felt particularly depressed. He kept thinking of his wife and the daughter he had never seen. He had not been able to phone them even though his

Shoot 14

Place	Date	Hour	Summary of Events and Information	References to Appendices
ARNHEM	25 Sep	0940	Maint Sitrep to Airtps Rear. No resup 24 Sep. Understand med stores, rations, some amn sent over river bu ducks, but unable distribute owing to enemy action and lack of transport. No sups now for 3 days. Water still scarce. Gun amn now very low. Div effective strength approx 2500 excl Poles 120. Resup required 25 Sep as for 23 Sep.	
		1030	Div Comd held conference of all Comds and gave out his orders for 'BERLIN'.	
		1800	A quieter day than yesterday, despite several local attacks, one of which drove in 156 Bn. Infiltration, however, went on steadily and by evening the enemy was firmly established in wood 795777 and at other points inside the perimeter. Most units were therefore to some extent encircled and cut off from their neighbours.	
		2145	First units to withdraw crossed starting line on rd between rd junc 792774 and CHURCH 796774.	
		2200	Crossing over river started, covered by very heavy pre-arranged arty concentration.	
		2230	Last tps of Div H.Q. moved out. Wounded under the care of Lt. RANDALL, RAMC, MO to H.Q., R.A., were left in the cellar of Div H.Q. A.D.M.S., other M.Os. and Senior Chaplain remained with wounded in the M.D.S.	
	26 Sep	0130	Guards of P.W. cage withdrew.	
		0550	Ferrying across river ends. Approx 300 personnel left on North bank. Arranged that boats should return the following evening for any survivors.	
NIJMEGEN		1200	Evacuation of Div H.Q. to NIJMEGEN completed from R.V. at DRIEL, where 130 Bde issued tea and rum, food and one blanket per man.	
		1430	G.O.C. held conference and issued orders re checking of personnel present, billetting, re-organizing and issue of clothing. Units ordered to make contact with seaborne lift, which had already arrived in NIJMEGEN.	

As shown in war diary page 14, General Urquhart ordered evacuation of Oosterbeek perimeter at 2145 on September 25th.

family lived only a few miles from the Hartenstein. The watch he had bought for his wife in England was still in his pocket; the Teddy bear he had planned to give his daughter was somewhere in a wrecked glider. If he was lucky enough to make it back to the river, Wolters would be leaving, probably for England, once more.

At the river the crossings had begun. Lieutenant Colonel Myers and his beachmasters packed men into the boats as fast as they arrived. But now the Germans, though still not aware that a withdrawal was taking place, could see the ferrying operations by the light of flares. Mortars and artillery began ranging in. Boats were holed and capsized. Men struggling in the water screamed for help. Others, already dead, were swept away. Wounded men clung to wreckage and tried to swim to the southern bank. Within one hour half the evacuation fleet was destroyed, but still the ferrying went on.

By the time Major Geoffrey Powell's men reached the river from their long trek down the eastern side of the perimeter, Powell believed that the evacuation was over. A boat was bobbing up and down in the water, sinking lower as waves hit against it. Powell waded out. The boat was full of holes and the sappers in it were all dead. As some of his men struck out swimming, a boat suddenly appeared out of the dark. Powell hastily organized his men and got some of them aboard. He and the remaining troopers waited until the craft returned. On the high embankment south of the Rhine, Powell stood for a moment looking back north. "All at once I realized I was across. I simply could not believe I had gotten out alive." Turning to his fifteen bedraggled men, Powell said, "Form up in threes." He marched them to the reception center. Outside the building, Powell shouted, "156th Battalion, halt! Right turn! Fall out!" Standing in the rain he watched them head for shelter. "It was all over, but by God we had come out as we had gone in. Proud."

As General Urquhart's crowded boat prepared to leave, it got caught in the mud. Hancock, his batman, jumped out and pushed them off. "He got us clear," Urquhart says, "but as he struggled to get back aboard someone shouted, 'Let go! It's overcrowded already!' " Irked by this ingratitude "Hancock ignored the remark and, with his last reserves, pulled himself into the boat."

Under machine-gun fire Urquhart's boat was halfway across when the engine suddenly stuttered and stopped. The boat began to drift with the current; to Urquhart "it seemed an absolute age before the engine came to life again." Minutes later they reached the southern bank. Looking back Urquhart saw flashes of fire as the Germans raked the river. "I don't think," he says, "they knew what they were firing at."

All along the bank of the Rhine and in the meadows and woods behind, hundreds of men waited. But now with only half the fleet still operable and under heavy machine-gun fire, the bottleneck that Urquhart had feared occurred. Confusion developed in the crowded lines, and although there was no panic, many men tried to push forward, and their officers and sergeants tried to hold them in check. Lance Corporal Thomas Harris of the 1st Battalion remembers "hundreds and hundreds waiting to get across. Boats were being swamped by the weight of the numbers of men trying to board." And mortars were now falling in the embarkation area as the Germans got the range. Harris, like many other men, decided to swim. Taking off his battle dress and boots, he dived in and, to his surprise, made it over.

Others were not so lucky. By the time Gunner Charles Pavey got down to the river, the embarkation area was also under machine-gun fire. As the men huddled on the bank a man came swimming toward the place where Pavey lay. Ignoring the bullets peppering the shore he hauled himself out of the water and, gasping for breath, said, "Thank God, I'm over." Pavey heard someone say, "Bloody fool. You're still on the same side."

Sergeant Alf Roullier, who had managed to cook and serve a stew on Sunday, now attempted to swim the river. As he floundered in the water a boat drew alongside and someone grabbed his collar. He heard a man shout, "It's O.K., mate. Keep going. Keep going." Roullier was totally disoriented. He believed he was drowning. Then he heard the same voice say, "Bloody good, old boy," and a Canadian engineer lifted him into the boat. "Where the hell am I?" the dazed Roullier mumbled. The Canadian grinned. "You're almost home," he said.

It was nearing daybreak when Signalman James Cockrill, still at his set under the veranda of the Hartenstein, heard a fierce whisper. "Come on, Chick," a voice said, "let's go." As the men headed for the river, there was a sudden sharp burst of noise. Cockrill felt a tug on his neck and shoulders. His Sten gun, slung over his back, had been split wide open by shrapnel. Nearing the bank, Cockrill's group came across a few glider pilots standing in the bushes. "Don't go until we tell you," one of the pilots said. "The Germans have got a gun fixed on this area, a Spandau firing about waist high." Coached by the pilots, the men sprinted forward one at a time. When Cockrill's turn came he crouched down and began to run. Seconds later he fell over a pile of bodies. "There must have been twenty or thirty," he remembers. "I heard men shouting for their mothers and others begging us not to leave them there. We couldn't stop." At the river's edge a flare exploded and machine guns began to chatter. Cockrill heard someone shout for those who could to swim. He went into the chilly water, striking out past panic-stricken men who appeared to be floundering all about him.

Suddenly Cockrill heard a voice say, "All right, buddy, don't worry. I've got you." A Canadian hauled him into a boat and seconds later Cockrill heard the boat ground on shore. "I nearly cried when I found I was back where I started," he says. The boat had gone on in to pick up wounded. As men all around helped with the loading, the craft started off again and Cockrill remembers a rush as men climbed in from all sides. Although their boat was weighted down and under fire, the Canadians made it to the far shore. After hours under the veranda and his nightmarish trip across the water, Cockrill was dazed. "The next thing I knew I was in a barn and someone gave me a cigarette." Then Cockrill remembered one thing. Frantically he searched his pockets and brought out his single piece of ammunition: the .303 dummy bullet with his cypher code inside.

Shortly before 2 A.M. what remained of the 1st Airborne's ammunition was blown up. Sheriff Thompson's gunners fired the last remaining shells and artillerymen removed the breech blocks. Lance Bombardier Percy Parkes and the remainder of his crew were told to pull back. Parkes was surprised. He had not thought about the withdrawal. He had expected to stay until his post was overrun by the Germans. He was even more amazed when he reached the river. The area was jammed with hundreds of men and someone said that all the boats had been sunk. A man near Parkes took a deep breath. "It looks like we swim," he said. Parkes stared at the river. "It was very wide. In full flood the current looked to be about nine knots. I didn't think I could make it. I saw men jumping in fully dressed and being swept downstream. Others made it across only to be shot scrambling out of the water. I saw one chap paddle across on a plank, still carrying his pack. If he could do it, I could."

Parkes stripped to his shorts, throwing away everything including his gold pocket watch. In the swift current his shorts slipped down and Parkes kicked them off. He made it over and, hiding by bushes and in ditches, eventually reached a small deserted farm cottage. Parkes went in to find some clothing. Emerging a few minutes later, he encountered a private from the Dorsets, who directed him to a collection point, where he was given a mug of hot tea and some cigarettes. It took the exhausted Parkes some time to understand why everyone was staring at him. He was dressed in a man's colored sports shirt and wore a pair of ladies' linen bloomers tied at the knee.

Private Alfred Dullforce of the 10th Battalion swam to the south bank nude but still carrying a .38. To his embarrassment two women were standing with the soldiers on the bank. Dullforce "felt like diving straight back into the water." One of the women called to him and held out a skirt. "She didn't bat an eyelash at my nakedness," he remembers. "She told me not to worry, because they were there to help the men coming across." In a multicolored skirt that reached to his knees and wearing a pair of clogs, Dullforce was taken to a British truck driving the survivors back to Nijmegen.

By now the Germans were flaying the embarkation area and mortar shells were screaming in. As Lieutenant Commander Arnoldus Wolters ran behind a line of men for a boat, there was an explosion among the group. "I was absolutely unharmed," Wolters recalls. "But around me lay eight dead men and one severely wounded." He gave the man a shot of morphia and carried him to the boat. In the already overloaded craft there was no place for Wolters. He waded into the water and, hanging onto the side of the boat, was pulled across the river. He staggered onto the southern bank and collapsed.

As dawn came, the evacuation fleet had been almost destroyed, yet the Canadian and British engineers, braving mortar, artillery and heavy machine-gun fire, continued to ferry the men across in the boats that remained. Private Arthur Shearwood of the 11th Battalion found Canadian engineers loading some wounded into a small boat. One of the Canadians motioned for Shearwood to get aboard. The outboard motor could not be restarted, and the Canadians asked all soldiers still carrying rifles to start paddling. Shearwood tapped the man in front of him. "Let's go," he said. "Start paddling." The man looked at Shearwood without expression. "I can't," he said, pointing to his bandaged shoulder. "I've lost an arm."

Major Robert Cain had put all his men across by dawn. With Sergeant Major "Robbo" Robinson, he waited on the bank so he could follow, but no more boats appeared to be heading in. In a group of other men someone pointed to a slightly holed assault craft bobbing on the water and a trooper swam out to bring it back. Using rifle butts, Cain and Robinson began rowing, while troopers who still had helmets bailed. On the south bank a military policeman directed them to a barn. Inside, one of the first men Cain recognized was Brigadier Hicks. The brigadier came over quickly. "Well," he said, "here's one officer, at least, who's shaved." Cain grinned tiredly. "I was well brought up, sir," he said.

On the perimeter's edge scores of men still huddled in the rain under German fire. Although one or two boats attempted to cross under cover of a smoke screen, it was now, in daylight, impossible for the evacuation to continue. Some men who tried to swim for it were caught by the swift current or by machine-gun fire. Others made it. Still others, so badly wounded they could do nothing, sat helplessly in the pounding rain or set out north—back to the hospitals in the perimeter. Many decided to hide out and wait until darkness again before trying to reach the opposite shore. Eventually scores succeeded in making their escape this way.

On the southern bank and in Driel, exhausted, grimy men searched for their units—or what remained of them. Sergeant Stanley Sullivan of the pathfinders, who had printed his defiant message on the school blackboard, remembers someone asking, "Where's the 1st Battalion?" A corporal immediately stood up. "This is it, sir," he said. Beside him a handful of bedraggled men pulled themselves painfully erect. Gunner Robert Christie roamed through crowds of men searching for troopers of his battery. No one looked familiar. Christie suddenly felt tears sting his eyes. He had no idea whether anyone but him was left from Number 2 Battery.

On the road to Driel, General Urquhart came to General Thomas' headquarters. Refusing to go in, he waited outside in the rain as his aide arranged for transportation. It was not necessary. As Urquhart stood outside, a jeep arrived from General Browning's headquarters and an officer escorted Urquhart back to Corps. He and his group were taken to a house on the southern outskirts of Nijmegen. "Browning's aide, Major Harry Cator, showed us into a room and suggested we take off our wet clothes," Urquhart says. The proud Scot refused. "Perversely, I wanted Browning to see us as we were—as we had been." After a long wait Browning appeared, "as immaculate as ever." He looked, Urquhart thought, as if "he had just come off parade, rather than from his bed in the middle of a battle." To the Corps commander Urquhart said simply, "I'm sorry things did not turn out as well as I had hoped." Browning, offering Urquhart a drink, replied, "You did all you could." Later, in the bedroom that he had been given, Urquhart found that the sleep he had yearned for so long was impossible. "There were too many things," he said, "on my mind and my conscience."

There was indeed much to think about. The 1st Airborne Division had been sacrificed and slaughtered. Of Urquhart's original 10,005-man force only 2,163 troopers, along with 160 Poles and 75 Dorsets, came back across the Rhine. After nine days, the division had approximately 1,200 dead and 6,642 missing, wounded or captured. The Germans, it later turned out, had suffered brutally, too: 3,300 casualties, including 1,100 dead.

The Arnhem adventure was over and with it Market-Garden. There was little left to do now but pull back and consolidate. The war would go on until May, 1945. "Thus ended in failure the greatest airborne operation of the war," one American historian later wrote. "Although Montgomery asserted that it had been 90 percent successful, his statement was merely a consoling figure of speech. All objectives save Arnhem had been won, but without Arnhem the rest were as nothing. In return for so much courage and sacrifice, the Allies had won a 50-mile salient—leading nowhere."[*]

Perhaps because so few were expected to escape, there was not enough transport for the exhausted survivors. Many men, having endured so much else, now had to march back to Nijmegen. On the road Captain Roland Langton of the Irish Guards stood in the cold rain watching the 1st Airborne come back. As tired, filthy men stumbled along, Langton stepped back. He knew his squadron had done its best to drive up the elevated highway from

[*] Dr. John C. Warren, *Airborne Operations in World War II, European Theater*, p. 146.

Nijmegen to Arnhem, yet he felt uneasy, "almost embarrassed to speak to them." As one of the men drew abreast of another Guardsman standing silently beside the road, the trooper shouted, "Where the hell have you been, mate?" The Guardsman answered quietly, "We've been fighting for five months." Corporal William Chennell of the Guards heard one of the airborne men say, "Oh? Did you have a nice drive up?"

As the men streamed back one officer, who had stood in the rain for hours, searched every face. Captain Eric Mackay, whose little band of stragglers had held out so gallantly in the schoolhouse near the Arnhem bridge, had escaped and reached Nijmegen. Now he looked for members of his squadron. Most of them had not made it to the Arnhem bridge; but Mackay, with stubborn hope, looked for them in the airborne lines coming out of Oosterbeek. "The worst thing of all was their faces," he says of the troopers. "They all looked unbelievably drawn and tired. Here and there you could pick out a veteran—a face with an unmistakable I-don't-give-a-damn look, as if he could never be beaten." All that night and into the dawn Mackay stayed by the road. "I didn't see one face I knew. As I continued to watch I hated everyone. I hated whoever was responsible for this and I hated the army for its indecision and I thought of the waste of life and of a fine division dumped down the drain. And for what?" It was full light when Mackay went back to Nijmegen. There he began to check collecting points and billets, determined to find his men. Of the 200 engineers in his squadron, five, including Mackay, had come back.

On the other side of the river remained the soldiers and civilians whose jobs and injuries demanded that they be left behind. Small bands of men too late to make the trip stayed too, crouched down in the now-unmanned trenches and gun pits. For these survivors there was no longer any hope. In the blackened perimeter they awaited their fate.

Medic Taffy Brace had brought the last of his walking wounded down to the river, only to find the banks now empty.

Huddling with them, Brace saw a captain coming forward. "What are we going to do?" the officer asked Brace. "There won't be any more boats." Brace looked at the injured men. "I guess we'll have to stay then," he said. "I can't leave them." The captain shook hands. "Good luck," he told them all. "I'm going to try to swim across." Brace last saw the officer wading out into the water. "Good luck yourself," Brace called. "Goodbye."

For Major Guy Rigby-Jones, a physician at the Tafelberg, "the division's leaving was a bitter pill to swallow," but he carried on his work. With teams of medics Rigby-Jones scoured the houses in the area of the hotel, bringing in wounded men. Often hand-carrying the casualties to collection points, the medics loaded them into German trucks, ambulances and jeeps and then climbed on themselves, heading into captivity.

Padre Pare had slept the whole night through at the Schoonoord. He awoke with a start, sure that something was terribly wrong. Then he realized that it was unnaturally quiet. Hurrying out into a room, he saw a medic standing at a window, in full view of anyone outside. As Pare came up the medic turned around. "The division's gone," he said. Pare, who had not been told about the evacuation, stared at him. "You're mad, man." The medic shook his head. "Look for yourself, sir. We really are prisoners now. Our chaps have had to retreat." Pare couldn't believe it. "Sir," the medic said, "you'll have to break the news to the patients. I haven't got the nerve to tell them." Pare made the rounds of the hotel. "Everyone tried to take it in good heart," he recalls, "but we were all in a fit of deep depression." Then in the large room where most of the wounded still sheltered a soldier sat down at a piano and began to play a medley of popular songs. Men started to sing and Pare found himself joining in.

"It was queer after the hell of the last few days," Pare says. "The Germans could not understand it, but it was easy enough to explain. The suspense, the sense of being left behind produced a tremendous reaction. There was nothing left to do but sing." Later as Hendrika van der Vlist and other Dutch civilians prepared to leave to help the wounded in German hospitals, Pare waved goodbye regretfully. "They had suffered with us, gone hungry and thirsty, and yet they had no thought for themselves." As the last ambulances disappeared, Pare and the medical staff loaded their meager belongings onto a German truck. "The Germans helped us," he recalls. "There was a curious lack of animosity. None of us had anything to say." As the truck drove off, Pare stared moodily at the blackened wreckage of the Schoonoord, "where absolute miracles had been worked." He was "firmly convinced that it was only a matter of a day or two, possibly this coming night, before the Second Army crossed the Rhine and took the area back again."

Across the street from the church, Kate ter Horst had said goodbye to the wounded, all now prisoners. Pulling a hand cart and accompanied by her five children, she set out to walk to Apeldoorn. A short distance away she stopped and looked back at the ancient vicarage that had been her home. "A ray of sunshine strikes a bright yellow parachute hanging from the roof," she wrote. "Bright yellow . . . A greeting from the Airborne . . . Farewell, friends . . . God bless you."

Young Anje van Maanen, also on the road to Apeldoorn, kept looking for her father as the Red Cross cars and ambulances passed, bringing the wounded from the Tafelberg. With her aunt and her brother, Anje stared at the familiar faces she had come to know throughout the week. Then, as a truck passed by, Anje saw her father, riding in it. She screamed to him and began to run. The truck stopped and Dr. van Maanen climbed down to greet his family. Hugging them all, he said, "We have never been so poor and never so rich. We have lost our village, our home and our possessions. But we have each other and we are alive." As Dr. van Maanen got back on the truck to care for the wounded, he arranged for the family to meet in Apeldoorn. As they walked among hundreds of other refugees, Anje turned to look back. "The sky was colored scarlet," she wrote, "like the blood of the airborne who gave their lives for us. We four all are alive, but at the end of this hopeless war week the battle has made an impression on my soul. Glory to all our dear, brave Tommies and to all the people who gave their lives to help and save others."

In Driel, Cora Baltussen awoke to a strange silence. It was midmorning Tuesday, September 26. Painfully stiff from her wounds and puzzled by the silence, Cora limped outside. Smoke billowed up from the center of the town and from Oosterbeek across the river. But the sounds of battle were gone. Getting her bicycle, Cora pedaled slowly toward town. The streets were deserted; the troops had gone. In the distance she saw the last vehicles in a convoy heading south for Nijmegen. Near one of Driel's ruined churches only a few soldiers lingered by some jeeps. Suddenly Cora realized that the British and Poles were withdrawing. The fight was over; the Germans would soon return. As she walked over to the small group of soldiers, the bell in the damaged church steeple began to toll. Cora looked up. Sitting in the belfry was an airborne trooper, a bandage around his head. "What happened?" Cora called out. "It's all over," the trooper shouted. "All over. We pulled out. We're the last lot." Cora stared up at him. "Why are you ringing the bell?" The trooper kicked at it once more. The sound echoed over the thousand-year-old Dutch village of Driel and died away. The trooper looked down at Cora. "It seemed like the right thing to do," he said.

You have read this Book through the auspices of one:

Donald W Caly

"In my—prejudiced—view, if the operation had been properly backed from its inception, and given the aircraft, ground forces, and administrative resources necessary for the job—it would have succeeded in spite of my mistakes, or the adverse weather, or the presence of the 2nd SS Panzer Corps in the Arnhem area. I remain MARKET-GARDEN'S unrepentant advocate."

—FIELD MARSHAL SIR BERNARD MONTGOMERY,
Memoirs: Montgomery of Alamein, p. 267

"My country can never again afford the luxury of another Montgomery success."

—BERNHARD, THE PRINCE OF THE NETHERLANDS,
to the author.

A NOTE ON CASUALTIES

Allied forces suffered more casualties in Market-Garden than in the mammoth invasion of Normandy. Most historians agree that in the twenty-four-hour period of D Day, June 6, 1944, total Allied losses reached an estimated 10,000–12,000. In the nine days of Market-Garden combined losses—airborne and ground forces—in killed, wounded and missing amounted to more than 17,000.

British casualties were the highest: 13,226. Urquhart's division was almost completely destroyed. In the 10,005 Arnhem force, which includes the Poles and glider pilots, casualties totaled 7,578. In addition to this figure RAF pilot and crew losses came to another 294, making a total in wounded, dead and missing of 7,872. Horrocks' XXX Corps lost 1,480 and the British 8th and 12th Corps another 3,874.

American losses, including glider pilots and IX Troop Carrier Command, are put at 3,974. General Gavin's 82nd Airborne Division had 1,432; General Taylor's 101st, 2,118; and air crew losses 424.

Complete German figures remain unknown but in Arnhem and Oosterbeek admitted casualties came to 3,300 including 1,300 dead. However, in the entire Market-Garden battle area, Model's losses were much higher. While no figure breakdown is available for the number of enemy killed, wounded and missing, from the breakout at Neerpelt, then along the corridor in battles at Nijmegen, Grave, Veghel, Best and Eindhoven, after interviewing German commanders I would conservatively estimate that Army Group B lost at least another 7,500–10,000 men, of which perhaps a quarter were killed.

What were Dutch civilian casualties? No one can say. Deaths in Arnhem and Oosterbeek are said to have been low, less than 500, but no one knows with any certainty. I have heard casualty figures— that is, dead, wounded or missing—given as high as 10,000 in the entire Operation Market-Garden campaign and as a result of the forcible evacuation of the Arnhem sector together with deprivation and starvation in the terrible winter that followed the attack.

THE
SOLDIERS AND CIVILIANS
OF
"A BRIDGE TOO FAR"

✿

What They Do Today

Following is a list of all those who out of their firsthand recollections contributed information to "A Bridge Too Far." First, the men of the Allied armies; then the Dutch who lived in the area during the battle; and finally the German military who fought there. Occupations may have changed since this book went to press, and where an asterisk follows a name it indicates that the contributor has died since these lists were compiled. All ranks given are as of September, 1944.

AMERICAN

Eisenhower, Dwight David,* Gen., Supreme Comdr. [SHAEF]. *Gen. of the Army, Comdr. in Chief, President of the United States.*

Bradley, Omar Nelson, Gen. [12th Army Group]. *Gen. of the Army; Company director, Beverly Hills, Calif.*

Abel, Leonard Edw., 2nd Lt. [82nd Airborne]. *Attorney, Bay Harbor Islands, Fla.*

Addison, William A. B., Major [82nd Airborne]. *V.-P. and trust officer, South Carolina National Bank, Columbia, S.C.*

Albritton, Earl M., Cpl. [101st Airborne]. *Rural mail carrier, Winnsboro, La.*

Alexander, Mark J., Lt. Col. [82nd Airborne]. *Real-estate broker, Campbell, Calif.*

Alhart, John Lamar, Capt. [82nd Airborne]. *Dentist, Rochester, N.Y.*

Allardyce, James R., P.F.C. [82nd Airborne]. *Engineer, Frankenmuth, Mich.*

Allen, James Mann, Lt. [101st Airborne]. *President, Allen Paint Supply Co., Denver, Colo.*

Allen, John Henry, P.F.C. [82nd Airborne]. *Upholsterer, Levittown, N.Y.*

Allen, Ray Carroll, Lt. Col. [101st Airborne] *Black Angus cattle rancher, Marshall, Tex.*

Altomare, John G., Cpl. [101st Airborne]. *X-ray worker for Westinghouse, Baltimore, Md.*

Anderson, Fred, Jr., Capt. [101st Airborne]. *V.-P. (Sales), International Corporation, Charlotte, N.C.*

Ankenbrandt, Louis E., P.F.C. [82nd Airborne]. *Ammunition plant mechanic, Baraboo, Wis.*

Antonion, Anthony J., P.F.C. [82nd Airborne]. *Shoe corrections, Long Island City, N.Y.*

Appleby, Sam, S/Sgt. [82nd Airborne]. *Attorney, Ozark, Mo.*

Arnold, George Wm., Sgt. [82nd Airborne]. *District manager, Detroit News, Birmingham, Mich.*

Asay, Charles Verne, Sgt. [101st Airborne]. *Linotype operator, Sacramento, Calif.*

Atkins, Lynn Cecil, Lt. [82nd Airborne]. *Asst. principal, Roosevelt Elementary School, El Paso, Tex.*

Badeaux, Nelson John, T/5 [82nd Airborne]. *Pipeline maintenance man, Tennessee Gas Pipeline Co., New Iberia, La.*

Bailey, Edward N., Cpl. [82nd Airborne]. *Claims counselor, veterans service, College Park, Ga.*

Bailey, Sam H., Jr., Lt. [82nd Airborne]. *Executive, Connecticut Mutual Life Insurance Co., Miami, Fla.*

Baldinger, Irving M., T/5 [101st Airborne]. *President, Legion-Olmer Bakery Co., New Haven, Conn.*

Baldino, Fred James, Cpl. [82nd Airborne]. *Postman, Burbank, Calif.*

Ballard, Robert Aye, Lt. Col. [101st Airborne]. *Grove owner and operator and Postmaster, Goulds, Fla.*

Barickman, John Hamilton, Sec. Sgt. [101st Airborne]. *Steelworker, Streator, Ill.*

Baugh, James Emory, Lt. [82nd Airborne]. *Medical doctor, Milledgeville, Ga.*

Baxley, George C., Pvt. [101st Airborne]. *Special representative, Southwestern Bell Telephone Co., Hewitt, Tex.*

Beach, Maurice M., Col. [9th Troop Carrier Command]. *Brig. Gen. (Retired), U.S. Air Force; consulting engineer, Garden Grove, Calif.*

Beaudin, Briand N., Capt. [82nd Airborne]. *Pediatrician, West Warwick, R.I.*

Beaver, Neal W., Lt. [82nd Airborne]. *Factory manager, Ottawa Rubber Company of Bradner, O., Wayne, O.*

Bedell, Edwin Allen, Major [82nd Airborne]. *Col. (Retired), U.S. Army; superintendent, Scientists' Cliffs Service Co., Inc., Port Republic, Md.*

Bennett, William A., Sgt. [82nd Airborne]. *Printer, Columbia, Pa.*

Bernardoni, August, P.F.C. [101st Airborne]. *Golf professional, Deerfield, Ill.*

Best, William Grew, Capt .[101st Airborne]. *Pathologist, Glen Mills, Pa.*

Besterbreurtje, Arie D., Capt. [82nd Airborne]. *Clergyman, Charlottesville, Va.*

Biekes, Tillman Edward, Cpl. [82nd Airborne]. *Packinghouse worker, Indianapolis, Ind.*

Bills, Lloyd Elvin, P.F.C. [82nd Airborne]. *Maintenance man, Capital City Telephone Company, Holts Summit, Mo.*

Birtwistle, Owen G., Col. [9th Troop Carrier Command]. *Col. (Retired), U.S. Air Force; Commandant, Extension Course Institute, Air University, Gunter A.F.B., Ala.*

Blackmon, Sumpter, Lt. [101st Airborne]. *Principal, Rigdon Road School, Columbus, Ga.*

Blanchard, Ernest Riley, P.F.C. [82nd Airborne]. *Machinist, Bristol, Conn.*

Blank, William Leonard, S/Sgt. [82nd Airborne]. *Management analyst, Veterans Administration Hospital, Richmond, Va.*

Blatt, A. Ebner, Capt. [101st Airborne]. *Physician, Indianapolis, Ind.*

Blau, Vincent Francis, Cpl. [101st Airborne]. *Electric-meter mechanic, Northern States Power Co., Minneapolis, Minn.*

Blue, James R., Cpl. [82nd Airborne]. *Retired, Dunn, N.C.*

Boling, Earl W., Cpl. [82nd Airborne]. *Security policeman, Security Dept., Veterans Administration Hospital, Akron, O.*

Bommer, Jack Louis, Cpl. [82nd Airborne]. *Salesman, Columbus Sign Co.; Columbus, O.*

Borrelli, Anthony N., 2nd Lt. [101st Airborne]. *Customer service man, Peoples Natural Gas Co., Glassport, Pa.*

Bowman, Bernard George, P.F.C. [82nd Airborne]. *Coal miner, Van, W. Va.*

Boyce, Robert Ignatius, Pvt. [101st Airborne]. *Postal clerk, Springfield, Mass.*

Brakken, Joyce Pershing, Pvt. [82nd Airborne]. *Carpenter, Minneapolis, Minn.*

Brandt, John Rudolph, Sgt. [101st Airborne]. *Warehouse foreman, Colma, Calif.*

Brennan, George F., 2nd Lt. [9th Troop Carrier Command]. *Director of Civilian Personnel, U.S. Dept. of Defense, Alexandria, Va.*

Brierre, Eugene Donnaud, Lt. [101st Airborne]. *Attorney, New Orleans, La.*

Brilla, Michael A., Pvt. [82nd Airborne]. *Parts manager, Grabski Ford, Inc., Garfield Hts., O.*

Brockley, Harold Raymond, Cpl. [82nd Airborne]. *Postal clerk, Connersville, Ind.*

Brown, Earl J., P.F.C. [82nd Airborne]. *High-school principal, Wilburton, Okla.*

Brownlee, Richard Harold, 2nd Lt. [82nd Airborne]. *Druggist, Yuma, Colo.*

Brunson, Ernest Merkle, Pvt. [82nd Airborne]. *Screen-room-department operator, Union Camp Paper Corp., Savannah, Ga.*

Bryant, Nelson, Pvt. [82nd Airborne]. *Outdoors writer, New York Times, Martha's Vineyard, Mass.*

Buck, Rex Douglas, Cpl. [82nd Airborne]. *Sales and service man, Jamestown Container Corp., Jamestown, N.Y.*

Buffone, Harry Joseph, Cpl. [82nd Airborne]. *Carpenter, Jacksonville, Fla.*

Burns, Robert G., Lt. [101st Airborne]. *College football coach, University of So. Dakota, Sioux Falls, S.D.*

Burriss, Thomas Moffatt, Capt. [82nd Airborne]. *General contractor, Columbia, S.C.*

Busson, Ralph Joseph, S/Sgt. [82nd Airborne]. *Farmer, Doylestown, O.*

Cadden, James Joseph, Pvt. [101st Airborne]. *Detective Lieutenant, Homicide, Baltimore City Police Dept., Cockeysville, Md.*

Campana, Victor Woodrow, Capt. [82nd Airborne]. *Schoolteacher, Lexington, Mass.*

Campbell, Richard Angel, Lt. [101st Airborne]. *Real-estate broker, Palo Alto, Calif.*

Cannon, Harold Felton, Lt. [82nd Airborne]. *Schoolteacher, Lakeside Junior High School, Anderson, S.C.*

Cannon, Howard W., Lt. Col. [9th Troop Carrier Command]. *U.S. Senator from Nevada, Washington, D.C.*

Carmichael, Virgil F., Lt. [82nd Airborne]. *Circuit judge, Cleveland, Tenn.*

Carp, Samuel M., Lt. [101st Airborne]. *Salesman, Rockford Standard Furniture Co., Rockford, Ill.*

Carpenter, Frank J., Sgt. [101st Airborne]. *Pharmaceutical representative, Upland, Calif.*

Carpenter, Lowell Keith, Sgt. [101st Airborne]. *Sales manager, Bend, Ore.*

Carroll, Jack Paul, 2nd Lt. [82nd Airborne]. *Appraiser, Riverside County Assessors Office, Riverside, Calif.*

Carter, Winston Owen, Lt. [82nd Airborne]. *Farmer, Helena, Ark.*

Cartwright, Marvin D., Pvt. [101st Airborne]. *Rural mail carrier, Elk Mound, Wis.*

Cartwright, Robert Stanley, Pvt. [82nd Airborne]. *Maintenance Dept., Detroit Metropolitan Airport, Detroit, Mich.*

Castiglione, Frank B., P.F.C. [101st Airborne]. *Hobbyshop owner, Orange, Conn.*

Cavanagh, Eugene, Pvt. [101st Airborne]. *Brakeman, Penn Central R.R., Croton-on-Hudson, N.Y.*

Chappell, Julian M., Col. [9th Troop Carrier Command]. *Retired, Americus, Ga.*

Chase, Charles Henry, Lt. Col. [101st Airborne]. *Maj. Gen., U.S. Army, Chief of Staff, Heidelberg, Germany.*

Cholmondeley, Jack A.,° M/Sgt. [82nd Airborne]. *Secretary, Kenwood Savings & Loan Assn., Cincinnati, O.*

Cipolla, John J., P.F.C. [101st Airborne]. *Finishing superintendent, Sargent & Greenleaf Inc. Rochester, N.Y.*

Clark, Harold L., Brig. Gen. [9th Troop Carrier Command]. *Brig. Gen. (Retired), U.S. Air Force; company director, Daedalian Foundation, San Antonio, Tex.*

Clarke, Richard Robert, Sgt. [101st Airborne]. *Deputy Information Officer, Office of the Information Officer, Hq., U.S. Air Force Southern Command, Curundu Heights, C.Z.*

Clemons, George W., Sgt. [101st Airborne]. *School principal, Fresno, Calif.*

Cockrell, James Knox, Capt. [82nd Airborne]. *Research engineer, Falls Church, Va.*

Colombi, Gerald, Sgt. [82nd Airborne]. *Real-estate broker and developer, Belmont, Calif.*

Connelly, John J., Pvt. [82nd Airborne]. *Construction electrician, East Islip, N.Y.*

Connelly, John W., Capt. [82nd Airborne]. *County extension agent, Richmond, Ind.*

Cook, Edgar L., 2nd Lt. [82nd Airborne]. *Copy editor, Northfield, Conn.*

Cook, Julian A., Maj. [82nd Airborne]. *Col., U.S. Army, Columbia, S.C.*

Copas, Marshall, T/Sgt. [101st Airborne]. *Sgt. Major, U.S. Army, A.P.O., San Francisco, Calif.*

Corcoran, James S., Sgt. [101st Airborne]. *Sales representative and group consultant, Hospital Service Corp., Chicago, Ill.*

Cox, X. B., Jr., Lt. Col. [101st Airborne]. *Rancher, San Angelo, Tex.*

Coyle, James J., Lt. [82nd Airborne]. *Accountant, American Tobacco Co., Hicksville, N.Y.*

Crabtree, Bernard Gilbert, T/5 [82nd Airborne]. *Teacher, Kissimmee, Fla.*

Craig, William H., Lt. [101st Airborne]. *Sales representative, Sentry Insurance, Pasadena, Tex.*

Cready, Raymond D., P.F.C. [101st Airborne]. *Masonry contractor, North Miami, Fla.*

Cronkite, Walter, News Correspondent. *CBS commentator, New York, N.Y.*

Damianov, George John, T/Sgt. [82nd Airborne]. *Plasterer, King of Prussia, Pa.*

Dahlin, John F., Capt. [101st Airborne]. *Aircraft engineer, North Hollywood, Calif.*

Davidson, Lawrence H., P.F.C. [101st Airborne]. *Owner, Davidson Meat Market, Franklin, Ky.*

Davis, Andrew James, Pvt. [82nd Airborne]. *Heavy equipment operator, Sun Valley, Calif.*

Davis, Robert, Pvt. [82nd Airborne]. *Assistant sales manager, Westport, Conn.*

Dawson, Buck, 2nd Lt. [82nd Airborne]. *International Swimming Hall of Fame, Ft. Lauderdale, Fla.*

De Paul, Leo J., Sgt. [101st Airborne]. *Salesman, Cleveland, O.*

Defer, Raymond Pierre, T/5 [101st Airborne]. *Owner, home appliance sales & service store, Warrenville, Ill.*

Demetras, A. D., Wire Chief [82nd Airborne]. *Attorney at law, Reno, Nev.*

De Vasto, Francis Alphonse, P.F.C. [101st Airborne]. *Contracts Administration, U.S. Government, Burlington, Mass.*

Dickson, Robert S., III, Lt. [101st Airborne]. *Col., U.S. Army, Defense Attaché, Teheran, Iran.*

Dietrich, Frank Leslie, T/Sgt. [82nd Airborne]. *Lt. Col., U.S. Army, Silver Spring, Md.*

Dispenza, Peter, Sgt. [82nd Airborne]. *Police officer, N.Y.C.P.D., Woodside, N.Y.*

Dix, Shirley H., Capt. [82nd Airborne]. *Dentist, Miami, Fla.*

Dobberstein, Hugo Paul, P.F.C. [101st Airborne]. *Laboratory technician, Kimberly-Clark Corp., Appleton, Wis.*

Dodd, Edgar Frank, Cpl. [101st Airborne]. *Minister, Crockett, Tex.*

Dohun, Charles J., S/Sgt [101st Airborne]. *Manager of resort motel, Topsail Beach, N.C.*

Donalson, John M., Col. [9th Troop Carrier Command]. *President, Tennessee Forging Steel Corp., Rockwood, Tenn.*

Donnewirth, George Adam, T/5 [101st Airborne]. *Carpenter, Clyde, O.*

Doxzen, George D., P.F.C. [101st Airborne]. *Installation supervisor, Western Electric Co., Baltimore, Md.*

Druback, William A., Pvt. [101st Airborne]. *Elevator constructor, Otis Elevator Co., Bayonne, N.J.*

Druener, Hanz Karl, 2nd Lt. [82nd Airborne]. *Lt. Col., U.S. Army, Carlisle Barracks, Pa.*

Duke, James Edward, Col. [9th Troop Carrier Command]. *V.-P., Electro-Medics Devices Co., Pacific Palisades, Calif.*

Duncan, John Richard, Sgt. [82nd Airborne]. *Schoolteacher, Quincy, Ill.*

Duva, August John, P.F.C. [82nd Airborne]. *Capt., Jersey City Fire Dept., Jersey City, N.J.*

Dwyer, Francis Patrick Thomas, Sgt. [82nd Airborne]. *Program director, Island Trees, N.Y.*

Dwyer, Robert Joseph, Lt. [82nd Airborne]. *Associate professor of sociology, University of Lethbridge, Alberta, Canada, Missoula, Mont.*

Eason, Bert C., Cpl. [82nd Airborne]. *House painter, Phenix City, Ala.*

Eatman, Harold Lee, Sgt. [82nd Airborne]. *Customer Services, Eastern Air Lines, Charlotte, N.C.*

Eisner, Julius, P.F.C. [82nd Airborne]. *Civil Service, U.S. Government, Miami, Fla.*

Elliott, Chester Harding, Pvt. [101st Airborne]. *Timber worker, Thomasville, Mo.*

Eubanks, Henry Edward, P.F.C. [82nd Airborne]. *Employee, Blue Bell Packing Co., DuQuoin, Ill.*

Felt, Robert H., T/4 [101st Airborne]. *Asst. train dispatcher, N.Y.C. Transit Authority, West Hempstead, N.Y.*

Fergie, Charles, Cpl. [82nd Airborne]. *Retired, Kearney, N.J.*

Ferguson, Arthur William, Capt. [82nd Airborne]. *Senior public health engineer, Warner Robins, Ga.*

Fielder, Robert Abbott, Lt. [82nd Airborne]. *Lt. Col. (Retired), U.S. Army, San Pedro, Calif.*

Finkbeiner, Theodore, Jr., Sgt. [82nd Airborne]. *Capt., Fire Dept., Monroe, La.*

Fischer, Russell W., P.F.C. [82nd Airborne]. *Senior instrumentation tech., Shell Development Corp., Lafayette, Calif.*

Fitzgerald, John E., P.F.C. [101st Airborne]. *Data-processing supervisor, Staten Island Community College, Staten Island, N.Y.*

Foley, John Paul, Lt. [82nd Airborne]. *Owner, picture-frame studio, Durham, N.C.*

Fosburgh, James Whitney, 2nd Lt. [9th Troop Carrier Command]. *Painter, New York, N.Y.*

Fox, James D., 2nd Lt. [9th Troop Carrier Command]. *Ass't. to V.-P., Pan American World Airways, Darien, Conn.*

Franco, Robert, Capt. [82nd Airborne]. *Surgeon, Richland, Wash.*

Franks, Darrell James, Cpl. [82nd Airborne]. *Construction engineer, Asheville, N.C.*

Fransosi, Arthur Arnold, Cpl. [82nd Airborne]. *Postal employee, Cranston, R.I.*

French, Donald J., Lt. Col. [82nd Airborne]. *Col. (Retired), U.S. Air Force; trucking and storage manager, Allied Van Lines, Vacaville, Calif.*

Fuller, Clark H., S/Sgt. [82nd Airborne]. *Cook, Jamaica, N.Y.*

Furey, Thomas Patrick, Lt. [82nd Airborne]. *Col., U.S. Army, Ryukyu Islands, A.P.O., San Francisco, Calif.*

Galvin, Wayne William, Pvt. [82nd Airborne]. *Journeyman painter, Fairview, Ore.*

Garber, Dean Landis, Lt. [82nd Airborne]. *Manager, Personnel & Labor Relations, Jeffrey Mfg. Co., Canal Winchester, O.*

Gariano, Vincent Paul, Pvt. [82nd Airborne]. *Bus driver, Englewood Cliffs, N.J.*

Garofano, Frank P., P.F.C. [101st Airborne]. *Investigator, Commonwealth of Massachusetts, Alcoholic Beverages Control Comm., Medford, Mass.*

Garzia, John, Pvt. [82nd Airborne]. *Owner, TV- and air-conditioning-service business, Hialeah, Fla.*

Gatlin, Hershel L., Sgt. [82nd Airborne]. *Farmer, Colfax, La.*

Gavin, James M., Gen. [82nd Airborne]. *Lt. Gen. (Retired), U.S. Army, Cambridge, Mass.*

Gelber, Aaron, Sgt. [82nd Airborne]. *Sgt. Major (Retired), U.S. Army insurance agent, Fayetteville, N.C.*

Gensemer, Harold Lester, Lt. [82nd Airborne]. *Sgt. Major, U.S. Army, Fort Hood, Tex.*

Gilbertson, Elmer, Sgt. [101st Airborne]. *Salesman, Wausau, Wis.*

Gilliam, Frederick Keene, Flt. Off. [9th Troop Carrier Command]. *C.P.A., Burlington, N.C.*

Goethe, James H., Lt. [82nd Airborne]. *Dentist, St. George, S.C.*

Gore, Tommy B., Sgt. [82nd Airborne]. *Retired, U.S. Army, Tahoe Vista, Calif.*

Gougler, Frederick W., S/Sgt. [82nd Airborne]. *Railroad conductor, Reading Railroad Freight Service, Clifton Heights, Pa.*

Grace, Jack, Pvt. [101st Airborne]. *High-school art teacher, Bartlesville, Okla.*

Graham, Thomas W., Lt. [82nd Airborne]. *Farmer, Bluffton, Ind.*

Gray, William Joseph, Pvt. [82nd Airborne]. *Bus operator, Vincentown, N.J.*

Grey, Thomas Charles, Jr., Sgt. [101st Airborne]. *Rural mail carrier, Macon, Ga.*

Hall, Raymond S., Capt. [101st Airborne]. *Retired minister, Falmouth, Me.*

Haller, Joseph, Jr., Cpl. [101st Airborne]. *Lithographing pressman, Detroit, Mich.*

Handelsman, Oliver, Major [101st Airborne]. *Physician, Pittsburgh, Pa.*

Hanlon, John Douglas, Major [101st Airborne]. *Newspaper columnist, Providence Evening Bulletin, Rumford, R.I.*

Hanna, Roy M., Lt. [82nd Airborne]. *Salesman, Berkeley Heights, N.J.*

Hannah, Harold W., Lt. Col. [101st Airborne]. *Law teacher, writer and researcher, Texico, Ill.*

Harmon, George E., T/5 [82nd Airborne]. *Shipping clerk, Wrightsville, Pa.*

Harrell, John Daniel, Capt. [101st Airborne]. *Druggist, Pensacola, Fla.*

Hart, Augustin S., Major [82nd Airborne]. *Exec. V.-P., Quaker Oats Company, Lake Forest, Ill.*

Hart, Leo Michael, Pvt. [82nd Airborne]. *Manufacturer's representative, North Miami, Fla.*

Hauptfleisch, Louis A., Capt. [82nd Airborne]. *V.-P., Halsey, Stuart, and Co., Summit, N.J.*

Heath, Stanley H., Lt. [82nd Airborne]. *Secretary, Masonic bodies, Fargo, N.D.*

Helton, Roy Francis, Sgt. [101st Airborne]. *President, J. D. Helton Roofing Co., Chattanooga, Tenn.*

Hennessey, Joseph S., Pvt. [101st Airborne]. *Millwright, Farrell Corp., Beacon Falls, Conn.*

Herkness, Frank G., Lt. [82nd Airborne]. *Supervisor, electrical installations, Railway Division, Budd Co., Philadelphia, Pa.*

Hogenmiller, Joseph James, Cpl. [101st Airborne]. *Glassworker, Crystal City, Mo.*

Holabird, John Augur, Jr., 2nd Lt. [82nd Airborne]. *Architect, Chicago, Ill.*

Hopkins, James Bernard, Flt. Off. [9th Troop Carrier Command]. *Ass't Director, County Health Dept., St. Petersburg, Fla.*

Horne, Thomas A., P.F.C. [82nd Airborne]. *Pipe fitter, Newport, Division of Tenneco Chemicals, Inc., Oakdale, La.*

Howell, James K., Pvt. [101st Airborne]. *F.B.I., Woodbridge, Va.*

Huebschen, Herbert E., S/Sgt. [82nd Airborne]. *Accountant, assistant office manager, Beatrice Foods Co., Wright & Wagner Dairy Division, Beloit, Wis.*

Hughart, Robert Ralph, P.F.C. [82nd Airborne]. *Steelworker, Kaiser Steel Mill, Fontana, Calif.*

Hull, Logan Ben, Capt. [101st Airborne]. *Obstetrician and gynecologist, Altoona, Pa.*

Hunt, Harold Lawrence, S/Sgt. [101st Airborne]. *U.S. Civil Service, household-goods inspector, Petaluma, Calif.*

Hurtack George J., P.F.C. [101st Airborne]. *Painting contractor, Plainfield, N.J.*

Igoe, Charles M., P.F.C. [82nd Airborne]. *Prop man, U.S. Army film production, Long Branch, N.J.*

Ihlenfeld, Edward W., T/4 [101st Airborne]. *Lieutenant, Milwaukee Police Department, Milwaukee, Wis.*

Ingalls, Wilbur Royce, Cpl. [101st Airborne]. *Signalman, Erie-Lackawanna Railroad, Wellsville, N.Y.*

Ireland, Alfred Warfield, Jr., Major [82nd Airborne]. *Sales executive, Woodland Hills, Calif.*

Irvin, James Morris, Lt. [82nd Airborne]. *District manager, Pendleton Tool Ind., Inc., Greensboro, N.C.*

Isaacs, Jack Roger, Capt. [82nd Airborne]. *Druggist, Coffeyville, Kan.*

Isenekev, Melvin Wm., Pvt. [101st Airborne]. *Rural mail carrier, Boonville, N.Y.*

Jackson, Schuyler W., P.F.C. [101st Airborne]. *Trucker, Bethesda, Md.*

Jacobs, Herbert, Capt. [101st Airborne]. *Physician, Glendora, Calif.*

Jakeway, Donald I., S/Sgt. [82nd Airborne]. *Manager, Export Orders, Ebco Mfg. Co., Johnstown, O.*

James, Lawrence F., Sgt. [82nd Airborne]. *Motorman, N.Y.C. Transit Authority, Brooklyn, N.Y.*

Jedrziewski, Anthony A., Capt. [82nd Airborne]. *Electrical engineer, Belle Vernon, Pa.*

Johnson, Harry F., P.F.C. [101st Airborne]. *Farmer, Arbuckle, Calif.*

Johnson, Joseph Bernard, Jr., Capt. [101st Airborne]. *Lawyer, Duluth, Minn.*

Johnson, LeGrand K., Capt. [101st Airborne]. *Regional manager, Central Region, Ryder Truck Lines, Atlanta, Ga.*

Johnson, Paul B., P.F.C. [101st Airborne]. *V.-P., insurance company, Ridgefield, Conn.*

Johnson, Wilton Harold, Cpl. [82nd Airborne]. *Mail carrier, Palo Alto, Calif.*

Jones, Alvin, Major [101st Airborne]. *Executive, Jones Motor Co., Inc., Allentown, Pa.*

Jones, Delbert Francis, Pvt. [101st Airborne]. *Mushroom grower, Avondale, Pa.*

Jones, Desmond D., Sgt. [101st Airborne]. *Inspector, Sun Oil Co., Brookhaven, Pa.*

Jones, Glynne M., Col. [9th Troop Carrier Command]. *Brig. Gen. (Retired), U.S. Air Force; Director of Aviation, airport manager, New Orleans, La.*

Jones, James Elmo, S/Sgt. [82nd Airborne]. *President, Industrial Plastics, Inc., and Industrial Fabricators, Inc., Greensboro, N.C.*

Jones, Robert Ellis, Capt. [101st Airborne]. *Col., U.S. Army, Bad Toelz, Germany.*

Jones, William I., Lt. [101st Airborne]. *Physician, Charlotte, N.C.*

Joyner, Jonathan S., Sgt. [101st Airborne]. *Civil-service employee, Lawton, Okla.*

Kaiser, James L., Major [82nd Airborne]. *Col., U.S. Army, Washington, D.C.*

Kane, Maurice T., Sgt. [101st Airborne]. *Police officer, Buffalo, N.Y.*

Kantala, Matthew W., Jr., P.F.C. [82nd Airborne]. *Quarry owner, Elberton, Ga.*

Kappel, Carl Wm., Capt. [82nd Airborne]. *Col., U.S. Army, Springfield, Va.*

Kartus, Charles Leroy, S/Sgt. [101st Airborne]. *Merchant, Rock Hill, S.C.*

Keefe, Jack Edward III, Lt. [82nd Airborne]. *Physician, Miami Shores, Fla.*

Keenan, James E., P.F.C. [82nd Airborne]. *Ass't V.-P., Chemical Bank, Hicksville, N.Y.*

Keep, Henry, Capt. [82nd Airborne]. *Hospital administrator, Villanova, Pa.*

Keith, Herbert Paul, P.F.C. [82nd Airborne]. *Tavern owner, Newcomerstown, O.*

Keith, John Marvin, T/Sgt. [101st Airborne]. *Repairman and installer, Mountain States Tel. & Tel. Co., Stevensville, Mont.*

Keller, John William, P.F.C. [82nd Airborne]. *Toolmaker, Sea Cliff, N.Y.*

Kinnard, Harry William Osburn, Lt. Col. [101st Airborne]. *Lt. Gen., U.S. Army, Ft. Belvoir, Va.*

Kirkwood, Robert S., Capt. [82nd Airborne]. *Lt. Col., U.S. Army (Retired); senior auditor, N.Y. Telephone Co., New York, N.Y.*

Kissane, Joseph M., Sgt. [82nd Airborne]. *Public accountant, Greenlawn, N.Y.*

Kjell, Clifford George, Capt. [101st Airborne]. *Letter carrier, Rockford, Ill.*

Klein, Richard Lionel, Cpl. [101st Airborne]. *High-school teacher, Huron, O.*

Knox, Clyde F., P.F.C. [82nd Airborne]. *Sgt. Major, U.S. Army, Fayetteville, N.C.*

Koch, Stuart H., T/Sgt. [82nd Airborne]. *General agent, Northwestern Mutual Life Insurance Co., Appleton, Wis.*

Kogut, Michael J., 1st Sgt. [82nd Airborne]. *V.-P., International Molders and Allied Workers Union, AFL-CIO-CLC, Ludlow, Mass.*

Komosa, Adam A, Capt. [82nd Airborne]. *Lt. Col. (Retired), U.S. Army; professor, North Michigan Univ., Jeffersonville, Ind.*

Kos, Rudolph, P.F.C. [82nd Airborne]. *Antique dealer, Deerfield, Ill.*

Kotary, William E., Lt. [82nd Airborne]. *Agency Dept. Philadelphia Life Insurance Co., Wayne, Pa.*

Kough, Frank L., Cpl. [101st Airborne]. *Correctional officer, Western Penitentiary, Pittsburgh, Pa.*

Krantz, Eugene A., P.F.C. [101st Airborne]. *Works supervisor, Chicago, Ill.*

Krebs, Frank X., Lt. Col. [9th Troop Carrier Command]. *Legislative ass't to Senator Cannon, Falls Church, Va.*

Kremer, Jean Harry, Sgt. [101st Airborne]. *Salesman, Westbury, N.Y.*

Kroener, Walter B., Lt. [82nd Airborne]. *Battalion chief, Huntington Park Fire Dept. and Asst. Civil Defense Director, Huntington Park, Calif.*

Kuehl, Delbert A., Capt. [82nd Airborne]. *Executive Asst. Director, Foreign Missions, Elmhurst, Ill.*

Kumler, Lyle Kay, Sgt. [82nd Airborne]. *Insurance business, Gibson City, Ill.*

Lachkovic, John Paul, P.F.C. [101st Airborne]. *Truck driver, Hagerstown, Md.*

La Magdeleine, Leslie Leo, Pvt. [101st Airborne]. *Die setter, Mundelein, Ill.*

Lange, William A., Sgt. [101st Airborne]. *Tenant farmer, Pleasant Plains, Ill.*

Langston, Ledford M., P.F.C. [101st Airborne]. *Industrial employee, Red Banks, Miss.*

Lappegaard, Ray Lenard, Cpl. [101st Airborne]. *Director of organization and personnel, Toro Manufacturing Corp., St. Paul, Minn.*

La Riviere, Richard G., Lt. [82nd Airborne]. *Construction superintendent, Chicopee Falls, Mass.*

Larkin, Bernard L., Pvt. [101st Airborne]. *Beer distributor, Levittown, Pa.*

Lassen, Donald Douglas, Pvt. [82nd Airborne]. *Plant mgr., Henderson Portion Pak., Miami, Fla.*

Lazenby, Harvill W., Sgt. [82nd Airborne]. *V.A. Hospital staff, Nashville, Tenn.*

Lee, John C. H., Jr., Capt. [82nd Airborne]. *Director, Office of Appalachian Studies, Cincinnati, O.*

Leebrick, Frank Lee, Jr., Cpl. [101st Airborne]. *Letter carrier, Silver Spring, Md.*

Lewis, Mike, T/4 [101st Airborne]. *Services machine tools for the Bendix Corp., North Hollywood, Calif.*

Lillyman, Frank Lewis, Capt. [101st Airborne]. *Deputy Operations Officer, U.S. Army Infantry School, Fort Benning, Ga.*

Lindberg, John Albert, Pvt. [101st Airborne]. *Sales representative, Oklahoma City, Okla.*

Looney, Frank J., T/4 [101st Airborne]. *Tavern owner, Albany, N.Y.*

Loveland, Glenn E., S/Sgt. [82nd Airborne]. *Employee, Board of Education, Shelby, O.*

Luiz, Charles, Cpl. [82nd Airborne]. *Engineering technician, Federal Aviation Administration, Manchester, N.H.*

Macchia, Rocco L., Lt. [82nd Airborne]. *Real estate, Ozone Park, N.Y.*

Machol, Robert Leonard, T/5 [82nd Airborne]. *Electrical foreman for Mafco Electric Co., of West Hartford, Simsbury, Conn.*

Mackey, Leonard Snow, Cpl. [101st Airborne]. *Runs mineral and lapidary shop, Colton, N.Y.*

MacLeod, Tom, Lt. [82nd Airborne]. *Postmaster, Columbia, S.C.*

MacNees, Frank J., Col. [9th Troop Carrier Command]. *Col. (Retired), U.S. Air Force; rancher, Travelers Rest, S.C.*

Maltese, Edward Vincent, Lt. [82nd Airborne]. *Col., U.S. Army, Washington, D.C.*

Mansolillo, Nicholas W., Pvt. [82nd Airborne]. *Works employee, Providence, R.I.*

Marohn, Robert E., P.F.C. [101st Airborne]. *Detective Lieutenant, Tonawanda Police Dept., Tonawanda, N.Y.*

Martin, J. Roy, Jr., Capt. [101st Airborne]. *Roofing contractor, Anderson, S.C.*

Martin, Orville S., P.F.C. [82nd Airborne]. *Laborer, Methyl Ware Corp., Two Rivers, Wis.*

Mason, Charles W., M/Sgt. [82nd Airborne]. *Airborne Historian, Fort Bragg, Fayetteville, N.C.*

Massei, Ernest Lawrence, Jr., Sgt. [82nd Airborne]. *President, Cape Fear Car Service Co., Fayetteville, N.C.*

Mastrangelo, William, Lt. [82nd Airborne]. *Tavern owner, Philadelphia, Pa.*

McCarthy, John T., M/Sgt. [101st Airborne]. *Employee of photoengraving plant, purchasing, estimating and billing, Chicago, Ill.*

McClain, Allen French, III, Lt. [82nd Airborne]. *City fireman, Coral Gables, Fla.*

McDavid, James Earl, P.F.C. [82nd Airborne]. *Construction superintendent, Hayward, Calif.*

McElfresh, John F., P.F.C. [101st Airborne]. *Clerk of Circuit Court, Deeds, Knox County, Edina, Mo.*

McFadden, Frank J., Lt. [101st Airborne]. *Lt. Col. (Retired), U.S. Army; Deputy Director, Tattnall County Civil Defense Unit, Reidsville, Ga.*

McGilvra, LaVerne Russell, P.F.C. [82nd Airborne]. *Beekeeper, Baraboo, Wis.*

McGinnis, Arthur J., P.F.C. [101st Airborne]. *Probation officer and real-estate broker, Elkridge, Md.*

McIlvoy, Daniel B., Major [82nd Airborne]. *Medical doctor, pediatrician, Bowling Green, Ky.*

McIntosh, Ben Charles, Pvt. [101st Airborne]. *Utility man for Board of Education, Bartlesville, Okla.*

McKeage, Donald Wm., Pvt. [82nd Airborne]. *Construction superintendent, Hemlock, Mich.*

McKearney, Bernard J., Lt. [101st Airborne]. *Ass't. Supt. of Schools, Hingham, Mass.*

McMandon, William T., Pvt. [82nd Airborne]. *Branch manager, Singer Company, Miami, Fla.*

McNiece, Jake, Sgt. [101st Airborne]. *Post office clerk, Ponca City, Okla.*

Meddaugh, William J., Lt. [82nd Airborne]. *Personnel specialist, I.B.M. Corp., Hyde Park, N.Y.*

Megellas, James, Lt. [82nd Airborne]. *D.S.C., Director, U.S. A.I.D. mission to Panama, Balboa, C.Z.*

Merlano, Louis P., Sgt. [101st Airborne]. *District sales manager, Hermes Business Machines Paillard Inc., Levittown, Pa.*

Meyer, Ralph F., Pvt. [101st Airborne]. *Union official and salesman, San Francisco, Calif.*

Meyers, James Joseph, Lt. [82nd Airborne]. *Col., U.S. Army, Columbia, S.C.*

Miller, Michael G., Sgt. [101st Airborne]. *Mailman, Edison, N.J.*

Miller, Walter Leroy, Jr., Capt. [101st Airborne]. *National Secretary-Treasurer, 101st Airborne Div. Ass'n., Greenville, Tex.*

Millsaps, Woodrow Wilson, Lt. [82nd Airborne]. *Lt. Col. (Retired), U.S. Army; civil service, Columbus, Ga.*

Mitchell, Charles A., S/Sgt. [101st Airborne]. *Insurance consultant, sales director, Talladega, Ala.*

Mitchell, Edward J., Cpl. [101st Airborne]. *Air-mail dispatcher, Oshkosh, Wis.*

Moe, Glenn Allen, Pvt. [101st Airborne]. *Sheet-metal mechanic, Toppenish, Wash.*

Morrison, Thomas J., Pvt. [101st Airborne]. *Advertising-specialty business operator, Ambler, Pa.*

Mulloy, Patrick J., Lt. [82nd Airborne]. *Employment counselor, Gary, Ind.*

Mulvey, Thomas Paris, Capt. [101st Airborne]. *Real-estate broker, stocks and bonds, Clarksville, Tenn.*

Murphy, Ernest P., 2nd Lt. [82nd Airborne]. *Law-enforcement officer, Kissimmee, Fla.*

Murphy, James J., Cpl. [82nd Airborne]. *Salesman, Indianapolis, Ind.*

Nadler, Philip H., Pvt. [82nd Airborne]. *Supervisor, Reichbold Chemicals, Inc., Westwood, N.J.*

Neill, Robert W., 2nd Lt. [101st Airborne]. *Retail-furniture dealer, Pullman, Wash.*

Nichols, Mickey, Sgt. [82nd Airborne]. *Insurance agent, Philadelphia, Pa.*

Nickrent, Roy Walter, S/Sgt. [101st Airborne]. *Town marshal and waterworks Supt. for village, Saybrook, Ill.*

Nicoll, Kenneth S., S/Sgt. [82nd Airborne]. *Ironworker, Montgomery, Tex.*

Norris, James Sherley, Pvt. [101st Airborne]. *Welder, Roanoke, Va.*

Nunan, Paul D., S/Sgt. [82nd Airborne]. *Sgt. Major, U.S. Army, Syracuse, N.Y.*

Oakley, Herbert L., P.F.C. [101st Airborne]. *Dry cleaner, Columbus, O.*

Oatman, William John, Pvt. [101st Airborne]. *Truck driver, Lancaster, Pa.*

O'Connell, Robert Philip, 2nd Lt. [101st Airborne]. *National accounts manager, Group Hospitalization, Inc., Bowie, Md.*

O'Hagan, Patrick J., Pvt. [82nd Airborne]. *Civil service, N.Y.C. Transit Authority, Brooklyn, N.Y.*

Oldfather, Earl Shively, Cpl. [82nd Airborne]. *Banking officer, Toledo Trust Company, Toledo, O.*

Olsen, William S., Lt. [101st Airborne]. *Asst. to the President, Florida Mobile Home Assoc., Madeira Beach, Fla.*

Olson, Charles Ray, S/Sgt. [101st Airborne]. *Asst. superintendent of the composing room of the Jamestown (N.Y.) Post-Journal, Lakewood, N.Y.*

Olson, Hugo, Lt. [82nd Airborne]. *Attorney, Moorehead, Minn.*

O'Neal, Russell Roy, S/Sgt. [82nd Airborne]. *Restaurant owner, San Anselmo, Calif.*

Osborne, Ernest William, Sgt. [82nd Airborne]. *Material expediter, Union Carbide, Charleston, W. Va.*

Parker, Arthur, Sgt. [101st Airborne]. *Retired fire fighter; television technician, St. Petersburg, Fla.*

Paterson, Charles, Lt. [82nd Airborne]. *Safety supervisor, Armour Agricultural Chemical Co., Winter Haven, Fla.*

Patton, Donald Vickrey, Acting Sgt. [101st Airborne]. *Architect, Allen, Patton & Associates, Rockford, Ill.*

Pearson, Donald T., S/Sgt. [101st Airborne]. *Supervisory Plant Quarantine Inspector, U.S. Dept of Agriculture, Bayside, N.Y.*

Peterson, Theodore L., Lt. [82nd Airborne]. *Manufacturers' representative, Bloomfield Hills, Mich.*

Phillips, Robert Hamilton, Capt. [101st Airborne]. *V.-P., Trust Company of Georgia, Atlanta, Ga.*

Pickens, Oren Clinton, Sgt. [82nd Airborne]. *Postal employee, Homestead, Fla.*

Piper, Robert M., Capt. [82nd Airborne]. *Col., U.S. Army, A.P.O., San Francisco, Calif.*

Prescott, William L., Sgt. [82nd Airborne]. *Artist, San Miguel de Allende, G.T.O., Mexico.*

Pritikin, Marvin E., Sgt. [82nd Airborne]. *President, Illinois Mutual Fire Insurance Co., Chicago, Ill.*

Prow, Robert F., T/Sgt. [101st Airborne]. *Manager of a Pennsylvania state liquor store, Ambler, Pa.*

Purcell, Warren Carver, P.F.C. [101st Airborne]. *Farmer; Deputy Commissioner of Revenue, Petersburg, Va.*

Quirici, Oreste, Pvt. [101st Airborne]. *Manager, Physical Testing Laboratory, Kaiser Steel, Rutherford, Calif.*

Ragland, Robert Eugene, Lt. [82nd Airborne]. *Western regional sales manager, Baldwin, Ehret, Hill Inc., Los Angeles, Calif.*

Randall, Charles H., Jr., Pvt. [101st Airborne]. *Highway engineering technician, Los Altos, Calif.*

Rankin, William J., S/Sgt. [82nd Airborne]. *Carpenter, Kingman, Ariz.*

Richards, Theodore S., Lt. [101st Airborne]. *Sgt. Major, USARSO, Canal Zone, Ft. Amador, C.Z.*

Richardson, William King, Lt. [82nd Airborne]. *Employee, Veterans Administration, Columbia, S.C*

Richmond, William K., Flt. Off. [9th Troop Carrier Command]. *Building-maintenance employee, Hicksville, N.Y.*

Ridgeway, Matthew B., Maj. Gen. [XVIII Corps]. *General (Retired), U.S. Army, Pittsburgh, Pa.*

Rippel, John Kenneth, P.F.C. [101st Airborne]. *Director, Electronics Mfg., Baltimore, Md.*

Roberts, James J., Col. [9th Troop Carrier Command]. *Col. (Retired), U.S. Air Force, Santa Barbara, Calif.*

Rocca, Francis A., P.F.C. [101st Airborne]. *Machine operator, Pittsfield, Mass.*

Rohr, Willis F., P.F.C. [101st Airborne]. *Carpenter, Hinsdale, Ill.*

Rosemond, St. Julien P., Capt. [101st Airborne]. *First Asst. County Attorney, Miami, Fla.*

Rosenthal, Hillel Z., P.F.C. [101st Airborne]. *Salesman, St. Louis, Mo.*

Rosinski, Harry F., P.F.C. [101st Airborne]. *Auto mechanic, Garfield Heights, O.*

Ruppe, Frank, Cpl. [82nd Airborne]. *Dental laboratory technician, Maspeth, N.Y.*

Ryals, Robert Wilson, Sgt. [101st Airborne]. *Sgt. Major, U.S. Army, Trenton, N.J.*

Sampson, Francis Leon, Capt. (Chaplain) [101st Airborne]. *Brig. Gen., Deputy Chief of Chaplains, U.S. Army, Arlington, Va.*

Sampson, Otis Little, S/Sgt. [82nd Airborne]. *Water company employee, Palm Springs, Calif.*

Sanders, Gus L., Lt. [82nd Airborne]. *Retired postmaster, Springdale, Ark.*

Santarsiero, Charles J., Lt. [101st Airborne]. *Pennsylvania Power & Light Co., Scranton, Pa.*

Scanlon, Wilbur J., 1st Sgt. [82nd Airborne]. *Customer-service manager, General Electric Supply Co., Baton Rouge, La.*

Scheaffer, John E., 2nd Lt. [82nd Airborne]. *Dairy sales manager, Camp Hill, Pa.*

Schmalz, Charles Edward, T/5 [82nd Airborne]. *Laborer, Wheeling Steel, Steubenville, O.*

Schmidt, Nicholas, T/4 [101st Airborne]. *Teacher of English and journalism, Twinsburg, O.*

Schneider, Frank, P.F.C. [82nd Airborne]. *Machine operator, Downers Grove, Ill.*

Schrader, Clifford W., Sgt. [82nd Airborne]. *Construction foreman, Hoffman Estates, Ill.*

Schultz, Arthur B., Pvt. [82nd Airborne]. *Counselor-therapist, San Diego, Calif.*

Schwaber, Sanford, P.F.C. [101st Airborne]. *President, S. & M. Quality Foods, and Tasty Mix Products, Brooklyn, N.Y.*

Schwartz, John J., P.F.C. [82nd Airborne]. *Fireman, Rochester, N.Y.*

Schweiter, Leo Henry, Capt. [101st Airborne]. *Brig. Gen., C.O., 173rd Airborne, A.P.O., San Francisco, Calif.*

Schwerin, William Fred, Jr., T/5 [101st Airborne]. *Medical doctor, Pittsburgh, Pa.*

Searrin, William D., Pvt. [82nd Airborne]. *Bell Flower, Calif.*

Sefakis, Manuel John, Pvt. [101st Airborne]. *Worcester, Mass.*

Sessions, Myron Guy, Sgt. [101st Airborne]. *College instructor, Spokane, Wash.*

Shapiro, Hyman D., Lt. [82nd Airborne]. *Ear, nose and throat specialist, East Lansing, Mich.*

Shennum, Merlin J., Cpl. [101st Airborne]. *Farmer, Brockway, Mont.*

Shepard, Robert B., Capt. [101st Airborne]. *Honda motorcycles, Memphis, Tenn.*

Shoemaker, Charles Harry, Sgt. [101st Airborne]. *Maintenance section of National Park Service, Boulder City, Nev.*

Shutt, Harry G., Jr., M/Sgt. [101st Airborne]. *Construction superintendent, Shreveport, La.*

Siegmann, George A., 1st Sgt. [82nd Airborne]. *District sales manager, Temple Terrace, Fla.*

Simmons, Cecil Lee, Capt. [101st Airborne]. *Traffic engineer for City of Grand Rapids and Commanding General of Michigan National Guard, Grand Rapids, Mich.*

Smith, Ralph R., Pvt. [101st Airborne]. *Post-office clerk, St. Petersburg, Fla.*

Smith, Raymond, Pvt. [101st Airborne]. *Owner and president of Smith-Elkhorn Coal Co., Thornton, Ky.*

Smith, William F., P.F.C. [82nd Airborne]. *Gas & Electric Utilities, New Castle, Del.*

Soper, Erwin J., Jr., P.F.C. [307th Engineers]. *Erection superintendent, Haarmann Steel Co., Feeding Hills, Mass.*

Speck, Roger Donald, Pvt. [82nd Airborne]. *Southern Bell Telephone Co. and V.-P. of Local 3204, Communication Workers of America, Atlanta, Ga.*

Stach, Stanfield August, Capt. [101st Airborne]. *Retired, disability, Houston, Tex.*

Stallbories, Robert Henry, Chief Warrant Officer [82nd Airborne]. *Life insurance agent, Equitable Life Assurance Society, Tulsa, Okla.*

Steed, James Thomas, Sgt. [82nd Airborne]. *Marketing manager, Southern Bell Telephone & Telegraph Co., Ft. Lauderdale, Fla.*

Steele, John M.,* S/Sgt. [82nd Airborne]. *Retired, Wilmington, N.C.*

Stein, Lester, Capt. [82nd Airborne]. *Eye surgeon, Steubenville, O.*

Steinfield, Manfred, S/Sgt. [82nd Airborne]. *Furniture manufacturer, Skokie, Ill.*

Strayer, Robert L., Lt. Col. [101st Airborne]. *Insurance executive, Springfield, Delaware County, Pa.*

Strieter, William L., Sgt. [82nd Airborne]. *Real-estate broker, Arlington, Va.*

Strunk, Willard M., P.F.C. [82nd Airborne]. *Carpet-store owner, Wheatridge, Colo.*

Sult, Vernon Ralph, S/Sgt. [82nd Airborne]. *Liquor salesman, Granada Hills, Calif.*

Swanson, James A., Flt. Off. [9th Troop Carrier Command]. *Material-control manager, Industrial Corporation, Park Forest, Ill.*

Swanson, Wallace Albert, Capt. [101st Airborne] *Geologist; general foreman & supervisor with W. S. Dickey Clay Mfg. Co., Fairfield, Ala.*

Sweeney, Neil J., Capt. [101st Airborne]. *Civil service, Villa Park, Ill.*

Sweeney, Patrick J., S/4 [101st Airborne]. *Public-relations coordinator, Wappinger Falls, N.Y.*

Taft, Chester Weldon, P.F.C. [82nd Airborne]. *Millwright-machinist, Seneca Army Depot, Clyde, N.Y.*

Tallerday, Jack, Lt. [82nd Airborne]. *Col., U.S. Army, Fort Bragg, N.C.*

Tallon, Robert M., Sr., S/Sgt. [82nd Airborne]. *Department-store owner-manager, Dillon, S.C.*

Tarbell, Albert A., Sgt. [82nd Airborne]. *Ironworks employee, Nedrow, N.Y.*

Taylor, Frank Curtis, Sgt. [82nd Airborne]. *Retired, Albuquerque, N.M.*

Taylor, John H., Sgt. [101st Airborne]. *Paint and floor-covering contractor and retail-store owner, Lufkin, Tex.*

Taylor, Maxwell D., Maj. Gen. [C.O., 101st Airborne]. *General, Chief of Staff (Retired), U.S. Army.*

Taylor, Ray Edward, S/Sgt. [101st Airborne]. *Plasterer, Ashtabula, O.*

Thain, Carl Ernest, Capt. [82nd Airborne]. *Contractor, McAlester, Okla.*

Tisdale, Paul Arthur, Lt. [9th Troop Carrier Command]. *Col., U.S. Army, Arlington, Va.*

Tomardy, Bernard Joseph, Sgt. [82nd Airborne]. *Washington Gas & Light Co., Vienna, Va.*

Travers, Thomas R., 2nd Lt. [9th Troop Carrier Command]. *Operator van and storage company, Berkeley, Calif.*

Tremble, Leonard G., P.F.C. [82nd Airborne]. *Staff assistant, petroleum company, Fort Worth, Tex.*

Tribe, Robert Wayne, Lt. [82nd Airborne]. *Specialist, U.S. Bureau of Reclamation, Sacramento, Calif.*

Truax, Kenneth W., P.F.C. [82nd Airborne]. *Agency manager, rural insurance companies, Wisconsin Farm Bureau affiliate, Ettrick, Wis.*

Tucker, Reuben H.,° Col. [82nd Airborne]. *Administrative department of The Citadel, Charleston, S.C.*

Tucker, William Humphrey, Jr., Sgt. [82nd Airborne]. *Attorney; formerly Chairman, U.S Interstate Commerce Commission, Washington, D.C.*

Tyler, John Norman, Major [101st Airborne]. *(Retired), Cleveland, Tenn.*

Vandervoort, Benjamin Hays, Lt. Col. [82nd Airborne]. *Col. (Retired), U.S. Army, Hilton Head Island, S.C.*

Van Duzer, Franklin Kenneth, S/Sgt. [101st Airborne]. *Owner of Ris-Van Realty Co., V.-P., Community National Bank; director, Guardsman Life Insurance Co., Clear Lake, Iowa.*

Van Ort, Richard M., Cpl. [82nd Airborne]. *Truck driver, Summit, Ill.*

Vanpoyck, Walter S., Capt. [82nd Airborne]. *Administrative officer, Eastern Air Lines, Miami, Fla.*

Vantrease, Glen Wilson, Sgt. [82nd Airborne]. *C.P.A., Gary, Ind.*

Veach, Donald, P.F.C. [82nd Airborne]. *Farmer, Manila, Ark.*

613

Vest, Hansford C., Sr., Cpl. [101st Airborne]. *Machinist, Boeing Co., Renton, Wash.*

Vuletich, Michael, S/Sgt. [82nd Airborne]. *Steelworker, South Holland, Ill.*

Wade, James Melvin, 2nd Lt. [82nd Airborne]. *Lt. Col., U.S. Army, Fort Bragg, N.C.*

Wagner, Richard Paul, S/Sgt. [82nd Airborne]. *Electric welder, Baraboo, Wis.*

Waldt, Anthony M., P.F.C. [101st Airborne]. *Clerk, Aberdeen, S.D.*

Webster, Leonard J., P.F.C. [82nd Airborne]. *Heating & air-conditioning engineer, Milwaukee, Wis.*

Weil, Bernard L., Lt. [82nd Airborne]. *Manager, furniture store, Norfolk, Va.*

Weinberg, Stanley, 2nd Lt. [82nd Airborne]. *Haberdasher, Jersey City, N.J.*

Wellems, Edward N., Major [82nd Airborne]. *Col., U.S. Army, Ft. Lewis, Wash.*

Welshons, Don R., Sgt. [101st Airborne]. *Minister, Sunland, Los Angeles, Calif.*

Wetsig, Chester J., S/Sgt. [101st Airborne]. *Micro-electronic engineering at General Electric Co., Marcy, N.Y.*

Whitacre, William B., Col. [9th Troop Carrier Command]. *Retired V.-P., American Airlines, Hot Springs, Ark.*

White, Myron A., P.F.C. [82nd Airborne]. *Farmer, Grinnell, Iowa*

Wienecke, Robert H., Lt. Col. [82nd Airborne]. *Major Gen. (Retired), U.S. Army; consultant and director of insurance company, Ventura, Calif.*

Wierzbowski, Edmund L., Lt. [101st Airborne]. *Special representative, insurance sales, Chicago, Ill. (NOTE: Uses name Edmund L. Weir for business.)*

Wilder, Thomas Patten, Capt. [82nd Airborne]. *Yacht consultant, Balboa, Calif.*

Williams, Adriel N., Col. [9th Troop Carrier Command]. *Brig. Gen., U.S. Air Force, Washington, D.C.*

Williams, John Henry, Pvt. [101st Airborne]. *Instructor in R.O.T.C. program at Central High School, Chattanooga, Tenn.*

Williams, Warren R., Jr., Lt. Col. [82nd Airborne]. *Director, U.S. Army Board for Aviation Accident Research, Fort Rucker, Ala.*

Winton, Walter Farrell, Jr., Lt. Col. [82nd Airborne]. *Brig. Gen., U.S. Army, Annandale, Va.*

Woll, Shepherd, P.F.C. [101st Airborne]. *Owner, Wholesale Drug Sundries, Rockville Centre, N.Y.*

Womack, Waymon W., Pvt. [101st Airborne]. *Dow Chemical, Freeport, Tex.*

Wood, Rev. George B., D.D., Capt. [82nd Airborne]. *Rector of Trinity Episcopal Church, Fort Wayne, Ind.*

Wood, Leslie Earl, 1st Sgt. [82nd Airborne]. *Laboratory technician, Wunda Weve Carpet Co., Travelers Rest, S.C.*

Wurst, Spencer F., Sgt. [82nd Airborne]. *Laboratory technician, General Electric Co., and Lt. Col., National Guard, Erie, Pa.*

Wyngaert, Julius A., P.F.C. [82nd Airborne]. *U.S. Army, 3D Special Forces, Fayetteville, N.C.*

Yates, Gorden Wyatt, S/Sgt. [101st Airborne]. *Assistant produce manager in a supermarket. Attends college nights, Phoenix, Ariz.*

Yedenock, William, Jr., S/Sgt. [82nd Airborne]. *Insurance broker, Berwyn, Pa.*

Yeiter, Robert D., P.F.C. [82nd Airborne]. *Restaurateur, Traverse City, Mich.*

Young, Charles H., Lt. Col. [9th Troop Carrier Command]. *Commercial airlines captain, Grapevine, Tex.*

Zagol, Walter Frank, P.F.C. [101st Airborne]. *State instructor, savings-bank life insurance, Taunton, Mass.*

Zakby, Abdallah K., Major [82nd Airborne]. *Middle-East representative, tractor company, A.P.O., New York 09694.*

Zapalski, Daniel J., 1st Sgt. [101st Airborne]. *Retired Army officer; field representative for Prudential Savings & Loan Association, Rosemead, Calif.*

Ziegler, Roland C., 1st Sgt. [82nd Airborne]. *Electrician, Baraboo, Wis.*

BRITISH

Montgomery, Sir Bernard Law, Field Marshal [21st Army Group]. *Viscount Montgomery of Alamein, K.G., retired, Hampshire.*

Adair, Allan, Maj. Gen. [Guards Armoured]. C.V.O., C.B., D.S.O., M.C., *General, British Army, retired, London.*

Allsop, D., Capt. [1st Airborne]. *Transport & dairy manager, Pontesbury, nr. Shrewsbury.*

Anson, Geoffrey F., Capt. [Guards Armoured]. M.C., *Area manager, Ford Motor Credit Co., Ltd., London.*

Ashington, George, Pvt. [1st Airborne]. *Tool setter operator, Birmingham.*

Ashley, Neville L., Sgt. [1st Airborne]. *Teacher, Cheshire.*

Ashworth, Walton, S/Sgt. [Glider Pilot Regt.]. *Watchmaker, Essex.*

Atwell, Douglas, S/Sgt. [Glider Pilot Regt.]. *Valuer, Somersetshire.*

Austin, John Edward, Pvt. [1st Airborne]. *Civil servant, Surrey.*

Axford, James Alfred, L/Cpl. [1st Airborne]. *Postman, Kent.*

Back, Harold E., L/Cpl. [1st Airborne]. *Post-office clerk, London.*

Bagguley, Reginald, Pvt. [1st Airborne]. *Snack-bar proprietor, Staffordshire.*

Ball, Donald, Pvt. [1st Airborne]. *Ambulance driver, Yorkshire.*

Barclay, W. J. J., Pvt. [Pathfinder, 1st Airborne]. M.M., *Major, Ndola, Zambia.*

Barnes, Frank, Sgt. [Guards Armoured]. *Hospital clerk, Belfast.*

Barnett, J. Patrick, Lt. [1st Airborne]. *Golf club secretary, Kent.*

Barry, Peter, Lt. [1st Airborne]. *Medical doctor, Somerset.*

Basnett, Edward F., Sgt. Pilot [Glider Pilot Regt.]. *Housemaster, Home Office Boys School, Salop.*

Baylis, George Sidney, S/Sgt. [Glider Pilot Regt.]. *Cargo superintendent, Kent.*

Beckett, Sir Martyn, Capt. [Welsh Guards]. *Architect, London.*

Bedford, Ronald G., F/Sgt. [R.A.F.]. *Salesman, Torquay, Devonshire.*

Beech, James W. A., Pvt. [1st Airborne]. *Agricultural store manager, Spalding, Lincolnshire.*

Bennett, Clifford J., Guardsman [Guards Armoured]. *Grocery manager, Rugby.*

Bennett, Frederick C., Pvt. [1st Airborne]. *Stock audit, Redditch, Worcestershire.*

Bennett, Henry, Pvt. [1st Airborne]. *Stockbroker's messenger, London.*

Bentley, Thomas C., Sgt. [1st Airborne]. *Warrant Officer, British Army Recruiting, Nottingham.*

Binick, Norman, Sgt. [Pathfinder, 1st Airborne]. *Entertainer, London, S.W. 14.*

Blunt, John Graham, Lt. [1st Airborne]. *Major, Zambia Regiment, Ndola, Zambia.*

Blyton, Henry, Pvt. [1st Airborne]. *Plant operator, Lancashire.*

Boldock, Walter, J. P., Pvt. [1st Airborne]. *Rodent operator, Lincolnshire.*

Boulding, George H. W., Sgt. [1st Airborne]. *Printing-machine minder, Kent.*

Bowden, T. D. L., Trooper Signalman [1st Airborne]. *Manager, the National Kenya Sweepstake, Nairobi, Kenya.*

Bowers, Reverend Raymond E., Chaplain [1st Airborne]. *Parish priest, Richmond Place, Bath.*

Bowles, Dennis A., Signaller [1st Airborne]. *Analytical chemist, Tewkesbury, Gloucestershire.*

Brace, Terry, Cpl./Medic [1st Airborne]. *Storekeeper, Kent.*

Breese, C. F. O., Major [1st Airborne]. *Brigadier, retired; Company director, Yorkshire.*

615

Breitmeyer, Alan N., Lt. [Grenadier Guards]. *Colonel, commander, Grenadier Guards, London, S.W. 1.*

Bridgewater, William George, Sgt. Major [Glider Pilot Regt.]. *Petworth, Sussex.*

Briggs, Bernard W., Capt. [1st Airborne]. *Lt. Col., British Army (Retired), Dortmund Station, B.F.P.O. 20.*

Brook, Henry, L/Cpl. [1st Airborne]. *Bank messenger, nr. Manchester.*

Brown, Francis Edward, Sgt. [1st Airborne]. *Porter, British Railways, Yorkshire.*

Bruce, David, Capt. [Guards Armoured]. *Stock jobber, London, S.W. 10.*

Bruce, Joseph Morrison, Sgt. [Irish Guards]. *Retired, Belfast 13.*

Bryant, Reginald, Pvt. [1st Airborne]. *Printing engineer, Bristol 5.*

Buchanan-Jardine, Rupert, Lt. [Guards Armoured]. *M.C., Farmer, Dumfriesshire.*

Burton, Arthur Edwin, Cpl. [1st Airborne]. *Assistant superannuation officer, Leicestershire.*

Butcher, John M., W/Sgt. [1st Airborne]. *Works manager, Manchester.*

Cain, Robert,° Major C.O. [1st Airborne]. *V. C., Retired, Oxted, Surrey.*

Callaghan, Harry, Sgt. Major [1st Airborne]. *O. B. L., Civil servant, Aldershot, Hampshire.*

Campbell, Alexander Wm., Cpl. [1st Airborne]. *Patrolman, County Durham.*

Campbell, Gordon, S/Sgt. [Glider Pilot Regt.]. *Order clerk, Workington, Cumberland.*

Campbell, P., Sgt. [1st Airborne]. *Motor parts manager, Johannesburg, South Africa.*

Cannon, Brian Frank, Pvt. [1st Airborne]. *Engineering foreman, Luton, Bedfordshire.*

Carr, B. D., Lt. [1st Airborne]. *Supervisor, trust company, Vancouver, British Columbia.*

Cassie, James, Signalman [1st Airborne]. *Bookbinder, Edinburgh 11, Scotland.*

Cawrey, Victor F., Pvt. [Pathfinder, 1st Airborne]. *Haulage contractor, Leicestershire.*

Chandler, William F., Trooper [1st Airborne]. *Instrument maker, London, S.E., 24.*

Chapman, Harry A., W/S/Sgt. [Glider Pilot Regt.]. *Electrical contracts manager, Cyncoed, Cardiff, Wales.*

Chatterton, George S., Col. [Glider Pilot Regt.]. *Retired brigadier, London, N.W. 8.*

Chennell, William, Cpl. [Guards Armoured]. *Carpenter, London, S.E. 4.*

Christie, Gordon, Sapper [1st Airborne]. *Bricklayer, nr. Spalding, Lincolnshire.*

Christie, Robert K., Gunner [1st Airborne]. *Life-insurance agency superintendent, Surrey.*

Christie, Valentine Brock, Flying Officer [Royal Canadian Air Force]. *Grain farmer, Alberta, Canada.*

Clark, R. J., Capt. [1st Airborne]. *Bank economic adviser, Hertfordshire.*

Clegg, Benjamin B., Capt. [1st Airborne]. *Managing director, Sheffield.*

Clegg, Eric, Gunner [1st Airborne]. *Universal miller, engineering workshop, Lancashire.*

Cleminson, James A. S., Lt. [1st Airborne]. *Company director, Norfolk.*

Cockrill, James D., Signalman [1st Airborne]. *Police sergeant, Norfolk.*

Cole, C. V., Pvt. [1st Airborne]. *Carpenter, North Queensland, Australia.*

Coles, C. J., Cpl. [Guards Armoured]. *Major, Royal Guards, Windsor, Berkshire.*

Consett, William L., Major [Guards Armoured]. *Retired, London.*

Conway, James J., L/Cpl. [1st Airborne]. *Driver, Ministry of Aviation, Camberley, Surrey.*

Cook, Ralph, Gunner [1st Airborne]. *Chemical operator, Grimsby, Lincolnshire.*

Cooper, Derek G. D., Capt. Major [Guards Armoured]. *County Donegal, Ireland.*

Cooper, Frederick S., Pvt. [1st Airborne]. *Driver, Hornsy Rise, London N. 19.*

Copley, Stanley G., Signalman [1st Airborne]. *Public-relations executive, Henley-in-Arden, Warwickshire.*

Corrie, Michael T., Capt. [R.A.F. Glider Pilot]. *Produce broker, London, S.W. 1.*

Cosadinos, George, Cpl. [1st Airborne]. *Barber, Stockport, Cheshire.*

Cosgrove, David Thomas, Pvt. [1st Airborne]. *Trimmer, motor works, Luton, Bedfordshire.*

Cox, Alan Harvey, Lt. [1st Airborne]. *Lt. Col., British Army, Warrington, Lancashire.*

Cox, David, Pvt. [1st Airborne]. *Machine-shop inspector, Hemel Hempstead, Hertfordshire.*

Cox, Ronald Charles Percy, Pvt. [1st Airborne]. *G.P.O. engineer, Hemel Hempstead, Hertfordshire.*

Crawley, Douglas E., Major [1st Airborne]. *Lt. Col., NATO, Kolsås, Norway.*

Creswell, J. N., Lt. [Guards Armoured]. *Lloyd's underwriter, nr. Polegate, Sussex.*

Cronk, Frederick J., W/O Pilot [R.A.F.]. *Coach works director, Nottinghamshire.*

Crook, John W., L/Bombardier [1st Airborne]. *Police sergeant, Shipley, Yorkshire.*

Dakin, John Leslie, Pvt. [1st Airborne]. *Telephone engineer, Spalding, Lincolnshire.*

Dalton, Austin D., F/Sgt. [R.A.F.]. *Compositor, Linotype operator, Belfast.*

Daniells, Frederick T., Pvt. [1st Airborne]. *Engineer, Dunstable, Bedfordshire.*

Dauncey, Michael D. K., Lt. [Glider Pilot Regt.]. *Lt. Col., British Army, Latimer, Chesham, Buckinghamshire.*

Davey, Harold Leonard, C.Q.M.S. [1st Airborne]. *Shopkeeper, nr. Selby, Yorkshire.*

Davis, George E., S/Sgt. [1st Airborne]. *Marketing (sales promotion) N.S.W., Australia.*

Dawson, Alan, Pvt. [Pathfinders, 1st Airborne]. *Company director, Wrington, nr. Bristol.*

Dawson, John Harold, Pvt. [1st Airborne]. *Tool setter, Wolverhampton, Staffordshire.*

Dent, Ralph, Pvt. [1st Airborne]. *Police sergeant, Scarborough, Yorkshire.*

Demetriadi, Springet, Capt. [Phantom Net]. *Member, London Stock Exchange, London, E.C. 2.*

Deane-Drummond, Anthony, Major [1st Airborne]. *D.S.O., M.C., Maj. Gen., Commander, 3rd Infantry Division, Tidworth, Hampshire.*

Dixon, George, Cpl. [1st Airborne]. *Production engineer, Crawley, Sussex.*

Doggart, James, L/Cpl. [Guards Armoured]. *R.Q.M.S. of Irish Guards, Birdcage Walk, London, S.W. 1.*

Downing, Robert W., Pvt. [1st Airborne]. *High-voltage cable jointer, Northampton.*

Drew, James R., Sgt. [1st Airborne]. *Engineer, Stafford, Staffordshire.*

Driver, John, Pvt. [1st Airborne]. *Catering officer, Ashton-under-Lyne.*

Dullforce, Alfred J., Pvt. [1st Airborne]. *Stockroom manager, London.*

Dunn, Pat., Pvt. [1st Airborne]. *Coal merchant, Leicestershire.*

Eagger, Dr. A. Austin, A.D.M.S. [1st Airborne]. *Retired medical doctor, Exeter, Devonshire.*

Edwards, Jimmy, F.O. [R.A.F.]. *Entertainer, Uckfield, Sussex.*

Edwards, Robert C. S., Pvt. [1st Airborne]. *Heavy-goods driver, nr. Coventry.*

Edwards, Roy Norris, Pvt. [1st Airborne]. *Electrician's mate, Barry, Glamorganshire, Wales.*

Egan, Rev. Fr. Bernard M., Chaplain [1st Airborne]. *Headmaster, Wimbledon College Preparatory School, London.*

Ellwood, Richard A., Sgt. [1st Airborne]. *Gas board staff officer, Hammersmith, London.*

Emery, Ronald T., Sapper [1st Airborne]. *Decorator, London.*

Essame, Hubert, Brigadier [43rd Infantry Div.]. C.B.E., D.S.O., M.C., *Retired Major General, N. Chichester.*

Fairclough, Thomas, Sgt. [1st Airborne]. *Civil servant, Lancashire.*

Falconer, Edward, Guardsman [Guards Armoured]. *Laborer, Montrose, Angus, Scotland.*

Faulkner, Maurice A., Pvt. [1st Airborne]. *Gear cutter, Tamworth, Staffordshire.*

Fenge, William J., Sgt. [Glider Pilot Regt.]. *Builder, London, S.W. 17.*

Fieldhouse, Stanley, Gunner [1st Airborne]. *Tailor's cutter, Leeds 16, Yorkshire.*

Firkins, Harold J., Sgt. [1st Airborne]. *Director, insurance brokers, Kings Heath, Birmingham 14.*

FitzGerald, Desmond R. S., Major [Guards Armoured]. *Merchant banker, London.*

Fitzpatrick, Francis "Pat," Sgt. [1st Airborne]. *Office manager, Coulsdon, Surrey.*

Formoy, Leonard, Cpl. [1st Airborne]. *Depot manager for sports manufacturer, London, S.E. 11.*

Foster, Raymond H., Sapper [1st Airborne]. *Shoe repairman, Farnham, Surrey.*

Frater, Les J., S/Sgt. [Glider Pilot Regt.]. *Civil servant, Weston-super-Mare, Somersetshire.*

Freemantle, Albert, Pvt. [1st Airborne]. *Superintendent, British South Africa Police, Rhodesia.*

Frost, John D., Lt. Col. [1st Airborne]. *Retired Major General, Oxshott, Surrey.*

Gammon, Peter John F., Sgt. [Glider Pilot Regt.]. *Chartered surveyor, Woking, Surrey.*

Garfield, Frank, Pvt. [1st Airborne]. *Transport driver, Birmingham.*

Gatland, George, Sgt. Major [1st Airborne]. *Technical assistant, London Street Lighting, Wembley, Middlesex.*

Gay, Robert D., Sgt. Major [1st Airborne]. *Construction manager, Burgh Heath, Surrey.*

George, J. H., Cpl. [1st Airborne]. *Metal engineer, Australia.*

Gibbons, Eric R., Cpl. [1st Airborne]. *Off-license manager, London, N. 7.*

Gibbons, Leslie N., S/Sgt. [Glider Pilot Regt.]. *Sales representative, B.E.A. Airways, Warwickshire.*

Gibbons, Harry A., S/Sgt. [Glider Pilot Regt.]. *Stock controller, Chippenham, Wiltshire.*

Gillie, Thomas, Sgt. [1st Airborne]. *Building foreman, Darlington, County Durham.*

Glover, J. W., Lt/QM [1st Airborne]. *Retired Lt. Col., British Army Administration, York, Yorkshire.*

Glover, Richard, Cpl. [1st Airborne]. *Company representative, Driffield, Yorkshire.*

Goldthorpe, Lawrence, Sgt. [Glider Pilot Regt.]. *Government service, Surrey.*

Gordon-Watson, Michael, Major [Guards Armoured]. O.B.E., M.C., *Stud manager, farmer, Dorsetshire.*

Gorman, John, Lt. [Guards Armoured]. C.V.O., M.B.E., M.C., *personnel director, B.O.A.C., Sussex.*

Gough, C. F. H., Major [1st Airborne]. *Insurance broker and company director, Lodsworth, Sussex.*

Goulburn, Edward H., Lt. Col. [Guards Armoured]. *Retired Major General, Surrey.*

Grafton, James, Major [43rd Division]. *TV script writer, company director, Strutton Ground, London.*

Grainger, Robert E., Co. Sgt. Major [1st Airborne]. M.B.E., *Racing manager, Greyhound Stadium, nr. Stroud, Gloucestershire.*

Gray, Donald James, Signalman [1st Airborne]. *Builder, Cleethorpes, Lancashire.*

Green, P. J., Pvt. [1st Airborne]. *Slatter, Morayshire, Scotland.*

Green, Thomas C., S/Sgt. [1st Airborne]. *Head remedial gymnast, Marston Green, Birmingham.*

Grieve, Duncan G., Signalman [1st Airborne]. *Rotary-press assistant, Grimsby, Lincolnshire.*

Griffiths, Frederick F., L/Sgt. [Guards Armoured]. *Miner, New Tupton, Chesterfield.*

Growe, Michael G., Pvt. [1st Airborne]. *Inspector of motor components, Sheldon, Birmingham.*

Hackett, John, Brigadier [1st Airborne]. D.S.O., M.B.E., M.C., *Retired Commander in Chief, British Army of the Rhine.*

Hall, Eric, Sgt. [1st Airborne]. *Sales manager, Schweppes, London.*

Hall, J. A., L/Cpl. [1st Airborne]. *Clerk, British Embassy, Louvain, Belgium.*

Halliwell, Stanley, L/Sgt. [1st Airborne]. *Builder, Cheshire.*

Hands, Lewis, Sgt. [1st Airborne]. *Company director, Nottingham.*

Hardman, Donald A., Pvt. [1st Airborne]. *Fireman, Northants.*

Harker, M., Capt. [Phantom Net]. *Director, wine & spirits merchants, London.*

Harris, Thomas H., L/Cpl. [1st Airborne]. *Grinder, Warwickshire.*

Harrison, Charles A., Capt. [1st Airborne]. *Stockbroker, London.*

Harvey, Bernard H., Warrant Off. [R.A.F.]. D.F.C., *Civil servant, Guildford, Surrey.*

Harvey-Kelly, C. William, Lt. [Guards Armoured]. *Colonel, British Army, London.*

Hatch, Roy Ernest, Sgt. [Glider Pilot Regt.]. *Motorcycle dealer, Caterham, Surrey.*

Hawkings, Angela [Red Cross]. *Buyer, New York, N.Y.*

Hay, Neville, Lt. [Phantom Net]. *General manager to a security organization, London.*

Haysom, James N., Signalman [1st Airborne]. *Engineer, Cardiff, Wales.*

Haywood, Bernard, Cpl. [1st Airborne]. *Legal executive, Cheshire.*

Haywood, Leslie N., F/Sgt. [R.A.F.]. *Retired police sergeant, E. Yorkshire.*

Hendy, Arthur S., L/Cpl. [1st Airborne]. *Bus driver, London Transportation, Kent.*

Hennon, Wilfred, Warrant Off. II [1st Airborne]. C.S.M., *Civil servant, Farnborough, Hampshire.*

Herman, Jack, Flying Officer [R.A.F.]. *Investment consultant, London.*

Hewitt, Jack, Signalman [1st Airborne]. *Assistant head postmaster, Yorkshire.*

Heyes, Stanley, Signalman [1st Airborne]. *Sub officer, fire brigade, Cheshire.*

Heywood, A. G., Capt. [Guards Armoured]. C.B.E., M.E., *Colonel, British Army, Wiltshire.*

Hicks, Philip H. W., Brigadier [1st Airborne]. *Retired Major General, Hampshire.*

Hicks, Thomas, Sapper [1st Airborne]. *Locomotive driver, British Railways, Yorkshire.*

Hill, Joseph J., W/Sgt. [Glider Pilot Regt.]. *Personnel officer, Staffordshire.*

Hogan, Patrick, Guardsman [Guards Armoured]. *Postman, Middlesex.*

Holburn, A. R., Pvt. [1st Airborne]. *Lt. Col., Zambia Army, Lusaka, Zambia.*

Hollis, Frank, Pvt. [1st Airborne]. *Oil company driver, Essex.*

Hollobone, Bernard, Sgt. [1st Airborne]. *Shopowner, Leicester.*

Holloway, John J., Signalman [1st Airborne]. *Engineer, Kennington, Oxfordshire.*

Holt, B. R., S/Sgt. [Glider Pilot Regt.]. *Engineering planning manager, Leeds 16, Yorkshire.*

Holt, Ronald C., Pvt. [1st Airborne]. *Managing director, flooring contractor, Saltney, Cheshire.*

Homfray, Frank R., Lt. [Guards Armoured]. *Farmer, Newbury, Berkshire.*

Hopkins, George, Cpl. [1st Airborne]. *Joiner, Tamworth, Staffordshire.*

Hopkinson, H. S., Lt. [Guards Armoured]. *Colonel, commanding Household Cavalry, East Hagbourne, Berkshire.*

Horsefield, James, Pvt. [1st Airborne]. *Planer, Whickham, Newcastle-on-Tyne.*

Hoskins, James, Sgt. [1st Airborne]. *Police constable, Manchester.*

Houghton, H. R., W/Sgt. [1st Airborne]. *Plasterer, Liverpool 7.*

Houston, Francis Wesley, Pvt. [1st Airborne]. *Clerk, Newcastle-upon-Tyne 3.*

Howson, Victor, Pvt. [1st Airborne]. *Heat and frost insulator, London, E. 17.*

Hudson, Frank, L/Cpl. [1st Airborne]. *Lodgeman, Stoke-on-Trent, Staffordshire.*

Humphries, Alan Peter, Lt. [1st Airborne]. *Partner in accounting firm, Esher, Surrey.*

Hunt, Stanley J., Flight Lt. [R.A.F.]. *Education officer, R.A.F. Squadron Leader, Aylesbury, Buckinghamshire.*

Hurst, William, W/Sgt. [1st Airborne]. *Foreman, nr. Bolton, Lancashire.*

Huth, William J., Sgt. [1st Airborne]. *Manager of jewelry shop, Morden, Surrey.*

Inglis, Walter, Sgt. [1st Airborne]. *Hall porter, St. Albans, Hertfordshire.*

Isherwood, Reginald, Sgt. [1st Airborne]. *Managing director, Brentwood, Essex.*

Isitt, Bernard C., Lt. [Guards Armoured]. *Insurance adjuster, Paris, France.*

Jeavons, Sidney T., Pvt. [1st Airborne]. *Machinist, Sheffield, Yorkshire.*

Jenkins, Walter, Pvt. [1st Airborne]. *Nurse, Derbyshire.*

Jennings, Robert, Pvt. [1st Airborne]. *Diesel-plant fitter, Farnborough, Hampshire.*

Johnson, Ronald O., Lt. [Glider Pilot Regt.]. *General manager, Hoover Co., Wien 19, Austria.*

Jones, Alfred, Pvt. [Pathfinder, 1st Airborne]. *Civil servant, British Army, Germany.*

Jones, A. G. C., Lt. [Guards Armoured]. *Lt. Col., British Army, London W. 8.*

Jones, C. P., Lt. Col. [Guards Armoured]. *G.C.B., C.B.E., M.C. Retired Army General, Rye, Sussex.*

Jones, Eric, Signalman [1st Airborne]. *Paper converter, Widnes, Lancashire.*

Jones, James F., L/Bombadier [1st Airborne]. *Detective inspector of police, Witney, Oxfordshire.*

Jones, James Henry, Pvt. [1st Airborne]. *Bus driver, Speke, Liverpool.*

Jones, Robert H., Sgt. [1st Airborne]. *Managing director, Transport & General Contractors, Kitwe, Zambia.*

Jones, William, Pvt. [1st Airborne]. *Electrician, Dudley, Worcestershire.*

Jordan, Ronald G., Arm/Cfn. [1st Airborne]. *Sales-office manager, nr. Birmingham.*

Jukes, G. W., Pvt. [1st Airborne]. *Telephone installer, Vancouver, British Columbia.*

Kane, John P., Pvt. [1st Airborne]. *Works foreman, Yorkshire.*

Keenan, James M., Pvt. [1st Airborne]. *Engineer, New Parks, Leicestershire.*

Kelly, Donald, L/Sgt. [1st Airborne]. *Hospital canteen manager, Bishopton, Renfrewshire.*

Kent, Ronald, Sgt. [Pathfinder, 1st Airborne]. *Solicitor, Cape Province, South Africa.*

Kibble, William H., Reg. Sgt. Major [1st Airborne]. *Caretaker, Twerton, Bath.*

Killick, J. E., Capt. [1st Airborne]. *Counselor in H. M. Foreign Service, Washington, D.C.*

King, Charles D., L/Cpl. [1st Airborne]. *Tannery foreman, Little Borough, Lancashire.*

King, Frank D., Capt. [1st Airborne]. *Major General, M.B.E., Whitehall, London, S.W. 1.*

King, Henry A., Flying Officer/Navigator [R.A.F.]. *Queen's Messenger Escort, London, N. 12.*

King, Leonard, S/Sgt. [Glider Pilot Regt.]. *Police sergeant, Barnet, Hertfordshire.*

Kitchener, Joseph H., S/Sgt. [Glider Pilot Regt.]. *Postal and telegraph officer, Lewes, Sussex.*

Knee, Frank, L/Cpl. [1st Airborne]. *Linotype operator, Coventry.*

Langford, Thomas, Pvt. [1st Airborne]. *Industrial buyer, Blaydon-on-Tyne, County Durham.*

Langton, Roland S., Capt. [Irish Guards]. M.V.O., M.C., *Colonel, British Army, Oxfordshire.*

Lankstead, William A., Pvt. [1st Airborne]. *Motor mechanic, Northwich, Cheshire.*

Lathbury, Gerald, Brig. [1st Airborne]. G.C.B., D.S.O., M.B.E., *Gerald, Sir, Governor and Commander in Chief of Gibralter.*

Lewis, Edward, Cpl. [Guards Armoured]. *Tool setter, Cheltenham, Gloucestershire.*

Lewis, Richard P. C., Major [1st Airborne]. *Corn merchant, Alton, Hampshire.*

Lindley, Francis William, Major [1st Airborne]. *Sub postmaster, Retford, Nottinghamshire.*

Line, Cyril, S/Sgt. [Glider Pilot Regt.]. *Surveyor, Wedmore, Somersetshire.*

Lister, Eric C., Sgt. [Guards Armoured]. *Fish merchant, Strood, Kent.*

Little, Kenneth E., Signalman [1st Airborne]. *Works employee, Bristol 4.*

Loney, Patrick A., Trooper [1st Airborne]. *Lorry driver, London, E. 6.*

Long, Michael W., Lt. [Glider Pilot Regt.]. *Manager, Technical Publications, Stratford-on-Avon, Warwickshire.*

Long, Richard C., S/Sgt. [Glider Pilot Regt.]. *Technical representative, Romford, Essex.*

Longland, Cedric James, Major [1st Airborne]. *Surgeon, Dumbartonshire, Scotland.*

Lonsdale, Richard, Major [1st Airborne]. *Private means, Jersey, Channel Islands.*

Lord, John C.,° Reg. Sgt. Major [1st Airborne]. M.V.O., M.B.E.

Love, Donald, Flight Lt. [Guards Armoured]. *Insurance agency superintendent, Eastbourne, Sussex.*

Luckhurst, Frederick A., Sapper [1st Airborne]. *Aircraft worker, Wooten Bassett, Wiltshire.*

Lumb, D., Cpl. [1st Airborne]. *Toolmaker, Rochdale, Lancashire.*

Lumb, Vernon, Sgt. [1st Airborne]. *Sales manager, Rotherham, Sheffield.*

Mackay, Eric M., Capt. [1st Airborne]. M.B.E., D.S.C., *British Army Colonel, The Maultway, Camerley, Surrey.*

Mackenzie, Charles B., Lt. Col. [1st Airborne]. *Secretary, T. & A.F.A., Glasgow, Scotland.*

Mahaffey, Rupert, Lt. [Guards Armoured]. *Bank director, London S.W. 3.*

Major, Sidney Francis, L/Sgt. [1st Airborne]. *Sales representative, Hatfield, Hertfordshire.*

Malley, Joe, Cpl. [1st Airborne]. *British Army, Hull, Yorkshire.*

Marples, Graham, Signalman [1st Airborne]. *Land investigator, Penistone, Yorkshire.*

Mason, Valery E. C., Sgt. [Glider Pilot Regt.]. *Official, Zambia government, Ndola, Zambia.*

Mayne, William Victor, Guardsman [Guards Armoured]. *Lorry driver, Newtonabbey, County Antrim, Northern Ireland.*

McBain, Ronald C., Sgt. [1st Airborne]. *Fish merchant, Whitehaven, Cumberland.*

McCardie, W. D. H., Lt. Col. [1st Airborne]. *Company director, Cheltenham, Gloucestershire.*

McClory, Owen D., Pvt. [1st Airborne]. *Records clerk, Billingham-on-Tees, County Durham.*

McGuinness, Hugh, Pvt. [1st Airborne]. *Docker, Whitehaven, Cumberland.*

McMahon, Thomas, Pvt. [Pathfinder, 1st Airborne]. *Turf accountant, Twickenham, Middlesex.*

McNeill, David W., S/Sgt. [Glider Pilot Regt.]. *Company director, Stirlingshire, Scotland.*

Milbourne, Andrew, Pvt. [1st Airborne]. *Civil servant, Newcastle-upon-Tyne.*

Miller, Claire [Civilian]. M.B.E., B.E.M. *Company director, Rickmansworth, Hertfordshire.*

Miller, Victor D., S/Sgt. [Glider Pilot Regt.]. *Technical representative, Walingham, Surrey.*

Mills, John C., Cpl. [1st Airborne]. *Auto association patrol, Scarborough, Yorkshire.*

Mitchell, Edward, Sgt. [Glider Pilot Regt.]. *Maintenance dept., Ford Motor Co., Liverpool 19.*

Mitchell, Gordon L., Pvt. [1st Airborne]. *Process engineer, Heanor, Nottinghamshire.*

Moberly, Richard J., Col. [1st Airborne]. *Retired Major General, British Army, Salisbury, Wiltshire.*

Mole, Joseph D., L/Cpl. [1st Airborne]. *Plasterer, Stepney, London, E. 1.*

Moncur, Francis W., Pvt. [1st Airborne]. *Educational adviser, publishing firm, Wellington, New Zealand.*

Montgomery, Hector, Capt. [1st Airborne]. *Sales manager, Woking, Surrey.*

Moore, Rodney, Lt. Col. [Guards Armoured]. G.C.V.G., K.C.R., C.B.E., D.S.O., *Gen. Sir. (Retired), Ascot, Berkshire.*

Moorwood, S. James D., Lt. [Glider Pilot Regt.]. *Solicitor, Shamley Green, Surrey.*

Morgans, Daniel T., Cpl. [1st Airborne]. *Storeman, Rhondda, Glamorganshire, Wales.*

Morris, Dave, R.Q.M.S. [1st Airborne]. *Security officer, Luton, Bedfordshire.*

Munford, Dennis, Major [1st Airborne]. *Retired Colonial Service official, Southwold, Suffolk.*

Murray, Iain, Lt. Col. [Glider Pilot Regt.]. *Retired, London.*

Nattrass, George, Sgt. [1st Airborne]. *Hotel manager, nr. Middlesbrough, Yorkshire.*

Nayler, Anthony E., Pvt. [1st Airborne]. *Lorry driver, Melton Mowbray, Leicestershire.*

Newbury, Edwin, Capt. [1st Airborne]. *Chief officer of Licensing Dept., London.*

Noble, Jeffrey F., Lt. [1st Airborne]. *Personnel director, Sussex.*

Nunn, Sydney R. G., L/Cpl. [1st Airborne]. *Photographer, Stevenage, Hertfordshire.*

Oakes, William, Sgt. [Glider Pilot Regt.]. *Civil servant, High Barnet, Hertfordshire.*

O'Brien, William A., Pvt. [1st Airborne]. *Salesman, Waltham Cross, Hertfordshire.*

O'Leary, Peter, L/Sgt. [1st Airborne]. *Sales-office manager, Goffs Oak, Hertfordshire.*

Overton, Leonard M., Sgt. [Glider Pilot Regt.]. *Police inspector, West Derby, Liverpool.*

Pare, G. A., Chaplain [Glider Pilot Regt.]. *Vicar, St. James Church, Warrington, Lancashire.*

Paris, Edward P., L/Cpl. [1st Airborne]. *Painter, decorator, Blackheath.*

Parkes, Percy, L/Bombardier [1st Airborne]. *Police superintendent, Derbyshire.*

Partridge, Felix F., Sapper [1st Airborne]. *Carpenter, Sudbury, Suffolk.*

Paterson, William, Signalman [1st Airborne]. *Managing director, Southport, Lancashire.*

Pavey, Charles, Gunner [1st Airborne]. *Painter and decorator, Crawley, Sussex.*

Pawsey, Jack, L/Cpl. [1st Airborne]. *Printer, London.*

Pearce, Kenneth J., Signalman [1st Airborne]. *Head of Science Dept., Longford School, Twickenham, Middlesex.*

Pearce, Thomas W., Sgt. [Glider Pilot Regt.]. *Driver, delivery man, Croydon, Surrey.*

Pearson, Dudley R., S/Sgt. [1st Airborne]. *Auctioneer and estate agent, Weston Favel, Northampton.*

Peatling, Robert, Pvt. [1st Airborne]. *Compositor, London.*

Phillips, Bernard, L/Cpl. [1st Airborne]. *Sales manager, Manchester.*

Phillips, Edward L., C.F. [1st Airborne]. *Vicar, Lewes, Sussex.*

Potter, George H., Cpl. [1st Airborne]. *Decorating contractor, Wednesfield, Staffordshire.*

Powell, Geoffrey S., Major [1st Airborne]. *Civil servant, London.*

Preston, Henry G. C., Cpl. [1st Airborne]. *Works employee, Syston, Leicestershire.*

Pritchard, Thomas, Pvt. [1st Airborne]. *Prison officer, Edinburgh, Scotland.*

Prosser, John E., Pvt. [1st Airborne]. *Security officer, Reading, Berkshire.*

Pyne, Gordon, Sgt. [Glider Pilot Regt.]. *Company secretary/accountant, Clophill, Bedfordshire.*

Quinan, B. P., Lt. [Guards Armoured]. *Oil company official, Baghdad, Iraq.*

Ralph, Edward E. S., S/Sgt. [Glider Pilot Regt.]. *Planning engineer, Eastleigh, Hampshire.*

Rate, John, Sgt. [1st Airborne]. *Coach driver/courier, Wigston Fields, Leicester.*

Rathband, Harry, Sgt. [Glider Pilot Regt.]. *Oil company service engineer, Oxford.*

Read, Victor H., Signalman [1st Airborne]. *Electrical contractor, Basingstoke, Hampshire.*

Reynolds, Alfred S., Sgt. [1st Airborne]. *Works foreman, nr. Dartford, Kent.*

Richards, John T., Sgt. [1st Airborne]. *Representative, Wilford, Nottinghamshire.*

Rigby-Jones, Guy, Major [1st Airborne]. M.C., T.D., *Orthopedic surgeon, London.*

Robb, Richard, L/Cpl. [1st Airborne]. *Lecturer in surveying, Nottingham.*

Robinson, Peter T., Sgt. [Guards Armoured]. *Excavator driver, Southend, Essex.*

Robinson, Wilfred H., Capt. [1st Airborne]. *Schoolmaster, Kenilworth Cape, South Africa.*

Rose, John William, Pvt. [1st Airborne]. *Postman, South Harrow, Middlesex.*

Roullier, Alfred W., W/Bombardier [1st Airborne]. *Restaurant manager, Egham, Surrey.*

Russell, Cyril, Lt. [Guards Armoured]. *Solicitor, London.*

St. Aubyn, Piers, Lt. [1st Airborne]. M.C., *Stockbroker, Ringmer, Sussex.*

Salt, Wilfred D., Pvt. [1st Airborne]. *Postman, Willenhall, Staffordshire.*

Savage, Gordon, Gunner [1st Airborne]. *Bus driver, Arrowthwaite, Whitehaven, Cumberland.*

Schofield, Allan, Warrant Off. [R.A.F.]. *Nurse, Dawlish, Devonshire.*

Scott-Barrett, David, Lt. [Guards Armoured]. M.B.E., M.C., *Colonel, British Army, British Forces Post Office 15.*

Seaford, Raymond G., Pvt. [1st Airborne]. *Executive director, Luton, Bedfordshire.*

Seccombe, Ernest, Capt. [1st Airborne]. *Senior tutor, Hospital Administrative Staff College, London.*

Seeckts, James, Co. Sgt. Major [1st Airborne]. *Machine operator, Skelmersdale, Lancashire.*

Shackelton, Ralph, Pvt. [1st Airborne]. *Wool broker, Shipley, Yorkshire.*

Shearwood, Arthur, Pvt. [1st Airborne]. *Docker, London.*

Sheath, Alfred H., S/Sgt. [Glider Pilot Regt.]. *Fishmonger, Kent.*

Sheriff, Gordon, Cpl. [1st Airborne]. *Telephonist, Gloucester.*

Short, Edward R., Pvt. [1st Airborne]. *Government housing employee, Westoning, Bedfordshire.*

Simpson, Walter T., Sgt. [R.A.F.]. *Engineering inspector, Cheylesmore, Coventry.*

Sims, James W., Pvt. [1st Airborne]. *Radio clerk, Brighton 6, Sussex.*

Small, Albert E., Pvt. [1st Airborne]. *Vehicle mechanic, Normanton, Yorkshire.*

Smart, Roy J., Pvt. [1st Airborne]. *Racehorse trainer, Johannesburg, South Africa.*

Smith, Arthur J., Sgt. [Guards Armoured]. *Charge Hand, Birmingham 31.*

Smith, Eric, Guardsman [Guards Armoured]. *Police officer, Coventry.*

Smith, Frederick J., Guardsman [Guards Armoured]. *Detective inspector, Bradford 2, Yorkshire.*

Smith, Frederick P., Pvt. [1st Airborne]. *Casualty orderly, London.*

Smith, Henry, Lt. Col. [Guards Armoured]. K.C.M.G., K.C.V.O., D.S.O., *Retired, Windsor, Berkshire.*

Smith, John S., L/Cpl. [1st Airborne]. *Communications engineer, Wolverhampton, Staffordshire.*

Smith, Thomas, Guardsman [Guards Armoured]. *Building foreman, Coventry.*

Southall, William J., Cpl. [1st Airborne]. *Recreational supervisor, Coventry.*

Spelman, Dennis G., S/Sgt. [Glider Pilot Regt.]. *Sales manager, Bromley, Kent.*

Spencer, Harold W., Pvt. [1st Airborne]. *Baker, Grimsby, Lincolnshire.*

Spicer, Gordon F., L/Cpl. [1st Airborne]. *Machine-tool worker, Portslade, Sussex.*

Spivey, Horace, Sgt. [1st Airborne]. *Textile executive, Dewsbury, Yorkshire.*

Stainforth, Peter, Lt. [1st Airborne]. *Chemical engineer, Knebworth, Hertfordshire.*

Standish, Harold, C/Sgt. [1st Airborne]. *Sgt. Major in S.A.S. Regt., Salisbury, Southern Rhodesia.*

Stanley-Clarke, J. Q., Capt. [Guards Armoured]. *Draper's assistant, Shepton-Mallet, Somerset.*

Stanners, Geoffrey, Cpl. [1st Airborne]. *Company director, Great Kingshill, nr. Wycombe, Buckinghamshire.*

Steele, Robert R., Capt. [Guards Armoured]. M.B.E., *Company director, Beaulieu, Hampshire.*

Stewart, Richard, Major [1st Airborne]. M.C., *Solicitor, Scotby, Carlisle.*

Storey, Charles, Sgt. [1st Airborne]. *Captain, Quartermaster, British Army, Bahrein Garrison, B.F.P.O. 63.*

Stretton, Arthur H., Cpl. [1st Airborne]. *Stamford jointer, Tamworth, Staffordshire.*

Sturges, Sidney A., Cpl. [1st Airborne]. *TV representative, Erdington, Birmingham.*

Sullivan, Thomas Stanley, Sgt. [1st Airborne]. *Managing director, Stockport, Derbyshire.*

Sunley, Ralph ("Joe"), Sgt. [1st Airborne]. *Head gardener, Farnham, Surrey.*

Swift, Norman, Sgt. [1st Airborne]. *Police sergeant, Maidstone, Kent.*

Swinfield, William A., Pvt. [1st Airborne]. *Butcher, Burton-on-Trent, Staffordshire.*

Taylor, Arthur Reginald, Sgt. [Guards Armoured]. M.M., *Police inspector, Ipswich, Suffolk.*

Taylor, George, Lt. Col. [43rd Wessex]. C.B.E., D.S.O., *Brigadier (Retired), British Army, Tilford, Surrey.*

Taylor, W. A., T/Capt. [1st Airborne]. *Lt. Col., British Army, Bournemouth, Hampshire.*

Tedman, Francis R., Sgt. [1st Airborne]. D.S.M., M.M., *Panel beater, Tadworth, Surrey.*

Thomas, D., Cpl. [1st Airborne]. *Foreman, TV cabinet firm, Croydon, Surrey.*

Thomas, Sir G. Ivor, Maj. Gen. [43rd Wessex]. G.C.B., K.B.E., D.S.O., M.C., *General (Retired), British Army, Salisbury, Rhodesia.*

Thomas, Thomas, C.Q.M.S. [1st Airborne]. M.B.E., *Major, British Army, Deringlines, Brecon, Wales.*

Thompson, William F. K., Lt. Col. [1st Airborne]. *Brigadier (Retired), British Army; military editor, Daily Telegraph, London.*

Thompson, William Peter, Sgt. Pilot [Glider Pilot Regt.]. *Company director, Gateshead, County Durham.*

Thorley, John Henry, Signalman [1st Airborne]. *Businessman, Barnstaple, Devonshire.*

Tilly, Gerald, Lt. Col. [XXX Corps]. D.S.O., T.D., *Board chairman, Coulsdon, Surrey.*

Tims, Eric Lawson, Sgt. [1st Airborne]. *Constable, Eccles, Lancashire.*

Toler, Thomas Ian Jodrell, Major [Glider Pilot Regt.]. *General manager, chemical company, Alvanley, Cheshire.*

Tomblin, Bryan Alan, Sgt. Plt. [Glider Pilot Regt.]. *Police superintendent, Duston, Northamptonshire.*

Tomlin, Edw. Geo., Pvt. [1st Airborne]. B.E.M., *Security officer, Acton, London, W. 3.*

Tompson, William Claude, F/Sgt. [R.A.F.]. *Shopkeeper, London.*

Travis-Davison, Kenneth, Sgt. Plt. [Glider Pilot Regt.]. *Company director, Leeds.*

Turnau, Godfrey Joseph, F/Lt. [R.A.F.]. D.F.C., M.S.C., *Civil servant, Salisbury, Rhodesia.*

Turner, Arthur J. B., L/Cpl. [1st Airborne]. *Chauffeur, Oxford.*

Turner, Desmond N. S., Lt. [Glider Pilot Regt.]. *Probation officer, nr. Bury, Lancashire.*

Turner, John, Pvt. [1st Airborne]. *Social-security administrator, Coventry.*

Tyler, E. G., Major [Guards Armoured]. M.C., Bar, *Company director, Wooburn Green, Buckinghamshire.*

Udal, E. R., Capt. [Guards Armoured]. *Legal adviser, banking group, Hong Kong.*

Umpleby, Kenneth, Guardsman [Guards Armoured]. *Textile foreman, Keighley, Yorkshire.*

Urquhart, Brian, Major [1st Airborne]. *United Nations, New York.*

Urquhart, Robert Elliott (Roy), Maj. Gen. [1st Airborne]. C.B., D.S.O., *Company director, Glasgow, Scotland.*

Vandeleur, Giles A. M., Lt. Col. [Guards Armoured]. D.S.O., *Privately employed, London.*

Vandeleur, J. O. E., Lt. Col. [Guards Armoured]. *Brigadier (Retired), British Army, Maidenhead, Berkshire.*

Van Zoelen, F. W. E. Groeninx, 1st Lt. [Guards Armoured]. *Investment consultant, Madrid, Spain.*

Vincent, Raymond, L/Cpl. [1st Airborne]. *Aeronautical worker, Little Stoke, Bristol.*

Vlasto, Robert A., Lt. [1st Airborne]. *Stockbroker, Worplesdon, Surrey.*

Waddy, John L., Major [1st Airborne]. O.B.E., *Colonel, British Army, Chelsea.*

Walch, A. G., Brig. Gen. [1st Airborne]. O.B.E., *Brigadier (Retired), British Army, Marlborough, Wiltshire.*

Walchli, Robin O., Capt. [R.A.F.]. *Chartered quantity surveyor, Sarratt, Hertfordshire.*

Walton, James, Sgt. [1st Airborne]. *Clerk, Bootle, Lancashire.*

Ward, George William, L/Cpl. [1st Airborne]. *Postman, Reading, Berkshire.*

Ware, Denis J., S/Sgt. [Glider Pilot Regt.]. *Headmaster, Huntingfield School, Mitcham, Surrey.*

Warnock, Geoffrey James, Lt. [Guards Armoured]. *Fellow of Magdalen College; tutor in philosophy, Oxford.*

Warrack, Graeme, Col. [1st Airborne]. *Dentist, Edinburgh, Scotland.*

Warrender, Alfred George, Pvt. [1st Airborne]. *Polishing ship inspector, Wolverhampton, Staffordshire.*

Watson, Arthur A., Pvt. [1st Airborne]. *Printer, London.*

Watson, Arthur E., L/Cpl. [Guards Armoured]. *Lorry driver, Sussex.*

Weallens, Arthur Edward, Sgt. [1st Airborne]. *Post-office employee, Northumberland.*

Wellard, Leonard Edward, Sgt. [Glider Pilot Regt.]. *Bank manager, London.*

Wells, William James, S/Sgt. [Glider Pilot Regt.]. *Administrator, London Electrical Board, London.*

Welsby, Cyril, Pvt. [Guards Armoured]. *Glazier, Manchester.*

Westbury, James Ernest, Pvt. [1st Airborne]. *Postman, Nottingham.*

Wheeler, Jack, Pvt. [1st Airborne]. *Retail grocer, Warwick.*

White, George, W.O.I. [1st Airborne]. *Verger and parish clerk, Bridlington, Yorkshire.*

Whitehead, James, S/Sgt. [Glider Pilot Regt.]. *Relay adjuster, Warwick.*

Wickham, John Thomas, Sapper [1st Airborne]. *Clerk, Leicester.*

Widdowson, G., Major [1st Airborne]. C.B.E., T.D., *Colonel (Retired), British Army; bank manager, Birmingham.*

Wilcox, Geoffrey, Sgt. [Guards Armoured]. D.C.M., *Works manager, Berkshire.*

Wilcox, Ivor, Sgt. [Guards Armoured]. *Welder, Bedfordshire.*

Williams, Cyril, Sgt. [Glider Pilot Regt.]. *Headmaster, School for Handicapped, Bristol.*

Williams, Gwyn, Sgt. [1st Airborne]. *Innkeeper, Cheshire.*

Williams, John James, Pvt. [1st Airborne]. *Steelworks mason, Tredegar, Monmouthshire.*

Willoughby, Michael, Capt. [Guards Armoured]. *Landowner, Yorkshire.*

Wilson, Norman Edward, Pvt. [1st Airborne]. *Works employee, Staffordshire.*

Winterbottom, Lord Ian, 2nd Lt. [Guards Armoured]. *Parliamentary secretary, Public Buildings & Works Ministry, Northamptonshire.*

Wood, Jack, Pvt. [1st Airborne]. *Laboratory assistant, Staffordshire.*

Wordsworth, Ferrers Robin, Lt. [Guards Armoured]. *Company secretary, Welwyn, Hertfordshire.*

Wright, Harry, Pvt. [1st Airborne]. *Structural-design draftsman, Transvaal, South Africa.*

Wright, Leonard, S/Sgt. [Glider Pilot Regt.]. D.F.M., *Schoolteacher, Whitehaven, Cumberland.*

Wright, William Charles, Sgt. Pilot [Glider Pilot Regt.]. *Sales representative, Bristol.*

Wrottesley, Lord Richard John, Capt. [Guards Armoured]. *Private means, Salisbury, Rhodesia.*

Wyllie, George, L/Cpl. [1st Airborne]. *Greengrocer, Warwickshire.*

Yerburgh, J. M. A., Lt. [Guards Armoured]. *Company director, Kirkcudbrightshire.*

York, Harold, L/Sgt. [Guards Armoured]. M.M., *Postman, London.*

Young, Arthur Vincent, Lt. [Guards Armoured]. M.C., *Company director, nr. Stourbridge, Worcestershire.*

DUTCH

Bernhard, The Prince of the Netherlands.

Aa, Rudolph van der [Ede]. *Photographer, Ede.*

Aeyelts, Lauren Daniel [Helmond]. *Staff employee, Royal Zwanenburg factories, Oss.*

Agt, Antonius L.G.M. van [Gemert, Eindhoven]. *Archivist, Eindhoven.*

Aken, Pieter van [Wolfheze]. *Dermatologist, Ede.*

Alsche-deKat, Hermina Jacoba [Elst]. *Housewife, Elst.*

Andriesse, Maurits [Dinther]. *Retired, Veghel.*

Ariëns, Theodorus Antonius [Arnhem]. *Retired cleric, Arnhem.*

Aspert-Doornakkers, Anna Maria van [Zeelst]. *Housewife, Zeelst.*

Assendelft, Leendert van [Huissen]. *Chemical engineer, Arnhem.*

Baak, Norbertus H. J. [Son]. *State policeman, St. Oedenrode.*

Backus, Johannes H.H.E. [Arnhem]. *Personnel manager, Nijmegen.*
Baltussen, Arnoldus J. A. [Driel]. *Burgomaster, Groesbeek.*
Baltussen, Cora [Driel]. *Teacher, Driel.*
Baltussen, Josephus Frans [Driel]. *Company director, Driel.*
Bartels, Willem F. H. [Nijmegen]. *Public prosecutor, St. Odilienberg.*
Barten, Johannes A. [Grave]. *Tailor, Grave.*
Bech, Niels [Wolfheze]. *Works inspector, Oss.*
Beek, Dirk van [Oosterbeek]. *Bakery salesman, Oosterbeek.*
Beek, Marius van der [Wolfheze]. *Psychiatrist, Bergen op Zoom.*
Beekmeyer, Adriaan J. P., Cpl. [British 1st Airborne, England/Arnhem]. *Veterinary-pharmaceutical firm employee, Amsterdam.*
Beermann, Victor Antonius M. [Nijmegen]. *U.N. Representative, Australia.*
Bemen, Bob W. van [Lent]. *Construction mason, Miami, Fla., U.S.A.*
Bergh-Braam, Anna H. M. van den [Gent]. *Housewife, Nijmegen.*
Bergh, Johannes G. van den, Commando [U.S. 82nd Airborne, England]. *Director, Students Housing Foundation, 's Hertogenbosch.*
Bernebeek, Franciscus J. H. van [Groesbeek]. *Printer, Groesbeek.*
Beyerbergen van Heneqouwen, Augustinus N. G. [Oosterbeek]. *Teacher, Amersfoort.*
Bijlsma-Lusschen, Maria [Oosterbeek]. *Oosterbeek.*
Bisterbosch, Heimrich [Arnhem]. *Alderman, Arnhem.*
Bitters, Jacob Johan [Nijmegen]. *Mechanic, Nijmegen.*
Bitters, Janna [Nijmegen]. *Housewife, Nijmegen.*
Blaauw-Baghuis, Fie [Eindhoven]. *Housewife, Arnhem.*
Blokland, Jan Jacob G. B. van Brig. Major [Princess Irene Brigade]. *Colonel (Retired), Dutch Cavalry, Oosterbeek.*
Bode, Nicolaas T. de [Arnhem]. *Supervisor, Netherlands Radio Union, Hilversum.*
Boekraad-Otto, Maria O. [Nijmegen]. *Housewife, Nijmegen.*
Bolderman, Cornelis [Arnhem]. *Sgt. Major, Netherlands Defense Forces, Arnhem.*
Bolle-deWijk, Jutta [Renkum]. *Housewife, Munich.*
Bossert, Gijsbert [Veghel]. *Translator and bank official, Amsterdam.*
Boyens, Jan Peter [Eindhoven]. *Teacher, Eindhoven.*
Brachten, Everardus [Driel]. *Retired, Driel.*
Bremen, Bertha [Oosterbeek]. *Housewife, Oosterbeek.*
Brevet, William Karel [Arnhem]. *Radiologist, Arnhem.*
Broekkamp, Elias Henricus [Nijmegen]. *Wine importer, Nijmegen.*
Brom, Johannes Hendricus [Valkenswaard]. *Caretaker, Town Hall, Valkenswaard.*
Brouwer, Jacobus G. [Nijmegen]. *Major, Royal Land Forces, Deventer.*
Brouwer, Jacobus, G. L. [Oosterbeek]. *Retired, The Hague.*
Brummelkamp-van Maanen, Anje [Oosterbeek]. *Housewife, Middelburg.*
Bruschetto, Peter John [Nijmegen]. *Security police officer, Ontario, Canada.*
Busch, Johannus J. T. [Driel]. *Hotel manager, Driel.*
Bÿen-van de Weerd, Jennie [Bennekom]. *Housewife, Richmond, Calif., U.S.A.*
Claassen, A. [Bladel]. *Teacher, Waalwijk.*
Clous-Veen, Ida Egbertina [Oosterbeek]. *Housewife, Oosterbeek.*
Companjen, Albert G. [Berg en Dal]. *Bookkeeper, Groesbeek.*
Coninx, Guillaume [Lommel, Belgium]. *Superintendent of Police, Lommel, Belgium.*
Deinum, Martijn Louis [Nijmegen]. *Director, Orpheus Theater, Apeldoorn.*
Derksen, Antoon [Arnhem]. *Retired, Arnhem.*
Derksen, Theodorus F. R. [Nijmegen]. *Headwaiter, Amsterdam.*
Deure, Jacob van der [Bennekom]. *Attorney, Ede.*
Deuss, Albertus J. P. [Arnhem]. *Liaison officer, A.K.U. (International), Arnhem.*
Dijk, Sister Christine M. van [Arnhem]. *Retired, Arnhem.*

Dijk, Frans van [Waalre]. *Company director, Waalre.*
Dijker, Reinold F. [Oosterbeek]. *Catholic priest, Sintang Kalbar, Indonesia.*
Does, Jacob van der [Arnhem]. *Retired surgeon, Arnhem.*
Donderwinkel, Jan Willem [Oosterbeek]. *Retired, Oosterbeek.*
Doorne, Herman van [Wolfheze]. *Retired, Wolfheze.*
Driessen, Jan, interpreter [30th Infantry Div.]. *Factory director, Veghel.*
Drost, Johannes C. [Arnhem]. *Physician, Arnhem.*
Edwards, Eric Stuart [Eindhoven]. *Painter, Eindhoven.*
Eerd, Johannes W. A. van [Veghel]. *Photographer, Veghel.*
Eijkelhoff, Jan Adriaan [Oosterbeek]. *Bank clerk, Oosterbeek.*
Eijnden, Lambertus H. van der [Eindhoven]. *Wage administrator, N. V. Philips, Eindhoven.*
Einthoven, Louis [Utrecht]. *Archivist, Lunteren.*
Elst, Evert Jan van den [Nijmegen]. *Retired, Nijmegen.*
Fabius, Kaeso [Doetinchem]. *Burgomaster, Bilthoven.*
Feenstra, Robijn [Kesteren]. *Fruit grower, Kesteren.*
Fischer, Wilhelmus Antonius [Berg en Dal]. *Company director, Bloemendaal.*
Fleskens, Leonardus Johannes J. [Aalst]. *Bank director, Geldrop.*
Gall-van der Heijden, Ida [Acht]. *Housewife, Eindhoven.*
Gelderblom, Jan [Oosterbeek]. *Head surveyor, Oosterbeek Gas Works, Oosterbeek.*
Gent, Jacob van [Nijmegen]. *Company director, Amsterdam.*
Giebing-van Kolfschoten, Geertruida W. [Oosterbeek]. *Housewife, Heelsum.*
Giebing, Willem H. [Oosterbeek]. *Café owner, Doorwerth.*
Gier, Dr. Johannes de [Eindhoven]. *Retired physicist, Eindhoven.*
Goossens, Adrianus [Bladel]. *Teacher at University, Bladel, Den Bosch.*
Goyaerts, Marinus Petrus J. [Veghel]. *Contractor firm employee, Rosmalen.*
Graaf, Kas de, Maj. [Netherlands Forces]. *Managing director, Netherland Shipping Council, Den Haag.*
Graaff, Pieter de [Arnhem]. *Surgeon, Arnhem.*
Gras, Jan Dirk [Princess Irene Brigade, Belgium]. *Captain, Artillery, Breda.*
Groot, Johannes A. de [Uden]. *Farmer, Uden.*
Groot, Johannes T. de [Uden]. *Retired, Rotterdam.*
Gysbers, Gerhardus Wilhelmus [Arnhem]. *Rare-book dealer, Arnhem.*
Haas, Henri Leonard de [Arnhem]. *Oculist, Arnhem.*
Hagens, Herman G. [Wageningen]. *Telephone company employee, Arnhem.*
Hak, Henri Johan [Arnhem]. *Retired minister, Dutch Reformed Church, Arnhem.*
Ham, Gijsbertus J. [Arnhem]. *Arnhem.*
Hapert-Lathouwers, Johanna Theodora M. van [Eindhoven]. *Housewife, Eindhoven.*
Harmsen-Gerritsen, Agnita G. M. [Ellecom]. *Housewife, Ellecom.*
Harmsen, Gerrit-Jan [Ellecom]. *Company director, Ellecom.*
Have, Frans van der [Wageningen]. *School headmaster, Wageningen.*
Heckman, Jacobus A. [Rotterdam]. *Medical doctor, Hilversum.*
Heestermans-Hendriks, Cornelia [Bergeijk]. *Housewife, Valkenswaard.*
Heijden, Jan van der [Netersel]. *Agricultural worker, Netersel.*
Heijden, Johannes A. van der, Sgt. [Netherlands Jendarmerie, Lent]. *Retired, Lent.*
Heijden-Otto, Magtilda J. M. van der [Nijmegen]. *Housewife, Nijmegen.*
Hendriks, Paulus Hendricus [Nijmegen]. *Director-owner, ironworks, Nijmegen.*
Henneman, Dr. Adrianus J. [Groesbeek]. *Retired medical doctor, Groesbeek.*
Henriette, Sister [Schijndel]. *Principal, St. Lidwina Hospital, Schijndel.*
Herbrink, Antonius M., 1st Lt. [Princess Irene Brigade]. *Colonel, Dutch Army, Eindhoven.*
Hezemans, Johannes W. [Aalst]. *Broker, Aalst.*
Hiddink, Dirk Jan F. [Arnhem]. *Photo-typist, Arnhem.*

Hielkema, Hielkem Johannus F., Sgt. [Princess Irene Brigade]. *Captain, Royal Army, The Hague.*

Hoefnagels, Hendrik W. [Arnhem]. *Medical doctor, Arnhem.*

Hoek, Herman Lodewijk M. [Groesbeek]. *Retired Roman Catholic priest, Groesbeek.*

Hoefsloot, Piet [Arnhem]. *Furniture-store owner, Arnhem.*

Hoof, Maria Cornelia van [Hoogeloon]. *Teacher, Hoogeloon.*

Hooff, Antoon Jacques J. M. van [Arnhem]. *Director of Zoo, Arnhem.*

Hooff, Johannes Antonius R.A.M. van [Arnhem]. *Scientific official, Utrecht State University, Bilthoven.*

Hooff, Johannes G. J. van [Veghel]. *Executive chef, Yonkers, N.Y., U.S.A.*

Horst, Jan ter [Oosterbeek]. *Lawyer, Oosterbeek.*

Horst, Kate ter [Oosterbeek]. *Housewife, Oosterbeek.*

Horstman, Albert Jan Carolinus [Arnhem]. *Architect, Amsterdam.*

Houtsma, Johannus H. [Achterhoek]. *Tax adviser, Haarlem.*

Hudd-van Bork, Hendrika [Heelsum]. *Velp.*

Huisson, Abraham [Arnhem]. *Captain (Retired), Royal Army, Utrecht.*

Hulleman, Coenraad [Arnhem]. *Bank director, Rotterdam.*

Hulsen, Johannes M. [St. Oedenrode]. *Bricklayer, St. Oedenrode.*

Hurkx, Joannes Aloisius [St. Oedenrode]. *Retired, St. Oedenrode.*

Hustinx, Charles [Beek en Donk]. *Retired, former Mayor of Nijmegen, Nijmegen.*

Huygen, Frans Josef Aloisius [Lent]. *Medical doctor, Lent.*

Italisander, Arie M. T., Cpl. [British 1st Airborne]. *Engineer, Bilthoven.*

Jans, Leonard [Venlo]. *Provincial commander, civil defense, Bunde.*

Jansen, Benjamin [Driel]. *Florist, Driel.*

Jonkers-Krimpenfort, Therese [Arnhem]. *Housewife, Eindhoven.*

Jonkers, Gerardus [Eindhoven]. *Office clerk, Eindhoven.*

Kaathoven, Franciscus van [St. Oedenrode]. *Retired, St. Oedenrode.*

Karel, Hendrik [Arnhem]. *Streetcar driver, Arnhem.*

Kelderman, Aart C. [Wolfheze]. *Mechanic, Wolfheze.*

Kerssemakers-Asselbergs, Johanna P. M. [Veghel]. *Housewife, Vught.*

Kersten, Jan Henri J. ['s Hertogenbosch]. *Foundation director, Naarden.*

Kip, Louis F. C. van Erp Taalman [Arnhem]. *Neurologist, Arnhem.*

Kippersluijs, Johan [Groesbeek]. *Medical doctor, Groesbeek.*

Kirchner, Gerardina Alexandrina [Arnhem]. *Bookseller, Arnhem.*

Knap, Henri A. A. R. [Arnhem]. *Newspaper columnist, Amsteveleen.*

Knopper-van Dijk, Maria Anna E. [Eindhoven]. *Housewife, Eindhoven.*

Knottenbelt, Maarten Jan [Arnhem]. *Writer, Australia.*

Knuvelder, Gerardus [Eindhoven]. *College president, Eindhoven.*

Kooijk, Johannes van [Eindhoven]. *Merchant, Eindhoven.*

Kooten, Bartholomeus J. C. van [Heerlen]. *Company director, Bussum.*

Kortie, Frans [Eindhoven]. *Municipal Information Dept., Eindhoven.*

Kraats, Wouter van de [Oosterbeek]. *Radio-TV shop owner, Oosterbeek.*

Krap, Charles Douw van der [Oosterbeek]. *Captain (Retired), Dutch Navy, The Hague.*

Kuijk, Joannes van [Arnhem]. *Squadron Sgt. Major, Govt. Police Staff Territorial Inspection, Arnhem, Velpe.*

Kuijpers, Theodorus Albertus [Veghel]. *Parish priest, Vught.*

Kuyper, Anthonius [Veghel]. *Cycle dealer, Veghel.*

Labouchère, Charles B. [Velp-Arnhem]. *Retired, Wassenaar.*

Lamberts, Jeanne W. P. C. [Arnhem]. *Arnhem.*

Lamers, Gerardus Johannes [Gennep]. *Archivist, Veldhoven.*

Laterveer, Anton Marie [Arnhem]. *Medical doctor, anesthesiologist, Arnhem.*

Lathouwers, Allegonda L. J. [Eindhoven]. *Teacher, nurse, Enshede.*

Ledoux, Lambert [Heelsum]. *Instrument engineer, South Africa.*

Leegsma, Agardus Marinus [Nijmegen]. *Bookkeeper, Arnhem.*

Leemans, Johannus A. J. [Lith]. *Dentist, Heesch.*

Leeuwen, Johannes C. van [Eindhoven]. *Company director, Sassenheim.*

Legius, Gerardus Laurentius [Eindhoven]. *Town Hall clerk, Eindhoven.*

Lenssen, Jan [Son]. *Miller, Son en Breugel.*

Los, Cornelis Bastiaan [Aalst]. *Engineer, Aalst.*

Luijben, Thomas Arnold J. [Oosteind]. *Municipal Tax Collector, Groesbeek.*

Luiten, Cornelis Hendrikus [Eindhoven]. *Company director, Nijmegen.*

Maanen, Hanno Paul van [Oosterbeek]. *Medical doctor, Heinkenszand.*

Maat, Franciscus van der [St. Oedenrode]. *Factory worker, St. Michielsgestel.*

Maria Veronica, Sister [Schijndel]. *Mother Superior, Schijndel.*

Marinus, Adrianus L. [Eerde]. *Asst. company director, Middlebeers.*

Marinus, Albertus A. J. [Eerde]. *Blacksmith, Veghel.*

Martens, Antonius Hendrik [Nijmegen]. *Retired, Nijmegen.*

Mason-Bremen, Johanna Dina [Nijmegan]. *Housewife, Fayetteville, N.C., U.S.A.*

Mast, Willem van der [Groningen]. *Medical doctor, Haren.*

Meddens, Joseph Ignatius M. [Nijmegen]. *Town Clerk, Nijmegen.*

Meer, Frits Gerben Louis van der [Lent]. *Roman Catholic priest; college professor, Lent.*

Memelink, Garrit [Arnhem]. *Chief Inspector, Royal Netherlands Heath Society, Arnhem.*

Meyjes, Lucretia [Velp]. *Velp.*

Mijnhart, Jan [Arnhem]. *Mortician, Oosterbeek.*

Minderhoud, Christiaan [Arnhem]. *Central Library chief, Eindhoven.*

Montfroy, Harry [Arnhem]. *Member, Arnhem City Council, Arnhem.*

Mortanges, Charles Ferdinand P. de, Lt. Col. [Princess Irene Brigade, Grave]. *General (Retired), Netherlands Defense Forces, Scheveningen.*

Muselaars, Joop [Eindhoven]. *Insurance company employee, 's Hertogenbosch.*

Nefkins, Petrus Antonius [Grave]. *Retired, Grave.*

Niesen-Otto, Elisabeth J. M. [Nijmegen]. *Housewife, Maastricht.*

Nijhoff-van der Meer, Dieuwke [Ede]. *Housewife, Ede.*

Nijhoff, Gerrit Jan [Ede]. *Labor cooperator, Ede.*

Nijholt, Gerrit [Oosterbeek]. *Painter, Oosterbeek.*

Nooy, Menno Antonie de [Ede]. *Paint manufacturer, Ede.*

Nooy, Cornelia de [Ede]. *Retired, Ede.*

Nooy, Willemina de* [Ede]. *Housewife, Ede.*

Noordermeer, Tiburtius Carolus [Oss]. *Rector, Oyen, N.B.*

Numan, Gijsbert Jan [Arnhem]. *Burgomaster, Harderwijk.*

Olivier, Agathes Willem [Eindhoven]. *Official (Retired), Netherlands Railways, Groenekan.*

Ommen, Gerrit Hendrik van [Delden]. *Warehouseman, Delden.*

Onck, Willem [Arnhem]. *Plumber, Arnhem.*

Onstein, Maria Josef F. L. van Grotenhuis van [Grosebeek]. *Retired, Nijmegen.*

Oorschot, Matheas C. van [Schijndel]. *Mineworker, Brunssum.*

Osterom-Janssen, Johanna C. van [Nijmegen]. *Housewife, Nijmegen.*

Otten, Antoinette [Erp]. *School principal, Erp.*

Otten, Gerardus [Erp]. *Soest.*

Otten, Harry [Erp]. *Erp.*

Oteen, Theodore [Erp]. *Heesch.*

Ouweneel-Coppens, Wilhelmina Bartholomea C. [St. Oedenrode]. *Housewife, Eindhoven.*

Oxener, Cornelis Gerard [Oosterbeek]. *P.T.T. official, Terborg.*

Passier, Johannes M. [Son]. *Retired teacher, Son.*

Peassens, Anne, Maj. [Princess Irene Brigade]. *Ministry of Foreign Affairs, The Hague.*

Peelen, Jan [Renkum]. *Chief of expedition, Krommenie.*

Peijnenburg, Henri Joan M. [Nijmegen]. *State Secretary of Defense, Royal Army, Wassenaar.*

Pennings, Jan [Renkum]. *Farmer, Renkum.*

Penseel, Johannes [Arnhem]. *Retired, Arnhem.*

Peterse, Wilhelmus Jozephus [Nijmegen]. *Curate, Rossum.*

Pieper, Jan Willem [Dodewaart]. *Headmaster, boarding school, Harderwijk.*

Pit, Hugo Frans [Oosterbeek]. *Engineer, Sterksel.*

Pol, Hendrikus van de [Ede-Bennekom]. *Deputy director of company, Ede.*

Pol, Leonardus Johannes van de [Son]. *Retired medical doctor, Enschede.*

Ponsioen, Jacobus [Nijmegen]. *Hospital director, Winschoten.*

Post, Hendrikus Jacobus [Arnhem]. *Station chief, central station, Rotterdam.*

Post, Tjerk, Lt. [Princess Irene Brigade]. *Lt. Col. (Retired), Royal Army, Diepenveen.*

Postulart, Johan Wilhelmus [Nijmegen]. *Garage owner, Nijmegen.*

Posthuma, Jan Pieter [The Hague]. *Director, telephone company, Leeuwarden.*

Praag, Simon van [Nijmegen]. *Retired, Nijmegen.*

Presser, Samuel [Arnhem]. *Photographer, Amsterdam.*

Putten, Theo van der° [Eindhoven]. *Municipal official, Eindhoven.*

Ravensbergen, Johannes [Arnhem]. *Retired, Bennekom.*

Remmerde, Dirk [Ittersum]. *P.T.T., Rijswijk.*

Reneman, Nico [Arnhem]. *Oosterbeek.*

Rietveld, Jan [Ede]. *Surveyor, Bennebroek.*

Ridder, Tony de [Oosterbeek]. *Housewife, Oosterbeek.*

Ringelenstein-van Stuyvenberg, Cornelia Elisabeth van [Arnhem]. *Tiel.*

Roefs, Martinus [Son en Breugel]. *Retired official, Son.*

Roelofs, Theodorus [Overasselt]. *Office manager, Eindhoven.*

Rooijens, Cornelis Joannes [Nijmegen]. *Municipal health clerk, Nijmegen.*

Roosendall, Rudolf Bartholomeus E. [Randwijk]. *Psychologist, Arnhem.*

Rooy, Petrus H. van [St. Oedenrode]. *School principal, St. Oedenrode.*

Sabel, Henricus H. G. [Eindhoven]. *School clerk, Eindhoven.*

Sanden, Johannes van der [Veghel]. *Veghel.*

Sanders, Petrus Antonius M. [Ledeacker]. *Civil servant, Eindhoven.*

Schaap, Lambert [Arnhem]. *Retired, Arnhem.*

Schalm, Leendert [Arnhem]. *Medical doctor, Arnhem.*

Schermer, Arjen [Arnhem]. *Retired, Arnhem.*

Schilfgaarde, Anton B. van [Arnhem]. *Retired archivist, Arnhem.*

Schmidt, Willem [Kesteren]. *Schoolteacher, Arnhem.*

Schoenmakers, Anna Maria P. [Groesbeek]. *Housewife, Groesbeek.*

Schol, Annie J. [Hoenderlo]. *Hoenderlo.*

Schouten, Antonius C. [Nijmegen]. *Retired, Nijmegen.*

Schrijvers, Leon [Veghel]. *Heart specialist, Eindhoven.*

Schulte, Marinus Jacobus [Arnhem]. *Doctor (retired), Arnhem.*

Schut, Jacoba Adriana [Oosterbeek]. *Housewife, Doorwerth.*

Schutter, Marinus [Elst]. *Retired, Elst.*

Schuurs, Wilhelmus Antonius [Tilburg]. *Bank manager, Wijchen.*

Six, Pieter Jacob [Amsterdam]. *Chairman, Combined Military Funds, 's Gravelande.*

Slingerland, Johannus C. [Deurne]. *Inspector of the P.T.T., Leidschendam.*

Smeenk, Bernard Daniel [Renkum]. *Protestant minister, Jerusalem.*

Smeets, Henricus Johannes J. [Roermond]. *Notary, Oss.*

Smulders, Robert M. [Utrecht, Nijmegen]. *Company director, Soest.*

Snoek, Johannes M. [Renkum]. *Minister, Israel.*

Snoek, Maria [Renkum]. *Church social worker, Schiedam.*

Soet, Frans de [Oosterbeek]. *Chief agricultural engineer, State Forest Administration, Zeist.*

Spaander, Jan [Amsterdam]. *General Director, Public Health, Ministry of Social Affairs and Public Health, Bilthoven.*

Spoormans-van Berendonk, Maria Josepha [Westerhoven]. *Housewife, Veldhoven.*

Sprangers, Waltherus [Nijmegen]. *Retired, Nijmegen.*

Steinfort, Johannes Bertus [Arnhem]. *Works employee, Den Haag.*

Stibbe-van Adelsberg, Elma Sara [Renkum]. *Psychiatric social worker, Israel.*

Stranzky, Antonia Maria [Arnhem]. *Nursing sister, Arnhem.*

Striker, Jan [Oosterbeek]. *Plumber, Oosterbeek.*

Struik Dalm-van der Stad, Maria Christina [Nijmegen]. *Housewife, Nijmegen.*

Symons, Sister M. Dosithèe [Nijmegen]. *Buyer of hospital supplies, Nijmegen.*

Tempel, Johannes W. [Nijmegen]. *Municipal employee, Town Hall, Nijmegen.*

Teunissen, Waandert [Velp]. *Coppersmith, plumber, Velp.*

Thomas, Carl Paulus Nicolaas ['s Hertogenbosch]. *Enterprise director, Switzerland.*

Thuys-Damon, Bernardina [Arnhem]. *Retired, Arnhem.*

Thyssen, Augustinus A. J. W. [Beuningen]. *Company director, Nijmegen.*

Tiburtius, Father Bernardus C. N. [Oss]. *Rector, St. Joseph Monastery, Oyen.*

Tiemans, Willem Hendrik [Arnhem]. *Architect, Oosterbeek.*

Tiemans, Cornelis Lieuwe [Oosterbeek]. *Director, Conference Center, St. Michielsgestel.*

Tigler Wybrandi, Adrianus, Lt. [U.S. 101st Airborne Div.]. *Company director, The Hague.*

Top, Gerrit van den [Ede]. *Retired, Ede.*

Uijen, Albertus Franciscus [Nijmegen]. *Municipal employee; head of Dept. of Information and Cultural Affairs, Nijmegen.*

Unck, Nicolaas [Arnhem]. *Schiedam municipality worker, Schiedam.*

Valk, Hendrik [Arnhem]. *Artist, Arnhem.*

Ven, Henricus Cornelis van de [Dinther]. *Company director, Dinther.*

Venderbosch, Anna Berendina [Oosterbeek]. *Social worker, Oosterbeek.*

Verhamme, Gerardus H. A. [Ravestein]. *Town official, Berghem.*

Verwegen, Wilhelmus J. [Vinkel]. *Works employee, Veghel.*

Visser, Cornelis Marinus de [Veghel]. *Elementary-school teacher, Loosbroek.*

Visser, Maria D. de [Veghel]. *Export manager, Den Bosch.*

Vliet, Leendert R. van, Sgt. [Princess Irene Brigade]. *Warrant officer, Netherlands Defense Forces, The Hague.*

Vlist, Hendrika van der [Oosterbeek]. *English teacher, Oosterbeek.*

Voskuil, Bertha [Oosterbeek]. *Housewife, Oosterbeek.*

Voskuil, Jan [Oosterbeek]. *Chemical engineer, Oosterbeek.*

Vries, Izak de [Oosterbeek]. *Librarian, Israel.*

Vromen, Abraham [Arnhem]. *Company director, Doetinchem.*

Vroemen, Lucianus Paulus J. [Arnhem]. *Sales representative, Amsterdam.*

Waard, Willem de [Vlaardingen]. *Office clerk, Voorburg.*

Wachters, Johannes Bernardus H. [Aalst]. *Insurance physician, Berg en Dal.*

Weerd, Nicolaas van de [Bennekom]. *Banking officer, Bennekom.*

Wely, Paul Agatho van [Zetten]. *Medical doctor, Son.*

Werz, Petrus Franciscus A. [Eindhoven]. *Entrepreneur, Roosendaal.*

Westerveld, Carel Christiaan [Amsterdam]. *State official, Rijswijk.*

Wiessing, George Efraim J. [Arnhem]. *Retired, Arnhem.*

Wijburg, Hendrik [Wolfheze]. *Retired, Ede.*

Wijdeven, Marinus Antonius van de [Mariahout]. *Contractor, Mariahout.*

Wijgerden, Antonie van [Geldrop]. *Information official, N.V. Philips, Eindhoven.*

Wijnbergen, Selma [Breugel]. *Textile worker, Eindhoven.*

Wijnen, Alphonse, 1st Lt. [Princess Irene Brigade]. *Lt. Col., commander of infantry, Garrison, Eindhoven.*

Wijt, Adriaan [Arnhem]. *Retired, Hoenderlo.*

Wit, Adrianus de, Sgt. [Princess Irene Brigade]. *Warrant officer, Royal Constabulary, Breda.*

Wit, Gerardus Johannes de [Zeelst]. *Retired, Zeelst.*

Wit, Karel de [Oosterbeek]. *Druggist, Oosterbeek.*

Woensel, Cornelis H. van [Eindhoven]. *Controller, Eindhoven.*

Woestenburg, Frederik J. [Schijndel]. *Roman Catholic priest, Leende.*

Voezik, Johanna Maria van [Eindhoven]. *Hotelkeeper, Eindhoven.*

Wolffensperger-van der Wegen, Helena Elizabeth [Vlokhoven-Woensel]. *Housewife, Heusden aan de Maas.*

Wolters, Arnoldus, Lt. Comdr. [Royal Netherlands Navy]. *Head Commissioner, Rotterdam Municipal Police, Rotterdam.*

Zanten, Wilhelmus Johannes van [Arnhem]. *Section official, electric company, Arnhem.*

Zweden-Rÿser, Suze van [Arnhem]. *Mathematics teacher, Arnhem.*

POLISH

Sosabowski, Stanislaw,[*] Maj. Gen. [C.O., 1st Polish Airborne Brigade].

Chwastek, Mieczyslaw, Pvt. [3rd Battalion]. *Turner, Manchester, England.*

Juhas, Woll W., S/Sgt. [Engineers]. *Slinger, Derbyshire, England.*

Kaczmarek, Stefan, 1st Lt. [Supplies]. *Bank clerk, Sydenham, England.*

Kochalski, Alexander, Cpl. [Engineers]. *Motor mechanic, Surrey, England. (Now known as Michael Alexander.)*

Korob, Wladijslaw, Cpl. [Brigade Hq. Co.]. *Car mechanic, Rotterdam, Holland.*

Lesniak, Jerzy, Lt. [1st Battalion]. *Goldsmith, London, England.*

Niebieszczanski, Adam, Cadet [Signal Co.]. *Office manager, Westbury, N.Y.*

Prochowski, Robert L., 1st Lt. [3rd Battalion]. *Senior control buyer, Chicago, Ill.*

Szczygiel, Wieslaw, Lt. [Engineers]. *Photographer, Leven, Fife, Scotland. (Now known as George W. Harvey.)*

Smaczny, Albert T., Lt. [3rd Battalion]. *Foreman, Cambridge, England.*

Wojewodka, Boleslaw S., Cpl. [1st Battalion]. *Underwriter for insurance company, Island Park, N.Y.*

GERMAN

Bittrich, Wilhelm, SS Lt. Gen. [II SS Panzer Corps]. *Retired.*

Rundstedt, Gerd von,[*] Field Marshal, Commander in Chief [OB West, Oberbefehlshaber West].

Student, Kurt, Col. Gen., C.O. [1st Parachute Army]. *Retired.*

Bang, Helmut, Pvt. [Ind. Eng. Battalion]. *Locksmith.*

Becker, Otto, Pvt. [2nd SS Panzer Antitank Regt.]. *Salesman.*

Berthold, Günter, Cpl. [Luftwaffe Flak Battery 591]. *Commercial traveler.*

Blumentritt, Gunther,[*] Maj. Gen. [OB West; Von Rundstedt's chief of staff].

Borkenhagen, Hans, Lt. [Infantry, Reg. 1036]. *Civil servant.*

Brandt, Georg, Cpl. [Luftwaffe RR Flak Unit]. *Civil servant.*

Brandt, Theo, Pvt. [Grenadier Battalion], *University purchasing manager.*

Burg, Wilhelm von der, Cpl. [Luftwaffe Flak Antiaircraft Unit]. *Merchant.*

Busch, Karl Martin, Pvt. [Kampfgruppe Knaust]. *Operates commercial-inquiry office.*

Dessloch, Otto, Col. Gen., C.O. [3rd Luftwaffe Air Fleet]. *Retired.*
Fiebig, Werner, Pvt. [SS Panzer Grenadiers Depot Battalion 16]. *Unknown.*
Fromm, Wolgang, Ordinance Officer [59th Infantry Div.]. *Horticultural business owner.*
Gehrhardt, Erwin, Sgt. [Artillery Regt.]. *Civil servant.*
Glücks, Paul, Sgt. [Regiment Jungwirt]. *Member of West-German Broadcasting Company.*
Haberman, Heinz, Sgt. [Luftnachrichteneinheit]. *Civil servant.*
Harmel, Heinz, Maj. Gen., C.O. [10th SS Panzer Div.]. *Manufacturers' representative.*
Harzer, Walter, Lt. Col., C.O. [9th SS Panzer Div.]. *Consulting engineer.*
Heck, Erwin, Liaison Officer [SS Training Battalion, Arnhem]. *Salesman.*
Heydte, Friedrich von der, Lt. Col., C.O. [6th Parachute Regt.]. *Professor, international law.*
Hilberg, Jürgen, Cpl. [Luftwaffe Comm. Battalion]. *Civil servant.*
Hoffman, Heinz-Jürgen, Gunner [15th Army Artillery Battalion]. *Dairy manager.*
Huck, Werner, Col. [Flakbrigade 19]. *Retired.*
Jansen, Georg, Pvt. [Engineers]. *Farmer.*
Jupe, Horst, Cpl. [9th SS Panzer Div.]. *Accountant.*
Knaust, Hans Peter, Maj., C.O. [Kampfgruppe Knaust, with 10th SS Panzer Div.] *Retired.*
Krafft, Sepp, Major, C.O. [Panzer Grenadiers Training and Reserve Battalion 16] *Police official.*
Lange, Hans, Maj. [Flak Unit]. *Retired.*
Laurenz, Josef, Pvt. [II Paratroop Replacement & Training Regt., Hermann Göring Panzer Div.]. *Store owner.*
Liermann, Werner, Sgt. [10th SS Panzer Div.]. *Painter.*
Linnenbrügger, Erwin, Pvt. [Infantry Regt. 364]. *Publishers' representative.*
Liss, Gerhard, Pvt. [II Paratroop Replacement & Training Regt., Hermann Göring Panzer Div.]. *Salesman.*
Majewski, Alfred, Maj. [Antiaircraft Unit 591]. *Office clerk.*
Moll, Jakob, Sgt. [Grenadier Regt. 520]. *Police official.*
Moll, Luise [Civilian]. *Housewife.*
Münks, Karl, Pvt. [84th Infantry Div.]. *Farmer.*
Nedel, Gerhard, 1st Lt. [Supply Battalion 801]. *Retired.*
Niemann, Charlotte, Red Cross nurse [Apeldoorn]. *Medical statistician.*
Pemsel, Max, Maj. Gen. [Chief of Staff, Seventh Army]. *Lt. Gen. (Retired), German Army.*
Petersen, Emil, M/Sgt. [Reich Work Service]. *Electrical engineer.*
Poppe, Walter, Lt. Gen., C.O. [59th Infantry Div.]. *Retired.*
Prümen, Josef, Pvt. [Reich Work Service]. *Insurance broker.*
Reichardt, Hans-Joachim, 1st Lt. [Luftwaffe]. *Captain.*
Ringsdorf, Alfred, Pvt. [10th SS Panzer Div.]. *Sales representative.*
Robeus, Hermann, Pvt. [Luftwaffe Paratroop Regt.]. *Tax consultant.*
Rohrbach, Wilhelm, Cpl. [Self-propelled Gun Brigade 280]. *Delicatessen owner.*
Rose, Heinz, Sgt. [Kampfgruppe Harskamp]. *Construction engineer.*
Savelsbergh, Matthias, Pvt. [Engineers]. *Retired.*
Schepers, Bernhard, Pvt. [5th Co.]. *Retired.*
Schmidt, Heinz, Cpl. [Luftwaffe Regt. 201]. *Telephone engineer.*
Sedelhauser, Gustav, 1st Lt. [Model's Hq., Transportation Chief]. *Brewer.*
Seesemann, Hans, Sgt. [Military Police]. *Printer.*
Sick, Josef, Cpl. [9th SS Panzer Div.]. *Truck driver.*
Skalka, Dr. Egon, Maj. [9th SS Panzer Div.]. *Physician.*
Stelzenmüller, Herbert, Cadet [German Naval Hospital, Cleves]. *Metallurgist.*

Strobel, Walter, Sgt. [Antiaircraft Unit]. *Retired.*
Tempelhof, Hans von, Col. [Model's Hq.]. *Retired.*
Tersteegen, Peter, Pvt. [Infantry Reserves Battalion—Wehrkreis—IV]. *Telephone engineer.*
Ullmann, Harry, Cpl. [10th SS Panzer Div.]. *Plant superintendent.*
Weber, Horst, Pvt. [10th SS Panzer Div.]. *Manufacturer.*
Weber, Max, Cpl. [15th Paratroopers Regt.]. *Physician.*
Wienand, Wolfgang, Pvt. [Antiaircraft Unit 591]. *Salesman.*

ACKNOWLEDGMENTS

At this writing almost thirty years have passed since World War II and, in spite of voluminuous Allied and German records, the trail is growing cold for the contemporary historian in search of survivors. Many leading personalities are dead, and gone with them are the answers to many baffling questions. Of all the major plans and campaigns following the invasion of Normandy none was more significant than Operation Market-Garden. Yet—apart from some personal memoirs and a few chapters in official and semiofficial histories—the tragic story is virtually unknown in the United States. The successful role of the 82nd and 101st Airborne in the battle—in particular, the crossing of the Waal by Gavin's troops—rarely merits more than a paragraph or two in British accounts.

The stand of the British 1st Airborne Division at Arnhem remains one of the greatest feats of arms in World War II military history. But it was also a major defeat—Britain's second Dunkirk. Thus, as bureaucracies often tend to hide their failures, documentation in both American and British archives is all too frequently scanty and hard to come by. To unscramble some of the riddles and to present what I believe is the first complete version of the combined airborne-ground-attack invasion from the standpoint of all participants —Allied, German, Dutch underground and civilian—has taken me the best part of seven years. There were times during that period, especially when I fell seriously ill, that I despaired of the book's ever reaching publication.

As in my previous works on World War II—*The Longest Day* (1959) and *The Last Battle* (1966)—the backbone of information came from the participants: the men of the Allied Forces, the Germans they fought and the courageous Dutch civilians. In all, some twelve hundred people contributed to the making of *A Bridge Too Far*. Unselfishly and without stint these military personnel, ex-soldiers, and civilians gave freely of their time in interviews, showed me over the battlefield and supplied documentation and details from diaries, letters, military monographs, telephone logs, carefully preserved after-action reports, maps and photographs. Without the help of such contributors (whose names are listed on preceding pages under the heading "What They Do Today") the book could not have been written.

For a variety of reasons—among them duplication, lack of corroboration and sheer bulk—not every personal story or experience could be included. Of the twelve hundred contributors, more than half were interviewed and about four hundred of these accounts were used. But after thirty years memory is not infallible. Certain strict guidelines, similar to research procedures used in my previous books, had to be followed. Every statement or quote in the book is reinforced by documentary evidence or by the corroboration of others who heard or witnessed the event described. Hearsay, rumor or third-party accounts could not be included. My files contain hundreds of stories that may be entirely accurate but cannot be supported by other participants. For reasons of historical truth, they were not used. I hope the many contributors will understand.

So many individuals helped me in reconstructing the nine terrible days of Market-Garden that it is difficult to know where to begin in naming them. At the onset, however, I want especially to thank His Royal Highness, Prince Bernhard for his time and aid in locating and suggesting people to be interviewed and for providing me access to both Dutch and British archives. My warm thanks goes also to De Witt and Lila Wallace of the *Reader's Digest*. They not only underwrote much of the cost of this history but made their reporters and researchers in bureaus both in America and Europe available to me. Among these I wish particularly to thank the following: Heather Chapman, of New York; Julia Morgan, of Washington, D.C.; Michael Randolph, of London; John D. Panitza, John Flint, Ursula Naccache and Giselle Kayser, of Paris; the late Arno Alexi, of Stuttgart; Aad van Leeuwen, Jan Heijn, Liesbeth Stheeman and Jan van Os, of Amsterdam.

A special paragraph must be devoted to the tireless, painstaking work of Frederic Kelly, who for two years acted as my assistant. His research, interviews and fine journalistic procedures in England, Holland and the United States proved invaluable, as did his photographs of the participants as they are today.

Thanks must also be expressed to the U.S. Defense Department's Office of the Chief of Military History under command of Brigadier General Hal C. Pattison (at the time of researching) and the assistants who aided me in developing the military framework—in particular, Ditmar M. Finke and Hannah Zeidlik. Another whose help and encouragement must be mentioned is Charles B. MacDonald of O.C.M.H., whose detailed *The Siegfried Line Campaign* contains a fine and accurate version of Market-Garden. I also depended greatly on *Breakout and Pursuit* by Martin Blumenson, whose work appears in the official O.C.M.H. historical series. And I express my thanks, once again, to Dr. Forrest C. Pogue for his detailed command structure in O.C.M.H.'s *The Supreme Command*.

For their help in locating veterans and arranging interviews throughout the United States and Europe, acknowledgment must go to the officers of he U.S. Defense Department's Magazine and Book Division—Colonel Grover G. Heiman, Jr., U.S.A.F. (Ret.), Chief of Division; Lieutenant Colonel Charles W. Burtyk, Jr., U.S.A. (Deputy); Lieutenant Colonel Robert A. Webb, U.S.A.F.; Miss Anna C. Urband; and, in the Office of the Adjutant General, Seymour J. Pomrenze.

For the German research I am indebted to the following in the U.S. Defense Department's World War II Records Division: Dr. Robert W. Krauskopf, Director; Herman G. Goldbeck, Thomas E. Hohmann, Lois C. Aldridge, Joseph A. Avery, Hazel E. Ward, Caroline V. Moore, and Hildred F. Livingston. Without a complete understanding of the German war diaries and monographs provided, it would have been almost impossible for me to accurately interview the German participants, particularly the SS commanders—Lieutenant General Wilhelm Bittrich, Major General Heinz Harmel and Lieutenant Colonel Walter Harzer—who for the first time told their version of Market-Garden to an American.

In the Netherlands my assistants and I received the most gracious cooperation from the Dutch archive authorities. I am most grateful to Professor Dr. Louis de Jong, Director of the State Institute for War Documentation; Jacob Zwaan, archivist; the curator of the Arnhem Airborne Museum, Mr. B. G. J. de Vries; and Dr. Eduard and Mrs. Emmie Groeneveld. In the Military History section of the Royal Army of the Netherlands pertinent research was made available to my assistants by many people, among them Lieutenant Colonel Gerrit van Oyen; Lieutenant Colonel August Kneepkens; Captain Gilbert Frackers; Captain Hendrik Hielkema. So detailed was the Dutch help that I was even provided with scale maps, drawings and photographs of the various Market-Garden bridges. Of particular help was Louis Einthoven, postwar Dutch security and intelligence chief, for his assistance in unraveling the story of Cornelius "King Kong" Lindemans, the Dutch spy.

Of vital importance were the municipal archives in Arnhem, Nijmegen, Veghel and Eindhoven, where an abundant amount of background material was located and examined. I am deeply indebted to the following in these centers: Klaas Schaap, Anton Stempher, Dr. Pieter van Iddekinge (Arnhem); Albertus Uijen and Petrus Sliepenbeek (Nijmegen); Jan Jongeneel (Veghel); Frans Kortie (Eindhoven).

Among the many contributors in Holland who deserve special mention are Jan and Kate ter Horst and Jan and Bertha Voskuil of Oosterbeek, who spent hours with me going over every detail of the last days of the 1st Airborne's ordeal in their village. Jan Voskuil took me over the battlefields, and Mr. and Mrs. Ter Horst unraveled the mystery surrounding the Driel ferry for the first time. In Driel the Baltussen family gave me hours of detailed interviews which proved invaluable. And for checking and reading Dutch interviews I must also express my appreciation to a magnificent journalist, A. Hugenot van der Linden, of the Amsterdam *Telegraaf*. Without his watchful eye I would most certainly have made many a mistake. So, too, for Lieutenant Commander Arnoldus Wolters, now Rotterdam's Commissioner of Police, who provided me with an almost minute-by-minute account of the happenings at General Urquhart's headquarters. In Oosterbeek the Maanen family provided extraordinary diaries and interviews, as did Hendrika van der Vlist, whose meticulous notes, like those of the Maanens, gave a clear picture of the situation in the casualty stations. Their vivid records and extraordinary help enabled me to re-create the atmosphere. I am deeply grateful to all of them.

Among the many military contributors who must be singled out for special thanks are General James M. Gavin, General Maxwell D. Taylor, General Roy Urquhart and Colonel Charles Mackenzie—all of whom sat patiently through countless interviews. Others who were most helpful were Major General John D. Frost; Colonel Eric M. Mackay; Major General Philip H. W. Hicks; General John Hackett; Brigadier George S. Chatterton; Brigadier Gordon Walch, Mr. Brian Urquhart; the late Major General Stanislaw Sosabowski; and Chaplain G. A. Pare, whose notes constitute an unforgettable, poignant document. Lady Browning (Daphne du Maurier) with her wit and common sense proved a delightful correspondent and set straight some of the myths of Arnhem.

In Germany I was assisted greatly in tracing survivors and locating background material, monographs and war diaries by Dr. Bliesener of Bonn's Press and Information Service; Lieutenant Colonel Siegel of the Ministry of Defense; Dr. Wolfgang von Groote and Major Forwick of the Military History Research Department; and Lieutenant Colonel Dr. Stahl of the Federal Archives.

There are many, many others whose support and assistance made this book possible. I must again thank my wife, Kathryn, a writer herself, who organized and collated research, edited and watched for my dangling participles. Also, when I was most seriously ill, I thank with all my heart the ministrations of my good friend, Dr. Patrick Neligan, together with Dr. Willet Whitmore, who in some miraculous way pulled me through and kept me going. Again, also my thanks to Jerry Korn, my chief "nitpicker"; Suzanne Gleaves and John Tower, who read the manuscript so carefully; Anne Bardenhagen, my valued friend and assistant; Judi Muse and Polly Jackson, who, at various times, worked as secretaries. My thanks also go to Paul Gitlin, my agent; Peter Schwed and Michael Korda of Simon and Schuster for their suggestions; and Hobart Lewis, President of the *Reader's Digest*, who waited patiently through all the travail.

BIBLIOGRAPHY

✧

Airborne Assault on Holland. Washington: U.S.A.F., Office of the Assistant Chief of Air Staff, 1945.

Allied documents from U.S., British and Dutch historical sources unpublished: plans, operational orders, logs, telephone and teletype messages, intelligence estimates, war diaries, commanders' reviews and after-action reports from *First Allied Airborne Headquarters; First British Airborne Corps; 1st British Airborne Division; 101st U.S. Airborne Division; 82nd U.S. Airborne Division;* Dutch underground messages, staff college studies, monographs and maps on "Operation Market-Garden"; *82nd and 101st Airborne Divisions* combat interviews.

Ambrose, Stephen E., *The Supreme Commander: The War Years of General Dwight D. Eisenhower.* New York: Doubleday, 1970.

Bauer, Cornelius, *The Battle of Arnhem* (on information supplied by Lieut. Col. Theodor A. Boeree). London: Hodder and Stoughton, 1966.

Bekker, Cajus, *The Luftwaffe War Diaries.* New York: Doubleday, 1968.

Bird, Will R., *No Retreating Footsteps: The Story of the North Nova Scotia Highlanders.* Nova Scotia: Kentville Publishing, 1947.

Blake, George, *Mountain and Flood: The History of the 52nd (Lowland) Division, 1939–46.* Glasgow: Jackson, Son, 1950.

Blumenson, Martin, *U.S. Army in World War II: Breakout and Pursuit.* Washington, D.C.: Office of the Chief of Military History, Dept. of Army, 1961.

Bradley, General Omar N., *A Soldier's Story.* New York: Henry Holt, 1951.

Brammall, R., *The Tenth.* Ipswich: Eastgate Publications, 1965.

Bredin, Lt. Col. A. E. C., *Three Assault Landings.* London: Gale & Polden, 1946.

Brereton, Lt. Gen. Lewis H., *The Brereton Diaries.* New York: William Morrow, 1946.

Bryant, Sir Arthur, *Triumph in the West: The War Diaries of Field Marshal Viscount Alan Brooke.* London: Collins, 1959.

Bullock, Allan, *Hitler: A Study in Tyranny.* London: Odhams Press, 1952.

Butcher, Captain Harry C., *My Three Years with Eisenhower.* New York: Simon and Schuster, 1946.

By Air to Battle: Official Account of the British Airborne Divisions. London: H. M. Stationery Office, 1945.

Carter, Ross, *Those Devils in Baggy Pants.* New York: Appleton-Century-Crofts, 1951.

Chatterton, George S., *The Wings of Pegasus.* London: MacDonald, 1962.

Churchill, Winston S., *The Second World War* (Vols. 1–6). London: Cassell, 1955.

Clay, Maj. Ewart W., M.B.E., *The Path of the 50th: The Story of the 50th (Northumbrian) Division in the Second World War 1939–1945.* Aldershot: Gale & Polden, 1950.

Cole, Lieut. Col. Howard N., *On Wings of Healing.* London: William Blackwood & Sons, 1963.

Collis, Robert, and Hogerziel, Hans, *Straight On.* London: Methuen, 1947.

BIBLIOGRAPHY

Covington, Henry L., *A Fighting Heart: An Unofficial Story of the 82nd Airborne*. Fayetteville, N.C.: Privately published, 1949.

Craig, Gordon A., *The Politics of the Prussian Army 1640–1945*. London: Oxford University Press, 1955.

Critchell, Laurence, *Four Stars of Hell*. New York: Macmillan, 1947.

Crosthwait, Maj. A. E. L., *Bridging Normandy to Berlin*. Hanover: British Army of the Rhine, 1945.

Cumberlege, G., editor, *BBC War Report, 6th June 1944–5th May, 1945*. Oxford: Oxford University Press, 1946.

D'Arcy-Dawson, John, *European Victory*. London: MacDonald, 1946.

Davis, Kenneth S., *Experience of War*. New York: Doubleday, 1965.

Dawson, W. Forrest, *Saga of the All-American* [82nd Airborne Div.]. Privately printed.

Deane-Drummond, Anthony, *Return Ticket*. London: Collins, 1967.

Dempsey, Gen. Sir Miles, *Operations of the 2nd Army in Europe*. London: War Office, 1947.

Ehrman, John, *History of the Second World War: Grand Strategy* (Vols V and VI). London: H. M. Stationery Office, 1956.

Eisenhower, Dwight D., *Crusade in Europe*. New York: Doubleday, 1948.

Eisenhower, John S. D., *The Bitter Woods*. New York: G. P. Putnam's Sons, 1969.

Ellis, Maj. L. F., *Welsh Guards at War*. Aldershot: Gale & Polden, 1946.

Essame, Maj. Gen. Hubert, *The Battle for Germany*. New York: Charles Scribner's Sons, 1969.

———, *The 43rd Wessex Division at War*. London: William Clowes & Sons, 1952.

Falls, Cyril, *The Second World War*. London: Methuen, 1948.

Farago, Ladislas, *Patton*. New York: Ivan Obolensky, 1963.

First Infantry Division: Danger Forward, with introduction by Hanson Baldwin: H. R. Knickerbocker, Jack Thompson, Jack Belden, Don Whitehead, A. J. Liebling, Mark Watson, Cy Peterman, Iris Carpenter, Col. R. Ernest Dupuy, Drew Middleton and former officers. Atlanta: Albert Love Enterprises, 1947.

Fitzgerald, Maj. D. J. L., *History of the Irish Guards in the Second World War*. Aldershot: Gale & Polden, 1949.

Flower, Desmond, and Reeves, James, editors, *The War, 1939–45*. London: Cassell, 1960.

Foot, M. R. D., *Special Operations Executive*. London: H. M. Stationery Office, 1967.

Freiden & Richardson, editors, *The Fatal Decisions*. London: Michael Joseph, 1956.

Fuller, Maj. Gen. J. F. C., *The Second World War*. New York: Duell, Sloan and Pearce, 1949.

———, *The Conduct of War, 1789–1961*. London: Eyre & Spottiswoode, 1961.

Gavin, Lt. Gen. James M., *Airborne Warfare*. Washington, D.C.: Infantry Journal Press, 1947.

———, *War and Peace in the Space Age*. New York: Harper & Bros., 1958.

Gibson, Ronald, *Nine Days*. Devon: Arthur H. Stockwell, 1956.

Gilbert, Felix, editor, *Hitler Directs His War*. New York: Oxford University Press, 1950.

Gill, R., and Groves, J., *Club Route in Europe*. Hanover: British Army of the Rhine, 1945.

Godfrey, Maj. E. G., and Goldsmith, Maj. Gen. R. F. K., *History of the Duke of Cornwall's Light Infantry, 1939–1945*. Aldershot: The Regimental History Committee, 1966.

Goerlitz, Walter, *History of the German General Staff*. New York: Frederick A. Praeger, 1953.

Guingand, Maj. Gen. Sir Francis de, *Generals at War*. London: Hodder & Stoughton, 1964.

———, *Operation Victory*. London: Hodder & Stoughton, 1947.

Gunning, Capt. Hugh, *Borderers in Battle*. Berwick-on-Tweed, Scotland: Martin's Printing Works, 1948.

Hagen, Louis, *Arnhem Lift*. London: Pilot Press, 1945.

Hausser, Paul, *Waffen SS in Einsatz*. Göttingen: Plesse, 1953.

Heaps, Capt. Leo, *Escape from Arnhem*. Toronto: Macmillan, 1945.

Heijbroek, M., *The Battle Around the Bridge at Arnhem*. Oosterbeek: The Airborne Museum Collection at Kasteel De Doorwerth, Oosterbeek, 1947.

Heydte, Baron von der, *Daedalus Returned: Crete 1941*. London: Hutchinson, 1958.

Hibbert, Christopher, *The Battle of Arnhem*. London: B. T. Batsford, 1962.

History of the 2nd Battalion, The Parachute Regiment. Aldershot: Gale & Polden, 1946.

Höhne, Heinz, *The Order of the Death's Head*. New York: Coward-McCann, 1970.

Hollister, Paul, and Strunsky, Robert, editors, *D-Day Through Victory in Europe*. New York: Columbia Broadcasting System, 1945.

Horrocks, Lt. Gen. Sir Brian, *A Full Life*. London: Collins, 1960.

Horst, H. B. van der, *Paratroopers Jump*. Privately published, n.d.

Horst, Kate A. ter, *Cloud Over Arnhem*. London: Alan Wingate, 1945.

Howard, Michael, and Sparrow, John, *The Coldstream Guards 1920–1946*. London: Oxford University Press, 1951.

Ingersoll, Ralph, *Top Secret*. New York: Harcourt, Brace, 1946.

Ismay, Gen. Lord, *Memoirs*. New York: Viking Press, 1960.

Jackson, Lt. Col. G. S., *Operations of the VIII Corps*. London: St. Clements Press, 1948.

Joslen, Lt. Col. H. F., *Orders of Battle, Second World War, 1939–45*. London: H. M. Stationery Office, 1960.

Kahn, David, *The Code Breakers*. New York: Macmillan, 1967.

Keitel, Wilhelm, Field Marshal, *The Memoirs of Field Marshal Keitel;* Walter Görlitz, editor. New York: Stein & Day, 1965.

Lederrey, Col. Ernest, *Germany's Defeat in the East—1941–45*. Charles Lavauzelle, France, 1951.

Lewin, Ronald, editor, *The British Army in World War II: The War on Land*. New York: William Morrow, 1970.

Liddell Hart, B. H., *History of the Second World War*. New York: Putnam's Sons, 1971.

———, *The Other Side of the Hill*. London: Cassell, 1948.

Liberation of Eindhoven, The. Eindhoven: The Municipality of Eindhoven, September, 1964.

Life, editors of, *Life's Picture History of World War II*. New York: Time, Inc., 1950.

Lord, W. G. II, *History of the 508th Parachute Infantry*. Privately printed, n.d.

MacDonald, Charles B., *Command Decision;* Kent Greenfield, editor. London: Methuen, 1960.

———, *The Mighty Endeavor*. New York: Oxford University Press, 1969.

———, *U.S. Army in World War II: The Siegfried Line Campaign*. Washington, D.C.: Office of the Chief of Military History, Dept. of the Army, 1963.

Mackenzie, Brig. C. D., *It Was Like This!* Oosterbeek: Adremo C. V., 1956.

Marshall, S. L. A., *Battalion & Small Unit Study No. 1: Kinnard's Operation in Holland*. Washington, D.C.: Office of the Chief of Military History, Dept. of the Army, 1945.

———, *Battle at Best*. New York: William Morrow, 1963.

————, *Men Against Fire*. New York: William Morrow, 1947.

————, Westover, John G., O'Sullivan, Jeremiah, Corcoran, George, *The American Divisions in Operation Market;* unpublished monograph, Washington, D.C.: Office of the Chief of Military History, Dept. of the Army, 1945.

Martens, Allard, *The Silent War*. London: Hodder & Stoughton, 1961.

Matloff, Maurice, *Strategic Plan for Coalition Warfare, 1941–2, 43–4*. Washington, D.C.: Office of the Chief of Military History, Dept. of the Army, 1953–59.

Milbourne, Andrew, *Lease of Life*. London: Museum Press, 1952.

Millar, Ian A. L., *The Story of the Royal Canadian Corps*. Privately printed.

Millis, Walter, *The Last Phase*. Boston: Houghton Mifflin, 1946.

Montgomery, Field Marshal Sir Bernard, *Despatch of Field Marshal The Viscount Montgomery of Alamein*. New York: British Information Services, 1946.

————, *The Memoirs of Field Marshal The Viscount Montgomery of Alamein, K.G.* London: Collins, 1958.

————, *Normandy to the Baltic*. Privately published by Printing & Stationery Service, British Army of the Rhine, 1946.

Moorehead, Alan, *Eclipse*. New York: Coward-McCann, 1945.

————, *Montgomery*. London: Hamish Hamilton, 1946.

Morgan, Gen. Sir Frederick, *Peace and War: A Soldier's Life*. London: Hodder and Stoughton, 1961.

Morison, Samuel Eliot, *The Invasion of France and Germany, 1944–45*. Boston: Little, Brown, 1959.

Nalder, Maj. Gen. R. F. H., *The History of British Army Signals in the Second World War*. Aldershot: Royal Signals Institution, 1953.

Newnham, Group Capt. Maurice, *Prelude to Glory: The Story of the Creation of Britain's Parachute Army*. London: Sampson Low, Marston, 1947.

Nicolson, Captain Nigel, and Forbes, Patrick, *The Grenadier Guards in the War of 1939–1945* (Vol. 1). Aldershot: Gale & Polden, 1949.

IX Troop Carrier Command in World War II. Washington, D.C.: U.S. Air Force, Historical Division, n.d.

Nobécourt, Jacques, *Hitler's Last Gamble: The Battle of The Bulge*. New York: Schocken Books, 1967.

North, John, *North-West Europe 1944–5. The Achievement of the 21st Army Group*. London: H. M. Stationery Office, 1953.

Not in Vain, Compilation by the People of Oosterbeek. Arnhem, Holland: Van Lochum Slaterus, 1946.

Orde, Roden, *The Household Cavalry at War: Second Household Cavalry Regiment*. Aldershot: Gale & Polden, 1953.

Otway, Col. Terence, *The Second World War 1939–45: Airborne Forces*. London: War Office, 1946.

Packe, M. *First Airborne*. London: Secker & Warburg, 1948.

Pakenham-Walsh, Maj. Gen. R. P., *History of the Corps of Royal Engineers. Volume IX, 1938–1948*. Chatham: Institution of Royal Engineers, 1958.

Patton, Gen. George S., Jr., *War as I Knew It*. Boston: Houghton Mifflin, 1947.

Paul, Daniel, with St. John, John, *Surgeon at Arms*. London: William Heinemann, 1958.

Phillips, Norman C., *Holland and the Canadians*. Holland: Contact Publishing Co., 1946.

Pictorial Biography of the U.S. 101st Airborne Division, A, Compiled by the 101st's Public-Relations Unit, Auxerre, France, 1945.

Pinto, Lt. Col. Oreste, *Spy-Catcher*. New York: Harper, 1952.

Pogue, Forrest C., *The Supreme Command*. Washington, D.C.: Office of the Chief of Military History, Department of the Army, 1946.

Rapport, Leonard, and Northwood, Arthur, Jr., *Rendezvous with Destiny: A History of the 101st Airborne Division.* Washington, D.C.: Washington Infantry Journal Press, 1948.

Reader's Digest, *Illustrated Story of World War II.* Pleasantville, N.Y.: The Reader's Digest Association, 1969.

Ridgway, Matthew B., *Soldier: The Memoirs of Matthew B. Ridgway.* New York: Harper & Bros., 1956.

Rosse, Captain the Earl of, and Hill, Col. E. R., *The Story of the Guards Armoured Division.* London: Geoffrey Bles, 1956.

Sampson, Francis, *Paratrooper Padre.* Washington: Catholic University of America Press, 1948.

Saunders, Hilary St. George, *The Fight Is Won: Official History Royal Air Force, 1939–1945* (Vol. III). London: H. M. Stationery Office, 1954.

———, *The Red Beret.* London: Michael Joseph, Ltd., 1950.

Seth, Ronald, *Lion With Blue Wings.* London: Victor Gollancz, Ltd., 1955.

Shirer, William L., *The Rise and Fall of the Third Reich: A History of Nazi Germany.* New York: Simon and Schuster, 1960.

Shulman, Milton, *Defeat in the West.* London: Secker and Warburg, 1947.

Smith, Gen. Walter Bedell (with Stewart Beach), *Eisenhower's Six Great Decisions.* New York: Longmans, Green, 1956.

Smythe, Jack, *Five Days in Hell.* London: William Kimber, 1956.

Snyder, Louis L., *The War: A Concise History, 1939–1945.* London: Robert Hale, 1960.

Sosabowski, Maj. Gen. Stanislaw, *Freely I Served.* London: William Kimber, 1960.

Stacey, Col. C. P., *The Canadian Army: 1939–45.* Ottawa: King Printers, 1948.

Stainforth, Peter, *Wings of the Wind.* London: Falcon Press, 1952.

Stein, George H., *The Waffen SS 1939–45.* Ithaca, N.Y.: Cornell University Press, 1966.

Sulzberger, C. L., *The American Heritage Picture History of World War II.* New York: American Heritage Publishing, 1966.

Swiecicki, Marek, *With the Red Devils at Arnhem.* London: Max Love Publishing, 1945.

Tedder, Lord, *With Prejudice: The Memoirs of Marshal of the Royal Air Force Lord Tedder.* London: Cassell, 1966.

Thompson, R. W., *The 85 Days.* New York: Ballantine Books, 1957.

Toland, John, *Battle.* New York: Random House, 1959.

———, *The Last 100 Days.* New York: Random House, 1965.

Trevor-Roper, H. R., editor, *Hitler's War Directives 1939–1945.* London: Sidgwick and Jackson, 1964.

Trials of German Major War Criminals, The (Vols. 1–26). London: H. M. Stationery Office, 1948.

Urquhart, Maj. Gen. R. E., *Arnhem.* New York: W. W Norton, 1958

Vandeleur, Brig. J. O. E., *A Soldier's Story.* Aldershot: Gale & Polden, 1967.

Verney, Maj. Gen. G. L., *The Guards Armoured Division.* London: Hutchinson, 1955.

Warlimont, Walter, *Inside Hitler's Headquarters 1939–1945.* London: Weidenfeld & Nicolson, 1964.

Warrack, Graeme, *Travel by Dark: After Arnhem.* London: Harvill Press, 1963.

Warren, Dr. John C., *Airborne Operations in World War II, European Theatre.* Washington, D.C.: U.S. Air Force, Historical Division, 1956.

Watkins, G. J. B., *From Normandy to the Weser: The War History of the Fourth Battalion, the Dorset Regiment.* Dorchester: The Dorset Press, 1952.

BIBLIOGRAPHY

Websters, Sir Charles, and Frankland, Noble, *The Strategic Air Offensive Against Germany, 1939–45* (Vols. 1–4). London: H. M. Stationery Office, 1961.
Weller, George, *The Story of the Paratroops*. New York: Random House, 1958.
Wheeler-Bennett, John, *Nemesis of Power*. New York: St. Martin's Press, 1954.
Wilmot, Chester, *The Struggle for Europe*. New York: Harper & Bros., 1952.

SELECTED ARTICLES

"Arnhem Diary," *Reconnaissance Journal*, Vol. 4, No. 1 (Autumn, 1947).
"Arnhem Was Their Finest Hour," *Soldier*, Vol. 13 (September 1957).
"Battle of Desperation, The," *Time* Magazine, October 2, 1944.
Best, C. E., M.M., "The Mediums at Arnhem," *Gunner*, Vol. 33, No. 1 (January, 1951).
Bestebreurtje, Maj. A. D., "The Airborne Operations in the Netherlands in Autumn 1944," *Allgemeine Schweizerische Militärzeitschrift*, Vol. 92 (1946), No. 6.
Breese, Maj. C. F. O., "The Airborne Operations in Holland, Sept. 1944," *The Border Magazine*, September, 1948 (Part 1), and March, 1949 (Part II).
Burne, Alfred H., "Arnhem," *The Fighting Forces*, 1944.
Chatterton, Brig. G. J. S., "The Glider Pilot Regiment at Arnhem," *The Eagle*, Summer, 1954.
Colman, D. E., "The Phantom Legion," *The Army Quarterly*, April, 1962.
Courtney, W. B., "Army in the Sky," *Collier's*, November, 1944.
Cousens, Maj. H. S., "Arnhem 17th–26th September, 1944," from *The Spring of Shillelagh*, Vol. 28, No. 322 (Spring-Summer, 1948).
Exton, Hugh M., "The Guards Armoured Division in Operation Market-Garden," *Armoured Cavalry Journal*, 1948.
Falls, Cyril, "Arnhem—A Stage in Airborne Tactics," *Illustrated London News*, October, 1945.
Fijalski, Stanley, "Echoes of Arnhem," *Stand-to*, 1950.
Gellhorn, Martha, "Death of a Dutch Town," *Collier's*, December, 1944.
Greelen, Lothar van, "The Puzzle of Arnhem Solved," *Deutsche Wochen Zeitung*, 1964.
Herford, M. E. M., "All in the Day's Work" (Parts 1 and 2), *The Journal of the Royal Army Medical Corps*, 1952.
"How the Supplies Reached Arnhem," *Journal of the Royal Army Service Corps*, Vol. 69, No. 2 (November, 1944).
Intelligence Corps, "With the Airborne at Arnhem," *Notes of Interest*, Vol. 8 (1945).
Lister, Evelyn, "An Echo of Arnhem," *British Legion Journal*, September, 1950.
McCulloch, C. A., "The Epic of Arnhem," *Springbok*, September, 1955.
Mackay, Maj. E. M., "The Battle of Arnhem Bridge," *Blackwood's Magazine*, October, 1945.
Montgomery, Field Marshal Sir Bernard L., "21st [British] Army Group in the Campaign in North-West Europe, 1944–45," *The Journal of the Royal United Service Institution*, Vol. 90, No. 560 (November, 1945).
Packe, Michael St. J., "The Royal Army Service Corps at Arnhem," *The Journal of the R.A.S.C.*, November, 1945.
St. Aubyn, Lt. The Hon. Piers, "Arnhem," *The King's Royal Rifle Corps Chronicle*, 1946.
Smith, Robert, "With the R.A.M.C. at Arnhem," *Stand-to*, Vol. 1, No. 8 (October-November, 1950).
Stevenson, Lt. J., "Arnhem Diary," *Reconnaissance Journal*, Vol. 4, No. 1 (Autumn, 1947).

Tatham-Warter, Maj. A. D., D.S.O., "Escape from Arnhem," *The Oxfordshire and Buckinghamshire Light Infantry Chronicle*, Vol. 48 (1946).

Taylor, Lt. Col. George, D.S.O., "With 30 Corps to Arnhem," *Ça Ira*, Vol. 8, No. 2 (June, 1949).

Tompkins, Col. Rathvon McC., "The Bridge," *Marine Corps Gazette*, April, 1951, and May, 1951.

Tooley, Lt. Col. I. P., "Artillery Support at Arnhem," *The Field Artillery Journal*, April, 1945.

Watkins, Maj. Ernest, "Arnhem, the Landing and the Bridge," *British Army Bureau of Current Affairs*, No. 83 (1944).

Williams, F. Lt. A. A., "I Was at Arnhem," *The Royal Air Force Journal*, December, 1944.

Wilmot, Chester, "What Really Happened at Arnhem," *Stand-to*, Vol. 1, No. 8 (1950).

Winder, Sgt. F., "Postscript" in "Arnhem Diary," *Reconnaissance Journal*, Vol. 4, No. 1 (Autumn, 1947).

Wood, Alan, "How Arnhem Was Reported," *Pegasus*, July and October, 1946.

———, "News from Arnhem," *Pegasus*, October, 1949.

Wooding, F. B., "The Airborne Pioneers," *The Royal Pioneer*, Vol. 7, No. 30 (March, 1952).

GERMAN MANUSCRIPTS, MILITARY STUDIES AND CAPTURED DOCUMENTS

Bittrich, SS General Wilhelm, CO II SS Panzer Corps., H.Q. Battle Orders; *Report on the Activities of the II SS Panzer Corps., Aug.–Nov. 1944*, together with maps; Bittrich's account of Arnhem Battle, September 17–26, 1944; Incoming reports from Commanders of 9th and 10th SS PZ Divisions; Personal papers, diaries and maps—as given to the author.

Blumentritt, General Gunther, *OB West, A Study in Command, Atlantic Wall to Siegfried Line*, Office of the Chief of Military History (hereafter referred to as O.C.M.H.), Department of Army, U.S.A., MS. B-344; Manuscripts, notes and maps as given to the author.

Buttlar, Major General Horst von, *OB West, A Study in Command, Atlantic Wall to Siegfried Line*, O.C.M.H., MS. B-672.

Christiansen, General Friederich, CO Luftwaffe, German Armed Forces in the Netherlands, Interrogation of, File No. 67 Nijmegen Archives; Testimony and trial proceedings, Dutch Ministry of Justice, July-August, 1948.

Feldt, General Kurt, *Corps. H. Q. Feldt and 406th Division from 17–21 September 1944*. O.C.M.H., MS. C-085.

Fullriede, SS Col. F. W. H., C.O. Replacement & Training Para. Brigade Hermann Göring. Utrecht. Personal Diary, September 1–October 5, 1944. Translated by Peter Ranger. Interrogation of, April 8, 1948, Nijmegen Archives, File 83.

Harmel, SS Major General Heinz, C.O. 10th SS PZ Division Frundsberg. Personal diary; maps, Orders of Battle; Operational Orders and pertinent sections of Official War Diary. All called the "Harmel Papers," as given to the author.

Harzer, SS Lt. Col. Walter, C.O., 9th SS PZ Division Hohenstaufen, H.Q. War Diaries, Operation Reports and Interrogations, all under "Harzer Papers." File #74; H.Q. Daily Reports, Document #78013/19. U.S., British and Dutch Archives.

Heichler, Lucien, *The Germans Opposite 30th Corps*, an account of the First Parachute Army on the Albert Canal. Research monograph. Washington, D.C.: O.C.M.H., Dept. of the Army, 1962.

Heydte, Lt. Col. Frederick von der, C.O., 6th Para. Regiment. *6 FS Jaeger Regiment in Action Against U.S. Paratroopers in the Netherlands,* September 1944; maps and overlays. O.C.M.H., MS. C-001.

Krafft, SS Major Sepp, C.O., Panzer Grenadier Depot Battalion 16 Netherlands, correspondence between Krafft and Heinrich Himmler; Krafft "War Diary"; "The Battle of Arnhem" as presented to Heinrich Himmler; British Intelligence Corps translation of Krafft Diary, with commentary.

Mattenklott, Lt. Gen. Frans, Report on Military Area 6 and The Rhineland, 15 September, 1944–21 March 1945. O.C.M.H., MS. B-044.

Meindle, General Eugen, C.O., II Para. Corps. *The II Para. Corps., 15 September,* tember, 1944. Document Nos. III H 15450 and 75145/5.

Model, Field Marshal Walter, OKW—AGpB War Diary, Operational Daily Reports, 1 September—15 October 1944. Document No. III H 15452/2; OKW—AGpB War Diary; Operations and Orders, September 1–September 30, 1944. Document No. III H 15453/2; AGpB–Situation and Weekly Reports; Telephone Log and Teletype Message Files, Proclamations for September, 1944. Document Nos. III H 15450 and 75145/5.

190th Infantry Division, Report of, Commitment 17 September, 1944–16 April, 1945. O.C.M.H., MS. B-195.

Poppe, Major General Walter, C.O., 59th Infantry Division. *2nd Commitment of the 59th Infantry Division in Holland, 18 September—25 November, 1944.* O.C.M.H., MS. B-149; War Diary and Operational Orders as given to the author.

Rauter, SS Lt. Gen. Hans Albin, Trial proceedings, Dutch Ministry of Justice, 1952; Interrogations of and testimony in Dutch Historical Archives and in the *Netherlands in Wartime,* Vol. 4, No. 1 (March, 1949). Rauter's Proclamations, Nijmegen Archives.

Reinhard, Gen. Hans W., C.O. 88 Corps., *Report of the Commander 6 June–21 December 1944,* O.C.M.H., MS. B-343 and MS. B-156.

Reinhardt, Maj. Gen. Hellmuth, C. of S. Wehrmacht Commander in Chief in Denmark. *Commitment of the 406th Division Against the Allied Airborne Assault at Nijmegen, September 17, 1944.* O.C.M.H., MS. C-085; Supplement to the Report, O.C.M.H., MS. C-085A.

Rundstedt, Field Marshal Gerd von, *OB West, Daily Reports of Commander in Chief West, September 2–30, 1944.* Document No. 34002; OKW—OB West War Diary, September–October, 1944, including Annex 2224–2476. British and Dutch archives; *OB West, A Study in Command, Atlantic Wall to Siegfried Line,* Vols. I, II, III, O.C.M.H., MS. B-633.

Scheidt, Wilhelm, *Hitler's Conduct of the War,* O.C.M.H., MS. ML-864.

Schramm, Major Percy E., *The West* (1 April 1944–16 December 1944), MS. B-034; *Notes on the Execution of War Diaries,* O.C.M.H., MS. A-860.

Skalka, SS Major Egon, Divisional Doctor, 9th SS Panzer Hohenstaufen, Official Headquarters Reports; Medical Estimate of the Arnhem Battle; Interrogation Reports. British and Dutch Archives. Diary, notes as given to the author.

Speidel, Lt. Gen. Dr. Hans, *OB West, A Study in Command, Atlantic Wall to Siegfried Line,* Vols. I, II, III, O.C.M.H., MS. B-718.

Student, Col. Gen. Kurt, C.O. 1st Para. Army, *Battles of the 1st Parachute Army on the Albert Canal;* and *Allied Airborne Operations on 17 September, 1944,* O.C.M.H., MS. B-717. Manuscripts, notes and maps as given to the author. Statement in Nijmegen Archives, File 35.

————, "Arnhem—The Last German Victory," from *The Soldier Speaks*, No. 5, 1952.

Tettau, Lt. Gen. Hans von, *Combat Reports 17 September–26 September, 1944 of Units Committed in the Netherlands*, Document No. 40649H. Dutch Archives.

Warlimont, General Walter, *From the Invasion to the Siegfried Line, 1939–1945*. London: Weidenfeld & Nicolson, 1962.

Zangen, General Gustav von, *Battles of the Fifteenth Army Between the Meuse-Schelde Canal and the Lower Meuse, 15 September–10 November, 1944*, O.C.M.H., MS. B-475.

Zimmerman, Lt. Gen. Bodo, *OB West, A Study in Command, Atlantic Wall to Siegfried Line*, Vols. I, II, III, O.C.M.H., MS. B-308.

Index

✧